W9-AOD-589

We Remember with Reverence and Love

Hasia R. Diner

We Remember with Reverence and Love

American Jews and the Myth of Silence
after the Holocaust, 1945–1962

Montante Family Library
D'Youville College

FEB 2 5 2010

New York University Press • *New York and London*

NEW YORK UNIVERSITY PRESS
New York and London
www.nyupress.org

© 2009 by New York University
All rights reserved

Library of Congress Cataloging-in-Publication Data
Diner, Hasia R.
We remember with reverence and love : American Jews and the myth of silence
after the Holocaust, 1945–1962 / Hasia R. Diner.
p.   cm.
Includes bibliographical references and index.
ISBN-13: 978-0-8147-1993-0 (cl : alk. paper)
ISBN-10: 0-8147-1993-7 (cl : alk. paper)
1. Holocaust, Jewish (1939–1945)—Influence. 2. Holocaust, Jewish (1939–1945)
—Historiography. 3. Holocaust, Jewish (1939–1945)—Public opinion, American.
4. Jews—United States—Attitudes. 5. Public opinion—United States.   I. Title.
D804.3.D58 2009
940.53'1814—dc22   2008052316

New York University Press books are printed on acid-free paper, and their
binding materials are chosen for strength and durability. We strive to use
environmentally responsible suppliers and materials to the greatest extent
possible in publishing our books.

Manufactured in the United States of America

10 9 8 7 6 5 4 3 2 1

D
804.3
.D58
2009

To Eugene

A wonderful addition to our family

Contents

Preface

I had long been bothered by the often repeated "truth" about post–World War II American Jewry's Holocaust avoidance, an assertion that to this day runs through the literature on American Jewish history. It struck me as wrong in and of itself and because it almost always came with little evidence to back it up. But since I had done no research on that era, I could not mount a sustained critique. I could only rely on feelings and my own recollections. Every time I taught the American Jewish history survey course, I confronted the well-worn statements in the books I assigned my students, and generally I mumbled something to the classes to the effect that I had my doubts as to the accuracy of what they had just read.

When Todd Endelman invited me to the University of Michigan to give the David W. Belin lecture in 2004 and recommended that I focus on some relatively contemporary aspect of American Jewish history, I decided that the time had come to try my hand at this topic. I set aside a few months to see what I could find and kept myself open to the possibility that the scholarship had been right all along. The opposite happened, and as a result of a summer's research to prepare for the Michigan talk, I had to buy myself a four-drawer file cabinet to house the material that demonstrated a widespread and intense American Jewish engagement with the Holocaust in precisely the years when silence had supposedly reigned, and this only after having gone through fairly obvious published material. So, my first thanks goes to Todd for inviting me and suggesting that I tailor my talk to the recent period.

At just about the same time, Paul Melrood invited me to Milwaukee to speak to the International Association of Yiddish Clubs on the theme of that year's conference, Yiddish and the Holocaust. A few more weeks of research to prepare a talk for this popular presentation provided me with even more material, more than my new, but already filled to brim, file cabinet would hold. Speaking to this group of ardent Yiddishists and local Milwaukee Jews convinced me of the importance of the topic, especially because the women and men of the audience, none of them historians, all of them active and engaged Jews, lovers of Yiddish, refused to believe anything I said. So deeply had the truth of postwar American Jewish Holocaust avoidance taken root that, as typical of such audiences, they bombarded me with heated statements of disbelief. Nothing I said could shake them from what they knew, with utter conviction, that in the years after the war, American Jews, in whatever language they expressed themselves, had little or no interest in the Holocaust.

I came away from this lecture with an equally strong conviction that the subject deserved a book. This then pushed me into years of research and sent me to an array of libraries and archives, and here I would like to thank the staff members of these various repositories who extended themselves to help me in my quest for materials.

Out of alphabetical order, I want to begin by offering my special gratitude to the librarians and archivists at the American Jewish Historical Society and the YIVO Institute for Jewish Research, both housed in the remarkable Center for Jewish History in New York City. I did the lion's share of my work there and am completely indebted to them. Having the two repositories in the same building, sharing a reading room, demonstrated the organic flow of Jewish history from and between eastern Europe and the United States. In addition, the American Jewish Archives in Hebrew Union College, Cincinnati, not only houses one of the richest collections in the field, but its staff knows how to accommodate scholars and to make them feel as though the facility exists for them.

I received excellent assistance and found massive troves of material at the Chicago Jewish Archives of the Spertus Institute of Jewish Studies, as well as its Asher Library, the Marvin Gelman Library of George Washington University, the Hebrew Union College–Jewish Institute of Religion's Klau Library in New York, the Fales Library and Special Collections of Bobst Library at New York University, and the Tamiment Library of the Robert F. Wagner Labor Archives, also at my home institution, New York University. Research trips to the Jewish Theological Seminary of America's Ratner Center for the Study of Conservative Judaism, the New York Public Library's rich Library for the Performing Arts and its Rare Books and Manuscript Division, the University of Wisconsin–Milwaukee Library's Manuscript Collection, the Administrative Archives at Yad Vashem in Jerusalem, and Yeshiva University's Archives all yielded remarkable material. I am deeply grateful to the librarians and archivists at each of these places. I wish I could name these staff members one by one, but the list would be too long.

Moving from institutions to friends and colleagues, I again express how thankful I am for their time and insights. The individuals whose names appear here encouraged me but also challenged me when they believed that to do so served my best interest. They had no problem telling me when they thought I might be off target, or when they decided that I had meandered in some problematic directions.

First in that long list is Lynn Gordon of the University of Rochester, who read a manuscript version of this book that ran even more pages than this one. She offered to read its subsequent, shorter versions, something I could not inflict on such a dear person. A critical reader and superb editor, she suspended her important role of friend to stand back and critique this work.

Tony Michels and Rebecca Kobrin also read the long and unwieldy first draft, and they offered important insights that helped me frame, redirect, and cut. I thank them. My wonderful colleagues Marion Kaplan and Ron Zweig worked through these chapters and provided me with many comments, delivered over copious cups of coffee at the Washington Square Diner.

The list goes on, and I hope that I will not leave anyone off. Diane Ashton and Rakefet Zalashik read all or parts of the manuscripts and told me exactly what they thought. Lawrence Baron played a role in chipping away at the dominant paradigm, and I learned much from him. Yigal Sklarin took a graduate seminar with me at Yeshiva University's Bernard Revel Graduate School on post–World War II American Jewish history. I assigned a version of this book in manuscript form, and while I learned much from the reactions of all the students in that class, Yigal, without my asking him to, marked the pages up, and he has continued even up to this late date to send me references germane to the world of postwar Orthodoxy.

Several of my students from NYU's Skirball Department of Hebrew and Judaic Studies supplied me with information that they found in their own journeys to archives, and they gave me leads to rich veins of material. In the process they asked me great questions that stimulated my thinking. Here I want to mention Natalia Aleksiun, Daniella Doron, Laura Jockusch, and Josh Perelman. Shira Kohn, Rachel Kranson, Lara Rabinovitch, and David Koffman all gave me important feedback and encouragement.

In addition, lengthy conversations and electronic communications with such scholars and colleagues as Alan Kraut, Dan Katz, John Bodnar, Gary Gerstel, Michael Meyer, Judah Cohen, Zohar Segev, Ofer Schiff, Michael Galashinsky, Derek Penslar, Jeffrey Shandler, Marc Saperstein,

Marsha Rozenblit, Odeda Arad, Robert Cherry, and David Levering Lewis made me feel that I had embarked on a project worth undertaking and that I had indeed asked an important question.

Vivian Mann helped me track down an elusive illustration. Mark Epstein did yeoman's service organizing my notes, preparing the bibliography, and tracking down wayward footnotes. Tina Tyrrell scanned images for me. Shayne Leslie Figueroa seemed to always be there to help me with a myriad of problems and pitched in with the many chores that multiplied as the process of writing this book went on its course. Despina Papazoglou provided great help as well.

Eric Zinner, my editor at New York University Press, gets a paragraph of his very own. He functioned as more than a good shepherd for this book. He expressed both enthusiasm and skepticism for what I did and how I did it. The former kept me going, and the latter made me clarify to myself, to him, and I hope to my readers what I was doing, and why.

I must note here the very special role played by Alex Goren in the making of this book. I cannot fully express how honored I am that the Cukier, Goldstein-Goren Foundation chose to fund a center for the study of American Jewish history at New York University in the Skirball Department of Hebrew and Judaic Studies. His generosity and belief in scholarship based on the vision of his father, Avram "Dolphy" Goldstein-Goren, is inspiring. In his lifetime Avram made a commitment to fostering the highest-quality Jewish studies scholarship here and in various places around the world.

As is customary in acknowledgments, one does not forget one's family, and I am blessed with an almost embarrassment of riches when it comes to the number of historians in mine, those closest to me who had no choice but to listen, read, and comment on all the details of this project, in its many stages. The next three names ought rightly to have been listed with the professional colleagues who helped me. But since my family in fact stands in a class by itself in my heart, they deserve to be singled out. My husband Steven Diner, way too busy as Chancellor of Rutgers University–Newark, not only read a draft but listened incessantly to me talk about this. With all his insights as an American historian, he asked probing and hard questions. My son, Eli Diner, now a student in the Ph.D. program in history at UCLA, had much to offer in our constant discussions of this book, and I derived much from our conversation based in part on his reading a lot of it. Eugene Sheppard, my newest "son," is a professor at Brandeis University, a scholar of German Jewish intellectual history. He is a great reader and sharp thinker. He simultaneously praised my work and cajoled me to go in directions that I had not thought to before. Finally Shira Diner and Matan Diner, my oldest and youngest children, may not be historians (or in Matan's case, not yet), but their constant interest, support, and love mean the world to me. These five truly make my journey a rich one.

New York City
May 2008

Introduction

Deeds and Words

THE JEWISH TEENAGERS who spent the summer of 1956 at the Reform movement's Camp Institute in Oconomowoc, Wisconsin, edited a literary magazine, a repository of their fond memories of a summer well spent. They could not possibly have known, as they cobbled together *All Eyes Are on the . . . Literary Magazine*—made up of mimeographed short stories, poems, humorous vignettes of camp life, mixed in with some serious pieces which speculated on the religious and cultural programs that they had just experienced—that, a half-century later, their camp yearbook would be used to show how American Jews went about the process, text by text, artifact by artifact, and act by act, of creating a communal culture that hallowed the memory of the six million Jews who perished in Europe during the Holocaust. Neither could they imagine that their deeds and words would play a role in undermining a widely accepted paradigm about post–World War II American Jews and the Holocaust, one which asserted that, on the whole, they remained silent about that catastrophe which had so recently befallen their people.

But their naive and youthful words show how profoundly the destruction of one-third of the Jewish people at the hands of the Germans infused the rhetoric and action of the Jews of America who, despite their distance in space and time from the tragedy, lived in its shadow. One camper, Sharon Feinman, said it most clearly as she focused in her piece on the summer's theme, "Naaseh v'nishma" [we will do and we will hear], the words drawn from Exodus, declaimed by the Israelites at Mt. Sinai as they accepted the Ten Commandments. In summarizing what she learned during those weeks away from home, she demonstrated how American Jews in the post–World War II period engaged with the horrendous events that had recently engulfed their people in Europe. Her brief essay's determined prose reflected the widespread concern of the Jews of the United States with the Holocaust, with their insistence that it be remembered and their understanding that it affected their lives.

1

"Everywhere," she wrote, wherever "Jews wandered, they established centers of learning in which the deed and word were enshrined in the life of the people. The waves of persecution beat against us but our spirit remained unbroken." That summer at Camp Institute, the teenagers contemplated the long chain of Jewish history and pondered "how today in the twentieth century, our people still affirm Naaseh v'nishma." During "the dark reign of terror when Hitler and the Nazis ruled Germany and plunged the world into a catastrophic war, when the people who called themselves the 'master race' murdered six million Jews," they had perpetrated "the worst slaughter in the history of mankind." The Reform youngsters had learned, however, that even amid this horror, "the light of 'Naaseh v'nishma' burned mightily. As the world watched, a miracle came to pass. Out of the bitter struggle, and against overwhelming odds, the nation of Israel was born."[1]

These words of a Jewish high school student encapsulated much about how American Jews after the war integrated the Holocaust into their communal lives. Jewish youngsters attending left-wing Zionist camps in California, Workmen's Circle Yiddish schools in the Bronx, or Orthodox Jewish day schools in Brooklyn would have recognized themselves in Feinman's essay. They would have articulated her feelings somewhat differently, each reflecting sentiments particular to their ideas as to the meaning of Jewish culture, but they would have, as she did, see this as a tragedy of "our people." So, too, would the adults who attended religious services, went to lectures in Jewish community centers, read the Jewish press, and participated in the public life of postwar American Jewry.

Metaphorically along with Sharon Feinman, America's Jews participated in building a culture that gave the Holocaust a prominent place. When they gathered in their myriad Jewish spaces and when they faced the larger American public, they invoked the all-too-horrendous devastation that had taken place in Europe. These American Jewish women and men, adults and young people, posed the catastrophic event in both deeply Jewish and broadly universal terms. Feinman's essay—just like the books and articles, sermons and literary works, liturgies and letters to public officials written by so many of the adults who ran Jewish institutions, staffed the organizations, officiated at synagogues, and published Jewish newspapers and magazines—blended a deeply felt anguish over this very particular Jewish tragedy with concerns for humanity writ large.

In the years following the end of World War II, that global conflagration which witnessed the destruction of one-third of the Jewish people,

American Jews, like the campers and staff at Camp Institute, found numerous times and places to publicly express their anguish over this horrendous reality. They devoted much of their communal rhetoric and institutional history to contemplating its effect on their lives and thinking about how it might shape them in the years to come. In the decade and a half following the war until the early 1960s, culminating in the capture, trial, and arrest of Adolf Eichmann, the gruesome details of the mass murder of so many Europeans infused every sector of American Jewry.

The vast repertoire of projects and texts created by postwar American Jews that incorporated the brutal realities of the Holocaust, like the little essay written by Sharon Feinman, on one level ought not to be considered particularly surprising or noteworthy. Since ancient times, human beings have memorialized tragedies and considered themselves obliged to keep alive the memory of their kin and compatriots who suffered at the hands of enemies who had inflicted great harm on them. At all times, in all places, societies and groups have employed the details of the great and painful losses they sustained to justify and shape behaviors and actions.

Memorializing tragedy underlay the Jewish tradition as it came down to the Jews of the United States by the middle of the twentieth century. At the broadest level, the Jewish women and men of America understood their history as a series of catastrophic events. These included the two expulsions from their homeland in 586 B.C.E. and 70 C.E., the Crusades with their bloody extirpations of the Jews of the Rhineland, the expulsion from Spain at the end of the fifteenth century, the vast massacres in Poland in the seventeenth century, the pogroms that commenced in the 1880s in Russia and sent so many of their families to the United States, and the quite recent mass murders that took place during and after World War I. Each of those tragedies entered into their communal lexicon and, by using words and images related to them, American Jewry remembered. The cycle of the Jewish calendar also moved from the recollections of one historic trauma to the next, each resonating with tales of past suffering and with liturgies that admonished Jews to always remember. These holy days include Passover, Purim, Hanukkah, Yom Kippur, and the Ninth of Av, the summer fast day that mourned the destruction of the Temples in Jerusalem first by the Babylonians and then the Romans.

However universal the urge to memorialize communal catastrophes and however deeply Jewish culture embedded such collective remembering, American Jews in the years after World War II, according to most later observers, behaved very differently when it came to the brutal deaths of the six million Jews. As regards them, a very different story has been told and has become accepted as the truth. The scholarship about postwar American and American Jewish history takes a decidedly unified view, asserting with utter certainty that American Jewry made little of the Holocaust, pushing it to the hidden corners and, indeed, under the rug of their communal lives. Nearly every historian, literary scholar, and cultural critic who has commented on the Jews of America in this era and their relationship to the Holocaust maintains that America's Jews had little interest in thinking about, engaging with, and memorializing the Holocaust.

That the Holocaust meant little to postwar American Jews has become an accepted truth, one holding that, until the 1960s—as a result of either the Eichmann trial early in the decade or the June 1967 Six-Day War in Israel—the story of Europe's destroyed Jews lay hidden through deliberate forgetting. American Jews could not, would not, and did not engage in acts of public mourning. This paradigm of American Jewish history postulates that, in the affluence of the postwar period, with the 1950s its epicenter, American Jews had nothing to gain from invoking the Holocaust. As most scholars and Jewish communal commentators see it, American Jewry suffered from an almost two-decade-long, self-imposed collective amnesia.

Statements as to the invisibility of the Holocaust in postwar American Jewish culture appeared in nearly every book written about that era, making this the dominant motif in the literature. Leon Jick, a scholar of American Jewish history, launched this historical narrative in a 1981 article, declaring that "American Jewry sought to forget" and "collaborated or at least acquiesced in [a] campaign to make the world forget." According to Jick, one of the first historians to treat postwar American Jewish history, until the 1960s, the Holocaust had been a "barely remembered, rarely mentioned event, of interest only to a limited circle of survivors."[2] In 1992, Edward Shapiro asserted in the first full-length scholarly book on postwar American Jewry that, in the 1950s, "there was little public discussion among Jews regarding the fate of European Jewry," to be then followed by the "unexpected emergence in the 1960s of the Holocaust into the forefront of American Jewish consciousness."[3] Gerald Sorin claimed in a widely used overview of American Jewish history that a "conspiracy of silence" reigned, not to be breached "until the 1970's" when, for the first time, American Jews would become conscious of "its enormity."[4] The Holocaust, literary scholar Alan Mintz declared in 2001, "and everything we now associate with it were not welcome guests" to American Jewish cultural life of the postwar period.[5] And in 2004, in his award-winning book on American

Jewish history, Jonathan Sarna postulated that in the period up to 1967 the Holocaust "incubated" below the surface of American Jewish public life.[6] Jack Wertheimer, a historian at the Jewish Theological Seminary of America, asserted that in the late 1960s, as "the communal agenda shifted . . . from universalistic concerns to a preoccupation with Jewish particularism . . . the trauma of the Holocaust buried in the American Jewish psyche . . . erupted into public consciousness."[7]

Instead, according to nearly all scholars then, in the aftermath of World War II, the Jews of the United States rushed to the suburbs, embracing the acceptance being proffered to them by an increasingly tolerant America. In this "golden age," they had everything to lose by associating themselves publicly with the horrendous event that made them so very different from the other white, middle-class Americans with whom they sought to integrate. In the bland suburban culture that American Jews created, the Holocaust could have no role because it so painfully differentiated them from others, precisely when they sought to highlight sameness.[8]

According to this truth, Jewish communal leaders in the postwar period did not "use" the Holocaust to inspire ordinary Jews to become more religiously or communally committed, to win support for Israel, or to alter the fabric of American life. Such deployments of the Holocaust, scholars both from left and right, from inside and outside the Jewish world, have repeatedly told, only surfaced in the latter part of the 1960s. Before that, American Jews believed they would derive no benefit from articulating their inner communal or external political agendas through the Holocaust.

If, according to this widely accepted view of the past, American Jews did say something about the recent tragedy, they did so obliquely by invoking universal concerns about evil in general, erasing the Jewish element of the tragic story. By stripping the Holocaust of its Jewish core they did not have to claim it as their own, and that suited them just fine. A variety of explanations for the invisibility have flourished. Some writers posed it as American Jewish self-defense. They did not talk about the Holocaust because they feared it would inspire more anti-Jewish activities. Yet another set of scholars, like Edward Alexander, offered that American Jews found themselves "unable to write about it afterwards" because they, "the most powerful, or at any rate, least powerless Jewish community in the world[,] had abnegated responsibility for its helpless brethren during their hour of utmost need."[9]

Nearly all who have written about this period of time in American Jewish history posited a causal connection between the Cold War and

American Jewry's avoidance of the Holocaust. In the period that witnessed the birth of intense Soviet-American rivalry, when the Federal Republic of Germany became an ally of the United States as a bulwark against the Soviet Union, American Jews refused to draw attention to the misdeeds of their nation's new best friend. The hysteria that reigned over the specter of domestic Communists and their purported infiltration of American institutions further suppressed any thoughts American Jews might have had about keeping alive the memory of what the Germans had done. In the poisonous atmosphere that pervaded America from the late 1940s onward, anti-Communism pushed American Jewry to self-censor and to avoid any kind of heated, passionate ideological rhetoric.[10]

To a person, scholars and the larger Jewish public accepted as true the proposition that Israel did much to bring the narrative of the Holocaust into prominence in American Jewish public life. Alvin Rosenfeld, a literary scholar, stated this premise quite succinctly: "For years after the end of World War II, Jews in America were unable or unwilling to face up to the horrors. . . . It was only in the 1960s, beginning with Israel's abduction of Eichmann," that American Jews undertook "an exceptional effort . . . to educate themselves and the public at large about the Nazi crimes." Israel's actions thus jolted the Jews of America into a forced encounter with the subject they had long buried.[11]

Writers and commentators attributed even greater transformative power to Israel's dramatic—indeed, lightning-speed—victory over the armies of several Arab nations in June 1967, a triumph that followed weeks of grave worry over its very existence. This confluence of events made it possible for American Jews to talk about the Holocaust for the first time. "Israel's vulnerability," opined Stuart Svonkin, "forced American Jews to consider the legacy of the Nazis' war against European Jewry." Israel, with its swift and decisive military action, handed American Jews something Jewish to be proud of, allowing them to revisit the era that had previously brought them shame.[12] With the resolution of that war, American Jews "suddenly" had, according to Seymour Martin Lipset and Earl Rabb, "a searing literature of the Holocaust."[13] Indeed, Kirsten Fermaglich declared, in the war's wake, "American Jews began more and more to view the Holocaust as a Jewish event, and to emphasize the connections between their own Jewish identities and the Holocaust."[14] "Israel's survival," wrote Michael Morgan, after 1967, "became for many Jews the core, if not the totality of Jewish identity," and with that came "an acknowledgement of the Holocaust, Auschwitz, the memory of catastrophe." It took that war to get

"the American Jewish community" to become "unburdened of its commitment to subordinate, even to *repress*, the death camps."[15] A consensus reigns
that, as a consequence of the war in which Israel, in six short days, went
from the brink of destruction to the heights of military prowess, American
Jewry became transformed and could then, at last, bring the Holocaust out
of the recesses of its cultural shame into its public displays.[16]

This particular understanding of the history of postwar America
and its Jews has been cast so widely through the literature and the public discourse as to constitute an accepted truth and has been picked up
by scholars writing on a variety of topics. In her ethnographic study of
the graduates of Newark's predominantly Jewish Weequahic High School
class of 1958, anthropologist Sherry Ortner took as a given the "fact" that
the Holocaust had had no impact on these young people; as she wrote, "it
seems to be the case that many parents did not talk about the Holocaust."
While Ortner admitted that she had no "detailed data on this point," she
still felt empowered to explain this silence by claiming that "many Jewish
parents were trying to protect their children from this awful knowledge"
and allow them to be "normal" and "just like everybody else."[17] Edward
Linenthal, a cultural historian specializing in the history of public memorials, declared that in the postwar period "the Holocaust lived . . . in the
subterranean anxieties." American Jews rendered it "virtually invisible."[18]
In a cultural history of postwar popular culture, Judith Smith affirmed that
"most mainstream Jewish organizations eschewed public discussion of
anti-Semism, Nazism, or . . . the death camps, because it seemed danger-
ous to call attention to Jewish victimization."[19] Sociologist Nathan Glazer
suggested that "the generation that experienced the Holocaust, either as
victims or as bystanders who did not or could not do enough, wishes to
forget it."[20] Tim Cole stressed that "it was not until the early 1960s that
anything like widespread awareness of the 'Holocaust' began to emerge."[21]
Even reference works, supposedly committed to presenting stripped-
down facts, and not venturing into analysis, have built this history into
their authoritative entries. A reference guide on the 1960s pointed out
to its users that "perhaps it was the Six Day War or perhaps it was only
that time had begun to make it possible to confront the past, but at the
end of the 1960s the Holocaust became a subject for examination," particularly within "American Jewish culture."[22] In the entry on "The Jews"
for Scribner's *Encyclopedia of American Cultural and Intellectual History*,
Stephen Whitfield posited that, "beginning in the 1960s, American Jews
stared into the abyss of the Holocaust and discerned meaning from that

catastrophe" and began to "memorialize the two out of three European Jews whom the Nazis murdered."[23]

Of the individuals who have disseminated this version of the past, none has equaled Peter Novick and Norman Finkelstein in terms of making it central to their arguments and in the amount of attention and publicity that their works garnered. None has asserted more vigorously the thesis of postwar American Jewish Holocaust avoidance. Finkelstein and Novick, like the American Jewish historians whose work they drew on, contended that American Jews, the leaders and the led, eschewed any kind of confrontation with the Holocaust. Novick's *The Holocaust in American Life*, published in 1999, and Finkelstein's *The Holocaust Industry*, in 2000, painted such a portrait of American Jewry in the postwar years. Too shallow, too compromising, too obsequious, and too eager to curry favor in the great age of anti-Communism to call attention to themselves as people with an agenda different from others, American Jews turned away from the Holocaust and embarked on the good life of suburbia and the 1950s. Even if the Holocaust mattered to them, they effectively silenced any Holocaust talk when facing the public.

The many public discussions that followed in reaction to these two books focused almost exclusively on their negative evaluations of late-twentieth-century American Jewish uses of the Holocaust. Both authors, harsh critics of American Jewry from the left, expressed contempt for contemporary commemorations and invocations of the Holocaust, lambasting the American Jewish community and its leaders for exploiting the Holocaust to a point of making it an obsession, a substitute for anything meaningful. The two contended that invocations of the Holocaust at the end of the twentieth century had little to do with the victims but everything to do with what they saw as the nefarious politics of contemporary American Jewry, particularly its uncritical advocacy of Israel, a state they believed did not deserve American support.[24] These works stimulated heated discussions, in print, at scholarly conferences, and in Jewish communal settings.

Yet none of the participants in the many debates surrounding these books interrogated the validity of their historical assertions, accepting as accurate the statements about postwar American Jews and the Holocaust. After all, that element of Novick's and Finkelstein's arguments seemed just right, dovetailing with the positions articulated by scholars and commentators from within the Jewish world. Novick's and Finkelstein's contentions about the postwar era fit perfectly with the communal myth.[25]

But, to put it quite bluntly, all who have participated in this discussion, from whatever political position, have erred grievously. They have built their arguments on a thin base of evidence, gleaned from few or no sources. Their descriptions hardly reflected the breadth and complexity of postwar American Jewry. Offering sweeping and highly judgmental generalizations about a complicated and divided group of people from a limited number of documents, they created this widely believed but deeply flawed truth. The paradigm of an amnesiac American Jewry during the postwar era had been built on slipshod scholarship that put ideology over evidence.

The errors of these historians served as the initial point of departure for this book, one that offers a very different history of American Jews in the postwar world. How could silence in actuality have dominated the American Jewish scene? What do the documents in the massive archives and mammoth array of books and periodicals on the library shelves have to say about when, where, and how American Jewry, reflecting its many inner divisions, talked about the Holocaust? What words did they articulate, and what deeds did they undertake in the name of Europe's murdered Jews? How did they define appropriate ways to memorialize the tragedy of the six million?

The sources, scattered across the United States and Israel, offered a set of answers that stand in stark contrast to nearly everything that has been written heretofore.[26] In this book, *We Remember with Reverence and Love*, I take my cues from the young camper in 1956 and the thousands—millions, actually—of American Jews, who wrote or read, scripted or watched, performed or participated in the postwar Jewish public sphere, arguing that they wove the catastrophe deeply into the basic fabric of community life and that they considered what they said and did as monuments to Europe's destroyed Jewish world. How they spoke and how they proceeded on their memorial efforts has a history worth telling, and it has to be the correct history.

But I go beyond merely taking to task those historians, literary critics, popular writers, and communal notables who have insisted on portraying a silent and purposefully forgetful American Jewry, which in the years from 1945 through 1962 tried to blot out the memory of the six million. I explore here the ways in which a group of women and men, the Jews of the United States, went about the process of shaping, from the ground up, a memorial culture.

Holocaust commemorations of the postwar era reflected a set of on-the-ground realities that deeply influenced how American Jews constructed their commemorative culture. They had no obvious precedent to guide them as they took first steps toward creating new ceremonies, writing new liturgies, setting aside days of mourning, and orchestrating pageants that confronted the horrendous story of death and destruction, mass murders, gassings, and cremations of millions of Jews. Almost nothing of this sort existed in the general culture that American Jews could adapt for their own uses to mark their catastrophe. They could not look around and see other ethnic communities presenting themselves to the larger society through the narrative of a devastating tragedy, particularly one perpetrated on foreign shores. No minority group in America had yet created a museum, erected a massive monument on public space, organized university courses, or held an annual and highly visible lachrymose commemoration open to all, which focused on the painful events in their pasts. American Jews had to embark on this on their own and with no domestic partners or models.

They also had no recent Jewish examples on which to rely, as they, step by step, experimented with language and genre to figure out which formulations worked best. Centuries had passed since the Jewish prayer book had incorporated the motifs of other cycles of sufferings, other holocausts, with the Crusades providing the last time this had been done. When American Jews in the years following *the* Holocaust, rabbis and religious leaders alike, discussed how to allow for liturgical innovations in memory of the Hitler Holocaust, they reflected that reality. No one could tell them where and how to open the seemingly sealed canon and interject the recent tragedy.

Talk of the tragic fate of the six million cut across the otherwise firm lines of Reform, Orthodox, Reconstuctionist, and Conservative Judaism. Despite fundamental differences about Judaism as a religious system, all made space for the Holocaust in their synagogues, seminaries, and publications. They did so differently, but they nonetheless did so. American Jews disagreed profoundly about Jewish culture and Judaism, and they also sparred among themselves as to what they ought to do as Jews and as Americans as a result of the Holocaust. But they agreed that it had permanently changed them and their worlds. In these years, the details of what had happened and what it meant to American Jews served as a basis for much that took place under the rubric of organized Jewish life.

American Zionists of every variant employed the Holocaust in their organizational works, as did the organizations that made up the building blocks of the American Jewish associational edifice, including the B'nai B'rith, the Jewish War Veterans, the Jewish Labor Committee, the American

Jewish Congress, the National Council of Jewish Women, Hadassah, Pioneer Women, and the American Jewish Committee, not to mention the youth movements, culture clubs, and Jewish community centers. Whether they expressed themselves in English, Yiddish, or Hebrew, they recalled the six million and contemplated the aftermath of the slaughter in ways that fit their identities. Whether in print or in oratory, they incorporated the catastrophe into the fabric of their public lives. American Jews who defined themselves on the political left, as well as those who participated in the Jewish defense, communal, and social service agencies on the local and national levels, all constructed a repertoire of words and deeds that took as their inspiration the calamity of the six million.

American Jews also performed their Jewishness by sending their children to some kind of Jewish school, contributing money to a Jewish philanthropy, or subscribing to a Jewish newspaper or magazine. The years after World War II indeed represented the high-water mark for synagogue membership and Jewish supplementary school enrollment and summer camp attendance. Never before in American Jewish history had such a large percentage joined congregations and exposed their children to some kind of Jewish education. And in those places, the tragic story of European Jewry under the heel of German Nazism reverberated deeply.

American Jews told and retold details of the catastrophe in multiple forms. Over and over, men and women asserted the necessity of revisiting it in their institutions and organs of public opinion, in all its horrors. By virtue of belonging to the people who had been targeted for extinction and as the victims' kin, both literal and metaphoric, they considered it their duty to recite the story of the six million.

Some attempted to construct grand narratives, describing the chronology of events that culminated in the massive slaughter. Most relied on particular aspects of destruction, referring, where they considered it fitting, to "Auschwitz," "Treblinka," and "Maidanek" and to the heroes of the Warsaw Ghetto, the partisans who had fled to fight in the forests, among others. Some believed that telling of the life and liquidation of the Jews in a specific town or city, particularly the one they or their parents had come from, amounted to narrating the tragedy as a whole. Regardless of the sweep, they joined in creating a memorial culture.

By putting words on paper, conveying emotions, facts, and ideas through oratory and sermons, crafting liturgies for synagogues and homes, they constructed a vast unorganized spontaneous project that sought to keep alive the image of Europe's murdered Jews. Some American Jews,

on their own or under the auspices of Jewish institutions, chiseled references to the tragedy onto cemetery markers and emblazoned them onto
the plaques that adorned the walls of Jewish communal buildings. Others turned to music, composing, recording, and performing what would
emerge as a familiar repertoire of works that stood for the Holocaust.
Those able to created dances, dramas, pageants, poems, scholarly works,
and graphic images that took as their subject something about the Jews
who had perished. An even larger number consumed these creations, making the catastrophe organic to American Jewish public culture of the postwar period. This creative output recalled the painful loss.

What American Jews created in the name of the six million slaughtered
Jews of Europe functioned on three interconnected levels. They fashioned
memorials of words, images, and music to keep alive the memory of the
Jews who had perished. By setting aside time to recall the massive number
who had endured such brutal deaths, so recently, American Jews believed
that they fulfilled a deep—indeed, sacred—obligation. They likewise invoked those deaths and the destruction of European Jewish communal life
as a rhetorical weapon in a series of campaigns to affect American politics,
to aid survivors, and to hold the guilty accountable for their crimes. American Jewry also had its collective eye trained on the future as it turned to the
tragic fate of the Jews under the yoke of Nazi rule and conquest to try to
bring about what they considered a better future, be it in matters of American domestic and foreign policy or in their efforts to strengthen Jewish life
and culture. Past, present, and future converged in the projects undertaken
by American Jewry as it referred to and considered the horrendous events
that had engulfed their co-religionists.

The women and men whose words and actions constituted postwar
American Jewish public culture and whose deeds and words serve as the
subject of this book did not consistently use the word "memorial" to describe their commemorative projects. But in all the places and times where
and when they wove the details of what happened to Europe's Jews into
their public works and as they contemplated what that destruction meant
to them, to the Jewish people, and to the world as a whole, in the past, the
present, and the future, they functioned as memorial builders. That word
"memorial" need not have been present in every text, on every page, in every pageant, concert, speech, or artifact, for them to have created a memorial repertoire that put in the foreground the six million murdered Jews of
Europe. They justified their political, communal, and philanthropic works
as a way to recall the six million, and they fashioned their memorials in

light of their concerns for contemporary realities and for the future. This organic blending of pure and simple memorializing and acting in the present in light of the memory of the catastrophe constituted a deep and powerful element in postwar American Jewish public life.

Debates over how to memorialize the Holocaust reflected the inner cleavages and the pluralistic nature of American Jewry. Jewish life got lived out in thousands of local American communities, each made up of multiple institutions, divided by ideology, function, class, language, and length of time in the United States. No national bodies directed "the group," and the utter disorganization of the American Jewish polity, its unwillingness to follow directions from any central agency, provided one of the leitmotifs of American Jewish history. Each organization and institution, each local community, did what it wanted and what its constituents deemed appropriate.

In that anarchic environment, no one opposed recalling the victims of the Holocaust, aiding survivors, and pointing out the evils of the perpetrators. No one disagreed with the basic premise that Jewish communal institutions, schools for young children through the seminaries which trained rabbis, the Jewish press, and the multiplicity of organizations philanthropic, cultural, political, and religious all had a share in remembering the six million and in using their memory to shape the postwar world. They did not converge on a single right way to do it, and, indeed, they bickered among themselves about this very issue. But since they had no authority to tell them how to do so and no central body to coordinate, each did it as it saw fit. They argued as to how, but not if, the slaughter of Europe's Jews ought to be part of their public culture.

In the inner discussions of the boards of their organizations, on school committees, in the sermons from their pulpits and the columns of their periodicals, in their radio broadcasts and television programs, American Jews experimented with various ideas as to the best, most appropriate, and most effective means by which to weave the Holocaust into their lives.

The words and deeds that constituted their memorial project can only be understood within the context of who they were and where they found themselves, as Jews and as Americans. As shareholders in the largest, wealthiest, most unfettered, most politically robust, and most institutionally elaborate Jewish community in the world, organized American Jewry undertook a set of monumental tasks that followed in the wake of the cataclysm. They, and pretty much they alone, raised the money to succor the survivors, starting immediately with the end of the war. They collected funds in the millions to support the liberated Jews in Europe's Displaced Persons camps, those who after 1948 went to Israel, as well as those who immigrated to the United States and those remaining in Europe. Only American Jewry had the resources to support the remnants of European Jewry, and, in the years that the survivors needed assistance, vast sums flowed for these projects. The fundraising juggernaut of American Jewry in the name of the remnant of Europe's Jews, who had outlived the Nazis' slaughter, went hand in hand with remembering, as each appeal for money relied on a rhetorical strategy that told and retold the Holocaust story.

The realities of postwar America also left their mark on how American Jews began the process of memorializing the Holocaust. America of the postwar era would wait for over a decade before the passage of any federal civil rights legislation, and the relatively weak one of 1957 had been the first since Reconstruction. Jews functioned in an environment in which private employers could, and did, refuse to hire Jewish applicants, where realtors could discriminate against Jewish families without fearing legal penalties, and in which private institutions of higher education made no efforts to hide their quotas against Jewish students and rarely hired Jewish faculty. This America admitted immigrants on the basis of national origins, unabashedly preferring white, northern and western Europeans.

The Jews who in the two decades after World War II sought to commemorate the lives and deaths of the six million did so in an America agitated at all levels of public life by an anti-Communist crusade. Some anti-Communists, in their broadsides and speeches, declared that "Jewish" and "Communist" could rightly be considered synonyms. Pamphleteers and orators claimed that the nation needed to protect itself against a Jewish threat to its coherence and viability as a Christian, white bastion.[27]

Postwar conditions exacted a price on all Americans of immigrant origins and their children, who felt compelled to use the public sphere to prove how American they had become and how little their ethnic cultures distinguished them from the national mainstream. In the postwar period, no university offered ethnic studies courses, let alone housed departments dedicated to studying the experiences of particular groups. American education idealized a common culture to which its component parts accommodated and submerged differences.

The liberalism of this America asserted that "Americans all" (the title of one book) should think of themselves as "brothers under the skin" (yet another publication) who, despite being religiously divided into "Catholic, Protestant, Jew" (a third book), had much in common. What differentiated them mattered less than what they shared. The postwar period, in which Jews accounted for about 4 percent of the American population, feared ideologies, particularly from the left, stressing compromise and consensus.

Throughout the period under consideration here, liberalism dominated American Jewish public life. With the exception of the dwindling Jewish far left, Jews subscribed to a political vision that stressed a belief in progress and a commitment to western values, to America, and to the idea that people of good will could together eradicate prejudice and foster a common culture that tolerated difference.

American Jewry's rhetoric and action took as its point of reference the catastrophe of the six million Jews who perished in Europe to reflect these realities. Comfortable in America, but not overly so, American Jews enjoyed the gradual erosion of some, but not all, the barriers that limited their access to American life. They fretted over the places where obstacles remained firmly fixed, yet they carved out political positions that made them different from other white, middle-class Americans, but did so in ways that reflected the powerful influence of the dominant culture. Their engagements with the Holocaust took their shape from those realities.

In the years from the cessation of World War II until the middle of the 1960s, these Jewish and American conditions influenced the ways in which American Jews played with words, phrases, genre, themes, and practices to contemplate the Holocaust and to discuss it among themselves and with their American neighbors. Their massive corpus of rhetoric and action fell into two types.

Some flowed from distinctly Jewish sources. Passover, Yom Kippur, and the Ninth of Av, among other ritual moments of the Jewish calendar, provided set times to invoke the most recent tragedy. Creators of postwar American Jewish works took advantage of the cycle of the Jewish year to recall the Holocaust. Jewish communal institutions also created and sponsored new texts and practices that provided platforms from which to think about the Holocaust. They produced textbooks for Jewish schools; wrote, published, and read memoirs and imaginative literature by survivors; scripted and performed plays in synagogue basements; delivered and listened to sermons; broadcast dramas on Jewish radio shows; fashioned new liturgical works; and restored and then displayed ritual objects salvaged from the destroyed Jewish communities of Europe. They staged and attended public memorial meetings, with the most common, although not the only ones, being those commemorating the 1943 uprising in the

Warsaw Ghetto and its suppression by the Germans. These performances of the Holocaust did not depend on outside events.

But throughout this period, the world intruded on American Jewry, and these intrusions provided a second force stimulating Holocaust performances. A string of events, both large and small, brought up the European tragedy over and over again, reinforcing the evolving commemorative culture of American Jewry. Among these, but hardly limited to them, were the declaration of Israel's independence; the publication of the diary of a young Jewish girl who perished in Bergen-Belsen, Anne Frank; the mass-market appeal of John Hersey's *The Wall*; the show trials and executions of Jewish political and intellectual figures in Czechoslovakia and then the Soviet Union; the finalization of an agreement with the government of the Federal Republic of Germany through the Conference of Jewish Material Claims Against Germany—the Claims Conference—in the early 1950s; the Sinai campaign of 1956; the Hungarian refugee influx to the United States that same year; the outbreak of swastika daubings and Jewish synagogue desecrations in Germany at the end of 1959; the rise of the American Nazi Party under George Lincoln Rockwell; the apprehension, trial, and subsequent execution of Adolf Eichmann; and the worldwide acclaim of "Babi Yar" by the Soviet poet Yevgeny Yevtushenko. All these allowed American Jews to incorporate new references into their telling of the Holocaust story. These events and numerous others in Germany, Israel, the United States, and around the world handed American Jews new particulars around which to commemorate the Holocaust, new pegs on which to hang the Holocaust narrative.

The American Jews who organized gatherings, reported on them in the Jewish press and in the bulletins, magazines, and newsletters of the Jewish organizations, wrote the books, crafted the sermons, arranged the concerts, gave the speeches, and compiled the songbooks, as well as those who consumed these works, took part in a massive, unorganized, and spontaneous memorial enterprise, which had political, cultural, and communal ends in mind. Their texts, projects, programs, and material objects that referred to the Holocaust, as a totality or to some individual part of it, constituted elements in a memorial repertoire.

They did not have a single idea of what constituted a memorial or a monument. Rather, the Jews of the United States produced commemorative works that fit the time and place in which they found themselves. That fit between postwar American Jews and their Holocaust commemorations serves as the central theme of this book. Here I argue that the ways a group of people remembers the past do not just happen: that commemorative cultures, like all elements of culture, evolve, change, and develop with shifting contexts. Far more common and analytically more important than hulking stone structures placed on the landscapes, memorials involve the full repertoire of words and actions that a group of people creates to enshrine something of its past and influence its present and future.

Memorial practices get made over time, and no one, scholars or others, ought to anachronistically expect them to be born whole and in final form. Because the memorial works of the postwar period differed from those of later decades does not mean that they did not exist.[28] The American Jewish women and men whose words and actions appear in the pages that follow developed their repertoire of remembrance out of a sense of obligation to recall the victims, aid the survivors, confront the guilty, and affect a new set of realities in the United States and around the world. As historical actors they deserve to be heard. While what they did and said changed incrementally and haphazardly, they actually laid the foundation for the better organized, bigger, and more elaborately funded Holocaust projects of the last decades of the twentieth century.

Perhaps the very grandeur and force of the Holocaust projects of the later era dwarfed the earlier, disorganized, scattered, and spontaneous ones. The prominence, mammoth funding, and colossal size of the later Holocaust commemorative projects may have done much to cast those of the postwar period into oblivion. Those later memorials also reflected a society and culture forged by the turmoil of the late 1960s and as such had to take a very different shape than those of the postwar period.

Postwar projects and texts can only be understood in their own terms and not in how they measure up to those of other, different times. The American Jews of the period 1945–1962 had no doubt that their words and actions vis-à-vis the European calamity constituted appropriate ways of remembering the one-third of their people who had been liquidated by the Germans. They did not avoid the tragedy, but, rather, as they could, they made their communities places to enshrine it and act on it.

1

Fitting Memorials

IN 1952, THE American Jewish Congress assembled a committee, chaired by author Rufus Learsi, charged with a unique task. Asked to compose a Passover text for both home and public ceremonial use that hallowed the memory of the six million Jewish victims of the Nazi catastrophe, the committee, which within a few years became independent, as the Seder Ritual Committee, did as charged. It produced in three English and Hebrew paragraphs a reading that encapsulated the labors of postwar American Jewry to keep alive the memory of Europe's slaughtered Jews.

The first paragraph of the Seder Ritual of Remembrance intoned that "we," those assembled who had been directed to stand, "remember with reverence and love the six million of our people of the European exile," who had been destroyed by "a tyrant more wicked than the Pharaoh who enslaved our fathers in Egypt." This line fit perfectly with the metahistoric event that brought Jews to their festive seder tables, the yearly gatherings at which Jews recalled the Exodus from Egypt. These recent villains, not the Egyptians, had attempted to "cut them off from being a people" so that "the name of Israel may be remembered no more." The past decade's "evil ones . . . slew the blameless and pure, men and women and little ones, with vapors of poison and burned them with fire." The reading refrained from saying more about the perpetrators, "lest we defame the image of God in which man was created."[1]

The second paragraph of the Seder Ritual of Remembrance marked a specific event, the already famous Warsaw Ghetto uprising. The text declaimed that "on the first day of Passover, the remnants in the Ghetto of Warsaw rose up against the adversary, even as in the days of Judah the Maccabee." These heroes "brought redemption to the name of Israel through all the world."

The third paragraph of the ritual, written "in memory of those who were lovely and pleasant in their lives and in their deaths they were not divided," ended on a hopeful note. In the English, the ritual concluded with a declaration that "from the depths of their affliction the martyrs lifted

Seder Ritual of Remembrance

FOR THE SIX MILLION JEWS WHO PERISHED AT THE HANDS OF THE NAZIS
AND FOR THE HEROES OF THE GHETTO UPRISINGS

Perform this Ritual
after the THIRD *of the Four Ceremonial Cups,*
just before the door is opened
for the symbolic entrance of the Prophet Elijah.

All rise,
and the leader of the Seder recites the following:

בְּלֵיל שִׁמּוּרִים זֶה נַעֲלֶה בְּדְחִילוּ וּרְחִימוּ אֶת זֵכֶר שֵׁשֶׁת מִלְיוֹנֵי אַחֵינוּ
בְּגוֹלַת אֵירוֹפָּה, אֲשֶׁר נִסְפּוּ בִּידֵי עָרִיץ וּמֵזִיד אֲשֶׁר הֵרַע לְעַמֵּנוּ
שֶׁבְּעָתַיִם מִפַּרְעֹה.

וְזֶה דְּבַר הֶעָרִיץ לִשְׁלִיחֵי מְזִמָּתוֹ: לְכוּ וְנַכְחִידֵם מִגּוֹי וְלֹא יִזָּכֵר שֵׁם
יִשְׂרָאֵל עוֹד. וַיַּהַרְגוּ תְמִימִים וּטְהוֹרִים, אֲנָשִׁים נָשִׁים וָטַף, בְּאֵד־יְרַד־עַל
וּבְמִשְׁרְפוֹת־כְּבְשָׁן. וְלֹא נִרְבֶּה לְסַפֵּר בְּרֹעַ מַעַלְלֵיהֶם פֶּן נְחַלֵּל אֶת
צֶלֶם אֱלֹהִים אֲשֶׁר בּוֹ נִבְרָא הָאָדָם.

וּפְלֵטַת עַמֵּנוּ בִּנְוָאוֹת וּבְמַחֲנוֹת־הַהַשְׁמֵד מָסְרוּ נַפְשָׁם עַל קִדּוּשׁ הַשֵׁם,
וְרַבִּים מֵהֶם לָבְשׁוּ רוּחַ גְבוּרָה וַיִּתְקוֹמְמוּ נֶגֶד הָרְשָׁעִים וַיַּפִּילוּ בָהֶם
חֲלָלִים. וּבְלֵיל הַתְּקַדֶּשׁ־חַג הַפֶּסַח קָמוּ שְׂרִידֵי הַגֶּטּוֹ בְּוַרְשָׁה וַיִּלָּחֲמוּ
עִם הַטְּמֵאִים כִּיהוּדָה הַמַּכַּבִּי בְּשַׁעְתּוֹ. הַנֶּאֱהָבִים וְהַנְּעִימִים בְּחַיֵּיהֶם
וּבְמוֹתָם לֹא נִפְרָדוּ וְאֶת כְּבוֹד יִשְׂרָאֵל עַל נֵס הֵרִימוּ.

וּמִמַּעֲמַקִּים פָּתְחוּ הַקְּדוֹשִׁים אֶת פִּיהֶם בְּשִׁירַת אֲנִי מַאֲמִין בְּבִיאַת
הַמָּשִׁיחַ.

All sing ANI MAAMIN (*"I Believe"*),
the song of the martyrs in the ghettos and liquidation camps:

אֲנִי מַאֲמִין בֶּאֱמוּנָה שְׁלֵמָה בְּבִיאַת הַמָּשִׁיחַ:
וְאַף עַל פִּי שֶׁיִּתְמַהְמַהּ, עִם כָּל זֶה אֲנִי מַאֲמִין!

English rendition of the Hebrew:

On this night of the Seder we remember with reverence and love the six millions of our people of the European exile who perished at the hands of a tyrant more wicked than the Pharaoh who enslaved our fathers in Egypt. Come, said he to his minions, let us cut them off from being a people, that the name of Israel may be remembered no more. And they slew the blameless and pure, men and women and little ones, with vapors of poison and burned them with fire. But we abstain from dwelling on the deeds of the evil ones lest we defame the image of God in which man was created.

Now, the remnants of our people who were left in the ghettos and camps of annihilation rose up against the wicked ones for the sanctification of the Name, and slew many of them before they died. On the first day of Passover the remnants in the Ghetto of Warsaw rose up against the adversary, even as in the days of Judah the Maccabee. They were lovely and pleasant in their lives, and in their death they were not divided, and they brought redemption to the name of Israel through all the world.

And from the depths of their affliction the martyrs lifted their voices in a song of faith in the coming of the Messiah, when justice and brotherhood will reign among men.

All sing ANI MAAMIN (*"I Believe"*),
the song of the martyrs in the ghettos and liquidation camps:

I believe with perfect faith in the coming of the Messiah:
And though he tarry, none the less do I believe!

ANI MAAMIN
(*"I Believe"*)

A-ni ma-a-min be-e-mu-no sh'le-mo
B'vi-as ha-mo-shi-aḥ, v'af al pi
She-yis-ma-mey-ha, im kol ze a-ni ma-a-min.

Issued by
SEDER RITUAL COMMITTEE
15 East 84 Street : New York 28, New York

Composed in 1952 by a small committee brought together under the auspices of the American Jewish Congress, the Seder Ritual of Remembrance had broad usage in American Jewish homes, schools, and community settings. The text presented the slaughter of Europe's Jews at the "hands of a tyrant more wicked than the Pharaoh who enslaved our fathers in Egypt" in both deeply Jewish and universal terms, as evinced by the English-language ending which claimed that "the martyrs" wished for a day "when justice and brotherhood would reign among men." Every year, both English-language and Yiddish newspapers carried copies of this text, and Jewish organizations distributed hundreds of thousands of copies to their members. *Courtesy American Jewish Historical Society.*

their voices in a song of faith in the coming of the Messiah, when justice and brotherhood will reign among men." After pondering the meaning of the European Jewish catastrophe, the brief memorial ceremony, whether held in the privacy of one's home or in some public space, drew to a close as participants sang, with the musical notes provided, the words of thirteenth-century Jewish thinker Maimonides, "*Ani Maamin* (*I Believe*), *the song of the martyrs in the ghettos and liquidation camps:* I believe with perfect faith in the coming of the Messiah: And though he tarry, none the less do I believe!"

Deeply rooted in Jewish religious tradition, this reading did not jar with the era's liberal and universalistic ideology. But the reverse also held true. The concluding words, imagining a more perfect world for all coming out of the Holocaust, did not sheer away the deeply specific Jewish idioms, setting, and meaning of their very particular tragedy. While later critics of postwar American Jewry claimed that these women and men eschewed making the Holocaust a uniquely Jewish tragedy, in this text as in the entire output of this era, concern for "all men" did not compromise the use of "we" and "our" as the operative pronouns.

One of many memorials created by postwar American Jewry, this reading's life extended throughout these years. American Jewish newspapers and magazines reprinted the Seder Ritual of Remembrance yearly so that readers could cut it out and have it at hand at their *sedarim.* Jewish organizations and community councils ordered copies of it by the tens of thousands, distributing them to members. Youth groups, synagogues, religious schools, community centers, organizations, and clubs annually included it in their "model seder" or "third seder" events, and without concern for copyright infringements, redactors of *haggadot* reprinted it in their booklets, so that each participant sitting around the holiday table could engage with these charged words. Rabbis and others made use of it at interfaith Passover programs and also on television shows intended to enlighten the general public about Judaism. It existed as a written, spoken, and sung text that traversed the public and the private, the Jewish and the American.

This reading, along with a wide range of other memorial texts, belies the accepted truth, which has posited that the Jews of America until sometime in the 1960s evinced nearly no interest in formally hallowing the memory of the victims of the Holocaust. To historian Jonathan Sarna, "it was Israel's capture of Nazi leader Adolf Eichmann in 1960, his trial in Jerusalem about a year later, and Hannah Arendt's disturbing book on the trial published in 1963" that unleashed American Jewry's memorial efforts.[2] Others have made 1967 the key date. Either way, all accepted with certainty the premise that devoting communal time, energy, and attention on remembering those who perished did not concern the Jews of the United States.

In trying out various ways to institutionalize the memory of the Jewish victims of the Holocaust, American Jews acted on their own. They had no single word that encapsulated the event, no single metaphor that stood for the phenomenon. Rather, they tried out words and images on their own as they made the remembering of the Holocaust a fundamental part of their public Jewish lives. So they employed a range of terms to connote this event. Sharon Feinman had called it "Hitler's dark reign of terror."[3] The composers of the Seder Ritual of Remembrance denoted "the six million of our people of the European exile." Such phrases as "Hitler times," "the catastrophe," "the Great Catastrophe," "the six million," and "the concentration camps" all worked, and American Jews invested little importance in the differences between them. In their publications, the printed programs of their communal events, the curricula of their schools, and their sermons, speeches, and press releases, they used these words, and others, interchangeably.[4]

The program notes, for example, for a concert of Jewish music staged by Chicago's Halevi Society in 1953, identified poet Mordecai Gebirtig, whose lullaby "Yankele" they would perform, as a "victim of the "Crematoria." The International Ladies' Garment Workers Union referred in its newspaper to "the accursed Hitler period," while a 1954 study guide, *What Do You Know About Jewish Religion, History, Ethics and Culture?* delineated Hitler's "ghastly program of extermination."[5]

The word "Holocaust," with or without capital letters, also resonated. In some texts it appeared as the "Hitler Holocaust."[6] The Jewish Museum, New York, in 1949 mounted a retrospective exhibit featuring the work of Abraham Walkowitz, a painter who had depicted the immigrant Jewish milieu of the Lower East Side of the early twentieth century. That world, the museum's brochure noted, of "half a century has passed. . . . These grandchildren [the paintings' subjects] have become grandparents. They have witnessed the Nazi holocaust, which threatened the very existence of the Jews."[7] Nine years later, the same museum informed the press that it would feature the work of artist Anna Walinska at the opening of its twenty-fifth season. The museum mentioned by name in its press release two notable pieces, "The Survivors" and "Holocaust," abstract ink drawings.[8] The 1953 *American Jewish Year Book* described Mark Zborowski and Elizabeth Herzog's 1952 *Life Is with People* as a "monument to a culture that flourished for many centuries, and which was destroyed only a short few years ago in the nazi holocaust."[9]

In Yiddish, journalists, poets, novelists, hosts of radio shows, orators, educators, and survivors who wrote of their suffering and the compilers of memorial books and pedagogical materials did not seize on any single word to trump all others. They invoked variously "Hitler *zeiten*" (Hitler times) or the "hurban" (the destruction, plain and simple), "unzer letzer hurban" (our most recent destruction), "der groisser hurban" (the great destruction), and "der dritter hurban" (the third destruction). They considered the one brought about by the Germans to be as cataclysmic and transformative as the destructions of the First and Second Temples in ancient times, which had altered the essential nature of Judaism. Hebrew writers also employed a number of terms, without pondering the epistemological significance and differences between "hurban," "shoah" (Holocaust), and "sheshet hamillionim" (the six million).

American Jews made the tragedy and the need to remember it a profound part of their collective communal existence, inscribing it in books and performances, in liturgies, and in the programs of their institutions. The leaders of their organizations invoked it as they assembled their meetings and public gatherings. The president of the National Conference of Jewish Communal Service, for example, called the 1955 annual meeting into session by declaring that "on this solemn occasion we call to our memory the millions of our brethren who perished at the hands of the Nazi tyrants only a few years ago," demonstrating how remembering the victims functioned as part of the very fabric of Jewish public life.[10]

As they convened their public meetings, celebrated joyous communal moments, and dedicated their sacred spaces, they made the memory of the six million manifest. At its 1946 convention, the Workmen's Circle asked all to rise as its president declared, "With bowed heads and with awe, we stand before the countless Jewish graves that are scattered over unknown fields in Europe, and before the ashes and the smoke in which millions of our brothers and sisters were destroyed by blood-drenched Nazism."[11] In 1947, the *Forverts*, the largest circulating Yiddish newspaper in America, rented out Madison Square Garden to mark a half-century of publishing. The *Forverts* Association acknowledged the incongruity of "celebrating the jubilee holiday in tragic times, when in our memory the horror . . . of the great Jewish folk tragedy is still fresh."[12] That year, members of Boston's Congregation B'nai Moshe, along with several local rabbis, the dean of Boston College, a Jesuit university, and an area Unitarian minister heard how the "new temple will be a Memorial Shrine," dedicated to America and "to the numerous Synagogues that were burned by the Teutonic Nazi fury."[13] When Label Katz assumed the presidency of B'nai B'rith in 1959, he, too, invoked the memory of the victims. "Our generation," he said, opening his acceptance speech with a paraphrase of Franklin D. Roosevelt, "has had a rendezvous with history. . . . We witnessed the tragic decimation of six million fellow Jews in the Hitler holocaust."[14]

Whenever the opportunity arose, American Jews expressed their obligation and desire to remember the six million. Oscar Handlin, professor of history at Harvard University, Pulitzer Prize winner, did so in his book *Adventures in Freedom* (1954), a key text of the Tercentenary celebrations of Jewish life in North America. "The year we commemorate is 1654," he declared in the introduction to this work commissioned by the American Jewish Committee, "but we cannot forget that the year in which we celebrate is 1954. Nor can we, in the midst of our joy and well-being, blot out the memory of the tragic decade that has just closed. Honesty demands that as we celebrate we have in our minds also the stark facts of our present situation. Jews have not recovered from the shock of the six million victims of the European catastrophe." His declaration that an inextricable connection bound American Jews and their history to the catastrophe, and that American Jews must remember the slaughter, represented the norm of this era, rather than an exception, as the dominant narrative has asserted. Remembering the catastrophe functioned as a profound aspect of their communal identities.[15]

The imperative to remember seemed obvious to them, for its own sake as they tied remembering to fundraising for the survivors, garnering support for Israel, forcing Germany to admit its guilt and offer financial restitution for the property and lives it had robbed, and advancing a particular liberal agenda. They also felt obliged to counter statements made, starting with the immediate end of the war, by individuals in Germany, France, the United States, and elsewhere that the mass murder of the Jews had not taken place, that Jews exaggerated the numbers who had been killed by the Germans, and that Germany had not embarked on a deliberate program of extermination. The phenomenon of denying the historicity of the Holocaust emerged early, and countering the arguments of the "hatemongers . . . [who] claim . . . six million Jews never died in the holocaust" provided an urgency to memorial projects.[16]

For these reasons and for the simple and profound human impulse to remember communal tragedy, the public culture of postwar American

Jews wove their memories into the essence of their public lives. American Jews remembered the victims, as reflected in the sum total of the magazines, newspapers, books of fiction, poetry, and essays, press releases, artistic products, liturgies, political tracts, pedagogic material, and sermons, as well as the publications of organizations—their newsletters, magazines, and fundraising brochures—and the speeches delivered by communal leaders.

Places to Remember

Postwar American Jews experimented with words and images to make manifest the memory of the Jewish victims of Nazi Germany. They did not build a single defining physical memorial, particularly one on public space. Indeed, if the definition of creating a memorial culture depended on unveiling a dominating monument on the cityscape of New York, Washington, D.C., Los Angeles, Chicago, or any other large American city, then they could be said to have not remembered the catastrophe.

But so narrow a definition of memorialization ignores the complex ways that humans, for most of history, have constructed their monuments to the past. It also wipes out the history of projects undertaken by American Jews to enshrine in physical space the memory of the six million. It ignores the numerous efforts, some successful and some not, of American Jews to mark the Holocaust onto the built environment. Indeed, even unsuccessful memorial projects, ones that some individuals labored for but failed to bring to completion, reflected an urge to build, a desire to transform the landscape by means of memorial structure.

The earliest and most notable of these involved the failed campaign in New York City to create an American Memorial to Six Million Jews of Europe, a charge led by Adolph R. Lerner, a refugee from Vienna, who had come to New York in 1938. As vice president of the National Organization of Polish Jews, he envisioned a large statue and eternal flame that would flicker in their memory. In 1947, he secured the help of New York's mayor, William O'Dwyer, and a vast throng, estimated by the *New York Times* at fifteen thousand, came to the cornerstone-laying ceremony at 84th Street and Riverside Drive in October of that year.[17]

The ceremony received extensive coverage in the press—local, national, and international—and it won the hearty endorsement of Jewish and non-Jewish notables. Complete with speeches, memorial prayers, and musical selections, as well as the symbolic burial of "ashes from various Nazi extermination camps," the public event seemed the first public step toward the eventual completion of the memorial structure. The *New York Times* devoted an editorial to the project at the time of the dedication of the cornerstone, declaring that "it is fitting that a memorial to the six million victims of the most tragic mass crime in history, the Nazi genocide of the Jews, should rise in this land of liberty." Fundraising material developed by the committee declared that the memorial would "honor the heroes of the Warsaw Ghetto, who, without outside aid, rose up against the might of the German Army in an epic battle of forty days and nights until nothing remained but ruin and smoke—to reaffirm those ideals of human liberty for which six million Jews sacrificed their lives."[18]

Lerner and his committee carried on their efforts for several years. They solicited design models from the well-known sculptors Eli Jacques Kahn and Jo Davidson, and in 1948 the Jewish Museum exhibited replicas of the proposed memorial. After the New York City Art Commission rejected these proposals, the memorial committee called for a competition and received submissions from William Zorach, Chaim Gross, Percival Goodman, and several other highly respected artists. The Museum of Modern Art staged a one-month exhibition of the plans in early 1950. Of these, the committee chose Goodman's, which involved a sixty-foot stone pylon crowned by a bronze menorah, situated on a plaza of flagstone bordered by a granite wall. Despite the enthusiastic response of the committee and the American Jewish press, which roundly applauded the idea of such a memorial, the Commissioner of Parks, Robert Moses, who had ultimate authority, rejected the plan.[19]

The following year, architect Eric Mendelsohn, a refugee from Nazi Germany, accepted the commission to design the memorial, along with Yugoslavian sculptor Ivan Mestrovic. Their plan resembled the earlier one, with the exception of a massive Ten Commandments replacing Goodman's Hanukkah menorah. The rhetoric justifying the memorial and the promotional material emphasized, as before, the importance of sustaining the memory of "Six Million Jews Martyred and Slain by the Nazis." From the time the committee accepted the new plan until Mendelsohn's death in October 1953, the Jewish press maintained a lively interest in it, and various individuals used radio and television programs to promise the public that the memorial would someday become a reality.[20] For example, several members of the committee appeared in May 1952 on Dumont Television's "Morning Chapel" program to talk about its progress. West Germany's

Chancellor Konrad Adenauer visited the memorial site in April 1953, at the committee's invitation, generating extensive publicity for the project and drawing attention to the German culpability for the tragic fate of the "Six Million Jews Slain by the Nazis."[21]

No structure ever rose above the ground-level cornerstone, as the project languished in the hands of government officials. Nevertheless, the publicity that attended it connected the American public with the Holocaust. The yearly ceremonies, marking the various subsequent anniversaries of the initial dedication, became opportunities when public officials, Jewish notables, foreign dignitaries, and the press confronted the history of the catastrophe. On the first anniversary of the dedication, New York's governor, Thomas E. Dewey, released a message to the press, declaring that the memorial will "remind us . . . and future generations that disregard for freedom and contempt for the dignity of the individual is invariably accompanied by disregard for human life. . . . Let us never forget that the sacrifice of these Jewish victims of the Nazi beast constituted another chapter in man's constant fight for freedom."[22]

The subject of the failure of the memorial project became the stuff of articles in the American Jewish press, of community gatherings, and of rabbinical sermons. In 1953, in a talk on the tenth anniversary of the liquidation of the Warsaw Ghetto, Rabbi Israel Tabak commented on the memorial's absence, telling his congregants that "all attempts that have been made in recent years to establish a fitting monument to the millions of our fellow Jews who have been burned and martyred by the Nazi beasts have ended in failure." That failure, he declaimed, did not reflect lack of interest or commitment, but "nothing so far contemplated has equaled the enormity of the loss; nothing so far proposed could heal the wound or reduce to memory that poignant pain that is still so keen and fresh." Lest American Jews, or at least those who listened to his sermon or read it in its printed form, think that no memorial of note existed, he showed them to be in error: "History . . . has already established that monument; it is nothing less than the State of Israel." History, he orated, "has decreed that for the Jews, a people reborn, Phoenixlike, out of the ashes of the concentration camps . . . only the reconstituted State of Israel can serve as their remembrance."[23]

The lack of progress on the memorial in the mid-1950s did not bring the issue to an end, however. In the early 1960s, the idea of creating a New York memorial entered a second, although no more successful, phase. Then two groups proposed competing memorials. Both groups commissioned

The American Memorial to

Six Million Jews of Europe

cordially invites you

to attend a

Reception

Monday, February 16th, 1953 at 5 p. m.

Hotel Pierre, Grand Ballroom

R. S. V. P.
American Memorial to
Six Million Jews of Europe, Inc.
165 West 46th Street
New York 19, N. Y.
Telephone: CIrcle 6-2880 or PLaza 7-8430

Despite the reality that the American Memorial to Six Million Jews of Europe never got built, the organizing committee held yearly receptions through the 1950s to raise money
and awareness for the project. Led primarily by A. B. Lerner,
the committee included such American non-Jewish notables
as U.S. Supreme Court Justices Hugo Black and William O.
Douglas, Reverend Harry Emerson Fosdick, former governor of New York State Averell Harriman, publisher Henry
Luce, journalist Herbert Bayard Swope, and Congressman
Franklin D. Roosevelt, among others, as well as a wide array
of American Jewish notables. The committee considered it in
its interests to make the story of the Holocaust known to a
wide swathe of Americans and to make them part of the effort to memorialize the catastrophe. *Courtesy YIVO Institute
for Jewish Research.*

sculptor Nathan Rapoport, who had created the epic statuary in Warsaw on the site of the ghetto. One group, the Committtee to Commemorate the Six Million Martyrs, made up heavily of Holocaust survivors, the Warsaw Ghetto Resistance Organization, and backed by three dozen Jewish organizations, battled for money, political clout, and the necessary sanction of the city government. A second, smaller group, the Artur Zygelboim Memorial Committee (named for the Jewish representative to the Polish Council who, out of despair over the millions of Jewish casualties, had committed suicide in May 1943) did the same.[24] The internecine squabbling over who should build the memorial, with its constant sniping, recriminations, and rumors, effectively killed both projects and soured Jewish public opinion on either, or any.[25]

In 1961, as debate smoldered over the question of who should sponsor a New York memorial, Bernard Richards, founder and director of the Jewish Information Bureau, placed an opinion piece in the *New York Times*, proposing that Lincoln Center, the soon to be opened performing arts complex on New York's west side, would make a fitting site for a "Jewish Memorial Library." Here Jews would find the "long-sought means and opportunity of assembling in one place all the records and chronicles, all the books and publications, all the writings in memorial volumes, all the outpourings of human experience that depict and testify to the cataclysmic destruction of European Jewry in World War II." Richards imagined this memorial, which, like the others, never moved beyond planning, as first and foremost "a shrine of reverence and homage to those who lived and died for the faith and honor of their people." With its wealth of books and other documents, it would serve as "a symbol and center that will stir the spirit" and would be a perfect "memorial to the hallowed victims of Hitler's assault on the Jews and on humanity."[26]

The towering statue and emotion-charged commemoration space that never came into being on the banks of the Hudson or the library-as-memorial which might have been prominently housed at Lincoln Center, had they been completed, would have taken their place alongside Holocaust memorials that came into being around the world in this period. The histories of the various Holocaust memorials in other countries, in fact, shed some light on New York's unbuilt ones.

When Bernard Richards came up with his plan, he referred to a global process of creating memorials to the "Hitler holocaust." The American ones would have functioned in that worldwide context. Richards made particular note of how the Jews of France had fulfilled their "high moral

WARSAW GHETTO MEMORIAL

Within the Warsaw Ghetto there was a building where the general staff of the Organization of the Jewish Fighters of the Jewish underground movement prepared in hiding the plans for the Warsaw Ghetto Uprising. This building was destroyed during the uprising, by the Germans. On this very site a monument designed and carved by the famous sculptor Nathan Rapoport was erected and unveiled on April 19, 1948, the very day (erev Pesach five years back when the Warsaw Ghetto rose against what was then the most formidable military power in the world.)

The monument is about 36 feet high. It is fashioned from Swedish granite. The World Jewish Congress Swedish Section was instrumental in getting this Swedish granite for the Monument. Ironically, this block of granite had been kept by Adolf Hitler in a port of Sweden destined to immortalize his expected victory and empire that was to last, he hoped, for at least a thousand years. Delegates from numerous countries attended the solemn unveiling of the Monument. The delegation from Israel brought Israel soil and it was enshrined underneath the Monument.

LEFT: ONE SIDE OF THE EPIC MONUMENT.

    PHOTO CREDIT: ISRAEL TODAY, AN INDEPENDENT FORTNIGHTLY SURVEY FOR AMERICANS, NEW YORK, N. Y.

ABOVE: ON THE OTHER SIDE OF THE MONUMENT IS THE PANEL DEPICTING THE MARCH OF THE VICTIMS.

    PHOTO CREDIT AND CAPTION: WORLD JEWISH CONGRESS, NEW YORK, N. Y.

Details from sculptor Nathan Rapoport's memorial to the Warsaw Ghetto, erected in Warsaw in 1951, graced the pages of American Jewish magazines and appeared in books on Jewish history published in the United States. Absent any other central icon to stand for the catastrophe as a whole, this image loomed large in American Jewish public works. *Furrows* and other Jewish youth magazines used it particularly effectively in their April editions, the month that the uprising had begun and when most American Jewish communities staged memorial events. *Courtesy Habonim Dror North America.*

obligation" by creating an institution not so different from that which he proposed for Lincoln Center. The Centre de Documentation Juive Contemporaine with its connected Tomb of the Unknown Jewish Martyr, dedicated in 1952 and opened in 1956, had been conceived by Isaac Schneersohn, a Polish Jew who relocated to France in 1920. During World War II he lived as a refugee in southern France and founded a research center within the underground resistance movement.

From a distance, American Jewry became a shareholder in the building of the Paris memorial. Starting in the late 1940s, Schneersohn actively and successfully solicited funds for the memorial and the documentation project among American Jews, from the American Jewish Committee and the Anti-Defamation League, in particular.[27] In 1953, he helped form an American Committee for the Friends of the Centre de Documentation Juive Contemporaine, dedicated to erecting "an appropriate monument or monuments to the . . . Martyrs of the Jewish faith," which would "revere and cherish the memory of the martyrs of the Jewish faith who were exterminated by the Nazis and their collaborators before and during the Second World War." He enlisted the support of American rabbis and leaders of communal organizations to reach the larger Jewish public. In 1953, Schneersohn wrote to Rabbi Louis Finkelstein of the Jewish Theological Seminary of America, with the proposition that the Paris Center gather the names of Jews who had been killed by the Nazis and that American synagogues collect from members the names of those who had lost "their dear ones."[28]

American Jewish publications actively tracked the progress of the Parisian project, the physical memorial in particular, detailing the dedication ceremony that established "in the heart of Paris" a "memorial to the six million martyrs of World War II."[29] Although many French Jews believed that their community faced more pressing needs, including the provision of material aid to the survivors and the rebuilding of Jewish communal institutions, the American Jewish press and the donors who gave money to the memorial considered Paris an appropriate place for a memorial in light of postwar Jewish realities.[30]

For one, the climate of public opinion in France gave Jews, both there and abroad, a sense of urgency about reminding the larger society about the tragic fate of French Jewry under German occupation. The Paris memorial and documentation center came into being in a place that had been a site of the Jewish tragedy and where the non-Jewish population played a role in its execution. Many French people had actively collaborated with the Germans in facilitating the extermination of the Jews, and the Vichy regime had expedited the Germans' murderous plans. In the years when the Tomb of the Unknown Jewish Martyr moved from the planning phase to its unveiling, France and French society said and did nothing to admit its own culpability.

Other postwar issues roiled French society, giving a sharp impetus to the memorial project. In the aftermath of the war, a heated controversy flared over the fate of French Jewish orphans there who found themselves in Christian homes and institutions, having been placed there for safekeeping by parents who had gone to their deaths in the camps. Jewish organizations from around the world pressed to have those children returned to Jewish relatives if they could be found or given over to Jewish institutions in the absence of family members. The Christian caregivers generally saw it differently and wanted to keep the children. The French government took the side of the latter, thereby reflecting the general consensus of the majority population. The Catholic Church also adamantly asserted the need for the children, many of whom had been baptized, to remain with the Christians who had opened their homes to these youngsters.[31]

In addition, shortly after the end of World War II, books began to appear in France, categorically denying the fact that six million Jews had been killed and that the Nazi program had involved systematic slaughter. In 1947, Maurice Bardeche published two books, *Letters to Francois Mauriac* and *Nuremberg or the Promised Land*, both contending that "I know that a lie has been put about," that being the lie of the Jewish Holocaust. In 1948, Paul Rassinier published *Le Passage de la Ligne*—crossing the line—a work that sold quite well, in which he commented on the "natural tendency of its victims to exaggerate" and undermined Jewish claims to having suffered so grievously at the hands of the Germans.[32] A memorial space in France thus had place-specific functions to play, ones absent from the American scene.

Other Jewish communities in Europe built Holocaust memorials, all in places where Jewish life had once flourished and then suffered from German brutality. The massive memorial in Warsaw with the prominent statuary of sculptor Nathan Rapoport quickly became an international shrine and something of a pilgrimage destination for Jews, as well as for American public officials. It literally marked the spot where the single largest Jewish city in Europe had flourished, where hundreds of thousands perished, and from which the Germans shipped so many to the gas chambers at Treblinka.

The Warsaw memorial, unveiled in 1948, captured the attention of the American Jewish press. Officials of American Jewish organizations, the American Jewish Committee, the American Jewish Congress, the Synagogue Council of America, and others attended its unveiling ceremony. In 1959, American Jewish publications took special note of Vice President Richard Nixon's visit to the memorial.[33] Photographs of the Rapoport statue graced the covers of Jewish magazines throughout the postwar years.[34] Publications issued by youth movements, such as *Furrows*, the magazine of Habonim, the Labor Zionist youth movement, or *Youth and Nation*, issued by Hashomer Hatzair, another left-wing Zionist youth group, nearly every April printed photographic details of the Warsaw statuary to mark the month's worldwide memorial events commemorating the Warsaw Ghetto uprising. Through frequent reproduction in Jewish magazines and other publications, the statue became iconic to a vast majority of American Jews, most of whom did not make the journey to Poland.

From afar, American Jewry continued to learn about other memorials to the victims of the Holocaust that arose on the ruins of Jewish sacred spaces, destroyed by the Nazis. In 1953, for example, the German city of Bremen rebuilt the Jewish chapel "with," and as, "a memorial for the 915 Bremen Jews murdered by the Nazis."[35] The 1961 dedication of the Sandhausen synagogue in the German province of Baden likewise typified this type of commemoration. The *American Jewish Year Book* actively tracked all such memorial projects and detailed how Jews had once worshipped in these places, and all of these German buildings had then come to a flaming end on Crystal Night, November 1938. By 1961, the Sandhausen synagogue, like many other Jewish places in Europe, had been rededicated in order to remember and recall the "victims of Nazism."[36]

American Jews paid attention to these many memorial efforts and saw them as part of a crucial project to ensure that the six million would not be forgotten. At times, American Jewish groups even tried to involve themselves in memorial efforts in Europe. In 1961, the Jewish Labor Committee wrote to the Department of Defense, urging Secretary Robert McNamara to "erect directional signs to the Dachau Concentration Camp Museum in Germany." Noting that visitors eager to see the former camp encountered difficulty getting there, the committee stated, "it would seem to us that the memory of those who died within the walls of Dachau would be better remembered if efforts were made by the United States Army to have proper directional markers within the army base itself and certainly on the outside." The Jewish Labor Committee officials stressed the need for making the memorial site accessible in order to engage with the "memory of those who died." Beyond that, the Dachau memorial served, as they saw it, a crucial political function. "There are many people within Germany," Adolph Held and Benjamin Tabachinsky pointed out, "and unfortunately in our own country who would like to forget that a Dachau existed. . . . Certainly the United States Army is the one force that can and should never let them forget it."[37]

These Holocaust memorials shared certain key characteristics setting them apart from any one that might have, or did, arise in the United States. All involved places where the destruction of Jewish life had taken place and in the war's aftermath had to be rebuilt, often from the ground up. This fundamental difference between America and Europe impressed American Jewry. It saw the creation of memorials in Europe as having greater salience than seeing them on the soil of the United States. Indeed, in 1947 while the New York planners began their doomed activities for a memorial on the Hudson, the Synagogue Council of America (SCA), a coordinating body of rabbis of the three American denominations, which supported the idea of an American memorial, noted that it considered it more urgent that "a monument be erected somewhere in Europe to all those for whom there is no identifiable grave, an idea which parallels that of the grave of the unknown soldier in both the first and second world wars."[38]

By not bringing to completion a monumental memorial in the United States, the Jews of America behaved like Jews all over the world, outside of Europe. No colossal statues or markers on public space went up in London, Toronto, Montreal, Johannesburg, Buenos Aires, or Melbourne, cities with substantial, free, and affluent Jewish populations. Like New York, none of these had been places where the Germans had marched in and destroyed Jews and Jewish communities. Similarly, unlike Amsterdam, Berlin, Florence, Warsaw, Budapest, and Paris, where memorials of various sizes got built, no non-European Jewish communities needed to be rebuilt, nor did any require that the new communal structures be linked to the destroyed past by a monument and a tearful plaque listing the names of those who had once lived there, used these spaces, and then, like the buildings themselves, were obliterated.

Yad Vashem in Jerusalem provided the one exception to the European locus of postwar memorial building. Its history sheds light on postwar American Jewry and its commitment to remembering the victims of the Nazi destruction. Plans for the memorial began in London at the tail end of the war, when the National Council of the Jews of Palestine set up the

Remembrance Authority, charged with creating a memorial institution, to be situated in Jerusalem. Committed to collecting the basic documents on the catastrophe of "the six million members of the Jewish people who died a martyrs' death at the hands of the Nazis and their collaborators," collecting their names, setting up an archive, stimulating scholarly research, staging exhibitions, and to be a memorial shrine, Yad Vashem dominated, or wanted to do so, the global process of remembering the Holocaust and its victims. Yad Vashem operated consistently with a firm and simple principle: to control all memorial activities, which emanated from the Jewish national center in Israel. Other Jewish memorial projects had to subordinate to it, and memorial planners had to defer to Jerusalem. It and it alone could determine who could speak for the memory of the victims.

Yad Vashem assiduously solicited money in the United States. As early as 1947, Yad Vashem communicated through the World Jewish Congress and its Palestine director, Arieh Tartakower, to the head of the New York office, Kalman Stein, a statement of principle that held for the entire postwar period, putting it quite bluntly: "the lion's part of the necessary funds will have to be raised" in the United States. Yad Vashem turned to the American Jewish press to make its case to the Jewish public, making it clear that, by supporting Yad Vashem, the Jews of the United States would fulfill their "important national duty."[39]

Yad Vashem's message linked the Jerusalem memorial and the Zionist enterprise. Yad Vashem repeatedly told American Jewry that "it is of common Jewish interest to concentrate" memorial activity, which included both the collecting of documents and the raising of a physical memorial, "to the martyrdom and heroism of our people in Palestine. Here it will be preserved as evidence of the events of those gravely important years."[40]

Yad Vashem officials insisted that American Jews not build any memorials of their own in the United States. From Jerusalem, they tracked the American Jewish press (in English, Yiddish, and German) and paid close attention to any hints of unwanted memorial activity. After reading about the proposed New York memorial slated for Riverside Drive, Yad Vashem staff members at a meeting agreed that the New York effort "will harm" the more important Jerusalem memorial site. "America," all at the meeting agreed, "is not the place where it is needed to put up such a memorial."[41]

This line of reasoning did not remain confined to the secret minutes of board meetings. In a stream of missives to American Jews, particularly to the heads of organizations, Yad Vashem stated its position in a direct and uncomplicated manner. To Joseph Tenenbaum, president of the American

Federation of Polish Jews, Tartakower referred to the plans for the New York memorial as evidence of "new trouble." He confronted that trouble, stating, "I am informed that a few persons started a drive in USA to have a monument erected there in commemoration of victims of Nazism in Europe and that a financial campaign for this purpose will be proclaimed or was already proclaimed in your country. This is clearly harmful overlapping of the work which is being done by Yad Vashem." Another time a Yad Vashem functionary stated bluntly, there "can only be one monumental project," and that meant the one in Israel. Similarly, Yad Vashem instructed the president of the Federation of Bessarabian Jews in the United States that he and his organization should undertake no memorial activities until receiving instructions from Israel. He, Moshe Shifriss, reported his willingness to go along with this, quoting verbatim from Yad Vashem, that "the land of Israel is the only and right place where such a significant monument should stand."[42]

The remembrance agency in Jerusalem reacted quickly and forcefully to efforts to construct even small, relatively unobtrusive Holocaust memorials in America. In 1946, the *Aufbau*, a New York newspaper launched by German Jewish refugees in the United States, announced that the New World Club, one of the organizations to which many of its readers belonged, had hoped to construct a memorial to the martyrs of Europe in Cedar Park, New Jersey—not exactly a place that would compete with Jerusalem. But Yad Vashem reacted anyhow. "I do not intend to restart discussion about Memorial Monuments nor do I want to deal with the merits of the plan," the letter stated, addressed to *Aufbau* editor Max Grünewald, but the American plan as described in the newspaper "will greatly interfere with the realization of the Palestinian institution."[43] Similarly, in 1946, when word came to Jerusalem that the Association of Yugoslav Jews in the United States wanted to erect a monument to their compatriots who perished at the hands of the Nazis, Yad Vashem stepped forward. We "must remind you," they wrote, that "there exists a special institution, on whose stationery the present letter is written and which was established in order to commemorate all Jewish victims of Nazism." Yad Vashem reminded the erstwhile memorial builders in the United States that "it is the duty of Yugoslav Jewry to join" in recognizing the sole right of Yad Vashem to memorialize the six million, or any subset of them.[44]

Yad Vashem's stance reflected its desire to make the "homeland" in Israel the center of world Jewish culture and to link the new state's legitimacy to the legacy of the Holocaust. "You will certainly agree," wrote a Yad

Vashem staff member to the Jewish Welfare Board in New York, on the eve
of Israeli statehood, that "it is of common Jewish interest to concentrate all
the material pertaining to this subject in one place, which is Eretz [the land
of] Israel."[45]

For the most part, American Jewish organizations and individuals deferred to Yad Vashem, buying into its argument that its activities constituted "holy work," echoing Moshe Shifriss of the Federation of Bessarabian Jews, and that scattered and decentralized memorial projects would
not serve the larger Jewish purpose, which at that point pivoted so closely
around Israel.[46] To what degree did American Jewry feel a sense of "survivor guilt," and to what degree did it agree with Yad Vashem's premise that
the Jewish state would, and did, function as the legatee of the destroyed
centers of Jewish life in Europe? The fact that most of the large memorial
projects never came about may indeed bear witness to the effectiveness of
Yad Vashem's rhetoric and the fact that it articulated a position that the
Jews of America themselves agreed with.

Though the grand, national monument never arose in America, the
desire to memorialize in physical space did not go unfulfilled. Instead,
American Jewry went about scattering small monuments in communities
around the country. Nearly all of the physical markers that American Jews
dedicated to the memory of the victims of the Holocaust went up in synagogues, the headquarters of Jewish institutions, and Jewish cemeteries. In
1953, for example, the Mizrachi Organization, religious Zionists, commissioned "the creation of a special memorial marker carved in marble from
the State of Israel to commemorate the death of six million Jews during
World War II," for its New York headquarters to celebrate the group's fiftieth anniversary.[47] The Associated Jewish Charities of Baltimore, Maryland, erected a "Memorial to the Six Million" paid for by the New Americans Club, in the Harry Greenstein Social Service Building, and the Akron,
Ohio, branch of the Workmen's Circle dedicated its "impressive monument
to the memory of the six million Jews martyred under Hitlerism," in the
building it occupied.[48] In 1955, when the Jewish Community Center in
Milwaukee opened its doors to the public, it included a room with a plaque
affixed to the wall, "in memory of all the relatives and intimate friends" of
the members of the New Home Club "who had become victims of Nazi
tyranny," the New Home Club being an organization of German Jews who
had fled from Hitler's Germany.[49]

Synagogues across the country also became sites for Holocaust memorial spaces. Congregation B'nai Israel in Millburn, New Jersey, made room

for a "memorial niche," consisting of two "white marble cornerstones from two synagogues destroyed by the Nazis in Mannheim, Germany." The stones carried an inscription: "To the heroes and martyrs, to the known and the unknown who died for the sanctification of the name," on one side, and, on the other, the names of destroyed German synagogues: "Hauptsynagoge, Mannheim" and "Klaussynagoge, Mannheim."[50] Har Zion Congregation in Philadelphia commissioned Louise Kayser and her husband to design a set of stained glass windows in the early 1950s. Kayser, who had fled to the United States from German-occupied Czechoslovakia, described her work in 1959 as inspired by the "memory of my departed sister, put into the gas chamber by the Nazis." She saw the windows—one of which stated simply "Auschwitz"—as "a tribute to the East-European communities, hundreds of years old, which were annihilated in our day." The Nazis, who had set out to "extinguish the vitality of Jewish life," had nearly succeeded since "six million Jews (60 percent of the total) had been wiped out." The windows in the Philadelphia synagogue would help, she believed, to recall all that had been so brutally destroyed.[51]

The availability of relics or artifacts from Jewish communities destroyed by the Nazis facilitated the construction of memorial spaces within American synagogues. The Synagogue Council of America had been asked by the Commission on European Jewish Cultural Reconstruction, headed by Columbia University professor Salo Baron, to take possession of thousands of Jewish ritual objects uncovered by the U.S. Army; restore these religious artifacts, if possible, for future use; and then distribute them to synagogues around the country. The Committee on Religious Objects began its work in 1950 and made available to congregations Torah scrolls, Torah covers, silver breast plates, and pointers used for the reading of the Torah, as well as Hanukkah candelabra, ritual wine goblets, and the like, all salvaged from destroyed European Jewish communities. The Synagogue Council launched a widespread informational effort, informing congregations about the availability of these objects, and many synagogues, if they had the space, set aside museum-like nooks to house these doubly sacred objects and to tell the story of the destruction of Jewish life in Europe.[52]

The displayed ritual objects functioned as small memorials, as did the spaces synagogues marked off to exhibit them. The Synagogue Council considered this kind of presentation to be a priority and suggested to congregational rabbis and chaplains serving Hillel houses on various university campuses that whoever accepted the scrolls or silver works became "the recipients of a legacy from the six millions of our people, the victims of a hate system."[53] As of 1952, over one hundred Torah scrolls had been "looked over" by experts. Thus, in a flurry of letters between the council and rabbis around the country, the process began by which the sacred objects made their way to congregations who would assign to them special places of honor.[54]

The Synagogue Council saw the salvage and distribution of the objects as more than a way to help congregations, in this era of tremendous institutional growth, acquire their Torah scrolls and other religious goods. It understood that by using these relics from the destroyed Jewish communities of Europe, American Jews would forge a bond with the past and would have a tangible way to memorialize the six million Jews of Europe. The council made this distribution of "holy vessels . . . rescued from the destroyed communities of Europe" a cornerstone of its work in the early 1950s and issued press releases to American and American Jewish newspapers about this kind of memorialization. It encouraged the congregations who accepted the Torah scrolls to hold dedicatory events at which the story behind the Torah—where it had come from and what had happened to the Jews who had once used it—become part of the consecration ritual and to commission plaques to be placed near the items to tell their story.[55]

Council officials encouraged synagogues to invite the local press (by definition, non-Jewish) to cover the various steps in the journey, to report as the Torah scrolls arrived by train from New York to the city, as congregational leaders received them, and as they were ceremonially dedicated. Rabbi Sanford Rosen of Temple Beth El in Bakersfield, California, negotiated for his synagogue some pieces of silver Torah regalia, and he reported back to the New York office that "the local newspaper has been giving exciting publicity to this forthcoming event. In tomorrow's edition they are running a feature story on it with photographs of the items mounted on the scrolls and being held by myself and officers of the congregation."[56] The *Newark Evening News* ran a story about the dedication ceremony of the Torah scrolls at the Wainwright Street Synagogue at which Rabbi Mordechai Ehrenkrants spoke about the Torah as a token of "memory of 6,000,000."[57]

Not to be forgotten after the dedication, the council wanted the objects to be prominently displayed as physical reminders of the Holocaust and to live on in the congregations as memorials. As Jewish institutions put in their requests for scrolls, they promised that, in fact, they would show them off. Members of the Religious Committee at the Hillel, which served Radcliffe College and Harvard University, made a particular case why it should receive a number of available items for simultaneous ritual and exhibition purposes, reporting that "an average of 400 to 500 persons visit Hillel House each week. Some of our visitors are non-Jews, many of them persons of note."[58] Those visitors, including the dean of Harvard College and a professor of the Divinity School, would as such have a chance to confront a memorial to the Holocaust through a salvaged religious object. This memorial effort served then a number of purposes. Though undertaken by a Jewish religious institution, the objects' memorial project meshed the serving of both Jewish and general ends. Housed in Jewish spaces and intended for Jewish ritual use, the memorial scrolls and other religious items played a role in American Jewry's effort to include the larger American public into its memorialization of the Holocaust.

Through the creation of memorial spaces, with or without salvage relics from the destroyed Jewish communities of Europe, synagogues in America blended memorialization of the Holocaust with the public practice of Judaism. However prominently they did so, they could not compete with Jewish cemeteries as the preeminent American locus for postwar Holocaust commemorations. In turning to cemeteries as venues to remember the victims of the Nazi onslaught, American Jews acted like Jews in the other countries that also had not suffered the ravages of the Nazi atrocities but wanted to set aside space to enshrine the memory of the six million. Throughout Latin America—in Chile, Brazil, Peru, Argentina, and Mexico, for example—Jews from the late 1940s through the 1960s consecrated markers and memorials "in memory of the Jewish . . . martyrs" in their cemeteries.[59]

In the United States *landsmanshaftn*, the hometown societies representing, particularly, the Polish cities, towns, and regions from which Jews had come to the United States in the late nineteenth and early twentieth centuries, provided the leadership in creating these cemetery-based Holocaust memorials. These men (these organizations by and large limited their membership to men) had come to the United States well before the devastations of the Nazi era, leaving behind family and friends. In the aftermath of the destruction, they wanted to hallow the memory of those who perished by erecting monuments in cemeteries, in the plots they maintained. The minutes of dozens of these *landsmanshaftn* detailed the efforts that went into raising the funds, designing the marker, arranging the unveiling ceremony, and then, every year, returning to the cemetery for a memorial event, usually scheduled to coincide with the day when the Germans had entered the town or when the final liquidation of the Jews had taken place.

The Busker Society in New York, a *landsmanshaft*, like many in America and around the world, started in the late 1940s to consecrate cemetery markers to recall those who perished "under the rule of the Nazi hordes." Placed in the Busker Society's section of the cemetery, the marker invoked the "God of Vengeance" in Hebrew and denounced "the most evil of the nations" responsible for "the spilling of blood." Burial benefits constituted one of the prime reasons for membership in a *landsmanshaft*, and this Holocaust marker stood in a central space among the Busker graves. A visit to the cemetery brought friends and family in constant contact with this reminder of the destruction of this town in the Tanopol region of Poland. *Courtesy YIVO Institute for Jewish Research.*

The memorials ranged from large to small, from those with only Hebrew text to those that also chiseled Yiddish and English into the stones. Some contained ashes brought to the United States from the crematoria, or, like the memorial erected by the First Zbarazer Relief Society at Beth David Cemetery in Elmont, New York, in 1947, included a bar of soap, which they believed had been made from human fat.[60] Those that represented smaller communities listed the names of all the Jews of the town who went to their deaths during the Holocaust. Others invoked not only their own beloved townspeople but also the six million as a totality. Some *landsmanshaftn* adorned their markers with graphic images, such as Stars of David, Eternal Lamps, Ten Commandments, and trees cut at the stump, while others relied on extensive text that provided the basic information as to the date and the manner of the devastating deaths. The words, in whatever language, all told the same story. "In holy memory of the ripped apart Grodner community," "For eternal memory shall be the holy martyrs, from the town of Drohobycz-Boryslaw who were killed, burned and slaughtered for the Sanctification of the Name of God at the hands of the Nazis, May the Almighty Avenge their Blood," and "In Eternal Memory of the Holy who fell at the hands of the Nazi Murders"—these typified the inscriptions on the dozens of markers that went up in the New York area alone.

These cemetery Holocaust memorials reverberated in the consciousness of ordinary American Jews, if they belonged to the *landsmanshaft* or not. Every time they went to the cemetery to bury a loved one, if they looked for it or not, they would have confronted a pylon like the one that read "The gate of this cemetery is dedicated to the memory of the holy martyrs from the town of Nova Ushitz who gave up their lives for the Sanctification of God's Name at the hands of the foul Nazis and may death disappear forever and may all who slumber in the dust awake." A trip to visit the graves of parents, a widely observed Jewish practice, on or near the anniversary of their deaths and in the month before the Jewish new year, Rosh Hashanah, meant an encounter with a stone such as the one that read "This monument is witness to the terrifying destruction, the handiwork of the wildly wicked and the satanic brutality of the Nazis and those that helped them." While these spaces lacked the public prominence of a city center, they existed at the heart of lived Jewish life.[61]

One particular cemetery event deserves special attention as a way of charting postwar American Jewish memorialization of the Holocaust. The Synagogue Council, which had arranged for the salvage and distribution of the ritual objects, realized that not all the scrolls could be restored for use. Some had been damaged beyond repair, and Jewish law stipulated that these once holy items had to be buried in the same manner as if they had been human beings.

In January 1952, the Synagogue Council of America held a public burial for a group of scrolls and "several thousand . . . ceremonial objects of silver, bronze, brass, copper, embroidered cloth," which could not be rendered acceptable or "kosher" for synagogue use. In a highly publicized ceremony at the Beth El Cemetery in Paramus, New Jersey, the SCA interred the "religious treasures looted by the Nazis," and a year later, on December 16, 1952, in a ceremony covered on radio and television, it unveiled a monument to "the Desecrated Torahs." Rabbis and cantors representing Polish, German, and Balkan Jewry, standard bearers of Jewish communities that had endured such tremendous losses, participated in the event. They spoke about their dead and intoned ritual prayers in memory of the six million, testifying to "the maniacal attempts made by the Germans to destroy the Jewish spirit."[62]

American Jews also participated in several global memorial projects. Two involved planting forests in Israel in the name of the victims. In the late 1940s, simultaneous with the development of Yad Vashem, the Jewish National Fund announced the planting of a Martyr's Forest in the Jerusalem hills, to be covered with six million trees. From its New York office, the Jewish National Fund enlisted American Jews through schools, synagogues, and organizations in this endeavor of remembering with trees "the six million Jews who perished in Europe."[63]

American Jewish organizations reacted enthusiastically, incorporating the tree sales into their organizational activities, articulating an organic and urgent connection between the planting of the Martyr's Forest, with its symbolic six million trees, the fact that the forest would be part of the Jewish reclamation of land in Israel, and the imperative that American Jews be part of the project. Collecting money in America to symbolically plant the six million trees tightened the rhetorical bond between politics—support of Israel—and the memory of the Holocaust. The *Jewish Spectator* editorialized about the linkage between the forest and the duty to remember. In support of the Martyr's Forest, the magazine's editor Trude Weiss-Rosmarin wrote in 1951, "If the doors of the Jewish homeland had been opened when the Nazis were engaged in the mass murder of the Jews of Europe, there would have been no need for the Martyr's Forest."[64] Those who contributed money received special certificates, which they could frame and hang on the walls of their homes and institutions. The certificate thanked the donor for having helped "establish a living monument to the 6,000,000 martyrs" in "a green shrine in which shall forever dwell the spirits of those who perished in the concentration camps and crematoria of Nazi Europe."[65]

Collecting money for the Martyr's Forest allowed American Jewry to participate in a worldwide memorial endeavor. The agencies and institutions of the community rallied members, along with all diaspora Jewry, to raise funds. American Jewish schoolchildren contributed their share for a special grove, a "Forest to the Unknown Child," set aside "in memory of one million Jewish children who perished in Europe." Educators urged American Jewish children to give from their allowance money and to ask others to do so as well, making them, along with the adults, facilitators of the Jerusalem project.[66]

A second linking of planting trees in Israel in the name of the victims also underscored how the memory of the six million sustained the ongoing activities of American Jewish communal groups. The B'nai B'rith, the oldest and most global of Jewish organizations, had had active lodges in Germany, Austria, Czechoslovakia, and elsewhere in central and even eastern Europe. It estimated that over one hundred thousand of its members had vanished in the cataclysm, and as early as 1947, over the objections of Yad Vashem, it conceived of the idea of dedicating a special forest to them.[67]

The organization initiated its fundraising drive among members in 1953, communicated around the country through its magazine and in a steady stream of material from the national office to regional, state, local, and individual lodges. Lodges formed special "Martyr's Forest Committees," each devising fundraising strategies and issuing certificates to donors, making remembering the victims an activity of the organization.[68]

The B'nai B'rith, like most of American Jewry, articulated an uncomplicated relationship between the Holocaust, itself, and Israel. "It is," wrote the organization's president, Philip Klutznick, in the *National Jewish Monthly*, "a memorial to our brothers and sisters in Europe who died in the great cataclysms of the Thirties and Forties; it is of material assistance to the people of Israel. . . . it is the expression of the special position the soil of Israel holds in our heart."[69]

Successful in its project, the organization dedicated the B'nai B'rith Martyrs Forest Memorial Shrine in May 1959. B'nai B'rith saw memorialization of its slain members as part of the larger imperative to keep in mind all the victims of the Holocaust, and to do so in Israel. "High on the hills of

Judea stands the "Martyr's Forest," declaimed the brochure describing the ceremony, "an evergreen memorial for the six million of our brothers and sisters who died *al Kiddush Hashem*." This forest could not and should not have been anyplace else: "Its trees . . . combat soil erosion, give employment to new immigrants and will . . . restore fertility to the land. On the approaches to the Holy City, this woodland bears witness to Jewish suffering and at the same time, symbolizes Israel's immortality."[70]

All of these memorials, whether in the United States or if supported by American Jewry but located elsewhere, challenge the dominant paradigm, which declares so emphatically that memorializing the Holocaust did not have a place on its communal agenda. In fact, the opposite constituted the reality. The Jews of the United States in the postwar era saw themselves as architects of a memorial culture, one that reflected the realities of the world they inhabited.

Memorials Beyond Space

American Jews did not limit themselves to consecrating the memory of the Jewish victims of the Nazis with buildings and physical markers. Rather, they undertook various projects that they deemed fitting memorials to the Holocaust. Sometimes this involved something as prosaic as making a financial contribution to a communal endeavor in the name of the victims. In 1956, for example, the New Home Club of Milwaukee raised $250.00 for the city's Jewish Welfare Fund, "in remembrance of all our loved ones who did not survive the holocaust of Nazi tyranny."[71] In May 1959, Chicago's Halevi Society performed at a local synagogue, and it declared in the program notes that its performance of Mordecai Gebirtig's song "Ess Brent" [It is burning] was "Dedicated to the martyred six million."[72] The gift, the musical offering, and countless scattered and spontaneous articulations of this trope demonstrated how postwar American Jewish communal life, pivoting around the narrative of Jewish suffering during the Holocaust era, permeated communal activities.

American Jews earmarked books as memorials as well, including volumes that had little or no direct connection to the catastrophe itself. Meyer Levin translated into English a collection of stories by the Yiddish author Sholem Asch in 1948. Published by G. P. Putnam, Asch in a Yiddish introduction and Levin in English "offered" the book "in commemoration of Polish Jews who were exterminated together with other Jews of Europe under Hitler's program."[73] In 1954, Irving Howe and Eliezer Greenberg edited a collection of Yiddish short stories. The anthology, published by Viking Press, began with the simple words, "Dedication: To the Six Million."[74] The year before, Emil Long offered a history of two millennia of anti-Semitism. He opened his book with his dedication, "To the memory of the six million martyred Jews, to their surviving relatives scattered across the world and to the sympathetic public."[75] Weighing in at 922 pages, Dagobert Runes's 1951 *The Hebrew Impact on Western Civilization* opened with a black-bordered box with the words, "To the sainted memory of the six million children of Israel who were put to the axe by the German nation because they were of the same blood as Jesus Christ."[76]

Sometimes the dedications told personal stories. Hayyim Schauss dedicated his 1962 *The Lifetime of a Jew*, a guide to Jewish life cycle events, "To the Memory of My Brother and Two Sisters and the Members of their Families Who Were Murdered by the Germans."[77] Rachel Wischnitzer consecrated her history of American synagogue architecture to "The memory of my father Wladimir Bernstein taken away from Paris on May 20, 1944,"[78] and Malka Lee, a Yiddish poet who had spent the war years in New York, inscribed her 1955 volume of verse, *Durkh kindershe oygen* [Through a child's eyes], to the memory of her family killed by the Nazis.[79]

Authors of yet another, large corpus of works, either survivors themselves or individuals documenting the carnage, made the point that by writing about the Holocaust they memorialized it. A group of survivors and others who had left Poland before the Nazi invasion put together a book to remember the teachers who had inspired them as youngsters. They opened their book with the dedicatory words, "In the ovens of the German concentration camps, in the Ghetto-camps from hunger, nearly all the teachers of the Jewish schools perished. Who knows if we will ever have the ability to tell about each one alone? Not just to list their names in a black list but to tell something about each and every one of them. Let this book be their collective monument."[80] Jacob Sloan published a 1958 English edition of the secret journal of Emmanuel Ringelblum, compiled in the Ghetto of Warsaw by the Polish Jewish historian who met his death there. Sloan claimed that the Ringleblum material convinced him that the Jewish experience in the Warsaw Ghetto constituted the "most important event of his generation," and in the book's dedication he declared that "to millions of people the Warsaw Ghetto will remain forever a symbol of man's inhumanity to man—and of the heroic resistance of the human spirit."[81] Finally, Koppel Pinson, a professor of German history at New York City's Queens

College and a Jewish communal activist, edited a group of essays by Simon Dubnow, Jewish historian and philosopher, murdered by the Nazis in 1941 in the Riga ghetto. Pinson dedicated his book "To the Memory of the Sainted Jewish Scholars who met their death at the Hands of the Nazis."[82]

For some books, the Holocaust existed as a kind of penumbra, shading and surrounding texts on other subjects, related certainly but not explicitly. Abraham Joshua Heschel's published lecture, "The Earth Is the Lord's," had been delivered in 1947 at the YIVO Institute for Jewish Research, which had been housed in Vilna until 1940. Only in the preface did the theologian who had come to the United States from Poland that same year refer to the catastrophe. "The story about the life of the Jews in Eastern Europe which has come to an end in our days is what I have tried to tell in this essay," he noted at the opening of the text. But Jewish readers and reviewers understood his words as a memorial to the six million.[83] Ludwig Lewisohn considered "The Earth Is The Lord's" "a great and poignant prose elegy on our martyrs—a commemoration, a monument, a prose *piyut* [liturgical poem]. It is . . . a humble yet unshaken reassertion of the nobility of our estate, despite our suffering and anguish."[84] So, too, Herman Kieval, reviewing "The Earth Is the Lord's" for *Conservative Judaism,* declared the book as evidence that "when the six million were destroyed," the Jewish people lost more than numbers. They lost a culture, a way of life. Their learning, their piety, their humanity, Kieval wrote: "This is the legacy they left along with their ashes."[85]

Excerpts from Heschel's elegy showed up as the introductory text of the 1947 collection of photographs published by Schocken Books, Roman Vishniac's *Polish Jews: A Pictorial Record.* As in the case of "The Earth Is the Lord's," the original work had no connection with the Holocaust. After all, the photographer had taken his images before the Nazi invasion of Poland. But the publisher, in a prefatory note, linked the photographs to the Holocaust, informing readers that the book needed to be seen as a visual record of a people, "only a year distant from catastrophe."[86] Reviews in Jewish publications saw the photographs and the words as memorials to "a community that no longer exists." The pictures "tell most effectively the story of a life so characteristically Jewish but now, alas, completely gone."[87]

Of all the books whose authors conceived of them as memorials to the victims of the Holocaust, and which commentators saw as such, none could equal the output and significance of *yizker bikher,* literally memorial books, mostly of Polish communities, which began to appear immediately at the end of the war and continued well beyond the 1960s.[88]

The *landsmanshaft,* or hometown society of Kolomey, like dozens of others, is-sued a memorial book as a way to enshrine their remembrances of their murdered friends and families. Kolomey enlisted the artist Chaim Gross to draw this cover for its 1957 *yizkor* book, which explored "the history, memories, characters, and destruction" of their former home. The image of the destroyed city in the center surrounded by the faces in flames made the Holocaust context of the book mani-fest. *Courtesy Renee and Chaim Gross Foundation.*

Published around the world, in Paris, Buenos Aires, Montreal, Tel Aviv, Johannesburg, Munich, and, of course, New York, these memorial books had some precedent in Jewish history. The chronicles of Jewish suffering during the Crusades provided one historical forebear, as did Natan Nata Hanover's *Yeven Metzulah,* a compilation of eyewitness accounts of the mid-seventeenth-century massacres of Jews in Poland.[89] The pogroms that ravaged the Jews of the Ukraine after World War I inspired a number of martyrological writings as well, producing books describing the carnage and naming the victims and perpetrators.

But the Holocaust *yizker bikher* differed from these earlier chronicles of Jewish suffering and pain in ways that fit the circumstances under which they came into being. They had multiple authors. The hundreds of such books that appeared between the end of the war and early the 1960s emerged from committees of survivors, as well as those women and men who hailed from these towns but had left years before.[90]

Unlike the earlier memorial books, the Holocaust-era ones typically took shape as the official projects of organizations. The writing of the books consumed much of the energy of the *landsmanshaftn,* which contacted possible contributors around the world, encouraging them to write down their memories. They tracked down photographs.[91] They raised the money to cover the cost of publication. Among themselves, they decided about including drawings or other kinds of imaginative artwork to complement the text.[92] Should some famous individual who had once lived in the town be asked for an introduction to add to the luster of the book?[93] How many entries and what language served the books' memorial function? Answering all these myriad questions took place on several continents and became a major task of the American *landsmanshaftn* in the postwar period, reinvigorating, if temporarily, these immigrant-era organizations whose original purposes had declined in the face of economic mobility, geographic dispersion, and the American nativity of their children.

The *yizker bikher* of the Hitler catastrophe differed from those of earlier catastrophes also in the fact that they not only narrated the deaths and destructions but also celebrated the lives of the Jewish communities that the Germans had obliterated. In large measure because nonsurvivors participated in these efforts, the books did more than tell how the Jewish denizens of these over two hundred places had met their brutal ends; they also invoked the images of how Jews had once lived there.

Not that the books' writers hesitated to share the details of the brutlity. Rather, the depictions of the invasions and exterminations, along with the names of those who had been killed and photographs of ruined cemeteries and synagogues, took on a particular poignancy when set against stories of life, often shorn of the real conflicts that had disturbed them during normal times. Jews from the White Russian city of Vitebsk titled their 1956 book *Vitebsk in the Past: History, Memories, Destruction, Essays*. Similarly, the 1957 *The Rise and Fall of Lomza* provided readers with both the life of the town and its devastating end. Jews in America and Israel who had once lived in Kurzeniec collaborated to publish, in 1956, *Megilat Kurenits: Ayara be-hayeha u-ve-mota* [The scroll of Kurzeniec: the town in its life and in its death].[94]

Who bought and read these town memorial books, and to what degree did they exist beyond the small circle of the townspeople who had once lived in these places that were no more? The number of copies actually sold had to be small because relatively few American-born Jews still belonged to the hometown clubs. As early as 1930, the majority of American Jews had already been born in the United States. But a larger swathe of American Jewry learned about these books, well beyond the close-knit *landsmanshaft* circle. American Jewish publications noted their emergence as a Jewish literary phenomenon. The Jewish Book Council of America, an agency of the Jewish Welfare Board, published an annual listing of the year's Jewish books accompanied by essays on the state of English, Yiddish, and Hebrew publishing in the United States and around the world. From the publication of the first of the *yizker bikher* and beyond, the *Jewish Book Annual* commented on their appearance, listing them as a genre of their own and as part of something it labeled "*hurban* literature," or "destruction literature."

Yudl Mark, a Yiddish writer, heralded the birth of this writing, this "effort to document the destruction in Europe and to perpetuate an image of the life that had been extinguished."[95] The *American Jewish Year Book* issued by the American Jewish Committee informed its readers about the appearance of *yizker bikher* in its annual discussions of the Jewish literary output of the United States, and *Jewish Social Studies*, the most scholarly of the English-language Jewish publications, paid attention to the memorial book enterprise, reviewing specific volumes as they appeared and regularly discussing the genre. Joseph Landis, a professor at Queens College, reviewed in 1957, for example, *Pinkes Kolomey*, and observed:

And still the number grows. Year by year the memorials increase, symbolic tombstones to the martyred towns of the Third Destruction. And in reading these Yiddish volumes, the details may vary but the essential story is always the same—settlement, suffering, contribution to the economic life of the land, more oppression; but always . . . the cultural life grows richer. . . . Over the numberless Jewish towns of eastern Europe a silence has settled. Only from a distance is pieced together the last testament to an epoch in Jewish history, its legacy of loyalty to the values and to the complex totality of a unique experience.[96]

Individual and groups of *yizker bikher* merited reviews, at times critical but always reverential, of the project as a whole. Historian Isaiah Trunk reviewed the Buenos Aires volume memorializing the town of Sidlice, and he remarked that the "yizkor book" had emerged as the dominant form in the "hurban literature."[97]

To many American Jews of these years, and unlike later historians, the appearance of books that functioned as symbolic tombstones, as paper monuments, meant more than the absence of physical ones on the American landscape.

Days to Mourn, Times to Remember

Specially designated books and cemetery markers, invocations at meetings and book dedications all provided American Jews with a set of tools to eternalize the memory of the six million and demonstrated their eagerness and sense of obligation to keep the image of Europe's murdered Jews alive. They also turned to the Jewish calendar to locate the memorial process in time, in the yearly flow of holidays and fast days. The Jewish tradition sanctified time more profoundly than space, investing greater meaning in temporal than in physical sanctity. And so American Jews, through their communal infrastructure, turned to the ritual cycle to engage with the memory of the victims of the Nazi Holocaust.

Even during the war, American Jews felt compelled to designate special memorial days to mark their anguish over the unfolding tragic fate of European Jewry. In May 1943, just a few weeks after word came to America of the final liquidation of the Warsaw Ghetto, the Synagogue Council of America "set aside" a "day of prayer and intercession for the 2,000,000 Jews who have been martyred at the hands of the Nazis within the year." Abba Hillel Silver, one of America's best-known rabbis, told radio listeners on Mutual Broadcasting System's Chapel of the Air, that the rabbis

Memorial Services

In tribute to the memory of the more than 6,000,000 Jews slaughtered by the Nazis in recent years;

will be conducted at the

Jewish Center of Forest Hills West

63-25 Dry Harbor Road

at the Sunday Morning Service, December 28, 1952.... Asarah B'Teves, the 10th day of Teves, 5713 at 9 A. M.

This Fast Day has been proclaimed as a Memorial Day for Jewish Martyrs of all times, with special reference to the victims of modern times.

Rabbi Samuel Geffen will conduct the Memorial Services.

It is your obligation to attend and participate in these services.

American Jewish congregations used the late-winter fast day of the Tenth of Tevet, here referred to as "Asarah B'Teves," both to memorialize "the more than six million Jews slaughtered by the Nazis in recent years" and to recall the "Jewish Martyrs of all times." The Synagogue Council of America, made up of Reform, Conservative, and Orthodox rabbis, had declared the Tenth of Tevet the day to remember the victims of the Nazi catastrophe even as the war raged, but the 1959 declaration of Yom Hashoah by the Israeli Parliament wiped this memorial day off the consciousness of American Jewry. *Courtesy American Jewish Historical Society.*

of the United States had decided, in light of the devastation in Europe, to mark for all Jews a time collectively "to remember" the millions of Jews already liquidated. After all, he noted, "The graves of our martyred dead are nameless. . . . No monuments will ever rise above them. Their lives must be their monuments and our hearts must be their final resting place."[98]

Only two years after the war's end, the issue of a memorial day became a matter of widespread Jewish communal discussion. Different organizations and swathes of American Jewry had their own ideas about when this day should be, and they communicated among themselves as to the need for such an annual event and the most fitting times for doing so. At times, they heard from Holocaust survivors still in Europe, who begged American Jewry to designate a memorial day, making claims that reflected their specific tragedies. In 1946, the Council of Jewish Communities for Bohemia, Moravia, and Silesia proposed to the Synagogue Council of America that March 13 would be a good day because "3,860 Jewish men, women and children . . . were destroyed in one night on that date in 1944 at the Birkenau Osveciem Camp."[99] The Central Committee of Liberated Jews in Germany suggested in 1946 the 14th of the spring month of Iyar, "the . . . anniversary of the liberation of our brethren, the shearith ha platah, the surviving remnant," to the Synagogue Council.

Various American rabbis had their own ideas as to what day would serve most perfectly as the memorial moment. Rabbi Isaac Schwartz of the Union of Orthodox Jewish Congregations, writing from Cincinnati, suggested in 1948 that "September 30 be proclaimed as an international day of mourning. On that date in 1938 the Pact of Munich sold millions of helpless people into slavery and death," while New York's Rabbi David da Sola Pool suggested the 20th of the Hebrew month of Sivan of the Hebrew calendar "be established as a fast day for the Jewish victims of the last decade."[100]

Jewish communal groups from around the United States made it amply clear that they wanted the council to come up with a day, designate and announce it, and then create appropriate liturgies for public ceremonies. In 1947, B'nai B'rith communicated with the Synagogue Council that the time had indeed come to "take action in the matter of a memorial day for the Jewish dead." The need for a memorial assumed particular urgency as Holocaust survivors began settling in American communities and wanted to recite kaddish—the memorial prayer—for their loved ones. These new American Jews often did not know the exact date when the deaths had taken place and therefore lacked an anniversary, a *yahrzeit,* to recite the memorial prayer, in accordance with traditional practice.

Such a date had in actuality come in 1947 when the Synagogue Council, in conjunction with rabbinical bodies around the world, decided on the mid-winter 10th day of the Hebrew month of Tevet, a fast day in the Jewish calendar. The day marked the beginning of the siege of Jerusalem by the Babylonians in the days of the First Temple. While this "minor fast" had been on the Jewish calendar for centuries, no evidence exists that American Jews paid it much attention. No doubt the most observant fasted on that day, but guidebooks for children and adults on the cycle of the Jewish year, sermons, and journalistic accounts of Jewish religious practice made no mention of it before the late 1940s. Most likely, like any number of the other minor holy days, it had faded into both general nonobservance and obscurity.

Only with the decision of the Synagogue Council to make it the reference point for the religious engagement with the Holocaust did it take on a new living form. The Synagogue Council could have chosen other dates. Rabbis within its executive committee debated other possibilities, with the Tenth of Tevet's closest competitor, the Ninth of Av, the summer fast day associated with the destruction of both the First and Second Temples in Jerusalem. In fact, in their sermons, rabbis throughout the postwar period conjoined the Ninth of Av with the Holocaust. Similarly, Jewish summer camps widely used the Ninth of Av, the only Jewish holiday to fall during the months when the children spent time away from home in their all-Jewish environment, to remember the recent European Jewish tragedy.

From the war years on through the postwar years, Jewish summer camps linked the Ninth of Av's commemoration of the traumas of the distant past with the all-too-close present. Every kind of Jewish organizational camp—Reform, Conservative, Zionist of every variant, Yiddishist, and Socialist—all devoted Ninth of Av programs to the memory of the slaughtered six million. Staff members of the Conservative movement's Ramah camps described at the end of the 1947 how "almost every camper wrote home about this service," which demonstrated the parallels between the ancient and the modern tragedies. Over the course of the 1950s, Conservative movement camp counselors prepared a special Ninth of Av prayer book, which included a "Kinoh [lamentation] for the Six Million."[101] Reform, Zionist, Socialist, and Orthodox camps all did the same, each putting its particular ideological stamp on the material. All, however, memorialized the Holocaust as the most recent manifestation of Jewish tragedy.[102]

Jewish adults, like their children in summer camp, blended the Ninth of Av and the Holocaust. Jewish organizations, institutions, and organs of public opinion commented on the connections between them, and they did so also when addressing audiences beyond the Jewish world. In July 1954, Rabbi Manuel Saltzman, speaking on national radio in the name of the Synagogue Council of America on a weekly show, "This Week in Religion," told his listening audience what the last week had held for Jews:

> This past week Jews the world over gathered in synagogues on the Holiday of Tisha b'Av [Ninth of Av] to commemorate the great calamities which befell our people in our past history and culminating in the tragic extermination of six million Jews in our day. We would never forget these martyrs and prayed that all mankind would likewise remember them, so that they will not have died in vain.[103]

But despite this widely recognized linkage, the Synagogue Council decided against the Ninth of Av as *the* day to remember the catastrophe, probably because it fell during the summer. Congregants might be out of town. Children would be at camp, and the synagogue religious school would be closed for vacation, meaning that teachers could not use classroom activities to participate in the memorialization. In addition, American Jews, in one way or another, recognized the Ninth of Av. Unlike the Tenth of Tevet, it resonated. It did not need to be rediscovered and recycled in the name of the six million, thus making the latter the more fitting vehicle for the new memorial moment.

With the Tenth of Tevet, the Synagogue Council could accomplish two ends. It could both memorialize the six million in Jewish sacred time and revive a pretty much moribund Jewish practice. The council wanted the observance of the Tenth of Tevet as a Holocaust memorial to take place on a global scale. The cables and letters it sent out to the chief rabbis of France, Palestine, Italy, and Great Britain testified to its vision of a worldwide Jewish project. American Jews, the Synagogue Council informed the rabbis of other lands, have clamored for "the establishment of a universal day of fasting, weeping and lamentation to commemorate the destruction of the millions of our people in the last decade."[104]

By the end of 1948, the rabbis proclaimed the Tenth of Tevet as the international Day of Memorial for the victims of Nazi persecution. To launch it and to make manifest its connection to the Holocaust, the Synagogue Council decided to unveil the memorial stone covering the grave of the unfit religious objects on that day and sought extensive television, radio, and newspaper coverage for the ceremony and for its designation of this sacred time to remember.

The council prepared a "Service of Memorial for the Six Million Jewish Martyrs of Nazi Tyranny," which included traditional mourning material, elements from Hebrew poetry, and new readings composed specifically for this sacred service. In 1949, the Synagogue Council had asked Leo Jung, an Orthodox rabbi, to prepare "a ritual for the observance of Asara b'Tevet [Tenth of Tevet] . . . as a day of memorial for the victims of the recent European holocaust."[105]

The liturgy prepared by Jung achieved wide usage. In the opening responsive reading from the congregation, the special prayer booklet declaimed: "No generation in Israel's long and sorrowful chronicle has known a destruction as immense as we have witnessed. . . . The household of Israel was devastated, its sanctuaries were desecrated, its houses of learning razed, its treasures looted; its elders and sages and guardians and people were slain." The prayer service made special room for the recollection of "the Martyrs and the Heroes . . . of Warsaw, of Bendin, of Tarnow, of Vilna, of Bialystok, of Treblinka, of the many lonely fighters in ghettos and murder-camps, who died with the last cry of Samson on their lips: 'Let me die with the Philistines.'" Finally, the service ended with the traditional dirge, the "El Moleh Rahamin" [God, full of compassion], and where in the liturgy the name of the deceased would be mentioned, the Tenth of Tevet ceremony invoked "the martyred, the tortured, the slain of Israel in the dominion of arrogance and cruelty."[106]

Congregations reported, randomly, back to the Synagogue Council on how they used this liturgy and how they involved the local media to publicize the memorial service for the six million. Rabbi Simon Konovitch of Congregation Sons of Israel in Newburgh, New York, for example, informed the council of the article that appeared in his town's newspaper after the memorial event at his synagogue. Konovitch clipped the full text of the newspaper article, which reported to Newburgh's residents, most of them non-Jews, that the rabbi had urged the town's Jews "to kindle a yahrzeit memorial lamp or candle on this day for the martyrs of Europe, to abstain from merriment and observe some token of mourning." In the service, Konovitch "likened American Jewry to Noah," the Bible's first survivor, and he "urged them to assume their responsibility in rebuilding a better world for themselves and their children, so that the sacrifice of the six million martyred Jews shall not be in vain." The rabbi of this small Hudson

River Valley synagogue also reported that the congregation had held a special children's assembly and that he had "conducted a special service over the local radio station in conjunction with this Day of Intercession and memorial."[107]

The use of the Tenth of Tevet as the day of mourning for the victims of the Holocaust made its way into books about American Judaism by the 1950s. In 1955, Abraham Katsch put together a bar mitzvah gift book "to encourage the Jewish boy who has reached" thirteen "to delve further into the spiritual treasures of his people." The book's description of the Jewish year devoted several pages to the "Day of Carnage" (the Tenth of Tevet), which commemorated Jewish tragedy "from the beginning of the siege of Jerusalem by the Babylonians in 588 B.C.E. through the slaughter of six million Jews by the Nazis." Jewish history, Katsch told his youthful readers, involved a "series of holocausts" marked by this fast day. "It was fitting," he continued, "that this day should . . . be designated by world Jewry to commemorate the slaughter of the last war," which saw "the destruction of the great Eastern and Central European Jewish civilization."[108]

The Synagogue Council considered its role in establishing the Tenth of Tevet as the "official" day to remember the six million one of its most important achievements. It took responsibility not only for getting it started but also for sending out press releases to the Jewish and the general American press informing them of the upcoming memorial day. Throughout the 1950s, it turned to the airwaves close to the day and retold how it had created the Tenth of Tevet as it chronicled the story of the tragic fate of the six million. Radio programs, directed at both Jewish and general audiences, yearly featured SCA officials connecting into one the triple tale of how it advanced the memorial process in the United States—indeed, the world —how it had buried the damaged religious objects, and how Europe's Jews had met their devastating end. As an organization of American rabbis, it therefore had the right, it claimed, to state that its constituents, American Jews, saw themselves as "the heirs from six million of our people who had synagogues in the Old World."[109]

Postwar American Jewish organizations and bodies, like the Synagogue Council, made use of the Holocaust to advance their own institutional interests. It did not take the Eichmann trial in the early 1960s or Israel's 1967 war to convince the leaders of American Jewry that the narrative of the six million could serve a profound memorial function and simultaneously enhance their institutional prestige. They recognized that American Jews responded to calls to remember and that the Holocaust provided an

THE DAY OF CARNAGE

From the beginning of the siege of Jerusalem by the Babylonians in 588 B.C.E. through the slaughter of six million Jews by the Nazis during the second World War, stretches a long period of suffering and ruthless extermination. The beginning of this series of holocausts is marked by a fast day on the tenth of Teveth (Asarah be'Teveth). On that day began the siege of Jerusalem by Nebuchadnezzar. It was fitting that this day should also be designated by world Jewry to commemorate the slaughter of the last war. The destruction of the great Eastern and Central European Jewish civilization was the culminating tragedy of the process begun by the Babylonians almost 2,600 years ago.

This catastrophe, marked officially by the fast day of Asarah be'Teveth, has already become the subject of a vast literature. In Hebrew it is referred to as *Hashoah*, the fearful destruction. As the story unfolds — in books, in memoirs, poetry, and fiction — we catch glimpses of the heroic spirit of Israel in the face of almost certain death. Hitler destroyed the bodies of millions of our brethren, but their spirit he could not cremate. In countless acts of resistance, culminating in the heroic Warsaw uprising, doomed Jews showed their kinship with the heroic forefathers who had defied the brutalitarians of their age — Babylonians, Assyrians, Greeks, Romans, Nazis.

May their memory ever recall the greatness of the prophet's vision of a united humanity, for which they gave their lives.

CHIEF RABBI OF ISRAEL, DR. ISAAC HERZOG, PLANTING THE FIRST TREE IN THE FOREST OF THE SIX MILLION MARTYRS, ISRAEL
Courtesy, Jewish National Fund, New York

The mid-1950s saw the publication of *The Bar Mitzvah Book* and *Blessed Is the Daughter,* marketed as appropriate gifts for teenage Jewish boys and girls as they marked their thirteenth birthdays and Jewish adulthood. Among the points in time around the Jewish calendar, both books included the mid-winter fast day Asarah b'Tevet, which the Synagogue Council of America had designated to be the day to remember a "series of holocausts," but particularly "the destruction of the great Eastern and Central European Jewish civilization" by the Nazis. Despite the festive nature of the bar and bat mitzvah, the authors of these books did not hesitate to provide in these volumes details of "the slaughter of six million Jews by the Nazis." *Courtesy Schreiber Publishing, Incorporated.*

attractive medium from which to proclaim their organizations' triumphs and importance.

Because of that recognition and its genuine belief that it had helped keep alive the memory of the slain six million, the Synagogue Council closely guarded the sanctity of the Tenth of Tevet, proclaiming the day as its creation and as the most fitting moment in time to remember in prayer the six million.[110] Annually, the council issued "official" calendars to Jewish organizations, and as late as 1958, it listed the Tenth of Tevet on it, calling it by then "Memorial Services for Nazi Victims."[111]

Despite the council's efforts, by the early 1960s the Tenth of Tevet diminished as a Holocaust memorial. Its demise, however, had nothing to do with a lack of American Jewish commitment to the memorial process. Rather, it demonstrates how outside factors complicated their endeavors. In 1962, New York's Society for the Advancement of Judaism (SAJ), a Reconstructionist congregation, printed an appeal to congregants to purchase special candles, Yad Vashem Memorial Lights, for home use, "for the express purpose of making the observance of the Yahrzeit for the victims of the Nazi holocaust universal in every single Jewish home." The SAJ suggested not one date, but two, to make use of this candle. One, the Tenth of Tevet, had been already fixed in the American Jewish consciousness through the efforts of the Synagogue Council. The other had a different history, one that spelled the death knell for the Tenth of Tevet as American Jewry's memorial day for the Holocaust.[112]

That date, the Twenty-seventh of Nisan, better known as Yom Hashoah, had been chosen by the Knesset, the Israeli parliament, after much debate and contention in 1951. Originally named Yom Hashoah U'Mered Hagetaot (the rebellion in the ghettoes), Israel had chosen this date for several reasons, which included the desire to memorialize the Holocaust, to assert the centrality of Israel around the Jewish world, and to project an image of physical bravery and resistance. The choice of the Twenty-seventh of Nisan made the 1943 uprising in the Warsaw Ghetto the defining image of the Holocaust. The rebellion had actually begun on the first night of Passover, the Fourteenth of Nisan. The rabbinate in Israel, Orthodox by definition, would not allow for a new "holy day" to conflict with Passover.[113] But to move the memorial time outside of Nisan would have detached the Holocaust narrative from that of defiance and armed resistance. Since the uprising had extended beyond the eight days of Passover, the later Nisan date satisfied all, avoiding conflict with the rabbinate but still allowing the concepts "shoah" and "mered" to be conjoined.

Over the course of the 1950s, observance of Yom Hashoah developed and took hold in Israel. Its name changed to Yom Hashoah V'Hagevurah —the day of the Holocaust and the heroism—but its purpose still connected the state, the memory of the Holocaust, and the idea of Jewish bravery in the face of oppression.[114] Whatever meaning and purpose Yom Hashoah achieved in Israel, in American synagogues it competed in the late 1950s with the Tenth of Tevet, complicating the memorial activities of American rabbis and congregations who had invested energy and political influence in creating the memorial day. The general disappearance of the latter—indeed, the ultimate amnesia that it ever existed as a Holocaust memorial day—dwarfed by Yom Hashoah, demonstrated the twin, and this case contradictory, goals of American Jewry: to memorialize the victims of the Holocaust and to be part of a global Jewish world with Israel a key player. Israel's declaration and institutionalization of Yom Hashoah may have obliterated American Jewry's use of the Tenth of Tevet, but the history of the latter bore witness to the desire of American Jews to have a day to remember and mourn for their co-religionists in Europe under the heel of Nazi rule.[115]

American Jews not only designated a day to memorialize their six million but also folded their memories into the broader flow of the Jewish calendar. The fall high holy days proved opportune. Jewish organizations of various kinds sent out special New Year greetings to members, and in the early postwar period, the tragic details of the catastrophe ran through organizational rhetoric. In 1946, the Kolbuszowa *landsmanshaft* extended its wishes to its constituency for a "healthy and happy New Year," tempering those familiar words with the fact that "as the Rosh Hashanah nears, we Jews turn our thoughts to the meaning of the last war that swept through half the world and count the toll of the Jewish victims: six million souls murdered, gassed in chambers, burnt in the crematoria, tortured, maimed. A tragic situation, this."[116] Rabbi Martin Kessler of Oak Ridge, Tennessee, also connected the New Year celebration with the European catastrophe in his holiday greetings to his congregants. In 1955, as the "days of awe" approached, he sent a letter to all the women of his congregation:

Dear Friend: It is customary for Jewish women at the time of candle-lighting, which in our tradition is a moment of divine good will, to pray. . . . My late mother . . . used to pray with greater fervor on Erev Rosh Hashanah than on the eve of other holidays. Please find below her candle-lighting prayer. . . . My mother was taken away from her home in April 1944 by the Nazis who later killed her. She has no grave. May her simple prayer be a memorial for her.[117]

Sermons given during the high holidays resounded with images, references, and invocations to remember the slaughtered Jews of Europe. A 1950 Yom Kippur sermon delivered in an Orthodox congregation in Wilmington, Delaware, admonished congregants, "If we should not forget the greatest catastrophe that smote our people, the death plague of the last decade, the rabbis must institute a ritual which will become part of our religion. If we should not forget the six million Jews who were killed, we must memorialize them in ritual. Only with ritual can the Jew remember."[118] Another Orthodox rabbi, Moshe Weiss, dedicated his 1959 Yom Kippur sermon to the theme of self-sacrifice, focusing on the liquidation of a particular town, Sandz, Poland. Once a great center of Jewish learning, it had been reduced to no more than eleven Jewish families, and even the community's cemetery had "practically disappeared, for the Nazis used these stones to make sidewalks and steps." One Jew, after the defeat of the Germans, at great risk to himself, recovered many of the cemetery stones, and now in the town one could see a "huge mass grave of four thousand Jews of Sandz who were burned and killed by the Nazis."[119]

Postwar high holiday sermons throbbed with grim references to the six million or to some detail of the larger catastrophe. Rabbis turned to the brutal deaths to inspire the women and men who flocked to the synagogues on these days, including the majority who rarely, or never, attended any other time of the year. The two new high holiday prayer books, *mahzorim*, issued during the postwar period incorporated the tragedy into the liturgy. For the first time, in 1948, the Reconstructionist movement produced a high holiday prayer book, and three years later, the United Synagogue of America, the Conservative movement, published its own, also a first. Both made room for the memory of the six million, in ways consistent with their ideologies.

The Reconstructionists, the youngest American Jewish religious movement, considered itself free to tamper with traditional texts. So for the Yom Kippur day service, which had for centuries included the "Martyrology" (in Hebrew, "Eleh Ezkerah," or "these I will remember"), a lengthy graphic paean to ten rabbis who suffered excruciating torture at the hands of the Romans who had forbidden them from ordaining new rabbis, the Reconstructionists excised the conventional words, substituting them with the following statement: "That the spirit of martyrdom is not dead among our people is attested by the way many Jews sanctified the name of God by their defiance of the demonic power of Nazism. Not even the overwhelming might of the fiendish Nazi regime could extinguish their loyalty to the moral order." The *mahzor* directed congregants to recite in unison a poem by Hannah Senesh, a Jewish woman from Palestine, a poet, who returned to her native Hungary to fight the Nazis. Captured by the Germans, who executed her, Senesh and her poetry inspired the American Jewish imagination, and her words entered into the sacred text. The Reconstructionists also included a declaration purportedly written by a group of Jewish girls of the Beth Jacob School in Krakow who committed suicide rather than be ravished by the invading Germans. Finally, the prayer book directed congregants to recite aloud "A Tribute to the Martyrs of the Bialystok Ghetto."[120]

Unlike Reconstructionism, Conservative Judaism did not give congregants or rabbis much leeway to change Hebrew liturgical texts. For its high holiday prayer book, the United Synagogue retained the "Eleh Ezkerah" in Hebrew with an English translation but added a lengthy composition, "We Remember the Six Million," a responsive reading that began with the invocation to remember: "Let us now pause to recall the bitter catastrophe which so recently has befallen our people in Europe. . . . Today we mourn . . . for . . . many . . . cities where six million of our people have been brutally destroyed." The reading ended with "Ani Ma'amin," the "hymn reaffirming their faith in the coming of the Messiah, when justice and peace shall finally be established for all men."[121]

Year after year in the postwar period, as Jewish holidays came around, Jews linked holiday observance with the gruesome fate of one-third of world Jewry. The Hillel rabbi at the University of Maryland contributed a piece to the student newspaper, *The Diamondback*, his 1960 Hanukkah message to the campus. He described "a small silver menorah" that had come into his possession. "Who its owner was," he continued, "we do not know. After the Nazi holocaust it was discovered among the loot and entrusted to us. It is not ours, but each year during the festival of Chanukah we light in it the little candles of the holiday." Purim plays, sermons, and articles likewise made the obvious connection between Haman, the fictive prime minister of Persia who set out to kill the Jews, and Hitler, the all too real German, who nearly succeeded.[122]

More than any other holiday, Passover became the moment on the Jewish calendar for American Jews to ritually remember those who had perished in the Holocaust.[123] As with the fall "days of awe," the vast majority of America's Jews participated in Passover events, including one or two *sedarim* in their homes with family and friends. Many attended some kind of community celebration, a third seder, sponsored by an organization, or a model seder, held in the Jewish schools that so many of their children attended.

Ironically, the holiday's theme should have rendered it particularly inappropriate for recalling the victims. The Passover narrative, the yearly repeated story of the deliverance of the ancient Hebrews from the rigors of slavery, jarred with what had befallen Europe's Jews under Nazi domination. The unprecedented murders, explicitly undertaken to extinguish the Jewish people, and the anemic world response to their plight represented the polar opposite of Passover's message of liberation. Passover, celebrating divine intervention, put God at the center. In the two decades after the Holocaust's end, the contrast could not be avoided. God had been noticeably absent from the end of the 1930s onward, and the cries of the trapped Jews in Europe, unlike those in Egyptian bondage, had gone unheard. Passover's miraculous story of plagues sent on evil Egyptians, the Exodus's glory, and the parting of the Red Sea should have had little resonance in the face of the crematoria of Nazi Europe.

But American Jewry twinned them, in large measure because the Warsaw Ghetto uprising had commenced during Passover. This chapter began with the Seder Ritual of Remembrance composed in the early 1950s. From its first publication into the early 1950s, this brief but emotional reading experienced wide distribution and use and was repeatedly printed in Jewish newspapers and *haggadot*. It received unalloyed enthusiastic response from the Jewish public.[124]

Some, although not all, Orthodox authorities could not endorse its use at the two seder nights. While they found the reading emotionally powerful, they refused to participate in its distribution because they believed that Jewish law took precedence over the power of modern words, and, as they saw it, Jewish law had fixed the Passover liturgy.[125] Nothing could be taken from it or added to it. One Orthodox rabbi, Samson Weiss of the Union of Orthodox Jewish Congregations, noted in 1962, in a letter to Rufus Learsi, that, while he had been "deeply moved, as surely every Jew has, by your endeavor," he felt unable to endorse it. "The Haggadah . . . which dates back in its major parts to Tannaitic times [approximately 200 C.E.], has not been changed for centuries." Other great Jewish tragedies, he pointed out, had not penetrated its closed covers. "Unless the inclusion of your Ritual of Remembrance were advocated by the recognized Torah authorities of our age, here and in Israel, I do not see my way clear in joining your committee."[126] Weiss, though, did not represent the totality of American Orthodoxy. Several years earlier, in 1955, Rabbis Hershel Lookstein and David da Sola Pool endorsed the Learsi text in a magazine article, encouraging congregations and individual Jews to contact the committee's offices directly to get their own copies.[127]

Those who communicated with Rufus Learsi or who commented on the Seder Ritual of Remembrance emphasized the grandeur of its language and their belief "that this is a much finer way of honoring our martyrs than by the erection of a monument," again demonstrating a sense that physical memorials did not constitute the only or even best way by which American Jews could enshrine the memory of the victims of the Holocaust. Few tombstones, wrote David Rudavsky of the Jewish Education Association of Essex County, New Jersey, to the editor of *Congress Weekly*, which yearly printed the reading, have "outlasted the century-old Haggada. The recitation of the memorial ritual year after year will . . . keep the memory of the six million victims of Nazidom alive."[128]

Individuals shared their personal experiences with the text, thanking its authors. Rabbi I. Usher Kirshblum of Kew Gardens, New York, wrote to Learsi immediately upon first using the text in 1952. After reporting that he "incorporated the ritual" into his sermon the Sabbath before Passover, he described his two seder experiences with it. On the first night, he had invited some guests to his home, "native Americans who sustained no personal losses through the Hitler holocaust":

> At the appropriate moment I informed my guests of the new ritual. I gave them no instructions whatsoever. As soon as I announced, "and now may I recite the prayer," all of them automatically rose . . . and with heads bowed listened most attentively. . . . When my wife, children, and I began to sing the immortal "Ani Maamin," a tune which they had never heard before, everyone of them made a serious attempt to join me. The solemnity, not sadness, lasted until we reached the favorite Seder melodies.[129]

Rabbi Kirshblum had a different, although no less positive or intense, experience the second night. On that night, he had at his "table a family of new immigrants who are the sole survivors of the Nazi persecutions":

> Strangely enough they had not heard of this ritual before. As I recited the prayer, this time in Hebrew, their tear ducts and mine refused to

remain dry. They found it most difficult to join me in the chanting of "Ani Maamin" which they knew, alas, so well. After awhile they expressed deep gratitude to me for having introduced it into my Seder for they felt that at last there was meaning to the death of their sainted martyred parents.

Rabbi Isaac Klein informed Learsi that he used it not just in his home and congregation but on "a local T.V. program," at which "we had a Model Seder and I incorporated the service into it." The executive director of the United Synagogue likewise let the author know that the Jewish chaplain at Keesler Air Force Base had used the Holocaust ceremony text in his seder, to which he had invited several Christian clergy.[130]

This Hebrew-English text achieved an impressive reach. In 1957, copies of the text had been mailed to 11,200 organizations; 18,500 had been directly ordered by individuals, and over three dozen Jewish newspapers had reprinted it. The National Women's League of the United Synagogue encouraged its branches to make use of it, suggesting that members "share this with your Adult Education and/or Judaism-in-the-Home Chairman." The Zionist Organization of America employed it repeatedly at communal events, as did Hillel chapters. Habonim, Hashomer Hatzair, and Young Judaea, youth movements, yearly printed it in their magazines. A number of *haggadot* did so as well.[131]

Other *haggadot* also remembered the horrendous fate of Europe's Jews, but in their own ways. Redactors of some added graphic images to bring the Holocaust onto the holiday table. A 1950 *haggadah* provided its users with three illustrations to accompany the "Pour Out Your Wrath" section. One engraving depicted Passover night among a group of Jews in Spain, captioned, "The Inquisition interrupts a seder." The other two images, illustrating the highly charged words imploring God to destroy those "who have devoured Jacob," showed "Oswiecim, where 4,000,000 were slain," with its portal "Arbeit Macht Frei" sign, and the other, a grainy black-and-white photograph, depicted a looming chimney, spewing smoke, labeled, "Treblinka, death house of 731,000 Jews."[132]

Some Passover seder booklets offered different possibilities as to where was best to insert the Holocaust.[133] A 1951 *haggadah* aimed at "young American Jews" instructed the leader of the seder to declare, after the youngest child asked the "Four Questions," that "Hitler diabolically gathered us from many lands, threw us into concentration camps and torture chambers. Pharaoh killed only infant boys: Hitler first cruelly tortured, killed with horrible death, young and old, little boys and girls, young men and women, old men and women—all—six million souls." In the "v'hee sheamda" [this which stood up for us] section, which pointed out that "not just one arose to end us, but in every generation, they arise to kill us," the editor reminded young American Jews that "tyrannical empires that have risen against us have fallen . . . most recently Hitler's Germany. Unfortunately, many of our people have been destroyed and exterminated."[134] A 1961 self-described "traditional" *haggadah* turned the "tzay u'lemad" (go out and learn) passage into a Holocaust memorial: "Hitler dreamed of world conquest and the annihilation of the Jewish people. Our generation experienced not only his dreams and hopes but quite a horrifying part of reality. A third of the Jewish people was slaughtered, a large part of Europe conquered." When participants partook of the bitter herbs, the leader, using this version of the text, intoned, "Life can at times be so bitter, miserable, and unendurable that death in comparison appears sweet. Inmates of concentration camps can testify to that."[135]

This *haggadah* most likely got its use at a school model seder or a youth group's third seder. Jewish institutions across the ideological spectrum staged such events, often composing their own Passover booklets to fit their specific political and cultural tastes.[136] Holocaust imagery abounded in these works. The Workmen's Circle, the Arbeiter Ring, a mildly socialist, Yiddish-oriented social and mutual-aid association, began producing *haggadot* as the war raged. Its school and its branch gatherings used these, variously titled *Di naye haggadah*, the new *haggadah*, *A naye haggadah shel Pesach* (here mixing Yiddish and Hebrew), or *Haggadah shel Pesach farn dritten seder*, as the Passover *haggadah* for the third seder. Regardless of title, the Holocaust loomed large.

In the 1958 Workmen's Circle booklet, for example, the leader, early on in the scripted ritual, declared the need to put celebration aside, declaiming, "In the hour of joy, in the festival days, our ancestors promised to mention our people's tragedy and destruction. We recall now the fate and the heroism, the deaths and the beliefs of the latest destruction." Celebrants, in unison, then read the poem "In the Warsaw Ghetto in the Month of Nisan" and sang "The Hymn of the Partisans."[137] Year to year, the ritual changed little, as these Yiddish Holocaust readings, among others, became canonical.

Elsewhere on the ideological spectrum, Labor Zionists, supporters of Israel's Labor Party and advocates of Hebrew, also hosted third *sedarim* and produced their own *haggadot*. Every year, a special committee of the

Chicago LZOA (Labor Zionist Organization of America) spent months fashioning their unique text in which the memory of the six million occupied a sacred space in songs, prayers, and discursive material accompanied by drawings and photographs.

In 1959, for example, those gathered around the tables, numbering over one hundred, read responsively an "Invitation to the Memorial," which began by depicting pre-Holocaust Jewish life in eastern Europe, intoning, "They strengthened and helped to develop the economy of the nations and they enriched the cultures. At the same time they created their own culture upon the basis of their rich and spiritual inheritance." The call to remember focused specifically on the Jewish children before their brutal end, recalling how "the Jewish word and song rang out on all the streets and under the green trees, carefree and happy, little Moshe and little Shlomo played." A soloist then sang "Unter the greene baymelach" [Under the green trees], a song written in Poland during the Nazi occupation. The leader then declaimed: "And then came the great catastrophe . . . among the six million destroyed Jews were a million innocent Jewish children." The soloist returned, with yet another song from the Holocaust repertoire, "Nishto mehr kein Moshe'le, Shloymele" [There is no more little Moshe, little Shlomo]. The memorial service continued. "YIZKOR! REMEMBER! Remember those of our people who died before their time . . . those who suffered hunger and thirst and perished under the sword of our enemies."[138]

Passover as a time to remember the six million pervaded postwar American Jewish culture. An Orthodox rabbi in 1953 extolled in his Passover sermon, "When Moses Wept," the fact that "in some homes a special mention was made at the Seder table . . . of those dreadful days . . . of . . . the catastrophe that overtook European Jewry. People were dragged by the thousands to gas chambers and crematoria, or to die in mass graves." To Rabbi Bernard Berzon, "when . . . the memory is evoked at the Passover Seder, the festive occasion is not marred or dampened. It is invested with new solemnity and dignity." Indeed, by 1961, Philip Goodman's *Passover Anthology* included dozens of examples of American Jewish programs and texts that meshed imagery of the spring holiday of the liberation from slavery and the Holocaust.[139]

That the Warsaw Ghetto revolt of 1943 had taken place during Passover offered American Jews of the postwar period a symbolic way to fuse their much-observed holiday's transcendent theme of the Jews' liberation from oppression with the tragedy of the Holocaust. This had given Rufus Learsi a particular rationale in creating the seder reading. His text devoted a third of its space to the heroism of the "remnants of the Warsaw Ghetto."[140] This reading indeed received some of its most visible attention at public observances to commemorate the uprising. Conversely, the reality that many American Jews annually confronted the Holocaust through the image of the Warsaw Ghetto as invoked at their home and community Passover *sedarim* set the stage for yearly Warsaw Ghetto memorial programs, held in communities around the country.

While ostensibly these ceremonies celebrated the heroism of the fighters and the resisters, they went far beyond that. The narrative of the uprising provided American Jewish communities with a vehicle to memorialize the victims as a totality and to retell the tragic details of the calamity as a whole. These public programs, held in Jewish communities throughout America and around the Jewish world every April some time after the end of Passover, involved months of planning. They encompassed a wide net of participants. In every city with a Jewish community, committees drew up plans, invited speakers, and solicited the participation of public officials to either appear in person or send words of greeting that would be printed in program books. Committees arranged for musical performers, rented halls, raised funds, and generated publicity in the Jewish and general press. They sent out mailings to the broad Jewish public about the time and place of the memorial event.[141]

Local Jewish communities and their multiplicity of organizations used the Warsaw Ghetto memorial programs to share their national catastrophe with a wide audience. In 1945, for example, Morris Blumenstock of the American Federation of Polish Jews, appealed to New York City's Mayor Fiorello LaGuardia to mention the upcoming "memorial meeting" on his radio broadcast and to address the meeting itself. Blumenstock reminded the mayor that, "after all is said and done, Polish Jewry has lost almost three and a half million souls and we know how you feel about it. May we then expect to hear this occasion mentioned on your program?"[142]

The involvement of prominent non-Jews, particularly elected officials, did not play an incidental role in the Warsaw Ghetto programs. Making them part of the program transformed these Jewish gatherings into political events. For the politicians, mayors, governors, and others in search of votes, these rites of mourning provided them with a chance to meet Jewish constituents in a seemingly apolitical context. New York's Governor Thomas E. Dewey had much to gain in 1945 from saying to the American Federation of Polish Jews, at its Warsaw Ghetto memorial event, that the "Polish Jews died as martyrs in a desperate resistance against the Nazi

FURROWS

Vol. XIV, No. 3
APRIL, 1958

Pesach in Warsaw, 1943   Published by HABONIM

Furrows, like most other magazines and newspapers that circulated among American Jews, whether written for and by young people or adults, devoted time and attention to the Holocaust. While this cover of the April 1958 issue depicted the heroism of the ghetto fighting, it also showed in the bottom left the monsters who devoured the city, the flames shooting up to the sky, and at the top of the drawing, the dead looking down.

oppressors. . . . I join in the fervent prayer of American Jews of Polish background that the Jewish culture of Poland may be revived."[143] Every year, the program book for Chicago's Warsaw Ghetto memorial ceremony contained words of greeting from the then sitting mayor of the city and the governor of the state.[144] So, too, in the spring of 1960, which marked both the seventeenth anniversary of the uprising and a heated primary for the Democratic presidential nomination, contenders for that coveted spot— Senators John F. Kennedy, Hubert Humphrey, and Stuart Symington—all courted Jewish voters by telling the thirty-five hundred of them who gathered at New York's Madison Square Garden for the memorial ceremony sponsored by the World Congress for Jewish Culture that they shared the Jews' pain. Kennedy continued in his years as president to use the Warsaw Ghetto moment to connect to the Jewish public. In 1962, he issued a proclamation, read at the Zionist Organization of America's Warsaw Ghetto commemoration, that declared that "time has not dimmed the heroism of the people of the Warsaw Ghetto, nor the cruelty that they were made to suffer."[145]

Jewish organizations invited other notables to such events. In 1952, the Jewish Labor Committee asked Philip Murray of the Congress of Industrial Organizations and William Green of the American Federation of Labor, rival labor organizations, to send words of solidarity to the memorial event. Both agreed, invoking the memory of the "slaughter of innocent men, women, and children" perpetrated by the Germans against the Jews. For the JLC, playing both sides of America's internal labor divide by getting the two presidents to address the same Warsaw Ghetto memorial event confirmed the continued importance of the Jewish organization in the "house of labor."[146] Harvard's Hillel House invited poet John Ciardi, a faculty member in the English department, to join historian Oscar Handlin in speaking at the campus's 1953 Warsaw Ghetto anniversary event, sponsored in conjunction with the Harvard Liberal Union, following then the national pattern of bringing non-Jews onto the dais and into the commemorative culture.[147]

The memorial programs' format varied little, year to year or city to city. Whether sponsored by a synagogue, a left-wing group, a Zionist group, or a coalition of liberal Jewish organizations, elements of the ceremony became fixed even during the war. A stirring speech telling of the horrific deeds of the Germans and their collaborators and speculating on the implication of those events for Jews in the present, reflections of a survivor, words of solidarity with the Jewish people articulated by the invited notable non-Jew, musical renditions by soloists and choruses, the participation of children, the lighting of six candles often by Jews who had lived through the catastrophe, the communal singing of canonical "ghetto" hymns, and the recitation of the kaddish all marked commemorations of the Warsaw Ghetto uprising.

While the programs quickly developed a fixed format, they differed as to sponsorship. Sometimes organizations created their own internal memorial ceremonies, making them part of their ongoing calendar of events. These small ceremonies allowed for ideological consistency and made it possible for a particular synagogue or a left-wing group, both of which sponsored such events, to control the performance. On April 14, 1961, for example, the Massapequa Jewish Center on New York's Long Island extended its weekly Friday night service to ritualize the Warsaw Ghetto uprising. It printed the Seder Ritual of Remembrance in the congregational newsletter mailed to members and handed copies out to those who showed up at services. After the congregation read the text in unison, the rabbi spoke on "The Heroism of Desperation." Together they sang "Ani Ma'amin" and stood as the cantor ended, chanting the memorial prayer "Ale Molay Rachamim."[148] Fanny Licht, representing the State Speakers Bureau of the Communist Party of New York State, had different ideas about how to commemorate the Warsaw Ghetto. But that date resonated as much for her and those American Jews who identified with the political left as it did for those who belonged to the Long Island synagogue. In 1947, she invited historian Morris U. Schappes to speak at a "rally" organized for the purpose of "commemorating the Warsaw Ghetto" in the Bronx at the Jewish Center of the Sholem Aleichem Houses, a left-oriented housing cooperative.[149]

Often local branches of large national Jewish organizations, such as the American Jewish Congress, the Jewish Labor Committee, the American Federation of Polish Jews, the Labor Zionist Organization of America, and the World Congress for Jewish Culture, staged large ceremonies in major meeting halls, hotel ballrooms, and other visible and prominent civic spaces. Starting in the early 1950s, American Jewish Congress sponsored the largest annual Warsaw Ghetto memorial ceremony in Chicago. Sponsorship helped the organization demonstrate its importance on the local organizational scene. It boasted yearly about the overflow crowds that jammed the ballrooms of the city's largest hotels.[150]

Not everyone agreed that the American Jewish Congress had the right to determine Chicago's Warsaw Ghetto memorial programming or that its event ought to be deemed the most important. The Mid-West Jewish Council, a left-of-center organization, challenged the American Jewish

Jews in Chicago in 1954 participated in multiple Warsaw Ghetto memorial events sponsored by the Jewish Culture Congress, in conjunction with such organizations as the Jewish Labor Committee, the Labor Zionist Organization, various *landsmanshaftn*, and reading circles, staged this one at the Douglas Park Theater. While ostensibly dedicated to the memory of the heroic uprising, as the name of the ceremony indicated, the flyer made no mention of the armed resisters. Instead, the box on the left exhorted attendees to remember "what the German Nazi-Amalek [the enemies of the Israelites in the Bible] did to your people. Remember the six million Jews who went to their deaths as martyrs at the hands of the German murderers, hangmen. Remember Treblinka. Remember Buchenwald. Remember Maidanek. Remember Dachau. Remember Auschwitz. Remember the gas chambers. Remember the crematoria. Remember. Six million." As such, the memorial programs served to commemorate the catastrophe as a whole, with the term "Warsaw Ghetto" employed to convey the totality of the horror. *Courtesy Jewish Archives, Spertus Institute of Jewish Studies.*

Congress by staging its own, alternative "Warsaw Ghetto Uprising" ceremony. The details of its commemorations in fact resembled those at AJC ceremonies. Every year, it also rented out a hotel room or some other large public hall. It also enlisted local non-Jewish public officials to send greetings, and it also used music, pageantry, speeches, and candle-lighting ceremonies to focus attention on the events that had transpired in Warsaw in April 1943. Other organizations also saw sponsorship of a Warsaw Ghetto memorial program as a way to bolster their public profile, indicating the degree to which the Holocaust functioned as an intra-Jewish political matter long before the late 1960s. No organizations wanted another, and competing one, to be able to claim a monopoly on remembering the tragedy of the six million.[151]

Therefore, the Mid-West Council's challenge spurred the American Jewish Congress to reach out to other organizations, to unite as many non-Communist Jewish groups as possible for its program.[152] So, in 1953, a symbolically important year marking the tenth anniversary of the uprising, the Chicago Council of the American Jewish Congress enlisted the World Congress for Jewish Culture and thirty other local Jewish organizations to create a citywide memorial event.

This represented a national trend. In the mid-1950s, communities around the country began to move away from several smaller separate, organizationally dominated memorial programs to a single, massive, citywide memorial program, at times organized by a body designated for that purpose alone. In Chicago, this meant the formation of the Chicago Yizkor Committee for Six Million Martyrs. The new organization's masthead proclaimed, "Chicago Jewry Unites to Commemorate the Fourteenth Anniversary of the Warsaw Ghetto Uprising." (Each year new stationery changed the number.) Where previously various organizations vied with each other over the Warsaw Ghetto program, now they began to go into coalitions with each other to stage a bigger and broader event than any could have on their own. In 1953 in New York City, the Club of Polish Jews joined with "two great American Jewish organizations, the B'nai B'rith and the American Jewish Committee," to create a mass memorial meeting at Hunter College's large auditorium. Their combined stature enabled them to secure General Telford Taylor, the chief prosecutor at the Nuremberg Trials, and "noted stage and screen star" Luther Adler as speaker and performer. The three organizations jointly proclaimed this event a "most solemn and sacred Anniversary, for on this day, we honor the memory of our dear departed ones who were the victims of Hitler's murders." The general and the actor would help "pay tribute to those who have no graves on which to place our wreaths."[153]

Elsewhere, rather than creating a new organization, the local Jewish community council (sometimes known as a Jewish community relations committee) filled that role. In 1955, the Jewish Community Council of Washington, D.C., which earlier had funded individual groups to stage their Warsaw Ghetto programs, began to discuss the logic of it, as the community's representative body, taking over sponsorship of "a *proper* observance of the Warsaw Ghetto uprising" for all Washington-area Jews. Noting that "the Yiddish-speaking groups in the community have done so for the past several years, as have other local Jewish groups including synagogues," the council believed it could do a better job, and a more elaborate event would draw larger crowds and more press attention. By 1958, it had taken over the memorial process.[154] This happened in Atlanta, Milwaukee, and Pittsburgh at the same time, creating as such a new era in Holocaust memorialization, one that emphasized coordinated community work.[155]

By the end of the 1950s, the ubiquity of Warsaw Ghetto memorial programs and their centrality to Jewish communal life garnered the attention of national Jewish organizations. They tracked such events, gleaned bits and pieces from the various programs, and provided communities with examples of outstanding ceremonies. Leah Jaffa of the National Jewish Welfare Board found impressive the script "Resistance and Redemption" written by Bernice Green, initially performed in Yiddish in Cleveland in 1960 by the Yiddish Cultural Committee of the Jewish Community Center. Jaffa offered other Jewish community centers an English version of the text, which linked the glory of the resistance to the memory of "our brothers, in the foul pits of Europe . . . Bergen-Belsen, Auschwitz, Treblinka. . . . The very names are fire on the lips / And gall to the speaking mouth / We remember you our brothers," victims of "the greatest holocaust / Which the Jewish people has ever endured."[156]

Planners of these events could count on the fact that American Jews repeatedly confronted images of the Warsaw Ghetto, grim accounts of the Jews penned in there, the murder in Treblinka of the vast majority of them, the heroism of the uprising of the few, and their ultimate defeat, in numerous places beyond annual memorial events. American Jewish publications did much to make the Warsaw Ghetto a central icon for the catastrophe as a whole and to use it as a prime part of their public culture.[157] The 1950 publication of *The Wall* by John Hersey and its transformation into a Broadway play a decade later helped solidify the Warsaw Ghetto's status.

When the play opened, theater reviewers for Jewish magazines seized on its importance. *Jewish Forum* recommended "the play for Jewish organizations because too many of us have in this era of good living, forgotten the lessons of World War II. We are too tolerant and unwilling to put out the fire before it becomes a conflagration." The reviewer pointed to recent political developments in the Middle East in particular and cited the "dangers to Jewish life now being quietly planned in many quarters of Europe and Egypt." *The Wall* (referring to the real wall which had immured the Jews of Warsaw), as a metaphor and a cultural event, the reviewer believed, could provide a fine countervailing force.[158] American Jews indeed had entered the postwar period primed to memorialize the Warsaw Ghetto, using it as the point of entry for remembering the victims as a collectivity.[159]

As a symbol, the Warsaw Ghetto uprising had become part of their communal culture as early as the days of the uprising itself. When the rebellion failed, Jews across America held tearful meetings. In October 1944, the New Jewish Folk Theater staged *Miracle of the Warsaw Ghetto*, with music composed by Sholom Secunda and actor Sam Jaffee offering the English commentary to the Yiddish play.[160] In 1945, the Jewish Labor Committee sponsored an art exhibition dedicated to the "Martyrs and Heroes of the Ghetto."[161] Just after the Germans suppressed the uprising, Arthur Szyk, a Polish Jew who arrived in America in 1940, painted *Defenders of the Warsaw Ghetto*, which the Jewish Museum exhibited in 1952 as part of a Szyk retrospective.[162]

In 1944, *The Eternal Light*, a weekly Sunday radio program sponsored by the Jewish Theological Seminary, showcased a drama, "The Battle of the Warsaw Ghetto," written by Morton Wishengrad.[163] Every year in April, and at other times as well, *The Eternal Light* featured the play, which ended with a eulogy for "the dead of the Warsaw Ghetto."[164] "The Battle of the Warsaw Ghetto," which began as a radio play, had a life beyond the airwaves, and it helped make the ghetto uprising a focal point of collective mourning. In 1952, for example, the Jewish students at Smith College, preparing for a combined Sabbath and Purim service, took the radio play, transformed it into a cantata, performed it on campus, and then took it on the road, staging it at B'nai B'rith chapters around the state.[165] Jewish students at the University of Maryland performed a reading of the play in 1953 at Hillel, as did the campers at Olin-Sang-Ruby, a camp sponsored by the Reform movement, in the summer of 1961.

American Jews heard the phrase "Warsaw Ghetto" repeatedly in speeches, sermons, and articles. The president of the National Federation

The National Federation of Temple Sisterhoods (NFTS), the organization of women from the Reform movement, offered this print, "a full-color reproduction," to members in 1952 at the special price of $3.95, encouraging them to buy it as a way "to pay homage to those who fell. . . . You will want to keep alive their memory." NFTS encouraged individual women and temple gift shops to order this piece of art, a testimony "from the hands of one who survived," as "it belongs in every Jewish home." *Courtesy American Jewish Archives.*

of Temple Sisterhoods (NFTS), the women's organization of the Reform movement, declared at the annual meeting of 1950 that "we have a magnificent double heritage. We are Americans. . . . We are Jews. We bear our burdens patiently but we emerge in triumph, be it from the land of Egypt, the walls of the Warsaw ghetto. . . . We always survive." In the middle of the 1950s, NFTS recommended that its members stock their synagogue gift shops with a print, suitable for framing. They suggested members display in their homes "The Ghetto Uprising in Warsaw, 1943," subtitled "The Walls Dripped Blood."[166]

Why did the Warsaw Ghetto become the prism through which American Jews performed the memory of the six million? Did the heroism of the ghetto fighters offer them something to be proud of rather than something that caused them shame? Did they use the Warsaw Ghetto as a magnet for community mourning because other images of the Holocaust inspired in them embarrassment and discomfort? The drama of the narrative cannot be denied, nor can the desire of American Jews and those around the world to be able to tell this story of consummate bravery. The fact that

Warsaw had been the single largest Jewish community in Europe certainly helped make it a central symbol. News of the uprising came to America as it took place, and the event became firmly fixed early into public Jewish consciousness. It occurred during Passover, the holiday of liberation, and that also enhanced its iconic status.

But the phrase "Warsaw Ghetto" did not always refer to the heroism of its last Jews. Just as often, it symbolized the death of the millions and their communities. As American Jewry experimented with ways to express its connection to the memory of the immense, impenetrable tragedy, it grabbed hold of the image of the Warsaw Ghetto as a metaphor for the catastrophe as a whole, and not just of the narrative of the poorly armed, but bold, fighters. Arnold Schoenberg set his 1948 musical offering *A Survivor from Warsaw* in a concentration camp rather than in the ghetto itself.[167] In 1954, the American Association for Jewish Education recommended a film, "Distant Journey (Ghetto Terezin)," as "especially useful in conjunction with the commemoration of the Warsaw Ghetto uprising of 1943." Sure to inspire viewers, the film, if shown at such community events, the educators' journal predicted, would be "good . . . for fundraising purposes and for inter-cultural programs." Notably, "Ghetto Terezin," a real historical place, had no particular connection to Warsaw, its ghetto, or its uprising.[168] In an analogous vein, historian Salo Baron in a 1958 essay used "Warsaw Ghetto" to encapsulate the entire extirpation of the European Jews and their civilization rather than to give rhetorical preference to the bravery of the few. In eastern Europe, Poland in particular, as in Germany, he wrote, "a great center of Jewish culture" had thrived. That cultural creativity, he noted, "flowered until the destruction of the Warsaw Ghetto." "Warsaw Ghetto" functioned here as the epicenter of Jewish doom rather than as a symbol of heroism.[169]

Even Warsaw Ghetto memorial programs did not actually privilege the resisters as deserving special memorialization, as opposed to the vastly larger number who had not engaged in armed rebellion. Programs pivoted around the symbolic use of the number six, embodied in the six candles, culminating in the dirges over all of the six million. Year after year, the Sholem Aleichem schools of Chicago sent out flyers and notices of the city-wide memorial event and also for its own special "ghetto yizkor evening" with speakers, singing, and candle lighting. Throughout the 1950s, after an abbreviated parent-teacher association meeting, the school performed its special ritual "to commemorate the Uprising of the Warsaw Ghetto . . . and the tragic extermination of six million Jews . . . the greatest catstrophy [*sic*] in Jewish History."[170] In announcing the 1951 Warsaw Ghetto Memorial Meeting in Los Angeles, the American Federation of Polish Jews elided the larger story with the smaller one, telling the Jewish public that "with the approach of Passover, the Jewish people, throughout the world again recall the heroic Uprising of the Warsaw Ghetto. . . . The last surviving Jews in Warsaw raised the banner of revolt against the armed might of Hitlerism, which had murdered six million of our brothers and sisters in concentration camps, gas chambers, and crematoriums."[171]

The widespread use of the number six in conjunction with Warsaw Ghetto memorial programs made it clear that the victims as a collectivity, rather than heroes and fighters, served as the real subjects of the commemorations. That same flyer, sent out by the Workmen's Circle for the World Congress announcing the Warsaw Ghetto memorial ceremony, made manifest that larger purpose. The World Jewish Congress "has come up with the idea of lighting six candles in every Jewish home and Jewish organization and schools for Jewish children . . . as a reminder of the perished martyrs. . . . We call upon all of our branches and every individual member of the Arbeiter Ring to light in their homes the six *yahrtzeit* lights. . . . If it is possible, the . . . candles should be in the windows. Let this be a strong and open manifestation of our sorrow and pain."[172] In 1954, the World Jewish Congress surveyed the ceremonies that had taken place across America and around the world, listing and analyzing how and where the meetings had been conducted. It concluded that *"the Warsaw Ghetto Uprising has already become a symbol of what might be called The Third Churban, the destruction of six million Jews."* The report continued: *"It is no accident, but rather profoundly significant, that the Warsaw Ghetto Uprising commemorations are now combined with the lighting of six candles, each for one million murdered Jews, thereby clearly indicating that the commemoration of the Warsaw Ghetto Uprising is accepted as a symbol of the whole Third Churban"*[173] (emphasis in original).

The desire for communal gatherings to publicly acknowledge the recent horrendous events could not be sated by a single day. American Jews found other moments in time to hold memorial ceremonies. The New Home Club of Milwaukee annually marked the anniversary of "Crystal Night of 1938" with speeches, prayers, and the recollections of those who had witnessed the horrifying event of the destruction of nearly every synagogue in Germany, the smashing of Jewish stores and places of business, and the violent murders of many Jews. German Jews, in particular, saw this event as the prelude to the Holocaust.[174] *Landsmanshaftn* organized

צינדט 6 יאָרצייט=ליכט

צום אָנדענק פון די 6 מיליאָן קדושים

דאנערשטיק, דעם 19 אפריל, 1951, 6 אָוונט

צום 8־טן יאָרצייט פון אויפשטאַנד אין וואַרשעווער געטאָ

זאָל מען אין יעדער יידישער שטוב, אין יעדער יידישער אָרגאָניזאַציע
און אין די שולן פאַר קינדער אָנצינדן 6 ליכט — אַ סימבאָל פון
אונזער אַלעמענס טרויער און וויי טיק.

אַלוועלטלעכער יידישער קולטור־קאָנגרעס

(יידישער אַרבעטער־קאָמיטעט, ציוניסטישער אַרבעטער־קאָמיטעט פֿאַר הילף און אויפבוי,
אַרבעטער־רינג, יידיש־נאַציאָנאַלער אַרבעטער־פֿאַרבאַנד, י. ל. פּרץ שרייבער־פֿאַראיין, פֿען
קלוב, „ציקאָ", שלום עליכם פֿאָלקס־אינסטיטוט, פֿאַראייניקטע יידישע געווערקשאַפֿטן, א. א.)

LIGHT 6 CANDLES

In Memory of the 6 Million Martyrs

on THURSDAY APRIL 19, 1951, at 6 P. M.

8th Anniversary of the Warsaw Ghetto Uprising

Every Jewish home, every Jewish organization and all schools should light
six candles as a symbol of our deep sorrow and mourning.

CONGRESS FOR JEWISH CULTURE

Jewish schools and other community institutions, including the Workmen's Circle, the Sholem Aleichem Folk schools, the Jewish Labor Committee, and various
Zionist groups, distributed these flyers to their members on behalf of the World
Congress for Jewish Culture, encouraging Jewish families and organizations to
light six candles as a memorial to the six million. The idea of lighting six candles
in homes and institutions represented one of many proposed ways to remember
the victims of the Holocaust which circulated in and around American Jewish
community settings. *Courtesy YIVO Institute for Jewish Research.*

annual memorial meetings at their headquarters and, if they had put up a memorial stone, in the cemetery on the anniversary of the German invasion of their towns.[175] The Committee of Jews from Czechoslovakia in New York held an annual service to mark "March 8, 1944," when "3,560 Czechoslvak Jews perished in the gas chambers of the extermination camp in Poland."[176] These programs had a relatively fixed format but also made room for new artistic and creative works to supplement traditional liturgies of mourning and first-person accounts of survivors. The postwar years witnessed an abundance of such rituals, sometimes competing, sometimes complementary, all of which reinforced American Jews' commitment to sanctifying the memory of those who had endured such brutal deaths.

Art as Memorial

American Jews created a corpus of artistic works that engaged with the memory of the six million through music, drama, pageantry, and dance. Creating, performing, and consuming these works linked American Jewish expressive culture with the memory of the six million. This took place in multiple genres and represented the broad-based sense of American Jewry that they had to, and wanted to, memorialize the calamity.

Jewish organizations, for example, issued songbooks, compilations of familiar and new pieces, Hebrew, Yiddish, and English, which they used at organizational meetings and in assemblies at community centers, schools, and camps. Jewish publishing houses also produced such texts. These songbooks, sometimes no more elaborate than pamphlets, others published by Jewish publishing houses, all included certain canonical Holocaust pieces. The two most familiar of these, "Ani Ma'amin" and the "Hymn of the Partisans," sometimes titled "Zog nit keinmol" (when translated into Hebrew, "Al nah tomar") [Do not say that you are on your last road], the opening line of the song, appeared in dozens of songbooks.

Entering into the American repertoire in the late 1940s, these songs became part of the warp and woof of Jewish community life. The editors of the "songsters" usually introduced the songs with explanations of their origins. In 1949, Bernard Carp prepared a songbook for Jewish community centers and for "every type of youth and adult Jewish organization, club, or group." He described "Ani Ma'amin" as "one of the Thirteen Principles of the Faith formulated by Maimonides and set to music by a nameless victim in the Warsaw Ghetto. It spread to guerrilla units and concentration

ANI MA'AMIN

The words and lyrics of songs drawn from the Holocaust showed up in postwar American Jewish songbooks, those published by organizations and those issued by publishing houses, as well as more informally produced song sheets used at camps and schools, with "Ani Ma'amin" and "The Hymn of the Partisans" most often included. Henry Coopersmith's 1950 *The Songs We Sing*, published by the Conservative movement, got wide usage in Jewish communal circles. Coopersmith made clear the Holocaust context of the singing of "Ani Ma'amin," although he erred grievously in the left-hand bottom explanation that "This song was sung by the DPs who were about to be cremated by the Nazis." No doubt the vast discussion among American Jews about the needs of the Displaced Persons caused his confusion. *Courtesy United Synagogue of Conservative Judaism.*

camps, giving hope and encouragement amidst unspeakable tragedy."[177] Harry Coopersmith in *The Songs We Sing*, published by the Conservative movement's United Synagogue of America in 1950, introduced "Ani Ma'amin," as "sung by the Nazi victims who were about to be cremated."[178] The songster *P'tsah b'zemer* [Break out in song] of 1959 considered the "Partizaner Lied" to be "the most stirring partisan song from the Second World War . . . written to commemorate the uprising by the Jews in the Vilna Ghetto. It has become a memorial symbol for all Jews destroyed during the Nazi era."[179]

Songbooks carried musical versions of two poems by Hannah Senesh, "Ailee, Ailee" [My God, my God], and "Ashre hagafrur" [Blessed is the match], which linked the poetry to her death at the hands of the Nazis. Other songs included in anthologies also carried deep emotional valence because of their Holocaust connection. Introducing the Hebrew version of slain poet Mordecai Gebertig's song "Ha-ayara bo-eret" [The town is burning], the editor of the Young Zionist Action Committee songbook told how "this song was written in Kharkov by the noted folk poet just before he was murdered by the Gestapo."[180] Camp Hemshekh, a summer camp founded in New York State by Holocaust survivors for their now American children in 1959, paid tribute to the ordeal undergone by the founders through its *"lieder bukh,"* songbook, which included the standard "Zog nit keinmol," as well as "Varshe" [Warsaw], "Yugnt-hymn" [Youth hymn], composed in the Vilna Ghetto, "Tsu eyns, tsvey, drey" [One, two, three], also collected in Vilna under German occupation, "Friling in Geto" [Spring in the ghetto], and "Oyfn lager" [In the concentration camp].[181] The repertoire had grown large enough and the songs so thoroughly woven into American Jewish life that the Union of American Hebrew Congregations in 1960 published a full-length book, *Songs of the Concentration Camps.*[182]

Not the exclusive domain of Jewish organizations, other songbooks engaged with the memory of the victims of the Nazi era. Chemjo Vinaver's *Anthology of Jewish Music* of 1955 placed original artwork by Marc Chagall on the jacket and the frontispiece. It included a liturgy using the words of Psalm 23 set to the music of "David Eisenstadt, choirmaster of the Tlomacka Synagogue in Warsaw. During the second World War he was killed by the Nazis." It also included a "Chassidic nigun" (melody), which Vinaver recalled, he had heard first in Warsaw in 1915, "sung by Reb Yechiel Alter . . . killed by the Nazis."[183]

Ruth Rubin, a well-known figure in both Jewish and American folk music circles of the 1950s and 1960s, helped spread Jewish songs outside of Jewish settings. Her 1950 *Treasury of Jewish Folksong* devoted a special section to "Partisan Songs," "songs composed during the catastrophic years of the Second World War . . . [that] sound the note of horror . . . songs of concentration camps, satiric songs full of hatred of the enemy, documentary ballads describing the hunger, exposure, inhuman labor, beatings, degradation and—finally—gas chambers, the Hebrew chants of Jews going to their death."[184]

American Jewish communal assemblies resounded with these songs. As early as 1947, a Milwaukee Yiddish newspaper described the "Partisans' Hymn" as "now very popular."[185] Communal programs often opened with these songs, and their performance erased vast ideological differences. In 1951, the Synagogue Council of America opened its silver anniversary dinner with "Ani Ma'amin," described by the master of ceremonies as "the melody and . . . words . . . sung by millions of our people in our day as they went on toward Kiddush hashem, the sanctification of G-d's [in the original] name."[186] Three years later, the Communist Yiddish newspaper *The Morning Freiheit* celebrated its thirty-second anniversary at Carnegie Hall, where the Jewish Peoples' Philharmonic Chorus sang the very same "Ani Ma'amin," described as a "Ghetto Song."[187] Two very different Jewish institutions—one bent on stimulating religious observance, the other on furthering a leftist agenda—considered this anthem of the Holocaust as theirs.

Jewish communal organizations fostered artistic memorializations of the Holocaust, blending music and drama into theatrical pageants. New York Rabbi Louis I. Newman of the Reform synagogue Rodef Shalom wrote and staged numerous plays in the late 1940s and 1950s. He recruited adult women and men of the congregation as actors and singers and included the children of the religious school. The congregants performed *Ein bereirah: No Alternative* during Hanukkah in 1949. It featured the "Vilna Ghetto Song" [The partisans' hymn], sung in Hebrew and English. *The Eternal Temple* of 1952 highlighted the other anthem of the catastrophe, "Ani Ma'amin." In the performance, after the Chronicler character declaimed to the audience how "the martyrs had gone to death by the myriads, singing the words of the hymn of faith," the airwaves resounded with the familiar words and music.[188] Samuel Citron wrote a set of plays for Jewish schools, and in *Darkness and Light,* a Hanukkah play for twelve- to fourteen-year-olds, he instructed the child representing the seventh candle to say, "there was darkness in Poland and Russia and all of Europe when we died in pogroms and as Hitler's victims, but the light came and we went free."[189]

New York's Society for the Advancement of Judaism, a Reconstructionist congregation that took the performing arts seriously, made performance a partner in remembering the Jewish victims of the Holocaust. In 1955, David Reiss, a young person who had grown up at the SAJ and now attended Harvard College, composed *For There Is Hope*, performed by the senior class as part of its graduation service. Based on words drawn from the Book of Job, "the scene of the students' presentation was the Ghetto in Warsaw under Hitler." This cantata blended a hopeful message for the future, embodied in its title, with the catastrophe's deaths and destructions.[190]

Most likely, no one other than the graduates' family and friends attended *For There Is Hope*, and the audiences for Louis I. Newman's cantatas extended no further than the congregation. But other works created by American Jews, supported and praised by Jewish organizations, cast their net more widely. In 1949, Sophie Maslow gave her first performance of *The Village I Knew*, a piece inspired by Marc Chagall's paintings and Sholem Aleichem's stories, at the American Dance Festival in New London, Connecticut, and in 1951 at the 92nd Street YM-YWHA. While ostensibly the dance had no Holocaust connection, Maslow wrote in the program notes that she considered it a memorial to the victims of the Nazi Holocaust. Their destruction had inspired her, and she danced it in their memory. In 1956, Maslow choreographed and performed *Anniversary*, described in *Dance Observer* as "a passionate and beautiful tribute to the Jews who perished in the Warsaw Ghetto during the Nazi liquidation," thereby providing a perfect example of "a time to mourn and a time to dance."[191]

Arnold Schoenberg's *A Survivor from Warsaw*, which premiered in 1947, brought the memory of the Holocaust to Americans through high culture. Conceived of as a "deliberate juxtaposition of helplessness, heroism, and faith" and commissioned by the Koussevitsky Foundation, *A Survivor from Warsaw* had its first performance in 1948 by the Albuquerque Civic Orchestra. The work employed an orchestra and a chorus and made use of a twelve-tone technique. It opened with the narrator saying, "I cannot remember everything. I must have been unconscious most of the time," and ended with the chorus chanting, indeed screaming, over and over again, the "Shema Yisrael." Jewish publications considered *A Survivor from Warsaw* to be a highly visible memorial to the Jews who had undergone the catastrophe, those who survived, and the vastly larger number, the six million, who did not.[192]

American Jews felt compelled to memorialize the victims of the European calamity, and at every level of their public lives, national and local, they did so. Invocations to remember the six million reverberated in their works, and calls resounded for them to remember more and better. Although they entered the postwar period with no firm idea as to how to do so or what constituted an appropriate form, they experimented with words, images, times, and places to inscribe the memory of European Jewry into their communal culture. Lacking a clear model as to the nature of a fitting memorial did not stop them from constructing many. Rather, they saw themselves as creators and participants in a vast memorial project that spanned the entirety of their public culture.

Postwar American Jewish life engaged with the memory of the brutal deaths of six million of their people, and this involved the women and men who belonged to Jewish organizations, sent their children to religious schools, tuned in to Jewish radio programs, attended Jewish theatrical productions, read a Jewish newspaper in whatever language, belonged to a Jewish organization, or contributed money to some Jewish cause. They participated in memorial activities, without always calling them that, and although the European catastrophe never represented the sum total of what being Jewish meant to them, neither did they avoid it. Instead, within the limits of their abilities, they found countless times, spaces, and means to weave the memory of the six million into their communal lives.

How stark the contrast between this vibrant and variegated memorial repertoire and the scholarly consensus, best summarized by historian Edward Linenthal, who declared that in the postwar period, "even in the American Jewish community, the Holocaust was virtually invisible."[193] Those who have written about this period and its American Jews have taken no notice of grassroots experimentations, organization by organization and community by community, the memorial effort that American Jewry lauched across all segments of the collectivity, regardless of ideology, class, language, or geography. The scholars who have written about this era have shut their ears to the voices of the Jews of America, as did Susannah Heschel, who claimed like so many later observers, that only with "the 1967 Middle East war . . . American Jews began to speak publicly about the Holocaust."[194] Such assertions, in the main based on sketchy or no empirical evidence, have drowned out the nearly ubiquitous invocations intoned by postwar Jews, offered by them in their communal settings and as they turned to the American public, on their need, indeed sacred obligation, to remember.

For some Jews in the years following the catastrophe, the project went beyond *just* remembering. They understood not only the limitations of remembering as an end in itself but that, in order to remember, Jews and others also had to know the facts and had to be reminded of them. In order for the memory of the six million to have an impact on the present and the future, those who could needed to extend their scope beyond memorializing, pure and simple. As institutions and individuals, they embarked on a set of activities for studying, teaching, writing, and displaying the facts of the European Jewish catastrophe. Memory would not suffice. They needed to balance pathos and mourning with information. They believed that they had lessons to learn and teach, and in order to do so, they had to make sure that the story of what had happened got told and retold.

2

Telling the World

"OF MAKING BOOKS there is no end," Shlomo Katz observed in 1962 in *Midstream*, the Zionist magazine he edited. Quoting Ecclesiastes in this survey of postwar American Jewish letters, he noted that the same compulsion to write which the biblical writer had observed "more than two thousand years ago" continued into the present: "This is also true of the great catastrophe that befell the Jews in Europe in our day. . . . A host of books have been written."[1] Commentators as a whole agreed with this assessment, noting that, since the end of World War II, American Jews as authors, editors, and publishers; lecturers and teachers; and producers of cultural works in multiple genres had created a corpus of works that presented details of the Holocaust to diverse audiences of Jews and non-Jews, who consumed them.

As they saw it, their world abounded in talk about the Holocaust. Trude Weiss-Rosmarin, editor of the *Jewish Spectator*, had deemed that literature large nearly a decade earlier than Katz, writing in 1953 in a note introducing Yossel Ostrover's short story "I Believe with Perfect Faith," a "touching memoir of a survivor of the Warsaw Ghetto." Readers, she asserted, had access to a "vast literature of recollections of men and women who experienced the hell of the Ghetto."[2]

Those who reflected on the state of American Jewry emphasized the broad penetration of the tragedy of the six million into their public sphere. In 1951, Rufus Learsi, the creator of the Seder of Remembrance, remarked that "the murder of European Jewry by the Nazis is a story that is no longer untold," while four years later, Leibush Lehrer, a Yiddish educator and communal activist, asserted that the recent calamity had produced a body of texts far surpassing those of earlier tragedies in Jewish history: "In the course of their long history of Jewish pain the Jews have not distinguished themselves with such productions known as 'in order that they might know,' as since the last greatest destruction of ours."[3]

None who evaluated the texts on the fate of the six million considered the task of telling about their brutal deaths to be devoid of daunting challenges. In the main, they considered ordinary modes of presentation unequal to its gravity. Known best as a humorist, Harry Golden, editor of Charlotte's *Carolina Israelite*, pondered in 1957 the near impossibility of such writing. "How," he asked, "could you begin to write of the slaughter of one-third of the Jewish population of the world? You cannot do it with statistics or with any recognizable form of fiction."[4] Samuel Charney Niger, a Yiddish writer, similarly saw the inherent limitations of conventional modes of writing when it came to the Holocaust: "Modern day Eliphazes and Bildads," Job's friends in the biblical text of suffering, "could not remain mute . . . to the destruction of the Old Home." Those who "had not been in Treblinka," and those who "*were* in Treblinka," faced "the difficulty, on the one hand, of finding words to express "the grief that was very great," coupled with, on the other hand, the overpowering need for unburdening their sorrow." To Niger, who had not been there, this made "ours . . . a literature of memoirs, documentation, history."[5] So, too, Dr. Max Grünewald, at the dedication of the Leo Baeck Institute in 1962, speculated on whether he and his generation might not be "altogether too close to the fire that consumed one-third of the Jewish people and do not in our situation the words of Shelley find their full application: 'Those graves are all too young as yet to have outgrown the sorrow which consigned its charge to each.' "[6]

Grünewald's rhetorical question, posed at the opening of an institution dedicated to conserving the documents of the destroyed Jews of Germany, might properly have been answered in the positive. Yes, postwar American Jews did live too close to the Holocaust's horror to adequately recount its details. But then they, the Jews of America who for the most part had been physically removed from the tragedy, might have rightly answered Golden's query by admitting that they could not write about such a cataclysm through available literary forms.

But as a collectivity, the Jews of postwar America answered both challenges in opposite ways. They found multiple opportunities to show, through a variety of means, what had befallen the Jews of Europe. They shared their insights about the Holocaust through books, magazine and newspaper articles, memoirs, poetry, fiction, and nonfiction of a scholarly and popular nature. Their magazines showcased short stories, poems, and essays that described what had happened, while book reviews tracked the emergence of a global literature on the catastrophe. They delivered lectures and taught classes that made the Holocaust a focus of Jewish public life. American Jews communicated with each other, with Jews around the world, and with the larger American public about the European cataclysm, integrating it into their communal culture by presenting its facts. Only a small minority created such works, but they did so for a public that consumed them and seemed to want even more.

Writers, scholars, rabbis, educators, editors, and others who wove the details of the Holocaust into their works rarely complained, as historians would later, that American Jews avoided the issue or that the leadership suppressed it. The writers, organizers of Jewish communal events, speakers, and participants might have been puzzled by Peter Novick's words written decades later, when he claimed that "between the end of the war and the 1960s, as anyone who had lived through those years can testify, the Holocaust made scarcely any appearance in American public discourse, and hardly more in Jewish public discourse."[7] They might surely have been surprised to read about their world as characterized by a "long . . . silence on the Holocaust."[8]

Instead, they remarked on American Jews' familiarity with the places, events, and terms that collectively made up the Holocaust. Repeatedly, writers invoked "Maidanek," "Treblinka," "Auschwitz," "the Warsaw Ghetto," "the crematoria," and "the six million" without explanation, assuming, rightly, that their readers knew what these meant. Art historian Alfred Werner, reviewing *Children's Drawings and Poems: Terezin 1942–1944*, the catalog of a Prague exhibit, opined in 1961 that "so much has been written in the past decade about Hitler's 'model ghetto,' Terezin, . . . that no Jew . . . can find it difficult now to trace on the map of his heart the location of this obscure fortress-town in northern Bohemia."[9] To Werner, then, the 1950s had been a time in which American Jews taught and learned the details of the catastrophe.

As on-the-scene commentators surveyed American Jewry and its reading habits, they saw how so much of what constituted their public sphere grew out of the Holocaust. In 1958, one constant observer of the Jewish book scene, Leo Shpall, reviewed Philip Friedman's *Their Brothers' Keepers*, a study of Christians who had rescued Jews from the Nazis. The "Jewish persecution and extermination by the Nazis," he wrote, has, "in the course of years, created a vast literature."[10] Another writer the following year, reflecting on Meyer Levin's novel *Eva*, assessed that "we have an abundance of books and articles on the story of the annihilation of the Jews of Europe. These books range from novels to source books containing valuable documentary material which gives evidence of the atrocities and cruelties inflicted by the Nazis."[11]

Presenting the Holocaust differed from memorializing it. Memorial materials, sermons, liturgies, *yizker bikher*, cemetery markers, and mourning ceremonies made the project of remembering the victims an end in itself, a sacred duty to those who had perished. Presentations of the Holocaust privileged the acquisition and diffusion of knowledge. Those engaged in this endeavor placed learning on a different plane than emotionally charged memorial works. They hoped to foster an understanding of how this ordeal had happened and, by extension, wanted to ensure that such knowledge could affect the present.

But no line sharply bisected texts and programs for remembering from those that told the history. The two depended on each other and together shaped the postwar American Jewish public life. The *yizker bikher*, perfect examples of memorials to the victims and their communities, depended on research and the collection of primary documents. These "paper memorials" presented extensive information, including the names of the victims, their photographs, and the grim details of invasions and liquidations. Memorial ceremonies drew on, and then stimulated, research. In preparing for Warsaw Ghetto memorial programs, organizers culled the available scholarship and enlisted speakers to lecture on the facts of the catastrophe. Their analytic words took their places alongside tearful liturgies and martyrological anthems. In 1953, in anticipation of the tenth anniversary of the doomed ghetto revolt, Isaac Schwarzbart of the World Jewish Congress issued a twenty-three-page analysis of the history of the Warsaw Ghetto uprising, including original documents, a day-by-day account of what had happened, and a bibliography.[12]

American Jews used these materials for a variety of ends. Writers and scholars aimed much of their work at fellow Jews, hoping that with this knowledge they would become more Jewishly engaged, whether by increasing their contributions to Jewish causes, participating more actively in Jewish communal life, or working harder to further Jewish political goals, as always, defined differently by different segments of "the community." Both the leaders and the rank and file wanted the broad American public to be exposed to these presentations as well. When they believed that the American media, for example, shunned the Holocaust story, they protested. For example, Mr. Tash of Aracoma Drive in Cincinnati dashed off an angry letter to WCPO-TV in 1962 because it had not broadcast a CBS special, *An Act of Faith?*, a drama concerning "the Danish people" who "rescued virtually their entire Jewish population from the Nazis." Why, he wanted to know, did the station make that decision? He claimed authority on the subject since "my ancestors came here to escape European 'ghettoes' just like those who escaped Hitler and the Nazis."[13]

Making the Presentations Possible

Those who created postwar American Jewish public culture believed that while the public had access to much material about the European tragedy, it needed more and constantly called for further expansion of the field of knowledge. Historian Solomon Bloom, in a 1949 piece in *Commentary* on the "Dictator of the Lodz Ghetto," declared that "it is imperative to know everything about the Holocaust," expressing the hope that his short article might stimulate more articles and books.[14] Philip Friedman, a historian who played a pivotal part in making Bloom's vision a reality, called on scholars not just to produce articles but to ultimately opt for big books that treated the totality of the Holocaust. Reviewing British historian Gerald Reitlinger's *The Final Solution: The Attempt to Exterminate the Jews of Europe, 1939–1945*, Friedman remarked that, as of 1954, "only a few attempts have been made to date to encompass the full scope of the great Jewish catastrophe during the Nazi era in a scientifically documented presentation." Hailing the book as a "pioneering enterprise," Friedman predicted that with time such work would follow.[15]

Friedman's and Bloom's wishes would have to wait until librarians and archivists collected, cataloged, and organized the millions of documents that constituted the Holocaust's primary material. Not the work of a year, a decade, or even several decades, only slowly did the vast and scattered material become available, and only step by step did archivists make it ready for researchers to use. Indeed, by the early twenty-first century, new archives still opened up, further extending the base of primary sources on which scholars could write their books about the fate of Europe's Jews.[16]

Yet, even given the necessary slowness of the archival process, postwar American Jewish communal organizations sponsored numerous projects to present the facts, albeit in piecemeal fashion, considering it in the political and cultural interests of American and world Jewry to reveal the history of the Nazi era and expose the extent of Germany's crimes against the Jews to the public.

A wide array of organizations, despite their divergent ideologies, facilitated the writing and dissemination of such books. Jacob Lestchinsky, a sociologist and demographer working for the Institute for Jewish Affairs, an arm of the World Jewish Congress in New York, researched and wrote *Balance Sheet of Extermination,* published in 1946. Two years later, the American Jewish Congress brought out his full-length study, *Crisis, Catastrophe, and Survival.* Other titles from the Institute for Jewish Affairs presses included Anatole Goldstein's 1950 *From Discrimination to Annihilation.* The institute revisited the Holocaust in 1956 by issuing *European Jewry Ten Years After the War.* The book's subtitle, *An Account of the Development and Present Status of the Decimated Jewish Communities of Europe,* made it clear that the Holocaust served as the booklet's point of reference.[17]

The American Jewish Committee, which during the war had published material about the unfolding tragedy, continued throughout the postwar period to advance its liberal agenda by facilitating the publication of Holocaust-related material. Committed for both ideological and strategic reasons to promoting the idea that prejudice and discrimination against any group harmed society as a whole, and that knowledge could reduce prejudice, it commissioned its Studies in Prejudice Series in 1949. Several of the volumes sought to explain the roots and consequences of the German campaign against the Jews, particularly Paul Massing's *Rehearsal for Destruction: A Study of Political Anti-Semitism in Imperial Germany,* which searched for the origins of the Holocaust in German history, looking back to the late 1860s. Other books in the series, like Nathan Ackerman and Marie Jahoda's *Anti-Semitism and Emotional Disorder,* emphasized psychological pathologies as the root causes of Nazism.[18] All the books in this series came out under the imprimatur of Harper Brothers, one of the country's largest publishing houses, as did Selma Hirsh's *The Fears Men Live By.* Hirsh, an American Jewish Committee (AJC) staff member, summarized for a general readership the themes of the scholarly volumes in the Studies in Prejudice Series.[19] In addition, in 1955 the AJC collaborated with Syracuse University Press to publish an English translation of Leon Poliakov's *Harvest of Hate,* a book that "uses primary source material in documenting the Nazi program for the extermination of the Jews."[20]

For some of the organizations on the American Jewish scene, presenting the Holocaust involved providing material assistance to those involved in collecting the basic documents that subsequent historians could then employ in their books. Since the end of the war, the American Jewish Committee had collaborated extensively with Isaac Schneersohn's effort in France to collect documents and place them in the Center for Contemporary Jewish Documentation in Paris. It also helped underwrite the first European conference on the study of the Holocaust, which took place in

November 1947, a gathering of researchers to which the committee sent representatives.[21] Documenting the Holocaust, nearly all realized, depended on gathering primary sources and also interviewing those who had undergone this ordeal. The Jewish Labor Committee (JLC) and the American Jewish Joint Distribution Committee as such helped underwrite a number of historical commissions in Europe, in the Displaced Persons camps. The commissions interviewed survivors and attempted to gather documents produced by the Jews themselves. The JLC provided much of the financial resources for the unearthing, processing, and transcribing of the hidden diaries kept in the Warsaw Ghetto by Emanuel Ringelblum, who had met his death there. Found after the war, the fragile documents had to be painstakingly exhumed and restored, becoming eventually the most important source of information on life for the Jews of Warsaw under Nazi rule. The infusion of funds from the American Jewish labor organization made that later scholarship possible.[22]

Detailing the Holocaust and disseminating that information took up much of the energy of the Jewish Labor Committee, starting as early as 1946 when it began to fund several "historical and research institutes, gathering material from the ghetto years." It acquired a list of names from the archives of Dachau, detailing those who perished there, and for years the Jewish Labor Committee maintained these records. Initially intended to help people in New York "see and verify the destruction of their brethren and friends overseas," the trade union group recognized that the material had importance beyond the personal.[23] As of 1954, it reported that these documents "possess an incalculable historical importance" and constitute a major source on "the fantastic destruction wrought by Hitler."[24]

Holocaust-related books also won prizes and benefited from the subvention of Jewish cultural institutions. The Jewish Book Council of America gave its 1952 award to Soma Morgenstern's *The Third Testament of the Lost Son*, published by the Jewish Publication Society of America, "a beautiful monument of the destroyed civilization of the East European Jews."[25] The L. Lamed Foundation of Detroit, founded in 1940 by Louis Lamed to advance "the best creative efforts in Hebrew and Yiddish by writers living in America," honored numerous books that took the European catastrophe as background, setting, and moral inspiration. In 1947, it bestowed its prize on Hayim Leivik's "In Treblinka bin ikh nit geven" [I was not in Treblinka], and the following year it honored a collection of poems by Aaron Glanz-Leyless, a work "spun out of the enormous tragedy Germany dealt the Jews. There is anger, indignation, the fist clenched in disconsolate mourning . . . the remorseless drive to see our enemy forever destroyed." Over the course of the late 1940s and 1950s, it honored creative work on the Holocaust, hoping that its awards would encourage further presentations of works on "the annihilation of East European Jewry."[26]

No institution on the postwar American Jewish communal landscape did more to foster the presentation of the Holocaust than YIVO (Yidisher Visinshaftlekher Institut), the Jewish Scientific Institute, which had fled to New York from Vilna, Lithuania, in 1940. In its pre-1940 incarnation, YIVO took as its mission the stimulation and dissemination of scholarship on the totality of Jewish history and culture. The war literally destroyed the world of YIVO, and it and some of its staff moved to New York, where it narrowed its scope of study to Yiddish and eastern European Jewish culture, those elements of Jewish life so brutally extirpated by the Germans. YIVO activists took upon themselves the task of telling about the Holocaust. Its September 1945 newsletter to members and subscribers, *YIVO Bletter*, included a fifteen-page listing of YIVO founders and members who had died at the hands of the Nazis, and the black-bordered pages, with the Yiddish/Hebrew word *yizker* (remember) repeated on every page, indicated how YIVO saw itself as a mourner and survivor, committed to continuing the work of those whose names appeared on the list, whose lives had been violently cut short.

In the years after World War II, YIVO became one of the world's major players in collecting and cataloging the primary documents of the Holocaust, in fostering scholarly research about it, and in telling the details of the catastrophe to the public. YIVO helped make a memorial culture possible by systematically preparing scholarly materials and presenting them. *Landsmanshaftn* used the institute's resources to create their *yizker bikher*, and television and radio show producers and the organizers of memorial pageants turned to its archives.[27]

The presentation of the catastrophe took center stage among YIVO's many projects. The pages of its various publications, *YIVO Bletter*, the *YIVO Annual*, and *Yedios*, a Yiddish and English newsletter, abounded with the details of the destruction. In these publications, YIVO described its efforts to collect the basic documents of the Holocaust era, sharing with readers in minute detail its progress in gathering, archiving, and microfilming primary materials, creating bibliographies, and assisting the scholars who used these resources. Photographs from the Holocaust appeared in nearly every issue, and even illustrations of pre-Holocaust Jewish life in

Europe bore captions that told directly that the people in the pictures had perished in the inferno, that the Germans had obliterated the places they had once occupied.

YIVO began collecting Holocaust material in the immediate postwar period. Between 1945 and 1954, it participated in a project in the Displaced Persons camps to create the "Archives on Jewish Life Under the Nazis." It worked in 595 locations throughout Europe to collect written material and conduct interviews with many Jews, including Jewish chaplains and soldiers in the U.S. Army, workers for Jewish relief agencies, particularly the American Jewish Joint Distribution Committee, and survivors themselves. YIVO brought these materials to New York, for cataloging, archiving, and eventually for public use. YIVO melded this collection with one found by the U.S. military. The American occupation forces in Germany had come across a massive trove of documents collected by the Nazis, intended to document their successful and complete destruction of the Jewish people. Their plans foiled, the American military transferred the material from Frankfurt to YIVO, and from that emerged the basis of the massive and constantly growing repository in New York.[28]

YIVO built its earliest exhibitions, conferences, and publications around this material. The first staging of the documents gathered in the DP camps took place in January 1947, when YIVO sponsored "Jews in Europe, 1939–1946," an exhibit of documents, photographs, and objects showing "the extent and ramifications of the Nazi crimes against the Jewish people."[29] YIVO launched "Jews in Europe, 1939–1946" at its annual conference, at which all speakers, most scholars, addressed the multiple ramifications of the Holocaust.[30] The material deposited in New York by the army also enabled YIVO's director, Max Weinreich, to produce one of the first postwar pieces of scholarship on the Holocaust era, *Hitler's Professors*, of 1946.[31]

YIVO recognized the pressing need to go beyond this material, which derived primarily from German sources. In 1953, it entered into conversations with Jerusalem's Yad Vashem to create a cooperative relationship that included sharing materials through microfilm, creating joint bibliographies, and collaborating on research projects—all to enhance and expand the scholarship. "Nothing can be done," noted a 1954 issue of *Yedios* announcing the conclusion of the negotiations with Yad Vashem, "to bring back to life the six million victims who were slaughtered in Europe. We cannot, however, be deprived of the treasures of that culture and spirit which enriched Jewish life . . . nor of their reintegration into the eternal and creative spirit of the Jewish people."[32]

YIVO displayed its Holocaust treasures at exhibitions in New York, Los Angeles, and Chicago, focusing on the catastrophe, directly and indirectly. In 1953, for the tenth anniversary of the Warsaw Ghetto uprising, it devoted its exhibition space, publications, and annual conference specifically to that ghetto, the life lived in it, its liquidation, and then the last stage, the uprising and its suppression.[33] Other YIVO exhibits did not put "catastrophe" in their titles, but it figured in the material displayed, the publicity produced, and audience reaction. In 1959, YIVO mounted a traveling exhibit on "The Shtetl," described as "the essence of Jewish life in Eastern Europe which is no more." YIVO hoped that the eight hundred objects and photographs it displayed would teach visitors about the way of life that had been typical of these Jewish small towns, while it highlighted "the fearful tragedy of the death of the shtetl," spanning the period "from the beginning of our century to its destruction at the hands of the Nazis."[34]

YIVO's work took place within a national and global project of collecting Holocaust documents, encouraging their use, and fostering an ever-expanding body of materials to present them. Other American Jews, as individuals and through their organizations, also played a role in gathering such material. In 1945, Boston librarian Fanny Goldstein, as an example, set up her own clipping file at the West End branch of the public library, on "the Jews under Nazi domination." She arranged for visits by local Jewish and non-Jewish notables, showing off her extensive documents, a project that one rabbi predicted "will be indispensable for the Jewish historian of the future who will attempt to make an objective study of the Jews in the Nazi years."[35]

Such scattered and spontaneous projects could make but a small dent on the massive collecting and archiving project that lay ahead of American and world Jewry in the years after the end of the war. Collecting Holocaust material, getting it ready for scholarly use, and producing the early scholarship owed much to the Conference of Jewish Material Claims Against Germany, known as the Claims Conference, which hammered out an agreement with the Federal Republic of Germany in 1953 for financial compensation to the Jewish people for the property stolen by the Germans. American Jewish organizations sat on the Claims Conference, including the American Jewish Committee, the American Jewish Congress, the American Jewish Joint Distribution Committee, the American Zionist

Council, B'nai B'rith, the Jewish Labor Committee, the Jewish War Veterans, and the Synagogue Council of America.[36]

The mandate of the Claims Conference included documenting the history of the Holocaust, and it facilitated such projects during the 1950s. By 1958, the Study Committee of the Claims Conference noted that this "documentation of the Catastrophe efforts" needed to be done because "evidence has begun to pile up that certain quarters may seek to rewrite the history of the Catastrophe from a point of view other than of objective history. An accurate record of the events to the period is indispensable. The consequences of a biased historical record are a danger to present and future generations."[37] By the middle of the 1950s, Claims Conference resources made possible YIVO's collaboration with Yad Vashem, the chief research beneficiary of the monies, and allowed YIVO to conduct several of its own studies.

So, too, the World Congress for Jewish Culture, founded in 1948 in New York as a response to the destruction of Jewish life in Europe, took upon itself Holocaust programming of both a scholarly and a commemorative nature. It considered its mission to present to Americans the history of the catastrophe in order "to immortalize for future generations Jewish nobility and courage in the face of Nazi brutality, through the collection and publication of documentary evidence of that tragic period." It republished the work of Yiddish writers and poets who had met their deaths at the hands of the Nazis; published fiction, poetry, and memoirs written by survivors; and issued discursive essays and pamphlets on the slaughter and its aftermath. It also received money from the Claims Conference, seeking to expand research on the experience of the Jews during the Nazi era. In 1957, it published a four-volume *Encyclopedia of Jewish Education*, which "carried factual material on the Jewish schools in the ghettos in a number of Nazi-occupied cities in Europe."[38]

The World of Books

The spread of knowledge about the European Jewish catastrophe by necessity proceeded incrementally. Most serious commentators who understood the challenges of research realized that authoritative books chronicling the full sweep of its history could not just spring forth. Their eventual publication depended on the careful and laborious collection of millions of documents, strewn over many countries, in multiple languages, as well as the meticulous compilation of bibliographies and the creation of archives, all of which took time. Until then shorter books would have to suffice.

Such books appeared, one by one, and the world of American Jewish letters hailed their appearance as paving stones on the road toward a full Holocaust literature. Without any self-consciousness on the part of the authors that their works constituted a genre, or that they made up a school of Holocaust writers, their books came out. Some discursive, some fiction, together they kept the details of the Holocaust vibrant in public consciousness. Mainstream publishing houses issued many of these books, which got marketed no differently than books on less-painful and less-Jewish topics.

The war had barely ended when Doubleday published Henry Shoskes's *No Traveler Returns: The Story of Hitler's Greatest Crime*, which juxtaposed the crimes with the fate of the Jews in the Warsaw Ghetto. At its conclusion it warned, "We must know . . . we must learn the facts of this greatest crime in history. Only if we know . . . will the fight of the Jews in the ghetto of Warsaw have the meaning they wanted it to."[39] In 1948, Beechhurst Press published Helen Waren's *The Buried Are Screaming*, in which the author presented herself as "born in New York City of Russian-Jewish parents," raised "completely divorced from contact with Jewish culture, history, and tradition." She wrote of her journey to Europe immediately after the war, which affected her deeply, and she drew her book to its end with the words, "Six million Jews have perished in a great flaming horror of pain and anguish."[40] The following year, Viking Press brought out an English translation of Bernard Goldstein's *The Stars Bear Witness*, a retelling of his five years in the Warsaw Ghetto.[41] In 1952, Philosophical Library published Joseph Tenenbaum's *Underground: The Story of a People*, the dust jacket of which read, "This is the story of a people, its origin, its history, its struggle for survival and its tragic end—the life-and-death story of Polish and other Eastern European Jewries."[42] His five-hundred-page *Race and Reich* came out in 1956, and journalist Boris Smolar, writing a syndicated column for the Jewish Telegraphic Agency, declared it "the most impressive book yet telling the story of the Nazi persecution and annihilation of the Jews . . . published in this country." Commenting on its "20 pages of bibliography" and "100 pages of reference," Smolar lauded the book, which "vividly presents a complete picture of every type of crime committed by the Nazis against the Jews."[43]

A chain of books played a role in telling the world. Hill and Wang published Gerda Weissman Klein's memoir *All but My Life* in 1957. Graced with a ringing endorsement by novelist Sloan Wilson, author of the popular *Man in the Gray Flannel Suit*, the memoir detailed the young woman's survival in a concentration camp. Wilson declared, "This is the incredible, but true, personal story of a young girl who emerged from the ghettos of Poland, the slave labor camps of Nazi Germany, to find love, happiness, and a new life. It is a deeply moving book."[44] Jacob Sloan turned to McGraw-Hill in 1958 to publish *Notes from the Warsaw Ghetto: The Journal of Emmanuel Ringelblum*, the chronicle of life in the Warsaw Ghetto.[45] Twayne Publishers may have wanted to capitalize on the furor caused by the Eichmann trial when in 1960 it published Randolph Braham's *Eichmann and the Destruction of Hungarian Jewry*.[46] A year earlier, Hill and Wang returned to the Holocaust with Elie Weisel's *Night*, endorsed by French writer François Mauriac.[47] Kitty Hart's retelling of her experiences in Auschwitz, *I Am Alive*, appeared in 1960, published by Coward-McCann, just before Bantam Press's release of *The Last of the Just* by Andre Schwarz-Bart, a lengthy novel that ended with its narrator's dramatic statement, "dead six million times."[48] In 1961, the first American-authored and published grand narrative of the Holocaust, Raul Hilberg's *The Destruction of the European Jews,* appeared under the auspices of Quadrangle.[49] Finally, Lippincott published in 1962 Meyer Barkai's *The Fighting Ghettos*.[50] Each book, with the exception of Hilberg's, as well as hundreds more, told a limited part of the Holocaust's enormity. Each pinpointed an aspect of the tragedy, and each presented to the public something about the annihilation of the six million Jews.[51]

The publication of books about that annihilation, in larger or smaller detail, became American Jewish news. Jewish publications, adult education programs, and lectures addressed the quality, meanings, and implications of book after book. Jewish magazines expended much attention on the 1950 release of *The Wall*, a novel about life in the Warsaw Ghetto written by John Hersey, a distinguished non-Jewish American author.[52] Jewish magazines and Jewish community groups for adults and young people devoted programs to it. Two years later, the publication of the diary discovered by Otto Frank, written by his daughter, Anne, while the family had hidden from the Nazis in an Amsterdam attic, grabbed the attention of the American Jewish public, as it did much of the rest of the world.[53] Jewish magazines hailed the unearthing and publication in English of Emmanuel Ringelblum's account of the day-to-day struggle for existence of the Jews in the Warsaw Ghetto. The Jewish press and communal commentators considered noteworthy, and positive, the American public's mass embrace of *Exodus* and *Mila 18* by Leon Uris, along with *Eva* by Meyer Levin, as well as Yevgeny Yevtushenko's poem "Babi Yar," all of which gave the American

and American Jewish public more images and information about the catastrophe.[54] The publication of these works stimulated Jewish communal
public programs, including lectures, sermons, and discussions.[55]

Hersey's *The Wall*, both the book of 1950 and the play a decade later,
provide a case in point. In a 1951 piece, Harold U. Ribalow asked, "Do
Jews Read?" He answered this question in the negative, as he lamented
what he considered American Jewry's low intellectual level. Ribalow found
one exception to the negative answer to the question he posed, that being
The Wall, "a novel on the Warsaw Ghetto." So, for a population that seemingly did not read much, the one book consumed widely and broadly had
been drawn from the Holocaust era.[56] Generally embraced by American
Jewish commentators, *The Wall* also provoked some critical responses. Despite its fictional form, some expressed outrage at its factual errors, as others wondered why "it had fallen to the share of a non-Jew to write the epic
novel of the Warsaw tragedy, which typified the tragedies of other Jewish
mother cities."[57]

These works of popular culture provided American Jewry, their producers and consumers, with a way to be part of an ongoing discussion of
the Holocaust extending beyond the group. But the outside American
world alone did not stimulate Jewish presentations of the catastrophe
through books. Jews and Jewish publishing houses took on this project.
The Jewish Publication Society of America brought out, in conjunction
with Random House, Marie Syrkin's *Blessed Is the Match*, in 1947, to much
acclaim, and Bloch Publishing Company, one of the Jewish houses, issued
in 1959 a translation of *A Cat in the Ghetto: Four Novelettes,* by Rachmil
Bryks, a survivor of the Lodz ghetto and of Auschwitz. In his volume,
Bryks listed the names of his "close relatives who were destroyed in the
camps. It begins with his father . . . and then his mother . . . and his sister
. . . and her husband and their two small children . . . and another sister
and her husband and child; and still another sister and her husband. All of
them were murdered in Treblinka in 1942." Bloch considered the book's
publication an important event and enlisted Eleanor Roosevelt, who had
also written the introduction to the American edition of *The Diary of Anne
Frank*, to provide a letter of endorsement for the frontispiece of Bryks's
book. Professor Sol Liptzin of Brooklyn College wrote the introduction,
and literary critic and Brandeis University professor Irving Howe, the
preface.[58]

Broadly reviewed in the Yiddish- and English-language Jewish press,
the American Jewish Congress deemed Bryks's book "required reading,"

while Boris Smolar saw it as "a monument to the 6,000,000 Jewish martyrs killed by the Nazis." Smolar predicted that the book would have a wide
readership and would be embraced by Jewish audiences, but "most unhappy over the book will probably be those Germans who still claim that
no millions of Jews were mass-murdered by the Nazis in gas ovens."[59] The
publisher made the catastrophe central to its advertising, identifying the
otherwise obscure Yiddish writer as "a survivor of the Auschwitz extermination camp, [who] portrays the experience of the Jews in both Auschwitz
and the Lodz ghetto in Poland." The *Farband News*, the newsletter of the
Farband-Labor Zionist Order, judged the book as an exemplary text of "An
Era That Must Be Remembered," and the reviewer, who simultaneously
reviewed Meyer Levin's *Eva*, noted that "both books are important and,
in a sense, they complement each others, as they "bring us back to . . . the
slaughter of 6,000,000 Jews by the Nazis."[60]

The American Jewish world took note of an array of books, considering them crucial to presenting the catastrophe. The *Jewish Book Annual*, a
source readily available to scholars, provided a yearly record of the world
of Jewish books, published by Jewish or general publishing houses, in
English, Yiddish, and Hebrew, for adult or younger readers. It offered in
dry alphabetical listings, and in interpretive essays, evidence of the year's
output of books, and each volume testified to the Holocaust as a constant
subject and to the incremental growth of a body of works that tackled the
catastrophe.

The Jewish Book Council, publisher of the *Book Annual*, had taken institutional shape after 1925 when Fanny Goldstein launched Jewish Book
Week for her West End Branch of the Boston Public Library. The first
volume of the *Annual* saw the light of day in 1942, as Jewish books, like
Jewish bodies, fell victim to the Nazis' torch. Edited by historian Solomon
Grayzel, the Book Council produced this reference volume for librarians,
book dealers, and book lovers and for program planners for Jewish schools,
community centers, and camps.[61]

As much as a reference book could, the *Jewish Book Annual* sought to
foster American Jewish culture, and volume after volume bore witness to
the efflorescence of interest in the Holocaust, identifying the European calamity as a powerful theme in American Jewish literary life. Indeed, in the
late 1940s, some Jewish community cultural activists started fretting not
that the catastrophe had been banished to the margins of the community
culture but that it had come too heavily to dominate it. Joshua Bloch, head
of the Jewish Division of the New York Public Library, in the introductory

essay to the 1948–1949 volume, speculated that "never have Jews been more painfully aware of the difficulties of Jewish survival. Never have Jews been more painfully aware of the 'Jewish problem' than they are now. The Jews are incessantly pre-occupied with . . . the abnormality of their existence." Bloch did not need to spell out the source of that "abnormality." Rather, he commented that this preoccupation "aggravates an already too widespread ignorance of matters of Jewish belief and religious practice." As he saw it, for the Jews of America "the experiences . . . in the last few decades" placed concern about Jewish survival, born of the Holocaust, above the inner contents of Judaism.[62]

What books did Bloch and the other editors of this volume mention as constituting that "preoccupation"? Although only three years had elapsed since the war's end, Bloch already devoted a special section of his essay to "The Literature of Martyrdom," noting that it could "not [be] merely a coincidence that so many fine books have come out of the tragedy of the Jews in recent years." He highlighted Marie Syrkin's *Blessed Is the Match*, "the story of Jewish resistance," published jointly by the Jewish Publication Society of America and Knopf ("It is a *Memoirbook* for the whole congregation of Israel"). He also discussed Jacob Pat's *Ashes and Fire*, translated from Yiddish and released by International Universities Press, an account of Pat's journey through "the ruins of Poland, the home of integral east European Jewry, for the past centuries" and the site of "the burial ground of nearly five million Jewish victims of Nazi brutality." These and the other books "hold grim fascination for every sensitive Jew." Bloch recommended for special attention *Between Fear and Hope*, originally in Yiddish, now available in English translation by S. L. Schneiderman, an American Jewish journalist who had gone back to Poland to record the voices of those who had experienced "the pogroms and the destructions wrought by the Nazis." Renya Kulkielko, "a young Polish Jewess now in Palestine," put her recollections together in *Escape from the Pit*, with a foreword by Ludwig Lewisohn. Bloch considered noteworthy Zvi Kolitz's *Tiger Beneath the Skin*, "stories and parables of the years of death . . . eleven stories . . . held together by the dual theme of death and faith . . . the men, women and children who were brutally tortured and destroyed by the Nazi monsters." He also pointed out for special mention *Five Chimneys*, the testimony of Olga Lengyel, who survived Auschwitz but "lost her parents and two children in the extermination chambers," and Eugene Weinstock's *Beyond the Last Path*, the record of a Hungarian Jew's time in Buchenwald, "hell on earth," among dozens of others.[63]

Books of poetry and drama also presented the Holocaust, and Bloch described the book-length *1933—A Poem Sequence*, which "gives expression to the reaction of a German Jew to the succession of events in 1933 . . . an intensely religious, almost apocalyptic attempt to explain 'the ways of God' to the Jewish people . . . when Hitler came to power." He singled out for consideration *I Cannot See Their Faces* by Leibel Bergman and Aaron Kramer's *The Thunder of the Grass*, "a powerful poetic narrative of the suicide of almost a hundred Jewish girls in a Warsaw boarding school about to be dishonored by Nazi officers."[64]

The Yiddish and Hebrew sections of the 1948–1949 *Jewish Book Annual* likewise made clear that the Holocaust shaped the postwar American Jewish book world. A special Yiddish essay specifically described a new category, "Yiddish Literature After the Destruction," noting that "in the destruction of the bloody Hitler-times entire communities were destroyed. And just as Jews were destroyed so the Jewish holy book and the Yiddish book were obliterated." But since Jews believed in the "holiness of the book," our "remnant pulls itself back to life and lives! So too the Jewish book, and so too the Yiddish language," commented the *Jewish Book Annual*, showing clearly how presenting the details of the Holocaust took on a deep purpose for community activists.[65]

In 1948–1949, the recent catastrophe's blows still smarted. The size of the literature may have reflected its unhealed freshness. If the regnant historical premise that dominates the scholarship actually worked, the flood of books should have ebbed markedly by the beginning of the 1950s. In fact, the writing continued unabated.

In 1950–1951, the editors discussed David Boder's *I Did Not Interview the Dead*, a psychological study based on interviews with survivors conducted by a professor from the Illinois Institute of Technology, and *The Root and the Bough* by Leo Schwarz ("The epic record of Jewish courage and heroism in the face of war and extermination, as revealed in stories by Jewish victims of Nazism"), as well as a study of "Nazi extermination squads" by Anatole Goldstein, titled *Operation Murder*. It noted the American Jewish Committee–sponsored *Rehearsal for Destruction*.[66] Three years later, the editor of the nonfiction section of the *Book Annual* observed how "books on the great catastrophe in European Jewish life, *khurban* literature, were [being] compiled by competent scholars who had personal access to original documents and to the events themselves. Thus stories of the Warsaw Ghetto and of the liberated Jews in Germany are now available in English for the first time."[67]

With time, the listings got longer rather than shorter. In 1959, the *Book Annual* gave special mention to Viktor Frankl's *From Death Camp to Existentialism*, Emmanuel Ringelblum's *Notes from the Warsaw Ghetto*, Ernst Schnable's *Anne Frank: A Portrait in Courage*, and Earl Weinstock's *The Seven Years*, "reminiscences of the tragic childhood and youth of a youngster who was sent to a concentration camp by the Germans."[68] Mary Kiev, writing for the *Jewish Book Annual*, remarked in 1960, before the Eichmann trial could have yet had any impact on the publication of books, that "of this year's titles . . . one-third of the books" connected somehow to the Holocaust "all depict memories of fear and turmoil and utter horror that cry out for an outlet." She cited as emblematic Meyer Levin's *Eva* ("True story of a young Polish-Jewish girl and her daring masquerade as a Gentile among the Nazis") and Rachmil Bryks's *A Cat in the Ghetto: Four Novelettes*, "a moving portrayal of the unspeakable and unimaginable horror of the Nazi holocaust, based on the author's experiences."[69]

The Yiddish section of the *Jewish Book Annual* also demonstrated the continuing magnetic appeal of the catastrophe to Yiddish writers, as well as the global dimensions of the literature that contemplated it. While the English-language section focused almost exclusively on American-written and published books, with an occasional British or Canadian title, the Yiddish section indicated the emergence of a worldwide Jewish Holocaust literature, with books published in Israel, Poland, France, Argentina, Canada, and South Africa joining those published in the United States.

The American works played an important part in that global literary project. The yearly compilations listed and commented on hundreds of works written in Yiddish, published in America, which dealt "primarily with the recent destruction of European Jewry." Dina Abramowicz, the YIVO librarian responsible for that section of the *Jewish Book Annual*, foresaw by the late 1940s that the "*Hurban* . . . will not disappear from Yiddish literature." The steady flow of books and poems "attest to the desire of writers to perpetuate the memory of the slain millions of East European Jewry." However much these Yiddish works sought to memorialize, they also served "without . . . melodrama . . . to describe the horrible experiences of the Nazi-era in a forceful and personal manner."[70]

As early as the late 1940s the *Book Annual* blocked off a section for "*Hurban* literature," including books of fiction, nonfiction, poetry, essays, and drama.[71] The yearly reference volumes listed and described the *yizker bikher* and the travel accounts of American Jews who went back to Poland to search for relatives or who journeyed to Germany to the Displaced Persons

Camps. Every issue of the *Book Annual* also drew attention to the "reissue of the writings that perished in the flames of the European holocaust." After all, noted one editor, "Yiddish books in Europe suffered the same fate that the millions who read them and the hundreds who wrote them met."[72]

New York occupied a key place in that Yiddish literary world, and a 1955 article commented on the fact that "during the postwar years a number of well known Yiddish writers came over to this country with the refugees. . . . Among them are Itsik Manger, Chaim Grade, Nachum Bomze, Joseph Rubinstein, B. Sheffner, and Ch.S. Kazdan. They chronicled their experiences of the Nazi destruction of European Jewry, thus giving greater prominence to the *Hurban,* the martyrdom and heroism of the Jewish victims."[73]

As it did for the Yiddish books, the *Jewish Book Annual* presented each year's Hebrew material in two forms and places, offering lengthy Hebrew essays with pages of bibliography of works produced in the United States and Israel. The *Annual* also summarized their contents for readers limited to English, highlighting the most important new works. American Jews, most of whom would have had halting, or no, ability to read Hebrew, got at least a sense of the richness and depth of the material. They could learn that in Hebrew, as in Yiddish and in English, the Holocaust functioned as a cultural bridge, connecting Jewish readers and writers across linguistic barriers and across time, as the deaths of the six million continued to reverberate in world Jewish culture.

Books that chronicled some aspect or another of the catastrophe grabbed the attention of the leaders of Jewish organizations, educators, publishers of Jewish magazines, and planners of Jewish communal events. They clamored to get advance copies, hoping to bring authors in for lectures, expecting to use the books for pedagogic purposes and, in turn, to stimulate public engagement with the European tragedy. In 1953, Farrar, Straus and Young published Leo Schwarz's *The Redeemers*, which told of the survivors of the Holocaust and those who rescued them, contextualized around the horrors that preceded the "redemption." The Israel Bond Drive, the Jewish Chaplains Committee, various Jewish community centers, Hadassah chapters, branches of the Jewish War Veterans, the Commission of Jewish Education of the Union of American Hebrew Congregations, Jewish bookstores, and more—all flooded the publisher with orders and requests for review copies. Jewish community newspapers requested the right, never granted, to excerpt lengthy sections of the book, "which is of such keen interest to Jewish readers." Trude Weiss-Rosmarin, editor of the *Jewish Spectator,* complained to the publisher that she wanted to incorporate material from *The Redeemers* into her lectures and to print sections of it in her magazine. She fumed over not having gotten a review copy for that purpose. Community activists as such let publishers know that Jews had a great interest in the Holocaust, and publishers, always looking for sales, discerned that Jewish audiences snapped up such books. Such projects fed on one another and advanced the production of books that treated the European Jewish catastrophe.[74]

Jewish communal groups, community councils in particular but also local chapters of the American Jewish Committee, often bought multiple copies of books they believed would spread goodwill toward Jews and distributed them to school and public libraries. They had begun doing this earlier in the century with other books.[75] Continuing this in the postwar period, they went out of their way to offer works that presented the Holocaust. They deliberated over which books told of that tragedy best and which books best suited which audiences. In 1958, the Cincinnati Jewish Community Relations Committee vetted a number of Holocaust-related books, debating which it should distribute free of charge to best serve Jewish interests. Committee members discussed Gerda Weissman Klein's memoir, *All but My Life,* "an autobiography of a young girl who endured the ghettoes of Poland and slave labor camps of nazi [*sic*] Germany," and decided that "although it is a remarkable volume and deserves our attention . . . [it] is too tragic in its . . . presentation for us to use it as an item for placement in the school libraries." They decided instead to provide free copies of the *Diary of Anne Frank* for its "superior public relations usefulness." They voted to buy multiple copies of "*Notes from the Warsaw Ghetto* . . . the history of the tragic decimation of the Jews of the Warsaw Ghetto, written by one of them, and hiffen [*sic*] in a tin box for future historians," for placement in all college and university libraries in the Cincinnati area.[76] Organizations like this believed that books about the Holocaust could serve the Jewish project of fostering tolerance and liberalism.

The idea of spreading goodwill toward Jews by the written word extended into books about Judaism in general, most of which incorporated into their texts details from the calamity. Authors of such books, many of them rabbis, found multiple places to fold the story of the Holocaust into their writings. They intended such texts for both the broad American public and for Jews who, the writers believed, knew scant little about Judaism. *On Being a Jew, What Is a Jew?, The Way to God, What the Jews Believe, Why I Am a Jew, I Believe: The Faith of a Jew, Judaism and Modern Man, Choose*

Life: The Biblical Call to Revolt, Judaism for the Modern Age, A Modern Treasury of Jewish Thought, among others, tried to explain Jewish traditions and values, and each incorporated the Hitler-era catastrophe into the text and as such into the essence of the meaning of Jewishness.[77]

Rabbi David da Sola Pool, for example, asked readers in 1957 to join him as he pondered *Why I Am a Jew.* He answered his own question: "In our generation we have seen how the unspeakable holocaust perpetrated by Hitler both strengthened the resolve of the loyal and often aroused in the passive Jews greater will to uphold their Judaism."[78] Rabbi Robert Gordis urged Jews in his 1955 *Judaism for the Modern Age* to redefine their religious thinking in light of "the brutal Nazi war of extermination against the Jewish people." That extermination involved more than just "the loss of a third of world Jewry in numbers." The slaughter executed by "Adolf Hitler . . . represented a body blow to the heart of world Jewry, the very center of every significant creative achievement."[79]

These two rabbis wrote their books to clarify Judaism to readers, and they considered the Holocaust part of their project. So did probably the most important book of this genre, Philip Bernstein's *What the Jews Believe.* In 1950, *Life,* one the nation's most widely read picture magazines, commissioned Rabbi Bernstein of Rochester, New York, who had served in Germany as Advisor on Jewish Affairs to the United States Military, to write a brief in-house document on Jewish beliefs and practices, so that when staff writers needed information on matters Jewish, they would have a quick guide to consult. According to Bernstein, that article constituted "a unique phenomenon in Jewish history. . . . Nothing on a Jewish religious subject, apart from the Bible, has reached such a wide audience."[80] Recognizing a market for such a book, Farrar, Straus and Giroux issued Bernstein's expanded version of the article as a book the following year.

Not written as a "Holocaust" book, *What the Jews Believe* referred repeatedly to that event and to the author's encounters with the "survivors of Nazi extermination," which he considered part and parcel of what the Jews today believed. As he described the cycle of the Jewish year, he remarked on how Holocaust survivors talked about the holidays, as they remembered them, both from their years of captivity under the Nazis and after liberation. In telling about the fall holiday of Sukkot, Bernstein remarked that "the Nazis, according to the survivors of the concentration camps, derived exquisite joy from cruelty," or, when explaining the holiday of Simchat Torah, he shared with his readers its celebration in a Displaced Persons camp among the "uprooted Jews . . . [who] . . . had suffered for many years. They had been tortured in concentration camps. They had been driven from land to land before the Nazi fury." To illustrate the centrality of synagogues in Jewish life, he told how, "on November 10, 1938, the synagogues of Frankfurt were desecrated, burned, and destroyed." Then, "in the fall of 1942 the end came [for Frankfurt's Jews]. Then began the deportation to Litzmannstadt, Lodz, where they were imprisoned in the ghetto, and ultimately exterminated." "We," noted Bernstein in the book, referring not just to himself but to all Jews, "are surrounded by memories today, by tragic memories of a greatness that was and is no more, and of a people who are no longer among the living."[81]

So, too, books on Israeli literature,[82] Jewish history, and profiles of Jewish communities around the world put the Holocaust up front. Leo Schwarz, in *Great Ages and Ideas of the Jewish People* (1956), began his book with a reference to Simon Dubnow, "one of the martyrs of 1941." Schwarz noted that "at the time of his death a new catastrophe was writing an epitaph on the tombstones of Slavic and German Jewries. World War II radically altered the map of the world and among the casualties were the ancient landmarks of European Jewry."[83] Jewish travel books also incorporated the Holocaust. These postwar books described the Jewish world as a place where travelers could see the ruins of Jewish communities destroyed by the Nazis, where memorial sites had been erected to consecrate their memory. A 1962 book published by Hill and Wang, *The Landmarks of a People,* noted that "more and more Jewish groups are regularly sponsoring organized tours," and Jewish "pilgrims come to honor parents and other kinfolk buried abroad . . . [and] former refugees from Nazi terror visiting their old homes." The guidebook narrated the history of the Holocaust by letting travelers know, for example, that if they went to Salonica, they could see the "JEWISH CEMETERY, in the suburb of Stayrouplis," with its "imposing monument to the 60,000 Jews killed by the Nazis." If visiting Budapest and its Great Synagogue, they should know that "during the Nazi occupation the synagogue . . . itself became a concentration camp."[84] Jewish travelers could consult this book for their journeys through Germany, France, Belgium, Greece, Poland, Romania, the Netherlands, and elsewhere, and in the book and on the tours they could connect with the European catastrophe.[85]

No matter the kind of Jewish book, if authors could bring the Holocaust in, they did. Some wrote special gift books for boys and girls about to celebrate a bar or bat mitzvah, and they included Holocaust material, despite the happy life cycle events for which these books were written.

They did not fear that articles and pictures drawn from the repertoire of the catastrophe would cut down on sales or alienate readers. Meyer Waxman, Sulamith Ish-Kishor, and Jacob Sloan compiled *Blessed Is the Daughter* to provide "young Jewish girls . . . with knowledge and information . . . to provide an outline of Jewish life in home and synagogue . . . to interest the reader and to sustain her loyalty." To do all this, the authors narrated the cycle of the Jewish year and included several pages on the Tenth of Tevet, which marked "the slaughter of six million Jews by the Nazis." They included there an excerpt from Hillel Seidman's "The Last Dance," a description of the final celebration of the fall holiday of Simchat Torah in the Warsaw Ghetto. Since the book's editors hoped to teach girls about Jewish women's special contribution to the history of their people, they made room for the stories of two girls, "Chajke and Frumke," Warsaw Ghetto couriers who played parts in the uprising, telling their stories and also recalling how "World War II saw the catastrophic extermination of European Jewry at the hands of Nazi Germany. Most of the hapless six million victims accepted martyrdom as inescapable. But there were exceptions," including these two young women and Hannah Senesh (here spelled Szenes). Her story also appeared in *Blessed Is the Daughter*. A thumbnail sketch of Jewish history rounded out the gift book's content, and it did not stint on the details of the "Catastrophe in Europe," which saw "six million Jews of Europe —more than one-third of all Jews in the world," killed "by the Germans under Hitler."[86]

Blessed Is the Daughter resembled Nathan Ausubel's *Pictorial History of the Jewish People* of 1953. Crown Publishers marketed it broadly, and it early became a standard bar and bat mitzvah gift. Lavishly illustrated, it began its narrative in antiquity, sweeping over the centuries to the postwar period. Directed not at scholars but at general readers, including "congregations, Hebrew schools, youth organizations," as well as those in search of presents for Jewish youngsters, Ausubel's book took on the history of the Holocaust. "Hitler over Europe" told of "The Nightmare," "The Warsaw Ghetto," "Bondage in Warsaw," "Battle of the Warsaw Ghetto," and "Uprising in Vilna," among other details of the catastrophe. Ausubel included photographs of "elderly Polish Jews, guarded by armed German soldiers, [who] are forced to dig their own graves before their execution"; "a pious Jew in a Galician town, standing beside the bodies of his murdered fellow-Jews [who was] allowed by the 'humorous' Germans a moment's grace to recite the prayer before death for himself and for those already slain"; "an eleven-year-old slave laborer, Fogal Abrahams, of Bialystok [who] shows

American war correspondent, Martin A. Bursten, the Buchenwald crematorium ovens in which his father and mother perished"; and more. Any youngster who received this history book as a gift or who encountered it in her Hebrew-school library would have no doubt that the Holocaust constituted a crucial chapter in Jewish history and that Jewish books offered them texts by which to learn about it.[87]

The rapidly expanding shelves of books written in the postwar period demonstrated the constant interest of American Jews in the Holocaust. A cadre of writers and an even larger universe of readers, rather than deeming the European catastrophe a taboo topic for public discussion, as historian Gerald Sorin contended,[88] actually placed it prominently in volume after volume. Those books represented a visible record of what that community produced and read, and they stand as clear evidence of the catastrophe's centrality in its communal culture.

The Catastrophe in the American Jewish Press

Those who wrote, edited, and published American Jewish periodicals, newspapers and magazines, also presented the facts, images, and idioms of the catastrophe.[89] Awash in a vibrant press, in English, Yiddish, and Hebrew, the world of American Jewry abounded in publications, some sponsored by organizations, some intended for a wider local or national Jewish audience. In 1950, some 225 publications—appearing either as dailies, weeklies, or monthlies, national or local—circulated among American Jews. Along with three national Jewish news syndicates, they made up the journalistic print culture of American Jews. Nine years later, the three syndicates remained in operation, and the number of publications climbed up to 244.[90]

These publications did not have to go out of their way to ferret out material on the Holocaust. Rather, the rush of contemporary events, including the production of literary and artistic works, made the catastrophe part of postwar American Jewish culture. Coverage of the Holocaust and its consequences spanned the gamut of articles in these publications. News stories, editorials, and features all provided opportunities for retelling something about the Holocaust. Local events, national issues, and international ones all offered opportunities for mentioning the Holocaust, presenting something about it. The catastrophe and what followed continuously functioned as news. Literary offerings, poems and short stories,

drew readers into the world of the Holocaust, as did commentary on theater, music, movies, and art exhibitions and the voluminous book reviews.
The Holocaust and its aftershocks ran so profoundly through American
Jewish journalism in the postwar period that it would have been impossible to have read any American Jewish publication in those years and not
confront the catastrophe in one way or another.

Just as later historians missed the memorial culture itself, so they
failed to consider the massive American Jewish journalistic output of the
postwar years which put the Holocaust and its legacy onto the pages of
their publications. These magazines and newsletters did not all write about
it the same way, given that they reflected an array of political and religious
ideologies, employed various languages, served specific purposes, and addressed particular audiences. But those differences aside, they all embedded the catastrophe into their words and into the lives of their readers.

Three very different national Jewish publications launched after the
war's end directly cited the deaths of the six million as a part of the rationale
for being launched. The American Jewish Committee inaugurated *Commentary* in 1945, and editor Elliott Cohen explained in "An Act of Affirmation: Editorial Statement" why the need for *Commentary* and why now.
"As Jews we live with this fact: 4,750,000 of 6,000,000 Jews of Europe," he
wrote on the first page of the first issue of the magazine, "have been murdered. Not killed in battle, not massacred in hot blood, but slaughtered like
cattle, subjected to every physical indignity—*processed*. Yes, cruel tyrants
did this. . . . But we must also record this fact . . . there was a strange passivity the world over in the face of this colossal latter-day massacre of inno-
cents." Cohen then offered as the first full article in the magazine's history,
"The Spiritual Reconstruction of European Jewry" by Columbia University historian Salo Baron.[91]

Ten years later, the Herzl Institute started *Midstream*, hoping to "promote the study and discussion of problems confronting Jews in the world
today." In its published mission statement, to convince readers why they
should choose this over other Jewish or Zionist publications, founding
editor Shlomo Katz acknowledged the "two overwhelming changes in the
context of our Jewish existence—on the one hand, the destruction of one-
third of world Jewry which has erased many of the political and cultural
landmarks, and on the other hand, the rise of the State of Israel."[92]

Like *Commentary*, *Midstream* began its journalistic life with a Holocaust-inflected piece, in this case, Julius Horowitz's "Dachau—1955," a
description of his journey to the German concentration camp which both

retold what had happened there to the Jews and how mid-1950s Germany still supported a virulent anti-Semitism. *Midstream* entered into the world of American Jewish journalism during the year of American Jewry's Tercentenary, and historian and Zionist philosopher Ben Halpern's "America Is Different" fittingly appeared in the premier issue. Halpern speculated on the irony that the "celebrations of the American Jewish community . . . chanced to come at a time when, we American Jews, after the destruction of the six million who were the main body of Jewry and the immediate source of our traditions, remain as the major part of all the Jews in the diaspora." Halpern considered that destruction to be the defining event of the American Jewish present, since "the destruction of European Jewry . . . a negative factor" had transformed Jewish life: "Without European Jewry, the face of the Jewish problem as it appears to American Jews is radically altered and in a way simplified. Hitherto, thoughts about the Jewish problem . . . were based upon our European traditions, and no less, upon our involvement with the European Jewish situation. But now we live in a Jewish world where essentially, we see only two main constituents: ourselves, American Jews, and the State of Israel." Like *Commentary*, *Midstream* became the venue for vast discussions of that phenomenon which Halpern grimly characterized as "anything but pleasant to remember."[93]

Finally, *Tradition: A Journal of Orthodox Jewish Thought* announced its birth in 1958 and explained itself to the public in light of the Holocaust. Yeshiva University professor Norman Lamm justified the new publication with a double-entendre title for the lead article, "The Need for Tradition," promoting both the magazine and what it advocated, traditional Judaism. "There have been," he declared, "changes on the world scene that have caused, particularly in America, a perceptible reorientation vis-à-vis Orthodoxy in the total Jewish community. The horrors of the Hitler era have profoundly shaken up man's confidence in the beneficent use of the power he has gotten."[94] His first issue foregrounded the Holocaust. In a piece on Jewish prayers and the efforts of liberal American Jews to change them to sound less harsh and condemning of other peoples, Emanuel Rackman asked, "Who but fools would not think of Hitler . . . as they read the verse of the Haggadah, 'Pour forth Thy wrath upon the nation's that knew Thee not'?" while a highly negative review lambasted an Anti-Defamation League booklet, *Your Neighbor Celebrates*, as too liberal, too upbeat, and out of step with tradition. After all, the article noted, "in view of the fact that in recent years six million Jews were exterminated," statements in the book that, "'in recent years, Tishah B'Ab [the Ninth of Av] has lost much of its tragic overtones' has a very hollow ring." Over the next decade, *Tradition* presented the Holocaust from an Orthodox perspective, offering its readers Holocaust heroes like Joseph Carlebach, the Chief Rabbi of Hamburg, who "died a martyr's death at the hands of the Nazis in Riga," and it discussed the ways in which the Holocaust affected *halakhah*, Jewish law in the present.[95]

These magazines differed little from other Jewish publications of the postwar period in terms of the extent to which the Holocaust appeared in their pages.[96] *Tradition* had little in common with the Communist *Jewish Life*, which in 1958 renamed itself *Jewish Currents*. But these two and others—including *Jewish Frontier*, an organ of the Farband-Labor Zionist movement; *Hadassah Magazine*, the official publication of America's largest Jewish organization; and *National Jewish Monthly*, sponsored by the B'nai B'rith; as well as Trude Weiss-Rosmarin's *Jewish Spectator*—revealed striking similarities when it came to the attention they focused on the Holocaust and the degree to which they wove it into their pages.[97]

Despite the magazines' contemporary focus and the brevity of the article format, they consistently brought up the Nazis' campaign against the Jews, using the news of the day to present the horrific past. Trude Weiss-Rosmarin in the *Jewish Spectator* of April 1953, in her monthly "Comments and Opinions" section, noted the impending fiftieth anniversary of the Kishinev pogrom, which had rocked the Jewish world at the century's start. "Fifty years have passed since the Pogrom of Kishinev," she recalled, but, "compared to the gigantic-scale mass murders of the Nazi period and especially the appalling tragedy of the Warsaw Ghetto enacted exactly forty years after Kishinev, the outrage of 1902 seems puny." How ironic, she marveled, that "the impact of the 47 who were slain in Kishinev, upon Jews and Christians alike, was infinitely more powerful than the impression created by the murder of the Six Million during the Nazi regime."[98] In 1951, when Hebrew University professor and philosopher Martin Buber accepted the Goethe Prize from the University of Hamburg, expressing his willingness to engage with postwar Germans, she spared no words in her editorial column in condemning him, deeming his act shameful. In her view, the Germans did not deserve any forgiveness. She also tracked the emergence of scholarship on the Holocaust, heralding books like Philip Friedman's anthology *Martyrs and Fighters* and Eli Cohen's *Human Behavior in the Concentration Camp* of 1954, both of which would keep the world aware of "what Amalek [the Israelites' arch-nemesis in the Bible] has done."[99]

Magazines like the *Jewish Spectator* employed every kind of article to imprint the history of the Jewish tragedy on their pages. Contemporary events in the United States, Germany, France, the Soviet Union, and Israel kept the memory of the Holocaust alive inasmuch as in all these places, Jewish survivors, German perpetrators, and the collaborators of other nations created news of keen interest to American Jews. Writers of travel accounts and memoir articles pondered in print the tragic Jewish past. For example, Joseph Schechtman told readers of *Midstream* in 1959 of his "Visit to Babi Yar," a Ukrainian ravine where in a short, two-day period in 1941 a German SS unit had slaughtered 33,771 Jews.[100] Andre Ungar, rabbi of Temple B'nai Abraham in Newark, New Jersey, had lived through the Nazi occupation of Budapest, and he offered that year a two-part retrospective of the last days of that community in the pages of the *Jewish Spectator*.[101]

American Jewish magazines also presented the Holocaust by showcasing new literature, short stories and poetry in particular. Some of the pieces had been written originally in Yiddish or Hebrew, and translations introduced general American Jewish readers to them. The *Jewish Spectator* probably devoted the most pages in this area. In 1959, it provided lengthy English excerpts from two of Hayim Leivik's most important Holocaust poems, *Di Khasene in Fernwald* [A wedding in the Fernwald Displaced Persons camp] and "In Treblinka bin ikh nit geven," in which he anguished over having escaped the fate of the victims. God, in this poem, appeared as a bedraggled beggar, mute and ashamed, unable to describe "the horrors of Treblinka and Maidanek."[102] Rachmil Bryks's Yiddish story "Rivka'le's kiddush hashem" [Little Rivka's martyrdom] appeared in the *Jewish Spectator* in June 1956, as did a medley of very short pieces by Avraham Sutzkever, in 1954, the first of which, "A Woman in a Straw Hat," bluntly read, "One day, during the time of the Nazi Slaughter, I sat in a small dingy room."[103]

Conservative Judaism did not typically publish imaginative literature, so in the spring of 1958 the editors explained their decision to do so: "While it is not our customary policy to publish fiction . . . the story which follows . . . is based, in large measure, on fact." The tale, "Ani Ma'amin—I Believe," had first appeared in Hebrew and "is, despite its brevity, one of the most penetrating and memorable pieces of literature to have emerged from the Catastrophe." The narrator in this story written by Fishel Shneirsohn directly addressed readers: "Do not fear, my friends, I am not going to recount the horrors which happened to me and to our brothers, the children of Israel, in the ghetto of Warsaw. Rather do I wish to tell you of the mysteries and wonders which my eyes beheld before the horrors came and after I was saved by a miracle from the death trains."[104] In 1960, Israeli writer Aharon Megged's Hebrew short story "The Name" appeared in English in *Midstream*, and he, too, told about the Holocaust through short fiction. The story is set in his grandfather's Ukrainian hometown, "which had been destroyed, and all of its Jews slaughtered by the Germans. . . . Nothing of all this is left," Megged lamented.[105]

English poetry touching on the Holocaust also showed up in the American Jewish magazines. Marie Syrkin marked the end of the war in *Jewish Frontier* with "My Uncle in Treblinka." About this "man of science in Berlin," Syrkin wrote,

> The Germans led my uncle to Treblinka.
> He went with his prayers and equations.
> His psalms and logarithms.
> At the door of the slaughter-house
> Both were with him—the angels at his side.[106]

Jewish Spectator took a particular lead in the poetry project, and Weiss-Rosmarin offered her readers, among other works, Elaine Toby Kaplan's "Poems," which despite the generic title began with the words

> I have not seen
> My mother or my father or my sisters or my brothers
> Dig their own graves amid jeers and ridicule and
> Giggling. . . . I have not seen
> Men and women and children
> Chanting the *Shema* in a creaking wooden cart
> . . . These things did not happen in America.[107]

Jewish Spectator also printed Harold Shapiro's 1957 poem "The Six Million Speak!" and Hilda Marx's 1959 "The Six Million to Job." Marx's 1959 words well represent the tone of this poetic corpus:

> Of us were millions, Job,
> What do you need
> As proof that we have suffered more than you.
> . . . Time alone may pin
> The martyr's medal to our memory.[108]

Yiddish magazines gave even greater space to the imaginative literature that followed the catastrophe. Many Yiddish poets active in the United States published in *Zukunft*, *Der Yidishe Kempfer*, and other magazines, which showcased the work of Jacob Glatshtaiyn, Hayim Leivik, Rachel Korn, Malka Haifitz Tussman, Kadya Molodovsky, Aaron Zeitlin, Chaim Grade, and Aaron Glanz-Leyless, among others. Their work pivoted around the Holocaust.[109]

American Jewish journalism presented the Holocaust. So did the *American Jewish Year Book*, which reasonably could be considered a periodical. The annual publication of the American Jewish Committee since the end of the nineteenth century, it functioned as a kind of "official" yearly text reporting on American and world Jewry. Based on meticulous research, its lengthy sections on domestic and global Jewish affairs, Jewish demography, geography, occupations, religious life, education, cultural affairs, organizational choices, and even the names and circulation data of their magazines and newspapers carried a stamp of authority. Its editors and staff writers expressed themselves in a terse economical style, rarely employing sensationalistic or emotional language. The American Jewish Committee sent the *Year Book* to public officials and libraries. Jewish magazines reviewed it. Rabbis, communal leaders, the staff of Jewish organizations and institutions, and journalists got it and referred to it.

Its reports on global Jewish affairs placed the Holocaust front and center. In its coverage of Europe, the fate of survivors and perpetrators, the *Year Book* made the catastrophe a constant point of reference, every detail drawing attention back in time to what had happened. In 1958, for example, the *Year Book* devoted much attention to the disbursement of funds to Israel and to Jews in the diaspora through the Conference of Jewish Material Claims Against Germany, a body whose very name announced the identities of the guilty party and the sufferers. It reported in minute detail on the ways and places that the "$10 million allocated for relief of Nazi victims" had been disbursed.[110] By reporting on these matters, it made a point. The Holocaust continued to affect world Jewry, and for any Jewish organization or individual Jew who paid attention, the Holocaust always hovered as a shaping presence.

Perusing that 1958 volume, readers could learn not just about the Claims Conference but about the whereabouts of those who had participated in the Holocaust's crimes. Reporting on France, for example, the *Year Book* remarked with alarm on "the bravura of former collaborationists" and opined that, "generally, French public opinion was not exercised by the activities of former collaborationists, and the emotions raised by the war had cooled down considerably. Thus for the first time since he was amnestied and returned to France . . . the pathologically anti-Semitic novelist Louis-Ferdinand Celine defended his attitudes." Recounting the "inauguration of the Tomb of the Unknown Martyr in Paris," the *Year Book* let its readers know that some people in France saw the memorial site as "a monument to the glory of Jewish domination of the globe."[111]

That year, the Federal Republic of Germany occupied a particularly prominent place in the *Year Book,* and like its sponsoring organization, the American Jewish Committee, the annual maintained a decidedly skeptical attitude about the degree to which Germany had shed its Nazi past. In 1958, it described, among other matters, West Germany's decision, with the cooperation of the United States, to rearm "Waffen SS officers up to and including the rank of lieutenant colonel . . . into the new forces," a rise in positive attitudes toward the Third Reich among Germans, the trials of former high-ranking Nazis, and the like. The *Year Book* reported even the smallest manifestations of Nazi sympathy. When it presented the fact that "a West Berlin court sentenced a locksmith to one month's prison after he had told a Jewish merchant, 'you are one whom Hitler forgot to burn,'" the *Year Book* helped keep alive the reality that Hitler had not so long ago burned Jews and that those actions still resonated with some Germans.[112]

It monitored developments large and small throughout Europe, moving from country to country, as it presented material about the Holocaust. It scanned developments in South Africa, Australia, Canada, and South America that dealt with the aftereffects of the Holocaust. In its coverage of worldwide Jewish news, the phrases "the six million," "the catastrophe," "Hitler holocaust," and "victims of Nazi persecutions" indicated that the editors considered that the Holocaust's aftermath continued to shape postwar Jewish life.[113]

The catastrophe also constituted a crucial part of the print world aimed at, and at times written by, children and young people. The publications of the Jewish youth groups testified to the widespread interest of American Jews in the Holocaust itself and its legacy. In the monthly magazines and newsletters of Zionist youth movements, Habonim, Hashomer Hatzair, and Young Judea, the echoes of the tragedy resounded. Each youth group employed the imagery of the six million to foster its ideology, to inspire its members to greater activism, and to recruit new young Jews to its ranks. These publications, like those read by adults, told the news, reviewed the literature, showcased occasional new pieces of imaginative writing, and depicted the status of Jews around the world—in particular, the circumstances of their own international movement—in light of the Holocaust. Like the adult publications, they integrated references to the catastrophe into articles on music, art, movies, and literature, demonstrating the degree to which these young Jewish activists could not separate the Holocaust from themselves.[114]

Certainly this would have been expected in the late 1940s, as these young people, still smarting from the loss of the six million, among whom had been Habonim and Hashomer Hatzair members, drew attention to the plight of the survivors, the need to rebuild their organizations in Europe, and the imperative for a Jewish state. *Furrows*, the Habonim magazine, reprinted a speech given at its 1947 annual meeting in which the speaker reminded those assembled that "it is not always we who determine our course of history. We have to develop within ourselves both the feeling for *tzar hauma*, for the sorrow of our nation, the full awareness of our tragedy, and of *ahavat yisrael*, the love of every Jew. . . . Not only the love of the Jew who fought in the Warsaw Ghetto, but of that same Berl and Shmerl who were so weak, who embodied all that we call *galut* [diaspora] characteristics, yet who possessed a tremendous amount of richness and power of endurance within them which we must try to recapture and which help us in our struggle." But this kind of rhetoric continued over time. For example, in the middle of the 1950s, a Habonim graduate, David Halperin, then serving in the U.S. Army stationed in Germany, communicated with his comrades in *Furrows*. He described how, with a number of other Jewish soldiers, he traveled to Worms, there visiting the grave of a great rabbi, the Maharal of Rothenberg, in an untended Jewish cemetery: "One of the boys . . . said a Kaddish at the Maharal's grave but broke down weeping in the middle and the rest of us had to finish it for him." Halperin reminded his fellow Habonim members about the "emotional impact of the figure 6,000,000," as he described what it meant to be in Europe, how even "one building or one cemetery actually seen in its starkness brings it all back." The news of the day also helped "bring it all back" to Habonim members. Carole Weiss, a member of the Cleveland chapter, reacted strongly in 1956 to President Eisenhower's order that Israel withdraw from the Sinai Peninsula during the Suez Campaign. Weiss shared with *Furrows* a letter to the editor she had successfully submitted to the *Cleveland Plain Dealer*. In it she chided both the U.S. president and Secretary of State John Foster Dulles. Sure, she wrote, "Israel could wait until Egypt and the other Arab lands start" a war "and then hope that the leaders of the United States would

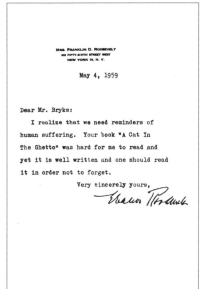

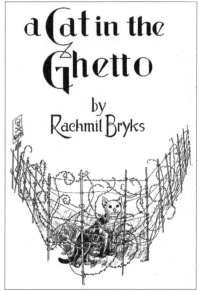

In 1959, Bloch Publishers, a Jewish publishing house, released a translation of *A Cat in the Ghetto: Four Novelettes* by the Yiddish writer, and Holocaust survivor, Rachmil Bryks. While hardly a major publisher with wide distribution beyond the Jewish reading public, Bloch's solicitation of a letter of endorsement by Eleanor Roosevelt demonstrated its desire to reach beyond its traditional audience. The book also came with a preface by Irving Howe, already a well-established figure in the American literary world. Howe ended his piece with the following statement: "And that, I hope, is what Rachmil Bryks' book will help us do; to remember what, in part of ourselves, we would all wish to forget. But we dare not forget—that right was not given to us." *Courtesy Bloch Publishing Company.*

have enough courage to help and supply arms." As this young Labor Zionist saw it, and as her movement peers could read about in the movement magazine, history did not warrant such a response. After all, "The Jews of Germany waited too; six million of them waited too long."[115]

The National Federation of Temple Youth (NFTY) enrolled a different membership than Habonim. Its participants came from families affiliated with Reform congregations. But its publications also served as vehicles for presenting the Holocaust. NFTY's magazine, *Youth Leader*, aimed at older members already in leadership positions, recommended that they immerse themselves in the books focusing on the catastrophe. In 1948, *Youth Leader* encouraged them to read and use for chapter programming Zvi Kolitz's *The Tiger Beneath the Skin* ("eleven moving stories about war-martyred Jews");

Ashes and Fire by Jacob Pat ("a story of Polish Jewry under the Germans"); the "diary of a survivor of Auschwitz and Birkenau," Olga Lengyel's *Five Chimneys*; and the sturdy favorite of these years, *Blessed Is the Match*.[116]

No one organization or segment of American Jewry controlled the print culture. A vast and variegated world of journalism stretched across the country as Jews consumed the magazines, newsletters, journals, and newspapers that appealed to them.[117] No one publication represented all of them, and no one could be deemed more influential in shaping the American Jewish public sphere. But, however different their orientations or modes of presentation, the Holocaust loomed as a dominating presence on their pages, demonstrating how much postwar American Jewish history cannot be disassociated from it and its implication.

Scholarship and the Writing of Jewish History

While all American Jewish publications provided room for presenting the Holocaust, its history and consequences, some took this task more fully and directly. A small community of scholars—whose work later historians have basically dismissed by literally ignoring them and what they accomplished—began immediately at the onset of the postwar era to begin the painstaking process of documenting, studying, and publishing its details.

They also engaged with the Jewish public in a variety of formats and forums but, in particular, used *Jewish Social Studies* to present their scholarship. Only the rare issue of *Jewish Social Studies*, published by the Conference on Jewish Relations, founded in 1933 by historian Salo Baron and philosopher Morris Raphael Cohen, failed to reference something about the catastrophe. Much appeared in article form, like Philip Friedman's "American Jewish Research and Literature on the Jewish Catastrophe of 1939–1945," Joseph Tenenbaum's "Auschwitz in Retrospect" and "The Einsatzgruppen," Julius Fisher's "How Many Jews Died in Transnistria," and Bernard Klein's "The Judenrat."[118] The January 1950 issue consisted solely of papers given at a Conference of Jewish Relations special conference held at New York's New School for Social Research in April 1949 on "Problems of Research in the Study of the Jewish Catastrophe 1939–1945." It included papers by Philip Friedman (described in the list of contributors as "one of the few surviving Jewish historians of Poland") and Samuel Gringauz ("a former jurist in Memel before World War II, is a survivor of the Jewish catastrophe"), who contributed "Some Methodological

Problems in the Study of the Ghetto." It published in this issue articles by Hannah Arendt on "Social Science Techniques and the Study of Concentration Camps" and Herbert Wechsler, "The Jewish Catastrophe and the Nuremberg Trials," as well as an introductory piece by Baron, which set the volume's themes against the background of the "unprecedented aspects of the Nazi attacks on the Jews." This conference marked the ten-year anniversary of the journal, and the scholars responsible for *Jewish Social Studies* chose to honor their academic achievements by means of the "Jewish Catastrophe." Baron clarified why the Conference undertook this task. "It is indeed our [Jewish scholars']duty to examine as rigorously as possible, the dissimilarities as well as the similarities which have existed between the great tragedy and the many lesser tragedies which preceded it."[119]

Jewish Social Studies fulfilled this "duty" in several ways. The Conference on Jewish Relations had participated, and indeed took a leading role, with the American Jewish Committee and the Joint Distribution Committee, in creating Jewish Cultural Reconstruction, Inc., to salvage Jewish materials left behind in Nazi-ravaged Europe, inventorying them, restoring them if possible, and distributing them to Jewish institutions around the world. Hannah Arendt played a key role in this effort, as did Joshua Starr, who served as the organization's executive secretary after he finished his service with the U.S. Army.

Several issues of *Jewish Social Studies* documented the results of this work, listing the relics piece by piece in the "Tentative List of Jewish Cultural Treasures in Axis-Occupied Countries." It also provided a "Tentative List of Jewish Educational Institutions in Axis-Occupied Countries" and a "Tentative List of Jewish Publishers of Judaica and Hebraica in Axis-Occupied Countries." While the lists appeared devoid of commentary, *Jewish Social Studies* informed readers that they constituted the remaining fragments of the "wholesale destruction of Jewish life and property by the Nazis."[120]

This journal, the only scholarly publication in the United States to treat the subject of Jewish history, also reviewed books and articles on the Holocaust published around the world.[121] Each review recounted elements of the history of the Holocaust, as it called for more scholarship. Additionally, contributors to the journal, on topics of all kinds, found ways to fold the Holocaust into articles that had either no or only the most tangential connection to it. Dora Edinger wrote a biographical article about the German Jewish social worker and feminist Bertha Pappenheim in 1958. Edinger detailed her subject's life, informing her readers that Pappenheim died in 1936, "and only a few years later all she had worked for vanished in the holocaust both in Germany and in the East."[122]

Jewish Social Studies filled its pages with articles and book reviews written by a small, yet growing number of scholars who took upon themselves the task of documenting the Holocaust and disseminating information about it. Two of them played a particularly formative role in this effort, historians Philip Friedman and Koppel Pinson. Their postwar American careers demonstrated the slow but steady emergence of Holocaust scholarship and the fact that audiences, Jewish ones in particular, existed for this kind of work.

Philip Friedman may very well be considered America's first professional Holocaust scholar. A Polish-trained historian, and a survivor, Friedman came to the United States in the late 1940s. At the time of his death in 1960, the *Jewish Book Annual*, of which he served as an associate editor, described his many activities and roles in the American Jewish community. "First of all," however, Friedman would be remembered "as the historian of the blood bath which drowned one-third of the Jewish people" and "will live on in the annals of Jewish life. His entire family was destroyed but he escaped the Nazi holocaust."[123] In the United States, Friedman taught as an adjunct professor at Columbia University and at the Jewish Teachers' Seminary. In both positions, he exposed students to the history of the Nazi campaign against the Jews. Scholars from around the world wrote to him for information about particular facts and for bibliographic and archival references to otherwise difficult to find Holocaust materials. Students contacted him as they pursued their projects.[124] Friedman helped make the case for studying the Holocaust among American scholars of Judaica who in the late 1940s and 1950s still concentrated on biblical, rabbinic, and medieval projects. In 1948 he challenged the members of the American Academy for Jewish Research, a body composed primarily, with the exception of Salo Baron, of classical scholars, with his paper on "European Research on the Recent Jewish Tragedy."[125]

Friedman helped foster the massive collaborative effort between Yad Vashem in Jerusalem and YIVO in New York, which resulted in the detailed and exhaustive bibliographies on the Holocaust, and his own bibliography of articles and books on the catastrophe in English, Yiddish, Hebrew, and Polish ran for pages.[126] Friedman the historian understood that scholarship on any subject could only proceed as documents became available through collection and annotation, and much of his work involved producing articles for scholars which listed archives, described sources, and provided information for others to use in producing monographs.[127] A "scholar's scholar," Friedman did not invoke sacred memories or issue heartrending calls to remember. Rather, he laid out historical narratives as the documents allowed him, meticulously checking facts and poring over citations.

While he saw himself as a scholar, committed to furthering knowledge, Friedman participated in communal memorial events. He addressed Warsaw Ghetto memorial meetings, corresponded with committees preparing *yizker bikher*, and assisted others involved in stimulating the commemorative culture. Synagogues and community groups around the country invited him to lecture, and he accepted these as his schedule allowed.[128] His 1954 book *Martyrs and Fighters* had been sponsored by the Club of Polish Jews in New York, and very positive reviews of Friedman's books appeared in nonscholarly Jewish magazines and newspapers. While he placed the scholarly project chief among his concerns, the Jewish public identified him as one of the architects of their scattered memorials to the six million.[129]

So, too, Koppel Pinson, a professor of history at Queens College in New York City, furthered the process of Holocaust scholarship. A specialist in German history, he wrote about the German past, particularly its nationalist tradition, and Simon Dubnow, the scholar murdered by the Germans in the ghetto in Riga. His synthetic *Modern Germany* of 1954, published by Macmillan, went back in time to the early nineteenth century but devoted several lengthy chapters to the evolution of the German campaign to exterminate the Jews and how it became a central element of Third Reich policy.[130] Similarly, by publishing in 1958 a collection of essays by Dubnow, Pinson provided readers with a scholarly work on secular Jewish nationalism and the Holocaust. Pinson opened the book of essays by noting, "It is a tragic irony of history that Dubnow, the first Jewish historian to rebel against the historiography that viewed Jewish history as primarily the history of literature and martyrdom, himself became one of the tragic martyrs in the Nazi war against the Jews." Most of Dubnow's essays had been written well before the Nazi era and dealt with unrelated topics, but, to Pinson, Dubnow's thinking on Jewish life and his tragic end during the Holocaust became indivisible.[131]

Friedman and Pinson did not act alone. Others participated in this scholarly endeavor. Usually not taking the catastrophe as the sole focus of their work, a range of Jewish scholars integrated it into their writings, making it a reference point for understanding and presenting the Jewish past.

Columbia University's Salo Baron, the first scholar of Jewish history to hold an academic appointment at an American university, wrote prolifically on the grand sweep of Jewish history. He interspersed details of what had happened to Europe's Jews under Nazism into his long list of articles and lectures. Known widely for his contention that the medieval period had not been the nadir of Jewish existence as commonly assumed, Baron made much of the Holocaust, showing that, instead, modernity had inflicted on the Jews their greatest suffering. Jews and their supporters, he noted, think of modernity as "all white against an abysmally dark background of 'medieval' suffering. So deeply had this misconception sunk into the minds of the Jewish people and their liberal non-Jewish friends, that when Hitler came to power . . . the Nazis and their opponents alike often spoke of the revival of the 'medieval' status of Jewry. . . . However, even in the 1930s and still more in the 1940s, it became manifest that through this comparison we were maligning the Middle Ages." The Nazis' "final solution to the Jewish question . . . the total elimination of Jews from Europe . . . their ruthless extermination of millions of Jews" persuasively proved that historians, and Jews generally, had to rethink the outlines of Jewish history.[132]

Philosopher Dagobert Runes wrote his 1951 *The Hebrew Impact on Western Civilization* to chronicle the Jewish contribution to western culture. His book of nearly a thousand pages detailed Jewish achievements in art, music, commerce, medicine, literature, publishing, science, and other fields, all contextualized around the reality that "six hundred thousand Jews of pre-war Germany produced as many Nobel Prize winners as sixty million Germans." As a result of that, "the *Herrenvolk* . . . showed its gratitude to the men who so tremendously helped in their growth by massacring the Jewish people of Europe. Six million souls in six years! . . . This is how one Christian nation repaid its debt to the people of Israel." Runes's book went back in time millennia, naming individual Jews who had enriched western civilization.[133]

While Runes's scholarship put German Jewry in the limelight and considered its demise at the hands of the "Herrenvolk," the master race, Uriel Weinreich's scholarship led him to analyze the Holocaust in terms of east European Jewry and the Yiddish language. In the preface to his 1954 study of Yiddish, published by Columbia University's Linguistic Circle of New York, he noted the importance of this study in light of "the German massacre" "of the larger part of Yiddish speaking Jewry." That slaughter "also destroyed the bulk of its scholarly personnel and the network of its institutions." His study of this language with its history extending back a thousand years, he believed, needed to be written and understood with the Holocaust as a point of reference.[134]

The American Jewish scholarly community in the postwar period did not have the benefit of well-organized archives or extensive bibliographies. Those would have to wait for later generations to complete. Nor did it have the backing of academic institutions, as would the historians of the future. No departments of Jewish studies then existed in American universities, and no history departments, with the exception of Columbia's with Baron ensconced in his chair, taught Jewish history. But with those limitations in mind, a growing cadre of historians and other scholars began the task of both writing the Holocaust and making the Holocaust a focal point in their studies of other aspects of the Jewish past.

Speaking of the Catastrophe

American Jews not only wrote and read about the Holocaust. Their organizations and institutions sponsored public lectures and adult education classes to explore it. Anyone eager to know what postwar American Jews said about the Holocaust in public and where they said it could readily hear their voices. The lectures and addresses they gave to both Jewish and general audiences bear witness to the degree to which the facts of the catastrophe reverberated in Jewish public spaces and in the places where Jews communicated with the broader American public.[135]

Anne Robison, for example, an officer and activist for the National Council of Jewish Women and the American Association of University Women (AAUW), addressed both audiences on matters growing out of the Holocaust. Robison had gone to Germany and France after the war, and she shared her experiences. She lectured at AAUW chapter meetings all over the country in 1948, sharing with them what she had seen in the Displaced Persons camps in Germany, how she had encountered survivors, who came "alive with excitement as our cars drove up the crowded streets. . . . These unfortunate people had each come as the one surviving remnant of his family, from the same community in Poland." Robison's late-1940s and 1950s speaking career made the Holocaust a central element in her public lectures, whether delivered to Jewish or general audiences.[136]

Koppel Pinson also lectured widely in the New York area to all sorts of groups about the Holocaust and its consequences. A mainstay of YIVO and a frequent lecturer at its gatherings, in 1955, he addressed the Queens,

New York, Americans for Democratic Action on the subject of "The German Problem," telling his audience that "the most awesome and most tragic fact of these years is the complete destruction and liquidation of East European Jewry. East European Jewry, from which the parents of most of us were derived, and from which all of us drew our chief religious, cultural and spiritual sustenance for the past four hundred years—East European Jewry is no more." In 1956, he accepted an invitation from the Herzl Institute on "The Future of Judaism," speculating on the meaning of the Holocaust, as he exhorted his listeners, mostly active Zionists, to "not fall prey to the violent reaction to emancipation that is in vogue among some Jewish circles . . . since the Hitler catastrophe." Temple Beth El of Manhattan Beach, New York, hosted him in 1959 to lecture on modern Jewish history. Here he presented material about the "liquidation of European Jewry" and its impact on the Jews of America.[137]

American Jewish organizations consistently invited non-Jews, national or local notables, to communal events where the Holocaust got talked about in formal lectures. At the 1957 American Jewish Committee (AJC) fiftieth anniversary celebration, for example, a five-day symposium with banquets, lectures, and roundtable discussions at New York's Waldorf Astoria hotel, a range of presenters addressed the theme "The Pursuit of Equality at Home and Abroad." Among others, the following attended the by-invitation-only event: Dag Hammarskjöld, Secretary General of the United Nations; New York City College's President Buell Gallagher; Union Theological Seminary's Reverend John Coleman Bennett; the editor of *America*, Jesuit priest Reverend Neil G. McCluskey; Sherman Adams, President Eisenhower's assistant; and newscaster Edward R. Murrow.

Talk of the Holocaust punctuated the lectures, with Judge Joseph Proskauer, former president of the AJC, setting the tone at the first session. This organization, he remarked, sought to foster "useful, valid scholarly research into those causes which have operated to make Catholics murder Protestants, Protestants murder Catholics, and both, in turn, from time to time, murder Jews, until we saw its culmination in the Hitler holocaust." Proskauer identified here various forms of group hatred, but only one, anti-Semitism, had culminated in a "holocaust." The assembled dignitaries, mostly non-Jews and leaders of the American Jewish Committee, heard the public reading of the resolutions adopted to mark this golden anniversary. The AJC described its financial and political obligations for Jews around the world, acknowledging the "vast changes that have taken place in the structure of Jewish communities" since 1906, the year of its founding, particularly "as a result of the holocaust of the Hitler period" in which "the great historic Jewish communities of Europe have been decimated."[138]

Communal rhetoric that resounded with the themes of the Holocaust abounded from the late 1940s through the early 1960s. Talk of Hitler, the Nazis, the destroyed Jews, and the catastrophe could be heard in the halls where community meetings took place. For example, attendees at the annual conventions of the National Federation of Temple Sisterhoods (NFTS) heard such references at every biennial, whether articulated by NFTS officials or by the invited speakers.[139] These meetings did not lend themselves to the presentation of history per se, but the Reform women found multiple ways to refer to the horrendous past and thereby to use the Holocaust to boast of their organization's accomplishments and advocate for contemporary issues. The delegates heard yearly how the sisterhood movement had brought several Holocaust survivors to Cincinnati to study at Hebrew Union College. When speakers referred to these students, they recalled the Holocaust's devastation. Isaac Neuman, introduced as "a student from the remnant of Polish Jewry," himself appeared at the NFTS 1957 convention, to personally thank the women for supporting him. As he noted, "it is not out of place to reflect on how much we are heirs to Jewish history. I, a survivor of Nazi concentration camps have become rabbi in Israel with your, American Reform Jewry's aid."[140] In 1959, the president of the Sisterhood Federation introduced another of these newly minted rabbis who had survived the Holocaust and then came to study at HUC under the organization's aegis. "After spending his youth in the dreaded concentration camp of Theresienstadt," he now belonged to the ranks of the Reform rabbinate.[141]

NFTS resolutions and political discussions justified their actions, when they saw fit, in light of the Holocaust. At the biennial meeting of 1961, as it had every year in the past, NFTS passed a resolution calling on the U.S. Senate to ratify the Genocide Convention. On what basis did it take this stand? "Mindful of the sanctity of all life and of the dreadful tragedy that swept over six million of our brethren in Europe during the Hitler era, as well as of the critical current need to affirm the dignity and equality of all people, [we] again urge" passage of the Convention.[142]

This kind of talk wafted through the air at meetings of the Labor Zionist Organization of America, B'nai B'rith, ORT (Organization for Rehabilitation Through Training), American Jewish Congress, Jewish Labor Committee, and Jewish War Veterans, among others. During the postwar period, speakers at Jewish organizational gatherings marshaled the history of the Holocaust to tell their own histories. In 1954, Isaiah Minkoff, speaking on "What Is Our Stake in the American Jewish Community?" at the Annual Conference of the Workmen's Circle Division of the Jewish Labor Committee (JLC), noted that when the JLC had been formed, "Hitler was in power and the Nazis exploited anti-Semitism as a fifth column activity in the United States." As time had gone by, the stake of the Jewish Labor Committee in the American Jewish community shifted as it responded to, serially, "the relief of the Jewish people throughout the world, . . . the tragedy of European Jewry and the gruesome extermination of 6,000,000 Jews."[143]

At the annual meetings of Jewish youth movements as well, during the postwar years, speakers invoked the Holocaust as those of the rising generation claimed that they would have to shoulder new responsibilities and bring about profound change because of the carnage in Europe. They did so prominently by stating that their organization—whether Habonim, Hashomer Hatzair, B'nai Akiva, Young Judea, National Federation of Temple Youth, or the like—faced the world as the heir to the six million. Each pronounced that it had a vision to enhance Jewish life in the face of the devastations of the Holocaust. In the early 1950s, the leaders of these Jewish youth groups attempted, unsuccessfully, to create a National Jewish Youth Council to strengthen Jewish life in America by erasing ideological differences. They met in the summer of 1951. Their conference, titled "Jewish Youth at Midcentury," began with a speech by historian Abraham Duker, who charged the young people with the task of achieving a unity that their parents had not. They, American Jewish youth, would inhabit a radically different world than previous generations. Not only had Jews become more secularized than "their Christian or Moslem neighbors," but also Jews had endured a devastating blow. "The Jewish people," Duker told them, had been "centered, only 11 years ago, in Central and Eastern Europe. Now due to the Hitler massacres . . . it is concentrated mainly in America." They, the rising generation, had to deal with that reality.[144]

As on the national level, so, too, on the local level across the country, if not more so, those who attended Jewish gatherings heard about the Holocaust. When in 1950 the Jews of South Carolina celebrated their two hundredth anniversary, they invited Rabbi Abba Hillel Silver, Zionist leader, to address an "overflowing audience" at an interfaith meeting on the meaning of that upbeat history. It, the renowned orator noted, had been shaped by the place where "brotherliness and tolerance and good will . . . existed, without the elements which have defiled the life of so many Jewish communities in the last 200 years." Silver, the *Charleston News and Courier* reported, had marveled over the fact that Jews, "the most persecuted community in history[,] should be the most optimistic, but he pointed out that despite centuries of oppression and the loss of almost 6,000,000 persons in Hitler's persecutions Judaism lives on, hungry for life."[145]

Jewish communal organizations also sponsored lectures, individual ones and series for the general Jewish public, on scholarly subjects and hosted discussions of current books and current events.[146] These directly named the catastrophe as their subject or, by virtue of the topic under consideration, dealt with it. Most lectures given at YIVO focused squarely on the Holocaust, and speakers there also worked it into presentations on other subjects. Lectures delivered at the Leo Baeck Institute took the calamity of European Jewry as their theme. After all, the institute, which described itself on the masthead of its journal as "named in honor of the man who was the last representative figure of Germany Jewry in Germany during the Nazi period," existed because of it. Starting in 1958, the annual Leo Baeck Memorial Lecture shared with attendees details of that cataclysmic event and how it differed from the others "which Jews have suffered throughout their history."[147]

A range of Jewish institutions made presentations of the Holocaust part of their programming.[148] The Wisconsin Society for Jewish Learning, from its founding in the middle of the 1950s into the early 1960s, invited numerous speakers on the subject, including University of Wisconsin historian George Mosse to lecture on "Roots of German Anti-Semitism" and Madison's Rabbi Manfred Swarensky, who spoke on Leo Baeck. Jacob Neusner, the first chair of the Hebrew studies department at the University of Wisconsin–Milwaukee, ended his inaugural lecture in 1961 by stating, "If we Jewish people had met utter destruction at the hands of the German Nazis between 1933 and 1945, the human West would doubtless take deep interest in the history and literature and philosophy of these ancient tragic men. What could be more pathetic or more tragic, or therefore, more interesting to men of culture than the story of what happened between Abraham and Auschwitz? Indeed there are some places where it is more respectable to exhume the dead than to examine the living. But the Jewish people live, endure, create."[149]

Jewish communal programming took place around the country, in institutions of various kinds, and these events gave prominence to the Holocaust. Young Israel, a network of Orthodox congregations, established an Institute for Jewish Studies and in 1950–1951 offered a course on "The Modern Period of Jewish History," with several of the sessions dedicated

Deborah Pessin's three-volume history *The Jewish People* may have been published by the United Synagogue Commission on Jewish Education, an arm of the Conservative movement, but Jewish schools of all kinds used it, making it one of the most widely adopted Jewish history books for youngsters in America. The third volume, which came out in 1953, dealt with the modern period and gave prominent place to the fact that "the Nazis began to murder the Jews of Germany and of the countries they had conquered. The people who called themselves 'super-men' and the 'master race' murdered six million Jews, the worst slaughter in the history of the world." The textbook also made much of the Warsaw Ghetto uprising. It illustrated the armed struggle not with drawings of the small band of young Jewish women and men with their makeshift arms but with this rendering of the destroyed city, the shattered synagogue, the abandoned book, and the absence of people. *Courtesy United Synagogue of Conservative Judaism.*

to "The Approach of the Hitlerian Era," "The Beginnings of Massacres," "The Second World War and Its Effects—Jewish Losses," and "The Concentration Camps and Nazi Torture."[150] From the late 1940s through the early 1960s, Chicago's College of Jewish Studies offered "Modern Jewish History" to both full-time students and adult learners. The course catalog specified that this class included a focus on "the Hitler Holocaust," taught by historian Moses Shulvass, who also offered "Migratory Movements of the Jews Until the Establishment of the State of Israel," with several sessions also devoted to "The Hitler Holocaust." In addition, the College of Jewish Studies offered special courses for "Sunday School Teachers and Club Leaders," and those enrolled during the academic year 1959–1960 could take "History 109," which covered "the struggle for emancipation . . . World War I and its aftermath, the Great catastrophe and the emergence of the State of Israel."[151]

Synagogues, clubs, and other Jewish institutions provided informal classes and lectures. The national offices of the National Federation of Temple Sisterhoods enlisted speakers to travel the country to speak at chapter meetings. The lectures offered included one by Eve Landau on Jewish music. Landau, originally from Germany, had, according to the speakers' bureau material, "escaped Hitler." She lectured for Reform women's groups on "Forbidden Music," music banned by the Nazis. Sisterhoods of Reform congregations in Alice, Texas; Bellaire, Ohio; Wichita Falls, Texas; Davenport, Iowa; Oakland, California; Cincinnati; and Buffalo held discussion groups on such topics as "Should Jews Return to Germany?" "The Spanish-Jewish Tragedy—Compared with the European Holocaust," "Conditions Prevailing in Europe—With Emphasis upon the Jewish People," and "An Unconquerable Soul—Dr. Leo Baeck Speaks to America."[152]

Adult education programs required course materials. NFTS provided these to its local groups, as did the Women's League of the United Synagogue, the women of Conservative Judaism. In 1947, Sarah Kussy and her committee prepared the *Handbook and Guide for Jewish Women's Organizations* for its synagogues and for use by "other Jewish Women's organizations desiring programs with Jewish content." When suggesting a model Hanukkah program, the *Handbook* recommended an episode of *The Eternal Light* about Hannah Senesh, "The Lantern in the Inferno," while for Purim, the *Handbook* proposed that women plan their events around the fact that "our own age has witnessed the rise to power of the arch-Haman of all times. It has also seen his complete destruction." Program planners, according to Kussy, could build activities around "Memorial Day," the Tenth of Tevet, for which they could use " 'Warsaw Ghetto,' a diary by Mary Berg; . . . 'Lest We Forget': the massacre of the Warsaw ghetto; a compilation of reports by the World Jewish Congress; . . . 'No Traveler Returns' by Henry Shoskes; . . . 'The Revolt in the Warsaw Ghetto' by Jacob Patt, in Magazine Digest; . . . [and] 'The Last Days of the Warsaw Ghetto,' a survivor's account of a heroic chapter in Jewish history."[153] B'nai B'rith's Department of Adult Jewish Education prepared two volumes in the 1950s, one on Jewish thought and one on Jewish thinkers, "to stimulate and promote the study of Judaism among adult Jews." Both volumes devoted full essays to Berlin's Rabbi Leo Baeck, "the heroic symbol of courage and spiritual resistance in the face of Nazi tyranny." They explored Baeck's philosophy, writings, and rabbinical career and highlighted how Baeck had refused to leave his congregations after Hitler had come to power despite numerous offers to escape to safety. Instead, "in 1943 he was sent to the concentration camp of Theresienstadt in Czechoslovakia where his teaching and religious activities set an example of hope and spiritual courage."[154]

Similar ideas emerged in Sidney Markowitz's *What Do You Know about Jewish Religion, History, Ethics and Culture?* a study guide for "youth centers, summer camps or army camps," intended for "Jews of all shades of opinion, . . . the curious youth and inquisitive child, . . . parents . . . who seek the proper questions asked by their children," and also for "non-Jews . . . who want a clear, unbiased and realistic picture." The booklet's history section explored the Holocaust. When writing about Germany, for example, Markowitz bluntly stated, "When the Hitler gang finally came to power, and the big lie of a super race was swallowed by the German people, the Jew became a perfect foil for the despots." This study guide pointed out that "up to and including World War II, most of the Jews in Germany, Austria and the other European countries conquered by the Nazis, were herded into concentration and slave labor camps. A ghastly program of extermination was put into practice, and over six million Jews were murdered."[155]

These scattered study materials reflected a desire on the part of their authors and editors to integrate the Holocaust into the world of Jewish adult education. They simultaneously recognized the broad and deep communal interest in the devastating subject and sought to promote its further study. Rather than functioning then as a matter of discomfort and shame, the Holocaust occupied a notable space in the American Jewish public world.

Teaching the Catastrophe

This same recognition influenced educators, those who ran Jewish schools and engaged in informal youth work. They, too, considered teaching the

European catastrophe a priority, although they did not have a clear idea how to do so. They discussed at length the best and most appropriate way to make the catastrophe part of the curriculum, but they realized that incorporating the Holocaust into the Jewish school presented them with a profound dilemma.[156]

They wanted to teach it, and did so. But this jarred with the basic premise of postwar Jewish education.[157] Education, they believed, should be undertaken in large measure to imbue children with a desire to embrace Judaism and Jewish culture. Jewish educators considered it crucial that children acquire cognitive knowledge, including Jewish languages (Yiddish or Hebrew), the Jewish Bible, Jewish holidays, the life cycle of the Jew, Jewish customs and traditions, and synagogue skills. But in the increasingly open and tolerant postwar years, they also hoped to give children affirmative attitudes about being Jewish. The schools, they believed, should stress positive Jewish values, upbeat Jewish themes, and the idea that people who maintained Jewish commitments benefited from them, while those without lacked meaningful identity and community. A National Federation of Temple Sisterhoods publication proclaimed the ethos of the era as it promised members involved with their congregational schools that "You Can Have a Happy School."[158]

To what degree did having a "happy school" and getting children to want to be Jewish conflict with educating them about the Holocaust? What could American Jewish youngsters derive from "the recent holocaust that has annihilated so much of our material and spiritual wealth," these words drawn from the "Declaration of the Sholem Aleichem Folk Institute" in 1949 as the raison d'être for its Yiddish-language-based schools? Michael Stavitsky, president of the American Association for Jewish Education in 1954, likewise charged educators and communities that "the most important task before us is the survival and revival of our people. . . . We have witnessed in our time . . . the slaughter of whole communities."[159] At their meetings and in their publications, Jewish educators anguished over the fact that, as Emanuel Gamoran, a pedagogue from the Reform movement, declared at the annual meeting of the National Council for Jewish Education in 1947, "as a result of Hitlerism over one-third of our people has been destroyed. No one can tell what a loss this is not only to the Jewish people but to Judaism."[160] The Jewish school played a crucial role in projecting of vision of how to make up for this calamity.

Educators recognized that, as a result of the "loss of the six million of our people," the world had changed, "and the balance of Jewry has now swung to the United States. The Jews of the world will look . . . to this country. . . . We can only meet this historic responsibility," said educator Uriah Engelman, when "our great material resources are joined with a far richer knowledge of Jewish history, traditions and problems than is possessed by the average American Jew." Education, clearly, seemed to him and others the key to making up for the "destruction of priceless spiritual and cultural treasuries . . . all . . . reduced to rubble and ashes."[161]

Jewish educators presented their ideas about how and where in the curriculum the Holocaust ought to be tackled in several ways.[162] First, in their professional journals they wrote articles about it, providing each other with information on educational projects that had worked, alerting each other on new texts to employ. Some thought that the study of Jewish heroism during the Holocaust years offered teachers a way to negotiate between the need to tell and the quest for positive symbols. Educators touted the pedagogic power of Marie Syrkin's 1947 *Blessed Is the Match*, which showed up on their suggested reading lists and in their pedagogic discussions.[163] Sholem Aleichem and Arbeiter Ring schools, which taught Yiddish, exposed their students to primary material in the original, drawn from the texts of the Warsaw Ghetto, the partisans, and from the writings of other Holocaust heroes who "fought back."[164] Educators emphasizing the heroism narrative used preparations for school Passover celebrations to teach students about the Holocaust. School Warsaw Ghetto ceremonies bridged the memorial and the educational, making it possible to teach something about the Holocaust to young children as they practiced for their pageants and model seder performances. In the Sholem Aleichem schools, fourth graders took part in "some observance of the anniversary of the Warsaw Ghetto," although only in the fifth grade when they began to study Jewish history did the curriculum go beyond the ceremonial and the heroic. In the fifth grade, the curricular guides noted that teachers should introduce "Hitler and German anti-Semitism. The destruction of European Jewry. Jews fight back. Warsaw Gretto [*sic*] Uprising. Partisans."[165]

The study of Jewish history seemed to many pedagogues the perfect vehicle for bringing the Holocaust into the classroom. A fairly new endeavor, teaching Jewish history in Jewish schools, had to be defended against those who considered the schools' job to teach Hebrew, prayers, Bible, and Jewish customs and to train boys for their b'nei mitzvah. Those who favored expanding the curriculum believed that studying the Jewish past could invigorate an enterprise they feared many youngsters found boring and antiquated. Among others, Alfred Freidman, Frieda Clark Hyman,

Deborah Pessin, and Milton Plesur considered Jewish history a new topic that could confer a sense of immediacy to school-age students.[166] Teaching the Holocaust figured into their *desiderata*.

In the pages of their professional journals, Jewish educators discussed how to teach the catastrophe. The Jewish Education Committee's *Bulletin* of May 1949 offered an example of such a learning project as it described how Brooklyn's Yeshiva Flatbush had taught the catastrophe by having students construct, as a Passover project, a replica of a concentration camp. In 1952, *Pedagogic Reporter*, the in-house publication of the American Association for Jewish Education, described a proposed full-length "Holocaust Curriculum Project."[167]

In addition, the journals reviewed books and drew teachers' attention to Holocaust texts, which they could then use in their classrooms, such as *No Traveler Returns, Balance Sheet of Extermination*, Renya Kulkielko's 1948 *Escape from the Pit* (the memoir of "one of the few young Polish Jewesses who survived the Nazi holocaust"), and *Notes from the Warsaw Ghetto: The Journal of Emanuel Ringelblum*, among others.[168] They touted the pedagogical import of such films as *Distant Journey—The Ghetto Terezin; Dr. Leo Baeck: Man of Faith*, with its particular "emphasis upon his spiritual and communal activities in Germany during the Nazi regime"; *Road to Israel*, a "moving film [that] tells of the heroic exploits of the defenders of the Warsaw ghetto"; and *Long Is the Road*, "an exciting feature film [in which], beginning with the German occupation of Warsaw, the journey to Auschwitz concentration camp . . . is dramatically portrayed."[169] *Distant Journey*, a Czech-produced film about Terezin, received elaborate praise from Jewish educational specialists as a "highly useful source . . . in the teaching of current events, the Jewish community and history." Warning that "the film is not considered suitable for very young children because of the horrors it portrays," *Pedagogic Reporter* downplayed potential criticism of the film. "There is nothing in it," the journal commented, "which would be objectionable to any religious grouping or to mixed audiences," as it maintained that Jewish youngsters ought to know about the Holocaust. These Jewish educators considered it their obligation, and that of the schools, to expose American Jewish children to the details of the Jewish catastrophe, to help them become conversant with its facts.[170]

Jewish educational institutions made ample use of the creative arts as a way to bring the Holocaust to their classrooms. Judith and Ira Eisenstein, through the Reconstructionist Foundation, created a cantata, *Reborn —An Episode with Music*, which Jewish educators considered well worth being staged in other Jewish schools. Based on "Life in a Bunker," a story in Leo Schwarz's *The Root and the Bough*, the cantata explored "the experiences of several Jews who were hiding in a forest to escape the Nazi terror." One educational journal recommended this as particularly appropriate for "children of confirmation age," around sixteen, and a fitting program for a confirmation ceremony.[171] In a similar vein, but serving a different denominational purpose, in 1948 the Union of American Hebrew Congregations' Commission on Jewish Education issued *We Must Rebuild* by Irwin Blank, "a playlet on the life of Dr. Leo Baeck, for children in elementary schools." Telling the life of Baeck, the Reform movement's icon of the Holocaust era, opened up the story of Nazism, Hitler, and the world of the concentration camp to Reform schools, and it added the arts to enliven the curriculum.[172]

Textbooks used in Jewish schools also brought the Holocaust narrative to children.[173] Rabbi Roland Gittelsohn prepared *Modern Jewish Problems* for high schoolers in 1949 and *Little Lower Than the Angels* in 1955, aimed specifically at the fifteen- to sixteen-year-old group in Union of American Hebrew Congregation Schools. The first of these, written in the first years after the war, focused on survivors, using their experiences to read back in time to World War II, when "one third of all the Jews in the world were killed." The second book posed the experiences of the war in the context of the emergence of Israel and the reality that "it is true that Hitler killed 6,000,000 Jews before he himself was destroyed. The fact that the Jewish people as a group triumphed over him and outlasted him may be of small comfort to the victims and their families but is enormously important in the light of history." Gittelsohn intended *Little Lower Than the Angels* to teach Jewish values rather than "facts," yet he presented information to illustrate ethical decisions and dilemmas. "You are probably already familiar," he addressed his teenage readers, "with the heroic story of the Warsaw ghetto." If not, he suggested they read Marie Syrkin's *Blessed Is the Match*. Gittelsohn also exposed students to the story of "the head of the Jewish Council," who, "when ordered by the Nazis to give them lists of Jews to be deported to extermination camps, steadfastly refused and in the end committed suicide rather than betray his fellow Jews."[174]

The Conservative movement also produced textbooks, with Deborah Pessin's four volumes of Jewish history, published in the 1950s, the most popular, used far beyond its own congregational schools. She brought the Holocaust in systematically and directly. What the Nazis did during World War II, when they "began to murder the Jews of Germany and of the countries they had conquered," constituted "the worst slaughter in the history of the world." She valorized the ghetto uprisings, the exploits of Hannah Senesh, the partisans, and the other acts of heroism undertaken by the Jews to resist the Nazis. But Pessin set against these presentations of the heroic her much longer sections, which traced how by the time the "the Second World War had ended in 1945 . . . the millions of Jews in Europe had been reduced to thousands."[175]

Through their schools and their informal educational programs, particularly summer camps, Jewish young people got a chance to present their own words, no doubt filtered through teachers, principals, and camp counselors, on the Holocaust. Students in the Sholem Aleichem Folk schools in New York wrote Yiddish essays to both hone their linguistic skills and express their ideas about Jewish history and culture. A batch of essays from the late 1950s included writings on such suggested topics as "The Heroic Uprising of the Warsaw Ghetto," "I Will Always Remember the Heroes of the Warsaw Ghetto," and "I Saw the Film 'The Diary of Anna Frank.'"[176] Malka Winters, age thirteen, provided a straightforward description of the Frank family in her theme and concluded, "The whole world knows that of the eight people" who hid in the Amsterdam attic, "only Mr. Frank remained alive. Anna died two weeks before the end of the war in Europe. She had a tragic life. I saw the film and read the book. I am ashamed for all the Nazis who killed so many people, so many children." Another student, with no name or age affixed to her essay, shared with her teacher and classmates that "when I saw the 'Diary of Anna Frank,' I cried bitterly. It is hard to believe that the Jews went through so much suffering during the World War. We Jewish children believe that it has always been as good for us as it is now and when our parents tell us how bitter it was for Jews in the old home at the time of the war, we do not believe them, because Jews in America live so well." Like so many postwar American Jews, she found an upbeat way to conclude: "I hope that the Jews will always live in peace and happiness and that never again will they have to run away from the hand of an enemy."[177]

The widespread embrace of Anne Frank, by Jews and non-Jews, Americans as well as people around the world, through the published diary, the play, and then the film, reflected itself in the activities of American Jewish youngsters in their educational settings, both formal and informal. During the summer of 1959, the Reform movement's Camp Olin-Sang-Ruby staged a "reading of The Diary of Ann Frank." Campers complained afterward, and counselors agreed, that not enough time had been allocated for the follow-up discussion, since "everyone seemed to have a lot to say."[178]

The yearbooks of Camp Hemshekh, the Yiddish-oriented camp founded in 1959 by Holocaust survivors, told how Anne Frank and the Holocaust functioned in the camp's educational work. Camp Hemshekh named its cabins after "Yiddish authors, pioneers of the Jewish labor movement, and . . . heroes of the Jewish fight and resistance in the ghettos." One bunk bore the name of Anne Frank, as campers read and wrote about her, "the Jewish child who was killed by the Nazi brutality. . . . Her name will live forever in world literature." Campers slept in buildings named Hirsch Glick, Mordecai Anieliewicz, Simon Dubnow, and Artur Zygelboim, all east European ghetto heroes.[179]

Even school yearbooks showcased the writings of Jewish children as they expressed their insights on the Holocaust. In 1953, the students at Brooklyn's Yeshivah of Flatbush, like millions of other children at schools around the country, ended the year with the publication of a book of memories, creative writings, and drawings. These children used their yearbook to present the connections they perceived between the catastrophe and various Jewish holidays, for example. One boy's Hebrew essay on Passover declared that "the last Pharaoh was in Germany, the evil one Hitler, may his name and memory be erased. By his orders six million Jews were slaughtered. This was the greatest national tragedy in all the generations of the Jews." Ruth Brenner made the Holocaust the background to her paragraph on Israeli Independence Day. How wonderful that "independence for a nation that suffered . . . in the ghettoes, in the concentration camps," while Rehavia Brisman expressed himself on the same event with the wistful "would that the Jews who suffered during the days of Hitler could be brought back to life and see the fulfillment of their hopes." Sixth grader Larry Goldfarb tried his hand at fiction with a very short story, "The Jewish Star," set in Germany. He created "a boy, named Jacob," who "while walking home . . . saw some Nazi soldiers marching through his village." Things went badly for Jacob. "The next thing he could remember was a concentration camp. Here he was told that his family was dead." The young author allowed Jacob a heroic fate. Jacob escaped from the camp, got to Israel, and rebuilt his life. Brana Haber, a seventh grader, moved to the realm of contemporary events, linking the fate of Jews in the Soviet Union with the evil deeds of the Germans. Titling her essay "Ghetto . . . Pogrom . . . Gas Chambers: Behind the Iron Curtain," she asked, "Can the Jewish people take any more?" and then answered her own question: "From Pharaoh to Hitler we have stood fast" and would persist.[180]

These words of some American Jewish children, influenced by their teachers, shaped by their youth, and harmonious with the dominant motifs of American Jewish culture, typified communal presentations of the Holocaust in the postwar period. Theirs, like all the other words written and spoken by the Jews of America in these years, demonstrated the depth of their interest in the catastrophe and their sense of obligation to keep writing and talking about it.

Presenting the Holocaust, Presenting Themselves

As postwar American Jews presented their history, they made the Holocaust a salient part of their texts, grappling with it and speculating on how it ought to be seen. Did it represent just the most recent example of Jewish suffering, or did it constitute an unprecedented event with no parallel in the Jews' long acquaintance with tragedy?

At times, as they recalled the narrative of their past—from the ancient period of the enslavement in Egypt through the destruction of the two Temples, the exiles, and the Crusades; expulsions from England, France, Spain, and elsewhere; seventeenth-century Polish massacres; Russian pogroms of the late nineteenth and early twentieth centuries—Jews claimed a history that made the Holocaust seem not so radically new. That their calendar moved from Purim, based on the story of Haman's plot to kill the Jews of Persia, to Hanukkah, which had introduced the concept of martyrdom into Jewish history, to the Ninth of Av's lamentations over the destruction of the two Temples and to Passover, which every year instructed them to retell how Pharaoh had decreed that all male Hebrew infants be killed, meant that they engaged annually with words and images of tragedy. They easily melded these with the recent cataclysm that had engulfed the Jews of Europe, positing a continuous history of suffering and, in the process, making the Holocaust an active partner in fostering Jewish historical consciousness.

The history they told themselves pivoted around episodes of suffering and pain and opened up places to talk about the Holocaust in Jewish historical terms. William Chomsky, a Hebraist, an advocate for modern Hebrew as the most potent resource to foster Jewish culture in America, made the connection in linguistic terms. Translation into English, he asserted, rendered the Hebrew "flat and insipid." Hebrew "expressions . . . stir in every conscious Jew feelings and images such as could never be evoked in any other language." He noted, "in the words of *Shema' Yisrael* [usually translated "Hear O Israel"] . . . we hear echoes and reverberations of the agonized cries of our martyrs from the days of Akiba [a rabbi executed by the Romans] down to the 'rebels' of the Warsaw Ghetto."[181] Judah Pilch, a prominent Jewish educator, considered that a new and better Jewish education required that young Jews be taught "the record of our martyrdom," telling teachers in 1962 that they should "recapitulate before them the story of the Inquisition, the banishment of Jews from one country after another, the yellow badge of shame, the ghetto walls, the Russian pogroms and finally—the Hitlerian holocaust."[182]

Presenting the Holocaust as the most recent link in a seemingly endless chain of Jewish suffering appeared everywhere in American Jewish public life, and these texts reminded American Jews that they had inherited that history. The 1948 Labor Day Conclave of the National Federation of Temple Youth included a dramatic reading before the recitation of the kaddish (memorial prayer) written by youth leaders George Kaufman and Phoebe Katz of New York's Rodeph Sholom Youth Council:

> And now, ere we part, let us call to mind the numbered hosts of Israel who have lived and died to sanctify God's name, and affirm their people's faith. . . . We recall . . . Crusaders swords and the Inquisition's rack. . . . We recall . . . the martyrs in the woods of Europe, the battlers of the Warsaw ghetto. . . . Let Israel remember: The vision is not yet lost![183]

Adults crafted such words as well. Rabbi Ely Pilchik of Newark's B'nai Jeshurun Congregation sermonized in the 1950s on the iconic song "Ani Ma'amin," derived from Maimonides's "13 Principles," sung by "Hitler's victims" as they "marched to their crematoria graves at Maidanek where 820,000 were burned, at Chmelno and Aischwotz [Auschwitz] where 1,3000,000 were gassed, and at Treblinka where two million were done to death." They sang this song, joining a chorus of Jews, slaughtered by "Roman Hadrian; Crusaders; under Ferdinand and Isabella; Chmelniecki [seventeenth-century Cossak leader]; and Petlura [the organizer of bloody pogroms in the Ukraine after World War I]." The "multi-million martyrs of Nazidom supplanted the Sh'ma with Maimonides' twelfth principle, as though to throw the torch of millennial faith to us who survived."[184]

When Yiddish writers called the Holocaust *der dritter hurban* (the third destruction), they showed how much they saw its devastation in terms of the extended history of the Jews. At YIVO's 1946 conference, those gathered together declared, "We believe in the strength of the Jewish people to survive the Third Destruction in our history."[185] In a 1961 book, *Basic Jewish Beliefs*, Louis and Rebecca Barish placed the Holocaust alongside the destructions of the Temples that had altered Judaism and Jewish life. "God," they wrote, "uses evil to rebuke, to chastise, to goad man to action." In historical terms, the authors remarked, "the prophets and sages of Judaism interpreted the military victories of other nations against the Jewish people in this light. The destruction of the Temple in Jerusalem taught the Jews that they had grown unworthy to possess a temple; the massacre of six million Jews by the Nazis, made Jews everywhere aware of their moral responsibilities toward their brothers and the need to support the rebuilding of Israel."[186]

They used Jewish history to think about the Holocaust and the Holocaust to contextualize Jewish history in the present. Gertrude Hyman of Temple Beth Sholom of Bayside, New York, prepared a "Leader's Discussion Guide for a Purim Workshop" for the National Federation of Temple Sisterhoods in 1955. She asked, "What . . . does make Purim a Jewish Festival?" Answering herself, she wrote, "The prevention of Haman's genocide plot through the vigilance . . . of Mordecai and Esther was as important for the survival of the Jewish people as the Exodus." She acknowledged that the festival and the Book of Esther probably had no basis in historical fact, but that posed no problem, "for the story in the Book of Esther happened many times and keeps repeating itself to this day." Hyman reminded Sisterhood leaders that, "when . . . Herman Goering heard he would die, he said a 'Purim 1946' would be celebrated—the Jews had gotten their Haman. He too recognized a repetition of the story of Purim."[187] To the compiler of a Passover anthology, the "long and dreary centuries of adversity" had earned a special place for that holiday in the consciousness of the Jews. "Passover," wrote Philip Goodman, "unites the generations of today with its ancestors of the days of Moses, the Inquisition, the blood libels of the Middle Ages, the cruel pogroms of benighted Russia, the uprising of the Warsaw Ghetto, and the unspeakable catastrophe of Nazi Germany."[188] In a talk to the National Executive Committee of the Anti-Defamation League in 1959, Label Katz posited the parallels of Jewish history, that "we had our Golden Age in Spain—then came the Inquisition. We had our Golden Age in Germany . . . and the crematoria exacted their ghastly price for complacency."[189]

Postwar American Jews drew many Jewish lessons from the catastrophe when they placed it into the extended Jewish history narrative. In 1959, Ben Stern, a writer for *Young Zionist*, told his readers that "the story of Hitler and Jews is almost an exact historical parallel of Maccabean times. There was pussyfooting among the Jews for Hitler's favors; many Jews intermarried and assimilated, many would rather be Germans and aspire to their culture, many forgot they ever were Jews—until Hitler 'reminded them'—and when the blow fell, 6,000,000 were *not* there to tell the tale." Writing for a Zionist publication, he discerned the meaning of the Holocaust in Jewish history, a history that showed, he believed, that Jews often lusted for other peoples' cultures. By doing so, they sacrificed group identity and solidarity, and that left them unprepared for the inevitable attacks.[190]

Others perceived in the Holocaust a triumphal message of survival, a theme linked to all of Jewish history. Samuel Rosenbaum, president of the Conservative movement's Cantors Assembly, noted in a 1958 speech that "in countless repetitions from Nebuchadnezzar [the king of Babylonia responsible for the destruction of the First Temple in Jerusalem] to Hitler, from the plains of Mesopotamia to the crematoria of Germany, how can we be less than convinced that Judaism is a supple, vibrant, living thing which calls us to itself and bids us to create again?"[191]

If many posited the Holocaust as a recent manifestation of a long history of suffering, others presented it as utterly unique, with no precedent in the Jewish experience. A 1953 Orthodox sermon offered for the special penitential service for the Sabbath evening before Rosh Hashanah, *selichot*, compared the Holocaust with previous eras of Jewish suffering and declared, "None has ever faced a darker hour than those in concentration camps, standing before the doors of the gas chambers."[192] Writers noted that the all-too-real Hitler, unlike the probably fictional Haman, came shockingly close to achieving his goal of obliterating the Jewish people. In February 1954, *Jewish Spectator* ran "Purim Thoughts 5714." Most Jews, the writer noted, compared Hitler, the "master demon," to the "villainous Haman. Yet the case of Haman is essentially the story of a plot which failed. . . . Hitler, however, almost wrecked the whole civilized world and hit the world Jewish community with dreadful cruelty by dwarfing anything ever attempted in the way of mass extinction."[193]

References abounded to the catastrophe of the six million as occupying a category of its own in the history of Jewish suffering, and scholars, writers, rabbis, and other commentators struggled to show the differences.

Political scientist Hans Morgenthau offered this view in his 1961 lecture to the Leo Baeck Institute on "The Tragedy of German-Jewish Liberalism." Focusing specifically on the fate of the Jews of Germany, Morgenthau told his audience, themselves primarily Jewish refugees from central Europe, that "the disaster which befell the Jews of Germany under the Nazi regime was not only a disaster of the kind which Jews have suffered throughout their history." It differed because "all previous persecutions and all previous decimations suffered by Jews were intimately connected with the Jewish religion." Not so the recent tragedy, which differed in the intent of its perpetrator, but also because it "laid bare the truth of the Jewish condition."[194]

Whether they presented the Holocaust as the most recent episode in their long tragic history or as something horrifically sui generis, they told of it wherever they could and described themselves as its legatees. Even writers, sometimes scholars, of American Jewish history found ways to weave the Holocaust into their master narrative, a tricky project that required intellectual ingenuity. Anita Lebeson in her 1950 *Pilgrim People* proved quite creative. When writing about the sympathy expressed by the broad American public to the pogrom victims at the end of the nineteenth century and the early twentieth, she interjected, "Perhaps some day the historian of the future will be wise enough to explain why Americans took the Jewish massacres of 1881–1906 to heart and not those of 1933–45." She dubbed the 1930s the eve "of destruction and annihilation," and in her chapter on that grim period, she celebrated American Jewry's rescue efforts, including that of Henrietta Szold, the founder of Youth Aliyah, which rescued children from Hitler's Europe. Szold, Lebeson wrote, "knew the anguish of deepest mourning for the millions who died in the crematoria and concentration camps of Germany."[195]

Elma Ehrlich Levinger's 1954 *Jewish Adventures in America* brought the Holocaust into communal celebration of three hundred years of American Jewish history. Writing about philanthropist Nathan Straus, who had been dead several years before Hitler gained power, Levinger described Straus's relief for European Jewry after World War I. "His death," she consoled her readers, "spared him the knowledge of the horrors of the Hitler persecution." To Levinger, the history of American Jewry could not be disassociated from recent history, when "six million Jews, not only those of German birth but . . . from German-conquered territory, perished in cattle cars, in concentration camps and crematoria."[196]

The American Jewish Tercentenary proved particularly opportune for Jews to write the Holocaust into their American lives. Historians looking back to that year and the festivities and programs sponsored to mark the three centuries of Jewish life in America have in the main believed it to have been devoid of any recognition of the recent slaughter of the six million.[197] They have, however, not paid attention to Levinger's book, to Oscar Handlin's somber introductory remarks to his *Adventures in Freedom,* or, indeed, to the actual records of the sermons and speeches that constituted the public programming of the year.

Rabbi Israel Goldstein delivered a set of lectures about the meaning of the anniversary over the course of 1954, publishing them as *American Jewry Comes of Age.* This one relatively small book abounded with Holocaust references, and their profusion indicates the degree to which those who thought about the experience of Jews in the United States in the 1950s refracted it through the lens of the catastrophe. Because of its fortunate history, Goldstein declared, "American Jewry . . . should bear its good fortune . . . with humility toward all other Jewries, and especially toward European Jewry at whose breast it had nursed. Alas, so many Jewish centers in Europe are only a shadow of their former selves—Vilna, Warsaw, Vienna, Prague, Frankfurt, Amsterdam, Antwerp. . . . Can American Jewry make up . . . for these casualties?" In valorizing American Jewish charity and communal activism, he bemoaned the fact that "no effort of ours could have availed to save the six million who were destroyed by Hitler," and as he described the first Jews who arrived in New Amsterdam in 1654, Goldstein noted, "They were refugees. After them there came successive waves . . . down to the recent chapter of our time with its black Hitler era."[198]

Historians even justified studying American Jewish history because of the Holocaust.[199] In 1947, when the Hebrew Union College in Cincinnati launched the American Jewish Archives, a repository of original documents and a library, it projected the Holocaust into its institutional rationale. The director of the archives, historian Jacob Rader Marcus, enumerated in the first issue of the archives' journal the reasons American Jewry needed to collect and study the documents of its past: "American Jewry is at this moment the largest surviving body of Jews in any one country." The fact of its "surviving" cast the founding of the research institution into the Holocaust context. Marcus extended this theme further, as he began his article: "These United States today shelter 5,000,000 Jews, almost one-half of the 11,000,000 who have survived the Hitler era."[200]

In the mid-1950s, as part of the Tercentenary, individuals called for the systematic study of American Jewish history, using references to the catastrophe. At the April 1953 conference to plan the nationwide history project sponsored by mainstream organizations—the American Jewish Committee, in particular—Rabbi Israel Goldstein reminded those assembled that, "in the midst of . . . progress, the greatest shock which these fifty years" since the 250th celebration at the beginning of the century "brought has been Nazi Germany's demonstration of the lowest depths to which human nature can sink. . . . The Jewish people . . . has felt the progress of these years and has suffered as the chief 'man of sorrows' from the tragedy of these years. . . . Of Europe's nine to ten million Jews, two-thirds fell victim to Nazi extermination." And "because of these casualties Jewish life can never be the same in the years and generations ahead." Therefore American Jews needed to contemplate their own past.[201]

Community programming that year paid homage to the Holocaust, integrating it into the history of American Jewry. A speaker at the February 1954 National Federation of Temple Sisterhoods Biennial Assembly acknowledged the anniversary, giving her version of American Jewish history. "With the advent of Hitler," the Reform women learned, "even the most apologistic [sic] Jew realized that whatever his status in the community in which he lived, no matter how he had or tried to assimilate, he was a Jew and Hitler and the world intended that he be constantly reminded of this fact. So, many ethnic and assimilationist Jews became intelligent, practicing Jews. They learned or re-learned the story of their people and became strong."[202] The Jewish Labor Committee's pamphlet *Scope and Theme: American Jewish Tercentenary 1654–1954*, a document for use by unions and other groups affiliated with the JLC "on how to celebrate" the anniversary, admitted that "history has made of the American Jewish community the largest Jewish community in the world. This community, in the American and the Jewish tradition, has had a record of concern for the rights and the well-being of Jews in other parts of the world," particularly as it helped the "refugees and displaced persons during and since the Hitler holocaust."[203]

Works of all sorts conjoined the Tercentenary and the Holocaust. YIVO historian Abraham Menes, writing for *Judaism*'s special three-hundredth-anniversary issue, put the American Jewish experience and the Holocaust together in demographic and nearly religious terms. "Tragic and painful beyond compare as the catastrophe in Europe has been for us," he mourned, "it would have been still more crushing to us as a people had it not been preceded by the miracle of mass immigration from Europe which commenced in the 1880's." Menes made the "pioneers of the East Side," the Jewish women and men who had settled in New York at the turn of the century, a kind of "saving remnant" since they "played a leading role in bringing about this miracle."[204]

Beyond 1954, postwar history projects on the experience of Jews in the United States, intended for multiple audiences, placed the Holocaust in that narrative. Morris U. Schappes, in his 1958 *The Jews of the United States: A Pictorial History, 1654–Present,* conformed to the dominant trope. He chronicled in detail what had happened and how "the six million dead, victims of Nazism, were two-thirds of the Jews of Europe, and more than one-third of all the Jews in the world." He invoked the "human ashes of the crematoria" and valorized the State of Israel as the by-product of the catastrophe.[205]

As American Jews wrote and spoke, as they presented their histories, and as they contemplated their present circumstances, they referred to the destruction of European Jewry by the Nazis. Rather than being women and men who sought to suppress this painful story, they searched for and found seemingly limitless opportunities to show what had happened.

Why Present?

Few American Jews, however, devoted much time to pondering why they talked or wrote about the catastrophe. It must have seemed natural and obvious to them that by presenting the details, they memorialized those who had perished. But some did articulate a very immediate and political reason for their words. Considering it crucial that Americans generally know history, Jewish commentators expressed little optimism that their American neighbors knew or even cared what had happened to Europe's Jews. Yet American Jewry depended on the larger public for myriad projects that grew out of the Holocaust's devastation, including aiding the survivors and bringing the guilty to justice. Writing in 1955, in an article marking the tenth anniversary of the downfall of Nazism, Alfred Werner maintained minimal hope that "Americans, a happy and lucky people," would remember.[206] Another writer, in a 1954 review of several Holocaust-related books, including Denise Dufournier's *Ravensbruck, the Women's Camp of Death,* published in England in 1948, worried that so many Americans considered the Nazi era a closed case. These Americans, Edward Grusd noted, considered the tragedy ancient history, not realizing that only nine years had passed and that many of those responsible for the atrocities had returned to respectable public lives in Germany.[207] Rabbi Judah Nadich made the same point in a 1960 *Jewish Social Studies* review of a biography of Goebbels. Goebbels, Nadich wrote, "had the power to destroy the Jews," and "he utilized it." Nadich praised the book's meticulous research and its ability to ensure that "the Nazi period . . . not be relegated to the forgotten past. Foul though the subject be, it must be subjected to continuing scrutiny and study."[208]

For these writers and other Jewish community workers, the possibility that the story of the six million would be forgotten with time meant that American Jewry had to prevent the erasure of memory. The charge that American Jews needed to spread the story of the six million became a theme of much greater proportion after the late 1960s, but its outlines took shape in the years from the late 1940s through the early 1960s. This charge coursed through their public culture, and they never questioned the task.

American Jews in speeches, sermons, and journalistic work fretted over the possibility that other Americans, those whom they depended on politically, would lose the memory of the catastrophe. This worrying took place against the reality that from the late 1940s onward, individuals, anti-Semites, claimed that the Holocaust had never happened. In the late 1940s and early 1950s, Gerald L. K. Smith and James Madole specialized in this line of argument, incorporating it into their publications and stump speeches. At the end of the 1950s, George Lincoln Rockwell propagated it, and Jewish communal workers paid attention to such talk.[209]

The *American Jewish Year Book*, as it tracked anti-Semitic broadsides, flyers, articles, and speeches, pointed out that anti-Semitic texts, when not justifying the Holocaust, declared that no six million Jews had perished at the hands of the Nazis. Jewish defense agencies investigated the dissemination of such materials nationally and locally. For example, in the 1950s, Bob Johnson of Dorchester, Massachusetts, wrote to the local Jewish Community Council, asking, "When are you people going to stop screaming about those communists Hitler had to remove from the face of the earth in Germany. There were no 6 million executed. Will you stop trying to convince us Christians; we know better." Mr. Johnson claimed expertise on the subject since he had been "a soldier over in Germany and I know from talking to those wonderful German people. Hitler had to execute about 200 thousand Communist traitors, criminals, thieves and other assorted trash. Naturally most of the Communists were Jews." Topping off his diatribe, Johnson added the words, "God bless Hitler."[210] Jewish community officials devoted meetings to the matter of what to do about such material, the extent of such sentiments, and how they, as an unofficial representative body of a voluntary community, might exert influence in this matter.

Local Jewish communal groups did not wait for Holocaust-denying letters to arrive in their mailboxes. The executive director of Chicago's American Jewish Congress reported to the board in 1955 that he recently "investigated the background of a German-American language newspaper in Chicago called the *Deutsch-Amerikanische Burger-Zeitung*. Several columns in this paper are notorious as regards anti-Jewish policy. . . . Particularly prominent are repeated stories about the 'myth of the six million Jews killed by Hitler.' "[211]

American Jewish communal workers tracked the proliferation of such material in Germany, the Arab world, and around the globe. Editors of the *American Jewish Year Book* made amply clear that they considered it their responsibility as "the eyes and ears" of American Jewry to know about, expose, and condemn such fabrications wherever someone uttered them. Jews had to counter statements questioning the historicity of the Holocaust. Alfred Werner declared in a review of Koppel Pinson's *Modern Germany* that it had appeared at just the right time, 1954, when "world opinion is being wooed by an avalanche of pseudo-historic writings intended to justify the Hitler experiment, or at least, to whitewash the surviving collaborators." Werner held up for particular opprobrium Peter Kleist's *You Too, Were Part of It,* which claimed that "only" a little more than a million Jews perished, and those merely as "part of the total war that was forced (*sic!*) on Germany." The false statement, that no Holocaust had taken place, that six million Jews had not lost their lives to the forces of German Nazism, Werner believed, would, in turn, foster widespread amnesia. Forgetting would set in as the falsehood spread. It behooved those Jews who could —writers, educators, and community leaders—to ensure that that did not happen. Werner had indeed opened his review by quoting Hitler: "Who still talks nowadays of the extermination of the Armenians?" Werner put a great deal of faith in historians, like Pinson, to set the record straight, and he returned to the Hitler quote at the review's end, with a hope that books like Pinson's, as well as articles, speeches, and all kinds of public works, would help ensure that Hitler's "own crimes will not be soon forgotten."[212]

Ironically, some on the American Jewish scene actually worried that the tragedy of the Nazi era occupied too much time in the schools in particular, and they fretted that overemphasizing the catastrophe harmed rather than helped American Jews, especially children, in sustaining positive Jewish feelings. By the early 1960s, Isaac Franck, the executive director of Washington, D.C.'s Jewish Community Council, considered that "the unrelieved recital of massacres, mass murders, persecutions, and disabilities inflicted upon Jewish communities" inspired in Jewish young-sters "feelings of inferiority and emotional insecurity." Franck thought he had an answer on how best to teach the Holocaust and advised that, "in teaching about the massacres," teachers must "get across the understanding that, except for the Nazi period, Jews always had a choice, they could have escaped these tortures by leaving Judaism."[213] During the Nazi era, they had no such choice. His view of how the Holocaust ought to be taught represented his opinion on a subject for which no consensus reigned, and teachers, like writers, editors, and speakers, differed not over *if* the catas-trophe ought to be part of the communal culture but, rather, *how.*

Their heated arguments among each other on the most appropriate way to tell themselves, their children, and the world as a whole about the devastating events that swept up their people in Europe reflected the de-gree to which they considered such telling to be a crucial part of their com-munal culture. Later historians notwithstanding, American Jews presented the details of the catastrophe. Their extensive efforts to offer the story of what had happened to Europe's Jews points to the inadequacy and error in statements such as "nobody," including American Jews and the leaders of their communal institutions, "in these years seemed to have much to say on the subject, at least in public."[214] Rather than constructing a communal culture of silence, American Jews made for themselves a world of words that, in one form or another, explored the matter of the catastrophe.

The world they inherited from the recent past engaged them deeply, as it also placed demands on them, inspiring them to produce a mountain of materials that explored what had happened to Europe's Jews. What they wrote and what they said reflected the reality that American Jewry, among all the Jewish communities in the world, assumed the burden of picking up the pieces of Jewish life left in the shambles of Nazism, the war, the slaugh-ter of the six million, and the destruction of their communities. The after-shocks of the Holocaust roiled the Jewish world continuously for the next two decades, and each reverberation forced—and allowed—American Jews to make that event a constant theme in the life of their community.

At a very practical level, they understood that many of the undertak-ings they needed to accomplish depended on their presenting the facts of the Holocaust. They understood that when it came to providing for the needs of the survivors, confronting the perpetrators, and engaging with new political challenges, American Jews could not go it alone. They needed to find sympathetic non-Jewish American partners to aid in the task of picking up the pieces left in the wake of the Holocaust. By invoking the tragedy of the six million, by telling of the calamity that had happened and of the needs that followed in its wake, not only did they shape their communal culture, but also they hoped to be able to reach out to the American non-Jews, on whom they depended and who could assist them in helping the survivors and in shaping the future of a forever-altered Jewish people.

3

The Saving Remnant

IN 1946, Ira Hirschmann, then a special envoy to the United Nations Relief and Rehabilitation Administration, published *Life Line to a Promised Land*, a harrowing description of the desperate plight of the Jewish survivors of the Holocaust. He dedicated this work, a scathing denunciation of both the United States and the British governments and their treatment of Europe's surviving Jews, "the remnants of a lost people," with the words, "To the survivors of Hitler's hate, who will most deeply love and live for freedom."[1] Like so many American Jews who participated in the public arena, Hirschmann focused much energy and attention on the Jews who emerged alive, but in great need, from the catastrophe perpetrated by the Germans and their allies. In expending that energy on the survivors and in bringing attention about them to the public, these American Jews both kept alive the memory of what the Nazis had done and endowed the survivors with a deep symbolic significance in postwar American Jewish life. To American Jewry across its many divides, aiding the survivors, telling of their ordeals, and holding them up as exemplars of Jewish endurance constituted an element in the memorial project.

In the aftermath of World War II, as American Jews struggled to come to terms with their greatly diminished people, they found a small solace. Some Jews had survived, a paltry number compared with the staggering toll of the six million destroyed. At the war's end, the Jews of the United States focused mightily on the needs of the approximately 1.4 million European Jews who endured the carnage. Addressing their desperate plight, the Jews in America orchestrated the largest nongovernmental philanthropic relief undertaking in human history, raising millions of dollars and collecting and shipping tons of foodstuffs and supplies to Europe. Fulfilling what they saw as a sacred duty, they joined together across ideological, geographic, and class divides.[2]

They invoked the image of the remaining Jews time and again, referring to them variously as "survivors," "the remnant," "the saving remnant," "the surviving remnant," the "sheerith hapletah" in Hebrew, "die geblibbene" (those left) in Yiddish, or "the Displaced Persons." These men and women reminded American Jewry of the enormity of Hitler's destruction, and in the American Jewish imagination, the survivors soon occupied a place of enormous importance. As the Jews of the United States talked about and acted on behalf of the "saving remnant," they repeatedly referred to what these Jews had endured, set against the stark fact that millions had been slaughtered.

What they did and what they said vis-à-vis the remaining Jews of Europe stands in sharp contrast to the conventional wisdom about the American Jewish postwar world. Rather than harboring "negative views of the survivors" or characterizing them in "hateful" ways, as Peter Novick has described the attitudes of American Jewry,[3] the Jews of the United States made their communities places to enshrine the memory of the Holocaust, in large measure by addressing the human crises of real Jewish women and men, left without homes and in desperate need of assistance. Similarly, the many times and places in which American Jewish organizations and publications made it possible for those who had lived through the catastrophe to share their experiences with those who had not calls into question declarations by historians like William Helmreich, who have asserted, repeatedly, that American Jews, particularly those involved in communal life, exhorted the survivors to keep silent and not relate the horrors they had witnessed.[4]

Calls to help the surviving Jews of Europe depended on references to the horrors that had preceded the liberation and, indeed, encouraged the survivors to relate their harrowing experiences. The Jews of America at one and the same time engaged in practical work for those who had not perished and kept alive the image of those who had.[5] American Jewish engagement with the survivors played itself out on both the practical and symbolic levels. The Jews of the United States made the remnant of European Jewry a symbol of the endurance of Judaism and the Jewish people. Sermons, speeches, books and articles, pedagogical works, and pageants emphasized that, despite the staggering six million Jewish casualties, some Jews had survived, portending, they hoped, that the Jewish people as a whole could endure.

In a 1946 speech, "The Disinherited Jews of Europe Must Be Saved," delivered at New York's Biltmore Hotel under the auspices of the American Jewish Conference, Judge Simon Rifkind declaimed that "it was not true that Hitler had won the war against the Jews. True, he multiplied their casualties, decimated their ranks, demolished their institutions, exterminated their leaders, but his war he did not win." As the civilian adviser to the commanding general of the U.S. Army, Rifkind had "visited the mass graves of these martyred dead, . . . viewed the instruments of torture, devised by the ingenious Germans, by which the innocent lives were crushed," forced himself "to look at the fertilizer manufactured by the thrifty Germans out of the human bones of their victims, . . . peered into the mouths of the evil furnaces." But after meeting his "brethren overseas," he realized that "there must be a life giving force in the Jewish tradition upon which these people had been nurtured which could not be burned out even in the super-infernos erected by the Germans. . . . There are 100,000 Jews who have courage to endure, who are determined to live as Jews, . . . are prepared to pioneer again and create again a Jewish civilization."[6]

Like Rifkind, American Jewry articulated a deep bond between itself and the survivors. As they gathered in communal settings and reflected on their present situation, American Jews acknowledged the immense emotional energy generated by the survivors and the sense of responsibility that they, who had not undergone the catastrophic ordeal, felt for those who had. Their organizations and publications, schools and camps, synagogues and social service agencies helped the survivors, negotiated for them in the political arena, and simultaneously celebrated their endurance.

They did it out of a sense of deep commitment and in the context of American political realities. The Jews of the United States lived in the nation that wielded nearly life-and-death power over the survivors. By 1946, the western sector of Germany housed nearly all Displaced Persons (DP) camps, which came under the direct administration of the U.S. military. American Jewry intervened on behalf of those in the camps under American control and participated in a heated debate about the admission of the DPs to the United States. They also injected themselves into global politics, demanding that Great Britain open the doors of Palestine to the survivors.

Survivors also came to America, about one hundred thousand of them, as of the middle of the 1950s. Their immediate needs affected American Jewry. They became the chief beneficiaries of American Jewish social service agencies, at the same time that the presence of the survivors, often called "new Americans," left their mark on American Jewish public life. American Jews, through their organizations and charitable bodies, saw themselves as agents for the survivors, reaching out to public officials, to their non-Jewish neighbors, and even goading fellow Jews to help the cause, never disassociating philanthropy from political action.

The years from the end of the war into the early 1950s constituted a period of intense, almost frantic, fundraising on behalf of the survivors of the Hitler Holocaust.[7] The exigency eased by the middle of the 1950s with the emergence of Israeli statehood, and as the flow of money to survivors, to the State of Israel, and to Jewish social service institutions around the world through the Claims Conference obviated the need for special fund-raising campaigns. But until then, the fate of the "saving remnant" functioned as American Jewry's central communal concern. And, as they labored on behalf of the survivors, American Jews believed that they fulfilled their duty to remember the victims. Memorialization and assistance operated in tandem.[8]

Negotiating for the Survivors

In the early postwar period, American Jews assumed the chore of representing the interests of the survivors, quickly realizing that the Allies would and could not meet their needs, neither as distressed human beings nor as Jews. While the United Nations Relief and Rehabilitation Agency, the underfunded, understaffed, and minimally trained UNRRA, had been charged with relieving the suffering left in the wake of the war, it faced tremendous difficulties in doing anything for the survivors as Jews.

Jews were hardly alone among Europe's displaced millions, but, unlike most, they had no homes to return to. Like the others in the camps, they endured shortages of food and medical care, cramped quarters, and disease. But the Jews could not and would not be repatriated to the countries where they had endured so much suffering, and the numbers of Jews in the camps swelled as Jewish survivors from Poland fled to the west to escape the rampant anti-Jewish violence that continued even after the Germans had been defeated. The Jews wanted to be recognized as a distinct group within the camp framework so that their circumstances could be addressed. Former New York governor Herbert Lehman, a hero to American Jews, recognized this failure on the part of UNRRA. He had taken on the job of administering it in 1942 and by 1946 felt so frustrated with its inability to deal with the unique crisis faced by Jews that he resigned, devoting his energies instead to finding a resolution to the Palestine problem, which he believed would provide Jewish survivors with a national home, a far better alternative than languishing in the DP camps.[9]

American Jewish periodicals and organizations closely tracked UNRRA and the conditions of the Jewish survivors who depended on it. In 1946, for example, Lieutenant General Sir Frederick Morgan, the British head of UNRRA's DP work in Germany, caused uproar among Jews when he complained that the Polish Jews streaming into Germany kept harking back to the "same monotonous story about pogroms." This infuriated American Jewry since anti-Jewish violence in Poland continued unabated, and Morgan's snide statements, according to Bernard Richards in a letter to Lehman, "added insult to injury: he has added most outrageous affront to the slaughter of six million Jews made all the more horrible and shocking by the British betrayal of her trust in the form of the Mandate over Palestine."[10]

American Jews articulated particular urgency over anti-Semitic violence perpetrated against the Holocaust survivors in Poland and UNRRA's insensitivity. Actor Eddie Cantor bought space in the *New York Times* to lambaste Morgan and UNRRA. Cantor's text, headlined "I Thought Hitler Was Dead," directly addressed Sir Frederick: "Are you one of those 'humanitarians' who believe that the only good Jews are dead Jews?"[11]

Descriptions of the appalling conditions of the Jews in the DP camps, including those run by the U.S. military, quickly appeared in the Jewish press, and rabbis and lecturers wove them into sermons and speeches, providing graphic details of the misery endured by the Jews. Living cheek by jowl in these camps with many former Nazi collaborators, the Jews experienced both fear and squalor. With no work, no way of making a living, and enduring dirt, overcrowding, and disease, the Jews in the DP camps also had to contend with physical violence and abuse from other DPs, many of them individuals who shared the anti-Jewish sentiments that had resulted in the Nazis' brutal behavior in the first place. American Jewry considered it its responsibility to intercede for the displaced Jews.

Interceding for the survivors with the American occupation forces in Germany became the project in large measure of American rabbis who served as military chaplains. Without being asked to do so, they monitored the conditions of the survivors in the camps, as well as those of Jews who lived in Germany outside the camps. Appointed by the Jewish Welfare Board to serve the spiritual needs of American Jewish soldiers, rabbis like Judah Nadich, Philip Bernstein, David Max Eichhorn, Eugene Lipman, Robert Marcus, Harold Saperstein, Abraham Klausner, and Joseph Shubow, among others, became witness to and mediator for the European Jews whom they encountered.[12] Nadich, for example, pointed out to General Walter Bedell-Smith, General Dwight D. Eisenhower's head of staff, the horrendous conditions in the camps, and suggested that staff members who worked with the Jewish DPs "be selected carefully," to screen out anyone with anti-Semitic opinions. Bedell-Smith, using Eisenhower's name, "ordered them to remedy the situation."[13]

Throughout the late 1940s and early 1950s, as long as the camps existed and Jewish survivors lived in them, rabbis associated with the military chaplaincy in Europe, Germany in particular, reported to the Jewish Welfare Board and to the Synagogue Council of America on the status of the Jews there. Rabbi Philip Bernstein, adviser on Jewish affairs to Generals Joseph McNarney and Mark Clark, spoke in New York in October 1946, reporting on the Polish Jews who had fled to the American Zone in Germany. Polish circumstances impelled their flight to Germany, seeking there the protection of the Americans. Bernstein had gone to Poland to see the conditions for himself: "I could understand their [the Jews in Poland] feelings. I was drawn to the Polish Ghetto," in Warsaw, and "it is the last word in desolation and sorrow. . . . I stood at the quiet, unused railroad siding at which each day Jews were loaded into locked box cars, and carried to the extermination chambers. . . . Every stone cried aloud the blood of their loved ones." Bernstein "could easily see why the Jews would want to leave Poland" for Germany, despite the reality that the "Jews . . . regard the Germans who despoiled them and murdered their families with an unforgiving hatred."[14]

Simultaneous with the chaplains' efforts in Europe, American Jewish organizations worried about how the many Jewish DPs would be able to immigrate to the United States. America loomed as an attractive destination for many survivors, but few could do so. Laws severely restricting immigration to the United States, passed in the 1920s, remained in effect. Of the Jews languishing in Europe, most fell under the very low quotas assigned to Poland and other east European countries. Most Americans, opinion polls revealed, preferred that the law remain unchanged. From the end of the war into the early 1950s, the immigration issue roiled American politics, with the American public opposing changes of the status quo. A Gallup poll of December 1945 found that only 5 percent of Americans wanted to see more immigrants admitted than had been in the years before the war, while 37 percent wanted fewer. No doubt they believed that more immigrants would increase unemployment and would complicate prospects for a smooth return to a peacetime economy.[15]

President Harry Truman shared the public's desire not to tamper with immigration policy, but in 1945 he proposed modest alterations to allow in some DPs. His efforts resulted in paltry changes, and in 1946 only about five thousand DPs gained the right to enter the United States, with

Jews making up a small minority. In October 1946, Truman announced that he would propose to Congress that Jews be admitted to the United States outside the quota system, a suggestion which a poll found 72 percent of the American public opposed. In 1947, Illinois Congressman William Stratton, a Republican who had once been associated with the isolationist America First movement, proposed an even further liberalization.[16] A 1948 bill authorized issuing 202,000 visas above the quota limit, and the 1950 Displaced Persons Act raised the number to 415,000, for Jews and for others who had been displaced by the war and could not return to their former homes, mostly ethnic Germans from countries that fell under Communist rule.[17]

In the political turmoil over the DPs, two matters in particular agitated American Jews. First, they saw how the laws and their implementation militated against easy entry for the Jewish survivors, making it clear that Jews who lived through the catastrophe had less chance of coming to the United States than did non-Jews, many of whom had actively collaborated with the Nazis. As of 1947, when the Cold War with the Soviet Union set in, non-Jews displaced from places like Estonia, Latvia, Lithuania, and the Ukraine, as well as "ethnic Germans" who had been expelled from Poland, received preferential treatment as refugees from Communism. In these places many local Christians had eagerly participated in the slaughter of the Jews. Many had served as guards at concentration camps.[18] But in the Cold War moment, they engendered the sympathy of the American public as anti-Communists, whereas the Jewish survivors did not. Will Maslow and George Hexter of the American Jewish Committee put it quite bluntly: the 1948 bill "might be entitled a bill to exclude DPs, particularly Jews, and to admit Hitler's collaborators."[19]

Second, the very details of the Displaced Persons legislation disadvantaged Jewish survivors. It stipulated particular preference for the admission of farmers, something that hardly helped Jewish DPs, nearly all of whom had lived in cities. The bill as passed also declared as eligible only those who had arrived in the American Zone as of the end of 1945. This seriously limited the number of Jews who could qualify, since so many of the Polish Jews who fled west to the American Zone did so after that date. The Displaced Persons legislation represented the furthest the American public would go on the matter of immigration. Their representatives in Congress recognized that the American people did not want to see admission of large numbers of immigrants, Jews in particular.[20] On this, the broad base of Jewish public opinion stood diametrically opposite that of other Americans. Indeed, when Stratton introduced his bill, an adviser warned him against taking such an unpopular stand. "Nobody in Illinois," he cautioned the senator, "outside of the Jews, wants any more Jews in this country."[21]

Jews as individuals and Jewish organizations marshaled their limited political strength, given their small number in the population, to make their case that so clearly went against the current. They wrote letters and editorial pieces, reached out to potential allies, and held meetings to discuss ways to make America more accessible to the survivors. American Jews recognized this reality and pressed when they thought they could for the survivors as Jews and in the name of the devastation of the Holocaust. The Jewish War Veterans cabled Truman from their annual meeting in 1947 about the DPs, begging him to "repay the moral debt owed by humanity to the survivors of the most cruel persecution known in history."[22] Jacob Pat of the Jewish Labor Committee wrote to President Truman in 1948, pointing out that the bill awaiting his signature "discriminates against Jews, the most tragic victims of Nazi inhumanity," but rewarded "Europeans of German ethnic origins. . . . It is scarcely possible," he chided the president, "to construe this as anything but a legislative embodiment of the abhorrent Nazi principle of race, a statutory preference for 'Aryans' over other groups."[23] Milwaukee's Rabbi Joseph Baron told his senator, Alexander Wiley, that "the only practical hope for those helpless victims, of Hitlerism, these pitiable remnants of once great Jewish communities, lies with the American government." The rabbi implored the senator to use his "influence towards the ultimate, human and just solution of an ancient problem," anti-Semitism.[24]

So, too, in the inner discussions of their community, American Jews minced no words when describing the DP issue as a crisis of the Jewish survivors of the Holocaust and that efforts to limit the number of new immigrants and to privilege those of German background and fleeing Communism constituted anti-Semitism. *Current Copy*, the monthly newsletter sent by the National Federation of Temple Sisterhoods to its chapters at Reform congregations around the country, declared in its late-summer 1947 issue, as it did every month that year, in bold letters that "THERE ARE FACTS TO KNOW." Among the matters it expected its members to discuss at chapter meetings and act upon politically, the Reform women of America alerted them to the fact that "hope died all over again this summer— hope for a home . . . hope for welcome and brotherhood. Yes, hope died in the hearts of 850,000 displaced persons in Europe when the Congress of the United States failed to pass temporary legislation permitting the emergency entry of some of these victims of the Nazi holocaust to the leading democratic nation of the world."[25]

Knowing that these survivors, here called victims, had been let down by the United States, the organization's leadership called the members of Reform sisterhoods to action: "YOU have to act! Direct action can be a powerful weapon for good. . . . Now, U.S. Congressmen are home. Visit them and tell them how you, the voter, feel about America's traditional responsibility to those who seek sanctuary." *Current Copy*, in urging its members to become politically involved over this issue, did not hide behind euphemisms. While they did not specifically name the victims as "Jewish," they identified the objects of their concerns as "victims of the Nazi holocaust" and "they, who have suffered most from tyranny." It also gave the number, approximate for sure, of Jewish DPs and not the total for all Displaced Persons. The Reform group likewise made it clear that, as its members went to see their congressional representatives, they did so as Jewish women representing a Jewish religious institution.[26]

A high school student from Rochester, New York, writing for the Young Judea *Senior* in 1946, also reflected the American Jewish consensus in her column, "Youth Speaks Its Mind": "To the starving desolate survivors, our theoretical discussions mean very little." They had just experienced the "inhuman barbarism of Nazi Europe." But now, vis-à-vis the United States, she and other American Jews contended with the parallel between "quotas in our country and mass murder in Germany! It seems that one could hardly mention these in the same breath."[27]

The paltry numbers of Jews allowed into the United States bore out American Jewish fears. From 1947 through the early 1950s, of the approximately four hundred thousand DPs who received permission to enter the United States after the passage of the 1948 legislation, Jews constituted about 16 percent of the total, about sixty-three thousand women, men, and children who had survived the Nazi slaughter. They joined the approximately thirty-seven thousand who had gained entry between 1945 and 1948.[28]

The situation of the Jewish DPs improved dramatically by late 1948. So many wanted to go to Israel, and with the declaration of Israeli independence and the removal of all barriers to Jewish entry there, they could do so. Even those who might have preferred the United States got the chance to leave Europe and begin their lives anew as Israel opened up to the masses of Holocaust survivors, from both inside and outside the DP camps. This relieved the urgency felt by American Jewry, which no longer had to engage in a hopeless political battle at home for a cause it knew it could not win. Yet it still pushed for the admission of Jewish refugees, and the meetings of communal organizations still resounded, even after 1948, with statements of regret over their powerlessness.

American Jews and their organizations expressed frustration at their inability to influence the legislative process or public opinion. Arthur Greenleigh, executive director of the United Service for New Americans (USNA), the Jewish organization that coordinated work for and with the survivors who did arrive in America, noted in his 1951 annual address that "1950 was a year of great disappointment." But despite that disappointment, he exhorted USNA, and American Jewry more generally, to keep up its work. "Too many Jews have already been destroyed," he told the assembled. "The souls of the six million so viciously exterminated at Buchenwald, Belsen, and Dachau cry out against any slackening in our effort. The obstacles must be removed."[29]

Serving the Survivors

Amid the frustration of navigating America's hostile immigration wars, American Jews did triumph when it came to attending to the physical needs of the survivors. On this matter, they did not have to depend on others. Caring for the survivors constituted a vast project of on-the-ground practical work undertaken by American Jewry through the panoply of communal organizations to which they belonged and to which they contributed money.[30] The *American Jewish Year Book* remarked in 1945 that "it would be beyond the scope of this brief report to detail the activities of every office" of just HIAS, the Hebrew Immigrant Aid Society, whose workers showed up in Europe immediately after liberation.[31] American Jewish rescue work for the Jewish survivors in the days, weeks, months, and years after liberation involved bringing food, medicine, clothing, books, and services of all kinds to the survivors, whether in Displaced Persons camps established by the American military or in cities around Europe where small clusters struggled to rebuild their lives. It took place in the United States as well, as American Jewish communities, locally and on a national level, put in place a network of social services to address as best as they could the needs of those who managed to immigrate to the United States, despite bureaucratic hurdles and popular opposition to their entry.

To the Jews of the United States, from those with limited means who made small contributions to survivor relief projects up to the massive organizations that existed for the purpose of ministering to the needs of the remnant of European Jewry, participating in this mighty Jewish humanitarian effort for the living constituted a memorial project for the dead. Campaigns pitched their calls to give in the name not just of those who survived but as a monument to those who had not. More urgent than planting a giant slab of marble in the ground, this philanthropy represented their living memorial to the six million.

This practical work can be measured empirically in terms of money raised by American Jews to succor the survivors. In 1945 alone, American Jews pooled their resources and collected $45 million, which went almost entirely to the Jews of Europe. The following year, that sum skyrocketed to $131 million, well above the $100 million goal set by the United Jewish Appeal (UJA), the preeminent fundraising body founded in 1939 to address the needs of the small trickle of refugees who had made it to the United States. In the next few years, the money pouring into the coffers of the United Jewish Appeal from the pockets of American Jews continued at this level, reflecting the ongoing sense of urgency and the real needs of the survivors. In the 1948 UJA campaign, three of its most critical beneficiary organizations, the American Jewish Joint Distribution Committee ("the Joint"), the United Palestine Appeal, and United Service for New Americans, collected $250 million for their work alone, and that work involved the survivors in Europe, Israel, and the United States.[32]

But in the early years, in particular, when tens of thousands of Jews lived in the DP camps, money needed to be augmented by goods and services. Lacking any commercial infrastructure, except perhaps the thriving black market, those who remained in the camps needed things rather than cash. They needed food, clothing, blankets, and medical supplies. Recognizing this, American Jewry mobilized itself to send material goods simultaneous with sending millions of dollars. Under the leadership of Blanche Gilman, the Joint in 1945 created an organization, SOS, Supplies for Overseas Survivors. In 1947 alone, SOS sent thirty-five thousand pairs of shoes, seven hundred pounds of equipment to provide for the dental needs of survivors, three million cans of food, and X-ray machines. By 1949, twenty-six million pounds of relief supplies had gone across the Atlantic from the Jews of America to their survivors in Europe. The initials "SOS" appeared repeatedly in the pages of the American Jewish press, in organizational bulletins, in flyers handed out to Jewish schoolchildren to take home to their parents, and in the minutes of organizations as they formed local committees to shoulder their part of this work.[33]

The SOS campaign went organizationally from the top down, but each group in each city came up with its own variant on the SOS campaign. Each crafted a message for its members and devised projects, activities, and materials to foster this monster collection effort. Yet despite this autonomy, little distinguished the campaign in one community from that in another or from one organization to another. "To All Friends in the Sholem-Aleichem and Amalgamated Houses" read a mimeographed sheet in Yiddish and English, distributed by the Jewish Labor Committee's Van Cortland Park Branch in the Bronx. "Winter has now passed. You are storing away your warm clothing. Consider a moment: Which of those things can you spare for our brothers and sisters, for our children in the camps of Germany, Italy, and Austria?" Remember, the flyer said, "they need everything. . . . *Our European brethren are starving! It is our duty to . . .* supply their needs."[34]

The Society for the Advancement of Judaism, Manhattan's Reconstructionist congregation, had a very different kind of membership from the Van Cortland Park branch of the JLC, but the SAJ also participated in SOS, and its bulletin exhorted, "We know that members of the S.A.J. will, as always, be prompt and generous in their response to this appeal. Through the extra help . . . it will be possible to bolster the diet of long starved men and women in former Nazi concentration camps; to provide milk for Jewish infants and children; and to bring hope and courage back to the hundreds of thousands of our fellow Jews in Poland, Rumania, France, and almost everywhere else on the continent."[35]

Young American Jews heard and heeded the SOS call. The national offices of the Reform movement's National Federation of Temple Youth sent out a one-page instruction sheet to all New York chapters, "An Urgent Appeal to Youth," imploring the youngsters to "help keep the remaining million and a half Jews in Europe alive." The national office let them know that "groups all over the city are asked to send out a call to their members asking them to bring at least one can of food to every meeting. Sunday school children are asked to bring school supplies . . . to school every week for the Collection."[36]

These three groups—the Jewish Labor Committee's neighborhood branch in the Bronx made up of working-class families of the immigrant generation; the highly educated affluent members of Manhattan's Society for the Advancement of Judaism, a Reconstructionist congregation whose ideology involved Zionism and innovative religious practice; and the young people of the Reform movement, the most American and comfortable portion of the Jewish community—may have had little in common in other ways and might have had few points of contact. But when it came to seeing themselves as responsible for "our European brothers," all those differences melted away. Individually and collectively, the fate of "our fellow Jews" bound these American Jews together as they engaged in a massive rescue effort on behalf of those who managed to elude the Nazis' plan to exterminate all the Jews of Europe.

Most responsible for using the millions of dollars raised in America and for bringing the basics of food, clothing, shelter, and medical care to the survivors, the Joint Distribution Committee, "the Joint," delivered the items and sent workers, child care specialists, doctors and other health professionals, and educators to the camps. They distributed the food, clothing, and medicine; set up hospitals and feeding stations; and helped the survivors track down relatives. The Joint arranged for Jewish community workers, socal workers, and others from the United States to go to Europe and work for its multiplicity of on-the-ground undertakings. In 1945, it asked Irene Lowy Arnold, a lawyer and director of the Women's Division of the American Jewish Congress, to help set up their operations in Buchenwald, the former concentration camp, which the Americans transformed into a Displaced Persons camp. Arnold, the first American professional woman to work in Buchenwald, stayed on until "the last trainload of Jews" left the camp. Also in 1945, the Joint tapped Joseph Levine, executive director of the Jewish Federation in Fort Wayne, Indiana, to go to Bavaria to provide whatever assistance he could; he stayed there as a Joint worker for a year. These stories could be replicated in the thousands.[37]

Other American Jewish organizations solicited funds in the United States and sent their personnel to work directly with the Jewish survivors. ORT, the Organization for Rehabilitation Through Training, took charge of providing job training for young people in particular, who, during their years in hiding or in concentration camps, had been denied an education. With the end of the war, they had to be helped, according to an ORT publicity pamphlet, to "Prepare for a Productive Life." ORT, which had been doing this kind of work among Jews in eastern Europe since the 1880s, recruited workers to go to Europe to open "schools, courses, workshops." It collected millions to purchase "tools, machinery . . . to give the survivors of Europe's holocaust, useful occupations."[38]

These Jewish communal workers, whether representing the Joint, ORT, or some other organization, went to Europe; provided direct services with the money raised by American Jewry; and then returned to the United States, where they wrote for their local Jewish community newspapers, for national magazines, and for the bulletins and newsletters of their sponsoring organizations, describing what they had seen. They lectured at Jewish gatherings, sharing their firsthand impressions of the survivors and the aftermath of the Holocaust. In the process, they helped raise even more money.

Queens College history professor Koppel Pinson left his teaching post in October 1945 and until September 1946 served as educational director for displaced Jews in Germany and Austria for the Joint. Returning to the United States in 1947, he published a detailed article in *Jewish Social Studies*, "Jewish Life in Liberated Germany." He also lectured widely to Jewish community groups on what he had seen there. He emphasized how, among the survivors, "their achievements, measured in terms of the insurmountable difficulties and enormous complexities with which they are confronted are heroic." Pinson, like some of the American Jews who went to Europe to work with the survivors, tended to overlook the organizations which the Displaced Persons themselves had created, leading him to declare that "they need leadership, which will only emerge once "they are resettled in normal communities." They need more from world Jewry, not so much in terms of "money and material. . . . they need *people,* warmhearted, full-blooded, intelligent and cultured Jews, who can supply that initial drive, that added push . . . that a leadership elite contributes to a society."[39]

Joint officials themselves spoke to Jewish organizations reporting on their work and on the survivors' continuing needs. In October 1948, the Joint invited some American Jewish notables, including officials of the National Federation of Temple Sisterhoods, to describe their activities among the survivors. In a talk titled "On the Road to Recovery," Joseph J. Schwartz declared, "You, who have seen the Jews through the worst—you, who have fed, clothed, housed them and nursed them back to health—will, I am sure, stand by a little longer. Today," six months after the declaration of a Jewish state and the beginnings of the mass exodus from Europe to Israel, "we are witnessing the beginning of the end. The goal is in sight but Europe's Jews still call forth our deep concern." The National Federation of Temple Sisterhoods, which sent a few representatives to the meeting, disseminated this information to all of its members around the country in its newsletter.[40]

A massive flow of information linked the leaders and workers of the American Jewish organizations who had seen the survivors to the masses of American Jews who funded these projects. They published booklets, magazines, fundraising flyers, press releases, and brochures, as well as produced films and radio broadcasts, documenting what they had done for "the Jews who have survived." A 1945 "kit" used by members of Women's American ORT to attract new members emphasized that, "from time immemorial, Jewish women have participated in giving help to the poor, the widow and the orphans." Women's ORT publicity material emphasized that "there are aspects of the Jewish problem which concern Jews only, and which Jews themselves must study and solve. For example, the Germans, in order adequately to feed their war machine, provided scientific and mechanical training for the natives of all the conquered countries. The Jews, on the other hand—those who were allowed to survive—were put to hard labor. In the postwar period, the Jews will be confronted with the competition of skilled labor, themselves being unprepared." In 1948, ORT mounted a traveling exhibit of "Articles Made by Students of the ORT Vocational Schools in the U.S.-Zone of Germany," testifying that the "exhibition is a witness to the goals for which we have striven. It mirrors the creative ability of the Shejrit Haplejta [Shearith Hapleta] and reflects our spiritual vitality. Every single exhibition article has been produced by the hands of former concentration camp inmates and persecutees. Though they are silent, their work speaks for them, and says: 'Am Jisrole chai'—the Jewish people lives!' "[41]

The places where Jews gathered for religious, educational, and social purposes became places to raise money for survivors. They even transformed the streets where they lived into philanthropic settings. Throughout the late 1940s, the Joint sent a truck around New York neighborhoods every Friday afternoon, picking up supplies at designated depots. The presence on the Jewish streets of these vehicles with the Joint's name emblazoned on their sides, as powerfully as the words in the flyers and in the phrases in the bulletins, confirmed the urgency of the moment and the involvement of American Jewry with the effort to Save the Overseas Survivors.

Smaller communities with fewer Jews did not have a Joint truck to collect their goods on a weekly basis, but they shared in this work. For example, Mrs. Silverstone in Washington, D.C., reported "eloquently" to

The United Jewish Appeal (UJA), founded in 1938 to deal with the gathering crisis of Europe's Jews, raised money in the postwar period in part through the horrific images of the Holocaust. The photograph of the little boy in the Warsaw ghetto with his hands held up in response to the drawn weapons of German soldiers became widely used as early as the late 1940s, and it appeared here on the cover of a fundraising brochure. The opening words of the appeal declared, "Let the dead sleep. . . . Let the chapter of murder be closed forever. Yes, we would bury the dead. But are our martyred millions dead?" The text went on to answer in the negative: "No, the dead will not depart. At this very moment they knock on the doors of our conscience—old men, little children and their mothers." The UJA solicitation material drew the connection between those deaths and the need to contribute money. Give, the brochure read, "to save us from falling into a trap—the trap Hitler set before his death. To save us from finishing his work of extermination." *Courtesy Yeshiva University Archives.*

It began in 1939, when Hitler's policy
of anti-Semitism became a policy of annihilation.
That year the United Jewish Appeal was born.

The United Jewish Appeal consistently linked its fundraising efforts with the imagery of the Holocaust. Like nearly all American Jewish organizations, it spent the postwar period showing the public that it had a Holocaust history, one that ultimately involved efforts to rescue European Jews. This 1962 UJA flyer declared to potential donors, "Those you could save were saved. But country after country succumbed to Hitler's onslaught. While civilization stood helplessly by, six million Jews were put to death. By 1945 all that remained of the great Jewish communities of Europe was a pitiful remnant." *Courtesy American Jewish Historical Society.*

the Delegate Assembly of the city's Jewish Community Council in the spring of 1949, when the SOS effort wound down, that over the course of the last few years, Washington Jews had completed their mission and that "hundreds of workers," volunteers, had collected tens of thousands of pounds of clothing, sewing goods, layettes, medical supplies, toys, and foodstuffs from around the Washington metropolitan area, an effort coordinated by the Jewish Community Council.[42] In Waukesha, Wisconsin, an even smaller community, the women's auxiliary of B'nai B'rith engineered the local SOS effort. They decided to concentrate on collecting canned goods, made their own arrangements to ship the food to New York, and announced at their December meeting that, that year, they had exceeded their goal.[43]

The postwar fundraising dynamo of American Jews on behalf of those in Europe linked Jewish organizations seeking the money and Jewish donors across the class spectrum. By and large, they alone asked for and gave that money. What funds flowed to the survivors—to feed, clothe, heal, and shelter them, let alone provide job training to face the future and resettle them away from the scenes of their suffering—came from American Jews as a cheerfully extracted self-taxation. The engines of the American Jewish world geared up to inspire American Jews to give even more than they had, and did so by telling the survivors' story, creating a narrative of what these women and men had endured. American Jewry, its press and organizations, schools and camps, clubs and synagogues, participated in the creation and dissemination of this message, and no segment remained unmoved.

Every medium they had available to them and every organization, at every level of Jewish life, transmitted the message that they, the Jews of the United States, had a responsibility to the Jewish survivors. Much of the fundraising emanated from the United Jewish Appeal (UJA), which determined how much each local Jewish community ought to give and assisted in their fundraising drives. UJA provided the information, and the local communities used the press to get the message out.[44] The UJA's drive in Newark, New Jersey, to offer one example, differed little from efforts in other cities or states. On May 10, 1946, the *New Jersey Jewish News*, a publication utterly typical of its time and genre, published that year's UJA message, in the form of an epistle from America's Jews to the Jewish children of Europe, obviously sympathetic symbols of need. "Dear Children," New Jersey Jews read, "We Will Not Let You Die." The article as letter comforted the children by telling them that "we in America have resolved that you shall live, that your broken bodies shall be mended, your broken lives made whole." It told the fictive children and the real residents of New-ark and the other cities of the Garden State that the UJA had set Newark's quota at $2,638,000. To ensure that the Jews of New Jersey met the goal, leaders of the local fundraiser launched the appeal: "We know that you are starved and frightened and ill—your eyes haunted with horror and your hearts torn with longing for parents you saw go into gas chambers and crematoria."[45]

The United Jewish Appeal and other American Jewish organizations turned to filmmaking to stimulate fundraising. *Passport to Nowhere* and *Where Do You Get Off?* both starring Hollywood star Edward G. Robin-son; *The Future Can Be Theirs, We Live Again,* and *Tomorrow's a Wonder-ful Day*—all used film footage of both the concentration camps and the DP camps, juxtaposing these images with the ardent desire of the survi-vors to rebuild their lives, something that could be done only with mas-sive amounts of American Jewish money. Jewish schools and community groups showcased these films, using them to raise awareness and money. In the summer of 1949, the first Summer Conclave of the Southern New England Federation of Temple Youth announced that it would host an eve-ning program, which would screen the "JDC film: THE FUTURE CAN BE THEIRS: 19 MINUTES," with Leo Lania, a foreign correspondent, on hand to answer questions.[46]

Radio also served the project of American Jewish organizations to tell of the needs of the survivors, of their horrendous experiences under the Germans, and of their hopes for the future. Samuel Gringauz took to the radio in 1948 on behalf of ORT, a beneficiary agency of the UJA, and de-clared that "the fate of the surviving Jewish victims of Hitler terror in the D.P. camps of Germany is hard and hopeless." Although three years had gone by, "nothing has been done, so far, to secure a permanent home." As to the survivors, "a deep wave of discouragement is sweeping over . . . the remnants who escaped the ovens and gas chambers of Auschwitz."[47] Veteran actor Paul Muni recorded a radio play, *How Can I Tell It?* for Ha-dassah, suitable, according to the organization, for "broadcast from a ra-dio station," as well as a dramatic presentation at a chapter meeting. Since Hadassah produced *How Can I Tell It?* it told of Youth Aliyah work among the survivors, including Naomi, who "could barely murmur the name of her mother without crying"; Sara, about whom, "the records indicate," that her "parents knew, even as they sent her on, that they were slated for deportation to a German labor camp, and that they would never see her again"; and, finally, "Lena, who saw her little brother die of starvation."[48]

Radio sermons and "sermonettes," *Eternal Light* episodes, and dramatizations sponsored by the United Service for New Americans all collaborated in the American Jewish mission to narrate the story of the survivors and inspire American Jews to dig deeper into their pockets.

In the narration of postwar needs, the details of the Holocaust occupied a prominent part. Rabbi William Rosenblum offered "The Message of Israel" in 1949 on New York's Station WJZ and ABC Continental Network, "in tribute to the Joint Distribution Committee." Titled "Operation *Nissim venifloos!*" [Miracles and wonders], Rosenblum's broadcast, accessible to anyone with a radio, Jewish or not, drew attention to the Joint's work and its efforts among the survivors. It recalled that "when millions of our people were being led to the Nazi crematories, we Jews in this land felt the scorching fires of Nazi bestialities." Rosenblum shared with his audience his encounter with a DP, a "thin, wan" survivor, in a Munich radio station from which he, Rosenblum, broadcast a speech "to the German people" on "JUSTICE TO THE JEW." The Joint had arranged for the man to practice on Radio Munich's piano, and "he played. There was genius in every note. His story was like so many others. One concentration camp after another, saved by his comrades who knew that he had been one of the greatest artists of Poland . . . so that his fingers might be saved for his art . . . when they would be freed . . . and get to Israel. Several of us in the studio were unashamed to weep as this young Jew played."[49]

Some Jewish agencies involved with fundraising for survivors recognized the power of the emerging medium, television, to generate sympathy. HIAS aired *Placing the Displaced,* filmed on location in Germany, on CBS television in 1948, and the United Jewish Appeal participated with NBC's *This Is Your Life,* which in May 1953 brought Hanna Konner, a survivor of Auschwitz, back into contact with some of her childhood friends and into the living rooms of millions of Americans. At the commercial break, cosmetic maker Hazel Bishop, a *This Is Your Life* sponsor, addressed "viewers of all creeds and colors," asking them to donate to the United Jewish Appeal, to which it announced it would contribute as well.[50]

The public world of American Jewry of the last half of the 1940s into the middle of the 1950s throbbed with the words and images of the survivors, whose very existence kept alive the images of the Holocaust's devastation. Looking back from 1958 to the early years after the end of World War II, HIAS and the Jewish Social Service Bureau of Rochester, New York, analyzed how it had conducted its work and how it had attempted to sustain and evoke the "impulse of generosity" for the newcomers, given

the "magnitude of the problem." HIAS and local Jewish social service bodies, like the one that issued the book *The Displaced Person and the Social
Agency*, recalled how, "apart from the . . . factual reporting through newspaper accounts, an apparatus was constructed whereby the message of
need was communicated through special channels—campaign speakers,
motion pictures, mass meetings and rallies . . . to dramatize in a way that
would evoke a desire for the community to help." In those early years, the
Jewish agencies sought out "pictures and eyewitness accounts of the physical condition of survivors of concentration camps" as the most "eloquent
testimonies that helped formulate and define the problem."[51]

Youth groups and adult organizations alike took tremendous pride
documenting what they had done for the survivors, the amounts they contributed, and the zealousness of their efforts. The Masada Zionist youth
group launched a "Skip-A-Meal, Buy-A-Meal" project in 1946, exhorting
its members to keep in mind that "our brethren in Europe are suffering the
deprivations of food and clothing. . . . We as young Zionists, interested in
the survival of our people and deeply affected by all their sufferings . . . resolve that so long as our brethren in Europe have need of assistance, we
shall sacrifice, in fast, at last one meal a week, and turn over the money
saved to the United Jewish Appeal."[52] The pronoun "we" referred to American Jews, and "our" denoted that American Jews saw a tight bond connecting them to the survivors. The ubiquitous use of the first-person plural
in fundraising material produced by the American Jewish communal institutions, the earlier part of it in particular when critical needs dominated
their agendas, indicated the degree to which American Jewry interpreted
its own existence through concerns for the survivors.

The organized community bombarded American Jews with two different kinds of appeals for money. The UJA as the centralized fundraising
body assigned quotas, expecting the thousands of organizations on both
the national and local levels to provide their fair share. Each organization,
in turn, tailored its appeal to fit its own constituents, although the essential message remained the same. In the name of those who perished and
for the sake of those who survived, American Jewry must give. The B'nai
B'rith Hillel Foundation called forth in 1947 a special Jewish Student Appeal, and on campus after campus, the word went out and the money got
raised. The combined appeal at Tufts University and Simmons College in
Boston featured a black-bordered pamphlet, which opened with the words
"Treblinka, 1947." The "Treblinka" letter appeared not only as a handout
distributed at Hillel but also as an advertisement in the Simmons campus

newspaper, accessible not only to those who frequented the Jewish student center but also to anyone on campus. "Dear Friend," this hypothetical letter from the notorious death camp read: "We who have been saved from death implore you. There is no time to lose. . . . Out of the DP camps of Europe, the voice of Israel's remnant cries—GIVE SO WE MAY LIVE. Give and give generously so that our children can eat and breathe again as free men." Signed by a generic and fictive "A Displaced Person," the Tufts-Simmons appeal differed from the ones at Harvard, Radcliffe, and the University of Maryland.[53] The Jewish Labor Committee sent out letters to its constituent unions and groups, reminding them that they had a responsibility to contribute not only to JLC's special survivor projects but also to the UJA, for "the urgent needs of our surviving flesh and blood in destitute and war-shattered Poland."[54]

Some Jewish organizations sponsored social events and hosted entertainments to meet their UJA quota, activities which on the face of it may have seemed inappropriate when considering the horrors of the context and even transgressive of Jewish tradition. But to those devising the fundraising activities, the money raised mattered most. They wanted to meet their goal by whatever means available. The Senior League and Guild of the Free Synagogue of Flushing, New York, organized in May 1949 a "Mardi Gras" for the benefit of the UJA appeal, with "music by Vic Lourie and His Orchestra," and however divergent the idea of "Mardi Gras," the pre-Lent bacchanalia, was from Judaism, the synagogue newsletter went straight to the Holocaust narrative to encourage members to come to the event. Giving to UJA, the flyer read, constituted "A Sacred Duty," and that year, 1949, the first full year of Israeli statehood, offered them a particularly meaningful way to fulfill that obligation, even if at a Mardi Gras festivity. "Every day," the newsletter *The Link* wrote, "men, women and children are streaming . . . through the gates of Zion. They show signs of what they have gone through in the torture chambers of Hitler's Europe, but there is hope in their eyes."[55] In 1946, the Los Angeles United Jewish Welfare Fund's Fairfax Division hosted a dinner with entertainment, under the theme of "Fight for Survival," with Orthodox rabbi Herschel Schacter, one of the chaplains in the U.S. Army who had met the survivors, as the featured speaker.[56]

American Jews received and reacted positively to the UJA's calls for money for survivors, while their own organizations maintained special projects funded by membership appeals, and these too fell on receptive ears. Workmen's Circle branches raised money to "adopt" Jewish orphans living in Jewish Labor Committee homes in Europe. Their newsletters listed the branches that had collected the most money, and as late as 1956 the Ladies' Clubs and Ladies' Branches touted their accomplishments for solving the "problems of the surviving Jewish children."[57] *Landsmanshaftn* heeded the UJA's appeal but also gathered money for their own survivors, the women and men from their towns and regions who had miraculously returned to them. The Kolbuszowa Relief Society held a fundraising event on December 8, 1946, at New York's Henry Hudson Hotel for the town's handful of survivors. The program book, paid for with advertisements, went out to the "several hundred of our Kolbuszower people," who "managed to survive the Hitler tortures and gas chambers. They are scattered all over Poland and Germany," reported David Saltz, president of the *landsmanshaft*, and "are in very desperate conditions." The dinner and book netted $50,000, and the evening's rhetoric made manifest deep and personal emotions: "The remnants of our brethren in Europe are facing a desperate situation, and we who but for the grace of God would now be in their place, owe them a tremendous debt. We are trying to pay off that debt to make up in part for the horror and heartbreak that has been their lot." The Kolbuszowa materials printed the names of townspeople who had been found, pinpointed their present locations, and drew attention repeatedly to the horrors these friends, family members, and, indeed, all European Jewry had endured. Think back, and "count the toll of the Jewish victims: six million souls murdered, gassed in chambers, burnt to bits in the crematoria." To the *landsleyt* sitting around the banquet table, the program booklet asked, "Think now about the present." The Jews, including their townspeople, can be found "trekking the roads of Europe, trying to find a roof over their heads. Many, their hearts and hopes turned toward Palestine." The Kolubuszower in America must "not only . . . do what we can . . . we must do more than we can."[58]

Rhetoric like this inspired generosity on the part of Jews who had come to the United States from Germany before the war. The New Home Club of Milwaukee worked among its members on behalf of the national organization Selfhelp of Emigres from Central Europe and in 1947 sent money, beyond what it gave to the local UJA drive, to the Combined Relief for Jews from Germany and Austria. They organized a local campaign, "Don't Let Them Perish," dispatching one of their members, Rabbi Manfred Swarensky from Madison, Wisconsin, to New York in May 1946 to help plan "a special campaign for the benefit of the remnants of the Berlin Jewish community and the Jews from other countries, chiefly Poland, who are at present in Berlin."[59]

Other American Jewish organizations devised special projects to relieve the suffering of survivors, making survivor relief central to the ongoing life of the association. The Jewish Labor Committee orphanages represented one such large-scale endeavor, which dominated its work through the early 1960s. The Jewish Labor Committee, created in 1933 as a direct response to Hitler's rise to power and the persecution of trade unionists, set up orphanages in France, Belgium, Poland, and Italy to care for Jewish children whose parents had perished during the Holocaust. In 1947–1948, these homes sheltered several thousand children with funds raised by its members in the United States. JLC staff members went to the homes, inspected the facilities, and met with the adult care givers.[60]

In order to shelter, feed, clothe, and educate the children under its care, the Jewish Labor Committee solicited contributions from members and, to do so, prepared material for distribution. The New York office sent out "Our Children," an illustrated English and Yiddish publication to its branches around the country. "Our Children" contextualized the organization's work with the orphans against the grim recent history that, "during World War II, a million and a half Jewish children perished. Only 100,000 youngsters remained. These were the innocent little victims whose parents had been deported, tortured to death, burned in the crematoria, annihilated in the gas chambers." JLC members should, the pamphlet suggested, "adopt" Jewish children in the orphanages. "These are the children," the pictures showed, "destined to survive who have been entrusted into our care. They look to us for help. We cannot forsake them in their need!" In the Yiddish text, the brochure reiterated this plea, declaring that "a million Jewish children went away in ash and fire, leaving behind these miracle children. Every child—a story unto himself. When you look in the face of such a child you see the suffering of a people." By the early 1960s, this rhetoric and work ebbed as the children reached adulthood, no longer needing to be cared for in orphanages, but until then, every year at JLC conventions and in its annual reports, in its monthly *JLC Outlook*, it enumerated the number of children cared for, their educational progress, and the cost involved. In the annual reports, like the one issued in 1954, *What the Jewish Labor Committee Has Done* [in Yiddish, *Voss ess tut der Yidisher Arbeter-Comitet*] it reminded its constituents of "the tragic history of our people during the Second World War," which "has given our Jewish general a great mission: *Building up Jewish life after the great destruction.*"[61]

Other organizations also zeroed in on survivor children as a particularly poignant symbol of Jewish suffering. Individual chapters of the

אונדזערע קינדער
ילדינו

I NOSTRI BAMBINI
NOS ENFANTS
NUESTROS NIÑOS

OUR CHILDREN

JEWISH LABOR COMMITTEE
CHILD "ADOPTION" PROGRAM

The Jewish Labor Committee (JLC) maintained homes in France, Italy, and Poland for Jewish children whose parents had perished in the Holocaust. The JLC raised money among its members and in the larger American labor movement to support these institutions. In the late 1940s and 1950s, it consistently offered pictures of the children under its care and provided testimony from them as to their progress. The fundraising material repeatedly told the story of what had happened to Europe's Jews under the Germans. Readers, potential donors, learned in this 1949 brochure, "Our Children," that Esther's "mother perished in Tremblinka," presumably Treblinka, the concentration camp to which the Germans had deported most of the Jews of Warsaw and where they met their deaths. *Courtesy Tamiment Library/Robert F. Wagner Labor Archives, New York University.*

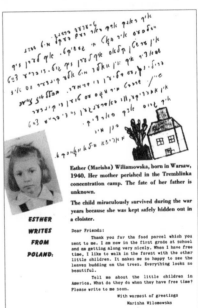

Esther (Marisha) Wiliamowska, born in Warsaw, 1940. Her mother perished in the Tremblinka concentration camp. The fate of her father is unknown.

The child miraculously survived during the war years because she was kept safely hidden out in a cloister.

ESTHER
WRITES
FROM
POLAND:

Dear Friends:

Thank you for the food parcel which you sent to me. I am now in the first grade at school and am getting along very nicely. When I have free time, I like to walk in the forest with the other little children. It makes me so happy to see the leaves budding on the trees. Everything looks so beautiful.

Tell me about the little children in America. What do they do when they have free time? Please write to me soon.

With warmest of greetings
Marisha Wilomowska

National Federation of Temple Youth, chapters as far apart as Mississippi and New York, started their own "Adopt-an-Orphan" project, raising $15.00 a month for the care of a Jewish orphan "somewhere in Europe or Palestine."[62] Pioneer Women, the Labor Zionist women's organization, launched its "Save a Jewish Child—Assure the Future of Our People," while the American Federation of Polish Jews inaugurated an orphan project for "the thousands of Jewish children who by some miracle escaped the Nazi death chambers where their parents and all their families died." This latter group sponsored *kinderheims* (children's homes) in Poland and France and asked members to give, "whether the amount . . . is big or small, we must all give something to fulfill the trust we inherited from the victims of the crematoriums—the care of their children."[63] In 1946, the American Association for Jewish Education came up with a School Adoption Plan, "the major purpose of which was to foster educational and fraternal bonds between the children in American and European schools." Jewish children in America raised money for books and other pedagogic material, as well as games and toys for about one hundred such schools, and "the individual pupils correspond with the European children," giving American Jewish youngsters a taste of philanthropy, in this case for peers, and providing for them a meaningful way to engage with Holocaust survivors.[64]

Not surprisingly, B'nai B'rith's Hillel program targeted college-age survivors. Marie Syrkin, an editor of *Jewish Frontier*, received permission from U.S. officials in 1947 to visit the camps in the American Zone, to survey the conditions of "the survivors of the Nazi holocaust." In conjunction with her trip, Hillel officials asked her to help identify fifty young survivors who might qualify for scholarships to come to the United States to pursue college education, charging her to "devise some method of gauging the qualifications of the countless applicants." As she reported back on this philanthropic venture, Syrkin lamented how few scholarships Hillel could give out and how cumbersome the procedure would be to get the lucky few into the United States. Interviewing potential scholarship winners made her painfully aware of the human aftermath of the catastrophe. None of the applicants could produce any documentation of their past schooling, since the schools they had once attended had been "destroyed together with their homes and families . . . their teachers fed into the crematoria," and the years spent in concentration camps had hardly furthered their formal learning.[65]

No more than one hundred survivors ever came to the United States on the scholarships, but the organization took this project seriously,

considering it one of its great accomplishments. Those few who did make it
to American colleges and universities found themselves cared for by Hillel
staff at the campus level and by the national office. The organization paid
their tuition and provided counseling, job placement, and legal assistance
in eventually navigating the naturalization bureaucracy. In 1949, Hillel
hired a full-time worker to run its Foreign Student Service office, to advise
the students and provide lawyers to shepherd them through the process of
regularizing their immigration status.[66]

American Jewish organizations took care of not just the physical but
also the cultural needs of the survivors, recognizing that after food, clothing, medical care, and shelter, the surviving Jews of Europe needed and
wanted books, religious objects, and the services of rabbis. Groups acted
on their own, deciding what they thought most appropriate, and went
about collecting objects and funds. Each time they went to their members,
they retold the story of Jewish suffering under the Nazis.

In July 1947, the Joint entered into an agreement with the Union of
Orthodox Rabbis in the United States "to coordinate relief and rehabilitation programs on behalf of Orthodox Jewry in Europe." The Jewish Central
Orthodox Committee, "An American Organization for the Religious Rehabilitation of European Jewry," as its letterhead proclaimed, named a European director headquartered in Paris, raised money, and sent to Europe kosher food, prayer books, and Passover *haggadot*. In May 1948 in its annual
report, the committee announced that it had shipped 6.5 million pounds
of matzah and matzah meal in anticipation of Passover. The matzah meal
got "baked in kilns by Jewish DP's at an AJDC ceramics works," and at the
Passover *sedarim*, sponsored by the Joint, the matzah came to the tables
on dishes that "bore the helpful legend, 'This Year in Jerusalem.'" Mindful
that the Nazi scourge had victimized not just Asheknazic Jews, the Jewish
Central Orthodox Committee printed special "Spanish," probably Ladino,
haggadot for Jewish survivors from Greece.[67]

Much of American Jewry, through its organizational network, involved
itself in this kind of work, and each organization did it according to its sense
of what the survivors needed. The Mizrachi Education Fund, representing
Zionist Orthodox Jewry in America, raised $100,000 in cash and collected
hundreds of boxes of what "Jewish DPs crave," including prayer shawls,
phylacteries, prayer books, Bibles, and volumes of the Talmud, destined
for "Our Brothers . . . in Europe's Vale of Tears." The American Federation
of Polish Jews, the Jewish Labor Committee, and the National Federation
of Temple Sisterhoods, all very different from the Orthodox groups, also

shipped books to the Displaced Persons camps. The Jewish Labor Committee placed an advertisement in the magazine *Zukunft* appealing to readers: "We beg you to participate in the book fund and help us by giving Jewish books and *seforim* [books of a religious nature] for the surviving Jews in Europe. The Nazis burnt along with the Jews, Jewish books. Those Jews who are still living are building back their lives and are asking us to help their spiritual hunger for a Jewish book."[68]

The National Federation of Temple Sisterhoods came up with a particularly novel project. In 1948 it formed a committee to support the work of the European Jewish Blind Survivors of the Palestine Lighthouse "to aid blind victims of Nazi atrocities." The monies it raised by means of special mailings and events went toward providing religious and secular Braille books and books on phonograph records to Holocaust survivors in Europe and Israel. Its fundraising materials stressed that, "of all the Nazi crimes committed against the human race, those which they perpetrated upon the European Jewish Blind cry out loudest among their acts of horror." Sisterhood members learned that "with the destruction of Jewish life in Europe . . . institutions for the Jewish blind were among the first and most completely destroyed." It took upon itself the chore of providing for "the surviving Jewish blind," who, "however eager they may be for ultimate resettlement and rehabilitation, have unfortunately by the very nature of their handicap relatively little opportunity to be accepted in the near future for such resettlement."[69]

The spiritual side to the rescue and relief work of American Jewry exceeded the collecting of books. As soon as the Allies beat back the Germans, first in France and then gradually over the rest of the continent, the Synagogue Council of America began helping in the rebuilding of synagogues for the liberated Jews. It created a committee dedicated to the Religious Rehabilitation of European Jewry and came up with a plan of twinning American synagogues with synagogues in France and then Germany. Within two months of announcing the adoption plan, over thirty American congregations responded, raising money and donating cartons of prayer books, Torah scrolls, Hanukkah menorahs, and other religious objects for their twin congregation which emerged from the ashes of the Holocaust. The Synagogue Council crafted a barrage of letters, flyers, and notices that went out to congregations around the country, announcing the undertaking, describing the nodes of Jewish communal revival in Europe, illustrating their religious needs, and then letting American Jews know how they might participate. In 1949, the Synagogue Council wrote about Germany, noting that "after the liberation of Jews from the concentration camps and from whatever hiding places they came out of . . . the Jewish community in Germany—small, scattered, leaderless, without synagogues—(they were burnt out during the Hitler days)—without any substantial form of organized religious or cultural activity—had to start all over again."[70]

In response to the material sent to the American synagogues, postcards and letters came to the council offices, detailing the efforts under way. All of the youth groups of the five St. Paul, Minnesota, non-Orthodox congregations pooled their efforts and held a charity ball for this project. Rabbi Abraham Rosenberg of the B'nai B'rith Jacob Congregation of Savannah, Georgia, claimed that his congregation had actually decided to undertake such a project even before it had heard from the Synagogue Council, yet "we shall be happy to do so if you would be kind enough to instruct me as to where to ship the *Sefer Torah* [Torah scroll]." From Tifereth Israel in Des Moines, Iowa, came an enthusiastic response: "We . . . can ship quite a number of Prayer Books, *machzorim* [prayer books for the high holidays] and *tephilin*." The rabbi of Brooklyn's B'nai Jacob congregation regretted that "we feel that our resources are too limited to obligate ourselves in that way," but the congregation still wanted to help. Instead, "we would like to be of help to our stricken sister Congregations. Would it therefore be appropriate to send a check . . . or prayers books and Taletim [prayer shawls] for an equivalent amount of money?"[71]

Participating in such efforts on behalf of the survivors became a mark of pride for Jews across the country. Organizations boasted to their members about the important work they had done and, often quite explicitly, how much more they had assisted in addressing the survivors' spiritual and physical needs than any other group. The Jewish Labor Committee proudly boasted of itself that "no other organization has accomplished as much in the field of Yiddish culture" for the survivors as the Jewish Labor Committee had. As of 1948 it took pride in saying it had "established 147 libraries in the various countries of Europe and in the camps of Germany, Austria, and Italy, which serve as the central agency for the circulation of Yiddish books sent by the JLC."[72]

Other organizations joined the Jewish Labor Committee in telling how much they had done on behalf of Holocaust survivors. Moses Leavitt of the Joint did not have to stretch a point in his 1952 history of the organization, in which he asserted that "at the moment of liberation, JDC threw its entire strength—and the strength of the American Jewish community—into a mighty effort to keep alive those Jews who had miraculously escaped the charnel houses of Auschwitz, Dachau, Buchenwald and the other concentration camps, or who had succeeded in remaining alive through years of hiding." In 1953 when the National Federation of Temple Sisterhoods celebrated its fortieth anniversary, it composed a ceremony, which it encouraged chapters to enact locally. For each decade of its history, it highlighted one notable achievement; for the fourth decade, it touted how it had brought survivors to America, providing this handful "from former concentration camps" with an education, helping them become Reform rabbis. Year after year into the early 1960s, it recounted this project as chief among its accomplishments.[73]

The desire to help the surviving remnant proved so powerful that it took on a competitive dimension. This happened because American Jewry recognized that it and it alone had the resources to alleviate the plight of those who had lived through the Holocaust ordeal. They raised money; shipped books, medical supplies, canned goods, food—everything and anything they could; and undertook projects because they believed they had to, that no one else would, and that they could do this on their own. To accomplish this mighty humanitarian project, they did not have to, in vain, lobby a hostile Congress for support, and they did not have to try to nudge Americans with no particular concern for Jewish survivors to change their minds about opening the country's doors to large-scale immigration. This lay within their means, and they understood it as an obligation to those who had perished, as well as to those who had not.

Throughout the postwar period, American Jewry expressed pride in what it had done for Holocaust survivors, seeing its financial generosity and volunteer activism as expressions of its unswerving commitment to the Jewish people. Indeed, boasting of service to survivors entered into the master narrative of its history, a visible project in the middle of the 1950s and the Tercentenary of Jewish life in America. Elma Ehrlich Levinger's 1954 history of American Jewry titled the chapter on the Holocaust years "American Jews to the Rescue."[74] Herman Stein in a history of American Jewish social work of 1957 noted that "the destruction of six million Jews by the Nazis produced a powerful effect on American Jewry, pervading all of their thinking and actions as a group."[75] In 1960, sociologist Nathan Glazer added to the chorus of praise, describing how "the last wave of immigration reached American shores . . . Jews who had survived Hitler. They came with nothing, or less than nothing, but they came to a community that was today able to spend tens of millions of dollars to establish them."[76]

Israel, the Survivors, and American Jewish Advocacy

Much American Jewish political action for survivors and the rhetoric it depended on, from 1945 through 1948, focused on Palestine as the solution to the desperate conditions of the remaining Jews in Europe. By the end of World War II, the vast majority of American Jews accepted the rationale for a Jewish state in some form, and even if they did not belong to a Zionist organization, as most did not, they still articulated a deep commitment to the idea that a Jewish homeland in Palestine represented the most appropriate way to address the desperate condition of the survivors.

Alone as an anti-Zionist organization, the American Council for Judaism rejected the idea of a Jewish homeland in Palestine. The organization had been founded in 1943, after the American Jewish Committee and the Central Conference of American Rabbis in the late 1930s, in the face of mounting terror in Europe, accepted the idea of a Jewish homeland in Palestine. With its tiny numbers and virtual banishment from the communal landscape, the American Council for Judaism stood by itself.[77]

Nearly all other American Jews who talked, wrote, lobbied, assembled, and raised money for the Jewish land did so by invoking the death camps, the gas chambers and crematoria, and then the exigencies of those who survived. In 1945, the American Federation for Polish Jews, an organization on the left of American Jewry, published *Peace for the Jews*, a book-length statement about the "Nazi horrors," emphasizing that "6,200,000" Jews had been "killed by the Nazi brigands." It declared: "We demand the Commonwealth now. No promises for post-war settlement will do. . . . The Jewish People demands a Jewish Commonwealth in Palestine."[78] Young Judea, a Zionist youth group that eschewed political ideologies, liberal or left, other than Zionism, inundated its readers with references to the Holocaust and the imperative of Jewish statehood. Rabbi Milton Steinberg offered to these young Zionists "A Voice from the Grave." Written through the voice of a "former textile jobber of Lodz, Poland, now reposing in the cemetery of an internment camp in the south of Italy," the article explained why he, the fictional Hayyim Rabinowitz, would not go back to Poland: "My synagogue is in ruins; the graves of my fathers have been obliterated, my friends are dead." But, with his people, he declared, "I am going home."[79]

Numerous American Jewish public works gave voice to the conjoined memory of the six million and the circumstances of the survivors as a rallying cry for Israel. The Mizrachi Organization of America, the religious

Zionists, dedicated its 1946 anniversary program book "To the Six Million of Our Martyrs in Europe and to the Yishuv in Eretz Yisrael Forging Heroically a New Life for Our People."[80] The Jewish Reconstructionist Foundation published and performed in 1946 a cantata, *Through the Open Door.* This "Fantasy for Informal Theater" invoked at its start the "six million who will never need to ask for visas now" and declaimed, "Be assured, O beloved dead! / We shall not falter!" The play came to its dramatic conclusion as the text read, "It's grown late, friends. It is later in the East. In Palestine . . . it will soon be dawn . . . dawn." The entire cast then sang the Zionist anthem, "Hatikvah."[81]

American Jewish cultural projects of all kinds, produced by individuals and organizations, repeatedly offered the message that Israel constituted the legacy of and compensation for the Holocaust. A phonograph record of the mid-1950s, *Israel Is Born: The Return of the Jewish Homeland —A Documentary Record,* was released by Caedmon Records. It included "The Actual Scenes of Kaddish for the Victims of the Concentration Camps." The mournful dirge "El Mole Rachimim," addressed to "God Full of Mercy," hallowed the memory, as the cantor intoned on the record, of "those who had gone to their deaths in Auschwitz, Treblinka, Maidanek, Bergen-Belsen, other concentration camps, and the ghettoes." The record cover carried endorsements from *Variety,* the *New York Herald Tribune,* and the *Cleveland Plain Dealer,* as well as Jewish publications and organizational newsletters, which suggested that the "record can be warmly recommended for every Jewish home." *Israel Is Born* presented the concentration camp tragedy as a crucial element in the fruition of the Zionist enterprise.[82]

The image of Israel as the place where the survivors would find both refuge and a place to start their lives anew linked American Jewish rhetoric in the period before May 1948 and beyond into the early 1960s. While Jewish survivors clustered in the Displaced Persons camps, Palestine lay beyond their reach. British policies limited the number of Jews who could enter legally. The White Paper of 1939, restricting Jewish entry into Palestine, still prevailed, making it nearly impossible for survivors to find permanent homes there. About seventy-two thousand set out for Palestine from Europe, and between August 1946 and the end of the mandate, British troops apprehended nearly all of them. The British sent most to holding camps in Cyprus, from which they allowed about fifty thousand to enter Palestine in small groups.[83]

As American Jews protested British policies and turned to their own government to indicate their rage, they invoked the moral debt owed to the Jewish people. Rabbi Joseph Baron, writing on behalf of the American Jewish Committee to Secretary of State James F. Byrnes, condemned Britain's refusal to honor President Truman's request that one hundred thousand European Jews be allowed into Palestine. In his letter, like statements sent to the U.S. government by the Jewish community councils of Cincinnati and Washington, D.C., among others, Baron expressed his hope that the United States would intervene on behalf of the survivors. "The sufferings of the decimated Jewish population of Europe are known to all," the rabbi wrote to the Secretary of State, and the one hundred thousand who might have entered Palestine needed to always be seen as the "survivors of a systematic persecution unprecedented in history."[84]

Books and other texts disseminated this message within the Jewish world and beyond it. Simon Rifkind, joined by a number of others including Abe Fortas, a partner in the prestigious law firm of Arnold and Porter and a close associate of Lyndon Johnson, issued *The Basic Equities of the Palestine Problem: A Memorandum* in 1947. They emphasized Palestine as the best way to "bring to a close the unhappy chapter in world history which opened with the advent of Hitler, proceeded with the unjust and unforgivable 1939 White Paper," and then saw how "nearly six million Jewish men, women and children—have been fiendishly exterminated." Rifkind and the others laid out how "the exterminations took place in Germany, Poland, Austria, Hungary, Romania, Jugoslavia, Greece, and even in some of the countries of Western Europe. To the surviving Jews these countries have become but graveyards of their slaughtered kin from which they shrink with horror. Their homes and property in most of those lands, their cultural, religious, educational and other communal institutions are no more: they were confiscated." Their "hopes for salvation are," the authors stated, now "so passionately linked with Palestine."[85]

Journalist I. F. Stone told this story in his 1946 *Underground to Palestine,* which he opened with the epigraph "*The Germans killed us. The British don't let us live,*" a statement he attributed to a "Jewish ex-Partisan." The book related an adventure story of the American journalist who went to see the illegal emigration from Europe to Palestine, a heroic emigration of women and men who had suffered "under Hitler." Stone personalized the fused Holocaust-Palestine narrative. "I am an American," wrote Stone, "and I am also and inescapably—the world being what it is—a Jew. I was born in the United States. My parents were born in Russia. Had they not emigrated at the turn of the century . . . I might have gone to the gas chambers in Eastern Europe."[86]

Novelist Meyer Levin produced several works between the end of the war and Israeli statehood that also linked the survivors, Palestine, and the Holocaust's horrors. *My Father's House* of 1947 told in fictional form the story of David Halevi, a ten-year-old concentration camp survivor, originally from Kracow, who made the illegal journey to Palestine, seeking his father. In Palestine, David met other survivors who took him along and told their Holocaust stories, harrowing tales of Auschwitz and Buchenwald, Bergen-Belsen and Dachau, juxtaposing these horrors with their new life in Palestine. The Jewish National Fund produced a film of Levin's novel, and Viking Press published a picture-book version titled *If I Forget Thee: A Picture Book of Modern Palestine*. Each version delivered the same message. After all the deaths and losses, the dislocations and the catastrophes, only in "the house of my father, Yisroel," as declared by David, could survivors find safety.[87]

Produced by the American League for a Free Palestine, the play *A Flag Is Born* ran from September 5, 1946, through the middle of December. Written by Ben Hecht, a supporter of Zionist Revisionism, the play brought the narrative of the Holocaust, the survivors, and the search for a home in Palestine to Broadway. Starring Paul Muni and introducing to theatergoers the young actor Marlon Brando, *A Flag Is Born* had pageant-like qualities. The actors spoke in soliloquies, orating against "the murderers called the Germans" and the nations of the world, "whose silence was a brother of murder." The script intoned, "And when the Jews of Europe died, when the six millions were murdered in the furnaces and gas chambers of the German, these cries were in their throats—'Where is Humanity? Where is the goodness of man that we helped create? Where are my friends?'" The answer, "They were nowhere," flowed into the next rhetorical question: "Where is Palestine? Which way does it lie? ... *Eretz Yisrael—Yerushalayim* [the land of Israel, Jerusalem]—these are the two words left in the dark night. All the other words are dead." The language of the play could not have been any less subtle as it preached why the Jewish survivors needed Palestine: "Does one open a shop under the gallows where one's father was hanged? Does one return to picnic near the lime pit where one's children were slain? Europe is a gallows and a lime pit. ... There are dead people under every road of Europe—dead Jews." In the final scene, David, Brando's character, meets a brigade of armed Jewish soldiers from Palestine, who exhort him "not to walk naked to a crematorium but to find manhood in the struggle." Inspired by this, the young man who had contemplated suicide picks up one of the other survivor's prayer shawl and turns it into a flag emblazoned with a Star of David.[88]

Numerous *Eternal Light* radio programs dramatized the survivors' yearning to leave Europe for Palestine. The dramas and the brief commentaries that followed conjoined the Holocaust, the survivors, and a Jewish homeland. In "To the Disinherited," aired on June 30, 1946, the narrator told the audience about an exchange between a young Jewish survivor and a general in the U.S. Army, who learned the truth about the survivors: "They know what they want. They want to quit Europe. They want to live together, no longer dispersed among a population trained to persecute them or to tolerate them. . . . In Germany and Austria, in Poland," their "civilization is dead. It was not only six million Jews who were slaughtered, it was Jewish scholarship . . . great academies of learning . . . Jewish music . . . poetry and painting that enriched a civilization which has made payment with bone ground into fertilizer." The narrator, after a pause, then made the political point: they "are determined to reach Palestine or to die."[89]

On the community level, speeches, sermons, rallies, school programs, and appeals to the American government relied on high emotion and on repeated references to "the surviving remnant of the 6,000,000 who were massacred by the Nazis" to make their case for Jewish entry to British mandatory Palestine, for an end to the mandate, and for the creation of an independent sovereign Jewish state. The United Jewish Appeal of St. Paul, Minnesota, cabled President Truman at the beginning of its fundraising appeal for 1946–1947, telling him—and St. Paul Jewry—that it had dedicated its campaign to the cause of helping "salvage the remnant of European Jewry —the 1,500,000 remaining of 7,500,000 Jews in Europe before the holocaust perpetrated upon the civilized world by Hitler." The Jews of St. Paul stand "prepared to do our part in terms of giving money to save the several hundred thousand displaced persons and the remainder of the million and a half still surviving who feel that they too are homeless and can no longer remain in the land where they are—the graveyards of the loved ones." Truman and the United States government should do its part, to see to it that Palestine's doors get opened for them.[90]

In the years following Israel's statehood and the mass exodus from the Displaced Persons camps, American Jewry turned its pageantry and political material, its public and pedagogical programs to celebrating Israel as the survivors' haven.[91] From 1948 through the early 1960s, it built a rhetorical edifice that brought together Israel and the narrative of the survivors as the living witnesses to the Holocaust. For the first Rosh Ha-shanah after statehood, for example, the Synagogue Council of America delivered its annual New Year message in writing and over the radio. The message conveyed the season's spiritual awe set against the extraordinary year: "Almost half of Israel's number is lost. The world's cruelest enemies have annihilated six and a half millions of our men, women and children. Great and ancient centers of Jewish piety and learning are no more." Having set the background, the message turned to the present: "We of the Synagogue Council extend New Year greetings to all our fellow Jews and our friends of other faiths. The newly established State of Israel, created by the heroism and self-sacrifice of our brothers, gives promise that the tortured and frustrated survivors of European Jewry may at length find security and peace."[92]

I. F. Stone followed up his pre-State book with *This Is Israel*, with photographs by Robert Capa. Stone took to task "the Wicked Midwives in . . . the State Department and the Foreign Office," who sought to "bring about a stillbirth" of Jewish statehood, and he retold the Holocaust story. "The end of the Second World War disclosed that 6,000,000 Jews had been killed, many of them by mass extermination devices," but he juxtaposed this with Israel. Describing the May 14, 1948, ceremony declaring the State of Israel, Stone wrote that those assembled talked about "the Exile . . . Herzl's vision . . . the achievements of the Return . . . the Balfour Declaration . . . the Nazi 'holocaust,' and the urgency it gave to the problem of Jewish homelessness." The photographs also told the Holocaust story, and one in particular made the connection between the Holocaust, the survivors, and Israel unmistakably clear. It showed two smiling little girls, and the caption read: "The Star of David on this little girl's dress, which Jews in German concentration camps were forced to wear as a badge of shame, is worn with pride as a badge of honor in Israel."[93]

Films, filmstrips, and other audiovisual materials, designed primarily for Jewish schoolchildren of the 1950s, made inseparable the narrative of Israel and the survivors. Journals and publications for Jewish teachers and boards of education advertised and lauded such materials as effective ways of communicating with American Jewish youngsters. For example, in 1954, a sixteen-millimeter, black-and-white film of forty-eight minutes, *Tomorrow's a Wonderful Day,* was produced by Hadassah, the Women's Zionist Organization of America. The organization encouraged Jewish schools to purchase this "moving story of the psychological rehabilitation of an emotionally scarred and anti-social D.P." who achieved "normalcy" in the children's village it ran in Beit Shemen. "Highly recommended for all age levels above the primary grades," *Tomorrow's a Wonderful Day* joined *Dream No More, House in the Desert,* and *Tent City* as cinematic works to show the Jewish children of America that Israel existed as the place of refuge for the survivors of the Nazi catastrophe.[94]

American Jewish journalism also pushed this theme throughout the postwar period. In 1957, *Jewish Spectator* reminded American Jews on the occasion of the celebration of the upcoming "Nine Years of Israeli Statehood" that the "calls for assistance which come to them from Israel are not for the benefit of the 'settled Israelis' . . . but for the New Immigrants, the survivors of the Hitler death camps." The next year, at the much celebrated tenth anniversary, the magazine observed that "Israel's achievements are unique . . . in that they have been attained in the face of crushing odds," which included the need to care for the "pitiful survivors of Hitler's death camps."[95]

Youth writing told the same story, and for that same tenth anniversary in 1958, Young Judea dedicated a special celebratory edition of its newsletter. The opening editorial, "A Decade of Growth," articulated a view that ran deeply through American Jewish consciousness. "American Jewry," wrote the young editor, "must continue to support Israel financially and politically," since it functions as the "haven for the ragged Jew displaced by a man named Hitler."[96]

Books written about Israel by American Jewish writers, hailed by Jewish community groups, constantly reinforced the idea that Israel existed as the haven for the survivors, the numerically few compared with the staggeringly great six million. Ruth Gruber, familiar to American Jews as the individual who during the war had engineered the rescue of a thousand Jews from Europe to a United States military base in Oswego, New York, wrote *Israel Without Tears* in 1950. The story of the Holocaust and its survivors ran through it. Those who made their way to Israel after the Holocaust "are now leading quiet, unsung, prosaic lives. . . . The graduates of Dachau and Auschwitz . . . have opened little tailor shops and gazoz (soda water) stands. . . . In rehabilitating themselves, the new immigrants are helping to rehabilitate the land." Israel, according to Gruber, had been built "on a Biblical vision and the cremated bones of the six million dead."[97]

Gruber's *Israel Without Tears* garnered far fewer sales or public attention than Leon Uris's 1958 blockbuster, *Exodus*, as well as the film version of 1960. But both made the nexus between the Holocaust, its survivors, and Israel inextricable from each other. The story of Dov Landau, a key character of one subplot of the sprawling book, took millions of readers and moviegoers into the Warsaw Ghetto, Auschwitz, Birkenau, and Treblinka. Through him they read about gas chambers, crematoria, skulls made into paperweights, dead Jewish bodies, Nazi medical experiments conducted on Jewish inmates, and "the memory of death" that Dov could never shake.[98] *Exodus* as a novel and a movie, a text about the founding of Israel, reached an immense American audience and depended for its pathos on the Holocaust and the story of its survivors, triumphant Jews who had faced the gas chambers but ended up building a homeland.[99]

Survivors as Symbols of Jewish Endurance

American Jewry in the postwar years read and heard much about the survivors, and not just as desperate people. American Jewish public culture witnessed the creation of a host of texts built around the image of survivors as symbols of Jewish endurance, as Jewish women and men who witnessed the catastrophe but whose very existence constituted miracles that bespoke the possibility of a Jewish revival.

Those who encountered the survivors in Europe and then wrote about their impressions offered the Jewish public a peek at the men and women who had endured and witnessed the catastrophe. They infused into their writing the notion of the survivor as witness and the survivor as hero, as symbols of Jewish determination. Leo Schwarz's 1949 *The Root and the Bough: The Epic of an Enduring People* highlighted the desperate plight of the Jews who had just undergone the murders of their families, the rigors of the life in ghettoes and concentration camps, but he also pitched his message in a decidedly Jewish triumphalist tone. Schwarz opened with "To the Sheerith Hapletah: My friends and kin among the surviving remnant who bid me make known what they experienced, this book which is theirs." He mingled his observations of what he had seen in Europe with the survivors' testimonies. In explaining the reason for such a book, he addressed both deeply Jewish and broadly universal themes. *The Root and the Bough,* he predicted, would have "prophetic meaning for our time" because "the small still voices which speak in these pages . . . bear witness that hatred is human but its works are short-lived; that one can bear the yellow patch with pride, knowing that it is a badge of human dignity." Schwarz valorized those who had somehow survived and "outlived the masterpieces of barracks and carnage." More than those who had undertaken "the Last Stand of the Warsaw Ghetto," Schwarz expressed awe that "the heroic resistance and survival of indomitable men, women and children in the face of a diabolical plan of extirpation" had led them to live on.[100]

Firsthand accounts of the survivors emphasizing simultaneously the horrors of the past and resilience in the present emerged in Yiddish letters as well.[101] A number of Yiddish works in the late 1940s and 1950s documented life among *di geblibene* in Poland, Germany, and elsewhere in post–World War II Europe. Jacob Pat spent two months in Poland, which resulted in *Ash un fayer* (*Iber di khruves fun Poylin*) [Ash and fire (about the destruction of Poland)], while Israel Efros sent *Haimloze* [Homelessness] articles to be published in New York's daily Yiddish paper, the *Morgen Zhournal*.[102] The most descriptive and powerful trove of Yiddish words about the postwar lives of surviving Jews, as witnessed by a nonsurvivor, came from poet Hayim Leivik, author of "In Treblinka bin ich nit geven" [I was not in Treblinka]. In 1946, he went to meet with and hear from the survivors. He had gone to Europe to attend the International PEN Congress, representing the Yiddish PEN. He went first to Germany to the DP camps, but, as he wrote to Joseph Leftwich, "It is impossible. . . . I can't leave. I am weighed down by the Jewish tragedy, the Jewish sufferings. I go from camp to camp. I find it hard to write about it."[103]

Yet he did. He translated the experiences of the survivors into a 1949 poetic drama of eleven scenes, *Di Khasene in Fernwald*, depicting a wedding in the Displaced Persons camp of Fernwald. Using a marriage ceremony between two survivors, both of whom had been previously married and both of whose spouses had been among the six million, the work celebrated the resilience of the survivors and their willingness to start up again, at the same time as it excoriated the Germans and mourned "our brothers lying under the monument-memorial."[104]

Representatives of a range of Jewish organizations went to Europe, beyond the Joint, ORT, and the Jewish Labor Committee. Each had its own reason for going; each had a particular focus. The National Council of Jewish Women sent representatives,[105] as did the American Federation of Polish Jews,[106] the Union of American Hebrew Congregations,[107] the World Jewish Congress,[108] the National Federation of Temple Sisterhoods,[109] the American Jewish Committee,[110] and numerous other organizations as they could. A group from Los Angeles that traveled to Europe under the auspices of the Joint saw an exhibition of artwork created by survivors and arranged to have over one hundred pieces in various genres brought to California in 1950. The Sarah Singer Art Gallery exhibited these pieces of

"Displaced Persons Art" at a showing sponsored by the city's United Jewish Welfare Fund.[111]

The observations of these travelers appeared then in the newsletters, magazines, and bulletins published by these groups and became the subject of reports and lectures at their annual meetings and at local chapter gatherings. These eyewitness accounts about the survivors as symbols of Jewish continuity became the basic stuff of the organizational life of the groups. In aggregate, they constituted a powerful unifying theme in postwar American Jewish culture.

Some organizations with only shoestring budgets could not send representatives to Europe to report back on the conditions of the survivors, but they did find ways to make contact and in the process joined in the celebration of the "saving remnant" as symbols of Jewish persistence. American Jewish youth groups like the Zionist Habonim and Hashomer Hatzair fell into this category. But young men from these movements serving in the American military sent back articles for their magazines, *Furrows* and *Youth and Nation*, which blended the details of the Holocaust with prospects of renewed life. They showed their members, all young American Jews, examples of Jewish determination as they chronicled their encounters with the survivors. One of the soldiers from Hashomer Hatzair published his piece in *Youth and Nation*'s monthly column, "Soldiers Write," in December 1945. He paid homage to "my Polish friends who were liberated from the German concentration camps" and described two girls he met, Leah and Bebah, both survivors of "the 'lager' of Osdzwieszm," a place which for most "'Juden' meant death within three or four days." The writer marveled how the girls, despite the fact that each had "a number indelibly tattooed on the left arm," "not only could . . . sing, they could laugh. I was to learn a great deal . . . from them. Most important I was to learn that this laughter was the secret of still being alive. It was the medicine that neutralized the poison of the concentration camp," of the "Gehimon" (purgatory) that they had endured.[112]

Some American Jews produced and many more consumed books and articles that portrayed the survivors as Jewish women and men determined to rebuild their lives. As American Jews encountered texts about the survivors' desire to start life anew, they expressed hope about the Jewish future. Ira Hirschmann's *The Embers Still Burn* (1949) made that message manifest in its title,[113] and *In Jewish Bookland*, a publication of the Jewish Welfare Board, commented on the large number of works written about how "the survivors . . . in the most abnormal conditions of camp existence . . .

began to rebuild their lives. . . . They redeemed themselves."[114] In 1946, *Congress Monthly* edited several articles from the recently launched *Unser Shtimme,* the newspaper of the Jewish internees in the Bergen-Belsen Displaced Persons camp. One article, "Risen from the Ashes," drew its readers' attention to the survivors' determination to affect their own destinies as Jews. "Here is the clue to the new Jewish personality," wrote *Congress Monthly,* about *Unser Shtimme.* It represented the words of the "new Jew" who "has emerged from the torture chambers and has risen out of the ashes of the crematoria. The scars on the body of this new Jew are an indictment against the world." The archetypical Holocaust survivor, as depicted in the American publication, "is not merely a man of Jewish birth or faith. He is a Jew who, because he is one of the few left of six million slain, feels that he and his like have become heirs to the collective self-awareness of the millions. . . . What separates them from us is the fact that Jewishness to them has become a consuming fire while to most of us it is at best a Sabbath candle."[115]

The image of survivors as Jewish culture bearers entered into American Jewish pedagogy from the end of the war, persisting thematically through the 1950s. A handbook for group leaders on how to use dramatics in Jewish community center youth groups suggested that club members "create dramatic situations . . . on material which is part of our own experience," and it offered a potential scenario of "a young girl of fourteen," who at the center "meets a refugee of her own age and tries to explain what a community center is."[116] Guides for Jewish teachers listed in the late 1940s and 1950s a variety of "Mimeographed and Pamphlet Literature" to use in their classrooms, including, among other suitable texts, "The Story of the Jewish 'DP'" by Gerhard Jacoby and "Headline Parade" by Samuel Citron, which dramatized for children the plight of the DPs.[117] Ben Edidin's *Jewish Community Life in America,* a textbook for young readers, described the situation of the surviving Jews in Europe and the organizational juggernaut of American Jewry to solve their problems, set against the background that "as many as 6,000,000 Jews in Europe were murdered by the Nazis for other reason than that they were Jews." Edidin told his readers, the young students, that "never again must Jews suffer as they did under the Nazi rule. The Jews of the United States are now the only large and strong Jewry in the world to fight for the safety and liberty of the Jews of Europe, and for the upbuilding of the Jewish Homeland in Palestine."[118]

Talk of the survivors and their special place in American Jewish consciousness percolated through classrooms at Jewish schools. In the late

**You saved him
from dying . . .**

**Train him
for living . . .**

through

O R T

The Organization for Rehabilitation Through Training (ORT), like many other Jewish organizations, spent the postwar period recruiting members and soliciting contributions through the medium of the Holocaust. ORT had been an active agent in the Displaced Persons camps, providing vocational training so that survivors could learn to support themselves. It had even maintained clandestine schools in the ghettoes under the Nazis, making it possible for some Jews to acquire those skills which might help keep them alive. In this mid-1950s recruitment brochure, ORT proudly proclaimed that history and hoped that, by telling of its accomplishments, it would add to its membership roster and to its coffers. *Courtesy YIVO Institute for Jewish Research.*

1950s, a student at one of New York's Sholem Aleichem Yiddish schools wrote an essay, "An Interesting Episode in My Life." The writer, a teenager, pondered the arrival in his home of a cousin he had never known before. The boy's grandfather showed inordinate love for this cousin, more than he bestowed on his own grandchildren. The young writer seemed surprised at his grandfather's obvious favoritism, since the cousin "was no different from the rest of us. His only difference was, he came from Europe after the Second World War." When the author of the little Yiddish essay asked his grandfather to explain, his grandfather promised that "when you are older and you go to a Jewish school and you learn what the Jews endured, I will tell you." When the student author finished fifth grade in Yiddish school, he approached his grandfather, pointing out that the time had come to learn the cousin's secret. The grandfather complied, and the two-page essay laid out the family's history: how it had become separated, with the grandfather comfortably living in America and the rest remaining in Europe. After the war, his grandfather explained, "We learned that my whole family had been killed by the Nazis." But then a miracle happened. Reading the Yiddish newspaper, which throughout the late 1940s and into the 1950s published the names of survivors seeking American kin, the boy's grandfather learned that a young man had come to America, seeking relatives. The newspaper printed his name, and he turned out to be "the only one of my whole family from Poland" who had not been killed. The Yiddish school essay ended with the grandfather's words, "Now you understand, my grandson, why I love him so much." Whether true or not, whether based on a classroom lesson or a real life experience, the fact of the essay's production as a homework assignment demonstrated the degree to which the presence of survivors in America shaped Jewish communal consciousness.[119]

Each swathe of American Jewry transformed the survivors into symbols of Jewish resilience, each according to its ideology and outlook. Reform Jewry, for example, consistent with its liberal orientation, used one particular survivor, Rabbi Leo Baeck, to talk about the Holocaust itself while celebrating progressive Judaism. The movement raised funds for all the remaining Jews through the image of Baeck, the survivor. The National Federation of Temple Youth (NFTY) named its special effort during the national SOS campaign "Fill a Box for Baeck." NFTY chapters competed among themselves as to which had collected the most, filling the greatest number in the name of the Berlin rabbi, the survivor of Theresienstadt. In 1948, NFTY's national office sent a sample flyer to chapters to encourage their members to "Fill a Box for Baeck: Celebrate—75th Birthday of Our

Heroic Rabbi." The eye-catching piece of organizational ephemera told the youngsters, "Any way you look at it—We know that—Here Is—A NFTY project that will satisfy—Displaced Persons in Europe—hungry for food and in want of clothing—All who participate in it—will congratulate themselves—and prove, in a concrete way, that America has not forgotten those who are sick and despairing of heart—that Youth can and will help—and that it will fulfill in actual deed—not merely talk about—the Mitsvo [obligation] of—DOING GOD'S WORK SAVING LIVES," and all in the name of "our Heroic Rabbi."[120]

The veneration of Baeck as the survivor whose story advanced the Reform ideology went beyond philanthropy. In 1952, the Reform youth organization earmarked an "Emphasis on Baeck Month," for which it created the script for a "Youth Shabbat Service," which wove his story into religious ritual.[121] Reform groups spoke about Baeck, created plays and filmstrips about him, dedicated religious services to him, discussed his ideas, and quoted him, paying homage to the narrative of how he, who could have saved himself from the concentration camp ordeal by emigrating, did not.[122]

A 1962 play about Leo Baeck, performed at the Leadership Conclave at Camp Olin-Sang-Ruby, offers one example. It began with the narrator, who intoned, "On Yom Kippur 1936, as the sacred notes of the Kol Nidre were all drowned out by the resounding clash of hopnail [sic] boots in the streets of Germany, Dr. Leo Baeck chief liberal rabbi of Berlin, rose to address his congregation." After recounting Baeck's decision to stay put, the drama ended with a description of the rabbi's ordeal in Theresienstadt, where "the Germans attempted to humiliate the Jewish leader. . . . But they could not break him." Baeck survived against all odds, and "on the birthday of Abraham Lincoln, before the Congress of the United States," the former concentration camp inmate declared, "God Bless America."[123] Reform rabbis devoted sermons to Baeck, and they, like the author of the playlet, told several crucial stories at one and the same time. One involved the story of dedication, of "the great German rabbi who remained with his people." Another focused on the Holocaust, with Baeck as the "witness to the annihilation by every barbaric means, of 6,000,000 of our people." But Baeck also allowed rabbis, like other American Jews, to tell a story of endurance, of an "indomitable faith."[124]

The small detail here that Baeck admired Lincoln and that he spoke in front of the Congress on Lincoln's birthday, invoking the "Great Emancipator," allowed the play's authors to also make an American connection to their survivor story. Through Baeck's Holocaust survival story, they demonstrated the deep connections between Jews, Judaism, and American liberal values.[125]

The theme of survivors as a "saving remnant" played itself out in American Jewish letters and in communal performances. According to the speeches, articles, books, and school lessons, this handful of Jews had not simply saved themselves physically, but their survival bespoke the possibility of also saving Jewish culture. As symbols, the collectivity of the survivors linked American Jews to a destroyed past and a more vibrant future. The story of the Jews who had eluded the Nazi Holocaust merged with the story American Jews told of themselves.

The notion that the very act of surviving the Nazi scourge could spark Jewish feelings went beyond the work of organizations. In texts of various kinds, American Jewish writers highlighted the inspiration they felt when confronted with the image of the Jews who somehow made it out alive and endured. Literary critic Alfred Kazin published a short memoir, *A Walker in the City*, in 1951. Originally four articles in the *New Yorker*, Kazin shared his bittersweet memories of growing up and leaving the dense Jewish world of Brownsville, bound for Manhattan's cosmopolitanism. Kazin's second chapter, "The Kitchen," connected his personal Jewish past with both the catastrophe and those who survived it. "The last time," he wrote, "I saw our kitchen this clearly," thinking back to his 1920s youth, "was one afternoon in London at the end of the war." Walking down the street, he had stopped "in the entrance to a music store. A radio was playing . . . and standing there I heard a broadcast of the first Sabbath service from Bergen-Belsen Concentration Camp. When the liberated Jewish prisoners recited the *Hear O Israel, the Lord Our God, the Lord is One*, I felt myself carried back to the Friday evenings at home, when with the Sabbath at sundown a healing quietness would come over Brownsville." The sounds of the "liberated Jewish prisoners" of Bergen-Belsen connected Kazin to his deepest Jewish memories, and, like so many other American Jews of the postwar era, he staked out a symbolic relationship to the Jews who had come through the Nazi catastrophe.[126]

The ability of the survivors to pick up and start again, as human beings and as Jews, seemed to American Jews to be a harbinger of a vibrant future for Judaism and the Jewish people. The *Jewish Spectator*'s Trude Weiss-Rosmarin implied this in a 1951 news article on the publication of a Talmud by a group of survivors in a Displaced Persons camp in Germany. The survivors had asked officials of the U.S. Army based in Heidelberg for their help in this effort. The army agreed and underwrote the costs. This small story meant much to Weiss-Rosmarin, whose unmistakable pessimism projected a gloomy future for Jewish life in America. Yet the story of the survivors who begged American military authorities to help them print a Talmud betokened a flicker of hope. "The cultural treasures destroyed by the Nazis," she wrote, "and the books which they burned can never be replaced, just as our 6,000,000 martyrs can never be restored to us." That the "Shearith Hapletah in Germany" had gone to great lengths to print a Talmud, however, "represents a small measure of moral restitution to the Jewish people for all they have lost."[127]

The Joint had played a pivotal role in negotiating between the survivors desirous of a Talmud to study and the American authorities who had the resources to make it possible. The Joint, in turn, offered a few copies of the Bavli, the Babylonian Talmud, to "institutions of higher learning as a token of appreciation of the help given by American Jewry . . . to rehabilitate the religious and spiritual life of our people." In his letter to one such institution slated to receive a set, the Boston Public Library's West End Branch, headed by Fanny Goldstein, Moses Leavitt, a Joint official, made clear that, very much like Weiss-Rosmarin had seen it, the Talmud project symbolized "the endeavor to revive Judaism and the Jewish spirit where Hitler sought to destroy them."[128]

Survivors: Real People in American Jewish Communities

It would have been impossible to belong to a Jewish organization, read a national or local Jewish publication, or even be solicited by a local Jewish federation and not hear about the "new Americans" or not learn how American Jewry aided them in family reunification, in getting them settled in apartments, in job placement, and in a multitude of other projects. In community after community, Jewish organizational efforts for survivors brought together professionals, usually although not exclusively social workers, and volunteers, rank-and-file members who gave their time and funds to serving the survivors. While no doubt more money could have been spent and greater sophistication in treatment could have been manifested, America Jewish agencies in the postwar period spent most of the resources that did not go overseas on, and devoted most of their professional attention to, the cause of the survivors who came to the United States.[129]

In Milwaukee, for example, aiding the survivors began immediately with the war's end. In November 1945, the head of the Jewish Social Service agency chronicled in the *Wisconsin Jewish Chronicle* how "the end of the war has seen a tremendous increase in the demands on the agency for migration services. Displaced, homeless, starving European Jews, often the only survivors of murdered families are desperately reaching out for ties with American relatives and friends. Aid on locating persons here and abroad, filing affidavits, transmitting funds and packages—these activities constitute a lifeline to many European Jews, a lifeline that extends to our agency office."[130]

As survivors arrived in Milwaukee, the Jewish Family and Children's Service, the local arm of HIAS, took on the immediate practical work in 1946, providing housing, jobs, clothing, and other services. It kept the city press, the *Milwaukee Journal* and the *Milwaukee Sentinel,* informed about the newcomers, presenting to Milwaukeeans details about the real people, with names and horrendous stories, now settling in their midst. In 1949, readers of the *Milwaukee Journal* read an article, generated by the Jewish charitable agency, featuring Abraham Oberzanek, his wife, and their children, who had just arrived in Milwaukee after years of suffering at the hand of the "Nazi hordes." Abraham had been "shipped to Lublin—marked for extermination at the nearby Oranienburg concentration camp." In Milwaukee the family met other survivors, including the Pelz family. The Jewish social service agency told their story to the city press: "In the German Flossenberg camp where 100,000 Jews, gypsies, Frenchmen, and others had been herded," Joseph Pelz "lost his first wife and two children, a girl of 5 and a boy of 3, who came to a tragic end, as so many others, in a crematorium. The Pelz family generally, fared badly. Of 250 in the family group, there are only 12 surviving today; seven of them face the future in America, in Milwaukee, with a growing confidence." Seven years later, the readers of that paper learned about another Jewish family, the Biringers, recently resettled from Hungary. The father of the family "recounted a story filled with atrocities and horrors under Hitler and later fear and regimentation under the Communists. . . . Biringer told how his first wife and three children were killed by the Germans and how he spent a year in Auschwitz and Dachau, notorious concentration camps."[131]

Because American Jewish communal leaders understood that the American public had little—indeed, no—interest in increased Jewish immigration, they mounted a public relations campaign on behalf of the survivors in the United States. American Jewish communal bodies, like the one in Milwaukee, pitched stories to the general press, issuing press releases that showed how the survivors who had endured great horrors stood poised and able to start over in America. In 1948, ORT placed an article in the *Indianapolis Star* about three men it had trained. "Rubin," the "sole survivor of a family of six," hailed from Warsaw; Joseph, born in Cluj, Romania, had been "tossed . . . from one concentration camp to another. When he returned to Cluj his family had vanished"; and "Icchok . . . born 30 years ago in Tomaszow, Poland, and once the manager of a textile plant . . . most of his family was wiped out in the Auschwitz concentration camp." In introducing the Jewish survivors to newspaper readers in Indiana, ORT hoped to personalize them to Americans, garner sympathy for them by making them more than statistics, and in the process allay fears that they would be unable to successfully adjust to life in America.[132]

Every American Jewish committee shouldered responsibility for the survivors. In Flint, Michigan, the local Jewish Community Council created a Resettlement Committee in 1943, already anticipating what would be a much greater need by the end of the war, and by 1945, this committee, directed by Rae Schafer, went to work. It had raised sufficient money for forty families, found and paid for apartments, stocked them with food and clothing, and located jobs.[133] In Washington, D.C., the Jewish Community Council sent out mailings to all of its constituent members, at the behest of the Jewish Social Service Agency, "enlisting their aid in finding jobs for D.P.'s who are brought to the Washington area."[134]

The Jews of Charleston turned to drama to advocate for the survivors being settled by HIAS in the South Carolina city. In the winter of 1950, they staged an elaborate, well-financed extravaganza marking the bicentennial of Jewish settlement. The planning committee hired New York playwright Sam Byrd to write a script on the community's history, resulting in *For Those Who Live in the Sun*, performed at Charleston's Dock Street Theater. The play involved a huge cast of costumed characters, including nineteenth-century poet Penina Moise; Francis Salvador, a hero of the American Revolution; and Judah P. Benjamin, the "Brains of the Confederacy." Actors performed the roles of Indians and British soldiers, late-nineteenth-century Jewish immigrants, and good-hearted, welcoming non-Jewish Charlestonians. Dancers and singers re-created an 1880s Purim Ball.[135]

The story for which *Those Who Live in the Sun* had been intended involved the survivors of the Holocaust who came to South Carolina. The play opened in "Barracks 17, Displaced Persons Center, Foehrenwald, Bavaria, and the Center Administrative Office. A November night, 1950."

On November 21, 1950, the Jews of South Carolina celebrated two hundred years of Jewish life there with the premiere of a play, *For Those Who Live in the Sun,* staged at the Dock Street Theater. The play involved the drama of a family of Jewish Displaced Persons, David and Lisa Schuman and their children. In the opening scene, set in the DP camp of Foehrenwald, the Schuman family learned about the wonders of South Carolina and the opportunity Jews had there to find their place "in the sun." The play, a historical extravaganza narrating the two centuries of South Carolina Jewish history, used the Schumans as witnesses to the evolution of Jewish rights and comfort in the American South. *Courtesy American Jewish Historical Society.*

As the play moved back to the mid-eighteenth century, narrating two centuries of "the Jews of Charleston," it simultaneously told, over and over again, "the story of the Schumans," the small displaced family from Poland "whose hope in life was to reach Charleston." David, Anna, and Lisa Schuman surfaced in every era as time-traveler witnesses to the evolution of this small piece of American Jewish history. The program book for the play, handed out to all who attended, included a piece written by the executive director of the local Jewish community center which made the same point but directly. Holocaust survivors have come to Charleston. They need services and should be welcomed. Thus, woven into the historical narrative of the Jewish experience in the Palmetto State, some survivors had begun to find there a new life "in the sun," and Charlestonians should help them make that a reality.

The dramatic device of making Holocaust survivors key characters in a pageant marking two centuries of a southern Jewish community spoke volumes about postwar American Jewry. The play allowed the local Jewish community to show how long it had been present in South Carolina and how crucial a role Jews had played in making American and local history possible. The play also allowed them to demonstrate to the estimated two thousand attendees of the three-hour extravaganza, and the larger number who read reviews in the local newspapers, how deeply they felt their responsibility toward the survivors of the Holocaust, some who in 1950 still found themselves in Fernwald, a real place, the last of the Displaced Persons camps, and those resettled in Charleston.

A range of Jewish organizations assisted in survivor resettlement. The Jewish Labor Committee used its extensive contacts with unions to negotiate jobs for survivors, either before, in order to secure visas, or after arriving in America.[136] The National Council of Jewish Women took on a lion's share of survivor resettlement work. Its Committee on Service for Foreign Born established branches around the country. In 1948, it estimated that its "volunteer services" that year alone expended "about 10,000 hours of work . . . or an equivalent of six-and-a-half paid professional workers." This one NCJW committee labored in four areas: naturalization work, international location efforts, port and dock work, and Americanization programs.

The port and dock work, as highlighted in the 1948 report, enlisted dozens of NCJW volunteers who met the boats at the docks, greeted the new arrivals, and facilitated the disembarkation process. "They frequently had to be on the pier at 8:00 in the morning and at times worked into the late evening," noted the report with pride. "A group of about 14 young women met the arrivals at the railroad stations at 6:00 P.M. and worked until 10:00 P.M., or later, to entrain immigrants for other communities. These women frequently left their offices just in time to report for duty. . . . We also provided a small group, among these some married couples, who were on duty at the railroad stations from 10:00 P.M. to Midnight."[137]

In addition, American Jewish social service agencies and other Jewish communal organizations helped survivors negotiate the process for filing Claims Conference applications. The *Wisconsin Jewish Chronicle* announced in 1950, after a smaller indemnification program had been negotiated with several German provinces, that "Sonya Essin, in charge of migration services at the Jewish Family and Children's Service announces that the migration department is now ready to provide information and consultation regarding the administration of the indemnification law which has been enacted in the four states . . . of the U.S. occupation zone in Germany." Throughout the postwar years, the newspaper informed readers that this

Migration Department "Offers to Help in Filing Forms and Claims," thus making the local Jewish communal agency and the local Jewish newspaper partners with the survivors in getting the financial compensation due to them as a result of their Holocaust ordeal.[138]

The survivors who came to America functioned as more than recipients of American Jewish aid or as abstract symbols of Jewish survival. The Jewish women and men who made their way to the United States after the Nazi catastrophe created organizations, participated in Jewish communal life, and told their stories, and in those ways made an impact on the American Jewish scene. Their words and actions entered into the communal culture. Survivors associated with particular religious and communal organizations, Zionist groups, Hadassah chapters, synagogues, and the like addressed audiences and spoke about their Holocaust experiences.

This fact stands in direct contradiction to the often repeated, nearly universally accepted assertion that the survivors of the catastrophe came to the United States and refused to talk about their brutal experiences. According to the dominant narrative, American Jews cajoled the "new Americans" into keeping quiet, demanding that they remain silent about the horrors that had befallen them. In an encyclopedia entry of the early 1990s, for example, Abraham Peck remarked that for the survivors and their place in American Jewish life, "a conspiracy of silence between Holocaust survivors and society" developed and that "silence . . . would characterize the lives of most survivors" for more than a quarter century.[139]

While historians cannot in actuality know about "most" survivors and cannot reconstruct what went on in their individual homes, in the American Jewish public sphere the survivors functioned as active architects of the memorial culture as they, along with nonsurvivors, attended memorial events and shared with audiences some details of their ordeals during the nightmare of Hitler's Europe. They created institutions and wrote works to commemorate their tragedy, simultaneously building their new lives in America. They invited nonsurvivors to learn about their harrowing pasts. The Jews whom they met in America who had not endured the catastrophe did not beg them to be quiet but listened to their public testimonies.

American Jewish publications paid attention to the activities of survivors in the United States and expressed admiration for their community building. In 1951, for example, the *Jewish Spectator* devoted a lengthy column to the dedication ceremony of a synagogue, whose membership "consists mostly of German and Austrian Jewish refugees." The congregants of Ohav Sholaum, New York, designated the building and the ceremony as a memorial to the synagogues Hitler destroyed in Europe, and the magazine editor described in loving detail how, "as the bearers of the Holy Scrolls marched through the aisles toward the open ark, there was audible weeping among the throng of a thousand people," those whose previous synagogues had been destroyed by the Nazis.[140] American Jewish publications opened their pages to survivors who shared with readers the details of their ordeals. Solomon Wieder, for example, described in the pages of the *Pittsburgh Criterion,* a local English-language Jewish weekly, how he, an inmate of Bergen-Belsen, had been "on more than one occasion . . . subjected to torture, to lashes as punishment." He recalled with anguish that, on his last day, before the liberation of the camp, "the Nazis burned alive my only sister and my two younger brothers." Wieder spared no details as he told his story to the Jewish women and men of his adopted new community.[141]

The activities of survivors in America functioned as an integral part of the larger Jewish community culture. Johanna Spector, as described by the National Federation of Temple Sisterhoods in a press release, "survived five years of concentration camp life during which she saw her husband killed." Before her ordeal, she had graduated from the Jewish Gymnasium of Libau, Latvia, and then enrolled at the State Academy of Music in Vienna, where she "majored in piano and music history." She fell into the clutches of the Nazis while pursuing a doctorate in musicology at the University of Frankfurt-am-Main, where she had embarked on a dissertation on the history of Jewish music. Spector survived and got a chance, through one of the National Federation of Temple Sisterhoods scholarships, to finish her studies in Cincinnati. Over the course of the 1950s, after completing her degree, she frequently spoke at Reform synagogues and at youth, women's, and young-adult clubs sponsored by these congregations. Described in the newsletter of one such group, the Schallek Club of New York's Central Synagogue, as "a young lady who spent the war years in a German Concentration Camp," Spector shared with them "some of her horrible, almost inconceivable experiences." She did so at a cocktail party "sponsored by the Youth council" of the synagogue, on "behalf of the United Jewish Appeal."[142]

Spector as a survivor not only spoke about her ordeal to and for the Reform movement that had enabled her to restart her career, but she also contributed to the creation of an American Jewish public culture on the Holocaust. In 1948, she oversaw the collection and editing of a book of songs, financed by the Joint, *Ghetto und KZ Lieder* [Ghetto and concentration camp songs].[143] In 1957, YIVO's *Yedios* reported that it had just received as a gift that same work, an illustrated volume of "ghetto and concentration camp songs." Johanna Spector, "through the good offices of the American Jewish Congress," had contributed the volume that she participated in creating. As it happened, a "young German anti-Nazi artist . . . heard the songs of the ghettos and concentration camps." Inspired, he "rushed home and painted for 36 hours without interruption." His work came to Spector's attention, and she "assembled and published—with music—the collection of 15 songs." The songs included not only the "well known Vilna Ghetto songs" but also various others, "sung in the Libau Ghetto" and in other camps. Johanna Spector, a survivor, had composed several of these.[144]

Spector's story revealed much about survivors in postwar America. No mere receiver of assistance, she helped fashion American Jewry's cultural life as scholar and survivor. She did not attempt to blend in and shed publicly her Holocaust experiences, and several, quite different, American Jewish organizations—including the Reform movement, the Joint, YIVO, the American Jewish Congress, and the United Jewish Appeal—all capitalized on her memories. They made it possible for her as a witness to the Holocaust to communicate her horrendous experiences to the American Jewish public.

In many communities, survivors, along with their American relatives and townspeople, organized Holocaust memorial events and invited others to join them. They participated in various citywide programs, planned and attended by others from the local Jewish communities. At those events, they told their stories, sharing their experiences of suffering and survival. Typically, Warsaw Ghetto memorial programs featured survivors, particularly in the ritualistic lighting of six memorial candles. In Chicago, for example, in 1957, the Chicago Yizkor Committee for Six Million Martyrs included the "New Citizens Club" among the sponsoring organizations, and it announced that, at that year's event, "the women who will light the six candles will remain on the platform throughout the evening's service. . . . each woman must be a Newcomer." Having survivors on stage made the ceremony more authentic, with the survivor, however referred to, functioning as a witness to the horrors.[145]

This ritual, with survivors prominently participating, took place across the country. It happened in Pittsburgh under the auspices of the Jewish Community Council. In the 1958 ceremony, staged at the Young Men's and Women's Hebrew Association building, "Abe Salem of the Newcomers in Pittsburgh . . . commented first, in Yiddish, on his memories of heroic comrades who died in the Warsaw Ghetto." He read the *"orders of the day."* He ended his speech "with a poem glorifying these martyrs." The audience rose, "while one of the other survivors of the ghetto lit memorial candles. *Mr. Jack Lipschitz,* of Warsaw, now of Pittsburgh, lit six candles in memory of the six million dead, following which Cantor Heiser chanted the memorial chant."[146]

Survivors addressed other communal gatherings, telling of their experiences. In 1951, "one of the last survivors of the Warsaw ghetto addressed [the] Temple Israel" Jewish youth group in Dayton, Ohio. In the early 1960s, David Wdowinski, a veteran of that same ghetto, spoke to both the annual Young Judea convention, held in Spring Valley, New York, and the Society for the Advancement of Judaism on the topic "My Credo as a Jew."[147] A number of Reform rabbis who had fled Germany before the final liquidation of the community but had spent time under the Nazi terror taught at the movement's summer camps. The staff introduced them to the children as Jews who had witnessed the destruction of Jewish life under Hitler. Rabbi Ernst Lorge spent the summer of 1959 at Camp Institute, and the youngsters learned that he had been "born in Mainz, Germany, the oldest Jewish community in the world outside of Israel. Mainz was completely obliterated by the Nazis." Survivors who lived outside the United States but had connections to American Zionist organizations came to the United States to engage with their colleagues and made their Holocaust narratives part of American Jewish communal discourse. Chaike Grossman and Itzhak Zuckerman, survivors of the Warsaw Ghetto uprising, came to the United States to address meetings of Hashomer Hatzair and the Labor Zionist movement, respectively. The newsletter of the Chicago chapter of the Labor Zionist Organization informed members of Zuckerman's upcoming talk. He, "a living symbol of the rejuvenation of a people once marked for extinction," had been known during his years in the underground as "Captain Antek." He had helped lead "the last ditch battle against Hitler's extermination squads."[148]

Some survivors founded their own organizations, which they often named New Americans Clubs. In New York, for example, some founded the Farband fun Yidishe Katzetler un Partizaner (Association of Former Concentration Camp Survivors and Partisans; formally, the United Jewish Survivors of Nazi Persecution). But they also joined other Jewish groups and participated in their ongoing activities. Of the six survivors who lit candles in that Chicago ceremony, one represented the New Citizens Club and one a Newcomers branch of the Workmen's Circle. The other four stood on the stage as members of Pioneer Women, Hadassah, the Women's Division of the American Jewish Congress, and the National Council of Jewish Women. A 1951 issue of *Mir Zeinen Doh* [We are here], the publication of the former concentration camp survivors, included a column on "involvements with other organizations." It declared that "the organization stands in a friendly camaraderie towards a large number of Jewish institutions. On the first level, the Jewish Labor Committee, the Workmen's Circle, and the Jewish Culture Congress," as well as with a number of unions, and with ORT, where two representatives of the survivor group sat on the executive board.[149]

Survivors' connection to these well-established American Jewish organizations meant that their activities did not take place in secret, nor did they obscure their personal histories. Survivors organized for themselves special branches of the Workmen's Circle and the Labor Zionist Organization. While they met separately, their activities were reported in the bulletins and reports of the larger organizations, and they participated in programs that cut across branch lines.

Survivors living in the Bronx in the early 1950s founded a Workmen's Circle branch, named after "ghetto hero" Michael Klepfitch. Although it sponsored its own kindergarten, it did so at the Workmen's Circle, School 10, a school attended by other Bronx Jewish children.[150] Similarly, survivors who in 1959 founded Camp Hemshekh placed advertisements in the Yiddish press, seeking to enroll nonsurvivor Jewish children. They made clear that Hemshekh had been founded by "former partisans and 'katseler' [concentration camp inmates] . . . to continue the programs and ideals found in the pre-war 'Tsisho' schools and the youth organizations 'SKIF' and 'Tzukunft,'" all Polish, Bund-oriented institutions, most of whose members perished in the Holocaust. The other children who attended and their parents who enrolled them as such became part of the cultural work of the survivors.[151]

Jews who had come to the United States from Germany before World War II straddled the world of survivors and that of the majority of American Jews who had been far removed physically from the scenes of carnage. The German Jewish women and men who had witnessed the evolving campaign of terror against them and found haven in America played a crucial part in keeping American Jewish attention fixed on the Holocaust and on Germany as the chief villain in this Jewish tragedy. For German Jews in America, telling the story of their suffering and that of their families and friends—most of whom had not survived—meant confronting the legacy

פֿאַרבאַנד פֿון געװעזענע ייִדישע
קאַצעטלער און פֿאַרטיזאַנער
אין ניו יאָרק
לוח
אױפֿן יאָר 1953

דערשײַנט צום 10טן יאָר-
טאָג פֿונעם אױפֿשטאַנד
אין װאַרשעװער געטאָ—
19. טן אַפּריל, 1943

✿ ● ✿

CALENDAR
for 1953

Dedicated to the memory
of the Warsaw Ghetto
uprising —
APRIL 19th, 1943

United Jewish Survivors of Nazi Persecution
31 East 7th Street, New York 3, N. Y.

The United Jewish Survivors of Nazi Persecution—literally
translated, the organization of former Jewish concentration
camp inmates and partisans in New York—issued yearly
calendars like this one, founded schools for its children in
conjunction with established Jewish educational institutions,
sponsored social events, participated in joint activities with
various American Jewish organizations, published a newspaper (*Mir Zeinen Doh*—We Are Here), and lobbied in Washington, D.C., with senators and representatives. As an organization, it created a vibrant and highly public culture through
which members recalled what they had endured in Europe
and shared those horrendous experiences with the larger
Jewish public. *Courtesy YIVO Institute for Jewish Research.*

of the place where they had enjoyed the full privileges of citizenship, where they had actively participated in the larger cultural and civic life of the nation. And then, their fellow citizens, neighbors, and colleagues voted into power a regime that demonized them.[152]

Bearing witness against Germany as the evildoer played as much a role in the life of German Jewish organizations like Milwaukee's New Home Club as did fostering social life and providing services for members. The club hosted lectures on subjects like "The German Jewish Dilemma." In 1956, Rabbi Manfred Swarensky from Madison, himself a German Jewish refugee, accepted the New Home Club's invitation to speak, and he suggested that, "in view of the fact that a discussion period has been suggested to follow my talk, I would think that a very heated discussion would be engendered if I discussed the rather delicate and complex question as to what the attitude of the Jewish people now and in the future would be toward the German nation." He played around with titles, offering "Remember Amalek" or "Should WE [capital letters in original] Forget and Forgive?" A frequent lecturer to the New Home Club, the Madison rabbi had spoken in German six years earlier on "Sollen wir vergessen und vergeben???" [Shall we forget and forgive], with the three question marks in his title, indicating the degree to which this group of German Jews now in Milwaukee carried complicated feelings about the place where they had been born and educated, and where many had achieved material comfort and professional respect, and then suffered as Jews. Furthermore, on a practical level, the New Home Club made manifest its moral claims against Germany as it served as a local clearing house where eligible Jews in Milwaukee could file their restitution claims against Germany.[153]

The New Home Club recalled Germany's crimes against the Jews as it engaged with the larger, non-Jewish public. In 1959, the New Home Club invited a number of local dignitaries, judges, members of the Board of Aldermen, and heads of civic organizations to participate in a symposium, "Human Relations: The Unfinished Business of Democracy." In its letter to these Milwaukeeans, the club described itself as "a group of newcomers from Germany to this country who have established themselves as fine citizens in a new land following the holocaust of Nazi oppression." Despite Milwaukee's large German American population, the New Home Club annually invited notable civic leaders and elected officials to its "Crystal Night" memorial ceremony.

In creating separate organizations, defined by place of origin in Europe as well as by ideology, the survivors behaved no differently than Jewish immigrants of previous eras had, and, indeed, like immigrants in general, who in their new-destination homes sought to re-create something of the ambience of "back home." That they gravitated toward others who spoke the same language, had intimate knowledge of the same places, and recalled common experiences made them more like "typical" immigrants than as refugees who had undergone a horrific ordeal. The tendency to form hometown associations, especially for men and women who shared premigration experiences, had been the norm in American Jewish history and in the histories of every immigrant group that came to the United States, rather than the exception for survivors of the Holocaust.[154]

A whole array of other survivor activities became, if momentarily, part of the larger American Jewish communal culture. Dina Blumenfeld, "famous Yiddish actress, star of the theater of the Warsaw ghetto," performed in New York in 1958. The Yiddish press advertised her performances, and actress Molly Picon devoted an installment of her weekly radio show to Blumenfeld, her artistry, and the fact that she "underwent the entire terror of the Warsaw Ghetto." "Today," Picon told her listeners, she wanted to talk "not just about the actress, but also about her survival."[155]

Individual survivors and groups of survivors began in the late 1940s to publish memoirs and accounts of their Holocaust ordeals. The *yizker bikher* provided one venue to share among themselves and their townspeople who had left decades earlier memories of the horrific events and details of life before the catastrophe. Other works in Yiddish included the memoirs of Aaron Tverski, *Ikh bin der korben un der eydes* [I am the victim and the witness], Shlomo Brynski's *Vehn fundamentn traisln zikh* [When foundations are shaken], and *Lerer-yizkor-bukh: Di umgekummene lerer fun Tzishe shuln in Poilin* [The teachers' book: the fallen teachers of the Tsisho schools in Poland].[156] These circulated only among Yiddish readers, although the English-language Jewish magazines and articles in the *Jewish Book Annual* paid attention to these books. Gerda Weissman Klein's *All but My Life*, on the other hand, came out in English under the imprimatur of Hill and Wang, a major publishing house.[157] Kitty Hart shared her Auschwitz ordeal in the 1960 book *I Am Alive,* a year after Romanian survivor Earl Weinstock published *The Seven Years.*[158] These were followed by S. B. Unsdorfer's 1961 *The Yellow Star,* the "memoirs of a boy whose childhood was broken by Nazism and who grew up in the concentration camps of Auschwitz and Buchenwald," and David Wdowinski's *And We Are Not*

IN COMMEMORATION OF THE

TENTH ANNIVERSARY

OF THE BATTLE OF THE

WARSAW GHETTO

THE AMERICAN
JEWISH CONGRESS

PRESENTS AN EXHIBITION

OF THE PAINTINGS AND DRAWINGS OF

LUBA GURDUS

MONDAY, APRIL 13 TO WEDNESDAY, MAY 13, 1953

STEPHEN WISE CONGRESS HOUSE
15 EAST 84th STREET, NEW YORK

Holocaust memorial events around the country, usually scheduled in the spring to coincide with the anniversary of the Warsaw Ghetto uprising, became opportunities both to retell the story of the revolt and to showcase art and music that took as their theme details from the Holocaust. Luba Gurdus, according to the program notes, "spent the entire war in Poland, escaped from a Nazi collections center, was captured and imprisoned in Maydanek." Her work included drawings titled "Gas Chamber," "Last Road," "One of the Nameless," and "Martyrs," among others. Gurdus created this particular piece to go along with Philip Friedman's "Ghetto Anthology." *Courtesy YIVO Institute for Jewish Research.*

Saved, a memoir dedicated "to the memory of my mother . . . my teacher, and to the unknown Jewish child, who symbolize for me the martyrdom of the Jewish people."[159]

In the ordinary course of postwar American Jewish public life, those who had survived the Holocaust found opportunities to tell their stories to those who had spent the horror years in America. Youngsters who attended Yeshivah Flatbush revealed their Holocaust experiences to classmates in the school's 1953 yearbook. Abraham Fuksman's "My Life Story" hid little: "I was born on May 1, 1940 in Baranowich, Poland. At that time, the Nazis started to attack Poland. I stayed with my parents a year and three months. On the sixteenth month, my parents gave me away to a Christian woman in order to save me. She baptized me, and I went to church every Sunday." He went on: "I did not know I was a Jew. I had no idea I had a real father or mother. As soon as the war ended with a casualty list of over 6,000,000 people, my mother and father came to take me back." His story continued: The woman who hid him refused to give him up. His parents went to court to regain custody. They fled to Vilna, then to "Hungary, Czechoslovakia, and other countries," and spent time in a Displaced Persons camp in Austria, and, finally, "on January 16, 1949, I arrived in Boston, Mass. . . . Now I study in the Yeshivah of Flatbush." This seventh grader's life story, as he presented it to his peers, evinced no shame, reticence, or discomfort at having gone through this experience.[160]

"MY LIFE'S STORY"

I was born on May 1, 1940 in Baranowich, Poland. At that time, the Nazis started to attack Poland. I stayed with my parents a year and three months. On the sixteenth month, my parents gave me away to a christian woman in order to save me. She baptized me, and I went to church every Sunday.

I did not know I was a Jew. I had no idea I had a real father or mother. As soon as the war ended with a casualty list of over 6,000,000 people, my mother and father came to take me back from the Christian woman. The woman did not want to return me. The only thing my parents could do was to take the case to court. There were three trials and we won them all, even in the Supreme Court. This all happened in Vilna. A few days later we left Vilna because we were afraid the woman would try to get us back. From there we traveled through Hungary, Czechoslovakia and other countries. We were put into a D.P. camp in Bad gastein, Austria. Later the Americans transferred us to another camp, by the name of Ebelsberg. There I went to school and studied Hebrew. We stayed in Austria from 1945 to 1949. And on January 16, 1949, I arrived in Boston, Mass. From there I went to New York. Later we moved to Lakewood, N.J. Now I study in the Yeshivah of Flatbush.

                                                      Abraham Fuksman

The testimonies of survivors, adults and children, entered into the American Jewish public realm. While not collected systematically, these narratives constituted an organic and constant element in the communal culture. A young boy, born in Poland and who survived the Holocaust by hiding with a Christian family, shared his personal story with his classmates in 1953 at Brooklyn's Yeshiva Flatbush in the school's yearbook. *Courtesy Yeshiva Flatbush.*

In these same years, survivors identified as such in prefaces and reviews and, in the very marrow of their texts, turned to creative writing and art to express something about their Holocaust experiences.[161] Fictional works penned by survivors over the course of the 1950s and into the early 1960s included, among others, those by Ilona Karmel, Herman Taube, and Norman Lipschutz, as well as Elie Wiesel's *Night* of 1960.[162]

Survivors turned to other art forms as well, and American Jewish institutions paid attention to their work. The artist Luba Gurdus "spent the entire war in Poland, escaped from a Nazi collection center, was captured and imprisoned in Maydanek," noted the pamphlet accompanying the exhibition of her work held at the Stephen Wise Congress House in 1953. The American Jewish Congress sponsored Gurdus's exhibit and drew attention to her experiences as a witness, in commemoration of the tenth anniversary of the Warsaw Ghetto uprising. Those who attended the exhibition should see her work, the guide to the exhibition suggested, as "striking, gruesome and extremely moving drawings of life in a Nazi concentration camp" created "by a former inmate of Maydanek."[163]

None of these narratives, nor those who offered them, existed in hidden or subterranean space. We cannot know how Abraham Fuksman's classmates related to his story, how the children of survivors and those of nonsurvivors interacted during their summers at Camp Hemshekh, or how those who attended Luba Gurdus's exhibit reacted and if they read the pamphlet accompanying it, but all these examples took place in the open and involved the survivors and the larger American Jewish public. The survivors who spoke and wrote, who joined general Jewish organizations, and who participated in the life of their Jewish communities did not seek to efface what had happened to them.

The work of the survivors on the American Jewish scene and the awareness of American Jews that those who had experienced the Holocaust had a particular agenda also emerged in the political realm as well. The clubs and associations they founded in their first years in America began with a political purpose. While the New York survivor organization reflected its members' desires to socialize with others who had endured a similar ordeal, and to join in "programs spent at decorated tables in a friendly environment," they also took up tasks involved with addressing the job, housing, and other needs of the newly arrived survivors, and they engaged with American and worldwide Jewish politics. They tracked the fate of Jews remaining in DP camps and paid attention to the work of the Claims Conference and the like. And they threw themselves into the political process. As of 1950, before the details of the Claims Conference had been hammered out, they "sent a memorandum to Senator Herbert Lehman" telling him they believed survivors should be compensated. That summer, a delegation of fifty members went to Washington and met with Lehman and his staff. As described in *Mir Zeinen Doh,* "Senator Lehman greeted warmly those who had been rescued from Hitler's hell and he showed much understanding of their needs and suffering."[164] These details of the survivor group's visit to Lehman's office and its memorandum on the restitution process offer a small window into survivors' understanding of themselves as political actors, who could and did speak for themselves. They learned the art of lobbying and did not shrink from stating quite clearly that they had a specific agenda, a result of their Holocaust experiences.

Starting in 1960, survivors in a number of American cities—New York, Boston, Cincinnati, Pittsburgh, and Washington, D.C.—publicly challenged the Jewish "establishment" as Jews who had endured "Hitler's hell." Two events rocked American Jewry. First, starting on Christmas Eve 1959 in Cologne, Germany, and then rapidly spreading around the world, including the United States, what Jewish community workers described as a "swastika epidemic" erupted. American Jews saw their synagogues and community centers defaced with the hated Nazi symbol. In a few instances, bombs ripped through Jewish buildings.[165] Second, at the same time, the American Nazi Party, led by George Lincoln Rockwell, the "American Fuehrer," blazed onto the headlines and into American Jewish consciousness. Clad in an S.S. uniform replete with a swastika armband and surrounded by similarly outfitted followers, whom he called "storm troopers," Rockwell organized rallies, addressing audiences with well-worn anti-Semitic canards, praising Hitler for his keen insights into the threat posed by "the Jews" and lauding his policies. In 1960, Rockwell threatened to set up pickets and disrupt showings of the movie *Exodus.* The swastika outbreak and the Rockwell problem took place against the backdrop of the Eichmann trial in Jerusalem, which focused attention on Israel, the Jews, and the story of the six million.

Rockwell, in fact, posed no threat to American Jews, and the swastika-daubing episode came and went. But the survivors shook up the American Jewish communal framework. Historically, American Jewish organizations such as the American Jewish Committee, the American Jewish Congress, the Anti-Defamation League, local community councils, and the National Community Relations Advisory Committee maintained a consistent posture on demagogues like Rockwell. Extending back to the 1920s, when

Henry Ford issued the *Protocols of the Elders of Zion*, the American Jewish consensus advocated quiet, behind-the-scenes action, but public silence. Anti-Semitic rabble-rousers, according to the regnant Jewish consensus, should be quarantined, ignored, and not allowed to command press attention. Counterrallies, protests, organized jeering, or any public confrontation only abetted their goal of generating coverage and drawing larger crowds. Most Jews had accepted this communal modus operandi.

But Rockwell generated a different reaction—partly because of his Nazi garb, partly because he popped up simultaneously with the Eichmann trial, partly because he strutted onto the American Jewish scene when survivors had become reasonably well integrated into their communities— and all of this simultaneous with the efflorescence of the civil rights movement. The established American Jewish organizations expected to proceed as in the past. NCRAC decided in 1961 that, since Rockwell constituted "a nuisance, not a threat," established practices should prevail.

This decision engendered fierce opposition from survivor groups around the country, particularly in the places where Rockwell appeared. He came to Boston with his storm troopers in January 1961 for the *Exodus* premiere. Local survivors insisted that his appearance not go unaddressed. The "New Americans' group" demanded a meeting with the Jewish Community Council to air its opposition to relying on quarantine and quiet in the face of Rockwell's advocacy of a "program for crematoria and gas chambers" for America.[166] In Chicago, the same controversy flared, and contrary to the community consensus, survivors picketed Rockwell, as they did in Philadelphia, Boston, and Washington. They carried signs reading "Remember Auschwitz."[167]

Their actions troubled council insiders. Those survivors who "bore mental and physical scars inflicted on them when they were inmates in Nazi concentration camps" engendered deep sympathy. Communal leaders recognized that the survivors had a unique perspective on this issue, different from most American Jews who had not experienced the Nazi ordeal directly. But the council, as Jewish defense organizations had long maintained, considered central to their conception of what best served the Jewish interest the defense of free speech, regardless of the words' odiousness. It also had an institutional stake in maintaining community discipline. The head of the Boston Jewish Community Council addressed this issue in January 1961 on his weekly radio show on WEEI, expressing concern for the survivors but maintaining the rightness of the communal position.[168]

The local Jewish press covered this internal Jewish disagreement that pitted survivors against the establishment. The newspapers editorialized, usually considering the council's well-trod path appropriate but, at the same time, remarking that "one has to sympathize deeply with those in our midst who directly suffered at the hands of the Nazis. Their emotional reaction is understandable when they see the Nazi symbols in this free land." Even leaders of the council recognized that the survivors' presence changed the communal calculus. Robert Segal, speaking for the Boston Jewish Community Council, noted, "you can't explain all that to the survivor of Dachau who came early to the scene of Rockwell's Boston operation and stayed late to be sure that the American who imitates the German Nazis was given no chance to picket the movie or peddle his line. You can't explain it to the Hitler era survivor. . . . Those with concentration camp experience cannot possibly be expected to adjust to the framework of a society dedicated to freedom to such a degree that even the most contemptible member of society is granted protection while uttering hatred. The man with the concentration camp serial number on his arm is wary of such nice distinctions."[169]

These articles ignited a storm of letters to the editor from survivors who, as Segal had reflected, had little interest in "such nice distinctions." One letter, from "Mrs. Fred M. Meyer, Brockton," published in Boston's *Jewish Advocate*, deserves attention. Mrs. Meyer took the council's executive director to task for his insistence on the conventional aloofness to anti-Semitic agitation. Mrs. Meyer not only argued against Segal's position, offering the opinion that "Rockwell has no right to appear in Boston and that he should have been stopped before he ever appeared," but wrote her letter as someone "who had left Germany." She blasted Segal's articles as an "insult" to "us, who have lost our mothers and loved ones in the gas chambers." She and Segal differed because he "does not have the experience we had." Having had that experience, she considered herself entitled to express herself, staking out a distinctive survivor position and announcing it as such to the community.[170]

The survivors, organized to confront the Nazis in America, did not just chide the basically powerless Jewish agencies for their lack of willingness to aggressively confront Rockwell in public. In New York, "concentration camp survivors deluged city officials with their protests," demanding that Rockwell not be granted a permit to hold a rally at Union Square. In other cities, individuals identified themselves as Jewish survivors of Nazi atrocities when interviewed by local, general newspapers.[171] The groundswell of protest by the survivor community represented the first time it had staked out a stridently particularistic position, divergent from American Jewry as a whole. This played a role in changing the communal response. Some Jewish agencies, historically committed to quarantine and now under the specter of Rockwell and the example of the militancy of the survivors, began to shift. In 1960, in anticipation of Rockwell's appearance in New York, the Jewish Labor Committee decided that "a request should be made by Jewish agencies of city authorities that they reject Rockwell's application for a permit," based on both the position that "the rights of freedom of speech did not include the right to advocate the extermination of an ethnic group" and "due to the nature of . . . New York city. . . . with its heavy Jewish population and its large number of persons who had either experienced the Nazi terror, or who had members of their immediate families killed by the Nazis, the holding of such a meeting would inevitably result in bloodshed."[172]

This statement of the Jewish Labor Committee reflected the growing prominence of survivors in the American Jewish postwar world. The women and men who had suffered during the Holocaust era functioned as political players in the American Jewish communities where they settled. They participated in the ongoing activities of those communities, but also they stood apart. As Jews who had endured a singular experience, they did not, as an organized group, shy away from discussing or sharing it with others.

The American Jewish collectivity, the organizations and organs of public opinion, the masses of American Jews who participated in one way or another in those institutions and consumed the information disseminated by the publications—all showed deep interest in and concern for the survivors. From the moment word came to American Jews about Europe's surviving Jews, they expressed through word and deed a commitment to doing practical work for the *shearith hapletah*, providing for their needs, advocating for them politically, and constructing them in their writings and performances as living embodiments of a Jewish past destroyed by the Germans, and as symbols of a possible Jewish future.

As it focused on the survivors, American Jewry itself became transformed. Its organizations and organs of public opinions articulated a deep sense of responsibility to those who had managed to emerge alive after the brutality of the Nazi era but also viewed these women and men as living witnesses to the event that so deeply defined postwar Jewish life. Not merely thinking of the survivors as Jews in need who provoked sympathy, the Jews of America described the very act of survival as testimony to the ability of Jews and Judaism to survive. As American Jewry focused on the survivors, whether it involved sending canned goods to them in the Displaced Persons camps or reading of their tribulations in the memoirs they wrote, it maintained a continuing interest in the catastrophe of European Jewry and in the fact that Germany and the Germans had perpetrated a momentous crime against the Jewish people.

4

Germany on Their Minds

IN A 1953 opinion piece in the *Jewish Spectator*, Trude Weiss-Rosmarin spewed vitriol at the "current tin-pan alley hit song" "Auf Wiedersehn!" and the Americans who enjoyed it. Since "popular songs must appeal to the sentiment of the masses by means of subconscious identification," she pondered why the songwriter had chosen for this lilting piece of music "a *German* refrain? And why," she asked, when "one probes further, is that *German* refrain so popular?" Weiss-Romarin detected sinister forces at work in an American culture which depicted "German characters . . . as such woeful and sympathy-deserving 'innocent' victims, unwilling instruments of the *bad, bad* Nazis, who are represented as if they had no connection at all with the 'good' Germans."[1]

Weiss-Rosmarin linked the song's mass appeal to an ongoing campaign, orchestrated by the U.S. government and postwar West Germany, to rehabilitate Germany's image, to convince the world that the latter had no connection to Hitler's Third Reich. The Jews of America, Weiss-Rosmarin predicted, would not be hoodwinked by this public relations ploy. She contrasted them with those Americans who enjoyed the song's catchy tune. Jews had been "gifted with a long and faithful memory." Their neighbors might fall for "Auf Wiedersehn" and by efforts of the German government to promote tourism to "Beautiful Germany." Jews would never "forget-and-forgive the concentration camps and the gas chambers, the Belsens and the Auschwitzes, the mass-graves which hold the remains of those buried *alive,* and the Jewish children asphyxiated by poison gas." Jews considered Germany "a country that still reeks with the blood of six million Jewish men, women and children murdered by *Germans.*" Who, she asked, could "expect Jewish tourists to come for 'pleasant travel' to the slaughter house of six millions of their sons and daughters" but "a people with a Nazi mentality"? Weiss-Rosmarin packed a punch in her words: "There is no 'Auf Wiedersehn' for Jews as far as Germans and Germany are concerned. We remember and shall always remember what this modern Amalek has done."

The magazine editor may have overestimated the significance of the silly song, but what she said and how she said it reflected American Jews' engagement with Germany, the German people, the German language, and, indeed, nearly anything "German." To them, Germany stood exposed as the murderer of one-third of their people, as bearing responsibility for the destruction of Europe's Jews and their communities. As American Jews confronted Germany in the postwar era, they kept that brutal truth in the forefront of their consciousness and placed it prominently in their public rhetoric. They never hesitated to label Germany as the culprit and asserted directly and indirectly that by keeping alive and exposed to public scrutiny the fact of Germany's culpability, they fulfilled a memorial obligation to their kin, literal and metaphoric, who had gone to their deaths at the hands of the Germans.

Every time it held up to public gaze the image of Germany as the wrongdoer and as a postwar nation that needed to admit its sins and rid itself of its Nazi past, American Jewry saw itself as carrying out its sacred task to remember and recall the six million. Its words about Germany and its efforts to get other Americans to listen functioned as monuments to the victims of the catastrophe, no less, but different, than did physical markers, liturgies of mourning, and dedicated books. By confronting Germany, the Jews of America not only expressed their anger and their need for justice, but they spoke for those who could no longer speak.

Historians of later generations would not see it this way. To Peter Novick, the very opposite kind of rhetoric and political action characterized American Jewry's stance toward postwar Germany. "In matters having to do with Germany," he wrote, "there was a virtual taboo on mention of the Holocaust," except in "private and in-house Jewish discourse." As he saw it, only the "Jewish left" invoked the Holocaust, thereby forcing the rest of American Jewry to remain mute when it came to casting blame on the culprit nation responsible for the systematic annihilation of so many Jews.[2]

The vast compendium of words and actions undertaken by American Jews tell a very different history. In their communal world, and as they turned to their non-Jewish neighbors and the American government, rather than being a taboo subject, Germany's responsibility for the Holocaust ran deeply and broadly through their public works. The sermons and articles in Jewish magazines, which might be aptly labeled "in-house," had a public function no less than the press releases they sent out to newspapers and television stations, inasmuch as these "private" works functioned as calls to action. Jewish communal leaders used the inner organs of Jewish news and opionion to mobilize the public to then go out into the larger world and let others know what the Germans had done to the Jews and how postwar Germany retained much of its Nazi past.

The matter of postwar Germany did present them a complicated challenge. Jews, as nearly every text they produced indicated, would have preferred to have no relationship with that place and its people. But they could not avoid it. Germany mattered in their world, and the era's unfolding realities required that they balance rage with facts over which they had little or no control. Their forced encounter with Germany came from three sources. First, after the Holocaust, worldwide Jewish bodies and, by the late 1940s, the State of Israel negotiated with the Federal Republic of Germany, founded in 1949, over restitution to the Jewish people for material damage inflicted on Jewish property and for reparations to individuals. Israel and West Germany entered into economic and commercial dealings with each other, leading to the eventual establishment of normal diplomatic relations in 1965. American Jews reacted to this development as Jews, with the Holocaust fresh in their minds and as supporters of Israel.

Second, in the Cold War, Germany occupied a key strategic and symbolic role in the struggle between the United States and the Soviet Union. American policy makers had no incentive to keep alive the history of Germany's unprecedented brutality toward the Jews. This meant that American Jews, as Americans, faced a potential dilemma about Germany. Their country, to which they expressed loyalty and devotion, now consorted with and celebrated Germany, the place that in their lexicon embodied the deepest evil.

Third, Jews continued to live in Germany. Small Jewish communities made up primarily of Polish Holocaust survivors had their homes in West Germany, and the public works of American Jewry, particularly when it came to ferreting out the not-so-hidden survivals of Nazi sympathy, took as context their fear and concern that these Jews would be the victims again of racist and ultranationalist violence.

But even facing those constraints, and despite their deep identification with the United States and the pressures of Cold War domestic American politics, on this matter, American Jews parted company with other Americans. They had to go it alone when it came to keeping a vigilant eye on Germany and the ways in which Nazism's legacy lived on despite defeat and military occupation. While Americans might have embraced "Auf Wiedersehn," American Jews did not.

No other country merited anything approximating the level of venom that American Jews expressed toward Germany, and they held no other nation up to such scrutiny. It stood in a class unto itself among nations. They described no other place in tones so laden with such negative visceral emotions. They saw only Germany as "the habitat of bloodshot nationalism and racialism."[3] Communal discussions and programs about the Soviet Union, and particularly its anti-Semitism, paled in terms of the numbers of such events, their frequency, and their rhetorical intensity when compared with those dealing with Germany. Certainly, American Jewish groups discussed problems of Soviet Jewry. Rabbis and writers emphasized that its Communist regime suppressed Judaism and Jewish culture, and they saw the Soviet Union as a political problem about which they wrote articles and organized conferences.

But the tone American Jews employed when focusing on Germany made it stand alone in its pariah status. American Jewish groups devoted a vast number of lectures and meetings, articles, books, and sermons to it and only it. A 1951 lecture delivered in Pittsburgh by Irving Kane intoned *the* phrase of choice for Jews of that era when referring to Germany, and to no other country and people: "We'll Never Forget, We'll Never Forgive," he declared.[4] American Jews worried about how only Germany's recent history got represented in American high school textbooks, and they protested only when German dignitaries came to the United States. Only Germany, they asserted, deserved no place in the family of nations.[5]

As the Jews of the United States saw it, only Germany had perpetrated so horrendous a deed as to have altered the basic character of world Jewry, Jewish history, and their own destiny. Germany alone conjoined politics with anguish and rage. So profoundly did they locate the source of evil in Germany that, as they referred to the Hitler era, they often mistakenly located the death camps in Germany, as opposed to Poland, where most had been. They described German soil as soaked with Jewish blood, a statement that fit Poland much better.

Many invoked the name "Dachau" as the synonym for the entire concentration camp experience, as the place where gassings had been perpetrated, where the crematoria had consumed the bodies of the millions of Jews. Dachau, in fact, had not been a death camp, and Jews had constituted a small portion of its inmates.[6] But its German setting made it a fitting icon for the killings as a whole. In a three-part radio broadcast on New York's WBAI, a medium hardly limited to Jewish listeners, and then reprinted in *Midstream*, Shlomo Katz used Dachau as the "Symbol of Our Terror." He disagreed with a tendency to employ Hiroshima as "*the* central and most meaningful symbol of the terror of our time." Katz offered a better symbol: "There is such a name, of a place . . . whose meaning and implications for the future of the human race equal and far outweigh those of Hiroshima." Katz had "not one but several. I have in mind Dachau, and Auschwitz and Treblinka." Of those, "for convenience sake, let us select Dachau." Repeatedly, Katz let Dachau, situated on the outskirts of Munich, represent "the distilled horror that took place in all the extermination camps." Rather than, in fact, doing this just for convenience sake, Katz, like so many American Jewish commentators, saw Germany as the incarnation of evil.[7]

He used that same theme in 1954, sharing with readers of *Jewish Frontier* his "Self-Portrait of an American Jew." Katz presented his composite portrait of what American Jews thought about themselves and the world through the medium of a guilty Germany. "As a Jew," he confessed, "I am not on speaking terms with Germany. Even if I cared to speak to Germany, I would not know how to begin." After all, he declared, "I cannot forgive it what it did, and I feel that it has done nothing to merit or to invite such forgiveness." But the world being what it was, Katz realized that he had to keep "a wary eye on it from a distance lest another calamity is cooked up for me somewhere between the Rhine and the Oder. My geography of Europe has a large area in the center that is stamped *taboo*, with all this implies of fear, untouchableness, threat and dark mystery."[8]

American Jews wanted to remind Americans that Germany had been the culprit responsible for the mass slaughter of European Jewry. Mr. H. Kudlowitz, principal of the Workmen's Circle I. L. Peretz School in Dorchester, Massachusetts, felt obliged to speak out on Germany and the Holocaust in his local press. In 1959, his enraged letter to the editor appeared in the *Boston Globe*, a newspaper that obviously went far beyond the city's Jewish population. His forthright identification of Germany as perpetrator typified American Jewish discourse:

> To the Editor—I am writing to tell you of a drastic error . . . [in the] May 4 Globe in the article covering the Warsaw Ghetto Memorial.
>
> It was printed "Children of the I. L. Peretz Arbeiter Ring School lighted the candles and later a reading in German gave a portrayal of life in the Ghetto and the massacre by the Nazis." In the first place, your reporter should have inquired as to the language used if it were unfamiliar to him. In the second place, it should have been apparent to the reporter that whatever language would have been used it certainly

would not have been German. This was a memorial observance paying tribute to 6 million Jews who died at the hands of the German Nazis. Therefore, it would seem incongruous to sing the praises of the martyred Jews in the German language. The children of the I. L. Peretz School rendered their portrayal in Yiddish, the language used by the Jews in Eastern Europe and taught at the school itself.

Since the appearance of your article our school has received numerous telephone calls questioning our use of German in the program. We would appreciate a retraction of your error.[9]

American Jews did not shrink from letting the non-Jewish public know about the Holocaust, how deeply they felt about it, and the centrality of the Germans in perpetrating it. Someone, after all, from the school must have informed the *Globe* about the upcoming memorial event in the first place, having wanted the school's memorial ceremony to become part of the public record, and they clearly did not hesitate to name the nation at whose hands the six million had been killed.

The "New Germany"

In their engagement with Germany after the defeat of Hitler, American Jews considered the Federal Republic, one of the two successor states to the Third Reich, to bear its predecessor's guilt. Immediately after the end of the war—indeed, before that, when it seemed clear that the Allies would triumph militarily—American Jews, in words and deeds, began to speculate about Germany's political fate. Jewish newspapers and magazines, the publications of organizations and sermons delivered from pulpits all weighed in on the shape of a future postwar Germany.

American Jewry in its communal bodies contemplated numerous ideas on what to do with Germany. In 1945, Henry Morgenthau Jr., Roosevelt's Secretary of the Treasury, published *Germany Is Our Problem*, proposing that Germany cease to exist and be converted into a patchwork of agrarian regions incapable of reindustrializing and remilitarizing. Morgenthau, not writing as the representative of any Jewish organization, used the word "Jewish" only once in the book. Up to that point in his life, he had maintained no connection to organized American Jewry, although he would in 1947 take over the leadership of the United Jewish Appeal and in that capacity raise millions of dollars for the survivors of the Holocaust.[10]

His detailed plan for the disintegration of Germany proved problematic for American Jewish communal leaders, particularly the American Jewish Committee. Committee leaders, who came from the same well-off social and cultural milieu as Morgenthau, rejected his plan as "neither feasible nor desirable." The National Community Relations Advisory Committee (NCRAC), which included most national Jewish organizations and all the local community councils, also dismissed this proposition, considering it more useful to revive Germany but "only under genuine democratic auspices" and achievable only "through support for the liberal-labor elements in Germany." They opposed the Morgenthau Plan, considering it unlikely to foster thorough and meaningful denazification and, most importantly, realizing that an economically degraded Germany could never make financial restitution for the millions in stolen property and the destroyed lives that it had robbed from the Jewish people. On a tactical level, they also realized that it would never win government approval, would generate intense ill will in America, and would "be fatal to any program put forward by Jewish organizations." NCRAC and local community councils knew full well that most Americans considered the Morgenthau Plan to be a "Jewish plan." "The erroneous identification in the public mind of the Morgenthau Plan with Jewish desires for vengeance" would not facilitate but would actually stymie denazification and generate hostility in America toward Jews, precisely when American Jewry assumed leadership of the world Jewish community in the wake of the Holocaust.[11]

Opposing the Morgenthau Plan on strategic grounds hardly meant that American Jews wanted to let Germany "off the hook" or that they considered its responsibility for the liquidation of European Jewry a matter only of the past. Rather, over the course of the entire postwar period and through their organizations and their press, American Jews made a number of points about what Germany had to do and what kind of nation it must become. It had to emerge as a nonmilitarized democracy and rid itself of all vestiges of its Nazi past. It had to admit its guilt. Those who had inflicted evil on the Jews had to be removed from public life and brought to the bar of justice. Germany had to pay, literally, for its crimes by recompensing the Jewish people for the property it had stolen from them and had to directly make restitution to individuals who lost their family members, their health, and their livelihoods. Germany would assume responsibility for underwriting care for, and rehabilitation of, the survivors, whether they remained in Europe, went to Israel, or moved to the United States. And as far as Israel went, German monies would be used to ensure the economic development of the new state, the place where, in fact, most of the survivors went. In turn, American Jewry set itself up as the monitor of these *desiderata*.

Into the 1960s, American Jews wrote and talked about the legacy of Nazism and the status of "former" Nazis in Germany. More than any other issue internal to Germany, the problem of incomplete denazification engaged them. American Jewry asserted that it had a profound stake in what happened within the borders of the new Germany. The slow but unabashed return of Nazi officials to civic respectability, the dismissal of judicial proceedings against abettors of the Third Reich, and a constant flurry of incidents of anti-Jewish violence in Germany galvanized American Jewry.

Even while American troops still occupied Germany and before the Federal Republic came into being, the pages of the Jewish press reported, constantly, on the ease with which Nazis regained respectability. In 1948, the American Jewish Congress created within its Commission on Law and Social Action a "Denazification Campaign Headquarter" to monitor, inform, and create programs on what it, and most American Jews, saw as a troubling reality. In the months that followed, the headquarter forwarded to its chapters three documents prepared by the national office for local use. The first provided text for a "sample postcard" chapter members should send to their senators, stating, "Dear Senator, I am deeply concerned over the evident failure of the denazification program in the American Occupation Zone of Germany. I should like to express my agreement with the resolution passed by the Executive Committee of the American Jewish Congress and urge the Senate to conduct a public investigation." Second, the national office composed a boilerplate news release for local papers, expressing "alarm at the virtual halt of denazification hearings and war crimes trials, commutations of sentences for such notorious war criminals as Ilse Koch." The news release continued: "The failure of the denazification program is reflected in the growth of anti-Semitic and anti-democratic trends in the U.S. Zone." Additionally, chapters received an accompanying document, "Let's Have the Facts," which stated, "The American Jewish Congress, alarmed by these symptoms, recalling that nationalist and anti-Semitic trends in Germany preceded the death of 6,000,000 Jews and made a war whose toll in lives and destruction has still not been calculated, feels that all facts be made known. It is calling for a Senatorial investigation of American policy in Germany."[12]

Local chapters responded to the call from the national office. The Chicago chapter issued its own press release, which announced the convening of an "Emergency Public Conference Against the Re-Arming of Germany." "De-Nazification," the notice that went out to the city's newspapers read, "has become *renazification*." The New England chapter prepared material on this, too, urging members to write to their senators in support of Senate Resolution 125, to establish a "public investigation of anti-semitic and anti-Democratic trends in Germany." A flyer went further: "Talk to your Neighbors. . . . Urge your neighbors and friends to gain the active support of SENATE RESOLUTION 125 calling for a probe of denazification in Germany. Get your clergyman to devote a sermon or service to this critical issue." The American Jewish Congress flyer could not have been clearer in terms setting the historical context. "Have you forgotten . . . Hitler? Buchenwald? Dachau?" the 1949 flyer shrieked, invoking the names of two concentration camps that had been on German soil and showing the graphic image of a cobra with a swastika on its head being hatched from an egg with "ANTI-SEMITISM" written on it, a dozen swastikas running along the top of the page and the bottom. It screamed out, "*YOU Must Stop the Renazification of Germany*."[13]

The Jewish War Veterans (JWV) took up this issue as well, and in 1949 urged the creation of a Senate investigating committee. It decried "resurgent German nationalism" and "the German problem" and suggested that "every JWV community meeting on the German problem should be given maximum publicity in your community press. Where feasible, efforts should be made to obtain public service radio time for round table discussions, etc. Newspapers should be invited to send reporters to every JWV meeting at which *The Nuremburg Trials*, a film made by the Jewish War Veterans, is shown."[14]

In 1951, the rabbis of the Conservative movement "went on record as viewing with apprehension the resurgence of chauvinism and its concomitant anti-Semitism in Western Germany." The rabbis, a patriotic group in the main, went further and expressed themselves to be "particularly uneasy over the current American policy of building a strong Germany," fearful that strengthening it without "the proper precautions" might easily lead to "the revival of German militarism."[15]

NCRAC, the closest body American Jewry had that could claim to represent a communal consensus, had called for the total denazification of Germany, its democratization and demilitarization. NCRAC sent a copy of this resolution to the president and the secretaries of State and Defense, demanding that the United States "take steps necessary for the revival of a democratic Germany." NCRAC's resolution reflected its awareness that "there are currently in Germany tendencies toward the revival of a way of life which was responsible for the greatest human holocaust in recorded history."[16]

The American Jewish Committee did not belong to NCRAC but engaged in the same kind of action, employing similar rhetoric as to the living legacy of Nazism in the Federal Republic of Germany. Delegations from the AJC met with senators, bringing with them copies of resolutions the group had adopted on the need for stemming the resurgence of Nazism, and every issue of its American Jewish Year Book provided in exquisite details facts about the reentry of Nazis into public life, commutations of sentences against Nazi officials, manifestations of anti-Semitism in West Germany, publication of Nazi-type material, and utterances in public that justified Hitler's actions.[17] In 1952, the American Jewish Committee issued a thirty-seven-page report that wondered "whether post-war Germany will become a truly democratic state or will revert to Nazism." In 1957, as part of its fiftieth-anniversary deliberations, among many resolutions, the AJC passed one on West Germany, which recognized that Germany would not, for a long time, be just one among the nations of the world. German "political developments," the resolution declared, "will be subject to the test of history," and among those troubling signs it saw "revivals of Nazi and totalitarian ideologies," against which it hoped the government in Bonn would provide "unfaltering vigilance."[18]

By the late 1950s, one way the American Jewish Committee attempted to act on this concern involved a project that began to systematically examine the curricula of German schools. Concerned by the failure of German educators to inform the rising generation of the evils that had been perpetrated by the Third Reich against the Jews, the AJC took it upon itself to do the work that it considered to be the responsibility of the West German government.[19]

Work on denazification, or the lack thereof, saw American Jewish community groups reaching out to other Americans as they sought allies in the large, liberal community. The Jewish Community Council of Boston devoted several meetings to "the deterioration of American policy on denazification in Germany" and wanted to "bring this community's influence to bear on our government in Washington toward the end of reordering our policy in Germany." Hardly able to do much on its own, it created a nonsectarian committee as "the best vehicle for achieving our objective." Council leaders called on Albert Sprague Coolidge, a former congressman from Pittsfield, Massachusetts; Professor Fayette Taylor of the Massachusetts

Institute of Technology; a professor of Christian ethics at Boston University, Walter Muelder; Harvard geologist Kirtley Mather; and the Reverend William Rice of Wellesley to join them. Each had been involved in other progressive causes and represented the local liberal elite, a fine set of coalition partners to help the Jewish Community Council of Boston take on the U.S. government's lax policy in policing resurgent Nazism in Germany. The council tried, unsuccessfully, to enlist a former commander of the statewide American Legion and Boston's newest congressman, John F. Kennedy. The council cast its net widely and as a body met with Harvard historian Arthur Schlesinger and Congressman John McCormack. One member contacted the state board of Americans for Democratic Action, which agreed to petition its national office on this matter. The Boston Jewish Community Council organized, finally, a mass meeting and placed in the local newspapers a statement "with as many signatures as possible."[20]

The issue of denazification and the role of the United States in turning a blind eye to it, by definition, forced American Jews to communicate with government officials. They did not just complain quietly among themselves. Adolph Held, president of the Jewish Labor Committee, sent an impassioned letter to Secretary John Foster Dulles in 1955, protesting the presence of vendors who sold "outspoken Nazi literature" at the Frankfurt Book Fair. "We were deeply shocked," wrote the chair of the Jewish Labor Committee, "that our government did not publicly protest to the fact that there are more than 20 West German publishing firms which issue, almost exclusively, memoirs of former leading Nazis, literature glorifying the barbarous acts of the Nazis." What gave Held and his organization the authority to lodge this protest? "The death stench," he wrote, "of the 6,000,000 Jews ... who perished in the concentration camps has not yet evaporated from the memories of those who have survived."[21]

Young American Jews got involved as well, and although they lacked such political contacts, they, too, wanted to be heard. In the summers of 1949 and 1950, representatives of a variety of Jewish youth movements spanning the cultural, political, and religious sentiments of American Jewry gathered at Camp Wel-Met in Narrowsburg, New York, for the Assembly of the National Jewish Youth Conference. These high school students passed a series of resolutions demonstrating the range of their concerns. In both years, they sent petitions to the Senate of the United States about Germany. They demanded in 1949 that the Senate "quickly establish its proposed committee to investigate the resurgence of Nazism in Germany" since "the resurgence of Nazism appears to continue unabated." If the senators in Washington wondered why these teenagers cared so much about Germany, the young Jews laid it all out in their 1950 petition. We, they intoned, "again call upon the government of the United States to do everything in its power to check the resurgence of a force which not only was responsible for launching a devastating war but for the murder of 6 million Jews, American war prisoners, and millions of all nations."[22]

American Jewish discourse at the end of the 1950s differed little from that of ten years earlier, and as anti-Jewish incidents occurred in Germany, American Jewry reacted. *Furrows*, the publication of Habonim, noted in 1959, in just one of a long string of statements on the resurgence of anti-Semitism in Germany, that "there is no need to express this publication's attitude toward Germany." But it did so anyhow: "We will never forget the murder of six million of our brethren at the hands of the Nazi brutes." The youth movement magazine noted that if "the German people" "realized their crimes against humanity [and] rid themselves of Nazi influences," they might "finally build a democracy." As far as these young American Jews saw it, Germans "are merely upset that" Hitler had lost the war for them, and they believed that "many Nazi officers maintain positions in local and state governments."[23]

Each year, something happened in Germany or some matter came up relating to relations between the United States and Germany that stoked the fires of American Jewish anger against the country. Each incident gave them an opportunity to tell, once more, about the catastrophe and Germany's role. Each incident inspired them to demand that the United States cease what they viewed as its coddling of Germany and its deliberate effacing of Germany's role in the perpetration of the Holocaust. When in 1950 the United States began discussing the rearmament of western-sector Germany in anticipation of an expected Soviet invasion, American Jewry reacted widely and swiftly. Chicago's various branches of the American Jewish Congress called an Emergency Public Conference in January 1950, and by featuring a survivor of Bergen-Belsen, Samuel Weintraub, to speak on the matter, the Congress publicly linked its concern about the present in Germany with the recent tragic history of Germany and the Jews.[24] American Jewish youth organizations launched their own discussions on the matter of putting weapons in the hands of German soldiers. *Furrows* characterized its position as "reluctant realism" in a symposium in its pages. On the premise that "German rearmament, in the final analysis, may become a realistic necessity," it declared that, "as Jews, we are unable to endorse it, for we cannot forget that it was Germany which destroyed European Jewry."[25]

Statements issued by Jewish organizations, articles in the Jewish press, lectures delivered at gatherings, and sermons all articulated some variant of this "reluctant realism" position. Groups further to the left, Communist-oriented ones and their publications, to be sure, took a harder line, largely echoing the stance of the Soviet Union, which occupied the eastern part of Germany. These Jewish groups questioned the morality of rebuilding western Germany. Mainstream Jewish organizations, however, laced their passionate language of mourning and pain with practical suggestions about the status of Germany. Germany, they declared in press releases, symposia, articles, sermons, and meetings, had to rid itself of Nazis and vestiges of Nazism. Its people had to be reeducated, and it had to admit its guilt because it had to be able to pay monetarily for its crimes.

Of all the matters involving Germany and the legacy of the Holocaust, American Jews discussed most widely and felt most intensely about restitution to the Jewish people. It surfaced as a communal concern when the U.S. occupation gave way to the newly created Federal Republic of Germany in 1949. That government entered into an arrangement with the Jewish world on the debt it owed to the Jewish people. In September 1951, Chancellor Konrad Adenauer addressed the Bundestag, acknowledging "the great suffering brought to the Jews in Germany and in the occupied territories in the era of National Socialism" and announcing the successful conclusion of discussions about financial payments to the Jewish people. Adenauer's speech unleashed a torrent of American Jewish words and programming. In his speech, while he owned up to the outrages perpetrated by the German government, stating forthrightly that "in the name of the German people . . . unspeakable crimes were committed which require moral and material restitution," he simultaneously proclaimed that most Germans had abhorred the Nazis' policies toward the Jews.[26] This provided American Jewish publications, whether in English, Yiddish, or Hebrew, an opportunity to condemn the German past, raise suspicions about its present, and express some tentative hopes about the future.

Most asserted that Adenauer's formulation of accepting responsibility and asserting the innocence of most Germans amounted to "whitewashing their sins, and performing an easy act of contrition." *Der Tog* editorialized the week after the address in the Bundestag in a piece titled "The German *Al Hayt*" (for the sin), referring to the prayer of contrition intoned by Jews on the Day of Atonement in which they confess their sins of the past year.

Declaring Adenauer's speech "the most important piece of German political rhetoric since the passage of the Nuremberg laws," the writer for *Der
Tog* faulted Adenauer's claim that most Germans had hated the crimes
committed in their name. The article argued simply that, had that been
true, Hitler would have never come to power. But the editorial continued.
The speech constituted a first step toward repentance, of which Jews understood two kinds existed. One form ushered in the doing of good deeds;
another, once articulated, got forgotten, and the sinner reverted to sinning.
The article ended with an uncertain but possible glimmer of hope, that Adenauer and the German people would follow the first path toward redemption. *Congress Bi-Weekly* greeted the speech with "mingled feelings." Despite the unanimous vote by the German parliament, "nothing the legatees
of Hitler's Germany will say or do can ever heal the grievous wounds inflicted on the Jewish people by the Nazi predecessors." Jews, "a people with
a highly developed sense of history, . . . will forever remember the wanton
destruction by Germans of a third of its human resources and the richest
reservoir of its spiritual strength." Like *Der Tog*, *Congress Bi-Weekly* choked
on Adenauer's declaration that the majority of Germans had despised Hitler's policies, speculating, "it remains to be seen what practical steps the
Western Government will take to translate its liberal professions into concrete realities." Real repentance will happen only if it takes actions that will
"bring a measure of justice to the principal victim of the Nazi regime." *Jewish Frontier* featured an article by Mordecai Shtrigler, a journalist and a survivor in Paris. "Frankly," he shared with the readers of the American magazine, "I am not very impressed. We have always known, and gladly admitted, that even under the Hitler regime there were thousands of Germans
who opposed the Nazis. Some of these Germans were at liberty and did
whatever they could. . . . A greater proportion were in the prisons and concentration camps. . . . We never denied that there were such Germans, but
the fact remains that they did not represent the collective face of the German people." Shtrigler dissected the details of the reparations agreement,
found them unimpressive, and chided Jews for their "urge to represent the
reparations agreement with Germany as a Jewish triumph." "Negotiations
with Germany had been unavoidable," wrote Shtrigler, but "the still fresh
Jewish sorrow over the fate of the six million should have found expression
in a more subdued reception of the results of the negotiation."[27]

In 1951, after West German Chancellor Konrad Adenauer offered his
statement about Germany's crimes against the Jews, the American Jewish
Committee reflected on his words in a documentary study it conducted on

The Recent Growth of Neo-Nazism in Europe. While the book examined all of Europe, Germany lay at its heart, and the AJC declared that "we cannot, of course, consider the Adenauer declaration to be anything more than a significant first step toward Germany's assumption of its moral and legal responsibilities for the unparalleled crime committed by the Third Reich against the Jews of Europe. . . . It now remains for the German people to make the spirit and letter of Chancellor Adenauer's words a reality."[28]

American Jews who had participated officially in the negotiations shared with the public their impressions of the process and its larger meaning. All used the occasion to justify the new reality, retelling details about the tragic history that had made restitutions necessary. Adolph Held of the Jewish Labor Committee had a particular stake in pointing out the positive implications of the negotiations' outcome. His organization sat at the bargaining table and had used its extensive contacts with the Social Democrats in the Bundestag to ensure the unanimous vote. With readers of the *New Leader,* a liberal anti-Communist magazine not published under Jewish auspices, he shared his emotions on the completion of the agreement and what it had meant to him to sit down with the Germans. "It is not easy to evaluate an historic event," he wrote, and "this is especially true when you are a participant" but even more so "when that event is underscored by deep emotion." He could not forget that "Adolf Hitler and his Nazi hordes . . . have achieved a catalogue of atrocities . . . in the main . . . aimed against the Jewish communities of Europe." Reflecting his anti-Communist *bona fides,* Held noted that Hitler had been "abetted during the Nazi-Soviet Pact by the Kremlin," but the Germans with whom he and the other Jewish leaders had hammered out the restitution agreement bore the sole blame for the truth that "not just human lives, crushed or cremated, but whole communities . . . were smashed. More than six million Jews were wiped out of the communities of Europe." That had been the historical reality against which "the Conference on Jewish Material Claims Against Germany was held."[29]

Bernard Bamberger of the Synagogue Council of America, also a participant in the negotiations, announced the position of his rabbinical body and sent a copy of its statement to the Secretary of State, John Foster Dulles, in 1952. The statement he forwarded to the press and to Washington made Germany's history central: "No mere financial reparation could ever compensate for the wanton extermination of six million human beings and the liquidation of great communities." But, and the same "but" followed in nearly all pronouncements, articles, speeches, sermons, and

radio programs, "the assumption by the German nation of some responsibility to the survivors of the Nazi persecution" went a distance toward
Germany's "desire to regain an honorable place among the nations." The
American Jewish Congress, also a party to the negotiations, justified its actions, reporting that the agreement struck between the various American
Jewish organizations, Israel, and Bonn over restitutions for the "vast material damage inflicted by the Hitler regime upon the Jews of Europe" had
been "undertaken not under duress" by the Germans, which exhibited a
"token of the genuine desire of the Germans to redress in some measure
the wrongs *they* committed against the Jewish people" (emphasis added).
Lest the Congress's words be construed as evidence that it wanted to let
the legacy of the past be swept away and that it wanted to decouple present-day Germany from the Holocaust, it declared, "no money payment by
Germany can atone for the millions of Jewish dead or heal the wounds for
the living."

A few phrases, then, from a single article encapsulated the American
Jewish engagement with Germany in the postwar period. Germany had
behaved in a horrendous manner to the Jewish people. That could not and
would not be erased. But the Federal Republic of Germany had to be contended with, and in this case, as far as the American Jewish Congress saw
it, it had done the right thing, albeit "partially and inadequately."[30]

American Jews beyond the leadership level engaged with this issue and
felt it viscerally. The extent of its treatment in the press and the number of
community meetings organized to explore its implications—to express the
prevalent mixture of great pain, a bit of hope, realism, and a sense of inevi-
tability—attested to that concern. Leaders of the organizations discerned
broad community interest in the issue. A fieldworker for the Jewish Labor
Committee reported to the national office after a visit to Sheboygan, Wisconsin: "The Jews" there, he informed headquarters, "are much concerned
with Israel . . . with German reparations."[31]

Concern about restitutions deepened because it conjoined the Holocaust with Israel, which had occupied a key place in the talks of the Claims
Conference, and received the bulk of the money pledged by West Germany. While many American Jews declared that they did not want Germany's "blood money," they recognized that those funds would subsidize
the staggering cost borne by the new state for the settlement of Holocaust
survivors and would hasten its economic development. This meant that
support for Israel and a willingness to accept the agreement operated in
tandem. One commentator, Reform rabbi Balfour Brickner, expressed a

widely shared feeling, in a coda to an *Eternal Light* radio drama on the subject of forgiveness: "Having innocently suffered at the hands of the world, forgiveness becomes a serious problem for the Jew. It is one thing not to forget and another thing not to forgive. Jews can never forget what the Nazis did to decimate six million of our people. But we cannot go on endlessly bearing hatred. It is in the spirit of our faith that the State of Israel and the people of Israel reconciled themselves to the acceptance of compensation from the German state in order to build Israel's economy."[32]

The range of positions expressed by American Jews as to how to engage with Germany, in light of the Holocaust, took part of its shape from the fact of Israel's role.[33] A debate raged in the pages of the Jewish press over what kind of relationship should, or should not, develop between Germany and Israel. However much they recognized the crucial need for the restitution money and the justice involved in the Jewish people extracting a monetary claim from the Germans, it galled many that Israel, their embodiment of redemption, engaged with Germany, their embodiment of evil. A 1951 article in *Jewish Spectator* predicted, and not happily, that an inexorable process had been set in motion in Israel: "Today—a concert in German; tomorrow trade with the Germans; and the day after—the approval of political relations," wrote Trude Weiss-Rosmarin. She dreaded the prospect that Israel would inch toward a policy whereby it would treat Germany like it would any other country because it occupied a category onto itself.[34]

Germany as news agitated the American Jewish world. The proper role of Israel toward Germany; the trials of high-ranking Nazi officials; plans by the United States to rearm Germany beginning as early as 1949; the continuing needs of the Jews who had remained in Germany; by the early 1960s, the chronologically linked phenomena of the reappearance of anti-Semitic groups in Germany, the "swastika epidemic" which began in Cologne and then spread around the world, and the arrest, trial, and execution in Israel of Adolf Eichmann—all caused American Jews to reiterate Germany's crimes and recall the Holocaust.

Articles and sermons on the Nuremberg trials (1945–1949), for example, detailed the court proceedings and related them back in time to the crimes perpetrated against the Jews, regardless of the fact that the "war crimes" trials only indirectly addressed Germany's slaughter of the Jews. Ben Halpern, writing for *Jewish Frontier* in late 1945 on the impending trials, believed that "the punishment of the leaders of an aggressor government . . . will mean at least, that the legal conscience of mankind is not completely dead," and since "all Germans share some guilt" for the events of the past decade, "getting the plot to exterminate the Jewish People in the Nuremberg indictment represents a moral victory for the Jews."[35]

In 1951, the youth of Habonim reacted angrily to the commutation of death sentences handed down against eighty-nine Nazi war criminals. In an article titled "A Feather in Hitler's Cap," the editors of *Furrows* expressed themselves quite openly: "Our human instincts and our Jewish consciousness want to cry out against this vile travesty . . . this disgusting 'leniency' to butchers and sadists." The sad truth about this reversal of justice meant to Habonim that "in whatever world Hitler and Goebbels reside, they must be having a hearty laugh."[36] That same year, Trude Weiss-Rosmarin expressed nothing but contempt for the pardoning of industrialist Alfred Krupp along with two dozen other Nazis, previously convicted and sent to prison. "The Nazi past," she wrote, "is not dead; it reaches out into the present and is feverishly at work building a 'Fourth Reich.'" To her, unlike President Eisenhower, whom she quoted on this matter, "bygones are not bygones."[37]

So it went on throughout the 1950s and into the 1960s, as trials, convictions, sentencing, and then, in many cases, pardons and releases of former Nazis in Germany made Jewish news in America and spurred communal reaction. The Eichmann affair, beginning with his apprehension in 1960 by agents of the Mossad, Israel's secret service, the trial that took place in Jerusalem, and his execution in 1962 produced a tidal wave of American Jewish writings, community programming, and public work not only to explain what Israel had done and why but also to retell the story of Germany's guilt.[38] Harry Golden provided a foreword to a hastily printed paperback book, *The Case Against Adolf Eichmann*, brought to market in 1960 by Signet Books for the New American Library, only four months after Israel's capture of the Nazi in Argentina. Golden squarely put the blame for Eichmann's crimes on all Germans. "What can we say," he asked, "to Herr Eichmann who carried out the orders of the Nazis to kill six million Jews in the twentieth century? What can we say of the Germans who empowered him?" Other nations besides Germany had a hand, admitted Golden, enabling Germany to accomplish its goal of killing the Jews. But "the Germans in the 1930s . . . persuaded Europe to turn its back on the pleas of the Jews," and the Germans "shaved the heads of these Jews to use the hair for mattresses; they pulled out the gold fillings of their teeth to send to the *Reichsbank*; they gathered up the toys of the Jewish children for use in the Nazi winter drive." The blame adhered to the German people, and Golden declared that "Germany today cannot be called a nation or a culture. It is only an economy." In conclusion, he noted, "Germany has always been torn between Beethoven and Hitler, between Goethe and Eichmann. But it is Eichmann who stands as the Nazi representative in the dock and when he pleads his case the Germans and Europeans must remember him before they find the memories of Goethe and Beethoven."[39]

In their public expressions in print and in community programming, American Jews squarely made the connection between Eichmann, the six million, and Germany's culpability. Boris Smolar's syndicated column appeared in local and national Jewish newspapers, and in January 1961 he speculated that "the forthcoming trial" might educate the world about the crimes perpetrated by the Germans against the Jews. He found this prospect compelling, given that "some efforts have been made recently by Germans to disprove the historicity of the execution by the Nazis of 6,000,000 Jews. . . . It is feared that . . . scholarly books may even appear giving a more pallid version of Hitler's 'final solution' of the Jewish problem. . . . And it now becomes more and more clear that, only when the trial of Eichmann is held in Israel, will the enormity of the Nazi crimes against Jews be securely established."[40] Similarly, in April 1961, as they did every year, members of the Labor Zionist Organization in Chicago came together to hold a Third Seder. They wrote the trial into their *haggadah*, making it central to their communal celebration. "Who Knows Twelve?" read the printed text, the familiar words of the holiday table song; "I know twelve! Twelve is the twelfth year of Medinat Yisrael [the State of Israel]." The hundreds of assembled Chicago Labor Zionists then together read aloud in unison, "On May 23rd of 1960 David Ben Gurion, Premier of Israel rose quietly from his place in the Knesset and said: I have to inform Parliament that a short time ago one of the greatest Nazi war criminals, Adolf Eichmann, who was responsible together with the Nazi leaders for what they called 'the final solution of the Jewish question,' namely the extermination of six million Jews . . . was found by Israeli security services."[41]

American Jews' interest in postwar Germany reflected their demand for justice in the memory of the six million. They also paid attention to it because some Jews lived there, survivors of the Holocaust, whom the Jews of the United States considered their responsibility. As early as August 1943, before the tide of the war had turned favorably enough toward the Allies to make predictions of Germany's defeat seem certain, the American Jewish Committee's Institute on Peace and Post-War Problems issued a study guide on the future of Jews in a vanquished Germany. While it did not envision a "mass return of Jews to Germany . . . it is likely that some may wish to go back. . . . Some . . . may want to return in order to regain their property. Others, identified with German culture, life and politics, may wish to participate in the introduction of a new social order. Still others believe that the absence of Jews from Germany would be a victory for Hitler after his defeat."[42] The compilers of the study guide rightly predicted Hitler's defeat but could not predict that at the end of war some Jews, mostly of Polish origin, who had been in the Displaced Persons camps, would decide to stay on in Germany.

Their presence on German soil fueled American Jewish discussions about resurgent anti-Semitism, giving them a particular urgency, and became the subject of much communal wrangling. Writing for the monthly magazine of the National Council of Jewish Women in 1957, an officer of its Pittsburgh chapters, "Mrs. Milton K. Sussman," shared her impressions of a journey she had taken to Germany on a fact-finding mission to assess the condition of the Jews there. She told of her encounters with the Jews in their small, struggling communities. "Notwithstanding the feelings of anguish, of hatred, of tragedy, and with a full realization of what it must mean for a Jew to live in Germany," she wrote after describing her own tears and the "sobbing which overcame" her as she walked around Dachau and Bergen-Belsen, "I cannot help but wish that again there be a strong Jewish community in Germany. . . . I am emotional enough to want to prove to the world and Germany, in particular, the indomitable spirit and the indestructibility of the Jew," thus stating the idea that a thriving Jewish community in Germany would be part of the Jews' revenge on Hitler.[43]

Others took a very different position. In a 1950 article attacking the restitution agreement as "blood money," poet Hayim Leivik declaimed that Jews should never dwell within Germany's borders, on principle. To remain there constituted an affront to the memory of the victims of the Holocaust. A number of Jewish gatherings and meetings from the late 1940s onward discussed the moral dilemma posed by a continued Jewish presence in Germany in light of the catastrophe. The National Federation of Temple Sisterhoods created a packet of materials for group meetings, which several of its chapters scheduled, for a "Congregational Town Hall Discussion" on "Should Jews Return to Germany?" leaving Sisterhood members to decide on the best course of action for German Jews. The American Jewish Congress's Chicago branches held a citywide symposium in 1950 on this subject. One speaker proposed a resolution in the name of the Jews of the United States to call "upon our fellow Jews to leave

Germany," a place which "only yesterday has been the charnel house of six million Jews." The resolution passed with only one dissenter, who "questioned the competence of Chicago Jewry to advise the Jews of Germany about anything," in particular, on where they ought to live.[44]

The debate over the appropriateness of Jews' living in Germany had no practical implications as Jews in postwar Germany made their decisions according to their own needs and proclivities. But American Jews— in the press, in meeting halls, and on the lecture circuit—worried about them because they believed a new Nazi-type Germany lay just around the corner. The American Jewish Committee, for example, reviewed surveys conducted in Germany in 1953 on the legacy of Nazism in the postwar present and expressed grave worry over the fact that 42 percent of those polled "considered that there had been more good than evil in Nazism."[45] German Jews would suffer from this. In addition, the Germans, never having really shed their Nazi sympathies, would export their venom to other places. At the beginning of the postwar period, American Jewry worried that "boys and men with the Army of occupation in Germany may return home infected with anti-Semitism caught from the Germans with whom they had been fraternizing," thus conveying to American soil the virus of Germany's anti-Jewish sentiments.[46] By the end of the next decade, their fears seemed to be substantiated. In December 1959, swastikas appeared on tombstones in the Jewish cemetery in Cologne, then spread across Germany, splattered onto Jewish buildings, and within weeks vandals painted the hated symbol on Jewish edifices around the world, including in the United States.

American Jews referred to this vandalism as a "swastika epidemic," and it hardly surprised them that the outbreak began in Germany. At the national level, Jewish organizations produced fact sheets and press releases and assembled meetings and task forces to track the swastikas and explore the appeal of the Nazi-inspired vandalism to American teenagers. They spoke of Germany as the incubator of the crisis, and Jewish community councils in Washington, Cincinnati, and Pittsburgh, as well as local chapters of the American Jewish Congress and the Anti-Defamation League, began to discuss the need to teach "the true facts about Nazism . . . and its bestial atrocities" in American public schools. Achieving this goal could not be accomplished by Jews alone, and, in fact, they made no progress in convincing public school officials of the urgency of this project. Fail as they did, they still made it clear that Germany's history of the mass murder of Jews ought to be part of the common American culture.[47]

Because of the intensity of American Jews' reaction to present-day Germany as the heir to the Germany of Hitler and the Holocaust, they expressed strongly negative feelings about Jews' traveling to the tainted land. In 1953, Norman Salit of the Synagogue Council went to Germany with an interfaith delegation to confer with Chancellor Adenauer. He also met with "the Jewish religious and communal leaders" in West Germany "to obtain a clear picture of how the Jewish communities of the Bonn Republic are managing their religious problems." He even met with leaders of the small Jewish community in East Berlin.[48] Despite his rabbinical position and the purposes of his trip, which included making contact with the Jews of both Germanies and their small struggling communities, a stream of angry letters from the Jewish public flooded his mailbox, questioning his motives and deriding his naivete, particularly after he held a press conference on his return praising Adenauer. "You might not know that you . . . are being used by the Germans in their propaganda drive to establish themselves as a pure and innocent people who never did harm to anyone," one letter writer wrote. Salit had been duped by the Germans, who now claimed that "the 6 million Jews that were killed by the Germans marched to the gas chambers voluntarily and any atrocities are fairy tales today." How could Salit, a rabbi, the letter writer continued, go about "shaking the hand of the German chancellor—the same hand that shook the hands of war criminals who killed thousands . . . millions of Jews."[49]

This kind of recrimination typified American Jewish discourse. Boris Smolar questioned the 1954 visit of Anti-Defamation League officials to Germany on the invitation of the government, and various Washington Jews criticized the executive director of the local Jewish Community Council, Isaac Franck, for his 1957 trip, a journey he admitted he had undertaken with "mixed feelings." Like so many participants in these Jewish delegations, he had been invited by the government, combining official meetings with opportunities "to learn what had been happening to the German Jewish community" and with a goal of seeing if, in fact, "democratization" had made any progress.[50]

Despite such heated words, American Jewish organizations sponsored "official" visits to Germany. Much of the work undertaken by these missions focused on the reparations, the failures and successes in denazification, outbreaks of anti-Semitism in Germany, Germany's relationship to Israel, the failure of German schools to educate its youth on the horrors perpetrated by the Third Reich, and the condition of German Jewry. Reports sent back and debriefings conducted after returning to America then became the subjects of organizational meetings and articles in newsletters and bulletins and in the Jewish press. These all made manifest American Jews' interest in the "German" problem and their belief that Germany's history under Hitler deeply influenced postwar West Germany.[51]

Typical of this interest, the B'nai B'rith sent a ten-person delegation in the summer of 1960, part of "an unprecedented exchange program of youth leaders and human rights experts concerned with the problem of democracy." The fifty-page report generated by the trip became part of the organization's work. It began with a foreword that told in no uncertain terms why the mission had been undertaken, how much the Holocaust lived in the consciousness of the organization, and the degree to which Germany as perpetrator agitated it. Alexander Miller, author of the report, set the stage:

> On Friday evening, members of the B'nai B'rith mission to Germany attended services at the Pestalozzi Street Synagogue in Berlin. Left in shambles by Nazi sympathizers on Crystal Night, wrecked by allied bombs, this edifice has been restored by the West Berlin government. As you enter the house of worship, your eye is caught by a stone table above the door. Its graven message is simple:
>
> In Memoriam
> Six Millionen Tote
> 1939–1945

Had he been a historian, Miller might have wondered why 1939 rather than 1933 had been chiseled on the stone and why the word "Jews" had been left off. But the words moved him and the other delegates deeply: "The message on the memorial tablet hung over our heads throughout our stay in Germany. It added emotional overtones to each interview, serving as an unseen visitor at every conference. It lay behind our every question. It caused nagging doubts and suspicions about the answers and the answerers." Before ending his report, Miller described the delegation's last stop, a "Visit to Dachau." "We dreaded the visit," he confessed, "yet felt impelled to make it."[52]

Miller's articulated "dread" of Germany, juxtaposed against his sense of being "impelled" to deal with it, corresponded neatly with the broad base of American Jewish communal response to the country that so recently had destroyed most of European Jewry. If they could have blotted it out of their minds, they no doubt would have, but they could not. World events pushed them toward engaging with Germany.

All this took place in the context of a postwar geopolitical reality in which the United States and the Soviet Union faced each other in a cold war of nerves and propaganda. Germany occupied a central place in that clash. The United States became the supporter of and advocate for the Federal Republic of Germany. The United States went to great lengths to revive the economy of its German client state, buttress its government, and portray it as having shed its Nazi past. After the Soviet blockade of Berlin in 1948, West Germany, America's strategic ally, emerged in American popular thinking as the beacon of democracy in central Europe, most of which lay in the Soviet orbit. The Soviet Union, on the other hand, had occupied Germany from the east, and its client state, the German Democratic Republic, served its political and propaganda interests.[53]

In the main, Americans identified the struggle between the United States and the Soviet Union, and the contrast between West Germany and East, in terms of a conflict between good and evil. American political culture took for granted this bifurcation of the world between democracy and godless Communism, and every medium in operation held up the specter of a rapacious Communist menace eager and able to deprive all "freedom-loving people," even Americans, of their liberties. In that world, Germany, divided between "red" Communism and freedom, functioned as a crucial battleground. From the days of the Berlin Airlift until the 1961 erection of the Berlin Wall, East Germany, the Soviet Union's surrogate, menaced West Germany in American rhetoric.

American Jews, with the exception of the shrinking number of Communists, had little regard for the Soviet Union and spent much of the postwar period fretting over the fate of its Jews. But they refused to buy into the regnant thinking that by and large expunged most of West Germany's Nazi past from public consideration. As American Jewry saw it, at least as expressed in mainstream publications, the struggle between the Soviet Union and the United States over Germany boded ill for the future and stymied the process by which those responsible for the Holocaust would ever have to truly admit their guilt. The *American Jewish Year Book* of 1953 summarized the general communal position: "The growing competition for Germany's military potential between the Western Powers and the Soviet Union has inevitably resulted in a strengthening of national self-confidence and the influence of nationalist and militarist elements, and to some extent of Nazi elements."[54]

However much American Jews concurred with public opinion about Stalin and then Khrushchev as bloody dictators of a totalitarian USSR, which denied its millions of Jews freedom of conscience as Jews, they continued to hammer away at Germany as the legatee of Hitlerism. American Jews doggedly refused to buy into the sanitization of Germany as a newly born ally in the fight against Communism and did not hesitate to name their own government as culpable.

Three small examples can represent this American Jewish reality. In 1955, while the American public accepted the premise that a Communist conspiracy threatened the nation, Harry Schnur, a member of Hashomer Hatzair, a left-wing, although not pro-Soviet, Zionist youth organization, offered in his movement's *Youth and Nation* newsletter his take on Germany, Communism, anti-Communism, and the Jewish catastrophe. "Yesterday's bloodthirsty barbarians," he wrote, "become today's 'gallant allies' in the shifting game of power politics. The world has long since forgiven Germany's crimes against the Jews, . . . and those of us who still harp on these things are accused of harboring resentment and of atrocity-mongering. Apologists tell us that the handful of wicked Nazis whose misdeeds tarnished Hitler's splendid anti-Communist record have been purged . . . and that after all, 'only' a couple of million Jews perished—but then, so did ten million Germans." Schnur told his readers, "The great whitewash is in full swing."[55]

High school student Steve Orlow, president of the Zionist youth group Young Judea, editorialized similarly in his monthly newsletter, the *Senior*, of December 1961 in "Forgive and Forget?" Unlike Hashomer Hatzair, Orlow's group assiduously avoided supporting any political position, had no left-wing leanings whatsoever, and focused its programming exclusively on Zionism. But Orlow sounded very much like Hashomer Hatzair's Schnur and expressed nothing but disgust as "the news media of our nation have been in the midst of a hero-worshipping campaign . . . to some poor, oppressed East German for an act of heroism." In that campaign, "people such as Jack Paar," long-time host of NBC's *Tonight Show,* "whined and sniffled over the tragic plight of the German people and they had nothing but praise for the 'determination and courage' which the Germans show in the face of such hardship." The Jewish high school student writing for his peers found himself "nauseated" at this. "Where," he asked, "were these hero worshippers just twenty years ago when Jewish mothers with their children . . . were carted off to concentration camps and eventually death?" Orlow took on Paar and American public opinion not just for having been silent during the Holocaust but for the fact that they, unlike American Jews, "did not realize that the ones they are making martyrs out of today were perpetrators of the most hideous crime ever committed in history just two decades ago; a crime in which one out of every three of our people perished because they committed the crime of being Jewish." The young Jewish communal activist chided the Germans and their American supporters for ignoring the fact that Hitler and Eichmann, whose trial already was in full swing, had not acted alone. The German people, now the objects of this veneration, "rounded up all those millions of people, marched them into the gas chambers and then pushed the buttons.... The Germans did a most efficient job, and their 'final solution' involved many thousands of Germans who today are alive and in many cases prospering but whose victims are either dead or in many cases scared [probably he meant "scarred"] for life."[56]

Lillian Friedberg, unlike Orlow and Schnur, occupied a sensitive position in the field of Jewish community relations work. She directed the Pittsburgh Jewish Community Council, putting her daily in conversation with public officials, Christian clergy, newspaper editors, educators, and the leaders of local civic institutions, most non-Jews. Unlike the leaders of the youth groups, she needed to measure her words carefully, ever mindful of the public relations implications of what she said. But when it came to Germany, she had no problem in making the Jewish position clear, despite its deviation from the American norm. In 1951, in her annual report on the year's activities, she noted the perverse impact that "the fear of Communism" has had. "We," presumably referring to American Jews, "have been subjected to the shocking spectacle of United States public officials kowtowing to the German populace, where the restoration of Nazis to places of influence is an acknowledged trend." She linked this directly to the Holocaust. "Military expediency," she noted, "wipes out the memory of the most hideous crimes in human history. Under these circumstances, the American Jewish community must feel apprehension and concern."[57]

Germans and Jews in America

Beyond the high drama of the Nazis returning to German public life, trials of Nazi officials, and the restitution agreements, a series of episodes involving Germany and Germans took place in America itself, providing American Jews with opportunities to again discuss Germany's nefarious past as played out in the present. Each consumed American Jewish public life, launching books and articles, press releases, symposia, mass meetings, letters to the editor of local newspapers and national magazines, letters of protest to public officials, radio programs, sermons, and programming for Jewish youth groups and clubs. Each exposed fault lines within the Jewish communities as to the "right" and the appropriate reaction, with each side acknowledging the imperative to respond but sparring over what constituted a fitting response. Each episode loosed a torrent of commentary on the inseparable bond between postwar Germany and the brutal deaths of the six million, making this avalanche of commentary itself memorials to the victims of the Holocaust.

Different segments of American Jewry reacted to particular reminders of the Holocaust embodied in postwar Germans and Germany, played out on American soil. In 1949, the American Federation of Polish Jews, a group to the left of the American Jewish spectrum, organized a picket line in front of the RCA building in New York to protest an exposition of German goods made by German manufacturers, organized by the U.S. government. To this Jewish organization, "a promotion of German wares is an insult . . . to American citizens whose relatives have made up most of the 6 million Polish Jews slaughtered, gassed and burned alive by the Nazis. People who mourn the loss of 6,000,000 of their brothers cannot be expected to support the industrial enterprises of the perpetrators." Picketers carried signs reading, "Six million Jewish men, women and children tortured, killed, gassed and burned alive by the Germans in Europe. Shall we forget and forgive???" and "Restoration of German industry will lead straight to new Death Camps and Gas Chambers." NCRAC and various other mainline groups opposed the pickets and the public disruption.[58]

In 1954 and 1955, various local and national Jewish organizations, particularly the community councils and the affiliates of NCRAC, reacted strongly to scheduled performances in the United States of the Berlin Philharmonic under the baton of Herbert von Karajan, in the words of the Jewish Labor Committee's press release, "a notorious Nazi."[59] In its statement to the press, the JLC called on the West German government to recall the orchestra and dismiss von Karajan and orchestra members "who have been affiliated with the Nazis," noting that, "while millions of Jews perished in the crematoria of the Gestapo, while many thousands of anti-Nazis, Jewish and non-Jewish, from Germany's musical and other cultural life were forced to flee from Nazi tyranny or were deported to Gestapo-run concentration camps, it was Herr von Karajan who helped Goebbels and Goering prostitute German cultural pursuits and condoned the murder and imprisonment of Jews."[60]

The Berlin Philharmonic issue agitated the Jewish communities in Washington, D.C., Boston, Baltimore, Detroit, Hartford, and elsewhere. Different factions, even within the same organization, offered different ideas about what kind of protest they should mount in light of the great acclaim of the conductor who had performed for the highest-ranking officials of Hitler's regime. Some called for pickets. Some thought letters to editors of the major newspapers might raise the consciousness of the general public, and others considered the possibility of convincing the management of the concert venues to cancel the contracts. But all agreed, in the words of Boston's *Jewish Times* of March 10, 1955, "It is not too far or out of line to imagine that if Hitler had won the war, perhaps" the orchestra and von Karajan would "be leading this same orchestra in Boston's Symphony Hall and probably two of the numbers would be the 'Horst Wessel Song' and 'Deutschland Uber Alles.'"[61]

In 1951, American Jewish organizations made much of the Hollywood movie *The Desert Fox*, a laudatory film about Field Marshall Erwin Rommel, which, as they saw it, lamented that a crazed Hitler with no tactical skills had stymied the brilliance of the "desert fox." Had Hitler not interfered with Rommel, he might have led his troops to victory rather than defeat in North Africa. The American Jewish Congress issued an "Action Bulletin" in November: "It appears that Americans are prepared to write off the Nazi holocaust as the unhappy work of a lunatic, and to cloak the infamy of Hitler's generals with the mantle of courage and good will." The Chicago branch of the Congress suggested that members "1. Call upon the Owner of your neighborhood theatre and a. Urge him not to show this motion picture! b. Protest if he is already showing it! 2. Write your protest to the maker of the film; Spyros Skouras, Twentieth Century Fox."[62]

Postwar American Jewish community groups paid close attention to the activities of German American groups, seeing them as defenders of Nazism and supporters of Hitler's memory. Jewish publications and defense organizations paid much attention to "the old pro-German groups" that functioned in the postwar period "under the guise of German-relief societies." The *American Jewish Year Book*, the community councils, the American Jewish Congress, and the Anti-Defamation League ferreted out and reported on publications, rallies, manifestoes, speeches, and other kinds of anti-Jewish material, regardless of their sources. These organizations gave particular attention to the "German Groups," which they considered as a category unto themselves. The 1950 *Year Book* included a special heading under "Anti-Jewish Agitation" for the work of "German Groups," describing their publications and meetings and detailing how "A. O. Tittman's Voters' Alliance for Americans of German Ancestry held a small meeting in a restaurant" and "Leonard Enders' Organized Americans of German Ancestry in Chicago . . . met regularly and issued a monthly bulletin."[63]

In a 1947 survey of anti-Semitism in the United States, the Anti-Defamation League noted that the "German papers," meaning the German American papers, "were particularly vehement" in linking Jews to Communism and making money—the old canards—but also "that Jews exaggerate Nazi atrocities and spread hatred of the German people to further their own ends." In 1955, the Chicago council of the American Jewish Congress informed its members that, among its activities, it had "investigated the background of a German-American language newspaper . . . the Deutsch-Amerikanische Burger-Zeitung. Several columns in this paper are notorious . . . particularly in reference to German relations with the Jewish people. Particularly prominent are repeated stories about 'the myth' of six million Jews killed by Hitler."[64]

While, in retrospect, the groups and their activities may seem trivial and exaggerated, they nonetheless reflected the deep association in the American Jewish imagination between Germans, the brutal reality of the six million, and the obligation they felt to defend the memory of the victims. By exposing pro-Nazi rhetoric in a German social club or showing that a German group, however obscure, claimed that the Holocaust had not happened, these Jewish organizations, which saw themselves as the defenders of the community, believed that they fulfilled a communal function.

Sometimes symbolic matters shaded into political ones. Cincinnati, for example, had a large German population, larger than its Jewish one, and in 1952 the city council decided to name Munich its "sister city." The National Community Relations Advisory Committee helped the upset Cincinnati Jewish Community Relations Committee devise a strategy to prevent that city from entering into this agreement. It advised lobbying with the city council, sending letters to editors of the local newspapers, and meeting with non-Jewish civic leaders, whose assistance they needed to sever the proposed bond between the city on the Ohio River and the city of the Beer Hall putsch.[65] Two years later, the Jewish Labor Committee telegrammed Attorney General Alfred Brownell, urging him to "Investigate American Firms Importing Ruhr-Manufactured Nazi Swastika-Decorated Daggers," while it, along with the Workmen's Circle, called on Dag Hammarksjöld, secretary general of the United Nations, "to reject the credentials of Peter Pfeiffer who has been designated by the West German Republic to represent his government as Observer-Representative at the UN." Pfeiffer's "Nazi record traduces the very ideals for which the UN was created." American Jewry alerted the world about Pfeiffer's background, the history of the Nazis and their "inhuman designs," and the callousness of the West German government.[66] In 1956, the Synagogue Council of America learned that "a local manufacturer of toy model airplanes was using swastikas on his reproductions of certain German airplanes," and in 1957, readers of Jewish newspapers could find a string of articles by Boris Smolar which reported with consternation that Alfred Krupp, the German munitions manufacturer, received a visa to come to the United States.[67]

Discussion about how to interact with Germany and Germans infused postwar American Jewish organizational life. One story that could be replicated for nearly any American Jewish community throughout this period can stand as an example of the inability to avoid Germany and the intensity of Jewish community reactions to it. In 1951, Isaac Franck, executive director of the Jewish Community Council of Washington, D.C., had been approached by the U.S. Department of State to participate in an "Exchange of Persons Program," which brought "a considerable number of German leaders" to the United States to acquaint "them with American life and institutions." The State Department asked Franck to lecture on "The Religious Life of America," alongside Catholic and Protestant speakers. A number of American Jewish organizations participated in this program, preparing material, translating key texts about Judaism and American Jewry into German, and the like.[68]

If he had been approached to lecture to any other group, he would not have felt compelled to secure first the permission of the council's executive committee. But this offer involved Germans, and that put it in a class by itself. Franck wanted to join his Catholic and Protestant counterparts in this project. He worked with them constantly on local matters and often turned to them when he needed partners and allies in a variety of civic projects affecting Jews. He also understood that American Jews had to deal with Germany, noting, "there are many indications, and strong opinions that this program already has proven helpful. A high State Department official . . . reported the repeated observation made by American officials, that the most hopeful signs in Germany center around the individuals who spent three to six months in the United States and then returned to Germany." Those who went through this "reeducation" would then help foster in Germany the kinds of changes that American Jews wanted to see.[69]

The State Department initiative sparked "an extensive and heated discussion" among the businessmen, lawyers, and government bureaucrats serving on the council's executive board. Some flatly opposed the plan or anything that involved a Jewish organization working with Germans. They did not want their communal body to be associated with anything having to do with Germany. They expressed profound opposition "in view of the history of Germany under the Nazis, in view of the destruction of six million Jews, in view of the lack of evidence of repentance and improvement on the part of the German, and in view of the manifestations of Neo-Nazism in Germany." This vociferous minority, which ultimately lost the vote, believed that "Jews should have nothing to do with Germany and with Germans." Those voting against the lecture criticized the problematic role of the United States government, which "has been guilty of a program of appeasement of Germany," and as a body, "we have no business cooperating with the State Department's program." The dissenters asserted that "many of the German leaders brought here are probably former Nazis who may have participated in mass murders; that our participation in the program stifles and waters down the Jewish cry for justice."[70] The proposal allowing Franck to participate and lend the Jewish Community Council's name to the program for visiting Germans passed fifteen to four, but the decision to do so did not reflect a willingness to "forgive and forget." Rather, it revealed the complex context in which American Jews faced Germany, defined their obligations to the six million, and participated in the civic life of postwar America.[71]

Germany, the Collaborators, and the Holocaust

As American Jews debated how to engage with postwar Germany, in their writings and speeches, they consistently retold the history of what Germany under Hitler had done. These words of history—sometimes streamlined into a few pages or sentences, sometimes extended into full-length books—told how the German people had willingly and knowingly endorsed Hitler's political agenda and had participated in the regime's assault on the rights and security of their Jewish neighbors. They reminded the world how Germany had extended its geographic grasp, capturing other countries and murdering millions of Jews throughout the continent.

Invocations to that German history ran through American Jewish public culture. Lectures, speeches, sermons, and articles, as well as creative works, repeatedly referred to the German Nazi past in general and, in particular, how it had so horrifically slaughtered Jews. Whether in biographical sketches of individuals, reviews of books, political commentary, or inspirational works intended to get American Jews to enhance the Jewish component of their lives or even to be better Americans, details of Germany's history as the crucible of the Holocaust came up again and again.

In the two decades following the war they wrote, read, reviewed, and gave much attention to a substantial corpus of work, which stated directly that Germany had committed the crime. Judah Nadich, for example, dedicated his book on General Dwight Eisenhower's sympathetic treatment of the surviving Jews of Europe to Eisenhower himself. Issued simultaneously with Eisenhower's 1952 presidential campaign, Nadich noted immediately in his introduction, "For what the Germans did to the Jews and for what the world let them do, there can be certainly no revenge and no atonement. Their crime was too colossal, the sin too great. There can be neither penitence or penance."[72]

So, too, the following books put Germany squarely into bold relief as perpetrator: *Hitler's Professors* by YIVO director Max Weinreich; Anatole Goldstein's two books, *Operation Murder*, a history of the Einsatzgruppen, and *From Discrimination to Annihilation*; Eva Reichmann's *Hostages of Civilization: The Social Sources of National Socialist Anti-Semitism*; Eugen Kogon's *The Theory and Practice of Hell: The German Concentration Camps and the System Behind Them*; Joseph Tenenbaum's *Race and Reich: The Story of an Epoch*; Leon Poliakov's *Harvest of Hate*; and Gerald Reitlinger's *The Final Solution* and *The SS: Alibi of a Nation*—all pointed to Germany. Randoph Braham published *Eichmann and the Destruction of Hungarian Jewry* in 1961, and Raul Hilberg's *The Destruction of the European Jews* rounded out this list of books.[73] Despite their various and conflicting interpretive frameworks, all began and ended with the statement that the tragic events culminating in the "annihilation," "destruction," and "hell" endured by the Jews had started in Germany. Germany had ruthlessly pursued a set of policies against the Jews, which constituted the Holocaust. Not all these books had been written by American Jews, or indeed by Jews, but all merited extensive commentary in American Jewish publications, which, even when reviewers disagreed with their emphases or quibbled with their conclusions, still hailed them as crucial indictments of Germany to be read by all.[74]

Other books of the postwar period explored Jewish history, the history of anti-Semitism, or contemporary Jewish life and in them revisited

Germany's behavior in the 1930s and 1940s, drawing their readers' attention to Germany's evil behavior toward the Jews. Nathan Zuckerman's anthology of 1947, *The Wine of Violence,* included excerpts from some available primary documents of "Nazi Germany—The Brown Terror," in his section on Jewish "Martyrdom." He documented the German responsibility for "the blood-spattered furnaces of Lublin and the unbelievable number of mass-graves of the martyred Jews of Europe . . . the sordid story of carnage and bestiality."[75] Ben Edidin's book on the American Jewish community, designed for younger readers, repeatedly referred to Germany, its actions, and the impact of its actions on American Jewry. One could not understand, he implied, "Jewish community life in America" (the title of his book) without understanding how "the Nazis brutally murdered about 6,000,000 in Europe." He blamed no generic "Nazis" but, rather, wrote, "There is hardly a Jew in the world who does not feel its [anti-Semitsm's] sting at some time in his life; while many, as in Germany, drank the bitter cup of blind hatred to the last drop."[76]

A handful of American Jews, professional historians and specialists in German history, also laid out the details of what that country, under Hitler, had perpetrated on the Jewish people.[77] No one's work exemplified this more than Koppel Pinson, author of *Modern Germany: Its History and Civilization,* a massive work published in 1954 by Macmillan. Born in 1904, he came to the United States at age three from Lithuania. Unlike many of the other scholars and writers who helped create in America the scholarly literature that focused on Germany's assault on the Jews, Pinson had not fled Nazi-dominated Europe before the war or survived the Holocaust. Pinson's book, a broad overview of German history, told that history on its own terms, detailing how Germany developed into a modern nation state, and posited that history in light of its end point, the rise of Hitler, the appeal of Nazism and its anti-Semitism to the German public, the Third Reich, and the brutal project undertaken by Germany and the Germans against the Jews. Jewish publications lavished praise on the book and on Pinson, known for his work with the Joint Committee after the war in the Displaced Persons camps, his involvement with *Jewish Social Studies,* and his assiduous labors for YIVO.[78]

According to Boris Smolar in Philadelphia's *Jewish Exponent,* Pinson's magnum opus on modern German history had made it impossible to write German history "without devoting at least a few pages to the Nazi brutalities against Jews and to the German extermination camps in which 6,000,000 Jews lost their lives." Smolar predicted and hoped that Pinson's book would "become a standard history book used by students in many colleges and universities in this country," thus ensuring that anyone who studied German history would also learn about its slaughter of the Jews.[79] Reviewing Pinson's book for *Congress Monthly*, art historian Alfred Werner considered it not just "a solid, scholarly work" but a book that will "make us understand . . . the geographic, social, economic and political factors which caused Germany to become a problem, not only for the world, but also for many Germans themselves." The book appeared at an opportune moment, when, "ten years after the Third Reich, . . . world opinion is being wooed by an avalanche of pseudo-historic writings intended to justify the Hitler experiment, or at least to whitewash the surviving collaborators." Werner considered Pinson's real contribution to be the discussion of how Hitler "could come to power in a highly civilized nation like Germany" and "how a nation as civilized as the German could indulge itself in the most sadistic brand of anti-Semitism."[80]

Throughout the postwar period, American Jewish journalism made it clear that Germany perpetrated the Holocaust. In March 1950 in *Congress Weekly*, Robert Kempner, the deputy chief prosecutor of the Nuremberg trials, wrote, "for the first time," in "Blueprint for Murder," the details of the meeting held in Berlin on January 20, 1942. At that auspicious meeting, on "the blackest day in Jewish history," Nazi officials met to hear "a progress report on the steps which already had been taken . . . in accomplishing the 'Final Solution' . . . the annihilation of the Jews of Europe." The document unveiled at that meeting, Kempner wrote, "The 'Wannsee protocol,' as we called this document in Nuremberg, . . . became the first genocidal instrument in world history. . . . In the files of the German Foreign Office we discovered numerous progress reports on the execution of the Final Solution in the various Nazi controlled countries."[81]

More often, articles about current events provided writers with segues to reference Germany's crimes during the 1930s and 1940s. In many of her writings in the *Jewish Spectator*, Trude Weiss-Rosmarin pointed an accusatory finger at Germany. In 1954, as one example, in "Lest We Forget," she condemned philosopher Martin Buber, since, as she saw it, by accepting a prize in Germany, Buber joined the ranks of those Christians, and even a few Jews, "who have forgotten-and-forgiven the slaughter of the Six Million . . . as if something had not happened, only yesterday, really, which will for always ever place Germany on a par with Amalek for Jews."[82]

A good deal of American Jewish historical writing tried to explain the behavior of the Germans, puzzling over the enigma of Germany's past as both an exemplar of "civilization" and as the seedbed of history's greatest crime against humanity as perpetrated on the Jews. "Germany was the most cultured and highly developed country in Europe," yet it, "the country of poets and thinkers," went about "mercilessly persecuting" Jews, "first in Germany, and then, after the Nazis' lightning conquest of most of Europe, in all Germany-occupied countries."[83] The conundrum of German history, the gap between Germany as the crucible of western culture and the Holocaust, infused postwar American Jewish works, whether crafted for internal consumption or for mass distribution. Rabbi Charles Chavel in a 1947 talk, delivered at an Orthodox synagogue in Edgmere, Long Island, declaimed to his congregants, "What a nightmare in the history of the world, and of Israel in particular! . . . Millions of our people . . . were tortured to death. Germans played the symphonies of Wagner and Beethoven in order to drown out the crying voice of children burning alive."[84]

Another rabbi pondered this conundrum in a radio sermon of January 30, 1953, given on the *This Week in Religion* program, a rotating spot shared by Catholic, Protestant, and Jewish clergy, noting the date and what it meant. "Two decades ago," the rabbi recounted, "on the 30th of the month" of January, "a monster in human form became the chancellor of a nation which had always prided itself on its poets and philosophers. When Adolf Hitler became Chancellor of the Reich on January 30, 1933, the world little realized that the raving maniac who spoke of conquest and enslavement meant every word of it." Hitler "bequeathed to mankind," the rabbi declaimed, "a heritage of suffering and hatred." But for Jews it meant much more. "The Jews of the world have particular cause to mark this day, adding a special prayer that a recurrence of such unbelievable and demonical insanity will never again be possible."[85]

The reviewer of Joseph Tenenbaum's 1957 *Race and Reich* put it simply: "When all the facts of Nazis are accounted for and analyzed . . . there still remains a large area of inexplicable mystery . . . what *really* could reduce a *civilized* nation like the Germans, civilized in the accepted connotations of the word, to beastly killers?"[86]

An American Jewish discussion took place, attempting to answer this question. Some commentators focused on the German "national character," contending that deep in the German soul lay the seeds for the Nazi horror. Jewish writers and rabbis frequently referred to the Germans' pagan origins. Jewish publications gave wide coverage to Adolf Leschnitzer's 1956 book *The Magic Background of Modern Anti-Semitism: An Analysis of the German-Jewish Relationship*.[87] Others discerned a distinctive Prussian character that venerated militarism, harshness, and hypermasculinity as the basis for Nazism. A 1948 sermon by Rabbi Leon Stitskin told how "the notorious Nazi Goebbels wrote a book of his speeches. He has this story in it. The Prussian people were very much concerned when Frederick the Great was a young prince. He liked to play the flute and write poetry. The Prussians wondered what will happen when this softhearted artist comes to the throne? . . . But, said Goebbels proudly, Frederick was a Prussian. The night that his father died, he broke his flute and changed it into a dagger. And then the Prussians rejoiced—the king was worthy of his country."[88]

Labor Zionist theoretician and editor Hayim Greenberg thought that Lutheranism served as the incubus for Hitlerism. In 1946 on the four hundredth anniversary of Luther's birth, Greenberg observed that the German Reformer "embodied the essentials of modern Nazism." Luther advocated the "sanctification of the state," synonymous with "the *Fuehrer* principle." That Luther, who preached violence against the Jews, allowed the possibility that Jews who converted to Christianity should be spared seemed to be "a residue from Catholic universalism." That did not obviate the fact that in his teachings could be found "almost all the features of a modern Nazi."[89] Writing in *Conservative Judaism*, Julius Guttmann also considered Lutheranism's contribution to Nazism. "Calvinism" had always remained "closest in spirit to Judaism," but Lutheranism, like much of Christianity, considered "the preservation of the state . . . the sole *raison d'être* of organized society." This played itself out in "the early days of Nazism," when the churches in Germany "merely . . . defend[ed] their respective spheres and . . . disclaim[ed] responsibility for whatever takes place in the political sphere."[90]

On a different level, the December 1962 *Bulletin* of the Society for the Advancement of Judaism included a piece by its rabbi, Alan Miller, on why Jews should not have Christmas trees in their homes. He saw "a connection between Christianity and the concentration camps," between the tree as an element of the "Nordic" tradition and Jewish suffering. In the "bestiality of the Nazis vis-à-vis the Jews," Miller opined, "a vile blend of German militarism with a sound Christian background of anti-Jewish indoctrination" came together. Urging his congregants to keep their homes free of any Christmas markers, Yuletide trees in particular, he reminded them to not "forgive and forget . . . out of respect for the Jewish dead."[91]

Others looked for a class explanation. Boris Smolar, discussing George W. F. Hallgarten's *Why Dictators?* a comparison of Nazism and Soviet totalitarianism, noted that the "German middle and lower middle classes were especially sadistic against the Jews whenever they found opportunities to be so." Solomon Landman and Benjamin Efron posited the initial source of Nazi support with the "wealthy industrialists and corporations" who "organized the anti-Jewish prejudices of Germany into a mighty political weapon."[92] Max Weinreich in *Hitler's Professors* explored the active role played by academicians in the Nazi program against the Jews. The *News of YIVO* noted the importance of the book, an effort "not to recount the tragic sufferings of the Jews under the Germans, nor to rehearse the bitter account of their extinction in the gas chambers, furnaces, and crematories of Oswiecim, Majdanek, Klooga, Treblinka and the many others, but . . . to present . . . the role of the German scholars in achieving this final aim of the Nazi regime."[93]

Whether the source was German paganism, Christianity, Lutheranism, or the basic character of the German people, American Jews in their cultural works speculated on the source of the Nazis' appeal, the ease with which the Germans succumbed to the Nazis' genocidal hatred of the Jews, and their willingness to support state programs for extirpating the Jewish people. American Jews also concurred that all Germans had lent a hand, with only a scant number of resisters and opponents. One could not disentangle the collectivity of the Germans and their history from the thinking about the fate of the six million. The American Jewish Congress's Office of Jewish Information issued a press release, "Extermination Was a German Cartel," and based on trials that had taken place in Germany, the Congress declared, "All Classes of German Society Participated."[94]

Knowing that whatever country the Germans went into, they found sympathetic individuals to help them in the perpetration of their crimes against the Jews, American Jewish discussions focused on the collaborators of other nations. The *American Jewish Year Book* reported on trials in the Netherlands, Belgium, France, and elsewhere of individuals who had assisted the Germans. It tracked the rehabilitation and "restoration of civic rights to collaborationists with the Germans" in those, and other, European countries.[95]

Through their organizations and magazines, American Jews kept their antennae attuned to the activities of individuals who in the various European countries had facilitated the murderous work of the Germans. The American Jewish Congress reported in 1951 that the American government had begun "extradition proceedings against" a Yugoslav, Anderija Artukovich, who as Minister of the Interior had been "primarily responsible for concentration camp brutalities and the annihilation of thousands of Jews" in Yugoslavia. It let its constituents know how effective it, the American Jewish Congress, had been in getting Artukovich arrested and bound for extradition, and it kept the history of the "annihilation" alive. It made clear how often Jewish organizations turned to the U.S. government to help in bringing perpetrators of the Holocaust to justice and informed the public that Germany had had helpers in perpetrating its crimes.[96]

In 1959, Boris Smolar reviewed for the Jewish Telegraphic Agency a recently published South African book on the Jews of Latvia. He noted, "in killing Jews, the Latvians have played no smaller role than the German Nazis. . . . In fact, the slaughter of Latvian Jewry was more a Latvian than a German affair." The Latvians as a people participated "not only in destroying their own Jews during the Nazi period, but also in helping the Nazis to destroy the Jews in Poland."[97] The American Jewish media produced similar reports on Hungary and the Hungarians, Poland and the Poles, Lithuania, the Ukraine, and the like.

Indeed, some of the harshest criticism leveled by American Jews at their own government involved its postwar policies toward would-be immigrants from the Baltic countries of Latvia, Lithuania, and Estonia, as well as the Ukraine, who had supported the Germans, working with them to murder Jews. The United States welcomed many of them as refugees from Communism. From the late 1940s through 1952, as Congress debated immigration, culminating in 1952 in the McCarran-Walter Act, American Jewish organizations and the American Jewish press kept in the public eye the fact that, in the words of the Jewish Labor Committee's press release and letter to the attorney general, "the opening of the gates of the United States to collaborationists especially to those who are still active or sympathetic to doctrines, is breaking faith with the millions of Jews and non-Jews whose lives were sacrificed in the crematoria of Nazi Germany."[98]

American Jewish communal relations workers also brought that same kind of vigilance to their own hometown communities. In May 1949, word came to the Jewish Community Relations (JCR) Committee of Cincinnati that the opera singer Kirsten Flagstad, a Norwegian, accused of pro-German and pro-Nazi sympathies, had been booked to perform. Historian Jacob Rader Marcus, a JCR Committee member, took the matter up with the group as a whole. He prodded the committee's chair to take a public position. As Marcus understood Flagstad's past, "the woman was at least a Nazi sympathizer," if not worse, and, "in order to preserve their sense of dignity and self-respect, the Jews of the community must be informed and advised not to attend the concerts." Marcus's note stimulated a flurry of letters within the Cincinnati Jewish community and between Cincinnati and the national offices of the American Jewish Congress, the Anti-Defamation League, and the Jewish War Veterans in New York. Marcus and the others wanted to see a Jewish communal response, "out of respect for the Jews that were killed." Marcus, his correspondents, and the committee as a body decided against picketing the concert, preferring that "a dignified note be sent to all heads of Jewish organizations and, in addition, an open letter be addressed to all Jews and published in the Jewish press." As to "the Gentiles," he expected they "will probably pick up this open letter," so "it must be phrased as to express our attitude with dignity." While not suggesting that non-Jews be invited "to join us in this withdrawal . . . it must be so worded that the average intelligent Gentile will agree that this is the only attitude a decent Jew can take with respect to this woman."[99]

American Jewish communal bodies, particularly those concerned with the reparations, paid attention to Austria, a nation that claimed it had been a victim of German aggression. As far as American Jewish public opinion went, Austria had eagerly joined with Hitler's Germany and had had a hand in the Holocaust. Negotiations between the Austrian government and the Claims Conference began in 1952 and did not result in a successful resolution until 1962. For that decade, American Jewry in publications, meetings, political efforts with civic bodies, and protests to U.S. government officials issued harsh condemnation of Austria, which had chosen to be part of the Nazi regime.[100]

In March 1955, on the anniversary of the *Anschluss,* the Synagogue Council of America, at the urging of the Claims Conference, declared a special Sabbath appeal for political action. "A request," the Synagogue Council's president Norman Salit declared, "will be made of all rabbis in America and other countries to devote a sermon . . . to arouse public opinion and exert influence on the Austrian government." It asked its rabbis to read a statement to their congregations that, while "Jewish organizations do not hold the present leaders of Austria responsible for the horrors perpetrated against the Jews under Austrian Nazism . . . it is a fact that the Jews were pillaged and exterminated. . . . It is a fact that large elements of the Austrian population participated in and benefited from these crimes." So, it declared, "it is therefore the moral obligation of the Austrian people . . . to make at least some amends."[101]

The Jewish Labor Committee enlisted the support of President George Meany of the American Federation of Labor to demand that Austria assume financial responsibility for its Nazi past and theft of Jewish property.

American Jewish magazines published articles with titles like "Ungenerous Austria," and speakers at communal events "sharply scorn[ed] the Austrian Government for its refusal" to deal with the issue of the settlement of heir-less property claims, claims on properties owned by Jews who had been killed and had no heirs who could come forward. The latter remarks came from a speech delivered by Israel Goldstein to the Chicago chapter of the American Jewish Congress, which the city press reported on. Goldstein declared that despite what the Austrians said, "the Nazi anti-Jewish cam-paign in Austria had been carried out with the active cooperation of large sections of the Austrian population." The Government of Austria "cannot postpone or avoid responsibility, since, no government has the right to profit from the murder of its citizens."[102]

In terms of how far the guilt for the Holocaust lay, beyond Germany's central role, Trude Weiss-Rosmarin forcefully articulated a position quite common among American Jews. In the first months of 1956 the Soviet Union denounced Israel in the United Nations, and the United States re-fused to sell it arms. Most observers predicted that Israel would be cen-sured by the world body. The editor of the *Jewish Spectator* used those facts in "The Nations Against Israel" to look back to the Holocaust. She speculated on "the political motives and calculations of the Western na-tions in forming a common front with the Communists against the young State of Israel." Despite the contemporary focus of the article, Weiss-Rosmarin drew her readers back in time, to show them that "the same ago-nizing questions troubled us during the years of Nazi domination." Weiss-Rosmarin detailed who did what to the Jews and where blame should be affixed: "Without the acquiescence of the German people as a whole . . . the Extermination Camps would not have been operated." But, she cau-tioned, "let us not forget, either, that in *all* countries conquered by the *Wehrmacht*, the populations cooperated gleefully with the Nazi policy of 'Death to the Jews.'" She then recited the list of people and places where this happened: "The Poles, the Czechs, and the Hungarians in the East, the French, the Belgians and the Dutch in the West, and the Danes and Nor-wegians up North nursed their own hatreds against the Germans, but they collaborated with the invader-tyrants in rounding up Jews and dispatching them to the death camps." Certainly "*some* men and women . . . preserved their humanity . . . by giving shelter to Jews," and she concluded that, like "the 'good' Germans," they had proven to be a rare exception: "In looking back upon those years of death-and-doom for European Jewry, one is led to conclude it was a natural latent dislike . . . of Jews and a natural, latent eagerness to see them suffer." Without this, she noted, "the Great Tragedy would not have happened."[103] In this piece, as in postwar American Jewish discourse as a whole, the Germans' culpability for the deaths of the six million was neither hidden nor played down, even when pointing out the culpability of others.

In this discussion of blame, two special groups captured the attention of American Jews in the postwar period, as they continued to pound away at Germany as the central perpetrator. The first involved the Arab world, particularly the Grand Mufti of Jerusalem. By drawing attention to this minor player in the Holocaust narrative, American Jewry reflected its overwhelming support for Israel and the ways it fused the narrative of the catastrophe with that of the Jewish state. In the postwar years leading up to 1948, Zionist and Jewish gatherings that called on the United States and Great Britain to allow for Jewish statehood recalled the active and energetic support of world Jewry and the Jews of Palestine in the military struggle against the Axis and pointed out that "the entire Arab world in the Near East, with the exception of a few individuals, was almost completely on the side of Germany." The name Amin al-Husseini, the Grand Mufti of Jerusalem, who broadcast pro-Nazi, pro-German speeches and beamed them out to the breadth of the Arab world, appeared repeatedly in American Jewish magazines, pointing out to readers the bond between the Nazis and Israel's enemies.[104]

In their publication of May 1946, members of the Masada youth group learned of the connection between Hitler's Germany, the Jewish catastrophe, and the Arab world. "During the Nuremburg [sic] trials of war criminals," the article noted, "the chief assistant to the head of the Gestapo's Jewish Extermination Bureau named the former Grand Mufti of Jerusalem as the one who had conceived of the idea of such extermination, and had 'sold' the idea to Hitler." When Minneapolis Zionist activist Jesse Calmenson cabled Truman, encouraging action on creation of a Jewish state in Palestine, he pointed out the pro-Axis sentiments of the "Arab states apparently stirred up by the Nazi mufti." Calmenson, like many American Jews, maintained that trope after 1948 and in a 1951 letter again to Truman referred once more to the "Arab Nazi-supporting nations." After 1948, Jewish journalists returned to the story of the Mufti and Arab support for the Germans as they reported on and advocated for Israel. Weiss-Rosmarin offered a 1956 article, "The Great Western Folly," which castigated the western powers in wanting "to outdo the Russians in winning the favor of the Arabs." She suggested that the diplomats "remember the failure of identical efforts on the eve and during the early years of World War II. Fifteen years ago," she reminded them, "it was totalitarian Nazi Germany which attempted to make the most of the Arabs' hostility to England." Germany had succeeded, and "the Mufti-spiritual head of the Palestine Arabs fled to Nazi Germany."[105]

Telling the history of Arab collaboration with and support for the Nazis fit well into American Jewish advocacy for Israel, which itself resounded with the theme of the Holocaust as a crucial reason for its need to exist. Irving Kane, a NCRAC activist who lectured to Jewish groups around the country in the 1950s, warned that "the Western World cannot count on allies," meaning the Arabs, "who had never shown the slightest interest in democracy, who maintained a pro-Nazi neutralism during World War II and who, if they could, would have been responsible for the loss of the entire Middle East and North Africa to Hitler." Rabbi Israel Breslau concurred in a letter to the editor of the *Washington Star* in 1953, claiming that the "Arab-Nazi connection" had "almost succeeded in opening the doors of the Middle East for the Nazis." Trude Weiss-Rosmarin reminded her readers that, during the war, the Mufti-spiritual leader of the Palestine Arabs escaped to Nazi Germany, "making him a culprit in the effort to exterminate the Jews." No dissenters spoke up to defend the behavior of the Grand Mufti or the Arab world, in general, during the Holocaust years.[106]

American Jewish publications, in contrast, sponsored a lively debate on the collaboration, or at least tacit support through silence, of the Vatican and Pope Pius XII with the Germans and their efforts to liquidate the Jewish people. Articles, editorials, and letters to the editor speculated about the responsibility he and the church bore for the Holocaust.[107] As early as 1947, this discussion began to appear in magazines, with occasional press articles indicating the contours of a larger discussion that would surface in later years. In his 1946 book *Essays on Antisemitism*, Koppel Pinson cited some Vatican efforts to subdue anti-Jewish sentiments during the Holocaust years and the various rescue efforts it undertook. This inspired a harsh negative reaction, launched by Abraham Duker on the English page of *Der Tog*. Duker equated Pinson's assertions with those of William Zuckerman in a book of that same year, *The Wine of Violence*. Duker considered both Pinson's and Zuckerman's statements nothing more than "prattlings," which flew in the face of such evidence as "the papal 'hechsher' (certification or approval) of Petain's Vichy laws."[108] When Boris Smolar reviewed Joseph Tenenbaum's *Race and Reich* in 1956, he pondered the activities of the pope during the time of "Hitler's slaughter of Jews." Tenenbaum, according to Smolar, praised "Pope Pius XI for his disapproval and con-demnation of Nazi persecution of Jews on more than one occasion." How-ever, his successor, Pope Pius XII, remained "painfully silent."[109]

Other, scattered writings in American Jewish magazines also tried to make sense of the actions, or nonactions, of the Catholic Church during the Holocaust years. In a 1950 *Commentary* article, Leon Poliakov wrote pointedly, "It is painful to have to state that at a time when gas chambers and crematoria were operating day and night, the high spiritual author-ity of the Vatican did not find it necessary to make a clear and solemn protest that would have echoed through the world." But even within that one article, a countertheme appeared. "One cannot say," Poliakov specu-lated, that "there may not have been pertinent and valid reasons for this silence," namely "the Pope's concern for protecting Catholics and the Church itself."[110]

No one in the discussion accused the papacy of active support of Nazi atrocities against the Jews. Rather, they noted his unwillingness to exert influence even when he knew the specific details of the slaughter and the fact that he did not use his considerable moral authority to condemn Ger-man actions, something that might have made a difference in those Euro-pean countries—Poland, Hungary, Slovakia, and Belgium—where Catho-lic majorities allowed the vast majority of their Jews to perish. Did silence constitute collaboration?

The pope's death in October 1958 led to a flurry of articles on this subject. An editorial in *Jewish Forum* two months after the death led the editor to ask, since no consensus existed, "What is the Jewish estimation of the recently deceased Pope who was in a strategic position during the period when six million Jews—men, women, and children—were barbari-cally done to death?" The editor included articles from a variety of Jew-ish publications, by such individuals as Rabbi Israel Goldstein, president of the Synagogue Council of America; Joachim Prinz of the American Jewish Congress; William Rosenblum, "who had gone to Rome 10 years ago to thank the Pope for rescue efforts"; and Hillel Seidman, a journal-ist and survivor of the Warsaw Ghetto. The editor shared statements by Israeli officials; Foreign Minister Golda Meir, who had had an audience with the pope; and President Yitzchak Ben Zvi and Chief Rabbi Yitzhak Herzog. As in the 1947 spat between Pinson and Duker, the quoted Jew-ish notables differed. Only Seidman, the sole survivor quoted, unequivo-cally condemned Pius XII, not just because "during the entire period of the murders, the Pope dropped not a single word of condemnation." Seidman characterized the Catholic Church as one "of the greatest collaborators" with the German Nazis.[111]

Readers of *Jewish Forum* then followed with a barrage of letters that went on for a year after Pius's death. With no scholarly credentials or access to primary documents, they nonetheless weighed in, voicing their position on the role of Vatican in the "greatest tragedy of all times that befell our martyr-people during World War II," as "Dr. Jacob B. Glenn, M.D." called it. Glenn told the history of "two trains on their way to Treblinka," which Pius knew about but "would do nothing" to stop. "Of course," Glenn wrote, "the Jews in those two trains went to their annihilation." Glenn hoped that the history of the Vatican, the Germans, and the Jews, "which await the gifted pen of the future historian," would put an end to "the appellation of the late Pope as a 'Pope of Peace.'" In concluding his letter, he reminded readers that "it was after all during the reign of Pope Pius XII, the 'Prince of Peace,' that six million defenseless and innocent men, women and babies found their eternal *peace* in the destruction camps of the Nazi-German hydra. . . . the Vatican can never wash away this greatest of sins and the guilt which they incurred by an attitude of inactivity and a policy of hands off from this greatest calamity of all times."[112]

Rescuers: Good Nations and Good Individuals

Postwar American Jewish discussions, whether in print or in public programs, made clear the centrality of Germany as the perpetrator and the helping roles played by a set of ancillary actors: the nations of Europe, the Arabs of the Middle East, and the Catholic Church. To highlight the sins of the many, Germany and the majority of its people, in particular, American Jewish institutions honored the handful of non-Jews who behaved heroically, rescuing Jews even at the risk of their own lives. While they offered their gratitude as thanks, pure and simple, they also used the examples of nations and individuals that risked much to defy the Germans as a way to highlight what exactly Germany had done. Drawing attention to the noble behavior of the few made manifest the nefarious behavior of the vast majority. Showing, as Philip Friedman did in his 1957 book *Their Brothers' Keepers,* that not all Christians and not even all Germans participated in the slaughter demonstrated even more clearly the active perpetration of the crime by the Germans as a collectivity.[113]

It took Friedman ten years of research to mount his evidence on the existence of that "other Germany," a counter to *the* Germany. He published several pieces on this subject in YIVO early in the 1950s, and even before *Their Brothers' Keepers* came out, the *Eternal Light* devoted a radio broadcast to material derived from various of Friedman's Yiddish articles. "In Dark Places" aired on February 17, 1957, with the concluding remarks offered by Charles Silver, president of the Board of Education of New York City, who offered a contemporary message about "brotherhood" and how it managed to survive even amid "the fear and degradation of Nazi Germany." Offered as a paean to America, where "brotherhood is part of our being every minute of every day," a place that looked "like . . . a rainbow . . . where many colors have fused and blended to fashion its blazing magnificence," Silver's words and the script based on Friedman's articles told one Holocaust-era narrative that took place in Vilna in 1941, when "the darkness spread over half the world" and where "walls of stone and barbed wire arose." The hero of the play, "Schmidt," declaimed to a Jew who slaved in the factory under his supervision, "I'm a German officer! But it doesn't mean that I brought you here, or that I want to keep you here. It doesn't mean that I believe that nonsense about Aryans, or that I think its right that Jews are to be beaten, murdered, thrown into concentration camps to rot!" The stage directions instructed the actor playing Schmidt to lower his voice as he said, "I'm not a person with complicated thoughts. I'll tell you what I believe. I believe that a man is a human being after all." Before the narrator brought the play to its end, observing that Schmidt had been one of the Germans who behaved humanely, radio listeners learned that "Anton Schmidt . . . of the army of the Third Reich . . . was taken by the Gestapo," because of his willingness to be "a man." Listeners should "write his name in your remembrance" because of his individual act of mercy.[114]

The publication of *Their Brothers' Keepers* later in 1957 became an event in itself, attracting attention beyond the reviews and commentary in the Jewish media. The Anti-Defamation League (ADL) sponsored a public ceremony in New York in November 1957, honoring Christian rescuers and dedicating a plaque to them at its headquarters. The ADL invited "top diplomats from eight European countries and . . . American religious and secular leaders" to the ceremony, at which Friedman spoke, presenting copies of his book, "the first documented and permanent record of Christian aid to Jews during the Hitler era." Friedman's words showed up in the city press. He explained what the book had meant to him: "After the Nazi Holocaust many of us were plagued by doubts and anxiety about the direction which it seemed mankind was taking. We wondered if all the enlightened centuries spent in the development of humanism and the fundamentals of religion had been in vain—all erased from human hearts and minds. For me, therefore, it was a great consolation to be able to lift hundreds of facts and episodes testifying to the contrary."[115]

Friedman not only wrote about "the other Germany" but also chronicled stories of rescuers of other nations. Indeed, in *Their Brothers' Keepers* non-German rescuers predominated, and he told of the Swedish diplomat Raoul Wallenberg, who helped thousands of Hungarian Jews escape certain death and then "disappeared" in the Soviet Union.[116] In 1954, *The Eternal Light* spotlighted Wallenberg in one of its radio dramas, "One Man," and that same year, Julius Fisher, a Hungarian Jew who had come to the United States in 1943 and served as a rabbi in Beaufort, South Carolina, offered a moving testimony to Wallenberg in "Not a Minor Saint" in the *Jewish Spectator*.[117]

While Friedman had been researching his book, occasional pieces appeared in the Jewish press telling of the same phenomenon. Like *Their Brothers' Keepers*, these articles demonstrated German guilt by focusing on lone heroes and solo rescuers.[118] C. C. Aronsfeld in an article in the *Jewish Spectator* in 1955 commented on the difference between "the damnation of all Germany," considering it utterly appropriate, and the principle that such damnation "does not doom every German." He valorized the few Germans who "braved the terror . . . the righteous among the Germans," contrasting their noble actions with the fact that "the German persecution of the Jews—the attempt to assassinate a whole nation—is a matter of history. The facts stand beyond challenge."[119]

Aronsfeld predicted that most Jews, so certain of the guilt of all Germans, would dismiss his piece as "whitewashing." They were less concerned with the truth that some Germans had behaved courageously and humanely, and Aronsfeld believed that, when it came to Germany, "the evidence has never been rated highly among Jews . . . [and] by those implacable preachers of vengeance." Aronsfeld defended his valorization of the few "good" Germans, since "the fact that they were German will not by an iota lift the curse that lies heavy on the name of Germany. But they at least have saved their souls."[120] As he saw it, in the middle of the 1950s, Jews, wherever they lived, could not conceive of a German innocent of crimes against the Jewish people.

Perhaps they also needed evidence that even in the midst of the brutality, humanity persisted, albeit in small places. Throughout the postwar period, stories in the Jewish press, programs at Jewish summer camps, and public ceremonies under Jewish auspices highlighted rescue efforts, recognizing the nobility of Christian helpers. Each event or article provided American Jews with opportunities to simultaneously thank the heroes and point their fingers at Germany. In 1945, after the war had ended, Hillel chapters at the Universities of Wisconsin and Minnesota, states with large Scandinavian populations, established special awards, presented with flourish to campus Scandinavian student groups in honor of King Christian X of Denmark and King Gustav V of Sweden, "as a tribute to the courage and humanness of the two Scandinavian sovereigns who, in the teeth of Nazi opposition had provided havens for refugees from Germany."[121]

Interest in the Danish rescue of its Jews became particularly widespread after the 1954 publication of Aage Bertelsen's memoir, *October '43*. Bertelsen and his wife, Gerda, helped engineer that rescue, and shortly after the book came out in the United States, American Jewish organizations and publications seized upon it.[122] Professor Samuel Sandmel of Hebrew Union College speculated on the Dumont network's *Radio Chapel of the Air* on "Religion and Good Will." Drawing from the recently released book, he described how, "when Hitler marched into Denmark and its Jewish community was under the threat of extermination, the Danes rescued virtually their entire Jewish population by . . . carrying them into safety into Sweden, and in Sweden the Jews were warmly and hospitably received."[123] In 1954, the Synagogue Council of America brought the Bertelsens to the United States, staging a public ceremony attended by diplomats from Sweden, Norway, and Denmark and the American press. The rabbis awarded the couple "with a Menorah retrieved from a Nazi concentration camp" and gave the diplomats certificates of tribute "to the Scandinavian peoples for their gallantry and humanity."[124]

The following summer, a delegation of American rabbis went to these Scandinavian countries to present "scrolls to the heads of these governments for their 'valorous and generous conduct' towards their Jewish populations during and since the Nazi terrorism." Two years later, *The Eternal Light* again returned to the theme of Christian rescuers in "The House with the Blue Curtains," a play about the Bertelsens' heroism against the Germans.[125] Danish diplomats stationed in the United States became featured speakers at Jewish lectures, Warsaw Ghetto memorial programs, and communal gatherings, and as these talks were reported in the Jewish and general press, the story took on a life of its own in the second half of the 1950s.[126]

A variety of other texts and performances gave American Jews opportunities to valorize Dutch, French, Italian, and Spanish rescuers. Every chance they could, they told the stories of brave Christians who, "at the risk of life and possessions, through THE TERRIBLE YEARS," saved Jews, in the words of a 1948 television program sponsored by the Synagogue Council of America. "The Pastor of Eindhoven" episode of *The Eternal Light*, broadcast in 1946, depicted defiance against the Germans through the dramatic medium of one Dutch cleric, Pastor Aadrian Von Hoogstraten, but the "VOICE" intoned that he, who at the end of the show was executed on the orders of the "Reich's Commissioner for the Netherlands," was not really the hero. That honor fell to "the people of the Netherlands. He was the deed that subordinated life to the message of life. He was Holland and the audacity of Holland," with the VOICE bearing witness as the collective spirit of "the Dutch Jew."[127]

American Jews celebrated the heroism of the rescuers because they felt gratitude toward these women and men who, despite the threat of punishment, had been moved by the horrors facing their Jewish neighbors and willingly risked much to aid those whom they could. They simultaneously used these narratives to retell what the Germans had done to Europe's Jews. That some European Christians, the occasional German, or, more boldly, the Danish people refused to go along with the slaughter made the behavior of the German people that much more reprehensible. In the texts produced by American Jews for their own consumption and for the American public, narratives of rescue became additional places to label the Germans as the perpetrators. Those uplifting stories about the nobility of the human spirit, just like those angry ones about collaborationists and abettors, laid bare a naked truth. Germany under the Nazi regime bore the responsibility for the deaths of six million Jews.

The corpus of work produced and consumed by American Jewry in the postwar years—whether immediately after the war, during the 1950s, or into the 1960s—never failed to tell of Germany's bloody history and the extermination it perpetrated on the Jews of Europe. Whether in their inner communal discourse or as part of their political work with the larger American public, whether articulated by those who advocated never forgetting and never forgiving, and as such advocated a virtual excommunication of Germany, or by the majority who asserted that present realities demanded engagements with the Germans, the Holocaust and Germany's role never vanished from communal prominence.

CONGREGATION BETH SHOLOM

Broadway and Washington Ave. — Lawrence, L. I.

COME TO OUR FRIDAY NIGHT FORUM

FEBRUARY 5, 1954 — 8:30 P. M.

•

HEAR

"WHAT IS LEFT OF JEWRY IN GERMANY"

•

An Address by

DR. NORMAN SALIT

PRESIDENT OF THE SYNAGOGUE
COUNCIL OF AMERICA

who has recently returned from a four week trip to Germany
at the invitation of the German government.

•

The Forum consists of a short devotional period, community singing,
good fellowshp and a question period and refreshments following the
address.

For A Sabbath Delight — Be With Us On Friday Night

Norman Salit of the Synagogue Council of America went to Germany in
the early 1950s, meeting both with Conrad Adenauer, chancellor of the
newly reconstituted postwar government, and with the small Jewish community still there. American Jews, like those who attended his talk at Congregation Beth Sholom, expressed interest and concern with the situation
of Jews still in Germany. Some suggested in print and at community meetings that Jews should not live there and that as a result of the horrendous
acts of the Germans under Hitler, the country ought to be considered a
taboo space by Jews. Salit's trip inspired a flurry of heated and angry letters
to the Synagogue Council. It also brought him invitations to speak at synagogues around the country, keeping alive the history of what the Germans
had done to the Jews and the implications of that history in the postwar
present. *Courtesy American Jewish Historical Society.*

When opportunities arose for American Jews in the present to refer
to the catastrophe, they did so because it served them as a people and because it reflected their deep anguish over their losses. Germany occupied
a problematic and unique status, not just in the agendas of Jewish communal organizations but also in the consciousness of ordinary Jews. Their
letters to the editor, their activities as the rank-and-file members of the

organizations, and their attendance at meetings and lectures on the subject of Germany indicated how profoundly Germany loomed in their minds as the perpetrator of the Holocaust.

They could do nothing for the six million who had been murdered by design. But by reminding themselves and the world of Germany's crimes, they simultaneously cried out for justice and constructed their rhetorical memorials. To honor the memory of those who had perished so brutally, American Jews through their organizations, synagogues, camps, and defense agencies, locally around the country and at the national level, kept vivid the brutal truth of what the Germans had done. They labored to ensure that their concerns resounded in the marketplace of American politics. To them, that constituted a memorial.

In their texts and political actions toward Germany, American Jews lived with the past. They believed the horrific years of the 1930s and the 1940s to be still very much with them. As they engaged with Germany, they did so mindful of the lack of clear boundaries between what had happened "then" and the world they lived in now. In large measure, they let the events of the Holocaust reverberate in their communal lives because they now shouldered a set of obligations and contemplated a set of issues that convinced them that the catastrophic past shaped their American present and their Jewish future.

5

Wrestling with the Postwar World

WITH THEIR EXPRESSIVE and practical works, postwar American Jews recalled the victims of the Holocaust, launched campaigns to aid the catastrophe's survivors, and confronted its perpetrators. Similarly, as they reacted to a set of political developments on the domestic scene, in Israel, and in Europe, they found ample opportunity to revisit the Holocaust and use its lessons to try to alter postwar realities. The projects that attracted them kept reminding them, as if they needed any such reminders, of the Nazis' barbaric deeds. They drew on images and metaphors culled from the horrors of the Holocaust to justify their actions, and they used these words repeatedly in their arguments as they sought to convince the larger public of the rightness of their positions. While debates raged within the ranks of American Jewry over the correct responses to take to an unfolding chain of contemporary concerns, all involved invoked the Holocaust, each differently and at different times. No one group could claim to be the preeminent custodian of the memory of the Holocaust, and none outdid any other in its invocations of the catastrophe. Likewise, none banished the Holocaust from its lexicon. Ironically, despite their different uses of the catastrophe, it served as a unifying context amid contentious community politics.

Whether they dressed their rhetoric up in the language of universalism or of Jewish particularlism, when it came to civil rights, the Cold War, the excesses of the anti-Communists, internationalism, and Israel, the Holocaust provided American Jews with platforms from which to articulate their views. In the causes they took up from the late 1940s through the early 1960s, they saw themselves as building their memorials to the six million. By working to change America and the world, the Jews of the United States acted in the name of the six million who had been killed by tyranny and racism. To them, this kind of engaged civic activism constituted monuments in political time.

As a small, internally divided people with no single voice to speak "for" them, America's Jews did not always agree on the Holocaust's lessons, but every segment of American Jewry reflected on how the Holocaust ought to be understood and acted on in light of postwar circumstances. Unlike the portrait offered by Norman Finkelstein of an "American Jewish leadership" that pursued "conformist policies" and as such conducted its campaign of "public silence on the Nazi extermination," the men and women who participated in Jewish communal life ardently worked to advance postwar liberalism, injecting the Holocaust often and energetically into pursuit of their agenda.[1] Active participants in the politics of the United States, they defined an agenda in part through how they believed the tragedy of the six million changed them and the world. Using their public works, newspapers and magazines, organizational bulletins, communal meetings, and the sermons of their synagogues, they framed the issues of the day around recollections of the Holocaust.

American Jews did not rush off to the suburbs and close their eyes to the challenges of the postwar era, nor could their politics, within the context of American realities, be rightly considered conformist. Rather, even with their increased affluence and despite the new opportunities that opened up and their high levels of suburbanization, they remained stalwarts of American liberalism, ardent supporters of liberal causes.[2] Lawrence Fuchs, one of the first political scientists to study American Jewish political behavior, writing in 1956, devoted a chapter of his book to the overwhelming support American Jews rendered to liberalism and internationalism. Rather than seeing the Jews he studied as having retreated to their comfortable postwar lives, Fuchs saw them as "anxious for the development and strengthening of the United Nations." They empathized "with others who are discriminated against and insecure" and placed themselves "in the forefront of civil liberties movements." Fuchs posited how "Jews sense that inroads on the freedom and well-being of others may soon be followed by onslaughts on themselves" and cited the example of the six hundred rabbis of the Reform movement who went on record in June 1954 to protest the loyalty oaths being enacted by local, state, and federal agencies to root out supposed left-wing subversives. To Fuchs, the behavior of the rabbis revealed something unique about Jews at that moment in time, and he wondered if one could "imagine a large body of Catholic and Protestant clergymen representing *well-to-do* congregations *unanimously* passing a resolution denouncing Senator McCarthy" (emphasis in original).[3]

Fuchs's portrait of a politically vibrant American Jewry willing to go against much of what constituted postwar politics stands in opposition to what some later observers would assert about it, which, in turn, they used to explain its alleged avoidance of the Holocaust. To literary scholar Alan Mintz, for example, the desire of Jews to enjoy the good life that unfolded for them after the war led them to create a culture that had "no room for a tragedy. The enormity of the catastrophe—what it meant for Jews and for the world that a third of the Jewish people had been murdered— simply could not be accommodated." For these postwar Jews, "an acute awareness of the Holocaust" would have "impeded the process of Americanization," so, instead, they went about "enthusiastically seizing the new opportunities."[4]

Fuchs rightly analyzed how Jews carried the liberal banner in America, and in that liberalism they found many opportunities to tell their American neighbors about the tragedy that had recently devastated their people. The pivotal phenomena of the era—the Cold War between the Soviet Union and the United States, the anti-Communist crusade that pervaded domestic life, the sprouting of a seemingly endless stream of right-wing groups, suppressions of civil liberties, the creation of the United Nations based on a vision of international cooperation and human rights, the flowering of the civil rights movement, and the constantly precarious security of Israel—all afforded American Jews occasions to invoke the Holocaust in their inner communal talk and in the messages they shared with others. Through their words and actions, American Jews revisited the European Jewish catastrophe, using it as an explanation for their actions, making it a prism through which they participated in and reacted to the events around them.

Some postwar issues that offered American Jews ways to talk about the Holocaust had concerned them well before the postwar era. Jews as individuals had participated in the quest for African American rights, for example, since the beginning of the twentieth century. Their Yiddish and English newspapers long articulated a deep bond of common concern between themselves and America's black people.[5] On the matter of the Soviet Union, a large swathe of American Jewry had for decades expressed hostility toward the Communist regime. This did not include just defense organizations like the American Jewish Committee, made up of the native-born, economically comfortable, politically well placed elite. It also included the socialists who constituted much of the American Jewish labor movement. The Workmen's Circle, with its network of fraternal branches and schools; the Labor Zionist movement; and the Forward, the largest circulating Yiddish newspaper—all placed themselves in the anti-Communist, anti-Soviet camp since the interwar period.

But on these and a host of other issues, the Holocaust deeply inflected post–World War II American Jewish rhetoric, with older arguments expanded to accommodate it. Previously, American Jews had justified their political positions by referring to the Jewish tradition, the trajectory of Jewish history, or Jewish self-interest. In the aftermath of the Holocaust, they expanded their rhetorical arsenal by means of the images of the slaughter of the six million Jews of Europe. Rather than being something that American Jews shunned in order to fit in while they "engaged in the energetic enterprise of entering American society," the Holocaust served them broadly in their works, as they critiqued practices they abhorred.[6] It became an object lesson they employed as they lambasted policies they loathed, serving as the moral yardstick against which they measured the individuals and institutions they despised. The Holocaust helped them navigate the new postwar world.[7]

As American Jews reflected on what it meant to be American and how they evaluated their country, they laced their words with Holocaust references, augmenting previous arguments in the name of Europe's slaughtered Jews. They peppered their public words with the "the six million," "the Nazi holocaust," and "the concentration camps" in general and with more specific ones: "Dachau," "Auschwitz," or "Maidanek." Likening some event, organization, or individual to "Hitler," "Hitler times," "the Nazis," or "Nazi Germany" connected American Jews' postwar political concerns to the calamity. Using German words like *judenrein* (free of Jews), *verboten* (forbidden), and *fuehrer* (leader), they alerted listeners to Jewish speeches and readers of Jewish articles that something in the present could be best understood in light of German Nazism and what it wrought on the Jewish people.

The issues of the day seemed to them naturally connected to the Holocaust, and discussing these matters provided opportunities to make the European Jewish catastrophe part of the larger common culture. Milwaukee's Rabbi Joseph Baron gave a Hanukkah address on a Sunday morning in 1946 on WTMJ, a local television station. American Jews, he said, owed a "debt due to the past," which had given them the holiday. But they also had "an obligation to the present and future." That obligation involved the reality that "freedom is not yet assured. As I think, for example, of the desperate innocent pitiable Jewish survivors of Belsen and Buchewald, waiting for home at last on the shores of Palestine . . . I think of the embattled patriots and bombed villages in many of the colonial areas of the world; . . . I think of the cruel economic and racial prejudices aflame in our country."[8]

In its 1950 annual report, the American Jewish Committee also fused some its issues with its belief that world events must be seen in light of the Nazi calamity. "Whatever touches the Jew," commented Jacob Blaustein, president of the committee, "or any minority group has an immediate reaction upon the concerns of the world. If Nazi persecutions and consequent cataclysm did not prove that point . . . what happens in England, in Egypt, in Morocco, in China . . . must concern us as much as the latest trends in German anti-Semitism. The admission policy of a fresh-water college in the Middle West and the denial of decent housing facilities to Negroes on the Eastern seaboard compete in interest with yesterday's manifestation of the Ku Klux Klan's strength in Georgia." Blaustein repeated himself: "What happens in Europe, in Asia, in Latin America or anywhere else in the world . . . vitally affects us both as American citizens and as Jews. Hitler . . . proved that for all times."[9]

Likewise in 1956, the American Jewish Congress issued an indignant press release chastising President Eisenhower for invoking executive power and allowing two hundred thousand Hungarian refugees seeking asylum after the failed uprising in their country into the United States, well above Hungary's 865 annual quota slots. However laudatory the AJC considered the Hungarians' stand against the Soviet Union, it questioned why such a welcome had been accorded only to "the victims of Communist persecution." Jews in Egypt also, at that moment, the American Jewish organization informed the president and the press, found themselves subjected to persecutions. Several thousand had fled their homes, unable to sell their property or take assets with them. "Nasser," declared the American Jewish Congress, "like Hitler is determined to make Egypt 'Judenrein.'" Nasser happened to also be the most powerful Arab leader in the coalition arrayed against Israel. So in one brief press release, the organization proclaimed its aversion to the Soviet Union, its criticism of the anti-Communist basis of American immigration policy, and its antipathy toward Egypt and Nasser, all hinging on a few words drawn from the Holocaust era.[10]

Contemporary events constantly kept American Jews focused on the Holocaust. Whatever issues they pondered, they connected the American present with Germany under the Nazis and its campaign against the Jews. During the 1960 presidential campaign, the American Jewish Committee's Community Affairs Department created a study guide for its chapters to use in discussing "Is There a Jewish Vote?" The booklet asked participants to consider various issues and pointed out that "Joseph R. [sic] Kennedy, *the presidential candidate's father took a 'soft line' on Nazi Germany when the U.S. Ambassador to Britain was a supporter of the isolationist America First Party and a financial supporter of Senator McCarthy"* (emphasis in original).[11] The high school participants at Camp Olin-Sang-Ruby in the summer of 1961 contemplated censorship in contemporary America. According to the Reform youngsters, suppressing unpopular political ideas, a strategy advocated and employed by the anti-Communists of the postwar era, could "be a tool of dictatorship. It is the method by which a particular point of view can prevent other points of view from being expressed." This resembled the time when "Adolf Hitler and the Nazis stayed in power by burning all subversive literature and censorship of free speech. They allowed no movements which would have caused internal unrest." Like many postwar American Jews, these teenagers and the camp's staff drew contemporary implications: "What is to prevent a recurrence of the same situation again" in the United States?[12]

American Jewish community groups used Holocaust and Nazi imagery, at times in shorthand form. At a Senate hearing in 1952, William Stern, the national director of the Workmen's Circle English-Speaking Division, testified in favor of legislation to create a Fair Employment Practices Commission. To the members of the Labor-Management Subcommittee, he stressed that, although seven years had passed since the end of World War II, "the American people would be shocked to learn that veterans . . . cannot get jobs . . . because some employers still have a psychological shrine for Adolf Hitler's 'Juden Verboten'—Jews Not Allowed philosophy."[13]

American Jews in the late 1950s and into the 1960s associated manifestations of anti-Semitism at home with the Holocaust. A spate of synagogue bombings in the late 1950s and early 1960s shocked them, and they posited them as the continued reverberations of the Holocaust in their American hometowns. Jews in Kansas City, Missouri, found a perfect way to show this connection after a bombing there in 1960. Their community council and eight Jewish groups decided to stage that year's annual "Memorial Service and yearly Observance and tribute to the Warsaw Ghetto Uprising" at "Kehilath Israel Synagogue. This is the house of worship recently bombed by the American type Nazi."[14] In other communities, local Jewish activists decided to counter the spike in anti-Semitic, Nazi-inflected activities in the early 1960s by asking public schools to start teaching about "the meaning of Nazism." When officials of the JCRC in Pittsburgh met with the superintendent of schools there on this matter in early 1960, they met resistance. The superintendent "seemed to feel" that the Jewish communal leaders "were asking for the introduction of horror material into the curriculum and that if this policy were to be followed," other, unspecified groups would demand that other "tragic things . . . fill the history hour." For their part, the small committee of Jewish leaders pointed out that "this very recent historic tragedy is very much closer to us than some of the others he referred to and that we consider it a serious lack in the curriculum if no effort is made to instruct the children about the meaning of Nazism."[15]

Into the early 1960s, as American Jews witnessed events, large and small, that seemed to them anti-Semitic or that seemed to propagate negative images of Jews, they protested by means of Holocaust references. When in 1962 CBS decided to televise Joseph Papp's Central Park production of Shakespeare's *Merchant of Venice*, Jewish publications and commentators took him, the park, and the television network to task for making manifest images of Jews that involved "a distortion and defamation of our people and faith that ranks with . . . the rantings of the late Julius Streicher of Nazi Germany." These words had been offered by a delegation of rabbis in testimony to a mayoral committee convened to consider the problems involved in the production of the play. Rabbi David Seligson of the Central Synagogue went further in his sermon, which the *New York Times* quoted at length: "Dr. Seligson drew a relationship between caricatures of Jews as vindictive, malignant and avaricious to the beginnings of the Nazi movement in Germany, producing a 'social climate' in which a generation of Germans could witness passively the extermination of 6,000,000 Jews." Hayim Leiberman, theater critic for the *Forward*, commented that "this agonizing play took two and a half hours, in which was heard a kind of echo of . . . the Hitler era. The only thing missing was a gas chamber."[16]

So ubiquitously did Jewish speakers and writers employ such rhetoric that others in the community began to assert that such language had gone too far and did not fit the circumstances. References to anti-Semitic pranks by juvenile delinquents or the fulminations of small groups of swastika-wearing "lunatics," some said, should not be equated with the European Jewish catastrophe. Minor episodes like these hardly warranted invocation of gas chambers, the six million, and Hitler. Isaac Franck of the Washington, D.C., Jewish Community Council, writing in 1961 at the height of the Rockwell affair, described the American Jewish community as being caught up in "hysteria and downright madness." After all, "Rockwell is not today, has not been at any time in the past, and unless the situation changes radically or appreciably, will not in the calculable future be a serious danger . . . any greater than . . . the other two or three dozen anti-Semitic leaders and groups now disfiguring the American landscape."[17]

Franck's counsel for restraint said much about how American Jews of the early 1960s processed the Holocaust. He found the "madness" displayed by American Jews about Rockwell and the swastikas to be "sad." "There must . . . still continue to be, in the inner mental recesses of substantial numbers of American Jews," Franck speculated, "reservoirs of fear, of emotional insecurity that the 15 years since the unspeakable agony of the Hitler holocaust have not drained or healed." To Franck, the seasoned Jewish community relations professional, American Jews of 1960—a community made up largely of American-born, economically successful, highly integrated women and men—lived with a severe disjunction "between the state of security it has *actually achieved* . . . and our recognition of that status, and our actions on the basis of such recognition." That chasm in large measure reflected the reality that the "Hitler holocaust" made it impossible for them to accurately see the security they lived with. Derived from his pivotal position as the executive director of a substantial local Jewish community relations agency, Franck's perception that 1950s Jews shaped their American lives in direct relationship to the "unspeakable agony of the Hitler holocaust" diminishes the regnant truth which has so broadly claimed that it meant relatively little to them.

But Franck may have been wrong about the issue of American Jewish insecurity as opposed to American Jewish confidence. That American Jews made so much about the Holocaust, that they analogized from it to their own lives, reflected their comfort in America. They sensed enough assurance that they could, when they wanted, describe and mourn what had happened to Europe's Jews during the Hitler years. They could take positions that deviated from the American consensus when perceiving parallels between something in the present and the Holocaust.[18]

Jews in Postwar America

These Jews lived with a set of contradictions about their place in America. When the era began, they still faced exclusionary practices in universities, the job market, and the housing field. By the end of the era, with the passage of civil rights legislation in 1964 and 1965, no such discrimination barred them from access to whatever they wanted. They benefited mightily from the affluence and openness of the postwar moment, joining their white non-Jewish neighbors in the rush to newly constructed suburbs on the edge of American cities. Indeed, they pioneered in the urban exodus.[19]

These years saw the almost complete passing of the immigrant-generation Jewish working class, as educated professionals became the American Jewish norm. They exulted in their educational and economic successes.

Despite economic mobility, American Jews still solidly allied themselves with liberalism, and an almost perfect synergy fused the American Jewish vision and the liberal one. These years saw the first important judicial and legislative victories of the civil rights struggle. Courts began to thicken the walls between religion, Christianity, and the state. The birth of the United Nations seemed to portend international cooperation, while debates over immigration reform resonated deeply with American Jews, promising that the hated quota system might soon crumble.

At the same time, though, liberalism came under attack. American Jews paid close attention to those assaults, recognizing that the assaulters considered Jews the chief agents of social and political changes. They heard quite clearly the diatribes charging Jews with subverting American values by destroying the nation's white Christian essence. Individuals, organizations, and publications from the political right challenged nearly every aspect of the American Jewish political agenda: civil rights, internationalism, strict separationism in church-state relations, support for labor unions, and the maintenance (indeed, expansion) of New Deal economic policies.

Many of these Americans linked Jews with Communism, an old canard, but revived with particular virulence as the United States and the Soviet Union engaged in a fierce ideological struggle and American society resounded with accusations of treason and disloyalty hurled at individuals and groups. Some argued that American Jewish liberalism constituted covert, even overt, Communism. American Jews tried to gauge the potency of the anti-Communist "radical right," believing that attacks on liberalism threatened Jewish interests. The fact that, through the middle of the 1950s, a small but vocal segment of American Jewry did sympathize with Communism and the Soviet Union complicated the American Jewish mainstream's arguments. To their detractors, this proved the point. Jews helped direct the international Communist menace, ready to destroy the American way. American Jewish communal agencies, in turn, attempted to prove that Jews opposed Communism, at the same time that they remained wedded to liberalism.

The sputtering of anti-Semitic organizations and publications, spewing anti-Jewish rhetoric, as well as sporadic acts of violence against Jewish sites, kept the symbols of the Holocaust alive in America. Jews could not help wonder about the number and potency of the anti-Semitic organizations that framed their words in Nazi metaphors, often accompanied by swastikas, Nazi salutes, and even storm-trooper-like uniforms. However minor and isolated, however skeletal the groups, they gave American Jews pause as they saw hated symbols of the tragic past pop up in their American present. American Jewish publications and the newsletters of their organizations covered in detail the rise of these anti-Jewish, Nazi-like groups. In covering them, the Jewish organizations put Holocaust idioms on the communal forefront.

American Jewry kept close tabs on anti-Semitism at home, seeing parallels between here and there, now and then. The National Federation of Temple Youth opened its 1945 national convention with a warning delivered by its president. "The conclusion of the war," he told his members, "does *not* mean that we do not have to continue the fight for the preservation of the democratic ideals of our forefathers. We know that Anti-Semitism did not die out with Hitler. It is at work right here in our own America."[20]

In 1947, the Anti-Defamation League informed members and the broader Jewish public about Maynard O. Nelson, operating in Minnesota and California, "wearing a full Nazi-type uniform." American Jews must have heard the echoes of Nazi Germany in the late 1940s in Jesse B. Stoner's words. Head of the Stoner Anti-Jewish Party of Tennessee, he proposed an amendment to the U.S. Constitution making it a crime to be Jewish in America.[21] The 1953 *American Jewish Year Book*, as it did annually, described the plethora of anti-Jewish groups and activities that surfaced around the country, including a rash of synagogue desecrations in the Philadelphia area, perpetrated by teenagers organized in "an imitation Hitler Youth group." That year, the *Year Book* highlighted James A. Madole and his National Renaissance Party, which held "weekly street meetings" in New York "at which praises of Hitler" could be heard. Two years later, Madole proposed that the United States needed "concentration camps like in Germany." He editorialized in his *Bulletin* of May 1953 that, "although Adolf Hitler is dead his philosophy lives again in the growing strength of Fascist forces in America, Europe, and the Middle East. What Hitler accomplished in Europe, the National Renaissance Party shall yet accomplish in America."[22]

The passage of time did not lessen the frequency or virulence of such rhetoric or American Jewry's monitoring of it. In 1953, Conde McGinley's *The Coming Red Dictatorship*, illustrated with "Streicher-like caricatures," told readers that, "in case you think we are prejudiced, history for more than 1,000 years indicates that wherever these people," the Jews, "have settled, it was necessary to evict them eventually—Babylon, Spain, France, England, and as recent as 1939, Germany, and it will happen in America." A 1961 ADL report told of a letter received by a Jewish fraternity from a "Neo-Nazi club, warning the young Jewish men to "REMEMBER BUCHEN-WALD: This might happen to you. . . . We don't want you JEWS to ruin us . . . as you destroyed the GERMAN spirit and dignity." By 1959, American Jews focused attention on George Lincoln Rockwell's American Nazi Party. Rockwell's publication *Stormtrooper* advertised the sale of "Nazi Stickers. Bright little hellraisers which do a wonder of good . . . and ANN FRANK SOAP WRAPPERS . . . Put it on regular cakes and delight your friends." A delegation from the Jewish War Veterans met with President Kennedy and "showed the President actual copies of the latest attempt at terror propaganda," crafted by Rockwell, including "postcards dispatched via U.S. mail, stating, 'Bring Back Auschwitz' and 'Juden Raus.'"[23]

Such rhetoric kept American Jews focused on the Holocaust. In the early 1960s, Jewish community workers discussed among themselves the appearance of bumper stickers reading "I Like Eich" and "Hitler Was Right!" When the "Hitler Was Right!" bumper stickers surfaced in St. Louis, with some "affixed to a temple and the YMHA," local Jewish community relations officials communicated with their counterparts in Detroit, Chicago, Cincinnati, Cleveland, and Pittsburgh, as well as the national offices of the Anti-Defamation League, on their experiences with the offending material.[24]

The cumulative effect of these incidents, all trivial but nonetheless terrifying, helped keep American Jews attuned to the Holocaust and convinced them that what happened in Europe in the 1930s and 1940s reverberated in the present. Even the most local of matters kept the Holocaust vivid. In 1962, the Jewish community of Hamden, Connecticut, became embroiled in a local controversy over public school Christmas celebrations. The Jewish Community Council of Greater New Haven had passed a resolution asking the Board of Education and town residents to "join us in abjuring any form of public sponsorship of religious exercises, celebrations and festivals" in the schools. This call for partnership fell on deaf ears. Instead, tempers flared, raucous meetings ensued, and the goodwill that Jews had worked to build seemed in jeopardy. Local Jews, describing the reactions of their neighbors to the suggestion that religious celebration had no place in public schools, turned to Nazi-era metaphors. The school board meeting, one Jewish resident wrote, seemed "comparable to a mob in Munich under Hitler." For their part, local non-Jews helped keep the Holocaust in the consciousness of the Jews. Jewish merchants started receiving letters threatening boycotts, swastikas sprouted on the walls of the high school building, placards displayed at the school equated Jews and Communists, and blackboard graffiti warned, "What Eichmann started, we'll finish."[25]

Activists in the Jewish communal infrastructure debated the extent of such thinking among Americans and the potential power of anti-Semitic groups to go beyond ugly words. In 1955, the Plenary Session of the National Community Relations Advisory Committee took up this issue. Attorney Joseph Rauh dismissed the speeches and publications of the anti-Semitic right as minor irritants. Joseph Barr of the Jewish War Veterans saw it differently, believing that small did not mean without danger. History offered Barr a particular lesson. "The Nazi Party in Germany," Barr noted, "between 1924 and 1930 was called a minuscule party and its importance was underrated because it was deemed a crackpot movement with only a few hundred members." To Rauh, on the other hand, constitutional guarantees of equality and justice rendered the historical analogy an inappropriate basis upon which to craft a communal response strategy.[26]

Despite the fears of many and their criticisms of America, the Jews of the United States celebrated America as hospitable, as a diaspora home unlike any others. They employed the Holocaust to do that as well. Novelist Herman Wouk brought his popular book *This Is My God* of 1959 to a close by remarking, "There will be no death camps in the United States.... The civilization we know will have to be obliterated before a Hitler can sit in Washington." Like so many other American Jews, Wouk measured the stark difference between the United States, a place where Jews, particularly in the postwar era, experienced acceptance, integration, and astonishingly high levels of economic mobility, with what had just transpired in Europe. In a 1954 article on "The Common Denominator Between the American and the Jewish Outlook," Nina Alderblum also posited the contrast with Germany. In America, that "common denominator" made it possible for Jews to become full Americans and remain involved Jews, but "the Jewish and the German way of thinking could not be coordinated." Those two world views had just been too far apart, and "that . . . has been proven by the complete Jewish assimilation on the one hand, and by Hitler's rapid dissolution of it, on the other."[27]

Postwar American Jewish texts hailed the liberal essence of America as the counter to the German Nazism that murdered European Jewry. They did so symbolically and rhetorically. Rabbi Norman Salit of the Synagogue

Council of America went to Germany in 1953 to meet with its small Jewish community and Chancellor Adenauer. He took along as gifts for both the Jewish survivors and the head of the Federal Republic of Germany framed copies of George Washington's 1790 letter to the Hebrew Congregation of Newport, Rhode Island, in which the first president greeted his new nation's Jews with the words, "the Government of the United States . . . gives to bigotry no sanction, to persecution no assistance. . . . may the children of the Stock of Abraham, who dwell in this land, continue to merit and enjoy the good will of other inhabitants."[28]

By hailing the United States, American Jews declared their loyalty to the nation and revisited the narrative of the Hitler era. Certainly Cold War circumstances played a role in this adulation of the United States, as did the reality that American Jews had prospered mightily from the accidents of their personal histories. They recognized on a visceral level that serendipity had put their parents or grandparents on ships bound for America, deciding not to remain in Europe, in the stretch of land from Poland to Lithuania and the Ukraine, the places from which most had emigrated and the epicenter of the Nazis' slaughter. The creators and consumers of American Jewish texts knew at a profound personal level that a different familial decision taken just a generation or two in the past would have meant that, rather than living in the beneficent affluence of liberal America, they might have been among those who had perished in ghettoes and gas chambers.

American Jews, the Soviet Union, and the Holocaust

Of the matters that dominated postwar America, few loomed larger than the complex of concerns involving Communism's "Iron Curtain," behind which lived the peoples of eastern Europe, and the United States' Cold War conflict with the Soviet Union. These issues blurred the line between foreign and domestic affairs, leaving their mark on every aspect of American life, and Jews in the United States resembled all other Americans in having to deal with them.[29]

But American Jews differed from other Americans in a number of ways on this subject. Those differences both reflected Jewish concern with the Holocaust and allowed them to keep its memory in the forefront of communal discussions. For one, Russia had long inspired loathing among Jews, and when they analogized between it and Germany's perpetration of the Holocaust, they did so in ways that had little, even nothing, to do with Communism. The Soviet Union, the successor regime to Czarist Russia, had a particular salience for American Jews. The forbears of the largest percentage of American Jews had four and five decades earlier immigrated to the United States from Russia. The American Jewish communal narrative attributed the great migration of over two million Jews to the waves of violence that, starting in the 1880s, periodically swept over Russia. That "old home" had been a midwife of modern anti-Semitism, and long before the words "catastrophe," "the six million," and "Holocaust" dominated Jewish rhetoric, the Russian word "pogrom" resonated in the Jewish lexicon. They had used "czar" and "czarist" as words of disdain before "Nazi" and "Hitler" embodied anti-Jewish evil, and the place name "Kishinev" predated "Auschwitz" or "Germany" as a site of Jewish suffering.

Furthermore, American Jews could not tell the history of the Holocaust without factoring in the actions of the Soviet Union. The 1939 pact between Stalin and Hitler opened up the western doors of Poland to the German invasion, exposing millions of Jews there to the brutality of occupation, ghettoization, eventual deportation to the concentration camps, and systematic murder. Germany's invasion of the Soviet Union in the summer of 1941 nullified the treaty, and the Jews of eastern Poland, Russia, the Ukraine, Lithuania, and Latvia, all under Soviet rule, found themselves exposed, terrorized, and slaughtered.

American Jewish writers, orators, rabbis, and community activists focused attention on the Hitler-Stalin pact and the behavior of the Lithuanians, Ukrainians, and Latvians, all Soviet citizens, toward the Jews during the German occupation. The Jewish Labor Committee, among the most stridently anti-Communist American Jewish organizations, constantly mentioned the two-year alliance between Nazi Germany and the Soviet Union as evidence of the evils of Communism. In 1950, the Jewish Labor Committee held a mass meeting, bringing together "more than 2,000 delegates" to New York's Astor Hotel under the rubric "Jewish Labor Fights Communism." The speeches, reprinted as a booklet, went out to unions and Jewish groups. In these speeches, the Hitler-Stalin pact provided ample evidence of the devastating impact of the Soviet Union's behavior. Adolph Held, the JLC's chairman, claimed that he and the others in the American Jewish labor movement "were not surprised by the Hitler-Stalin pact. We knew better from previous events—when the German Communists made pacts with Nazis to destroy the free trade unions, and break the strikes aimed at defeating the rising power of the Nazis. And we were not blinded to the nature of Bolshevism when it became America's military ally." One speaker, Herschel Himmelfarb, "one of Stalin's former slave laborers and a pre-war head of the Polish Needle Trade Union," had fled the Nazi zone "when Stalin and Hitler made their infamous pact." Nathan Chanin, educational director of the Workmen's Circle, told how, "in 1939 after the Nazi-Soviet Pact, with Stalin's help, Hitler created the Ghettoes which cost the lives of 6,000,000 Jews."[30]

Yet even in the most anti-Communist text, when discussing this historical event, American Jews directly or indirectly rank-ordered the perpetrators, naming as evil the Germans far more than the Soviets. For example, a 1954 installment of *The Eternal Light* dramatized the destruction of the Talmudic academy in Volozhin, "in the corner of Poland near Russia." The drama began "that summer of 1939 when Hitler and Stalin made an agreement and the German army began to overrun Poland." Volozhin came under Russian control. The play, a rare *Eternal Light* drama about the Soviet Union, focused on the destruction of this center of Jewish learning by the "Commissars." The drama's protagonist, "Shlomo," challenged "Comrade Granovsky," landing him "in the prison labor camp in Siberia," where he "slaved and froze and hungered for seven years." Shlomo survived and got to "have the last word" in the play. Given the date of the play, 1954, a highwater mark in Soviet-U.S. tension, his last word could easily have been an anti-Soviet diatribe. On the contrary, he turned his attention to the greater villain: "You know how many died . . . when Hitler's understanding with Stalin expired and Hitler's armies swept over Poland?" he asked listeners. The *Eternal Light* commentator, Myron Weinstein, returned to the Volozhin story in his concluding remarks, contrasting it as an educational institution based on "freedom of inquiry—freedom of assembly—freedom of the spirit" with the "the police state" that destroyed it. Listeners might have expected that Weinstein had Stalinist Russia in mind. Rather, Weinstein blasted "the tactile swords of Hadrian, Nero and Hitler."[31]

Similarly in 1955, in an impassioned article condemning the American rearmament of Germany, Trude Weiss-Rosmarin opined on the aptness of the aphorism "politics makes strange bedfellows," predicting that the "Democracies will have to rue this choice of what is considered 'the minor evil,'" a remilitarized Germany as a buffer to Soviet expansion plans into the west. She likened this decision to the Nazi-Soviet pact and asked, "What assurance is there that Western Germany, armed to the teeth and in command of a strong army, will not join forces with Soviet Russia, so as to bring about the unification of the Reich? If Hitler and Stalin could manage to unite so as to advance their respective aims, it is certainly possible that the Bonn Government and Malenkov will get together." The article, "Thinking About Germany," began, "We have our own case to plead —the case of SIX MILLION Jews bestially done to death by Germans." To Weiss-Rosmarin, Stalin and the Soviets occupied a rung of evil well below Germany.[32]

American Jewish references to the evils of the Soviet Union also took their shape from the fact that an estimated million and a half Soviet Jews had perished at the hands of the Germans, particularly in western Russia and the Baltics. American Jewish articles, speeches, and public meetings which discussed the liquidation of Jews in the Soviet Union focused on the collaboration of local Russians, Ukrainians, Lithuanians, and Latvians with the Germans. In 1959, in "Khrushchev and the Jews," Leo Heiman, like other writers, tried to pin down the actual number of Jews who had been murdered by the Nazis within the Soviet Union. "In 1941," he wrote, "there were at least one million Jews in Western Ukraine and in Kiev, Odessa, and other population centers." Khrushchev organized the unsuccessful defense of the Ukraine against the German armies, and Heiman considered him, to a degree, responsible for the massive slaughter of the Jews in his zone of authority. After all, "most . . . were killed, largely by Ukrainian-Nazi police, Ukrainian Nationalist guerrillas, pogrom-running mobs and Ukrainian units of the German security police," with the oversight and help of the "SS shock troops." By the end of 1943, "only 100,000 Jews remained in ghettos and labor camps. They were killed that year by Germans and Ukrainians."[33]

Questions about how many Jews had been murdered in the Soviet Union during the Nazi occupation and how many survived showed up repeatedly in American Jewish writings, allowing writers and community activists to highlight the role of Soviet citizens and, some asserted, the state in the slaughter of the Jews.[34] In its relentless propaganda war against the Soviet Union, the Jewish Labor Committee offered a several-page mimeographed fact sheet on "How Many Jews Survived in the Soviet Union Following World War II?" "One, two or three million?" it asked, contrasting statements about the heroic rescue effort undertaken by the "Red Army," which boasted of having "saved the Jewish people at the most critical hour of its history," and the "ever increasing amount of evidence" showing that "there was no appreciable evacuation of Jews from Lithuania, Latvia and Estonia. Over two thirds of the Jews in Bessarabia and Bukovina were left behind to certain extermination by the invading Nazis." The fact sheet presented material from an article by Vassily Grossman, "Ukraine Without Jews," in which the writer estimated that "Hitler killed all the Jews he met in the Ukraine, everyone without exception. No less than a million."[35]

Jewish community texts highlighted the fact that Soviet commemorations of the German occupation suppressed the truth of the Jews' particular suffering and annihilation. The 1960 annual convention of the Jewish Labor Committee featured a speaker who said that "the people of the USSR were never told of the bestialities committed by the Nazis against Jews in Poland or in the Soviet Union itself. And whenever they accused the Germans of atrocities against Russian citizens, they never mentioned that those citizens were Jews."[36] Jewish publications and sermons lamented the fact that "Soviet authorities do little to protect and care for the graves of Jewish victims of the Nazi mass murders, particularly in the Ukraine where there had been over one million Jewish victims of the Nazis."[37]

In 1961, Soviet poet Yevgeny Yevtushenko handed American Jewry a new golden opportunity to tell this story when he published "Babi Yar." The poem excoriated Soviet officials who failed to put up a marker over the collective grave of the more than forty thousand Jews from the Kiev area, all machine-gunned to death or just buried alive and dumped in the ravine of Babi Yar over the course of a few days. The Jewish press covered the poem's publication, offered English translations of it, and hailed the poet as someone who with a single stroke told graphically of the Germans' barbarities and exposed the anti-Semitism rampant in the Soviet Union. "The Soviet authorities," wrote Boris Smolar for the American Jewish press, "have—for reasons known only to themselves—attempted to wipe out every possible memory of this huge field." Today, Smolar wrote, "it is difficult for a tourist even to get to Babi Yar. . . . Intourist officials tell tourists that 'they have never heard' of Babi Yar. . . . The mention of Babi Yar in connection with the massacre of Jews became an offense," and the "only ones who remember the Babi Yar tragedy are the Jews of Kiev. On Yom Kippur eve, regarded as the anniversary of the great massacre, they go stealthily to the site of the slaughter to mourn their dead and pour out their hearts."[38]

That several million Jews lived in the Soviet Union during the postwar period further made American Jewry's Cold War different from that of most Americans. Just as American Jews fretted over outbreaks of anti-Semitism in postwar Germany, Argentina, and the Arab Middle East, they organized meetings about the plight of "Iron Curtain" Jews. The fact that the Soviet Union housed the world's second largest Jewish population and little communication linked them to American Jewry complicated the situation.[39] American Jews monitored the fate of the Jews in the Soviet Union and Soviet policies vis-à-vis the practice of Judaism, Jewish culture, and the freedom of Soviet Jews to immigrate to Israel. During the postwar period, Jews also lived, in obviously greatly reduced numbers, in the Soviet satellite countries, Poland, Czechoslovakia, Hungary, Romania, and the German Democratic Republic. Their situations troubled American Jewry. American Jewish organizations and publications kept track of anti-Semitism in those Communist-dominated places, paying attention to Jewish communal and cultural life there, following closely and commenting on, for example, the execution of a group of Jewish writers, artists, and intellectuals in Moscow in 1948, the trial and execution in Czechoslovakia of Rudolf Slansky in 1952, and the 1953 "Doctor's Plot" in Moscow. American Jewish organizations carefully tracked the Communist governments' use of anti-Jewish and anti-Zionist rhetoric.[40]

American Jews roundly condemned eastern-bloc anti-Semitism, often folding in Holocaust references, comparisons, and linkages. When they brought the Holocaust into discussions on the Soviet Union, they tended to do so more in the form of questions than as statements of fact, pondering possible similarities between German anti-Semitism and that of the Soviet Union, hinting, rather than predicting, that maybe the Soviet Union might become the site for the next Jewish catastrophe. In 1952, the American Jewish Congress's Commission on Law and Social Action expressed itself on this subject: "Are we to see the annihilation of another two million Jews? Will the Communist powers finish the all-but-completed job of the Nazis? Will the world again sadly shake its head but lift no helping hand?"[41] The 1954 annual report of the American Jewish Committee articulated its fears about a possible "merger of world-wide anti-democratic forces: the Communists, the Germans in Europe, the Arabs in the Middle East, [and] the fascist countries in South America." "For the second time in a generation Jews may well become the scapegoats of restive and fearful peoples any where in the world. The further fact that 2,500,000 Jews now living in Iron Curtain countries are in the most immediate and extreme danger" exacerbated its foreboding.[42]

American Jewish public programs and projects contemplated the likelihood that the Soviets under the right circumstances could "finish what Hitler had no time to carry out," as articulated by Hayim Leivik in *A Decade of Destruction: Jewish Culture in the USSR*, written to commemorate "the ruthless destruction by the Soviet government of the last vestiges of Jewish culture along with the remaining Jewish writers in the Soviet Union."[43] Lucy Dawidowicz, writing for the *American Jewish Year Book*, chronicled a wide range of protest activities undertaken by American Jews over anti-Semitism in the Soviet bloc countries. She put the matter in a clear histori-cal context: "With the memory of Nazi Germany's murder of 6,000,000 fresh in their minds, American Jews were in the main convinced that only a tremendous world-wide protest could stop the further development of the Communist anti-Semitic campaign."[44]

Words involved calls to political action, framed in the memory of what had happened to Europe's Jews during the Nazi era. In a letter to her "co-workers," offering suggestions for political action by Reform women, the president of the National Federation of Temple Sisterhoods, Mrs. Abram V. Goodman, noted about the Slansky trial, "Purges are no novelty in Communist history, yet the Czech purge has introduced a new note. Anti-Semitism is now added to the other invidious weapons of the totalitarian arsenal, and the world shudders at the possibility of this trend's presaging another nightmare like Hitler's Jewish extermination policy." She suggested possible activities around this, speculating why anti-Semitism had surfaced so sharply in the eastern-bloc countries: "Are the Jews being made scape-goats to distract from the failure of the Communist internal economic pro-gram? Is this Stalin's way of linking arms with the renascent Nazi move-ment or wooing the Arab states to enlist under his banner? Could this be the prelude to a new war as Hitler's anti-Semitic program anticipated his aggression?"[45]

Perceived parallels between the Holocaust and Communist poli-cies that targeted Jews drew the attention of young people as well. Young Judea's newspaper, the *Senior,* devoted a front-page article to the Slansky trial. "Genocide—1953" detailed the trial, describing Czechoslovak Jewry as "the weak and vulnerable remnant" of the once-thriving Jewish com-munity: "There is good reason to fear that the anti-Semitism now being whipped up behind the iron curtain may be the prelude to a pogrom [of] a genocidal nature and proportions. *The spark of anti-Semitism generally ig-nites the conflagration of the crematorium*" (emphasis in original).

Most American Jewish commentary and communal programming dealing with Soviet Jewry focused not on a physical threat to Jews in Com-munist countries but on the dangers posed to religion and Jewish cultural life. The editor of the *Senior* notwithstanding, Jews would be allowed to survive physically, but not Jewish culture. American Jews reflected on how

"Communist Russia uprooted Yiddish cultural institutions and imposed linguistic-cultural assimilation upon Soviet Jews," bringing about the "liquidation within the Soviet Union of both Jewish cultural personalities and institutions." They contemplated a "cultural genocide" perpetrated on the Jews by the Communist governments.[46]

In their texts, they conjoined this fear with the legacy of the Holocaust. In a series of lectures given to mark the three hundredth anniversary of Jewish settlement in America, Israel Goldstein noted, "World War II decimated" the Jewish people. "Of Europe's nine to ten million Jews," he enumerated, two-thirds fell victim to Nazi extermination. "And of the surviving remnant, the largest part have come under the Communist regimes where their fate is"—then he turned to Hebrew—"*Srayfat neshamah veguf kayyam*" (the soul is burnt but the body persists).[47] The editors of a proposed book on the Jews of Bessarabia invited Jewish Labor Committee official Jacob Pat to contribute an essay. He described the Bessarabian Jew as "twice ripped apart: the Nazi-Rumanian evil carried out upon him . . . in Transdnisteria [*sic*]. The Soviet evil cut him up spiritually."[48]

However passionately American Jews condemned Soviet policies toward the Jews, they emphasized that Jewish culture and not Jews suffered, highlighting the nonracialist basis to Soviet anti-Semitism. That differentiated it from Nazism. In 1953, Isaiah Minkoff lambasted the Soviet Union for its propaganda against Israel; for disseminating the specter of "an internal, imperialist, bourgeois conspiracy under Zionism"; and for using Jews "as a scapegoat, as did decades ago the Czarist regime and later Hitler." Yet, Minkoff added, "they did not adopt the racist Nazi theory."[49]

Comparison between the Germans and the Soviets even received a *halachic* (legal) analysis, again with the Nazis emerging as the clearly worse villains. In a 1962 issue of *Tradition*, Maurice Lamm examined the proposition, so commonly heard in America in those days, " 'Red or Dead'? An Attempt at Formulating a Jewish Attitude." To Lamm, the answer involved only "whether he," the observant Jew, "is capable of observing the fundamentals of the Basic Moral Life, or whether he must violate them in order to survive." Since in the Soviet Union, "while the Jew is not openly permitted to observe his religion . . . unlike under the Nazis, there Jews are not coerced to kill or to commit acts of immorality. . . . Under such circumstances the individual must consider the inherent sanctity of life itself: Better Red than *Dead*. . . . Unlike the Nazis, the Soviets do not want to destroy the *lives* but rather the *spirit* of the Jews. A completely assimilated,

Russified Jew may be able to get along very well in Russia, despite some minor discrimination."[50]

None asserted that the Communists even remotely equaled the Nazis in brutality. American Jews explicitly declared that the latter far outdid the former. Editorials and articles in Jewish publications minced no words in their opposition to Communism. In their assessment of Stalin and, in a milder form, Khrushchev as totalitarians responsible for the suppression of Jewish life and culture, American Jews depicted them as far different, and less physically menacing, than Hitler and the Nazis. In 1953, Weiss-Rosmarin put recent Soviet anti-Semitism in historical perspective: "Whatever political motives . . . may inspire the current Soviet hate-campaign against Jews," she suggested, "one thing is certain; that campaign is gleefully supported and enjoyed by Russians, Czechs, Hungarians, Rumanians and other Iron Curtain peoples." But "the communist Satellites enjoy anti-Semitism no less than the French, the Belgians and the Dutch did under the Nazi regime," although "with moderation." She then compared them all to the archvillains of Jewish history, commenting that none demonstrated "fortunately . . . the bestial lust with which the Germans responded to 'Jewish blood dripping from the knives.' "[51] The following year in a speech in Pittsburgh, Isaiah Minkoff, condemning "totalitarianism whether red or black or brown or even silver," warned that "the Soviet brand of anti-Semitism is not to be compared to the bestial extermination methods of the Nazis," although the "Red regime knows how to exploit anti-Semitism for its own political and conspiratorial purposes."[52]

The temporal proximity between the Holocaust and manifestations of anti-Semitism in the Communist world shaped postwar American Jewish rhetoric, whether within communal circles or beamed to other Americans. Pointing out the parallels between the Holocaust and Soviet anti-Semitism continued into the 1960s. At the Reform summer camp Olin-Sang-Ruby's Leadership Conclave of 1962, the youngsters held a study session on Soviet Jewry, learning that "the terrible nightmare was over; Nazi Germany was no more. The Jews around the world could take a breather. Never again, Judaism hoped, would such persecution" take place. But, now, "it appears that we may soon see another Germany in the making" in the Soviet Union.[53] A speaker at a Labor Zionist gathering in Chicago in 1960 remarked on the "very fundamental changes in the total structure of our people the world over, such as the destruction of the major part of European Jewry by the Nazi holocaust," as well as "the enforced assimilation of Russian Jewry under the heel of Communism."[54]

Specter of Anti-Communism

American Jewish political projects that rhetorically linked Stalinism and the Soviet Union with the imagery of the Holocaust existed in tandem with fears of the growing power of a rabid brand of American anti-Communism.[55] American Jews knew well that Americans on the right considered "Jew" and "Communist" synonyms and that much anti-Communist rhetoric conflated them. Texts produced by their organizations fretted greatly about the number of speakers, organizations, and publications that made this point. The 1952 *American Jewish Year Book* noted with alarm, "In the atmosphere of mounting world tension that prevailed . . . anti-Semitic agitators intensified their typical attacks upon American Jews as Communists and Soviet agents." And in what must have seemed reminiscent of early Nazi agitation in Germany when Hitler attracted supporters by appealing to anti-Communist fears, the *Year Book* found troubling "the tendency of certain respectable elements in the United States to be more tolerant of patently anti-Semitic individuals and themes because they were anti-Communist." In this charged atmosphere, American Jews' efforts to prove their anti-Communist *bona fides* constituted in part an attempt at self-defense.[56]

American Jews constructed a public message that, they hoped, disproved popular beliefs about Jews as Communists. As they saw it, the degree to which American Jewry could draw the public's attention simultaneously to its antipathy to Communism and Nazism, the safer they would be. The Jewish Labor Committee particularly perfected this rhetorical strategy. In its anti-Communist documents, it always mentioned that it had been founded to combat Nazism, and its anti-Communist work flowed logically from that. It cited the rallies it staged against Communism as naturally following those that it had organized against Hitler.

So, too, in 1950, B'nai B'rith issued an article, "Jewry an Old Foe of Communism." The article began with the words, "The time was October, 1935. Adolf Hitler had just deprived the Jews in Germany of their rights as citizens," and then recalled how it, along with the American Jewish Committee and the Jewish Labor Committee, had in 1935 crafted a "Public Statement on Communism and Jews." The 1950 article reprinted the 1935 one, written to prove the falsehood of Hitler's propaganda which asserted the singularity of the Jewish and Communist threats, and concluded with the words, "Is it not plain that his thunderbolts against Marxism are only a smokescreen for his sinister designs upon the liberties of the German

"YOUR HONOR, SIR. AFTER OBJECTIVELY CONSIDERING THE EVI-
DENCE PRESENTED BY THE STATE, AND FINDING IT INSUFFICIENT
TO CORROBORATE . . . BEYOND A REASONABLE DOUBT . . . THE
GUILT OF THE DEFENDANT, WE THE JURY FIND THE DEFENDANT
NOT GUILTY OF BOMBING THE JEWISH TEMPLE AT . . ."

On January 26, 1959, George Bright was acquitted of the charge of the bombing, in 1958,
of the Temple in Atlanta, Georgia. The state's witnesses testified that Bright hated Jews
and that he had plotted the bombing of a synagogue. The jury gave the "not guilty" verdict
because the state of Georgia did not prove its case "beyond a reasonable doubt."

Jewish youth publications like *Furrows*, the magazine of the Labor Zionist youth group Habonim, just like American Jewry broadly, linked
manifestations of anti-Semitism in the United States with memories of
the Nazi era. While the 1958 cartoon depicted the bombing of a synagogue in Atlanta, the posters on the floor read "Exterminate the Jew"
and "Why Hitler Was Right!," demonstrating the constant playing out
of the Holocaust in postwar American Jewish life. American Jews did
not have to be overly imaginative to see this connection since many of
the anti-Semitic groups themselves invoked Hitler, the six million, and
their desire to continue this murderous work in America. *Courtesy Habonim Dror North America.*

people and the peace of the world?" The authors of the 1935 document could not know what the B'nai B'rith officials did in 1950—that is, where Hitler's propaganda line about Jews as Communists would lead. By reprinting the historic statement, it sought to prove that most Jews abhorred Communism, yet despite that, this malicious lie had just recently resulted in the wholesale slaughter of European Jewry.[57]

In their discourse about Communism and its evils, American Jews also tried to turn American anti-Communism on its head by pointing out the far greater evil perpetrated by the Nazis compared with the Soviets and how Cold War anti-Communism led to absurd and frightening results. In 1955, Adolph Held wrote to Secretary of State John Foster Dulles. He opened his letter by invoking the era's dominant rhetoric about the need "to combat Soviet imperialism" and stating that the "Hammer and Sickle" symbolized "totalitarian power." Although his letter said nothing about "Soviet imperialism," it had everything to do with the legacy of the Holocaust and Nazism in a less-than-denazified Germany. This allowed Held to criticize the ineffectiveness and ludicrousness of the anti-Communist moment: "If we are to combat Soviet imperialism, we cannot do it effectively by permitting West Germany to give official sanction to the deification of another totalitarian power." The United States must, Held wrote, actively root out "publishers or firms responsible for perpetuating the companion symbol of the Hammer and Sickle—the Nazi Swastika." The Jewish Labor Committee and American Jewry "urge an immediate investigation and a full public report and administrative reprisals" by the U.S. government.[58]

American Jewry's reaction to Communism and the Soviet Union reflected a complicated reality. It included within its ranks uncountable numbers of former Communists. These Jewish women and men had once belonged to the party itself or to organizations sympathetic to Communism, or they merely approved of its ideology and had admired the Soviet Union. They added their voices to the chorus of American Jewish commentary on Communism, creating a discourse that conjoined Communism and Nazism. Novelist Howard Fast remained with the Communist Party until 1956 and contributed an article to the Zionist magazine *Midstream* shortly after renouncing his membership. He pointed to his intimate knowledge of Communism and its rhetorical strategies. The orthodox Soviet position deemphasized Jewish suffering in the Holocaust, he pointed out, and he hoped to set the record straight. "I have lived through the Jewish experience," he wrote, and "I have tried to cope . . . with the fact that of all modern peoples, the Jews have suffered most savagely at the hands of reaction and fascism. Their loss was the greatest, fully one third of their number done to death, their pain the cruelest. . . . The Soviets' desire to deny this cannot change it." He chided Americans who considered Communism history's greatest evil and the Soviet Union as the perpetrator of civilization's most heinous crimes:

> For all its evil resemblances to Nazi anti-Semitism, this Russian variety is not the same. The Nazi goal was the elimination of all Jews through the direct and brutal action of mass murder. The Russian purpose . . . is to grant Jews at least a fair amount of equality, opportunity and security, provided they cease being Jews. Whereas the Nazis . . . declared Jewishness to be an ineradicable blood taint, even unto the fifth generation, the Russians . . . say that Jewishness is merely a rather offensive religion and can be cast off as easily as a garment.[59]

While American Jewry's participation in postwar anti-Communism provided a way to narrate the Holocaust, a small but vocal number dissented. Some postwar American Jews, whose numbers defy easy enumeration, supported the Soviet Union and, despite the hysteria sweeping the United States, championed Communism. Jews had been a mainstay of American Communism since the 1920s, although the number dwindled over time. Many Jews had left the party in 1939 with the Hitler-Stalin pact, while the immigrants who had made up so much of the party's leadership and rank and file in the 1920s and 1930s had not replicated themselves politically by moving their daughters and sons into the liberal camp. Among American Jews, however, Communism still found its adherents. By 1947, New York's Yiddish-language Communist daily newspaper, the *Morgen Frayheyt*, boasted a daily circulation of about twenty-one thousand, equivalent to the readership of the English *Daily Worker*, whose readers likely also included many Jews. The Furriers' Union, a predominantly Jewish union, articulated pro-Communist sympathies, as did the Jewish Peoples' Fraternal Order, the Yiddish-speaking wing of the International Workers' Order.[60]

Battles between the small, declining Jewish far left and the rest of American Jewry dated back to the 1920s when struggles between Communists and socialists rocked the Jewish labor movement and immigrant organizations like the Workmen's Circle. By the postwar period, while the Communists had become vastly reduced in number, such conflicts persisted and drew the attention of mainstream communal bodies nationally and locally. Both sides in this inner-Jewish war relied on Holocaust imagery.[61]

The Jewish Communists and the rest of the organized community differed publicly over a range of issues, including Soviet anti-Semitism. The Communists claimed that it did not exist and that "reactionary" Jewish organizations had created this bogeyman to curry favor with the American public. In 1954, the *Daily Worker*, reporting on the massive American Jewish protests against Soviet anti-Semitism, claimed that no anti-Jewish policies prevailed in the Soviet Union and that the U.S. government and Jewish labor leaders like David Dubinsky had cooked up these accusations, hoping to reap "profits out of the ashes of Auschwitz."[62]

The American Jewish pro-Soviet left, like their anti-Communist (or at times just non-Communist) Jewish foes, employed Holocaust references, making their case in part in the name of the Jewish catastrophe. In their communications with the American public and government officials, and in letters to the editor of general publications, they analogized between troubling contemporary events and what had transpired in Europe in the 1930s and 1940s and the tragic fate of Europe's Jews. In 1953, Louis Harap, the editor of *Jewish Life*, a Communist magazine, testified before the House Un-American Activities Committee, which he loathed: "This Committee is doing its utmost to subject America to a repeat performance of Hitlerism." Harap claimed the right to make his statement "as a Jew, whose people has suffered so terribly from nazism, to which this Committee has a fatal resemblance."[63] Simon Federman, the president of the pro-Communist American Federation for Polish Jews, echoed this sentiment in his testimony before HUAC, as a representative of the "people who still mourn the loss of six million of their murdered kin."[64]

The American Jewish left equated anti-Communism, both foreign and domestic, with the Germans' brutality toward the Jews and boasted that they most zealously conserved the memory of the six million. They excoriated other American Jews, the liberal organizations and the communal mainstream, for their seemingly tamer, more compromising stance toward Cold War suppressions of civil liberties, and by this diminishing the legacy of Europe's slaughtered Jews.[65] The American Federation for Polish Jews sent an impassioned letter to B'nai B'rith in 1950, expressing its disgust at B'nai B'rith's participation in the "All American Conference Against Communism," recently held at New York's Hotel Astor. This amounted to a "betrayal . . . of the interests of the Jewish people" on the part of "the great organization that always claimed leadership in defending Jewish rights. . . .

As an organization of American Jews," the letter began, "who from the experiences of their murdered kin in Europe have learned the full meaning of anti-Semitism and reaction," it, rather than B'nai B'rith, kept alive the memory of the Holocaust and, by asserting its pro-Soviet sentiments, derived the more fitting lesson from the catastrophe.[66]

So, too, Morris Schappes, a key figure on the American Jewish far left, wrote to Senator Herbert Lehman in 1950, warning him against the Mundt bill, a sweeping piece of legislation aimed at reducing subversive activity by barring Communists from holding office and requiring that they register with the Justice Department. Lehman, one of the Senate's fiercest critics of anti-Communist suppressions of civil liberties, hardly needed to be chided to vote against it. Indeed, all the Jewish defense organizations lobbied actively for its defeat, informing their members of its dangers. Schappes, however, exhorted Lehman to realize that "this Bill is aimed at you . . . as much as at me." The passage of the Mundt bill would "legislate fascism in this country as directly as did the Nuremberg laws. And, when such 'laws' are on the books, are the crematoria far behind?"[67] Schappes, an editor, writer, and lecturer, made this argument around the country to Jewish groups, stressing that the anti-Communist right threatened Jews in ways that should remind them of Nazi Germany.[68]

But the American Jewish left did not have a monopoly on using the Holocaust as it condemned the era's rampant violations of civil liberties. American Jews, from within the communal bodies, speaking for these groups to the public, also described and condemned postwar American anti-Communism, whether government policy or right-wing agitation, as something frighteningly reminiscent of Hitler's Germany. The Boston Jewish Labor Committee, in conjunction with the Boston Labor Committee to Combat Intolerance, which it founded and funded, produced a 1946 film, *Don't Be a Sucker*. The "powerful film," as the Jewish Labor Committee described in its promotional material, "points out the parallel between the rise of Nazism in Germany and the Fascist menace in the United States." The film dramatized the experiences of "a young man returning from the war to his home town," who "hears some rabble-rouser in the park denouncing Jews and other minority groups. In a series of flashbacks, the synonymous danger of race and religious hatred in Germany and America is made clear." This organization inundated civic and religious groups in the Boston area with announcements of an upcoming meeting, featuring the executive director of the Boston Jewish Community Council whose talk would show that "the war against Hitler still has to be fought in

America." It named as the agents of that domestic Hitlerism the lynching of African Americans, "the revival of the Ku Klux Klan, and the mouthings of Nazi lies by the Bilbos, Rankins and Gerald L. K. Smiths"—the first two U.S. senators prominently associated with militant anti-Communism and the third one of the early postwar period's most notorious anti-Semites and anti-Communists.[69]

Rabbi Israel Levinthal offered a sermon, which he then reprinted in his congregation's magazine, the *Brooklyn Center Review,* in 1952 that took to task the anti-Communist crusade in general and as embodied in the activities of Senator Joseph McCarthy and reflected in legislation like the Mc-Carran Act of 1952. McCarthy and McCarran resembled the demagogue of the 1930s, the Catholic priest from Michigan, Father Charles Coughlin. These three, like "Goebbels for Germany," used the "method of smear, of half-truth, of innuendo."[70] In his 1956 *Political Behavior of American Jews,* political scientist Lawrence Fuchs quoted an informant, "one rabbi, probably repeating the thoughts of many Jews," who "compared McCarthy to Hitler."[71]

The fact that Jews in America, both from the left and from within the communal establishment, saw parallels between the anti-Communist hysteria sweeping the country and the tragic fate of Europe's Jews demonstrated the degree of extremes converging, as well as the salience of the Holocaust in American Jewish life. All participants in communal debates over the implications of extreme anti-Communism heard the echoes of the Holocaust all around them in America. They heard it differently and acted on their fears differently, but across the board, they discerned in the postwar years a looming threat that reminded them of the events which had unfolded in Germany starting in the 1920s and culminated in the deaths of the six million.

The Holocaust, American Jews, and the Liberal Agenda

Liberal politics, civil rights in particular, inspired American Jews operating through their communal institutions and articulated in their communal press to look back to the Holocaust, using it to justify their political interventions. Their energetic and vocal work on civil rights and immigration reform, undertaken under the official sponsorship of their organizations in the years after 1945, represented a departure. In the prewar era, American Jews as individuals had assisted in civil rights endeavors, and Jewish publications passionately condemned racism against African Americans and the quota system in immigration. But the communal organizations limited themselves to quiet, behind-the-scenes tactics in tackling nasty political problems. As formally constituted Jewish organizations, they had generally stayed focused on specifically Jewish matters.

The brutal murder of the six million turned this around. Jewish agencies at the local and national levels became vigorous and highly prominent partners in the civil rights struggle, and Jewish organizations assertively confronted the racially based immigration system. They did this boldly in the name of American Jewry and put the Holocaust into prominent relief as they articulated their positions. They made these subjects the focus of programming within their community groups and the goal of their political actions by which they projected the image of the six million to the American public.

In the meeting rooms and offices of their community agencies, they recognized this profound shift, talked about it, and thereby reflected on how events in Europe had transformed them. Arthur Plaut of the Cincinnati Jewish Community Relations Committee considered the agency's history in 1954, describing in actuality a national trend. Plaut began his look backward in the present, a time when real estate interests in Cincinnati's South Avondale neighborhood began stirring up fear among white homeowners about the impending influx of "members of another racial group," which would lower property values. These real estate agents with financial interest in newer suburbs hoped to steer frightened homeowners to sell in panic, at deflated rates. But South Avondale did not succumb to this scare tactic, in this JCRC narrative, because "one of the residents of this neighborhood had heard of the work of the Community Relations Committee of the Cincinnati Jewish Community Council." The CRC sent in "trained workers" who explained to the homeowners that only the real estate dealers would profit from the hysteria and rumors. In this human relations success story, as told by the Jewish agency, some families from that "other racial group" moved in, most longtime residents stayed put, and "panic had been avoided."[72]

Plaut then turned back to the early 1930s when a group of local Jewish volunteers came together informally as they "sought to protect the rights and help solve the problems of members of our Jewish community. They shuddered at the rise of Hitler in Germany" and worried about the "ripples of the Nazi movement" being "felt in many places—including Cincinnati." This "small group of Cincinnati Jews," who "recognized the dangers of the

Nazi movement, . . . sought to counteract Nazi propaganda by presenting factual information showing the contributions made by American Jews to our traditional American way of life." With the "outbreak of war in Europe in 1939 . . . the organization realized that the job could not be done secretly by volunteers." They formally constituted themselves into the Community Council, hiring an executive director. By war's end, though, they "realized that defense was not enough," having learned that "any threat to democracy in the United States was a threat to Jewish life" and that "the security of Jewish communal and religious life depends on the safeguarding of the rights of all minority groups." This led the JCRC into coalition with the Urban League, the National Association for the Advancement of Colored People, and others, in advocating for the creation of an Ohio Fair Employment Practices Commission and the repeal of discriminatory laws in housing, education, and employment.

This brief prosaic insider document had been written to tout the work of the Committee to the local Jewish community; it boasted that it had prevented "block-busting" in South Avondale and had also led the campaign against "the controversial Sister-City Plan which was proposed in early 1951 by a group of Cincinnatians who would have had Cincinnati officially adopt Munich, Germany." Jews had reacted viscerally to this plan, "shocked at the plan to 'adopt' a city linked so closely with the Nazi movement." The JCRC had aborted the plan.

This unexceptional text, recounting the history of a local Jewish agency so as to boost its communal profile, made several key points about the postwar period. It could not tell its history or justify itself in the present without the background of Hitler, the Nazis, and Germany. What those proper nouns conveyed to Jews did not have to be labeled "Holocaust" or "six million," just as the "other racial group" needed no name. Everyone knew exactly what these referred to, and without the Holocaust, the basic organizational character of the local Jewish community would have been very different. Likewise, like many postwar Jewish community organizations, it posited no clear divide between its Jewish and liberal work. The tragic events in Europe pushed it to work with other Americans, involving it in advocacy action for liberal causes, some that specifically affected them as Jews, others only indirectly. Either way, the Holocaust functioned as background, context, and justification for actions taken.

Accordingly, Jews challenged American practices by which the state divided people on the basis of race, nationality, and ethnicity in the public sphere. Such invidious distinctions smacked to them of "Hitlerism." They used whatever opportunities appeared to condemn polices that considered "race" a natural and appropriate basis for meting out privileges and liabilities. Doing so had in the very recent past led to the deaths of one-third of the Jewish people and the destruction of the centers of European Jewish life. Columbia University professor Salo Baron noted in his presidential address to the American Jewish Historical Society that "many of the Nazi enactments could conceivably [have been] placed on American statute books . . . if a Nazi-minded party were to control a majority in Congress, or in one or another state legislature. Have not our Negro compatriots suffered from much legal discrimination in several states despite the constitutional provision for equality? . . . We recall how quickly the outspokenly liberal constitution of the Weimar Republic was swept away by the Nazi upheaval."[73]

American Jews described, explained, and twinned their involvement with civil rights in reference to the European Jewish tragedy. That watershed event did not provide them with the sole rationale or appear in every text and program Jews produced to do away with racial discrimination. They also cited the Judaic tradition of social justice and the long sweep of Jewish history and suffering. But in their compendium of words, written or spoken, the image of the slaughter of European Jewry during "Hitler times" surfaced often and clearly, making it a rhetorical partner to their other themes. At public programs, at the annual meetings of Jewish communal and religious organizations, and in publications, American Jews talked about these two matters, the Holocaust and civil rights, one after the other. Even when not articulating an explicit connection, their proximity to each other as topics on a meeting's agenda, for example, indicated the degree to which Jewish community activists perceived an organic connection between the two.

The two issues clearly existed in tandem with each other in the minds of American Jews. In 1947, for example, the national staff of the Intercollegiate Zionist Federation of America sent a memorandum to its chapters, offering ideas for campus programs. It suggested two recent texts it thought would appeal to Jewish college students. First, it cited an article from *Jewish Affairs*, by Elmer Gertz, from the Commission on Law and Social Action of the American Jewish Congress: "*American Ghetto* . . . it deals mostly with the problems faced by Negroes in finding housing rather than that of the Jews since of course the Negro problem is a much more serious one." Immediately after that, the memo suggested "*Lifeline* by Ira Hirschmann—An Eternal Light Script from the broadcast of January 5,

1947. LIFELINE tells the story of Mr. Hirschmann's super-human effort . . . to open the doors to the persecuted Jews of Europe. It portrays his feeling of frustration at the continuous slamming of possible doors of escape until finally he managed to get some Jews out of the Nazi-satellite countries. This script could be the basis for an excellent meeting." The leaders of this Zionist college society assumed, when it came to program planning and membership recruitment, that Jewish students would want to know more about discrimination against African Americans and the events of the Holocaust era, at one and the same time.[74]

So, too, the Jewish Labor Committee in 1946 perceived a bond between American Jewish consciousness of the tragedy of the Nazi era and the continuing denial of civil rights in the United States. It created a Committee to Combat Intolerance, and through it the JLC conducted workshops and conferences with trade unionists to educate them on the imperative of antidiscrimination work, to lobby for civil rights legislation, and to root out racism in the labor movement. At a meeting held by this group in Bridgeport, Connecticut, in the fall of 1946, Adolph Held told the predominantly non-Jewish audience about why he felt obligated to "combat intolerance." He declared to them that "the Jewish people have an important stake in our democracy. We have suffered severe losses. We can count to our chagrin four million martyrs of Hitler's barbarism, but we are also realistic trade unionists, and we know that not only were the Jews exterminated, but also were the trade unionists of Germany, Austria and other central European countries dominated by the Hitler philosophy." Held had not yet incorporated the more accurate number of six million into his speech, but he echoed the dominant American Jewish rhetoric that drew few boundaries between the specificity of their tragedy and universal concerns. Turning to the audience, he urged them to "keep building your committees. Keep educating your rank and file. You are conducting a noble experiment."[75]

If at times American Jews linked the Holocaust and civil rights by inference, they just as often connected them explicitly, doing so because they believed that Jews and blacks had common enemies and suffered to different degrees, but suffered nonetheless, from the same pernicious forces at work in American society and that the tragedy of the Jews of Europe contextualized them. Testifying to a Senate committee in 1952 on discrimination in employment, William Stern of the Workmen's Circle and the Jewish Labor Committee condemned employers who "still have a psychological shrine" for Adolf Hitler's "Yuden [sic] Verboten" policy. He asked the senators, then, about the disabilities endured by both Jews and African Americans: "Do former World War II pilots who are Jewish fly the planes of our airlines? Who can name the Negro WAC who was rewarded with a job as a stewardess on our airlines?" In 1958, at a celebratory dinner marking a quarter century since the founding of Boston's Jewish Labor Committee, with Senator John F. Kennedy and Congressman John McCormack present, Adolph Held described a spate of recent anti-Semitic publications, "mouthing the sort of calumny against Jews and Negroes that is in the best tradition of Hitler."[76]

Throughout the postwar years, American Jews bundled the Holocaust and the contemporary American civil rights revolution together. In 1950, Rabbi William Rosenblum offered a sermon on the Synagogue Council's MBC's *Chapel of Air* slot, "There Is Happiness in Numbers." He reported to his radio listeners that he had just returned from the annual convention of the B'nai B'rith, at which delegates discussed the imperative of "securing rights for others who are targets of discrimination because of their color." Rosenblum lauded the convention for not limiting itself to the welfare of its members or to Jews alone but, instead, "expressed sorrow that color . . . still bars many Americans from jobs in factories, offices and marts and pleaded for Fair Employment laws." Rosenblum explained that this concern reflected American Jews' "remembrance of the six million Jews who were burned in the furnaces of Nazism," which, "still fresh in American Jewish minds," caused them to think beyond "taking care" of themselves alone.[77]

In 1955, Louis Ruchames, a Reform rabbi and a scholar of African American history, addressed the Grand Street Boys Club for Negro History Week. Made up of Jewish men who had grown up on New York's Lower East Side, prospered, and moved away, but who still maintained a lively interest in the "old neighborhood," the club had invited the rabbi, who was Hillel director of the colleges of western Massachusetts, to also offer some thoughts about the Tercentenary of Jewish life in America. Ruchames posited his remarks about the American Jewish past and that of the "Negro people" in "Parallels of Jewish and Negro History." He pointed out the present condition of "persecution, of segregation, and of the deprivation of elementary human rights" endured by "the Negro." He opened his speech (which later appeared in the *Journal of Negro History*) by asserting that "we Jews have known within our lives and the lives of our fathers the problems which have confronted the Negro." In particular, "in our own day, the lesson that men have had to relearn in every generation, that the rights of all men are inter-related, that no minority group is safe while others are victims of persecution, has been seared into our minds and hearts through the burning flesh of six million of our brethren in Europe." In this organic blending of the particularly Jewish and the broadly universal, the rabbi offered to Jewish and African American audiences his understanding of the lessons of the Holocaust.[78]

Jewish public figures, writers, and community workers declared that they saw connections between what had happened to the Jews of Europe, the discrimination Jews faced in America, and the need to overturn America's racial system. They resembled one another in making this fusion prominent in American Jewish culture. Morris U. Schappes delivered an address for the Jewish Peoples Fraternal Order in 1952 on "The Truth About Jewish-Negro Relations." Inspired by "the twelve unpunished bombings of Negro homes, Jewish Temples . . . and the *murder* of HARRY T. MOORE, Negro leader of the NAACP in Florida," Schappes gave his talk at Detroit's Jewish Center. The handbill advertising his lecture noted that "Rabbi Abba Hillel Silver," the Reform rabbi and Zionist leader, "denounced the murder and bombings and declared that the American people must put an end to racist bands emulating the Hitlerite murderers." Schappes words, if he intended them or not, demonstrated the degree to which American Jews, regardless of political ideology, concurred in seeing parallels between the murderous actions undertaken to stymie civil rights for African Americans and the murderous actions the Nazis had visited on Europe's Jews.[79]

Otto Kleinberg, a social psychologist and long a foe of racialist thinking in America, addressed the American Jewish Committee's jubilee conference on the subject of "Equality of Opportunity." He saw a "close connection between our handling of the problem of equality at home and our international relations," not just as a matter of "obtaining good propaganda weapons in the cold war." To demonstrate how the United States' denial of equality of opportunity for all Americans negatively affected its "relations with the people of Africa, . . . Asia and elsewhere," he turned to history and to "the German treatment of Jews," which "modified and transformed the relationship of Germany and other countries."[80]

The civil rights struggle grew and attracted increased public attention in the late 1950s, emerging as a powerful political issue by the early 1960s. But as far as the American Jewish political agenda went, it had been prominent since the end of World War II. Throughout these years, it had been framed around the metaphor of the Holocaust. Abraham Feinberg, a rabbi, exhorted readers of B'nai B'rith's *National Jewish Monthly* in early 1959 that "we must never forget . . . the 6,000,000 . . . because they were ours." But since "the story of Nazism reveals how low mankind can sink into depravity," Jews ought to consider how "anti-Negro segregation" constituted "a sick fragment of Nazi racism," which, in turn, should make them see how "the horrors of the Holocaust must serve as a lesson that human life is the most important value and has to be preserved."[81]

Jewish organizations kept up the rhetoric and action they had adopted in the late 1940s. In 1960, the Jewish Labor Committee issued a pamphlet marking its role in a "Quarter-Century of Human Rights Progress." It recounted its founding "as the new barbarism of Nazi fascism was rising to power in Europe. . . . As Jews we protested the most concentrated persecution of Jewish people in all their history." The page glided next to the present as the Jewish trade unionists declared that they now had taken up "civil rights for Negroes." "Racism," it declared, "is still too deeply rooted in American life for self-satisfaction or a letdown in effort."[82]

Jewish youth activities reflected the same insistence that the struggle for African American rights needed to be understood in relationship to the tragic fate of Europe's Jews. Conversely, one way to understand what had happened to the six million would be to pose it in terms of the plight of black people in America. The teenagers at Camp Olin-Sang-Ruby in the summer of 1961 experienced this fusion. The Junior Session devoted time to "Campers Relive Jewish History," staging a mock Eichmann trial. The campers created artifacts, including "diaries, pictures, Torah pointers and burned out matches," symbolic of the Holocaust era. The next day they discussed "Separate but Equal." Those in the Intermediate Division participated in a role-play staging of the history of racial oppression in America. The camp became a faux plantation. Some campers spent the day as slaves, forbidden "to go to the washroom or to take a drink from the drinking fountain" without the permission of "the Plantation Master." Throughout the day, "if any slave is walking on the sidewalk going toward" the "Master," the rules decreed that "the slave would have to get off the sidewalk." In the segregated dining hall, the youngsters ate food based on their racial status, with "white" campers getting the better dishes. After the play acting ended, "a discussion of slavery was held." A few days later, the same campers turned to the history of the Joint Distribution Committee and learned in a discussion session that the Joint had been "about to close operations when the Hitler holocaust erupted and renewed need for food, repatriation of refugees and saving of lives." These activities—the Eichmann trial with its symbolic use of Holocaust details, the plantation play that sought to make manifest African American history, the history of the Joint, and the "Hitler holocaust"—logically connected to the summer's educational agenda, which demonstrated the Reform movement's belief in the intimate connections between liberalism and recent Jewish history.[83]

Members of Young Judea read in 1960 in their movement's monthly magazine a cynical critique of "Brotherhood Week." Set against the background of the bombing of Miami's Jewish Community Center, the editorial recalled "the wounds of six million dead" and exhorted its readers, in boldface lettering set off from the rest of the editorial, to "face facts—discrimination cannot be wiped out in a week, and since the great majority of Americans seem perfectly content to talk about it and think about it only one week each year, during February, Jews, and Negroes, and all other minorities had better start walking around with protective suits of armor." The editorial ended with a confession: "Sorry, but this week at least, with Brotherhood ringing in my ears, I can't come out and say, as Anne Frank did, 'In spite of everything I still believe that people are good at heart!' I close my eyes and see"—and here a swastika had been drawn—"1960!"[84]

Invocations offered by American Jews on the interconnectedness of the Holocaust and the denial of rights to African Americans could be heard as they declared their commitment to universalism, appealing to Jews and to other Americans to end the hated system of inequality. Economist William Haber delivered the Kol Nidre sermon at the University of Michigan's Hillel in 1962, and he too wove together insights from the Holocaust with a universal call for human rights. Haber, who had worked directly with survivors in the Displaced Persons camps through ORT, told the students that European Jewry now "is over. Hitler saw to that." That should inspire them to fight for a society that recognizes that "no faith or race is free when there is no freedom for all faiths and races." "True," he said to the students, "whether in Mississippi or Michigan, Judaism as a living ethic affirms the *essential equality and unity of mankind*. . . . Deprivations of the humanity and dignity of *one* group is a sickness that threatens all."[85] A Jewish Labor Committee speaker at the National Trade Union Conference on Civil Rights held at Unity House in 1961 believed that civil rights could not be achieved in America for African Americans without the American public knowing about the Holocaust: "We cannot speak about Anniston, Alabama," he declared, "if we have forgotten Auschwitz."[86]

In a way, American Jewish community leaders had no choice but to see and make the connection between the civil rights movement and the legacy of Hitler and the Nazis. Their enemies—avowed racists, anti-Semites

—crafted a rhetoric that made that point as well. Many opponents of civil rights, reacting violently to the movement's progress, blamed Jews for creating "restiveness" among African Americans. They also put the Holocaust into the discussion. Joseph P. Kamp, one of these segregationists, published a pamphlet in 1957 during the integration crisis in Little Rock, Arkansas: *Little Rock and the Plot to Sovietize the South.* Jews stood at the vanguard of that "sovietization," and, according to Kamp, "some intemperate Southern leaders have compared Dwight Eisenhower to Adolf Hitler. . . . They are wrong. . . . Hitler had the constitutional right to use Nazi storm troopers in a way that he pleased. Eisenhower had no such right to use Federal troops in Arkansas."[87]

Jews paid attention to this kind of talk. Anyone even casually perusing the *American Jewish Year Book* in the 1950s and early 1960s would have known of the currency of such thinking and would have recognized Jewish anxiety about it. Label Katz, the national president of B'nai B'rith, told readers of the Anti-Defamation League's *Bulletin* in 1958 that "the Citizens Councils," white groups formed throughout the South to resist strides toward integration, "have re-echoed the ideas of Nazi Germany." Their scurrilous charges against Jews sound like, he declared, "the statements of Hitler and Goebbels," which "produced the vilest, darkest consequences in history."[88] The Jewish War Veterans reported to its members in 1961 on the spread of "Hate Propaganda," noting that "the organ of the National States' Rights Party," the *Thunderbolt*, had attacked what it called "Today's Jewish Rape of the South." "That same hate sheet defends Gestapo Colonel Eichmann." That same "hate sheet" dedicated to opposing civil rights for African Americans also "maintained that the Jews had caused the war, faked atrocity stories, and were now 'persecuting Eichmann.' "[89]

American Jews put into bold relief Holocaust imagery as they tackled immigration reform as well. In the early 1950s, their engagement with immigration legislation focused on their efforts to defeat the McCarran-Walter Act (the Immigration and Nationality Act of 1952), Cold War legislation which on the one hand abolished the ban on Asian immigration, thus liberalizing 1920s policies, but on the other hand kept the quota system intact and expanded the power of the attorney general to deport immigrants and naturalized citizens deemed subversives. It made special allowance for potential immigrants fleeing Communist countries and defined subversion as something that only Communists did, as opposed to those responsible for the deaths of "the millions of Jews and non-Jews whose lives were sacrificed in the crematoria of Nazi Germany."[90] These words drawn from a press release sent out by the Jewish Labor Committee to the national press reflected the anger of American Jewry at the legislation. The United States has endorsed "the admission of Nazis and Fascists," wrote the Washington bureau chief of the Jewish Telegraphic Agency, as he described McCarran-Walter as the "First U.S. Nuremberg Law" since it opened "the doors wide to former Nazis," some of whom had "records . . . so bad that they were previously refused admission," and included "former Gestapo men and S.S. troops."[91]

American Jewish organizations all opposed the bill in its original form and over the course of the 1950s lobbied for drastic revisions. The annual meetings of their religious, communal, labor, and defense organizations resolved that Congress amend or repeal the law, calling on members to work for this outcome.[92] Organized American Jewry had much more to say about McCarran-Walter. American Jews invoked the Holocaust in their scathing denunciation of it, its authors, and their twin ideologies of anti-Communism and racism.

The liberal Jewish organizations came together to draft in 1952 "A Statement of Principles in Regard to American Immigration and Naturalization Policies Including Some Suggestions for Basic Revision of the Immigration and Nationality Act of 1952." Signatories to this document, submitted as a formal statement to the Senate and House Judiciary committees and the President's Commission on Immigration and Naturalization, took as their point of departure the fact that, as Jews, they had "no special private cause to plead . . . no special self-interest in the improvement of our immigration laws save that of Americans concerned with the reformulation of basic law to accord with democratic principle." American Jewry, they declared, had no group interest in the radical revision of the legislation because of the "tragic fact that such betterment" could not benefit "prospective Jewish immigration," nor would it be "to the special advantage of the Jewish community in this country."[93]

In case members of Congress, other government officials, the press, and the readers of any newspaper that covered the Jewish manifesto on immigration did not immediately recall the "tragic fact" which precluded Jews from benefiting from liberalized immigration policy, its authors spelled it out with no shame, fear, or desire to bury the very Jewish origins of their emotions: "More than six million Jews in Europe were exterminated in Nazi gas chambers and concentration camps," wiping out the masses of Jews who might have sought admission to the country. This theme resounded through the American Jewish discourse on McCarran-Walter. One rabbi testifying before a very public House-Senate subcommittee dealing with immigration, explained, "The European reservoirs of potential Jewish emigration" no longer existed, having been "depleted through extermination." Notably, some in the organized American Jewish world hailed McCarran-Walter's removal of the ban on Asian immigration as both a positive step and a way to recall the nefarious impact of the National Origins Act on the Jewish people. The *Jewish Forum* editorialized in 1955 that the legislative change "will eliminate recism [*sic*] and national discrimination, the advocacy of which also preceded the slaughter of our 6,000,000 brethren abroad."[94]

The argument advanced by Jewish organizations over McCarran-Walter took place at a particular moment in time. By 1952, the Displaced Persons camps had been emptied out and indeed closed as Holocaust survivors flocked to Israel, thus obviating the Jewish refugee crisis in Europe. American Jewry defined Israel as the place of refuge for Jews in distress who needed to find new homes. In the early 1950s, whole communities of Jews from North Africa and the Middle East, who would have been utterly unable to immigrate to the United States as a result of still-operative immigration policy, did make the move from Iraq, Morocco, Algeria, Yemen, and elsewhere to Israel.

As such, when rabbis and community leaders claimed that they had no special Jewish agenda in mind when they advocated against the racially based quota system, they did so sincerely and also as a way to remind Americans of the tragedy of the Holocaust. In framing their argument this way, the Jewish organizations accomplished several political goals, although they failed to block or change the policy. They demonstrated their universal and liberal credentials. They had, they claimed, nothing to gain from the political position they staked out, operating only to advance anti-racism and progressive Americanism. They could condemn long-abhorred restrictionist policies, which they believed had enabled the Holocaust to have happened. In their attack on McCarran-Walter, they could also condemn the nation's anti-Communist mania. And, they could hold up to the American public images of concentration camps, gas chambers, and the extermination of the European Jews.

Liberalization of immigration laws could not bring back to life the slaughtered Jewish victims of the Nazi inferno, but arguing for such legislation provided American Jewry with a double platform from which to advance the liberal political agenda and simultaneously remind Americans about the Holocaust. Similarly, American Jews, starting before the war had ended, used the brutal details of the destruction of European Jewry to press for international guarantees to protect human rights. With that grim reality as the backdrop, they argued for the adoption by the United Nations of both the Declaration of Human Rights in 1945 and the Genocide Treaty, which the United States did not sign on to until 1987. In pressing for both international human rights documents, American Jews, rather than obscuring the Holocaust as the reason for their embrace of universalism, instead held the catastrophe up as a powerful stimulant for their actions.[95]

The American Jewish Committee and its president, Joseph Proskauer, in conjunction with forty-one other civic groups, took the lead in drafting the Declaration of Human Rights. The document submitted made it clear that this Jewish organization, along with the B'nai B'rith, the Jewish Labor Committee, and the other Jewish communal and defense organizations, thought about the future of the world in light of their people's tragedy. They did not need to specify their Jewishness or that of the victims, but describing the state of the world left in the wake of "Hitlerism" made its Jewish and Holocaust contexts manifest. The document began with "the inevitable end of Hitler" and then declared that "Hitlerism has demonstrated that bigotry and persecution by a barbarous nation throws upon the peace-loving nations the burden of relief and redress." For "those who have been driven from the land of their birth there shall be given the opportunity to return, unaffected in their rights by the Nazi despotism," while "To those who wander the earth unable or unwilling to return to scenes of unforgettable horror shall be given aid and comfort to find new homes and begin new lives in other parts of the world."[96]

American Jews, in their discourse on this document, made the extermination of European Jewry the linchpin of their political action. Adolph Held had participated in a meeting of the trade union groups from around the world who met in San Francisco at the end of the war. Held discussed the Human Rights document with the group, showing American Jewry's interest in it. Their work constituted a "mission entrusted to us by our millions of brothers and sisters who perished in the Nazi-enslaved lands. Their blood still cries out. They perished with a message to the world against national hatred, animated by the spirit of the battle for human rights."[97] The Synagogue Council of America issued a memorandum to all American delegates to the San Francisco conference, entitling its statement "JUSTICE TO THE JEW." "The desperate need of the Jewish people, despoiled, disenfranchised and decimated in the twelve long years of Nazi barbarism," it wrote, "must challenge the conscience of humanity." The Synagogue Council of America released this document as a press release and asked rabbis to deliver sermons based on it, hoping to stimulate their congregants to act politically upon this matter.[98]

American Jewry also weighed in heavily on the Genocide Convention, formally known as the Convention on the Prevention and Punishment of the Crime of Genocide, which had been drafted by Raphael Lemkin, a Polish Jewish jurist who had fled to safety in the United States in 1941 and lost forty-nine family members to the catastrophe. He had become interested in the phenomenon of genocide well before the Nazi era, when during the interwar period he started reading the details of the massacre of Armenians by Turkey. Working in the waning years of World War II for the Carnegie Endowment for International Peace, Lemkin coined the term "genocide" to encapsulate the Germans' program for the Jews. He submitted the Convention in 1948 to the General Assembly of the United Nations. Its passage required ratification by twenty member states, a milestone achieved in 1951.[99]

American Jewish communal organizations in their public works made much of the fact that Lemkin had lost so many family members to the Nazis. Interviews and articles about him drew attention to the Holocaust, making it impossible to unmoor the Genocide Convention from the Jewish genocide. Gertrude Samuels profiled him in the *New York Times Magazine* in 1949, informing readers that "Hitler's plan to annihilate European Jewry . . . cost Lemkin several members of his family." Quoting him, she wrote, "I think it would be an inspiration to the world if the United States Senate showed the way and ratified it first. . . . It's a funny thing that some people still believe that Dachau, Auschwitz, Buchenwald are manufactured propaganda." Anne Robison profiled Lemkin for readers of the National Council of Jewish Women's magazine, *Council Woman*. She, too, in part attributed his crusade to the grim reality that he had "lost forty-six [actually, forty-nine] members of his family in Poland."[100]

Over the course of the early to mid-1950s, American Jewish organizations bestowed awards on Lemkin, using presentation ceremonies to advocate for the Genocide Convention and to recall the Holocaust.[101] National Jewish organizations mobilized members to work on behalf of the Convention and urged them to raise money to defray Lemkin's expenses. The National Federation of Temple Sisterhoods, in its official publication, *Current Copy*, commented, "at the risk of repetition we must once more ask the constituent Sisterhoods . . . to urge upon the U.S. Senate ratification of the Convention on the Prevention and Punishment of the crime of Geno-cide." It provided a laudatory sketch of "Dr. Raphael Lemkin, the man who almost single-handedly is responsible for the adoption by the UN of the Genocide Convention." Now, "in need of funds to carry on his fight," NFTS encouraged members to give and asked rhetorically, "Who better than the Jew can understand the awful catastrophe which can result when any na-tion sets out on a path to wipe out whole communities or peoples?"[102] A Jewish Labor Committee press release in 1953 informed the media that it had adopted a resolution praising the United Nations for adopting "resolu-tions condemning genocide, after viewing the ruins wrought by the Nazi holocaust and witnessing the wholesale murder of 6,000,000 Jews."[103]

Had Lemkin not been a Jew or suffered personally so many losses at the hands of the Nazis, American Jews would likely still have seen in his crusade a way to improve the world and simultaneously hold vibrant mem-ories of the Hitler catastrophe. They demanded more than the Genocide Convention's passage by any twenty nations of the world. They labored as-siduously, across the organizational spectrum, for the U.S. Senate to ratify it. Communal organizations nationally and locally, religious bodies, and the defense agencies all passed resolutions calling on the U.S. Senate to pass it. The American Jewish Congress, Synagogue Council of America, National Community Relations Advisory Committee, local Jewish com-munity councils, National Federation of Temple Sisterhoods, Jewish La-bor Committee, Workmen's Circle, and Jewish War Veterans, among other Jewish groups, declared that the world community ought to be governed by such a document and found it shameful that the United States had not joined the list of its signatories.[104]

They organized letter-writing and telegram campaigns to their sena-tors, testified on the document's behalf to the Senate Foreign Rela-tions Committee, and held community meetings to discuss strategy. The American Jewish Committee had worked with Lemkin on drafting the document, thereby making it a key item on its organizational agenda. The National Community Relations Advisory Committee created a special Sub-Committee on Genocide in the fall of 1948 to spearhead Jewish lob-bying with government officials and with non-Jewish civic groups.[105] The National Council of Jewish Women took the American Bar Association to task in the fall of 1949 at its national convention for its failure to "ap-prove the U.N. treaty outlawing *genocide* or mass killing." Throughout the postwar period, in the middle of the 1950s and in the early 1960s when the Convention came up again in the Senate, the women of Reform passed resolutions, organized chapter meetings on the subject, wrote to public officials, and expressed their disgust at how their American "fellow citizens" had failed to be moved by the issue. On the local level, Jews organized as well. Cincinnati's Jewish Community Relations Committee, for example, collected and distributed pamphlets and other printed material on "Genocide: An Antidote to Barbarism" and "A New International Crime."[106]

Hitler and the Holocaust loomed large on the American Jewish landscape as organizations, journalists, and rabbis spoke in favor of the Genocide Convention.[107] Jacob Blaustein of the American Jewish Committee could not have been clearer in his testimony to the Senate Foreign Relations Committee and its Subcommittee on the Genocide Convention on January 23, 1950, on the Jewish stake in this matter in light of the Holocaust, couched simultaneously in universalistic terms. After introducing himself and his organization, he explained why he had come before the senators. "We are concerned," he declared, "with genocide not only because six million Jews were recently murdered, but also because genocide is a crime against humanity." His sixteen-page statement, published for distribution by the American Jewish Committee, wavered back and forth between recitations of crimes visited on other peoples—Armenians by the Turks, "the mass extermination of Slavic populations by the Teutonic Knights, the excesses of Ghengis Khan," among others—and those substantiated by "former Gestapo officers at the Nuremberg trials," which "revealed that four million Jews were murdered in the Nazi death camps, while two million more were killed in other ways."[108]

The next day, David Ullman spoke to the senators on behalf of NCRAC, making the same points: "The Jewish people have been perhaps more often than any other the victims of genocidal crimes. Not fewer than six millions of them were destroyed by the Nazis." In the name of the "six major national Jewish organizations . . . and the . . . twenty-eight Jewish community Councils," he predicted that if the nations of the world, including the United States, subscribed to the convention, "it will stand as a statute to all future generations and will mark the time when the nations in noble unison resolved that such ghastly carnage as the Nazis wrought should not again be visited upon any of the peoples of the earth."[109] To these American Jews, advocacy for the Genocide Convention amounted to an act of memorialization for the victims of the genocide their people had endured.

The Holocaust's connection to the political work involved in passage of the Genocide Convention echoed in American Jews' publications, organizational meetings, and synagogues. In late 1949 and early 1950, the Synagogue Council of America called on the Senate to pass the Convention in the name of the Jews, "among the chief victims of genocide." In that context, Rabbi Leo Jung, chairman of the Asarah b'Tevet [Tenth of Tevet] Memorial Day Observance Committee, wrote to all American rabbis, urging them to highlight the genocide document in sermons delivered at the "Sabbath of Asara b'Teveth," thereby weaving this political project into the sacred service of remembering the "recent victims of the European holocaust."[110] Jung and the Synagogue Council followed up the letter to the rabbis with a press release, hoping that the American press would also note this "memorial for the six million victims" and its connection to the Genocide Convention. Jung made the point that passage of the treaty would "certainly be hastened if the Senators hear from their constituents throughout the country."[111]

Such talk swirled around the American Jewish world of the early 1950s, bringing together political action and Jewish community work, memorializing the victims, and changing the world. The American Jewish Congress (AJC) communicated in September 1951 with the presidents of other Jewish organizations, sharing its concern that the Senate would not pass the Convention: "It means very much to all civilized mankind" but "especially to we Jews who lost 6,000,000 of our brethren," the AJC wrote.[112] In 1953, the AJC, B'nai B'rith, Hadassah, the Jewish Labor Committee, the National Council of Jewish Women, and the Union of American Hebrew Congregations, among others, created an Ad Hoc Committee on the Human Rights and Genocide Treaties, producing educational materials and press releases on history's many genocides, particularly the "killing of 6,000,000 Jews . . . by Hitler."[113]

American Jewish action on and attention to the Genocide Convention became particularly urgent in 1954 when the Federal Republic of Germany passed it. The Jewish Labor Committee of Boston reacted, drafting a resolution that it distributed to the press and to the state's senators, which shamed the United States. "WHEREAS: This Treaty—which the United States took the lead in drawing up—has been ratified by 44 nations, including Germany—which was guilty of genocide in destroying 6 million Jews under Hitler . . . and WHEREAS: this treaty—which is in keeping with the finest American traditions—has received no action from the Senate Foreign Relations Committee," so, the Jewish trade unionists declared, the time had come "to secure prompt Senate ratification." Despite Jewish efforts, the Senate did not pass the treaty, and the United States did not join

Germany in signing this document, which to American Jews bridged a gap between memorial and political work.[114]

They had yet one more chance to try, however. The burst of global attention to the Holocaust and the Jews accompanying Eichmann's capture in Argentina and trial in Israel awakened in American Jews hope that they might finally accomplish what they had labored for so unsuccessfully. NCRAC expressed this hope in February 1961, and Boris Smolar, writing his syndicated column for the American Jewish press, pointed out in April that "American Jewish organizations are preparing to utilize the effects of the Eichmann trial . . . in order to arouse more interest among Americans toward the international Genocide Convention." Like the journalist, the organizations recognized that, among Americans, the "virtual disappearance of interest" in the matter set American Jews, those who participated in the affairs of the community and read the Jewish press, apart from their non-Jewish neighbors. The leadership of the organizations sought to capitalize on the trial, anticipating that it "will bring the subject of genocide before the public again." Jewish communal groups defined the international agreement on genocide as their issue, a specifically Jewish one, and as a political matter that would be well served by the explosive and much-reported-on trial of a key architect of the Final Solution.[115]

The connections Jews made between their hopes for a revival of interest in the Genocide Convention and the Eichmann trial ironically resembled arguments advanced by their enemies, who claimed that Jews sought to gain support for the Convention through the proceedings taking place in Jerusalem. The *Thunderbolt*, a racist publication published in Birmingham in the early 1960s, reported that "the Jews are not spending millions for nothing" by orchestrating the Eichmann trial. The "plot" hatched against him constituted an "effort to secure the worldwide ratification of the Genocide Convention," a document much abhorred by the writers and no doubt readers of *Thunderbolt*.[116]

While probably few Jews perused the *Thunderbolt*, they could access it in edited form in local Jewish papers. They could read Boris Smolar in June 1961 in one of his numerous "Eichmann Echoes" articles in his weekly "Between You and Me" column. Smolar quoted from *Thunderbolt* and from the National Renaissance Bulletin, "organ of the neo-Nazi James A. Madole, who advised readers to study the 'hate-crazed statements' by Jewish leaders with regard to the Eichmann trial and the necessity for ratification of the Genocide Convention."[117]

The energetic campaign undertaken by American Jewish organizations, the groups that constituted the mainstream of the community on behalf of the Genocide Convention, revealed much about them, their constituents, and American Jewry as a whole. They understood their political work in terms of the Holocaust and how it reverberated in the present. They considered themselves obligated to "fix the world" in light of the brutal deaths of the six million, not just for themselves but for others, but always with an understanding that the world needed to remember what had happened to the Jews of Europe under the dominion of the Nazis. They, the Jews of America, may very well have enjoyed the affluence of these years, participating enthusiastically in the new opportunities open to them, but they did not do so by forgetting the six million, who very much accompanied them on their journey through the postwar period.

Israel, the Holocaust, and American Jewry

American Jews, the organizations and publications, synagogues and other communal institutions, blended Jewish and universal themes when contemplating civil liberties, civil rights, immigration reform, and international human rights. They did not consider them binaries and handily traversed the particular and the general. Yet when it came to Israel and its relationship to the Holocaust, they expressed themselves differently, making their pitch for it in purely Jewish terms.

Certainly, they emphasized to Americans that Israel, a small democratic nation, threatened by larger undemocratic ones, deserved their support. At times, they projected metaphoric parallels between Israel, founded by small bands of determined "pioneers," and America, which liked to hark back to its origins as the destination of settlers, intrepid newcomers searching for a haven.[118] But more overarching than these themes, American Jews approached the American public with a message that Israel ought to be seen as both the survivors' place of refuge and, on a metaphoric level, as the Jews' compensation for the loss of the six million. They did not separate the reality and need for Israel from the memory of the destruction of six million Jews in Europe. Their rhetoric about it, directly or indirectly in support of their political work, never wavered, and no serious divisions existed within American Jewry.

The Holocaust and Israel had become so melded into one idea in American Jewish discourse that some commentators described Israel as the catastrophe's living memorial, and political work for Israel as such

Israel, both before and after the 1948 declaration of statehood, served as a way for American Jews to tell the details of the Holocaust. The Holocaust functioned as a potent justification for support for the Jewish homeland. The protesters at this Philadelphia rally, in front of City Hall, made manifest the linkages between the Holocaust and their demands for a Jewish homeland. The prominent location of the protest meeting made this much more than a Jewish communal event. *Courtesy Temple University Libraries, Urban Archives, Philadelphia, Pennsylvania.*

amounted to memorial building.[119] Yeshiva University professor Isaac Lewin, a spokesman for American Orthodoxy, writing in 1950, in *Noch'n Hurban,* "after the destruction," postulated that Israel had made this "hurban" different from previous ones. It, "the greatest destruction of Jewish history," led to Jewish sovereignty, and when "the mourning for the six million martyrs had hardly begun . . . the Jewish people have taken up the task for which there is no precedent—to build their home in Israel. Without help from the outside . . . the old wandering nation has come back to its home." That "the wild beasts," the Germans, "did not leave behind even the smallest reminders of the victims" mattered less now since "the Jewish people can put up a memorial in the new home. Let the new settlements be named after the martyrs. Let the streets of Jerusalem, Tel Aviv and Haifa and all the other cities in Israel be the memorial markers for the ripped away sons and daughters of our people."[120]

American Jews asserted that the Holocaust and Israel, singly and together, changed them. Even though only a minority joined or paid dues to a Zionist group or sent their children to Zionist camps, with the most minimal exceptions, all embraced the proposition that the Jewish people deserved a place of their own.[121] Their massive financial support of Israel and their advocacy for it with the American public reflected that feeling, as did the words they crafted to describe themselves in exploring their identities. In a sociological study of a "typical" American Jewish suburb, Marshall Sklare and Marc Volk's 1957 *Riverton Study* noted that respondents overwhelmingly "reported affirmative feelings about Israel." The sociologists explained: "Almost all Riverton Jews, even those coolest to Israel and most indifferent to Zionism as an ideological movement feel favorably disposed toward the State. They see it . . . as a place of refuge for homeless Jews, and they feel favorably disposed to help their co-religionists." One respondent put it in personal terms. He had had "little positive contacts with Jewish affairs until the advent of Hitlerism." Hitlerism changed him and led him to see Israel as a place of refuge.[122] A 1958 article in the *Yad Vashem Bulletin* described how all diaspora Jews, the largest number of whom lived in the United States, manifest "interest and devotion . . . towards Israel [which] stems primarily from the feeling of a common destiny which was awoken and underscored as a result of the great catastrophe."[123]

While community programming about Israel could be seen as an internal Jewish matter, the leaders and rank and file of American Jewry understood that they needed to reach out to the American public. In matters large and small, they had to stimulate broad public support for Israel. Its fate lay not just in American Jewish hands but in that of the government of the United States and as such with the American people. How they spoke about Israel among themselves segued into presentations of Israel to Americans—in particular, the opinion molders and policy makers. In this task, the Holocaust occupied much space, attention, and emotion.

Much of what they produced about Israel as the obverse of the Holocaust grew out of this practical political reality. They reached out to Americans—non-Jews, liberals in the main, those in office, and those active in civic organizations—with the message that Israel deserved America's support. The material American Jews generated for the general press emphasized how Israel had come into being as the answer to Hitler's savagery. They did this at an opportune time when liberal Americans, non-Jews, also embraced Israel and saw in the new state an embodiment of hopeful progressivism. This meant that the Jewish discourse about Israel and the Holocaust fit neatly within a larger political vision, further solidifying the connection between American liberal values and the vision of American Jews.[124]

Israel, they articulated, ought to be seen as the Jewish people's revenge, their solace for the loss of the six million. In their thinking, these two epiphenomena could not be seen as anything but inseparable. Rabbis articulated this idea in religious terms. Reconstruction Rabbi Milton Steinberg created for the Synagogue Council of America a "Service of Thanksgiving" to mark the first anniversary of the establishment of the State of Israel. The pamphlet for the service, aptly named "The Miracle," began with a responsive reading:

> RABBI: Has there been such a thing as this from one end of Heaven to another, that a people shall so long be mindful of its lost land?
> CONGREGATION: But in spite of humiliation and homelessness, of ghettoes, inquisitions, pogroms, Jew badges, gas chambers, and crematoria, the Jews persisted and found in Israel "The Fulfillment," "The opening of graves, a doomed people arising to life, to light, to youth."[125]

The entire repertoire of American Jewish sermons of the postwar years resounded with such images.[126] The chronology of events, the destruction of one-third of world Jewry, and the emergence, so soon thereafter, of a sovereign Jewish state following millennia of statelessness inspired American Jewish rhetoric, which consistently referred to and essentially sanctified them as inextricably connected events. As American Jews saw it, Israel had come into being through the "blood of the six million," the phrase intoned by Nahum Goldman, president of the World Jewish Congress, in 1955, at a Madison Square Garden assembly:

> We are the survivors of a generation of Jews that has witnessed not only the greatest tragedy in our people's history, but also the perpetration of the greatest crime humanity has ever permitted against the Jewish people. The blood of the six million Jews massacred by Hitler has tainted all mankind. . . . The strongest motive behind the U.N. vote for the establishment of a Jewish state was humanity's bad conscience, its conviction that it shared the guilt for the Nazi massacres and that it

was morally obliged to prevent the recurrence of catastrophe and to enable the Jews to possess a country of their own, where all Jews who needed or desired to do so could pursue a sovereign life in dignity and self respect.[127]

One 1950 *haggadah* included a copy of Israel's Declaration of Independence and pointed out to seder participants that the Jew "has seen six million Jews sacrificed and though their memories will never cease, he recognizes that with their saintly lives they paid the price for the emergence of the State of Israel."[128]

Creators of American Jewish religious texts experimented with formulations that simultaneously avoided blaming God for the slaughter but allowed divine intervention to explain the political "miracle" of Israel. On the first anniversary of the United Nations' vote on partition, the Synagogue Council of America told the American press that, "coming, as this glorious event does, after the most brutal and conscienceless campaign of extermination known to man, it restores our faith in the moral government of the universe."[129] A 1955 installment of *The Eternal Light* titled "The Hour of Forgiveness" featured the voice of Joseph, a victim of the Nazi slaughter, telling his story from the grave. Rabbi Andre Unger, himself a survivor from Hungary, offered the concluding observations: "In a world that begrudged him life," Joseph "refused to die. So with Joseph's people. . . . For a God of Mercy and justice would not have permitted the world to exist without providing comfort to Joseph, a home of his own." The liberating and apocalyptic return of Jewish sovereignty enabled Unger to situate Israel as the locus of God's actions in the Jewish world.[130]

In the words of Workmen's Circle Branch 244 in 1958, Israel emerged as "the only ray of light . . . the fulfillment of the prophecy 'out of Zion will come forth Torah,'" set against the "most tragic era in the history of the world and of our Jewish people," when "mad dogs attacked and destroyed our nearest and best."[131] A Jewish college student writing for *Ha-Oleh*, the publication of the Intercollegiate Zionist Federation of America, declared that "the Jewish state is necessary," an antidote to "being shipped off to the gas chambers without the minimal chance for self-respect."[132] Trude Weiss-Rosmarin wrote that "the void left by the virtual annihilation of the European Jewish center is somewhat relieved by the rise of Israel," while Norman Lipschutz, author of a 1960 Holocaust memoir, *Victory Through Darkness*, juxtaposed "the horrible massacre of my people by the Nazis . . . the disappearance of most of relatives and friends of my childhood" with "the establishment of Israel," which "somehow compensated for the loss of my dearly beloved."[133]

This kind of rhetoric engulfed the American Jewish public sphere. A Conservative rabbi in Brookline, Massachusetts, Herman Rubenvitz, dedicated his 1955 Rosh Hashanah sermon to this theme, telling congregants that "there is much to mourn over but . . . ours is the privilege to help rebuild new Jewish communities for those destroyed, new Jewish life in Israel in place of the millions slaughtered in Europe."[134] Chicago's Labor Zionist Organization braided together the Holocaust and Israel in its specially crafted *haggadot* for third seder usage. For Peretz Tauman and Danny Greenberg, who compiled the booklets, and the hundreds who annually assembled and read from these mimeographed texts, connections between the two barely needed justification. "We who sit at this table," exclaimed the 1954 *haggadah*, "have been privileged to view the restoration of the people of Israel to the land of Israel in our day. There were those who within our lifetime dreamed the dream and perished before they could see it materialize. It is appropriate that at this time when we are approaching the 11th anniversary of the Uprising of the Warsaw Ghetto . . . [we] remember our holy dead."[135]

American Jews ubiquitously fused these two metaevents of modern Jewish history. Warsaw Ghetto memorial programs typically asked the assembled to rise and sing Israel's national anthem, "Hatikvah." Communities, at times, commemorated the Ghetto uprising and Israel's independence at one large event. The Jewish Welfare Board's 1960 pamphlet *Resistance and Redemption*, a model for such community pageants, based on a program held at the Cleveland Jewish Community Center, blended the images and implications of two events, the uprising in the Warsaw Ghetto and the emergence of the State of Israel.[136]

What did this fusion mean in political terms? How did it impact the ways American Jews reached out to the larger American world? In an overwhelming communal project, they took this fused Holocaust-Israel imagery and embedded it in the flood of materials they produced for public consumption, for government officials and the press. The leadership, the rabbis, the writers for Jewish publications, and the producers of other kinds of texts constantly reminded rank-and-file American Jews about that bond, expecting that as they behaved politically they would make sure that that message went forth to those who could affect Israel's security and welfare.

Israel, the antithesis of the Holocaust, seemed to be suspended in perpetual insecurity, living under an existential threat. Over the entire course of the postwar period, from the drive for statehood through the 1956 Sinai campaign into the early 1960s, one crisis after another provided American Jews with the chance to write and read, orate and hear, the message that they had to garner support for Israel and that the tragedy of the six million lay at the heart of their project. One threat might illustrate this message and represent the discourse as a whole.

Starting in the middle of the 1950s, American Jews, through their communal institutions, began to discuss the nexus between Germany and the Arabs, particularly Egypt, the most powerful of the nations arrayed against the Jewish state. In fact, this political matter provided Jews with an opportunity to fulfill a number of tasks. They could show Israel's vulnerability and the need for American support. They could retell details of the history of the Holocaust; and they could, once again, hold up a guilty Germany, responsible for the destruction of European Jewry.

Arab opposition to the reparations agreement between West Germany and Israel, and Egypt's threatened economic boycott of German goods because of it, provided American Jews with an opportunity to ponder similarities between their two antagonists. The Jewish press amply reported news about trade agreements between Arab countries and Germany, the sale of German military hardware to Arab countries, and the spread of anti-Semitic propaganda out of Egypt and elsewhere in the Arab world, described repeatedly as "Nazi-like."[137] The latter provided American Jews, in meetings, publications, and sermons, a particularly fertile field to use Holocaust imagery in light of current political matters. The National Federation of Temple Sisterhoods urged members to come up with political action programs to raise public consciousness about the fact that a "Nazi war criminal who had obtained shelter in Egypt, had been asked by the Egyptian regime to set up a Nazi-style 'Jewish Department,' which would produce anti-Semitic propaganda, targeting both Israel and the Jews of Egypt."[138]

Jewish Forum reported in 1959 on the Egyptian publication of the *Protocols of the Elders of Zion*, "one of Hitler's chief means of arousing somewhat civilized people to the murder of Jews." Boris Smolar reported in 1961 on how "even the Talmud is injected into the new wave of Arab propaganda which can only be compared in its vulgarity with the notorious 'Der Stuermer,' the Nazi publication edited by Julius Streicher."[139] In the middle of the 1950s, American Jewish communal groups reported on the influx of German scientists to Egypt to work on arms programs. They labeled the scientists not just "Germans" but "Nazis."[140] In his column in the *Senior*, the president of Young Judea described his outrage after learning about the "German scientists in Egypt. . . . One begins to wonder whether the German people actually *are* repentant for their crimes of World War II."[141]

Each incident allowed American Jews to recall the Holocaust as embodied in Israel's present. When in 1954 the Jews of Egypt began to be subjected to arrests, property confiscations, and deportations—followed by the swift expulsion of nearly the entire community, numbering between twenty-three and twenty-five thousand—American Jews took up their cause. They wrote, lobbied, and organized rallies to protest.[142] Their words and actions resonated with statements about the parallels between Egypt under Nasser and Germany under Hitler. In 1956, the American Jewish Congress issued *The Black Record: Nasser's Persecution of Egyptian Jews*. The book's title, style of presentation, and format mimicked *The Black Book of Polish Jewry* (1944), an account of the mounting toll of Jewish losses. One chapter in *The Black Record*, "Nasserism and Hitlerism," began unmistakably: "The parallels between Hitler's campaign against the Jews of Germany and Nasser's attack upon the Jews of Egypt are too close to be accidental." *The Black Record* described Nasser's skill at "adapting the Nazi methods to the Egyptian scene": the "'Egyptianization' program under Nasser was reminiscent of the Nazi slogan 'Germany for the Germans' and of the Nazi technique for pauperizing the Jews and forcing them out of the country."[143] The Jewish Labor Committee issued a press release about the book's publication and sent a copy of the book to Eisenhower.[144]

American Jewish texts dealing with Nasser, the Jews of Egypt, and threats to Israel replayed the Holocaust. They invoked names of Nazis, relying on German phrases throbbing with Holocaust references. The Arabs at the United Nations, wrote the American Zionist Council of Atlanta, spoke lies about Israel "in [a] most unscrupulous manner and with utter disregard for the truth. . . . It is the well known Goebbels technique of repeating lies until the liar himself believes them." Boris Smolar in 1956 warned that "the possibility of an Egyptian 'blizkreig' [*sic*] against Israel is not excluded," and Nasser's 1958 effort to unify all Arabs by forming the United Arab Republic smacked to a contributor to *Congress Weekly* of an "Ominous Anschluss," referring to Hitler's annexation of Austria.[145] German, Nazi-inflected words revealed the degree to which the two sets of images folded into each other, as did an address by the president of the Zionist Organization of America, Emanuel Neumann, who on ABC radio in 1956 called Nasser "the little Hitler of the Nile." Columnist Harold Debrest labeled him "the Egyptian Hitler."[146]

Writers and rabbis searched for opportunities to show this parallel. In early 1956, after reciting the history of the 1930s and 1940s, "when the Jewish Homeland was most needed as a refuge by the hapless victims of the Nazis," Weiss-Rosmarin shifted to speculating about the future. "Henceforth," she thundered, "the Western democracies which deny Israel the right of self-defense will be partners in guilt with the Arabs who are rehearsing for their Second Round. . . . This is a great and terrible responsibility, but not greater and more terrible than that which the democracies flaunted when they did not help the Jews under Nazi rule at the time when help was still feasible." To her, as with so many Jews, threats to Israel from Egypt loomed ominously as harbingers of another great catastrophe, something that could be staved off only by American Jewish advocacy. Only by marshaling their political clout as Americans could the Jews of the United States forestall this "Second Round."[147]

The Jewish War Veterans distributed to the press and to all its posts the text of speeches given at its 1957 Madison Square Garden rally, "protesting any thought of sanction against Israel" by the United Nations in the wake of the Sinai Campaign and Israel's foray into Egypt. National Commander William Carmen reflected the communal consensus. Threats to Israel, direct or indirect, resembled the tragedy of the Holocaust, and any action against Israel needed to be understood in light of the cataclysm. "Thirty-six years ago," he declared, "there was introduced in the world a new cancer. It came in the form of the man by the name of Adolf Hitler." The "fulminations of this great monster of the 20th century" brought about "unimaginable horrors . . . upon the Jewish people," and American Jews from afar saw "our people butchered and slaughtered." All the help that came through the might of the American military had been offered "too late[,]" for the stench of the gas chambers and ovens had already putrefied the air of Europe." Now "a new embryo of evil has risen in the world—disregarding morality and decency as Hitler had done." Nasser, like Hitler, "has come as a reformer for his starving, illiterate and impoverished people," but he, too, "brings wrath upon our people with the same hatreds that our generation knows so well." He "has made his ultimate goal clear—to push the democratic nation of Israel off the face of the earth" and, in league with the Soviet Union and "with the Nazi remnants of the leadership of Adolf Hitler," threatens to bring about "the elimination of world Jewry."[148]

The task of staving off this threat fell on their shoulders, they believed. As citizens of the United States, one of the world's two great powers, they had no choice but to speak up for Israel, the homeland they saw as the memorial to the six million. To accomplish this goal, just as surely as securing the liberal agenda, they had to work with others. And as they went about crafting a message to make this possible, they assertively and publicly employed the imagery of the Holocaust, making it a crucial explanation for their political projects. They understood that they could not accomplish any of their political tasks by quietly and privately mourning the Holocaust.

Historians of later generations failed to see how prominently postwar Jews held up the Holocaust in all their political works, as advocates for Israel with the government and the press and as supporters for liberalism, working with partners, in particular, the liberal churches, labor unions, civil rights organizations, and civic bodies. These postwar challenges pushed them into alliance with others, and in those alliances they projected the image of the Holocaust into the larger public sphere.

But, when it came to the Jewish challenges imposed on them by the Holocaust, American Jews had to go it alone. The violent destruction of six million Jews and the extirpation of the great centers of Jewish learning and culture thrust on the Jews of the United States a staggering responsibility to somehow fill the Jewish void. This project worried them greatly, and they faced that burden with little confidence that they could do so.

6

Facing the Jewish Future

THE HOLOCAUST MOVED American Jews as they participated in the American world, using it to advance liberalism by invoking it to advocate for the political agenda they considered in their own and America's best interests. The catastrophe also shaped their understanding of themselves as Jews, providing them with a rationale by which to articulate their responsibilities to the Jewish people and the Jewish tradition, believing that the destruction of the six million Jews of Europe marked and changed them.

In their public works, American Jews acknowledged the incontrovertible fact that the loss of the great Jewish population center of Europe made America the largest functioning Jewish community in the world. This momentous shift imposed a burden on them as the extermination of the Jews of Europe and their cultural institutions had unwittingly thrust American Jewry onto the center stage of the Jewish world.

Mrs. Sheldon Black, a lecturer for the National Federation of Temple Sisterhoods, ushered in the postwar period with exactly this message in her talk and article sent out to temple sisterhoods around the country, "The Child in the Jewish Home." "The times are grave," she wrote, articulating the tragic atmosphere that pervaded much of American Jewish life. "It is really not for me to speak of this now," she went on, indicating, rhetorically, a reticence to confront the middle-class, white, privileged American Jews of Reform with gloomy reminders of the past and the serious contemporary issues facing the Jewish people resulting from that tragedy. "And yet it is," she continued, declaring what Reform, and American Jews, women, and men, ought to do:

> From the destruction of European Jewry to American Jewry, upon whose shoulders the burden of responsibility now rests, to the sanctuary of our individual homes, these are stepping-stones. There is no halfway when we walk on stepping-stones, we take them or we sink and are no more to be counted among our people. . . . The home, the ordinary American Jewish home is the beginning of salvation.[1]

"The Child in the Jewish Home," an ephemeral document in an ocean of articles, papers, speeches, sermons, books, and other texts produced by postwar American Jews, exemplified how they saw the implications of the Holocaust for themselves as Jews. They believed that the phenomenon Mrs. Black called "the destruction of European Jewry" imposed a duty on them. It brought them, the Jews of the United States, into the center of the Jewish world, asking them to become custodians of the Jewish future. Despite agreeing among themselves that this tectonic change in Jewish life had occurred, they could not agree on how to assume these obligations or what compensating for the six million actually meant. Having been forced into this position, they argued and debated the catastrophe's legacy. Could they, they asked, adequately shoulder the painful burden that they had never asked for?

The catastrophe came in the postwar period to serve a number of decidedly inner-Jewish communal projects. As communal leaders called for increased religious observance and enhanced Jewish education, they put in the foreground the destruction of European Jewry. Those slain Jews, as communal leaders reminded the American Jewish public, had been pillars of authentic Judaism, their communities the wellsprings of Jewish culture, and the fountains of Jewish inspiration. With the destruction of European Jewry, American Jewry now had to pick up where the "martyrs" left off.

American Jews had no physical place to represent authenticity to them. Only the memory of the Europe that the Nazis destroyed could serve as their imagined source of Jewishness. On a practical level, no place existed any longer from which American Jewish institutions could recruit fresh batches of scholars, teachers, or rabbis to provide them with Jewish "high culture," including scholarship, fiction, plays, poetry, and the polemical works representing socialism, Orthodoxy, and Zionism, ideologies that had bound the Jews of America to those in Europe.

For centuries, American Jewry had rightly seen itself as a net importer of Judaica from Europe and had self-critically believed that in terms of Jewish culture, religious or secular, the Europeans did it better than the Americans, occupants of the backwater of the Jewish world. Now the denizens of the Jewish hinterland, the United States, had no one to rely on. If they sought a vibrant Jewish life, they had to do it themselves. The postwar American Jewish project, they said, had to be understood against the backdrop of the grievous loss of European Jewry. Reform rabbi William Berkowitz, in a 1961 book, a collection of speeches given at Congregation

B'nai Jeshurun and its Institute of Adult Jewish Studies, opened with "A Message to the Twentieth Century Jew," articulating a common sentiment of the postwar years: "We, today, have witnessed one of the darkest chapters in our long history. Our mighty centers of culture have been destroyed, the Yeshivoth [academies of higher learning] of Poland, of Austria, of Hungary are no longer on the map. . . . In the span of our lifetime we have witnessed the massacres of one third of our nation." He then asked, "Are we," the Jews of the United States, "prepared and willing to assume a dominant role in Jewish cultural activities?"[2]

Appeals directed at ordinary American Jews to become "more Jewish" as a memorial to the six million necessitated the creation of a new Jewish history. The Jews murdered by the Nazis had to represent Jewish piety, intensity, and traditionalism, all lived out and exterminated in profoundly Jewish settings. It mattered little that so many of the six million had been thoroughly modern people who, like American Jews, had become highly secularized. It mattered little that among the six million had been cosmopolitans who had lived in cities, partaken of twentieth-century culture, spoken the languages of the lands where they lived, and articulated complicated, and often tenuous, connections to their Jewishness. In the postwar years, in the communal rhetoric, those whom the Nazis murdered had died *al Kiddush hashem*, as martyrs who went to their deaths for the sanctification of God's name. American Jewish communal activists transformed Europe's Jews into the dwellers of "the shtetl," a mythically imagined all-Jewish space where all-Jewish warmth, life, learning, and communal cohesion flourished.

Across the ideological spectrum of American Jewry, the leaders asserted that the Jews of the United States had to compensate for what had been demolished. Only more Jewish knowledge, greater Jewish commitment, and deeper understanding of the destroyed world of European Jewry, they exhorted, could even begin to make up for the grievous losses. Nearly all statements of this sort ended with a question rather than with confidence about the Jewish future. Did American Jews, they asked, have the cultural wherewithal to step into the chasm left by the brutal departure of the six million? Did they have the Jewish stamina to fill the void created by the destruction?

The Holocaust lent urgency to long-heard exhortations hurled by Jewish communal leaders at the rank and file for them to become more Jewish. It offered moral immediacy to communal projects, allowing advocates for both well-established and new undertakings to present their visions in nearly sacred terms, as memorials to the six million. The catastrophe provided the leadership of American Jewry with a powerful tool as it pondered how to construct self-sustaining intense Jewish life in America. While those who invoked the Holocaust to remind American Jews of their new role in the world differed radically among themselves as to what constituted a robust Jewish existence in America, they shared a powerful belief that the Holocaust made their project more compelling than before.

The Holocaust and a Changed American Jewry

American Jews, both youth and adults, faced an unprecedented reality in the postwar era. Divisions derived from decades earlier persisted, but the fundamental changes, some wrought by the Holocaust, others by the affluence, suburbanization, and liberalism of the era, meant that different strands of Jewish life each had to decide how to cope with the new environment. Religiously, American Jews divided between Orthodox, Reform, Conservative, and the very small Reconstructionist variants of Judaism.

Since the latter decades of the nineteenth century, Reform had been shedding much of the trappings of Jewish distinctiveness and began to embrace ritual practices it previously had discarded, like the bar mitzvah, and increasing amounts of Hebrew could be heard in the liturgy in its temples. As a movement, it now wholeheartedly embraced Israel as a pillar of American Jewish identity, whereas before the 1930s, support for a Jewish homeland had been a minority position, particularly among its rabbis.

A product of the early twentieth century, the Conservative movement became more secure in the postwar era as the middle ground of American Judaism, in part because, in the aftermath of World War II, it emerged as the largest of the country's Jewish denominations. That newfound preeminence allowed it to issue its first denominational prayer books, and its Law Committee took bold steps in demonstrating a willingness to blend Jewish law with American reality. In the early 1950s, for example, it ruled that Jews could drive to synagogue on the Sabbath, reflecting Jewish suburbanization and its own institutional élan.

Orthodoxy on the one hand experienced an influx of immigrants, particularly Hungarian Holocaust survivors, who settled into places like Lakewood, New Jersey, and established their self-described "Torah-true" institutions of higher learning. The first of the many hasidic sects that arrived after World War II, they helped make the profile of American Jewry quite different from what it had been before. On the other hand, American-born middle-class Orthodox Jews found multiple ways to embrace postwar changes and incorporate them into their religious framework. In 1954, for example, at a time when increasing numbers of American young women opted for college education, Yeshiva University opened Stern College for Women, declaring that Orthodox girls, like American girls in general, could partake of higher education. Orthodoxy and American culture need not be seen as antithetical.

In addition to their religious groupings, American Jews in the postwar years also divided along a variegated cultural and ideological spectrum, between Zionists of various persuasions, Yiddishists who sought to protect and even build up an American Jewish culture based on the Yiddish language, socialists, communal activists, and "just" Jews, the women and men who may never have joined a Jewish organization but nonetheless contributed money to their local Jewish federation, bought Israel bonds, subscribed to their local Jewish newspaper, sent their children to a Jewish supplementary school, lived in Jewish neighborhoods, and the like. In these endeavors as well the postwar period witnessed Jewish institutional vigor, measured in terms of membership and financial support.

These years witnessed a religious revival in American society. Jews joined this "return," which brought their Christian neighbors in record number back to churches. American Jews affiliated with synagogues to an unprecedented degree. Their religious landscape transformed as congregations mushroomed, particularly in "better" city residential neighborhoods and new suburbs. Established congregations embarked on ambitious building projects, often as they relocated from older urban areas to newer, more affluent ones, replacing modest structures with imposing edifices to announce boldly the Jewish presence. Young Jewish couples who moved to the suburbs decided to form congregations, and the various denominations courted these families trying to get them to affiliate with either the Reform, Conservative, or Orthodox branches. Whatever choices these women and men made, they planted new congregations in their new neighborhoods. Parents sent their children to Jewish supplementary schools as never before, and Jewish summer camping and youth programs grew into substantial enterprises undertaken by the religious bodies and by other Jewish organizations. Jewish community centers multiplied and, particularly in suburbs, became hubs of Jewish activity. From the point of view of buildings, institutions, and communal activity, American Jewry enjoyed a "golden age."[3]

That postwar American Jewish world—replete with its synagogue-building boom, its burgeoning school enrollments, and its institutional growth, all made possible by highly successful fundraising campaigns—believed that the Holocaust had profoundly changed it. Both those who studied American Jewry and those who hoped to motivate American Jews to be more actively involved in community life assumed that the catastrophic events of Europe moved them as nothing else had. In 1955, the directors of the Jewish Publication Society of America assessed that "the impact of the annihilation of six million of our brothers and sisters in Europe—the frightful tragedy in our tragic history"—had made a difference, and "the Jewish consciousness of our people here, particularly that of our youth, has been powerfully aroused in recent years."[4]

Texts written by and for American Jews returned to this theme, whether contemplating American Jewry as a whole or examining the life stories of individual American Jews. In an introduction to a book on synagogue art and the career of A. Raymond Katz, philosopher Horace Kallen noted that when Katz started out, "he was a painter who happened to be a Jew, but he could then in no sense be called a Jewish painter." Things changed: "Like so many Jews in the arts of the intellect and imagination, the Nazi abomination seems to have reawakened his Jewish interests."[5]

Postwar American Jews created a public culture in which they revealed the Holocaust's impact on themselves. Speaking to the American Jewish Congress in November 1949, Max Lerner recounted how he had recently run into a former Harvard student "at a Zionist gathering in Boston." The student marveled: "Mr. Lerner . . . I am terribly surprised to find you at this kind of meeting and saying what you do, because as I remember you fifteen years ago you were not interested in this sort of thing." Lerner agreed, saying simply, "You are right. You know, I have had a very expensive education. Before I could get educated six million of my brothers and sisters had to die." He had, he admitted, acquired his education "in the furnaces of Auschwitz and Dachau . . . [in] the shower room where they were stripped . . . the gas chambers where they were gassed . . . the furnace room . . . where the names of the victims [were] written by their friends."[6]

Others discerned a collective communal transformation in the aftermath of the Holocaust. Stuart Koff won first place in the B'nai B'rith Youth Organization's 1956 oratory context on the assigned topic, "Trends in Judaism." Jewish self-consciousness had swelled as a result, he asserted, of "Hitlerism." The young speaker claimed that it had "scared American Jews into organizations in World War II," and in the present, in the aftermath of catastrophe, Jews in America had become different. "Today," he observed, "organized Jewish life is built upon positive qualities and appreciation of the beauties of the Jewish heritage."[7] Those attending Jewish communal meetings heard this kind of talk repeatedly. Bernard and Nathan Lander addressed the 1957 General Assembly of the Synagogue Council of America: "The Hitler holocaust and the failure of the philosophy of assimilation . . . have profoundly affected the thinking of American Jewry," they said. Jews, they believed, "are identifying themselves more and more with Jewishness. Synagogue membership is increasing, especially in suburban areas. More and more Jews are giving their children a maximum of Jewish education."[8]

Scholars also discussed the proposition that the Holocaust had made American Jews more Jewish. Albert Gordon, a rabbi and trained anthropologist, made this point in his 1959 study of suburban Jewry, based on empirical evidence drawn from the observations of rabbis serving suburban congregations. They discerned new behaviors and intuited sharpened Jewish sensibilities. Gordon had studied eighty-nine Jewish communities, conducted interviews, and tabulated results from survey questionnaires sent to the rabbis, who, he reported, "note that the Passover Seder services in the home are more popular and even better attended than they were a decade ago, with approximately seventy-five to eighty per cent of Jewish families conducting or attending a Seder." Gordon quoted one of his rabbinic informants, who knew why this change had come about: "What lesson can have greater meaning to Jews in these days who remember Hitler?" The suburban Purim, Gordon observed, "is charged with meaning for the Jew of today who remembers Hitler's crematoria and concentration camps." He discerned grassroots theological shifts. While the suburban Jew "believes that there must be a God who created this world, he cannot understand His continuing association with the Jews or, for that matter, with mankind. He has seen so much misery and wretchedness. . . . The fate that recently overtook six million Jews in Europe has shaken what little faith was left in him." Anguish, though, did not push them away from Jewish identification. Rather, the Jewish suburbanite "turns to his people, the Jewish people, and hesitantly seeks to understand his ancient Torah. His quest is real, and the challenge to organized religion and its spiritual leaders is great."[9]

Such observations about the Holocaust's profound effect on American Jewry resonated broadly and deeply. Morris Schappes, representing the American Jewish left, a consistent critic of the communal mainstream, concurred with nearly everyone else in his 1958 history of American Jewry: "The Jewish community in America is Americanized, but it is distinctive. Jews have neither allowed themselves to be melted down, nor have they been willing to melt away." Documenting escalating rates of organizational and institutional affiliation at midcentury, Schappes saw that "they are more highly organized than ever before." Why, he asked rhetorically, did these changes happen? "The Hitler horror and the birth of Israel have contributed to the expansion of Jewish consciousness that is at the base of this move to organization."[10]

This kind of thinking continued unabated into the 1960s. C. Bezalel Sherman picked up on it in his 1960 volume *The Jew Within American Society*. "The Nazi catastrophe," he wrote, "reinforced the community bonds between them and the Jews in other lands, at a time when the ties of individual kinship were becoming looser, thus strengthening the urge among the former to belong." To the Jews of the United States, Sherman wrote, who had been "helpless to prevent or halt the slaughter of millions of their kin in Europe and cruelly disappointed by . . . the democratic world in the face of this slaughter . . . the Jewish people . . . ceased being an abstract concept and became a living reality."[11]

The nearly universal use of the pronouns "we" and "our" to describe both the victims and themselves, and the degree to which they divided their lives into a "before" and "after" the catastrophe, made manifest an American Jewish self-understanding that the catastrophe lay deeply embedded in their lives. Upon accepting the presidency of B'nai B'rith in 1959, for example, Label Katz made that point in his speech, "Creative Jewish Living." "Our generation," he declared, borrowing liberally from Franklin D. Roosevelt's first inaugural, "has had a rendevous [*sic*] with history. . . . We witnessed the tragic decimation of six million fellow Jews in the Hitler holocaust."[12]

American Jews believed that the Holocaust had made them. They took this as a given, and this belief circulated so widely as an assumed truth that sociologist Nathan Glazer felt compelled to show otherwise. In the definitive synthetic work of the era, *American Judaism*, a volume in the University of Chicago's History of American Civilization series, Glazer noted that "there seems to be no question that there is much greater interest in religion among Jews today than there has ever been before." Referring to the plethora of books being published on Jewish topics, he stated that "commercial publishers find it worth their while to publish books on Jewish theology, and the fact that there are today such books written by Americans to be published is itself revealing." He dissented from the conventional interpretation as to what lay behind this trend. Nearly everyone else believed that this upsurge in Jewish interest among Jews stemmed from "Hitler and Zionism." Glazer disagreed: "The two greatest events in modern Jewish history, the murder of six million Jews by Hitler and the creation of a Jewish state in Palestine," played a less important role than suburbanization in changing Jewish behavior. Glazer may or may not have offered the more plausible explanation, but he admitted that everyone else placed the Holocaust at the center of American Jewish self-understanding.[13]

Some commentators actually worried that, in fact, the catastrophe had left too deep a mark on the Jews of America, overshadowing Judaism, a religion with a centuries' old core of law, canonical texts, ethics, ritual practices, and learning, which should transcend the obsession with the Nazi Holocaust. In 1956, one Orthodox rabbi, Milton Polin, considered a swathe of American Jews to be "Hitler Jews"—those whose "Jewish biographies consist of a series of catastrophe after catastrophe." Polin warned that Jews who "need the pressure of a Hitler" to awaken in them their Jewish consciousness could not be counted on to sustain Jewish survival. He recognized, though, how profoundly the communal ethos took its shape from the recent tragic history, and while it disturbed him as a religious leader committed to the verities of the tradition, he understood that the fate of the six million shaped the Jews of postwar America.[14]

The Holocaust and American Jewish Anxieties

Yet for all the changes that took place and the many individuals who claimed that the Holocaust had transformed them and American Jewry as a whole, rabbis, teachers, writers, and community workers wondered, quite publicly, what this all meant, pondering the nature of Jewish life in America and fretting about its future. The pages of their magazines resounded with deep self-criticism, bristling with a sense that all the activity amounted to little more than hollow conformity and meaninglessness. Jews may have joined synagogues in greater numbers than ever before, but commentators disdained this empirical fact, believing that most did so for social rather than spiritual reasons. Jewish children attended Jewish schools at levels unmatched in earlier eras, but they seemed to learn very little about the Jewish religion and culture. Economic prosperity enabled Jews to invest in their grand physical infrastructure, but some believed that this material prosperity threatened Jewish values. What got built and done seemed vapid. Jewish learning appeared woefully low, superficial at best.

Sermons and books, speeches, articles in the journals of Jewish educators, and pedagogical works reflected this disquiet about American Jewry, posing questions that belied the high levels of affiliation and ambitious building booms. What could the American Jewish leadership do to really invigorate Judaism, to make it meaningful for American Jews? How deep did Jewish commitments go? How could they create a self-sustaining Jewish culture in America? What kind of education would ensure a knowledgeable and committed American Jewry? What would the next generation, a thoroughly American one, several steps removed from the European experience of parents and grandparents, feel and do as Jews, as barriers in American society peeled away?

Communal organizations invested time, energy, and money in contemplating this issue, launching a broad discussion about American Jewry's failings, juxtaposed against proposals as to how to overcome them. In 1952, the Fraternal Order B'rith Abraham, in collaboration with the American Association for Jewish Education, established a prize worth $500.00 for a "worthy student in the pursuance of advanced studies in Judaica in an accredited American college, university, or other school of higher learning." The successful candidate had to submit an essay on "Jewish Life in America as I See It—Its Problems and Needs."[15]

American Jewish communal leaders had worried about the future of Jewish life in a free, democratic, and seductively inviting society, not just for decades but for several centuries. This lament had been the communal leitmotif for the full sweep of American Jewish history, starting in the seventeenth century. Nearly every institutional innovation of American Jewry, whether Reform, Modern Orthodoxy, Conservativism, or Reconstructionism, whether Zionist youth work, Jewish summer camping, or the Jewish center movement, arose in part to grapple with the problem of Judaism and Jewish identity in America's overly hospitable climate. Each response expressed a distinctive view, yet all tackled the same concern.[16]

The Holocaust added a new layer of questioning and urgency, expanding the repertoire of anxieties about the Jewish future. It provided a new lexicon by which to pose such questions and articulate possibilities. Would American Jews ever produce texts and institutions, teachers, leaders, and a committed laity to assume a place in the chain of tradition so violently ripped asunder? Could American Jews ever fill the vast cultural chasm left empty with the destruction of the great Jewish centers of Europe? Would America's individualism and materialism, attributes of the larger society that had benefited the Jews, trump the passion for learning and the intensity of collective identity, which they saw as the hallmark of Jewish life, a way of living that, with the six million, had gone up in smoke?

That the burden for sustaining Jewish culture had been involuntarily transferred to the United States troubled them. For most of its history, American Jewry recruited its Jewish teachers and texts from abroad. Regardless of ideology, the consensus among European Jews—intellectuals, political activists, rabbinical authorities, writers, culture makers, and educators, some of whom immigrated to America—maintained that American Jews lacked authenticity, passion, and seriousness of purpose. European Jewish intellectuals had long maintained that the Americans had created a shallow, derivative culture. The destruction of European Jewry made these Jews, long viewed as woefully inadequate, now responsible for the future of the Jewish people. They had to do this on their own.[17]

They asked in myriad ways and places if they could actually accomplish very much. Isaiah Minkoff shared this vision, pointing out to the Jewish Labor Committee in 1951 that this body now had to deal with "the problem of the future of the Jewish community in America." For the first time in its history, Jews considered the need to undertake Jewish cultural projects because of "the virtual disappearance of the great European Jewry of 6,000,000 souls." This "annihilation of European Jewry" meant not just the devastating loss of life but "the obliteration of many of the centers from which we had drawn spiritual and cultural values and inspiration." The Jewish Labor Committee, for one, decided that it had to now devote more attention to Jewish cultural projects, something it had not undertaken before.[18]

American Jews articulated this concern about themselves. Trude Weiss-Rosmarin, praising the work of the poet Aaron Zeitlin, underscored that just as "He will not forget and thus cannot forgive the Germans," he also "will not accept 'American Jewish culture' as the successor of the Jewish culture centers of the past."[19] It was not only Zeitlin who did not see anything hopeful in American Jewish culture. In her journalistic work of the postwar years, Weiss-Rosmarin repeatedly drew stark contrasts between the six million, pious and intensely Jewish, and the appallingly lackadaisical Jews of America, who seemed to care little for authentic Judaism.

"America Is Not Babylon," she wrote in a 1953 article, not to compliment the former. Rather, she predicted, America would never produce anything of compensatory spiritual or intellectual worth that might make up for what had been lost after "the great Eastern European Jewish centers . . . were destroyed by the Nazis." Babylonia had made up for, and rivaled, Jerusalem in its day, but America, she predicted, would not come close to equaling the "Jewish centers of gravity" that had been "annihilated."[20] An ardent champion of intensive Jewish learning in America, Weiss-Rosmarin chided American Jewry for its educational failures, repeatedly lambasting it in the name of that which the Germans had obliterated. In 1959, she exposed what she defined as the superficiality of "The American Jewish Revival," commenting, "We create much motion, but generate little spiritual power. What the Pharaohs and the Czar, the Hamans and the Hitlers failed to accomplish ignorance, apathy and indifference threaten to achieve" in America, as demonstrated by low levels of Jewish education.[21]

Rabbis, writers, educators, and community workers continuously took up the issue of American Jewry's ability—or, better, inability—to shoulder this burden. Books, articles, sermons, pamphlets, youth group activities, and camp programs all wondered about it. The young leaders who met in the summer of 1952 at the Leader Training Institute of the National Federation of Temple Youth pondered past and future. "Our generation," their study guide told them, "has witnessed two unprecedented phenomena— the destruction of 6,000,000 Jews in Europe and the emergence of the new State of Israel—which have affected our 'Jewish' look. What is involved in being a member of the Jewish community," they speculated, "in our home towns, in our country, in our world today?"[22]

The Eternal Light dramatized this conundrum in a 1955 radio broadcast of a short story by Isaac Bashevis Singer, "The Little Shoemaker." In the commentary offered at the play's end, Joseph Unger, a member of the Board of the Jewish Theological Seminary from Youngstown, Ohio, discerned "the moral of the story": "Despite the fact that Abba Schuster's sons went to America and there became successful businessmen who were able to rescue their father from the European massacre, they were unable to enable him to enjoy life despite the many luxuries that they provided for him." Like "the shoemaker's children," Unger told radio listeners, "our forefathers were blessed with great material prosperity so that when their loved ones were engulfed by the terrible tragedy of the Hitler era, they were able to snatch them from the inferno and bring them to this land." But physical survival did not suffice: "It soon became apparent" that the shoemaker's sons, stand-ins for America's comfortable Jews, had to "reestablish their will and maintain [a] . . . desire to live . . . as Jews." Unger urged, "We must do more than simply provide physical comforts." Jewish learning had to be invigorated in response to the "inferno."[23]

These questioners exuded little confidence about the possibility of a positive answer, and they focused in the main on American Jewry's weaknesses and shortcomings. Perhaps because of the magnitude of the destruction and the horrendous way it had been executed, they believed that they hallowed the memory of the six million by admitting their own inadequacies. Each time they verbally flagellated themselves for the anemic state of their Jewish commitments, their lack of learning, and the silliness of their culture, they declared how learned the six million had been, how intense the Jewish culture of the "martyrs," how zealous the Jewish commitments of Hitler's victims. Herman Kieval reviewed Abraham Joshua Heschel's book *The Earth Is the Lord's* for *Conservative Judaism.* As an elegiac farewell to the Jews of eastern Europe, the volume performed "a sacred task" by "telling the story of the 'inner life' of the East European Jew." Kieval intoned a dominant trope of postwar American Jewish culture: "This is the kind of thing we lost when the six million were destroyed. Statistics do not bleed but the cutting out of such a spirit, such a holiness from our world bleeds like a mortal wound." The Jews of that world, Kieval declared, "had something else in their culture which—for all our education and culture—we lack. They had a pattern and a purpose for living. They had their own etiquette and manners whose guiding principle was not beauty but holiness, not correct form but inward feeling." Unlike the Jews who perished "when Warsaw and Vilna, Lemberg and Lublin became the funeral pyres of those six million," American Jews "see no reason to exert ourselves to preserve the Yiddish and Hebrew languages and literatures in which these people expressed themselves, the Chasidic stories and songs, the works of learning and ethical behavior." Whether it was accurate or not mattered less than the frequency with which American Jews offered this assessment of the six million as better Jews than themselves, revealing the degree to which they memorialized the victims by confessing their own failures as Jews.[24]

The World That Is No More

All of American Jews' fretting over their deficiencies and all the laments over their weaknesses reflected a particular understanding of the relationship between American Jewry and those whom the Nazis had destroyed. American Jewry in the past—writers, educators, rabbis, and communal workers assessed—had depended on European Jewry for teachers and texts, Jewish ideas, and, essentially, anything of value in Jewish culture. In 1956 in a keynote address to B'nai B'rith's Grand Lodge Number 7, Label Katz stated it succinctly: "In a real sense, the American Jewish community has been an importer from Europe and other parts of the world of Jewish learning, pedagogues and Rabbis. No longer can we be importers. Our source has been destroyed. The cataclysmic destruction of European Jewry, a citadel of Jewish learning, culture and art, suddenly brought to an end our ability to be importers. We must relearn the lessons of history." In fact, a more complicated flow of ideas, books, and cultural practices had connected the Jews of America to those in Europe, but all postwar public commentators asserted that the culturally backward American Jewry had received, while the Jewishly authentic Europeans had given.[25]

The embrace by American Jewry of a sweet, if not overly sweet, image of the world of east European Jewry, as a place that once throbbed with a vibrant culture of intensely lived Jewish life, reflected its violent demise at the hands of the Nazis. The postwar period witnessed the emergence of a nostalgic romance about Jewish eastern Europe, witnessing the production of texts that offered American Jews glimpses of it, set against the background of its destruction. The vast majority of American Jews descended, one or two generations back, from the great migration from eastern Europe that had commenced at the end of the nineteenth century. As such, in venerating the now-destroyed world of the Jews of eastern Europe, American Jews honored their own antecedents.

Shlomo Katz made this point in the first issue of *Midstream* in 1955, a publication which, given its Zionist orientation, in the prewar period would have found little of value in the Yiddish-based culture of eastern Europe. But in 1955, Katz discovered that, since the late 1940s, affection for the world of eastern European Jewry swept through American Jewry. Trying to understand it, Katz wondered whether it was "because American Jewry suffered from a burden of guilt that it had, through no merit of its own, been spared from sharing the fate of its kinsmen, or because it suddenly became aware that Old World Jewry was now dead, not as one dies slowly, but murdered in cold blood—in any case the wave of nostalgia was overwhelming. Memory of the *shtetl*, which for decades had been relegated to the back of the mind . . . now came into its own in the thinking and writing of American Jews. It was recalled vividly and with love."[26]

Publishers recognized a market for Yiddish works in translation, books that spoke for that world. Maurice Samuel presented *Prince of the Ghetto,* an anthology of Y. L. Peretz's essays, in 1948, through Alfred A. Knopf. He introduced the book with the "destruction of Polish Jewry." The women and men Peretz wrote about, Samuel noted, the "Polish Jews who were the objects of Peretz's passionate and scrupulous concern have been wiped out by the modern world. Of the three and a quarter million, three million were done to death—gassed, machine-gunned, bombed, burned or buried alive." Samuel's translation played a role in bringing them, as it were, back to life. In 1962, Knopf also rereleased Samuel's 1943 book, *The World of Sholom Aleichem,* a translation of short stories. This collection also took as its deep context the Holocaust that killed that world. Looking back in time, Samuel remarked that "in the innocent childhood of our century the Russian-Jewish Pale of Settlement was the disgrace of Western humanity, the last word in reaction and brutality." But "we have traveled far since then." In that journey from the past, Jews had come to realize the insignificance of the "occasional slaughters" of that world, which had "never amounted to more than a few hundred men, women, and children at a time." The Russian Pale where Sholem Aleichem's short stories took place, had, Samuel told, worked on the principle that "everything was forbidden to Jews unless specifically permitted. But by an oversight which Germany has since corrected, the right to remain alive was not challenged."[27]

Texts venerating the culture of eastern European Jewry flourished in the postwar period. In 1949, Farrar, Straus, Giroux issued Abraham Joshua Heschel's YIVO lecture, a paean to east European Jewry, *The Earth Is the Lord's.* Without chronicling its horrific end, Heschel described the Jews' inner lives. He opened his eloquent narrative with the declaration, "The story about the life of the Jews in Eastern Europe which has come to an end in our days is what I have tried to tell in this essay."[28] Three years later, International Universities Press offered Mark Zborowski and Elizabeth Herzog's *Life Is with People.* Graced with a prefatory statement by the country's leading anthropologist, Margaret Mead, *Life Is with People* made the eastern European *shtetl* a singular place, with distinctive ways and characters, values and expressions. Regardless if lived "among Poles or Russians, Lithuanians or Hungarians," the Jewish small town of eastern Europe supported a special culture. "Only the wars and revolutions of the twentieth century," she wrote, "with the final destruction of six million lives, put an end to its role as the current home of the tradition." The Jews of all these places ultimately suffered a similar fate at the hands of the Nazis, and postwar American Jewish culture conveniently flattened out differences between them, rendering them all dwellers of "the *shtetl*" and all their host countries "eastern Europe."[29]

The embrace of the world of the slaughtered Jews of eastern Europe and a simultaneous romance for Yiddish by postwar American Jewry played broadly in the postwar period. Translation into English of the works of Isaac Bashevis Singer did not directly connect to the Holocaust, but his books began to appear in American bookstores and libraries. Knopf released *The Family Moskat* in 1950, followed by *Gimpel, the Fool* in 1952, *Satan in Goray* in 1955, *The Magician of Lublin* in 1960, and *Spinoza of Market Street* in 1961. The popularity of these books demonstrated how much the American Jewish public embraced Yiddish texts in translation, in a way and to a degree not witnessed in the pre-Holocaust period.[30] The immense acclaim of the 1954 Broadway production of *The World of Sholom Aleichem* and its 1959 television adaptation paled when compared with the 1964 sensation *Fiddler on the Roof.* But the appeal of these performances reflected the sentimental valorization of Yiddish and the emergence of a culture of nostalgia for the lost Jews of eastern Europe.

In the pre-Holocaust period, many American Jewish institutions and organizations had either looked down on Yiddish as "jargon," a relic of an "old world" in need of replacement, or just paid it no attention. After the Holocaust, they expressed warm feelings for the language. A writer for Habonim's magazine *Furrows*, despite the organization's commitment to Hebrew as the living language of the Zionist enterprise, reviewed with reverence Irving Howe and Eliezer Greenberg's anthology of Yiddish stories in 1955. "The tragedy of the Jewish people in the last two decades," asserted the reviewer, "is also the tragedy of the Yiddish language. Hitler destroyed not only six million men, women and children; he destroyed—or almost so—a language and a culture." Recommending the book to the Zionist youth whose movement made Hebrew a sine qua non for active participation, the writer lamented the poverty of English translations of Yiddish and admitted that, in the face of the near total destruction, secondhand would have to substitute for the original.[31]

Reform movement summer camps in the 1950s and early 1960s turned to Sholem Aleichem, Peretz, and other Yiddish writers for material for music, dance, and drama programs. Reform had long emphasized English as the dignified language of religious worship, and its comfortably American members came from families where Yiddish had never been spoken or had been spoken so long ago in the families' pasts as to not constitute part of their lived culture. But in the postwar period, the movement looked to the world of Yiddish literature to inspire young people. They prefaced camp activities with grim reminders that the literature they would be performing had emerged in an eastern European Jewish world which "is no more" and how indebted they felt to "a European Jewry now extinct."[32]

Those involved in Jewish education also found room in new curricula for that world. The Jewish Education Association of America in 1953 distributed a filmstrip, *Grandfather's World*, for school use. "A visualization of four stories of Jewish life in Eastern Europe," recommended for all between the intermediate grades and adult learners, used black-and-white illustrations of life in the destroyed "Old Home" as a tool in teaching American Jews about the holidays. Simultaneously, it used the holidays to make that now-destroyed world palpable in 1950s America.[33]

In tandem with hallowing the memory of the ruthlessly murdered world of east European Jewry, American Jews developed a rhetoric that defined the six million as saintly by virtue of having undergone their ordeal. The editor of the *Jewish Spectator* articulated this most forcefully in her September 1954 issue, in the spirit of the upcoming high holidays, in an appropriately entitled article, "Inscribe Us in the Book of Life":

> The chronicles and reports of the survivors of the Nazi Holocaust show that even in the death camps, Jews believed . . . in the Coming of the Messiah, the symbol of life. Although they knew themselves doomed, the hapless victims of the Nazis continued to concentrate on life. More heroic than the Revolt of the Warsaw Ghetto was the steadfastness with which its inhabitants—hundreds of thousands—resolutely shut their eyes to death and dedicated themselves to LIFE by heroically going about their tasks and pursuing their ideals, although they knew that their days, even their hours, were numbered.[34]

To use such language, alongside the iconization of the images of eastern European Jewry, and the telling of their story as one throbbing with sweetness, authenticity, piety, and intensity fulfilled two functions. This cultural product of the postwar years provided American Jewry with yet another way to memorialize the six million. It also made more manifest exactly what had been lost, and as such it rendered more challenging, nearly daunting, the role that American Jews had to play in making up for what had been destroyed.[35]

That world had been killed. Communal voices asked if American Jewry would and could compensate for what had been killed. Posed bluntly as a question or indirectly as speculation, the issue of American Jews' ability or inability to pick up where European Jewry had been forced to leave off echoed in communal discourse. Speaking to his fellow Conservative rabbis in 1960, Rabbi Israel Goldstein charged them not only to remind their congregants that "the Jewish people [had] lived through the destruction of one-third of its numbers, its choicest part . . . the alma maters which nourished the Jewish present and future" but also to tell them that they, American Jewry, now constituted "the largest remnant," who must "try to fill the spiritual-cultural voids."[36]

God, American Jews, and the Holocaust

The need to fill the empty Jewish spaces influenced the ways in which American Jews contemplated the theological implications of the horrendous slaughter. The tragic fate of European Jewry found its way into their speculations about God, God's place in human history, the relationship between good and evil, and the conundrum of how God could allow such vast suffering. Where had the God whom they blessed been when the Germans conducted their nearly successful genocidal campaign against the Jews? Since such pondering could not be answered, commentators used American Jewry's new role, thrust upon it by the Holocaust, to justify religious participation. If they could not use God and God's commandments to explain their Jewish commitments, they could use the legacy of the six million to do so.

For all of its history, American Jewish culture had devoted relatively sparse time and minimal energy to systematic thinking about the existence, meaning, and nature of God. Scholars agree that up until the late 1960s, theology occupied a minor place in American Jewish intellectual life, and even the rabbinical seminaries had paid scant attention to it.[37] A study of the Jewish Theological Seminary of America (JTS), for example, put this matter in comparative terms. Because Judaism, particularly as constructed by the Conservative movement, focused on observance, wrote Glenn T. Miller, JTS, unlike the nation's Catholic and Protestant seminaries, "invested few resources in the teaching of theology." As the leaders of America's largest Jewish denomination saw it, Miller asserted, "doctrinal clarity is not central to authentic Jewish practice," and, therefore, "given the relatively small place of doctrine in Jewish practice, the type of theology taught at JTS has logically tended toward the philosophy of Judaism rather than toward the systematic exposition of Jewish teachings."[38]

But even with that in mind, the problem of God and the Holocaust surfaced in Jewish public forums. In 1951 and 1952, the Jewish Theological Seminary sponsored a series of lectures at Carnegie Hall by Martin Buber, the German-born philosopher who taught at Hebrew University in Jerusalem. Speaking to an overflow crowd for his third lecture, on "The Dialogue Between Heaven and Earth," Buber asked his New York listeners, "Dare we recommend to the survivors of Auschwitz, the Job of the gas chambers: 'Give thanks unto the Lord, for he is good: for His mercy endureth forever'?" Buber distinguished between two "Jobs," the "Job of the Bible" and the "Job of the gas chambers," and in doing so defined the way to respond theologically to evil and, as such, God's absence.[39] In *God in Search of Man*, issued in 1952 by Farrar, Straus, Giroux, a mainstream publishing house, Abraham Joshua Heschel declared that "in trying to understand Jewish existence a Jewish philosopher must look for agreement with the men of Sinai as well as with the people of Auschwitz." Later, in his 1956 article, "A Confusion of Good and Evil," the Polish-born Jewish thinker, then teaching at JTS, questioned not God but human reason in the face of the enormity of the Holocaust.[40]

At a popular level, removed from the philosophic speculation of trained theologians, postwar American Jews offered their views on God, God's hand in history, and both in relationship to the destruction of European Jewry. They asked painful questions about how the Holocaust could have happened if a "God full of compassion" actually existed. Camp programs, congregational sermons, magazine articles, and books directed at general, not intellectually sophisticated, audiences struggled with this question.

In 1958, the National Federation of Temple Brotherhoods asked Rabbi Morton Applebaum to prepare an adult education kit for congregations. Applebaum took his material and made it into a question-and-answer book, *What Everyone Should Know About Judaism*, a slim volume prefaced by Reverend John Haynes Holmes, the Minister Emeritus of the Community Church of New York. Most questions addressed purely empirical or informational issues, like "What does 'Kosher' Mean?" "What is a 'Yarmulka'?" and "What is a 'Shofar'?" Rabbi Applebaum also fielded conceptual matters like "Why are Jews such a persecuted people?" and his answer involved the Holocaust and its theological underpinnings. "This question," the rabbi shared with his Jewish and non-Jewish readers, "smacks of an antiquated belief in divine retributive justice which conceives of 'good for good' and 'bad for bad.' According to such thinking, the persecution of Jews through the ages must be proof of the punishment that fits the crime, God-sent suffering for Jewish sinfulness." Applebaum rejected such thinking: "What persecution the Jewish people has suffered can neither be attributed to God nor punishment for sinfulness. To imply that the recent 'liquidation' of six million Jews by the Nazis was the will of God would be an impeachment of His goodness, and to absolve the murderers of any guilt. It would be to accept any and all forms of persecution as divine intent, and absolve all persecutors." This, he asserted, "is not reasonable."[41]

Some rabbis, pondering the meaning of God in the context of the Holocaust, juxtaposed its brutality with the idea of God as good and a possible source for human improvement, despite the omnipresence of evil. Albert S. Goldstein of Boston's Ohabei Shalom Congregation engaged with this idea in a poem he printed in the congregational bulletin:

> I am no child, afraid of the dark
> God has led me through so many
> Nights with a light of fire,
> Surely no darkness is too dark—with Him.
> When I walk with Him, even the
> Night shineth as the day,
> The darkness is as the light. . . .
> Egypt, Babylon, Greece, Rome. . . .
> Crusades, Black-Death, Exile, Crematorium,
> Pharaoh, Haman, Nero, Hitler. . . .

Despite this arc of suffering, when God could have saved the Jewish people, the rabbi told his congregants,

> This night too shall pass
> And in the morning light
> We shall behold Thy face,
> O Lord, in righteousness
> And in Thy light shall we see light.[42]

Goldstein's words reflected the postwar American Jewish engagement with God and the Nazi catastrophe. God's goodness existed, but human beings —the German Nazis, perpetrators of the Holocaust—alone bore responsibility for the slaughter.

The contrast between God's beneficence and human beings' ability to be utterly evil, along with the need for faith in God despite evil, ran through American Jewish religious material. Laying out for readers the Jewish "Quest for God," Sidney Greenberg in his *A Modern Treasury of Jewish Thoughts*, a 1960 compilation of excerpts and snippets from Judaic works spanning the canon from the Talmud and prayer book through contemporary sermons and other recent works including synagogue bulletins, made room for the Holocaust. Greenberg began the "Quest for God" section with a quote from Zvi Kolitz's *Tiger Beneath the Skin*, a 1947 collection of stories and "Parables from the Years of Death." "I believe in the sun," Kolitz had written, and Greenberg quoted him, "when it is not shining. I believe in love even when not feeling. I believe in God even when he is silent."[43] This quote came from an "inscription on the walls of a cellar in Cologne where Jews hid from the Nazis." Of all the entries included in "Quest for God," Greenberg gave the most space to an excerpt from Kolitz's "Yossel Rakover Talks to God," a parable from *Tiger Beneath the Skin*, which began with the words, "In the ruins of the ghetto of Warsaw, among heaps of charred rubbish, there was found, packed tightly into a small bottle, the following testament, written during the ghetto's last hours by a Jew named Yossel Rakover." The fictional Rakover's testament ended with the following:

> I have followed Him even when He repulsed me. I have followed his commandments even when he castigated me for it; I have loved Him and I love Him even when He has hurled me into the earth, tortured me to death, made me an object of shame and ridicule.
>
> And these are my last words to You, my wrathful God: Nothing will avail You in the least. You have done everything to make me lose my faith in You, but I die exactly as I have lived, crying:
>
> "Hear, O Israel, the Lord our God the Lord is One.
> Into Your hands, O Lord, I consign my soul."[44]

Some American Jews derived different messages about the relationship between God and the Jewish people as a result of the Holocaust. In the summer of 1962 the young Reform Jews who gathered at Camp Olin-Sang-Ruby pondered this problem.[45] The high-school-division campers staged a mock trial at which "G-d" (in the original) had been handed an "indictment . . . for negligence, cruelty, and murder." In the play, God stood trial for these crimes, with Job, Rabbi Akiba, and Anne Frank testifying for the prosecution. One camper from the older, advanced Torah session shared his thoughts about that summer's discussions. In the camp newsletter, he remarked, "Through the many hectic and unsteady years of existence of Judaism, specifically in terms of its encounter with prejudice and attempted continual genocide, I am brought to the point of contemplation on what type of god, if any, rules the Jew." Steve Rosenberg wrote, "It is puzzling to think of the Jews as the 'chosen people' if we consider the seemingly unconnected chain of events that have befallen our people from the giving of the Ten Commandments through the massacre of six million Hebrews." This conundrum forced Rosenberg to conclude, "We are not even sure" if God exists, but still we "should devote our strength and energy to the betterment of our earth and people."[46]

The most committed of the movement's young people who attended the Mid-Atlantic Federation of Temple Youth Leadership Training Institute met with a rabbi from Allentown, Pennsylvania, Rabbi Stephen Schaefer, who admitted that the Holocaust caused him to doubt. He "uttered the nightmarish fact [that] . . . millions of Jews were killed" and engaged the young leaders with the question, "Why did this happen?" The rabbi told them that they, "the youth of the camps[,] must face this and other questions."[47]

Filling the Void?

Of those "other questions," none, including discussion about God and the catastrophe, received greater attention than those that asked how they, the Jews of America, could change themselves to make up for the horrendous losses endured. As soon as the war ended and the fact of six million destroyed European Jews became fixed in American Jewish consciousness into the 1960s, leaders and community activists exhorted American Jews to compensate for what had been lost by becoming better, more knowledgeable, more active Jews. Statements that questioned their ability to do this commanded attention in the Jewish press, lecture halls, publications, and synagogues.

David Petegrosky, writing for the American Jewish Congress executive committee in 1946, told the defense organization that its activities must now constantly be based on the fact that the "magnitude of the Jewish catastrophe in Europe had imposed on American Jewry an ever-increasing

share of the responsibility of the security and status of Jews everywhere."
He prescribed "an intensive program . . . to develop among American Jews
a far more adequate understanding of Jewish values and culture."[48] The
Jewish Publication Society of America issued a press release in 1948, advertising Lee M. Friedman's *Pilgrims in a New Land,* a history of American
Jewry. That document stated directly, "History has now forced us, for the
first time, into a dominant role in the life of world-Jewry. Whether we are
mature enough or not . . . leadership is ours. . . . The heart-rending duties
of fund-raising for our brethren in the DP camps and for resettlement in
Palestine will demand . . . less of our time and energy." The time had come,
JPS said, to "develop our genuinely creative American Jewry." Only such
a Jewry could assume adequately the obligations that history had thrust
upon it.[49]

The trope of the Holocaust's imposition of a burden on the Jews of
America could be heard most everyplace they discussed the Jewish pres-
ent and future. Abraham Neuman, speaking to the National Conference of
Jewish Communal Service, the organization of social workers who staffed
Jewish service agencies, on "The Evolving American Jewish Community"
put it in epic terms:

> We are the last of the great Western Jewries. . . . We are the heirs of
> Israel's prophets, sages and seers. We are successors to the scholars of
> Babylon, the creators and redactors of the Talmud. . . . We have seen
> with the mind's eye the inexpressible Jewish tragedy of all time: the
> battle to death of the immortals behind the Ghetto walls of Warsaw
> . . . the ashes and ruins of countless Jewish communities that mourned
> the brutal desecration of Sifre Torahs and the destruction of houses of
> worship and sacred study.

Having anchored Jewish social workers' responsibilities in terms of the
"inexpressible Jewish tragedy of all times," Neuman asked them, "How do
you visualize the goal of the evolving Jewish community?"[50]

This question, in one way or another, dominated American Jewish discourse throughout the postwar period. The sermons and speeches American Jews heard, the magazines they read, lobbed this challenge at them.
World Jewry, said Israel Goldstein in a 1951 speech, "Some Current Problems of Jewish Life in the United States," stood at a "crossroads, since eastern European Jewry is no more."[51] Trude Weiss-Rosmarin said it as well in
1959, as she called on American Jews to recognize that the "contemporary

burden of making restitution for the void left by the virtual annihilation of the European Jewish center" rested on them.[52]

Individuals and institutions representing the spectrum of Jewish ideologies and worldviews volunteered to guide the Jews of America in taking up the challenge handed to them by Hitler. In 1947, in addition to all of its other Yiddish publications, YIVO brought out an English-Yiddish anthology of essays by Y. L.Peretz. Sol Liptzin provided the introductory material, explaining that the end of the war "marks a definite turning point in Jewish history. It marks the end of the East European era and the beginning of the American era. At the dawn of our century, Eastern Europe, between the Elbe and the Dnieper, contained more than half of Jewry. By 1945 . . . Eastern Jewry lay prostrate and decimated." While Hitler, Liptzin asserted, had failed at his "supreme effort at annihilation of the Jews," he "succeeded in definitely shifting the center of Jewish cultural life, even as Pharaoh and Nebukadnezar had done before him." Hitler had transferred it to the unprepared Jews of America. In the Peretz pieces, Liptzin hoped, American Jews might "find the key to an understanding of themselves in the realization that they are the heirs of the Jewish cultural tradition."[53]

On a different note, Nahum Goldman, president of the World Jewish Congress, speaking at a 1954 dinner sponsored by the Histadrut Ha-Ivrith of America (Hebrew Language and Culture Association) in honor of Columbia University's Hebrew program, promoted that language as the most effective way for American Jewry to strengthen itself. "Let us face the truth," Goldman orated in his after-dinner speech; "Jewry's continuity is in greater jeopardy today than ever before in Jewish history. Six million Jews were physically lost to us as a result of Nazi Genocide." He exhorted the audience to realize that "Hebrew alone, living Hebrew, can assure survival. This language, communicating the ideas and values of living Jewish tradition, must become the acquisition of a majority of the American Jewish community."[54]

That community had no guide or precedent to assist it as it tried to take up the challenge of compensating for what had been so violently destroyed. How would American Jews change their lives, and how would those changes lead to a flowering of Jewish culture in America? How much money and energy should they contribute, and to what, in order to most effectively instill new vigor into the battered and traumatized collectivity of the Jewish people?

Writers and rabbis, community leaders and commentators did not leave it up to the rank and file of American Jewry to answer these questions.

They suggested a slew of ideas, each designed to best equip American Jews to step into the footprints of European Jewry. Many proposals came from institutions and organizations already in existence, each claiming that it could direct American Jewry in this compensatory project, thus linking their own institutional raison d'être to the awesome task at hand. The jumble of voluntary organizations and institutions that constituted the infrastructure of American Jewry, a myriad of synagogues and denominations, all competed for the membership, loyalty, and financial support of a fixed population, and each stressed how much it could do to make up for the great cultural losses sustained by world Jewry.

For example, in its first postwar fundraising campaign, launched under the slogan "There Is No Dignity Without Religion," the Union of American Hebrew Congregations, along with Hebrew Union College, appealed to members for financial support. The recent tragedy created many immediate exigencies in its destructive path, and American Jewry, the solicitation letter noted, had risen to the challenge for "the deliverance and rehabilitation of our Jewish brethren in DP camps abroad." But American Jewry ought not forget its own needs, "when the destruction of European centers of Jewish learning places a vastly increased responsibility for the spiritual welfare of world-Israel upon American institutions." Hebrew Union College (HUC) had played its part and deserved the support of the Jewish public, he said: HUC has provided "a haven . . . for eleven famous scholars driven from their homes by Hitlerism, the last remnant of the great Jewish culture of Europe." Money contributed to the Cincinnati school as such assisted American Jewry in becoming the next link in the chain of Jewish "spiritual welfare."[55]

Advocates for Jewish projects of all sorts promoted their undertakings in the name of the Holocaust. In 1947, Rabbi Abraham Scheinberg, editor of *American Jews: Their Lives and Achievements*, justified his book in terms of the "six million European Jews [who] have perished in an orgy of mass murder unparalleled in history" and the fact that "the five-and-a-quarter millions of American Jews" who constituted "a half of the total world Jewish population" are "the most numerous, the most prosperous, the freest among all the Jewries of the Diaspora." Scheinberg asked the era's ubiquitous American Jewish question: "Now that European Jewish life lies in ruins, what do we here in the United States have in the way of human material that makes for Jewish vitality and Jewish survival here and elsewhere? What are we contributing to Jewish life in our own country?" To find the answer, he suggested, not surprisingly, that American Jews learn more about themselves by turning to his book.[56] Two years later, the American Jewish Historical Society announced the first "observance of Jewish History Week," taking as its cue the interrelated phenomena that most of the "great communities of Europe . . . have ceased to exist" and the "coming of age of the American Jewish community."[57]

Both the Conservative and Reform movements created institutions for the advancement of liturgical music, and both did so in the name of the Holocaust. The Reform did it first. In November 1948, the Hebrew Union College Jewish Institute of Religion in New York announced to the press that, with a grant from New York's Temple Emanu-El and supported by the Society for the Advancement of Jewish Liturgical Music, it was launching the School for Sacred Music, a nondenominational academy, under Reform auspices. Nelson Glueck, the president of the Reform seminary, connected the new musical institution with the recent tragedy. "This school," he said to the press and to those assembled at the inaugural ceremony, "will help to fill the void caused by the disappearance of the great centers of Jewish culture and learning in Europe during the occupation by the Nazi horde. Many artists and intellectuals," he recalled, "were among the 6,000,000 Jews who were slaughtered. . . . In consequence, Europe has lost her position as the richest source of Jewish cultural tradition." In 1948, only American Jewry could claim that position.[58] In 1954, the Conservative movement established its Cantors' Institute, and in heralding this, it, too, cited the Holocaust: "With the disappearance of many European Jewish communities, American Jewry is assuming a major role in preserving and enriching the total Jewish musical tradition." A concert marked the school's opening, and the school noted in its program, "With the disappearance of Jewish life in Europe . . . we in America have become the heirs to their musical tradition. Ours is the duty to collect, to codify and to transmit this tradition so that it may continue to flourish."[59]

Advocates for numerous American Jewish cultural projects and innovations from the late 1940s onward claimed that their effort to stimulate Jewish creativity in America drew its inspiration from the reality of the Holocaust's devastations.[60] Ira Eisenstein, a key figure in the Reconstructionist movement, had published *Creative Judaism* in 1936, for use by "adult study groups and college students" interested in the movement. When he, and the Reconstructionist Foundation, reissued the book in 1953 in revised form, they acknowledged the great changes wrought in the "intervening years," which "witnessed the tragedy of Hitlerism at its worst," as well as "the triumphant establishment of the State of Israel." These two together changed American Jewry and necessitated new creative ways of thinking about Judaism and Jewish life.[61]

Rabbi Joachim Prinz encapsulated this kind of thinking most persuasively in a 1958 article in *Conservative Judaism*, appropriately, or ironically, titled "Creative Catastrophe." "It might not be entirely out of order to think of Jewish history in terms of creative catastrophes," wrote the Newark rabbi who had fled from Germany in the late 1930s. "This is, of course, neither a legitimate nor a delicate approach when we stand at the mass graves of Bergen-Belsen and Dachau, or look at the ash containers of Auschwitz." But, he offered, this most recent catastrophe, like those that preceded it, could be a source of renewal through new cultural work crafted to confront the tragic. "In terms of Jewish *life* (as distinct from mere *survival*)," he continued, "the creative reaction of our people to all the miseries from Mitzraim [Egypt] to Hitler is of great importance."[62]

Those who observed the state of American Jewry, who diagnosed its ills and then prescribed remedies, saw in the devastating details of the Holocaust a possible platform for regeneration. The unfathomable horrors that had been visited on the Jewish people, they believed, could be expressed through creative work which, in turn, had the potential, as they saw it, to inspire. Art, music, new liturgies, and other forms of imaginative expression would serve double duty by both breathing life into American Jewish practice and, at the same time, serving as a memorial to the vanished six million.

American Jewish Youth: Legatees of the Holocaust

Much of the discourse about the catastrophe's legacy for American Jewry got articulated through communal concern about youth and Jewish education. Adults discussed among themselves the prospect that a new generation born and raised in the years after the war might not be moved by the slaughter of the six million and would also be less Jewish. They concurred that they, the Jewish women and men who had lived through the 1930s and 1940s, continued to be influenced by the slaughter.

C. Bezalel Sherman noted in a 1954 article, "Three Generations," that "the desire for identification with the Jewish group is very strong among the members of the third generation. Psychological factors have combined with sociological developments to stimulate this desire." He identified them: "First there was the tremendous impact of the Hitler misfortune which strengthened the community bonds between American Jewry and the Jews in other lands at a time when the ties of individual kinship were becoming looser. The Hitler tragedy has also enhanced the sense of responsibility that Jews in this country feel for Jewish well being the world over. For the first time in history the survival of the Jewish people was literally placed in the hands of American Jewry."[63] Like most of his generation, however, Sherman had less faith in the rising ones.

When American Jewish communal leaders diagnosed the problems of young people, whether involving specifically Jewish concerns like their Jewish knowledge and levels of religious observance, or when involving more general contemporary problems facing adolescents and youth, they looked to the Holocaust to make their arguments, hoping its memory would inspire positive changes. They employed it as the measure by which to think about their young people and to exhort the community that much work needed to be done. Graenum Berger, a social worker associated with the Federation of Jewish Philanthropies of New York, played an active role in Jewish youth work and Jewish community centers, and he lectured widely during the 1950s and 1960s on these topics. He laced his speeches, even when delivered to professional audiences, with analogies to the European Jewish calamity in the context of the era's perceived youth crisis.[64]

A 1959 talk he gave to young adults interested in Jewish community centers considered alcoholism, suicide, drug addiction, and other pathologies. "Jews," he told his audience, "have so far produced few alcoholics. Studies indicate that it is our Jewish cultural attitude toward drinking which keeps us from going to pot." Berger fretted, though. As traditional patterns eroded, would Jews continue to avoid this problem? He looked at an increase in suicide rates, again wondering about the Jewish future. "Suicide," he reminded the audience, "is culturally proscribed in Judaism." How to show this to his audience? Berger took his listeners to "the Kovno Ghetto of 1941, a time when life was considered worthless, when we Jews were already on the way to losing 6,000,000 of our brethren." Berger quoted at length from a rabbinic responsum issued in that ghetto about suicide, "when tens of thousands of men, women, and children were being slaughtered."[65]

Inner-Jewish discussions about American Jewish teenagers, their Jewish commitments, and the role of the Holocaust began early in the postwar period. Jewish publications evaluated cultural works that dealt with the catastrophe in relationship to their power to influence young American Jews.

A reviewer in *Jewish Social Studies* in 1949 lauded Marie Syrkin's *Blessed Is the Match* for its possible impact upon "our Jewish youth, who so often hunt for its idols among the literature of other nations." They could in this book about ghetto fighters and partisans who confronted the Nazis, the reviewer hoped, "find beautifully written pages about heroes that by now have already become legendary."[66]

Leaders hoped that young American Jews would be inspired by stories drawn from the Holocaust era. Reform rabbi Albert Vorspan published *Giants of Justice* in 1960, biographical sketches of American Jews who paid heed to the "prophetic tradition," which exhorted "the Jew" to live by the words "justice, justice shalt thou pursue." He made much of the tragedy of European Jewry in his portraits of American Jews who combined love of their people with public service. Louis Brandeis, Vorspan described, had retired from the U.S. Supreme Court in 1939 but would not "rust away his last years in a rocking chair. There was still too much to do. Even before his retirement, the Nazi extermination of Jews had compelled him to break his customary judicial reserve and appeal to the President to do all in his power to prevent the impending termination of immigration to Palestine." Brandeis failed but did not give up, and "even in the grim moments of Nazi butchery, he never despaired of the ultimate triumph of the democracies and of the imperishability of Jewish ideals and aspirations."[67]

Lillian Wald also spent her final years of life consumed with the "deathly tragedy of Nazism," while Henry Monsky of the B'nai B'rith lobbied, organized, pleaded, and spoke out as he tried to do something about the "savage massacre of European Jewry by Hitler." So, too, as chronicled by Vorspan, had Henrietta Szold, David Dubinsky, Stephen Wise, Abraham Cronbach, and Herbert Lehman, all American Jewish "giants of justice," led public lives that touched on the Holocaust. Vorspan wrote this book not purely as history. He hoped to inspire his audience, "native-born . . . and middle class" Jews who "have imbibed the values of middle-class America; conformist, complacent, acquisitive, with success and money the gods to be worshipped." He wanted them to advocate for justice in America, not to lapse "into guilty silence and moral neutrality." And, he asked, "What of the future?" Not so upbeat about that, Vorspan noted, "this generation has been moved and shaped . . . by the profound experience of Hitlerism and the destruction of 6,000,000 Jews." As to the future, he hoped young American Jews would also consider that tragedy so that when they became adults they would think about "the survival of Jewish identity and ethical values in Judaism."

Calls for increased Jewish education, for greater commitment by parents for their children's formal Jewish learning, for more professionalized schools and curricula, backed up by greater communal expenditures, came to the Jewish public through Holocaust-inflected arguments and language based on the idea that the Jewish future lay in their hands. In the late 1940s, speakers at Jewish communal gatherings and educators sharing their concerns converged on a single point. Abraham Millgram stated it most succinctly in 1947: "That the pulse of Jewish life is rather low is known to most of us, . . . the appalling wide-spread ignorance in the field of Jewish learning" being one of the key indicators of the weakness, despite the fact that "Jewish Community life in America is supposedly thriving." An enhanced "field of Jewish education . . . as the first line of defense" in the Jewish people's "war for survival," he believed, existed in light of "the extermination of Jewish community life in Europe."[68]

In 1948, Salo Baron charged Jewish communities, as opposed to synagogues or independent schools, to foster Jewish education in the new postwar world. American Jews could no longer "delegate a major share of responsibility for Jewish education to other countries, especially Poland, Russia and Germany." He noted that American Jews should have figured that out "even before Hitler." But Hitler utterly changed Jewish reality: "We can no longer look to European Jewry as a source of our leadership."[69] Meir Ben-Horin, a faculty member at Boston Hebrew College, described the realities of contemporary American Jewish education in historical terms in 1959: "We do not see Jewish education in proper perspective until we view it against the background of . . . the destruction of much of European Jewry in World War II . . . [and] the emergence of American Jewry as the world's leading Jewish community."[70] Finally, Rabbi William Berkowitz pointed out that the great centers of learning "are no more on the map." American Jewish adults, denizens of "the only remaining Jewish cultural center, outside of Israel," have been "charged with the task of imbuing our youth with the teachings of our forefathers." To his rhetorical questions, "Have we in America fulfilled our adult obligation towards our youth? Are we prepared and willing to assume a dominant role in Jewish cultural activities?" he answered with a resounding negative.[71]

The belief that American Jewry needed to strengthen itself to make up for the massive losses endured during the Holocaust reverberated in its community programs as justification for projects of all kinds. Simon Rawidowicz, historian and Jewish thinker, came to Chicago in 1947 to teach at the College of Jewish Studies. He delivered the keynote address at the opening convocation in the fall of 1948. Rawidowicz, born in Poland, had lived in England since 1933, but he introduced himself to his audiences as "one humble member of the European *Sheertih Israel* [remnant of Israel] of the forties in our so advanced 20th century." That century and decade witnessed history's "most barbaric inhumanity, perpetrated upon 'six million Jews,' 'martyrs' . . . gassed or buried alive without leaving any mark." The martyrs had lived "noble lives," constituted "some of the finest" Jews of all times, and had served as "the bearers of the tradition of our learning."[72]

Rawidowicz retold the details of the catastrophe to those assembled, the faculty, financial backers of the college, community notables, and students, those engaged in either full-time or part-time advanced Jewish learning, some already teachers in Chicago's Jewish schools, others preparing for careers in Jewish education. The lives and deaths of the six million offered an "unforgettable lesson for Diaspora Jewry, everywhere, at all times." Those martyrs, according to Rawidowicz, "our brethren in the Polish ghettos under Hitler kept up the traditional idea of Jewish Learning," and "the way they learned, youth and aged, up to the last moments of their lives, until they were thrown into the gas-chambers, will stand for ever as one of the glorious pages of our history." The legacy of their learning in the face of death imposed a burden on diaspora Jews, including those who studied and taught at the Chicago College of Jewish Studies and in the community's many Jewish schools: "The blood of our brothers and sisters cry out from under the foundation of Europe. Will the world ever be able to bring that blood to rest. . . . Is there any 'compensation' in the world for such slaughter?" Rawidowicz had taken upon himself the mission to "tell my brethren in the New World . . . to exhort them never to forget those millions . . . but to build up their tradition, to go on weaving the web of the generations." The message could not have been clearer to the stakeholders of the College of Jewish Studies. The advancement of Jewish learning in Chicago would make it possible for the six million to "live with us forever." To Rawidowicz, and the others who participated in this discussion about postwar Jewish education, fostering that learning amounted to providing a basis for the Jewish future and memorializing "those millions" who had been killed.

A vast postwar discourse about the Holocaust as a profound matter that had made all the difference for American Jews and that in particular impacted young people swirled around American Jewish public culture. The Chicago College of Jewish Studies hosted a local Youth Forum in the winter of 1951, bringing together young people from organizations that otherwise never met together, spanning the Orthodox B'nai Akiva, Reform's National Federation of Temple Youth, the left-wing Zionist Hashomer Hatzair, Habonim, and socialist Zionists, as well as Junior Hadassah, the B'nai B'rith Youth Organization, and Hillel of the University of Chicago, among others. They listened to a lecture by Professor Louis Gottschalk and discussed the question he posed: "Destruction of European Jewry . . . How Does It Affect Us?"[73]

Whether discussing Jewish education in general or specific new Jewish educational ventures, the Holocaust bubbled up in the rhetorical caldron of images and words, as justification for actions taken or urged. Not surprisingly, the schools that individual commentators considered best and most likely to compensate for the horrific losses reflected their own ideologies. Different schools, conversely, only intensified the spiritual loss visited on the Jewish people by the Nazis. An Orthodox rabbi in a 1959 sermon charged his congregants to "read . . . the countless volumes of the 'Churban Europe' [Destruction of Europe] literature . . . and there you will find the unspeakable crimes perpetrated against our people." In the next paragraph and breath, he asked them to consider the fact that "reliable statistics reveal that only eight percent of Jewish children in America receive a full and complete Jewish Education." Given the fact that a majority of Jewish children in 1959 attended some Jewish school, he considered "full and complete" to be only those conforming to his ideal, which emphasized traditional text study under Orthodox auspices. Anything else he considered empty and incomplete, furthering the devastation wrought by the Nazis.[74]

This rabbi no doubt would have considered Yiddish schools inadequate to the task of providing a "full" education, and as such unable to compensate for that which had been destroyed. But advocates of Yiddish-language education believed that what they taught actually best fit the pedagogic needs that grew out of the catastrophe. The American Jewish children who enrolled in Workmen's Circle and the Sholem Aleichem schools, Yiddishists asserted, learned the language of the extirpated Jews of Europe. By studying the language of the six million, American Jewish children really prepared to take the place of those who had been so brutally liquidated and kept alive the memory of Europe's Jews.

In their publications, partisans for this kind of schooling claimed that "the war, which brought destruction to East European Jewry, placed upon the Yiddish schools the burden of continuing the culture which was created in that center."[75] Yiddish educators praised their own efforts, declaring that "the tremendous catastrophe of East European Jewry has had a greater and more noticeable repercussion in it [the Yiddish school] than in other schools which are established on more traditional foundations." Yudl Mark, one of those educators, touted his schools as places in which "the children . . . may be said to have lived through the happenings themselves. For them the gruesome tortures, the march through the crematories and gas chambers did not remain a secret. The teachers never stopped telling the children what happened. . . . It may be that we sinned thereby against child psychology; nevertheless we permitted ourselves to be influenced by the urge to take our children in as partners in our harsh fate." Mark wanted other Jewish educators to recognize that the schools which taught American Jewish children Yiddish taught "the language of the recent martyrs."[76]

The Holocaust transformed Yiddish schools, in operation since the 1910s. Once avowedly secular, one observer noted in 1953, "the [Yiddish] school movement assumed," after the war, "a traditional temper and showed interest in religious values," as it had not before. "Hitler Germany's destruction of East European Jewry accounted for the transition. It was predicated on the premise that American Jewry must rescue and preserve our cultural treasures that were created and accumulated by the martyred millions of Yiddish speaking Jews."[77]

This preservation project provided Yiddish schools with a marketing tool in the 1950s and early 1960s. They publicized the proposition that they, more than others, linked American Jewry with the martyred millions. In the 1950s, the Workmen's Circle issued Yiddish and English flyers and pamphlets, "Shule Propaganda" [School propaganda], to convince parents to send their children to Jewish schools, particularly its institutions. "Don't neglect your child's Jewish education," intoned one brochure. "The Workmen's Circle School acquaints the child with Jews in America, who in so short a time trod the path from the sweatshop to great accomplishments; with Jews in Palestine who turned swamps and wilderness into a fruitful land and a home for persecuted brethren; with the Jews of Eastern Europe from which we or our parents came and where despite the terrible Hitler atrocities Jewish life will again flourish." Fused together, these three forces—Jewish success in America, the flowering of Jewish life in Israel, and the "Hitler atrocities"—provided the rationale for educating Jewish children.[78]

American Jews, the Yiddish educators asserted, should not only recall the memory of the victims, but by living a better, richer, fuller Jewish life, they engaged with the six million victims. "In these perilous times, during which our people have suffered the greatest catastrophe in our long history;

when six million Jews have been annihilated by our enemies, when all our spiritual values have ... been brutally trampled under the Nazi boots," the Workmen's Circle education director, N. Chanin, wrote in a circular to parents, "We appeal to you! Send your children to our schools. Also see to it that your neighbors' children and the children of your friends join them. Help us build a healthy Jewish spiritual life."[79]

Yiddish schools in the 1950s constructed a sharply focused Holocaust-centered rationale for their existence. The Sholem Aleichem school system adopted a declaration of purpose at its 1949 annual banquet, forging a link between itself and the catastrophe: "We are living in a time when the struggle for our survival as a people has become intensified in the lands of the Diaspora. ... We have lived through the recent holocaust that has annihilated so much of our material and spiritual wealth." While acknowledging the importance of "ancient and modern Hebrew ... both active and living forces," the Yiddish educators declared the primacy of Yiddish, since "we are intimately bound to living Yiddish, the tongue of the last thirty generations." Only Yiddish "keeps alive the hallowed memory of the millions of our brothers and sisters who have perished." The Sholem Aleichem schools consistently made manifest the connection between what they did and the Holocaust. In 1960, at the end of the school year, Mr. I. Goichberg celebrated his fortieth year as a Sholem Aleichem teacher, and upon accepting an award for his service, he reflected on the last four decades of his life and of the Jewish people: "The Holocaust let fall Elijah's heavy cloak on the still weak shoulders of our American Elisha, but the tragedy also stirred and aroused the half-atrophied limbs of the people." The event, a testimonial to him, a morale booster for the school, also became a time to remember the Holocaust.[80]

Advocates for Yiddish education, which despite all the institutional activity actually declined in the postwar period in terms of the numbers of students who attended, broadly linked their schools to the Holocaust. In 1959, the Jewish Labor Committee's Research Department prepared a lengthy report on "Jewish Culture and the American Jewish Community," reprinting the document in its membership magazine, *Outlook*. It began forcefully, stating, "The problem of Jewish survival has assumed new significance in the light of the extermination of 6,000,000 of our brothers in Europe. For centuries Jewish communities all over the world looked to European Jewry for cultural and spiritual guidance." The report detailed the woefully low level of funding for Jewish education generally, and specifically for Yiddish education, seeking to make the case for the latter to the

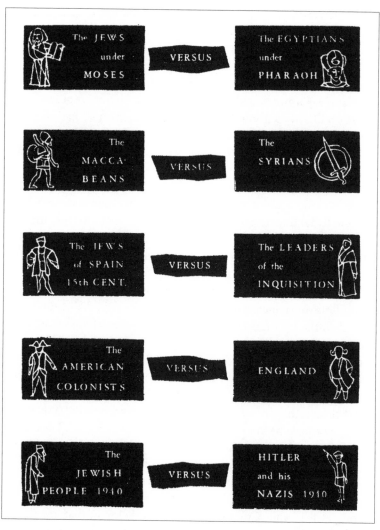

Typical of postwar renditions of Jewish history, the Holocaust fit into a narrative of centuries of suffering, of Jews being pitted against a succession of enemies. In *Little Lower Than the Angels,* a 1955 book for young adults, Reform rabbi Roland Gittelsohn instructed his readers to think of Jewish history in those terms, with "the Jewish People 1940 versus Hitler and his Nazis 1940" as the most recent manifestation of a long chain of persecution followed by Jewish survival, a chain that began with "the Jews under Moses versus the Egyptians under Pharaoh." The penultimate oppositional in Gittelsohn's schema, "the American Colonists versus England," reflected the positive embrace of America by most Jews in the postwar period. *Courtesy Union of Reform Judaism Press.*

Congress of World Jewish Organizations by posing the question of why Yiddish education as opposed to Hebrew. The answer flowed from the recent tragic past, reminding the community that "Hitler burned out Jews and Yiddish at the same time." American Jewry, carrying the responsibility to make up for that loss, should turn to Yiddish: "Time is short and the labor great. May it not already be too late! May we not witness the rise of a generation of Jews without Jewish conscience! *We have not survived persecution and atrocities, and lived thousands of years dispersed to all corners of the globe only to perish now, in the heart of prosperity and on the threshold of a new Jewish era!*"[81]

In this call for better funding for Yiddish schools, the Jewish Labor Committee made a point that went beyond advocacy for more Yiddish education. It demonstrated how the Holocaust and the memory of its victims inspired American Jewish communal leaders and institutions to valorize the language: "When millions of Yiddish-speaking Jews perished in the crematories it was thought . . . that the language had perished with them," the report told. As Yiddishists described the emergence of new language undertakings, including the inauguration of Yiddish courses at the college level, the creation of Yiddish clubs in some of New York's junior and senior high schools, preliminary to what they hoped would be the introduction of the study of Yiddish as part of the "regular language courses," it turned to the touchstone of the Holocaust. Quoting at length from the announcement of the formation of the clubs by the Committee for Yiddish in High Schools, the JLC noted, "In a generation when 6,000,000 Yiddish-speaking Jews have been exterminated by Hitler . . . we . . . Jews living in a free America dare not remain indifferent to the fate of the Yiddish language, its literature and its culture in our country." And these "free Jews" had a "national historic obligation" to preserve the language and its values.

Like other advocates for Yiddish learning as a counter to the Holocaust, the Jewish Labor Committee conveniently forgot that not all the six million had spoken Yiddish. The Jews of Germany spoke German; French Jews, French; and Italian Jews, Italian. Jews in the Balkans expressed themselves in the languages of their host countries, and Ladino served as their Jewish language. By the 1930s, in fact, many Polish, Czech, and Hungarian Jews comfortably spoke those languages and did not use Yiddish. But these historical specifics paled in comparison with the powerful image of Yiddish as the martyrs' tongue.

Orthodox, Reform, Conservative, and Zionist educators also made use of this exact formulation, in nearly the same terms, as did this proponent of Yiddish, still secular-oriented, despite the greater attention they paid to Judaism in the postwar period. The ideology being advanced mattered little when it came to invoking the victims. All found it fitting to remind their constituents of the fact of the horrific Jewish losses and to connect them to particular programs and projects at hand. Participants in a workshop sponsored by the Reform movement's National Association of Temple Educators in 1959 discussed the "important psychological effect on American Jews" wrought by "the destruction of European Jewry." Echoing the point made across the spectrum of American Jewry, the Reform temple educators contemplated the fact that, "before World War II, the American Jewish community had to depend almost exclusively for its religious, spiritual and intellectual community leadership on the European Jewish community. We can no longer depend on outside forces," thus making American Jewry dependent on its own teachers and schools.[82]

Whether they called for immersion in canonical texts, mastery of "synagogue skills," gaining fluency in Hebrew, developing an understanding of Jewish history, or becoming proficient in Yiddish, each swathe of American Jewry believed that its educational program represented the most efficacious means to make up culturally for the devastating losses endured by the Jewish people. All converged on the premise that American Jews had to confront the enormity of what had happened and then figure out how to remedy the loss of the six million and their Jewish cultures.

Fears of Forgetting

Amid all the writings, speeches, and performances that claimed that American Jewry had been changed by the tragedy of the six million, a small counternarrative could be heard. In random places, scattered through the communal discourse, individuals either criticized American Jews for beginning to forget the catastrophe or articulated aloud their fears that forgetting would set in as affluence, comfort, and acceptance grew in America. Accusing other Jews of having forgotten, or standing on the precipice of forgetting, constituted one of the most barbed forms of self-criticism hurled during the postwar era.

Individual writers, rabbis, and community workers found moments to castigate the masses for letting the Holocaust fade from their collective memory. Some predicted that, although in the present the Holocaust still resonated with American Jews, amnesia lurked in the immediate future.

Rarely the central point of an article, sermon, or book, the theme of forgetting and the sin of not thinking about the Holocaust enough, as defined by the author, crept in as an ominous warning, one that later critics picked up on as they claimed that postwar Jews as a whole consciously suppressed the story of the six million.

Rabbis and writers, educators and community activists not only held up American Jewry as pathetic, as deficient in Jewish learning, but also accused each other of having "forgotten" the tragic fate of the Jews of Europe because of their weaknesses as Jews. In the arsenal of condemnations that one Jewish group used against another—that a writer, rabbi, or activist hurled at American Jewry, young people in particular—none was articulated with greater venom and rage than statements that some, or all, American Jews had shelved the catastrophe of European Jewry to the recesses of their consciousness. The mammoth compendium of speeches, sermons, articles, books, radio broadcasts, camp programs, institutional brochures, and other texts showcasing the catastrophe notwithstanding, some American Jews at one time or another asserted that the memory of the six million had ceased to move American Jewry. Heard as early as the late 1940s and continuing as a rhetorical counterpoint, such accusations served as didactic clubs, intended by some American Jews to shame others into becoming better Jews. How Jews ought to improve, how they should remember and honor the six million, required conformity to the accuser's vision. Other ways missed the mark, and by not offering the correct proposal to foster greater Jewish commitments, they did not remember well enough or in fact remember at all.

The fear that American Jews would soon begin to forget peppered the communal discourse. *Jewish Forum* opened up its pages in 1959 to a symposium, "Problems Worrying Our Youth." One participant, Albert Baumgartner, about to enter Columbia College, told how "we have suffered." Baumgartner reminded his readers, "We have been cremated. Our bodies were defiled. The gas was 'scientifically' picked. We were tortured. Our bodies were mutilated for the sake of 'science.' Our skins were made into lampshades and our fat into soap." For Baumgartner, the legacy of that horror mandated that "for every cadaver there should be a tongue crying out against this injustice. For every dead child, a mind that does not forget." But "this is not so," and "in the present era of fun and frivolity memory is almost as painful as thought." He took to task the world "that condoned this genocide." Segueing to the political implications of the memory of the Holocaust, he noted, "we have achieved certain concrete results by remembering. The United Nations has set itself firmly against genocide." But the task of American Jewry could hardly be said to be complete. "If Jews begin to forget the awful price extracted upon them by Hitler, as our youth is doing, who should remember?" he asked, charging his generation with the project of fulfilling "our mission as Jews," which "lies before us. Inspired by the memory of our dead, we must re-inspire our youth."[83]

Each ideological swathe of American Jewry set itself up as the one most vigilant in remembering and in acting on those memories in the best way. To Zionists, it meant ardent support for Israel, embracing it as the locus of Jewish cultural identity. To educators, it meant furthering Jewish learning; to Yiddishists, support of Yiddish language programs; and to partisans of the religious denominations, participating in synagogue life. As advocates for any and all of these positions made their arguments, they held up the image of the Jews of America as shallow in their Jewish commitments, overly eager to conform to the American mainstream, and forgetful of the Holocaust. Partisans for each vision of a better Jewish future lambasted American Jews for their Jewish failings and their quest for assimilation, which combined to cause them to defame the memory of the six million whom they had forgotten.

Since American Jews lacked any authority structure that could tell them how to remember the six million and how to act as Jews in the present in light of that memory, they aired a range of ideas, plans, and arguments. This debate took place in publications, sermons, and meeting rooms. Community activists essentially held up behaviors they did not approve of and claimed them to be proof that American Jews had banished the Holocaust from their consciousness. Like many Jewish intellectuals who had come to the United States from Europe, Jacob Lestchinsky held American Jewry in low regard. In 1949, commenting on intermarriage and assimilation, he expressed skepticism that American Jews remembered the Holocaust deeply enough to change their behavior. He doubted "whether the great catastrophe in Europe . . . will retard the rate" of Jewish melding into the American mainstream.[84] In the early postwar period, despite his leadership in B'nai B'rith, a non-synagogue-based Jewish organization, Label Katz touted synagogues as the most effective vehicle for enhancing Jewish survival. Survival required the commitment of American Jewry, which no longer, Katz warned, felt emotionally "the plight of our brethren in Europe. . . . Six millions of our Jewish people were subjected to unbelievable torture and indescribable suffering," he recalled. American Jews, he claimed, manifested only "insensitivity and callousness" to the memory of those victims and to the fact that "the eradication of these six million Jews also meant that the greatest reservoir of Jewish learning and Jewish culture was eliminated." Only synagogue membership and attendance would make up for that.[85]

Into the 1950s, this countertheme cropped up as American Jews took each other to task for purportedly committing the twinned sins of forgetting and not fulfilling their obligations, which the memory of the six million imposed on them. Orthodox sermons played on this theme in particular, as the rabbis urged greater observance. In 1953, on the tenth anniversary of the Warsaw Ghetto uprising, Israel Tabak chided the community: "We American Jews . . . one decade removed from the great catastrophe which has befallen our people . . . are going about our business as though we have completely forgotten." Ironically, he delivered this sermon to congregants assembled at a special service in memory of the liquidation of the ghetto, Jews who had taken time out of their ordinary business to gather to remember. Rabbi Julius Hoffman picked up this theme the following year, describing how he visited a college campus at which the Hillel chapter seemed to only muster handfuls of Jewish students to its programs. This constituted "Jewish amnesia," a pathology that took many forms and that existed throughout the community. "You and I," he told his congregants, also "are frequently guilty" of Jewish amnesia: "When we forget in our daily life that less than two decades ago, six million of our brothers and sisters were exterminated by a man, so depraved that he does not deserve the designation 'man,' we too are victims of this historical amnesia." Not content with lobbing just one salvo at his congregants, he condemned them to think about the six million every day. Rabbi Hoffman went on: "Ten years have not yet passed since six million Jews—our own fathers and mothers, sons and daughters, brothers and sisters, uncles and aunts and cousins—were murdered in gas chambers and crematoria, and already we have forgotten."[86]

Zionists employed the specter of this creeping amnesia about the Holocaust in advocating for their cause. Nahum Goldman addressed the World Zionist Congress in 1956 on "Let's Avoid Being Normal!" Speaking of the increasing dangers of "assimilation" of Jews "in the Diaspora," an article published by NCRAC reported that "Goldman credited the Hitler persecutions with slowing down the process. Then the . . . leader of the World Zionist Movement added, 'But the impact of the Hitler period in deepening Jewish emotions is fading away and Jews are beginning to return to normalcy.' Goldman offered only one powerful solution to this ominous drift. 'Of course, Israel . . . now the State of Israel is to take up where the ebbing impact of Hitler left off.' "[87]

But Leibush Lehrer, a Yiddish educator, speaking on behalf of Camp Boiberik, a summer camp sponsored by the Sholem Aleichem Folk schools, told a similar but different story. At a 1958 gathering of the adult supporters of the camp, meeting on the Ninth of Av at the Rhinebeck, New York, facility, Lehrer lectured on the connection between past and present, memory and forgetting, holding up this camp as the only antidote for the latter. Some object, he told those assembled, to "the idea of the dramatization of sad memories for children." But he believed the camp had an obligation to remind the youngsters every summer that "only some fifteen years ago, a catastrophe befell our people, a tragedy the likes of which in magnitude and inhumanity, is not known to recorded history." Yet now, at the end of the 1950s, he discerned among the Jews of America an "appallingly callous indifference . . . a lack of connectedness to the Jewish past." Boiberik's vision of engaged secular Yiddish-based youth programming would best serve as "an antidote to forgetfulness."[88]

No matter what they wrote, said, or created on the matter of the European catastrophe, it never could be enough or right. Someone would, and did, find fault with it. Solomon Bloom reviewed a number of books on "The Great Unsolved Crime" in *Commentary* in 1955. He found fault with United States Jewry for its failure to "square itself with . . . the destruction of nearly all European Jews." How did he measure this failure? "Not a single general work in English by an American has yet appeared," he wrote. Then he praised Leon Poliakov, a French scholar of the Centre de Documentation Juive Contemporaine in Paris for his book that had just come out in the United States, and Gerald Reitlinger, an English historian, whose *Final Solution* had recently been published in America. Bloom bemoaned the fact that neither book had been written by an American or had been released by a major publisher and that both had been "little publicized, advertised, or reviewed." American Jewry, as such, forgot and failed.[89]

This criticism continued unabated into the 1960s. "Strange as it may seem," Graenum Berger observed at a Labor Zionist gathering in New York in 1962, "except in Israel, there is no evidence that Jews want to make up for the loss of some 6,000,000 Jewish dead in the European holocaust." Berger referred here to the demographics of American Jewry and to the fact that "Jewish women tell researchers that they want a family size of '2.4 children,' " not enough to compensate for the vast number of Jewish lives lost. He pointed to a study in the *Annals of the American Academy of Political and Social Science* on "Jewish Teen-Age Culture." The adolescents evinced little "sense of uniqueness, of special destiny. . . . Jewish life is conceived of as middle class, non-ideological, and entirely consonant with the dominant modes of American life." Berger derived from the article that "even the mass atrocities of the Nazis have undergone a curious softening in the minds of Jewish teenagers, who, to be sure, have no recollection of these events." As an antidote, Berger opined that "perhaps American Jewish youth needed the Eichmann trial more than the so-called dejudaized Israeli youth." As to the intellectuals of the community, the "younger" ones who participated in a 1961 symposium sponsored by *Commentary*, Berger expressed contempt for their avoidance of the Holocaust as a motivating force in their lives. That avoidance reflected the "flabbiness" of their Jewish commitments. "One can only turn from these pages," he lamented, "with despair."[90]

Berger's despair, as well as Hoffman's and Tabak's, actually had little to do with how American Jews remembered and memorialized the Holocaust. They despaired, rather, that American Jews did not behave as they, the communal guides, wanted them to as Jews. They worried about the future as these young people—born after the war and for whom "Hitler is a name almost as remote in the past as Haman," then raised in a hospitable American environment in which they felt increasingly comfortable and at ease—would have to take charge of the Jewish community.[91]

That the occasional rabbi, writer, or communal orator lambasted American Jewry for not remember the European catastrophe well enough, or not acting in a fittingly appropriate Jewish manner as a result of it, indicated the degree to which they recognized the Holocaust's power in shaping communal discourse and identity. These critics knew how deeply the Jews of America engaged with that cataclysmic event, and they hoped to shame the masses, the ordinary American Jews, into behaving better, as each individual critic defined better, by accusing them of forgetting, making them feel that their weaknesses as Jews defamed the memory of the six million who had been lost. These critics, regardless of ideology, realized the potency of the Holocaust as a rhetorical device and used it when they thought it would inspire behaviors they wanted.

They joined a chorus of self-appointed Jewish critics, who for centuries had been lamenting the failings of American Jewry. The masses of American Jews were not Jewish enough, not serious enough, and not conscious enough of the obligations that Jewish history and Judaism had imposed on them. These postwar denunciations constituted merely another chapter in a long history of self-criticism, launched from the top down. They also anticipated the scholars of the later decades of the twentieth century who retrospectively sneered at postwar American Jews for the sin of Holocaust avoidance.

Those in the postwar years who asserted that the Jews of the United States did not remember well and not enough—this sprinkling of rabbis, writers, and organizational leaders—constituted a distinct minority. They recognized that in the voluntary, almost anarchic, world of American Jewry, women and men participated in institutions, acknowledged leaders, and consumed texts only as they wanted to. They subscribed to magazines, joined organizations, affiliated with synagogues, attended cultural performances, and sent their children to summer camps and schools that conformed to their vision of what Jewishness meant to them. The leaders wielded little authority and had minimal power to shape behavior. Rather, ordinary American Jews opted for practices and modes of being Jewish that worked for them, and they rejected those that did not.

That the publications and books, youth programs, meetings of communal organizations and religious institutions, representing not just one ideology or iteration of Jewish culture, made room for the Holocaust, and that they all explained themselves by virtue of the catastrophe's impact—all these indicated the depth of meaning that the tragedy of the six million had for American Jews of the postwar period. Had these projects been undertaken by only one swathe of American Jewry—the Yiddishists or the Zionists, the Orthodox or the survivors, Hebraists or the leaders of Reform—these works could easily be dismissed as idiosyncratic and not representing the "community" as a whole. But those who made the Jewish public culture of America, across all these divides, knew full well that from the end of World War II into the 1960s the memory of the six million deeply resonated with American Jews. It motivated them in both their Jewish and their American lives. They used it to explain their liberal and Jewish agendas.

What would have been a proper memorial and what might have been the right amount of time, energy, and emotion to expend on their recollections of the six million victims of the Holocaust could not be answered by those who asserted that what American Jews did fell far from the mark. It also cannot be assessed retrospectively by historians who hold up a particular standard from a later era and evaluate the Jews of the postwar period accordingly.

American Jews in the years from the end of the war into the early 1960s responded to the Holocaust in ways that fit their place in American society and in the Jewish world. Communal critics and later historians notwithstanding, postwar American Jews built a public culture that they considered to be the fitting memorial to the Holocaust. They could do no less. But since they operated within the context of a specific time and place, they could also do no more.

Conclusion

The Corruption of History, the Betrayal of Memory

AMERICAN JEWS IN the years from the end of World War II into the early 1960s had much to say about the European Jewish catastrophe, doing so in a multiplicity of ways. Whether in liturgy or journalism, in pedagogy or sermons, in staged ceremonies or in the deliberations of their organizational meetings and the discussions of their youth groups—in all of these, the tragic fate of European Jewry coursed prominently through their public culture. It moved them, frightened and angered them. It stirred them to action, and they consistently designated times, places, and ways to say so.

They reflected on the horrific set of events, the Holocaust, to remember it for its own sake and to teach and learn more about the fate of its victims, with whom they identified, referring to them as "we," "our," and "us." They incorporated into their communal cultures images, words, names, and references to the Jewish catastrophe.

The Jews of America in the postwar years had practical reasons not to consign the tragic events into obscurity. Instead, they held up to public gaze images of the concentration camps, gas chambers, and ghettoes, pictures, both metaphoric and graphic, of numbers tattooed into Jewish flesh, of families ripped asunder, lives destroyed, and yet a hopeful "saving remnant." They did this in order to encourage the broad public to help them in aiding survivors, exposing perpetrators, and winning support for the State of Israel, as well as advancing liberal political causes they supported. Because they believed that practical and necessary results would flow from their telling of the tragedy of the six million to the American public at large, they did not repress or suppress it.

Within the Jewish community, references to the destruction of European Jewish culture, the liquidation of the great centers of Jewish learning, and the violent deaths of the women and men who had been the source of Jewish creativity served a decidedly communal purpose, as the leaders of

American Jewry tried to inspire the American Jewish masses to give more, care more, and do more to strengthen Jewish life in the United States.

Spontaneous and disorganized, lacking a single icon to symbolize the catastrophe or a central address to coordinate programs and publications about it, American Jews, through their local and national bodies, religious, educational, associational, and political, incorporated into their many endeavors the details of the *hurban*, the great destruction of European Jewry. Not always appearing under the rubric "Holocaust" or "the six million," the European catastrophe wound its way into their culture organically, yoked to Jewish texts on nearly every cultural and political issue, to Jewish history, civil rights, the observance of Jewish ritual, and a host of other concerns.[1] Books, radio broadcasts, and sermons on a range of topics told about the tragedy. The Holocaust pervaded their lives. They wove it into their works.

In their publications and speeches, these American Jews differed among themselves as to how best to narrate the catastrophe and what lessons should be derived from it. Those differences reflected the degree to which it weighed on them. They experimented with language, texts, images, and pageantry, casting about for answers to some ineffable questions: Why did it happen? Did it constitute a new reality, or did it represent "merely" the latest and worst link in a long chain of Jewish suffering? How did the destruction of the six million impinge on their American lives? How did it structure their relationships to other Jewries? How did it define their connection to Palestine, then Israel? What constituted heroism and resistance? Where had God been?

Most participants in this unstructured discussion did not come from the ranks of an intellectual class. They registered little awareness of the possible epistemological implications resulting from the usages of such phrases as "the six million" versus "catastrophe," or "Holocaust" versus "Hitler Holocaust," "Hitler times" versus "concentration camps." They did not fret over the linguistic and philosophic ramifications of referring to the slaughtered Jews of Europe as "victims" or "martyrs," or *kedoshim*, if they expressed themselves in Yiddish or Hebrew. Indeed, they used all these terms interchangeably, sometimes in the same text. They knew that because most of Europe's Jews had been murdered, they, the Jews of the United States, bore some kind of posthumous responsibility toward them.

Directly and indirectly, they pondered how to memorialize the tragedy, confronting questions that had no right or wrong answers and for which they had no authorities from abroad or rules from the past to follow.

When it came to the practice of Judaism—celebrating holidays, conducting synagogue services, performing life cycle rituals—they did have such guidance, which they could obey, improvise on, or reject. But they knew what such occasions demanded of them. When it came to figuring out how to create a communal culture to memorialize the six million, they traveled solo, in terms of both time and space. Just as their rabbis, educators, and other community activists warned them, they, the Jews of the United States, alone had to pick up the pieces left in the wake of the cataclysm, on the practical level, of politics and fundraising, and on the cultural level, of creating a vital new center of Jewish life to make up for the vast destruction.

The Holocaust did not provide them with the only rationale for any of their undertakings, but neither did they bury it out of shame, discomfort, lack of a fixed terminology, or a desire to appear just like all other white, middle-class Americans. Instead, among the arguments they made for their cultural and political projects and among the images they invoked to describe themselves, their community, and their tradition to American non-Jews and to their own children born into the liberal and affluent postwar years, they turned to the catastrophe.

They did not produce a single work by which to remember it, nor did they agree to say what constituted the best and most meaningful way of recalling the catastrophe and learning from it. Rather, in a jumble of projects incorporated organically into a sea of scattered books, prayers, songs, pageants, poems, articles, ephemera, press releases, pamphlets, and ceremonies, they believed that by their actions they sustained the memory of the six million and that in this they somehow improved the world for themselves and for others.

American Jews, journalists, rabbis, writers, educators, camp counselors, youth group leaders, functionaries of communal agencies, and the many others, including the "ordinary" Jews who wrote letters to the editor, sent their children to the camps, attended meetings, sat in the audiences, listened to the concerts, and contributed money to the causes promoted in the name of the catastrophe—all these wove the cataclysmic slaughter of the six million European Jews at the hands of the Nazis into the lived texture of their communities. The sum total of these efforts constituted American Jewish public culture, as consumed by congregants, readers, students, campers, and the dues-paying members of voluntary associations, the masses of American Jews. In every sector of the American Jewish collectivity, Jews told the story. In large cities and smaller communities, in programs for adults and for young people—those which survivors created, those undertaken by refugees who had left Europe just as the horrors began, and those that reflected the sensibilities of Jews with long and deep roots in America—all assigned a place of significance to the European catastrophe. Whether they articulated their feelings in English, Yiddish, or Hebrew, they crafted words about the six million. Orthodox, Reform, Conservative, and Reconstructionist institutions all produced materials and created practices that contemplated the catastrophe and reminded American Jews of their responsibilities toward its memory.

Even when they used the image of the six million to expose American Jews for their spiritual weaknesses and cultural deficiencies, they made the story of the tragedy a vital part of the life of the community. Articles, sermons, radio shows, and speeches took American Jewry to task for forgetting, and they helped keep the memory alive. They placed in the public consciousness the fact that, in the years of the 1930s and 1940s, one-third of world Jewry had been exterminated by Germany and its accomplices, who had hoped to slaughter them all. All of this constituted their memorial project.

Yet, from the vantage point of a widely believed, unquestioned, conventional understanding of the past, regnant at the end of the twentieth century and the early years of the twenty-first, none of this took place. This prevailing orthodoxy has been articulated by historians and by other scholars, by individuals from within the Jewish community, and by critics of contemporary Jewish politics and practice, as well as by those who define themselves on the left of the political spectrum all the way across to those who sit on the right. All of these converge on a single historical assertion. According to that "truth," the Jews of postwar America had had little or nothing to say about the Holocaust. They lacked interest in it and did not trouble themselves to think about it. They made no space for it in the life of their community and went out of their way to avoid it.

Susannah Heschel has correctly assessed the historical writing on this subject, which has coalesced around this flawed narrative. "Most historians," she wrote, "agree that the 1967 Middle East war became an important moment for American Jews, who, emboldened by Israel's military victory, began to speak publicly about the Holocaust."[2] Indeed, literary critic Ruth Wisse's words can stand for the entire range of discourse that has posited postwar American Jewry's disinterest in the Holocaust and the condemnatory tones in which such statements have been cast. "American Jews," wrote Wisse, "were not only spared the Holocaust, they unwittingly drew from the moral credit that accrued to its victims." Jews benefited from the catastrophe as domestic anti-Semitism plummeted and opportunities to Jews opened up, inspired by Americans' revulsion against what Hitler and the Nazis had done. Yet despite being the beneficiaries of this sea change, American Jews, Wisse declared, entered the postwar world "with almost total oversight of the events," including the loss of "one third of their numbers," which had "transformed their people."[3]

The story, regardless who has told it, runs along a standard track. According to the dominant paradigm, the American Jews who came out of the World War II experience, witnessed the emergence of a Jewish sovereign state in Israel, lived through the Cold War, moved to the suburbs, helped finance a synagogue-building boom, and participated in the coalescence of the modern civil rights movement had no room in their public culture for the tragedy of European Jewry.

Written off as callousness, apathy, or cowardice, historians, literary scholars, and journalists have taken as a given the truth that the Jews of postwar America did not care to talk about the tragedy of the six million or care enough to make it part of their community culture. Even memoirists who themselves lived through those years have asserted that in the Jewish families and communities they grew up in during the 1950s and early 1960s, no one talked about the European catastrophe.[4] All have looked back to the postwar years and characterized them by the deafening silence of American Jews who went about their upbeat lives, oblivious to the tragedy that had so recently encompassed their people.

Historians have offered all sorts of explanations to show why American Jews refused to speak out about the Holocaust or to enshrine its victims into their memory culture. To some, the Cold War made Germany America's ally in the struggle against the Soviet Union and created an environment in which Jews felt constrained from naming it as the perpetrator of the immense crime. As long as Americans valorized the Germans as the brave heroes who stood on the ramparts of Berlin facing Russian tanks, Jews silenced themselves, constraining themselves from pointing an accusatory finger at the successor state to Hitler's Third Reich.

Others have stated that American Jews, as part of their shallow quest for acceptance into the world of the white suburban middle class, eagerly participated in a conspiracy of silence, refusing to remember the victims of Hitler's slaughter in exchange for the privilege of securing a comfortable life of American conformity, one requiring that they not appear in the eyes of others as members of a community of "victims" whose people had undergone a diabolic slaughter. Since no one else had such a story in their past, or at least no one whom they aspired to emulate and be accepted by, then they had a powerful reason to engage in a highly organized, effective campaign of self-censorship.

Their efficient and widely respected organizations to which the masses deferred and which controlled what American Jews said and did in public, particularly the American Jewish Committee, according to this rendition of the history of postwar American Jewry, ably quashed efforts by the Jewish public to know about the Holocaust, remember it, and share its tragic details with others. This assessment of postwar American Jewry assumes not only that, across the board, the Jews of America followed the dicta of the "establishment" that ably enforced community discipline but also that the Jews cared more than anything about acceptance by the American mainstream. They lacked any kind of Jewish authenticity.

According to the prevailing narrative, in fact, they only began, on a piecemeal basis, to embrace the images and details of the European Jewish catastrophe in the early 1960s because other Americans, those whom the Jews lusted to be like and be accepted by, began to consume bits and pieces of Holocaust history and popular culture. When their non-Jewish neighbors embraced, for example, the movie *The Diary of Anne Frank*, Jews then decided that they could gradually come out of their enforced amnesia and admit, gradually, that yes, this had happened to their people. The fact that American newspapers and television networks covered the Eichmann trial in Jerusalem in the first two years of the 1960s meant, according to this version of history, that the Jews felt able to emerge from hiding and take the dormant narrative of the Holocaust out of its metaphoric slumber.

Yet other analysts have asserted that since Israel mattered so little to the Jews of the United States and that they took its existence for granted until June 1967, they had no reason to focus on the destruction of European Jewry. Until that watershed month and year, American Jews paid Israel scant heed. They did not worry about it, nor did they consider its existence to be in jeopardy. They also did not posit a connection between it and the six million or see it as the apotheosis of the brutal slaughter of the Jews under Hitler.

But 1967—more precisely, June 1967—changed all that. Israel's dramatic military victory had, after all, been preceded by fretful days and weeks dominated by a chilling rhetoric that emanated from Egypt and Jordan, threatening a campaign to drive the Jews into the sea. Images of a second Holocaust electrified the American Jewish public. Those two combined, the dazzling victory that had followed the apocalyptic rhetoric of imminent destruction, jolted them "suddenly" into a renewed acquaintance with the horrific events of 1933–1945.

The reasoning that places the 1967 victory at the center of American Jews' consciousness about the Holocaust begins with the specifics of their elation over the victory, set against the frightening prelude that predicted doom. The six days in June, the argument runs, made American Jews proud of being Jewish for the first time, willing to go public with their ethnic identity. Now Jewishness could be associated with something positive, strong, and triumphant, rather than with weakness and passivity. In essence, then, the military might of Israel made it acceptable for American Jews to look back to that ghastly era in which their people had "been led like sheep to the slaughter." After all, after 1967, no one could doubt that Jews could fight.

From this moment, then, according to the conventional wisdom about American Jewish history, American Jewish institutions and organizations became obsessed with Israel, pushing it to the top of their political agenda. They used every argument they could to work for it in the political arena. The narrative of the tragedy of the six million now had a place in the American Jewish repertoire as powerful American Jewish organizations went to work reminding the American public that when there had been no Israel, six million Jews had been killed. Only Israel stood as a bulwark against this happening again.

Other commentators have marshaled the Israel factor to prove that postwar American Jews had no interest in or role for the destruction of European Jewry but in a contrary way. The tellers of this tale have asserted that American Jews in the postwar period had actually spent so much time on Israel, expended so much of their energy to get support for it, and labored so assiduously to assert the image of the virile, brave little state that they purposely suppressed the history of the Holocaust with its images of Jewish weakness and powerlessness.

With few exceptions and across an array of ideological divides looms this widely believed myth that takes as a given the fact that the Jews of the United States during the period 1945 until 1967 had been unwilling, unable, and uninterested in hitching their public culture to the tragedy of European Jewry. Either they would not or they could not incorporate it into their communal consciousness.

Why and how did the postwar American Jewish experiments in language and performance disappear from the historical record? How have historians, among others, come to accept as true the assertion that, until the mid-1960s, American Jews avoided the horrific history of their people? The full explanation for that must be derived from a thorough and systematic exploration of the history of the later period, and as such it lies beyond the scope of this book. Here I have sought, instead, to document and analyze the multiple venues, times, and modes by which American Jews from 1945 into the early 1960s engaged with the Holocaust in their communities and in their interactions with the larger American world. But some possibilities suggest themselves.

To some degree, the community activists, rabbis, educators, intellectuals, and writers who during the postwar years criticized American Jewry for its moral weaknesses planted the seeds for the false history that would later take hold. They had begun almost immediately at the war's end to chide American Jews for their failure to live up to their obligations as Jews. In so doing, they claimed, they defamed the memory of the martyrs. That defamation, the rhetoric went, involved not being good-enough Jews and, simultaneously, forgetting the six million who had been the exemplars of authentic Jewishness.

Another important part of the explanation for the emergence of the belief that postwar Jews chose not to remember the six million lies in the fact that, later, a mammoth Holocaust output so overshadowed the earlier one as to render it nearly invisible. From the vantage point of the early twenty-first century, postwar American Jewish Holocaust works may seem so unsubstantial as to have basically not been there. Since the 1970s, the Holocaust has become a vastly enlarged, amply funded, and well-coordinated element in American Jewish community life. Jewish communities have created "Holocaust resource centers" and put up monuments on prominent public spaces in cities around the country. Professors sit on endowed chairs at American universities and teach the Holocaust. Educators who have attended special seminars on this subject teach courses labeled "Holocaust education" in Jewish schools.[5] American Jewish teenagers go on pilgrimages to march triumphantly through the ruins of Poland's concentration camps.[6] Synagogues, Jewish community centers, federations, and community councils have designated "Holocaust" committees to coordinate programming, and, by the 1980s and 1990s, a vast outpouring of books advertised in publishers' catalogs under the "Holocaust Studies" rubric came to be the norm.[7]

After the 1970s, American Jews went aggressively public with their catastrophic narrative, and their campaign fell on sympathetic ears. They successfully lobbied states like New York and New Jersey to require teaching the Holocaust on the secondary level. They used their political clout to create state-sponsored Holocaust councils and memorials. In 1979, they persuaded President Jimmy Carter to organize a national commission to oversee government-sponsored Holocaust programs. In 1993, the U.S. Holocaust Memorial Museum opened in Washington, D.C., situated visibly at the edge of the mall, the nation's sacred space, in close proximity to the Lincoln and Washington monuments. These moved the Holocaust into American prominence.[8] Cities, states, and the federal government sponsor Holocaust remembrance ceremonies.

The late-twentieth-century public consumed the Holocaust through such popular culture texts as the television series *Holocaust* of 1978 and acclaimed box-office hit movies like *Schindler's List* and *The Pianist*. In 2006, television personality Oprah Winfrey announced that Elie Weisel's novel *Night* would be sold with her name and seal of approval on its cover as part of her book club. All these provided Jews with opportunities to share their particular history with millions of other Americans.

This proliferation of Holocaust memorialization inspired the historians and commentators of the 1980s and beyond to assert that something new had happened, that, for the first time, the Holocaust had entered American consciousness. Some have stated, in fact, that American Jews, as the agents of this public awareness, engaged with it too much and that the society had become oversaturated with these many performances of the Holocaust.[9] The size, scope, and funding of Holocaust projects in the period after the 1970s certainly dwarfed the spontaneous, grassroots, and unorganized modes of commemoration that characterized the earlier era. That the American public responded so widely and positively to programs, projects, and texts about the Holocaust also conspired to render earlier ones nearly invisible.

The place the Holocaust came to occupy in American life in the decades after the 1970s also reflected much about that America and those Jews, revealing the pressures and opportunities of a specific era. In this, it resembled the postwar period, inasmuch as in both periods of time, American Jews engaged with the Holocaust in ways that fit the needs, concerns, and challenges of the time and place in which they lived. Yet comparing them has obscured history and ignored the very different realities that shaped postwar American Jewry and its performances of the Holocaust.

Postwar engagements with the Holocaust emerged spontaneously as American Jews contemplated a vastly altered Jewish world and confronted an array of immediate practical problems left for them to deal with after the whirlwind had subsided, while the latter period took place in a "post-Holocaust" world, when most, although certainly not all, of its issues had been resolved. The passage of time made these two periods different from one another.

In the postwar period, the survivors of the catastrophe who came to the United States had to plunge into the immediate chores of finding work, making homes, raising children, and learning a new language. By the time the latter era commenced, they could begin to start telling their stories in a more focused way, particularly as their children entered into young adulthood, joining their peers, the other young American Jews in the American universities, and entering into the world of communal activism. That next generation of the American-raised children of the survivors entered into the American Jewish world, carrying the legacy of its parents' horrific experiences. By the 1980s, these children had become adults, and, mostly all professionals, they sat on the boards of synagogues, federations, community centers, communal agencies, and the like and could push those institutions to enshrine the Holocaust experience as they saw fit, differently than their parents had. American educated, these children of survivors could turn to the academy, literature, art, and other media and in so doing confront the legacy of their parents' suffering in ways that their parents as struggling new Americans could not have even imagined in the postwar period.

The differences between the two eras could not be more striking. The Jews of postwar America created from nothingness the commemorative forms—literary, liturgical, political, and rhetorical—to memorialize, and they described what had happened to the Jews of Europe, building the memorial edifice from the ground up. With no obvious models to emulate and no ready-made language to draw on, the Jews of America in the postwar years cast about for modes of expression that recalled the calamity. They could only draw on the words and images that made sense to them in their own time and place, and as such they could only create the memorials, broadly defined, that fit the world in which they lived.

In large part, the American Jews of the post-1967 era, who made and consumed the massive Holocaust project of their time, benefited from the spadework undertaken by their forbears of the postwar period. Those American Jews who confronted the cataclysmic changes in the Jewish world of 1945 and beyond until 1967 (and who directed the affairs of the community, organized the meetings, gave the lectures, wrote the study guides, arranged for the ceremonies, taught the classes, crafted the sermons, and met with public officials on matters growing out of the European tragedy) confronted the events that had taken place in Europe. They then incorporated their thoughts and insights into their works. They cobbled together the first liturgies, staged the first memorial ceremonies, wrote the first chapters to appear in textbooks, taught the first courses, and approached the American public first with this tragic history.

Later American Jews, living in a very different world, could accept elements of what had been created before or could reject, if they so chose, the products of that earlier period, but they had a repertoire of words and images to react to. They could build bigger and better, as they may have defined it, memorial projects, but they did not start out devoid of precedents from which to draw. The Holocaust memorial culture of the later part of the twentieth century did not emerge, as it were, fully formed from the efforts and ideas of its late-century creators alone, without reference to and guidance from that which had been produced before. They had the work done in the early postwar period to cull and to modify as they saw fit.

The kinds of public ceremonies, for example, that came to predominate in the late twentieth century to mark Yom Hashoah, Holocaust remembrance day, employ some of the very same rituals that Warsaw Ghetto memorial meetings of the late 1940s and 1950s relied on: lighting six candles by survivors, singing "The Partisan's Hymn" and "Ani Ma'amin," communal recitation of kaddish, and the spoken words of one who had been there and lived to tell about it. While many of these ceremonies now have governmental sponsorship, unlike in the postwar era when Jewish communities invited public officials to watch, the ritual details of the commemorative programs bear a striking resemblance to each other.[10] At the beginning of the twenty-first century, Jewish summer camp Ninth of Av programming pairs the destruction of the two Jerusalem Temples in the ancient world with the Holocaust. These programs differ not at all in intensity and imagery from those same programs staged at those very camps in the 1950s. Calls by Jewish community leaders for teaching the Holocaust in public schools in the 1980s succeeded mightily, whereas the efforts in the late 1950s and early 1960s by Jewish community councils in various cities had not. But those later successes built on the earlier failed efforts. The triumph of the later efforts did not mean that postwar American Jews had not attempted to accomplish the same end. It did not mean that they did not consider it crucial for American children, Jewish and non-Jewish, to know something about what Hitler had perpetrated on Europe's Jews.

From a research perspective, much of the Holocaust-related material produced in the late 1940s and into the middle of the 1960s did not appear in archives and libraries, in the indices of books or in card catalogs under the heading "Holocaust." To get to that material in its breadth and depth, a historian must undertake a more circuitous journey into the records of the past and into the community lives of postwar American Jews. Most of those records at first blush, and in the descriptions of archival catalogs, seemingly had nothing to do with the tragedy of the six million. Going into the boxes and opening the folders, however, told a very different story, and the words included in those collections indeed had everything to do with it.

More profoundly, in order to understand how the nature of American Jewish rhetoric about the catastrophe changed in size and scope, why the larger American public began to listen more attentively to what Jews had to say, and why the myth of the postwar silence came to be accepted can only be explained in historical terms.

Both America and its Jews changed together, and together they collaborated in the emergence of a highly visible, publicly prominent culture, which converged on the term "Holocaust" to name what had happened, and in the process to make it seem as though all of this emerged de novo at the end of the 1960s. Changes in "the Holocaust" and its place in American and American Jewish life cannot be disentangled from the great transformations of American society since the late 1960s. Changes in thinking and talking about the Holocaust went hand in hand with changes in thinking and talking about nearly everything else in American public and private life. Starkly put, in fundamental ways, America at the start of the twenty-first century looks, acts, and thinks differently than America in 1950 or even 1960. After all, how Americans, Jews among them, now discuss and experience on a lived level such profound issues as family, gender, sexuality, race, education, communal authority, and religion, among other matters, underwent a literal revolution.

It should not therefore be a matter worthy of wonder, and certainly not condemnation, that later American Jews engaged with the destruction of the six million Jews of Europe differently than their parents and grandparents did sixty years earlier. Assertions that the Jews of 1950s America used different words, invoked different metaphors, and derived different lessons from the catastrophe than their children and grandchildren would in the 1990s reveals not only a lack of historical consciousness and a failure to confront the vast and scattered sources but a politically driven need to assume that, on that particular matter, the Jews of the earlier era should have resembled their descendants in a later and very different era.

What forces had been at work that enabled the Jews of America from the late 1960s onward to produce a different and vastly larger culture of Holocaust commemoration? What changes in American society meant that the American public responded positively to texts prepared by Jews about the Holocaust?

The Jewish community that existed in America from the late 1960s and forward, for one, had more resources, political and financial, at its command with which to endow all kinds of projects and to press for public recognition of Jewish concerns than did that of the late 1940s. The later community also had fewer pressing economic demands on it, particularly since the vast human undertaking that had consumed its energies and involved both aiding the survivors of the Holocaust and establishing the State of Israel had been resolved. By the late 1960s, most Jewish social service agencies no longer served Jewish clients. The virtual disappearance, with some scattered exceptions, of the Jewish poor and even the working class, meant that communal monies, contributed by the upper-middle-class majority of them, could be directed elsewhere.[11]

The Jews of America from the late 1960s into the early years of the next century also lived in an America governed by civil rights legislation, which they benefited from and which made anti-Jewish discrimination a historical fact rather than a lived reality. The Jews of the 1950s had still faced quotas in American universities, lived with explicit employment restrictions, and could on their travels see hotels advertising that they served "Gentiles Only."

In the closing decades of the twentieth century, the Jews of America lived in a very different country, one in which they felt comfortable asserting their Jewishness in public, to a degree that would have been breathtaking a decade or two earlier. Jewish college students began to organize kosher eating facilities on campuses and started enrolling in Jewish studies courses, something that did not exist before the late 1960s. Some adorned themselves with Jewish symbols; young men began, for example, to comfortably don skullcaps in classrooms and other public settings. In doing this, they behaved differently from their fathers and grandfathers of the postwar years, who had continued to follow the old dictum offered to Jews during the age of emancipation: "Be a man on the street, and a Jew at home." That formula, inherited from the nineteenth century, still operated in the postwar period but could be said to have died in the late 1960s.

After that date, the Jews of America felt no need to bifurcate their world into a private Jewish sphere and a public American one.

The later generation had few reservations when it came to declaring that Jews had particular interests that made them different from others and that they could perform their identities in public as they chose. They could do so because they lived in a society in which "identity politics" flourished and the society as a whole listened to the demands and declarations of various minority communities. Society accommodated the concerns of people who defined themselves as outside of the mainstream and tried, as far as possible, to be sensitive to difference. Jews in that later America had no need to garb their group concerns in the clothing of universalism.

The history of the name of one organization might illustrate this point. The National Community Relations Advisory Committee, cited throughout this book by its acronym NCRAC, had been founded in 1944 to deal with the multitude of crises and concerns that confronted American Jewry in the face of the European catastrophe, the war, heightened anti-Semitism, the quest for a homeland, and a host of other matters. Made up of the representatives of most of the large national organizations and the local Jewish community councils, it liked to think of itself as the public face of the Jews of America and that it spoke for them, particularly as they faced the national press, policy makers, and the public. Conspicuously absent from its acronym, however, was the letter "J," to stand for the missing word "Jewish." A press release issued by NCRAC, for example, could essentially masquerade as being the words of a general, liberal civic organization. In 1971, it dropped this pretense and renamed itself the National Jewish Community Relations Advisory Committee, and while in its new acronymic form it became unpronounceable, the change of nomenclature revealed the degree to which the 1960s liberated American Jews from some of their fears about being labeled "too Jewish" in public.[12]

The emergence of Jewish studies at the university level also provided another case in point. Starting in the 1960s, American colleges and universities began to provide academic space, almost always funded by Jewish donors, for the study of subjects that had previously been limited to the handful of Jewish seminaries and teachers' colleges, along with the two Jewish institutions of higher learning, Yeshiva University and Brandeis University, founded in 1948 as a nonsectarian university under Jewish auspices. Fewer than two dozen scholars came together in 1969 at the first meeting of the Association for Jewish Studies, and most of them came from the seminaries, as well as from Yeshiva and Brandeis. By 2007, the

scholarly body claimed fifteen hundred members, representing faculty
and graduate students from public and private colleges and universities in
nearly every state.[13]

This growth amounted to a sea change in both Jewish learning and in
the American Jewish public persona. That by the 1970s a student could
attend an American university, whether public or private, including some
of the nation's most elite, which a decade or two earlier still had quotas on
Jewish students, and there take courses in Yiddish, medieval Jewish history, Talmud, and by the end of the 1970s, the Holocaust represented a
profound change in Jewish and American academic life. Similarly, in 1950,
only two Jewish museums existed in the United States, the Jewish Museum
in New York and the Klutznick Museum in Washington, D.C., a project of
B'nai B'rith. By 1977, enough such institutions had come into being to
warrant the creation of the Council of American Jewish Museums, which
in 1991 had thirty-five members.[14]

In addition, by the latter decades of the twentieth century, American
Jews realized that they did not alone carry the burden for the creation
of Jewish culture and for the production of Jewish texts. American Jews
began to rely on Israel for that. Despite the fact that millions of dollars
flowed from American Jews to Israel, teachers, youth group leaders, and
counselors known often as *shlichim* (messengers) from Israel served Jewish
schools, community centers, and summer camps, lending to these places a
stamp of Jewish authenticity, a connection to the land, and forging a bond
between the two Jewries. The greater ease of travel abroad, coupled with
widespread American Jewish affluence, made Israel a real place within the
reach of Jewish youth groups, synagogues, community centers, and federations, all of which sponsored their "missions."[15] On a very profound
level, in the face of a perceived increase of Jewish illiteracy in America, the
rabbis, educators, and community leaders admitted that American Jews
once again had to depend on other Jews for at least some of their Jewish
resources.

All of these developments made the world of American Jewry a very
different entity than the one that had been in existence during the score of
years after 1945. The post-1967 American Jewish world consisted in large
measure of women and men even further removed from their European
origins than their parents had been. To them, in fact, the old city neighborhoods like New York's Lower East Side and Chicago's Maxwell Street
served as the "old home," with the towns and cities of eastern Europe the
subjects of Broadway musicals rather than the stuff of family stories.[16] They

spoke English almost exclusively and functioned with nearly total comfort almost anyplace in America. Communal leaders worried about rising levels of intermarriage, the increasing ease of melding into the American mainstream, and the dazzlingly high rates of acceptance that other Americans offered them. By definition, then, the kinds of memorial texts that Jews, starting in the late 1960s, created for the Holocaust would have to have differed from the ones that their parents had created and participated in in an earlier era.

American Jews changed in large measure because America had changed. The nation that came into being in the late 1960s contrasted dramatically with the one that postwar Jews had lived in and in which they took the first steps to create a commemorative culture for remembering the six million. Historians who have begun to build the literature on post-1960s America have almost all agreed that nearly every aspect of American life destabilized and went through the process of redefinition and that the society that grew out of the turbulence of the late 1960s bore little resemblance to the confident and optimistic postwar years.[17]

Much of what changed affected the ways American Jews engaged with the Holocaust and shaped how the larger society became part of that engagement. The confrontational politics of the 1960s, the latter part of the decade more dramatically than the earlier, for one, created a new America in which many groups—including students, feminists, antiwar activists, African Americans, Asian Americans, Hispanics, Native Americans, gays and lesbians, the disabled, and the elderly, among others—pressed their political and cultural cases, volubly and demonstratively, to the larger public. Certainly, this helped shape historical thinking. The insurgents did not ask but demanded that the "establishment" or the "power structure" recognize their particular grievances, acknowledge their plight, and remedy the injuries bequeathed them by past injustices. They did not appeal to universal principles of goodwill, nor did they emphasize how much all Americans who shared a culture and destiny would benefit from any of the changes being proposed.

Rather, by asserting group interest and calling for the recognition of "the group" as a matter of policy, they reflected the dissolution of the liberal consensus that had so characterized much of the postwar rhetoric and that American Jews had been so thoroughly part of. The Jewish liberalism of the postwar period, the one on which the early Holocaust commemorations had been based, fell apart in the late 1960s. It unraveled as a result of assaults from both the right and the left.[18]

Those who opposed it from the right, who long had seen liberalism as "communistic" and at odds with the values of the real America and its white, Christian, business-oriented majority, had little impact on American Jewry and its subsequent Holocaust project. Rather, attacks on liberalism from the left influenced it greatly. Many of the nation's young people, Jews among them, rejected the liberal ethos as too slow, too celebratory of American values, and too compromising with evil when it came to rectifying the problems of racism, militarism, and poverty, among many other injustices.

The upheavals that swept the campuses of American universities and spilled out onto the streets consumed the energy of much of the generation that came of age in the 1960s. They expressed disdain for the institutions then in existence and doubted the legitimacy of the leaders and cultural arbiters of the society. The women and men born after the war, who like so many young American Jews participated actively in this volcanic upheaval, had been raised in the affluence of the 1950s and its suburban culture. They rejected these.[19]

At the heart of the minority insurgencies—and, indeed, fundamental to the cultural revolution of the late 1960s—lay a rejection of the ideal of cultural pluralism, first articulated in the early twentieth century by people like Jane Addams and Horace Kallen, who described a model for American society that assumed the fundamental sameness of all, despite difference. The philosophers of cultural pluralism marginalized the specifics of the group, subordinating the cultural practices and values of the ethnic communities to the needs of the larger society. Cultural pluralism asserted that America derived its strength from ethnic differences, but only insofar as those differences did not threaten the common culture. Being "different," cultural pluralists advised, could be tolerated if those differences did not go too far and did not make any demands on the society as a whole.[20]

The cultural revolution of the 1960s had nothing but contempt for this way of describing American reality or applying it as a blueprint for the future. Differences, the post-1960s rhetoric proclaimed, should not be hidden or made subservient to the common culture. The larger society, through schools and the agencies of the state, had no right to affix such a price tag to citizenship. Not only did the critics of the era eventually claim that no common culture existed, or ever had, but that people of the minority communities should not be required to give anything up.

As culture critics in general and college students in particular pressed their specific agendas, they challenged the modus operandi of schools, churches, government institutions, and the "family," as they envisioned new and better kinds of relationships between whites and blacks, adults and youth, women and men. They brushed aside the optimistic and conciliatory rhetoric of the postwar period, and in the process they deliberately hoped to disrupt America's "business as usual."

Their arguments grew out of an across-the-board generational chasm, a critique hurled by the young at the values and institutions of the world in which they had grown up and the adults who ran their societies. The adults who administered the universities, the school systems, religious institutions, and bureaucracies had created a flawed world that lacked passion and compromised with evil in order to keep society working smoothly. They, the young people of America, engaged and committed to change, claimed repeatedly in political and cultural works that they saw through the sham of the liberal consensus. They could and would do it better. In their words and actions they extended this argument to their teachers, clergy, and others who had played a role in their upbringing. While in retrospect veterans of the 1960s, historians among them, have probably overstated the degree to which America in, say, 1968 stood on the brink of a revolution, at the time, no one could ignore the idioms of revolt and resistance or the barbed rejections of liberalism and suburban conformity that throbbed in America.

The young people of the minority communities had a particular argument to make in this context. As they saw it, the leaders of their communities had put up with injustices for too long, had accepted crumbs from those in power rather than boldly daring to demand total respect from the oppressive majority, and had forced on their communities a culture of accommodation. The older generation had spent too much time proving their loyalty as Americans, worrying about the goodwill of the majority, and showing their oppressors how much they had achieved despite the discrimination. The rising generation of young African Americans, Native Americans, Japanese Americans, and Mexican Americans rejected the liberal politics of compromise imposed on them by their community elders in collaborating with the very forces that kept them powerless. Younger and more militant elements of the minority communities charged that ethnic group "leaders" had suppressed the true history of their group in America in order to fit in and curry favor with the white power elite.[21]

Other matters changed in America, which left their mark on how Jews would engage with the Holocaust after the late 1960s. In the confrontational politics of the late 1960s, the term "Holocaust" came to be used by numerous groups to describe their own oppression in America. But perhaps more formative, or transformative, to American Jews, some Americans—particularly those on the left and specifically from the ranks of African American nationalists—began to use Holocaust imagery against American Jews. In the summer of 1967, the newsletter of the Student Non-Violent Coordinating Committee ran an article condemning Israel's "massacre" of Palestinians in the course of the recent war and included a photo captioned, "This is Gaza Strip, Palestine, not Dachau, Germany."[22]

During the tumultuous teachers' strike in New York in Brooklyn's Ocean Hills–Brownsville neighborhood, black radicals like Sonny Carson and his followers chanted, "The Germans did not do a good enough job," as they taunted their antagonists, the predominantly Jewish teachers' union. Julius Lester, a commentator on New York's radio station WBAI, read a poem written by a student in one of the schools that lay at the center of the controversy:

Hey, Jew boy, with that yarmulke on your head
You pale-faced Jew boy—I wish you were dead.

Lester continued for his listeners with the words of the young black student:

I'm sick of seeing in everything I do
About the murder of six million Jews.
Hitler's reign lasted only fifteen years
My suffering lasted over 4000 years, Jew boy.

Another critic of the union, and its Jewish leaders, commented on Lester's show, "Hitler didn't make enough lampshades out of them."[23]

As the 1970s and 1980s wore on, a seemingly endless stream of disputes between Jews and blacks produced an equally lengthy discourse by some African American militants on the Holocaust, challenging Jews' right to claim a special status of victimhood. Jesse Jackson, running for the Democratic nomination for president in 1984, shared with *Washington Post* reporter Milton Coleman that he had become "sick and tired" of hearing about the Holocaust from Jews. Previously, complaints about American Jewish usages of the Holocaust had come from the right wing, from Germany and pro-Nazi German American groups. Now such language emanated from African American sources, representing a segment of the

American population with whom Jews had been politically allied throughout the postwar years. This turn of events also played a role in sharpening organized American Jewry's desire to hold on to and broadcast more systematically and more widely the truth of the Holocaust and its vast brutality.[24]

Young American Jews took all this in. They not only inhaled the rhetoric of their non-Jewish peers, but also they participated in large numbers in campus revolts, led many of those uprisings, and counted themselves among the activists of the late 1960s. With others, they wrote the manifestoes, coined the slogans, and brought the message of confrontational radicalism to public attention. They played a not insignificant role in dislodging the liberal ethos of cultural pluralism and community compromise.

Some of them conveyed this same stridency of generational confrontation to their Jewish communities. Those who did so—whether they called for heightened religious observance, deeper identification with Israel and Zionism, more assertive Jewish behavior in public places, more militant action on behalf of Soviet Jews, the embrace of Yiddish and east European Jewish culture, or greater emphasis on Jewish cultural creativity in America —found what existed on the American Jewish ground devoid of intensity and lacking real Jewish content.

The American Jewish mainstream came to be wracked by dissent from young people, college students in the main, who took to task the Jewish establishment for its lack of militancy vis-à-vis the plight of Soviet Jewry and who found existing programs in Jewish education boring, too assimilationist, too accommodating to America and its values, and basically not Jewish enough. As they saw it, the Hebrew schools taught a watered-down, vapid curriculum, and the community centers spent too much of their resources on sports and fitness. Neither offered enough of real Jewish substance. In 1969, a group of Jewish students staged a noisy demonstration at the General Assembly of the National Council of Jewish Federations and Welfare Funds. They charged that the umbrella fundraising body paid too little attention and devoted too few resources to fostering Jewish identity, promoting Jewish education, and strengthening the Jewish core of community life. On the local level in the early 1970s in Washington, D.C., a group of Jewish young people, Jews for Urban Justice, invaded a luncheon meeting of the Jewish Community Council, chiding the communal elders for not doing enough to address the needs of the city's black poor. On the far right of the American Jewish political spectrum, but still evincing the same disdain for the liberal values of the community mainstream, the creation in 1968 of the Jewish Defense League by Meir Kahane also demonstrated the degree to which Jewish communities at the national and local levels became agitated settings for conflicts between insiders and insurgents.[25]

The "new Jews" of the late 1960s also created new Jewish practices and called for the restructuring of synagogue life in ways that would have startled the Jews in the middle of the 1950s. Some launched a movement to grant women greater and even equal rights and roles in public worship. In 1972, Hebrew Union College graduated the first woman rabbi, Sally Preisand, a veteran of the Reform movement's summer camps. Women in the Conservative movement in the 1980s organized themselves into Ezrat Nashim, going around the country enlisting support to persuade the Jewish Theological Seminary to admit women to its rabbinical program. Feminists called for new religious rituals, like baby-naming ceremonies for girls, and called for new texts that used gender-neutral language, stripping God, as it were, of masculinity.

Starting in the late 1960s, a small but visible number of American Jews rejected conventional synagogues altogether because of their emphasis on decorum. These young Jews, mostly on university campuses but in New York, Boston, Washington, and Los Angeles as well, opted to create the *havurah* movement, small, loosely organized bands of young Jews who experimented with new modes of worship and who disdained the hierarchy of the conventional synagogues with their robed rabbis standing on raised stages, facing passive congregants who sat quietly below.[26] The late 1960s also saw the increase in Jewish day schools, with parents in communities all over the United States rejecting not just public education but the Jewish supplementary school system, considering both inadequate.

In dozens of publications, manifestoes, and public programs, the engaged young Jews of the late 1960s found much fault with the actions and affect of American Jewry. "In America," wrote Arthur Wakow in the 1969 *The Freedom Seder: A New Haggadah for Passover*, "we have been both coerced and cajoled into abandoning the prophetic legacy. . . . Our people have been frightened into allowing themselves to be purchased, and have forgotten to be angry."[27] Sherman Rosenfeld, a veteran of the Radical Jewish Union in Berkeley, published a piece in 1971 in the *Jewish Radical*, a publication of its time, in which he took the American Jewish adult world to task. He claimed that "traditional Jewish values have been divorced from action" in the Jewish community. "Most American Jewish parents don't seem to give a damn about living Jewishness in their houses. . . . The contemporary American synagogue seems to intensify the split between Jewish values and actions. . . . The leaders of the Jewish Establishment . . . have no deeper commitment to Jewish education." Of all the sins of American Jewry none loomed larger for Rosenfeld and his peers than "the most fatal compromise of all," which "was made when American Jews, wanting to believe in the dream of the melting pot, defined themselves solely as religious beings, trading in their political souls in the process."[28]

They examined the practices of the institutions in which they had been raised—the schools, synagogues, and community centers—and scrutinized the workings of the communal institutions that constituted the Jewish establishment, applying to them the same standards of criticism that they used when looking at the larger society. They found the American Jewish world equally wanting. Like the deficiencies they saw in American society as a whole and with the same disdain that the young people of other groups directed at their communities, young American Jews considered American Jewish institutions to have become too consensus-oriented, too unwilling to assert Jewish distinctiveness, and too concerned with avoiding confrontation with others.[29]

Of the many images that the activists employed in the context of their condemnation of contemporary American Judaism, few resonated with them more deeply than the Holocaust. Here, for one, they had a tragedy that they could cite as their own, one that made their story utterly unique. Here they confronted a trauma of nearly unfathomable proportions. And in its name, they could not only demand that the larger society take note of them as Jews, but they could lambaste established Jewish institutions. Those communal bodies, according to the young Jewish activists, had rarely talked about the Holocaust and had memorialized it only obliquely and quietly. These critics, "the new Jews," perceived a gaping chasm between how their communities memorialized the Holocaust and how they believed it ought to be treated. One activist "new Jew," Alan Mintz, who later became a scholar of the Holocaust and helped create the history of the silence of the postwar period, noted in a 1971 anthology, *The New Jews*, that "as of late consciousness of the holocaust has been decisive," functioning as an opposite to the earlier era's "suppression of emotion," when presumably the catastrophe had not been so salient. His coauthor James Sleeper defined himself as a product of an "age in which we who would not retell the Jewish story have learned how to sigh-not . . . from the hollowness of an affluence and a freedom which surrounds us with glibness, detachment, and meaninglessness."[30]

These activists of the late 1960s created a set of texts, articles, books, pamphlets, newsletters, and broadsides that claimed that, despite their own emotional anguish over the Holocaust, the generation which held the reins of power in the Jewish community had acted with shallowness when it came to engaging with its enormity, that the Jewish community had been so concerned with being like all other Americans that it had forgotten to draw attention to the missing six million of its people. The leaders of the community institutions had so lusted after acceptance into a corrupt America that they forgot the lessons of the Holocaust.

In *Never Again! A Program for Survival* of 1971, Meir Kahane went so far as to say that "there are in the end, only two groups who continue to maintain that they know nothing of the death camps then. The Germans there and some Jewish leaders here." Among his plans for "survival" he demanded "an in-depth study of the Holocaust." So, too, in his condemnation of the Jewish community centers, which he saw as shallow and meaningless, evidenced by the fact that the members have never been "interested in Talmud classes, in Jewish Holocaust programs, and in studies of Judaism." The clientele want "basketball, games, dances, and *fun*." Clearly, the Jewish leaders and institutions he pointed his fingers at could not have been considered worthy custodians of the memory of the Holocaust. He and his Jewish Defense League, however, would fulfill that role. After all, in his "Movement Handbook," he declared that his organization, "whose hallmark is action," represented a "new philosophy . . . born as a new Jew arose from the mound of corpses at Auschwitz, Treblinka, and Buchenwald." The JDL, as opposed to all the establishment organizations, emerged "from the ashes of decay of the holocaust."[31]

That generation of activists had hardly been known for its commitment to nuance in its rhetoric or subtlety in its polemics. It could not have been so, given the project it had undertaken as it sought to remake America and, in this case, American Jewry. The versions of the "truth" that the activists articulated and that then became enshrined in American Jewish history and memory had been constructed in the late 1960s, in that singular era of engaged cultural confrontation. At that time, on their college campuses and in the other places where the Jewish youth culture flourished, these young Jews, the products and critics of the postwar era, challenged the adult leaders of the American Jewish world to become more Jewish, more radical, less liberal, and more focused on the Holocaust. They claimed that they, unlike the generation that they wanted to dislodge, had essentially discovered the Holocaust. They—not their teachers, not the writers of the textbooks they used, not their summer camp counselors, nor the magazine editors, rabbis, or community center workers—put the catastrophe onto the Jewish communal agenda. They—not the functionaries of the "Jewish establishment"—had brought the images and metaphors of the Holocaust to the attention of other Americans.

The insurgents in the American Jewish world that came into being in the late 1960s issued, for the first time, a blanket condemnation of the previous generation which during the war did nothing to halt the slaughter. No more "American Jews to the Rescue," as Elma Ehrlich Levinger had put it so exuberantly in 1954.[32] Instead, Meir Kahane in 1971 linked the "Jewish establishment" of his own times with the leadership of American Jewry in the 1930s and 1940s. "Why," he asked in one of his many polemical works, "were we silent? Why do our organizations condemn Jewish militants today? Why were *the very same groups* stricken with political laryngitis as millions died in Auschwitz?"[33]

The newsletters, broadsides, pamphlets, and articles of the youthful insurgents throbbed with a rhetorical trope linking the contemporary Jewish politics of the mainstream Jewish organizations with Holocaust avoidance. Those organizations which have, according to the manifesto of a Washington, D.C., group, Jews for Urban Justice, "collaborated with the American empire to control, cajole, and oppress the Jewish people" may on the surface seem to be Jewish, but they did everything they could to downplay "real" Jewishness, including a systematic repression of Jewish sensibilities and concerns, including a project to temper historical consciousness.[34] Aviva Cantor Zuckoff, a leading figure in Jewish feminism and a founder of one of the left-leaning groups, the Jewish Liberation Project, pointed her finger at the "Assimilationist Jews" in 1970 who "have led us to believe that it is 'paranoic' to recognize anti-Semitism in the U.S." "Jews are taught to feel guilty about harboring these feelings," she asserted, and "this is one of the reasons Jews feel so uncomfortable about and unwilling to confront the implications of the Holocaust."[35]

"New Jews" also confronted in their polemics their peers who seemed to identify only with the left and with other minority causes, eschewing any interest in Jewish matters and expressing no Jewish pain. M. J. Rosenberg took on this group in a piece in the *Village Voice* in 1969, "To Uncle Tom and Other Jews." In his call for a new consciousness, an awakened assertive Jewish ethos among the young in America, he called out to "you who are so trapped by your Long Island split-level childhood that you can't see straight. You who fight against everything you are. . . . In the aftermath of the crematorium, you are flippant. In the wake of Auschwitz, you are embarrassed. Thirty years after the Holocaust, you have learned nothing and forgotten everything. Ghetto Jew, you'd better do some fast thinking."[36]

They demonized the ethos of the postwar period—in particular, the ways Jews experienced it. In that, they joined the chorus of voices from the postwar period which also claimed that somehow American Jews failed as Jews because they neither measured up to the six million or remembered the martyrs well enough. They continued the discourse that claimed, even in the immediate years after the end of the war, that American Jews had somehow blotted the catastrophe out of their minds.

Many of these activists persisted in telling the story as the century wore on and came to an end, and as they participated in the construction of the next, larger, commemorative culture that fit other circumstances. In the works they accomplished in their later lives, they held fast to the truths they had enunciated in the heady days of their youthful rebellion. Those who went on to become rabbis, leaders of the communal agencies, and journalists remembered the message of the engaged era which commenced in the late 1960s, and they incorporated many of its ideas into their professional work. Other veterans of the "Jewish counterculture" of the late 1960s, who did not devote their subsequent careers to Jewish community work, however, became the adult women and men who participated in Jewish community life on the membership level. They, too, did not forget the ethos of the late 1960s, and they, too, accepted a particular and very flawed version of the postwar era as a time when the establishment did not care, when the community only sought integration, and when the horrendous story of the Holocaust was pushed to the side.

Scholars, some of whom participated in the counterculture, have also taken these words seriously. Over time, they used these statements to provide the basis of a widely shared truth about the past, one that became so deeply embedded into the communal consciousness as to require nearly no other proof or documentation. The politically charged utterances of the late 1960s and 1970s came to be used by historians, literary critics, journalists, and others in later years when they started to write the history of the Jews of postwar America and how they had, or actually had not, memorialized the Holocaust. They turned to these texts so full of disdain and rage for the postwar generation and accepted them at face value, reading them as historical reality rather than as the political expressions of anger offered by a generation at odds with its elders.

The process by which the activists' rhetoric became a profoundly held communal orthodoxy about the past happened partly because some of the activists went on to become academics, rabbis, journalists, and communal leaders, both professional and lay. Some of them, as well as the others who had watched from the sidelines but still imbibed the radicals' words, went on in subsequent decades to become the Jewish women and men of America who participated in and supported the mammoth Holocaust culture of the late twentieth century.

Inherent in that later culture of Holocaust remembrance lay the belief that, in the postwar period, American Jews had turned their backs on the harrowing images of the destroyed six million. Yet, by telling the history the way they did—by claiming that the shallow, assimilating Jews of America in the two decades that followed the end of World War II had shunned the Holocaust and had made it utterly marginal to their community lives—historians and others produced a flawed history and perpetrated an injustice to the past. By ignoring the full and variegated historical record, they essentially defamed a group of Jewish women and men who, in fact, had confronted the enormity of the losses, taken note of the gravity of the cultural destruction, picked up the pieces of a shattered Jewish world, and experimented with language and modes of expressions to create memorial projects that fit their time and place. The Jews of postwar America, rather than ignoring the Holocaust, opened up the possibility of fitting it into their communal lives. They searched for ways and times to weave it into their Jewish projects, and what they created they believed to be fitting memorials to the six million. They did what they could and took pride in having done so, believing that they simultaneously hallowed the memory of what had been lost and helped improve America, its Jews, and the world at large.

Notes

Notes to the Introduction

1. *All Eyes Are on the . . . Literary Magazine*, n.p., in American Jewish Archives (AJA), Hebrew Union College, collection 266, National Federation of Temple Youth, box 3, folder 2.

2. Leon Jick, "The Holocaust: Its Uses and Abuses in the American Public," *Yad Vashem Studies* 14 (1981), pp. 308–9.

3. Edward S. Shapiro, *A Time for Healing: American Jewry Since World War II* (Baltimore: Johns Hopkins University Press, 1992).

4. Gerald Sorin, *Tradition Transformed: The Jewish Experience in America* (Baltimore: Johns Hopkins University Press, 1997), p. 217.

5. Alan Mintz, *Popular Culture and the Shaping of Holocaust Memory in America* (Seattle: University of Washington Press, 2001), pp. 1, 5.

6. Jonathan D. Sarna, *American Judaism: A History* (New Haven, Conn.: Yale University Press, 2004), p. 333.

7. Jack Wertheimer, *A People Divided: Judaism in Contemporary America* (Hanover, N.H.: University Press of New England, 1993), p. 7. See also Ruth K. Angress, afterword to Ilona Karmel, *An Estate of Memory* (New York: Feminist Press, 1969), p. 445.

8. Seymour Martin Lipset and Earl Rabb wrote broadly that "American Jews . . . along with everyone else, were fully engaged in 'making it' in a benign postwar America" (Lipset and Rabb, *Jews and the New American Scene* [Cambridge: Harvard University Press, 1995], p. 117).

9. Edward Alexander, *The Resonance of Dust: Essays on Holocaust Literature and Jewish Fate* (Columbus: Ohio State University Press, 1979), p. 122. Susan Gubar contends that a "number of assimilated American Jews worrying that any attention to the disaster would bring further harm to Jewish people," participated in a "highly effective . . . conspiracy . . . to nullify the Holocaust" (Gubar, *Poetry After Auschwitz: Remembering What One Never Knew* [Bloomington: Indiana University Press, 2003], pp. 2–3).

10. Linda Gritz states with utter certainty that "for at least two decades, the Holocaust was a taboo subject, too raw for most to contemplate. The Warsaw Ghetto Uprising was a proud moment . . . but it was a drop in the bucket compared with the magnitude of six million murdered." Gritz, "Commemorating the Uprising: Challenges Throughout the History of Warsaw Ghetto Uprising Observances," *Jewish Currents* (March–April 2006), p. 24. Like writers from a leftist perspective, Gritz asserted with absolutely no evidence that "the leftwing organizations that publicly embraced the Uprising . . . were shunned by mainstream Jewish organizations as McCarthyism gripped the country. Against this backdrop, the path to memorializing the Holocaust was not clear" (p. 24).

11. Alvin H. Rosenfeld, "The Assault on Holocaust Memory," in *American Jewish Year Book: 2001* (New York: American Jewish Committee, 2001), pp. 6, 9.

12. Stuart Svonkin, *Jews Against Prejudice: American Jews and the Fight for Civil Liberties* (New York: Columbia University Press, 1997), p. 179.

13. Lipset and Rabb, *Jews and the New American Scene*, p. 119.

14. Kirsten Fermaglich, *American Dreams and Nazi Nightmares: Early Holocaust Consciousness and Liberal America, 1957–1965* (Waltham, Mass.: Brandeis University Press, 2006), p. 170.

15. Michael L. Morgan, "To Seize Memory: History and Identity in Post-Holocaust Jewish Thought," in *Thinking About the Holocaust: After Half a Century*, ed. Alvin H. Rosenfeld (Bloomington: Indiana University Press, 1997), p. 158.

16. According to Jacob Neusner, American Jews seized onto the idea of the Holocaust in 1967 as a direct reaction to the new realities in Israel. That new iteration of Judaism put the Holocaust and Israel into the center of spiritual life (Neusner, *Death and Birth of Judaism: The Impact of Christianity, Secularism, and the Holocaust on Jewish Faith* [New York: Basic Books, 1987]).

17. Sherry B. Ortner, *New Jersey Dreaming: Capital, Culture, and the Class of '58* (Durham, N.C.: Duke University Press, 2003), pp. 300, 309.

18. Edward T. Linenthal, *Preserving Memory: The Struggle to Create America's Holocaust Museum* (New York: Columbia University Press, 1995), pp. 7, 8. The word "subterranean" to describe postwar American Jewish engagements with the Holocaust surfaced repeatedly. See, for example, Eli Lederhendler, "On Peter Novick's *The Holocaust in American Life*: A Review," *Jewish Social Studies* 7, no. 3 (Spring/Summer 2001), p. 163.

19. Judith Smith, *Visions of Belonging: Family Stories, Popular Culture, and Postwar Democracy, 1940–1960* (New York: Columbia University Press, 2004), p. 140.

20. Nathan Glazer, "Hansen's Hypothesis and the Historical Experience of Generations," in *American Immigrants and Their Generations: Studies and Commentaries on the Hansen Thesis After Fifty Years*, ed. Peter Kvisto and Dag Blanck (Urbana: University of Illinois Press, 1990), p. 109.

21. Tim Cole, *Images of the Holocaust: The Myth of the "Shoah" Business* (London: Duckworth, 1999), p. 7.

22. Richard Layman, ed., *American Decades: 1960–1969* (New York: Thomson International, 1995), p. 418.

23. Stephen J. Whitfield, "The Jews," in *The Encyclopedia of American Cultural and Intellectual History*, ed. Mary Kupiec Cayton and Peter W. Williams (New York: Scribner's, 2001), vol. 2, p. 381.

24. Peter Novick, *The Holocaust in American Life* (Boston: Houghton Mifflin, 1999); Norman G. Finkelstein, *The Holocaust Industry: Reflections on the Exploitation of Jewish Suffering* (London: Verso, 2000).

25. In some cases, historians have moved a bit forward the date of the birth of Holocaust consciousness to the earlier years of the 1960s under the impact of the Eichmann trial (e.g., Svonkin, *Jews Against Prejudice*, p. 180). Even the revised date, however, allows the late 1940s and the 1950s to remain as the years in which Holocaust silence predominated.

26. One of the major exceptions to this paradigm is in a chapter in Michael E.

Staub's *Torn at the Roots: The Crisis of Jewish Liberalism in Postwar America* (New York: Columbia University Press, 2002), pp. 17–44.

27. Will Herberg, *Protestant, Catholic, Jew: An Essay in American Religious Sociology* (Garden City, N.Y.: Doubleday, 1955); Carey McWilliams, *Brothers Under the Skin* (Boston: Little, Brown, 1943); Benjamin A. Heydrick, *Americans All: Stories of American Life* (New York: Harcourt Brace, 1941).

28. This book joins a growing body of scholarship that is interrogating the myth of postwar silence about the Holocaust in Israel. Scholars and other public commentators have asserted that Jews in Israel, like those in the United States—but for different reasons—had buried the tragedy of the six million, only to exhume it decades later. For example, see Anita Shapira, "Hashoah: Zikaron prati v'zikaron tzibui" [The Holocaust: Private memory and public memory] (pp. 527–40), and Dalia Ofer, "Mah v'ad kama lezkor mean hashoah: Zikaron hashoah b'medinat Yisrael b'assor harishon l'kiyuma" [What and how much to remember about the Holocaust: The memory of the Holocaust in the State of Israel in the first decade of its existence] (pp. 171–93), both in *Atzmut: 50 shanim harishonim* [Independence: The first fifty years], ed. Anita Shapira (Jerusalem: Mercaz Zalman Shazar L'Toldot Yisrael, 1998).

Notes to Chapter 1

1. The collection of the Seder Ritual of Remembrance, including various drafts, correspondence, publicity, and distribution materials, is in the American Jewish Historical Society (AJHS), New York City, I-50. The decision not to name the perpetrators and to quickly pass over the most brutal details has a degree of resonance in traditional Jewish texts and in many postwar narratives about the Nazi extermination of the Jews. According to the authors of *The Black Book*, the earliest comprehensive recitation of the brutal facts of what the Germans and their allies had done, "the chronicler of a Jewish catastrophe in the Middle Ages ended his sad tale with the following charitable words: 'And much more had come to pass than we have recorded here . . . but we have refrained from telling them out of our respect for the human race, which is the crown of the Lord's creation, and not to undermine the faith of the future generations of mankind'" (Jewish Black Book Committee, *The Black Book: The Nazi Crime Against the Jewish People* [New York: Jewish Black Book Committee, 1946], p. 456).

2. Jonathan D. Sarna, *American Judaism: A History* (New Haven, Conn.: Yale University Press, 2004), p. 333.

3. Sharon Feinman, essay in *All Eyes Are on the . . . Literary Magazine*, n.p., in American Jewish Archives (AJA), Hebrew Union College, collection 266, National Federation of Temple Youth, box 3, file 2.

4. Leon Jick made much of the terminology used and not used. He asserted that "in the early 1960s, slowly . . . the introduction of a new term of reference: Holocaust" betokened a sea change in American Jewry and its new willingness to think about the European tragedy (Jick, "The Holocaust: Its Uses and Abuses in the American Public," *Yad Vashem Studies* 14 [1981], p. 309).

5. *Jewish Music Concert Programs as Performed During the 1953 Jewish Music Festival* (New York: National Jewish Music Council, n.d.), n.p.; clipping, International Ladies' Garment Workers Union, *Justice*, September 1, 1948, in YIVO Institute for Jewish

Research (YIVO), ORT (Organization for Rehabilitation Through Training) Papers, RG (Records Group) 130, box 12; Sidney Markowitz, *What Do You Know About Jewish Religion, History, Ethics and Culture? A Comprehensive Book Covering Every Phase of Jewish Life for the Past 3500 Years* (New York: Saphrograph, 1954), p. 41.

6. Stephen Whitfield has boldly asserted that in the postwar era "not even the term 'Holocaust' was in use" (Whitfield, "Value Added: Jews in Postwar American Culture," in *A New Jewry: America Since the Second World War*, ed. Peter Medding [New York: Oxford University Press, 1992], p. 74).

7. "Abraham Walkowitz Exhibit," brochure, October–November 1949, in Ratner Center, Jewish Theological Seminary of America, Jewish Museum Papers, RG 25, box 7.

8. Clipping, "Art: By Anna Walinska," *New York Times*, September 13, 1957, in Ratner Center, Jewish Theological Seminary of America, Jewish Museum Papers, RG 25, box 17.

9. *American Jewish Year Book: 1953* (Philadelphia: Jewish Publication Society of America and American Jewish Committee, 1953), p. 581. Hereafter cited by year only.

10. Judah Pilch, "President's Message at the Opening Session," *Jewish Social Service Quarterly* 32 (Fall 1955), p. 3.

11. Judah Shapiro, *The Friendly Society: A History of the Workmen's Circle* (New York: Media Judaica, 1970), p. 188.

12. "Our Holiday of Today," program, "Forward 50th Anniversary, May 25, 1947," in Fales Library, NYU, Sholom Secunda Papers, box 89.

13. "Temple B'nai Moshe: Ceremony of Ground Breaking," in Ratner Center, Jewish Theological Seminary of America, archive 99, box 8, "Communal Relations" folder.

14. Label Katz, "Acceptance Speech: Creative Jewish Living," in AJHS, P-492, Label Katz Papers, box 1, "Election as President" folder.

15. Oscar Handlin, *Adventure in Freedom: Three Hundred Years of Jewish Life in America* (New York: McGraw-Hill, 1954), pp. vii–viii.

16. *American Jewish Year Book: 1962*, p. 196.

17. Rochelle G. Saidel, *Never Too Late to Remember: The Politics Behind New York City's Holocaust Museum* (New York: Holmes and Meier, 1996), pp. 3–5, 20, 44–55; James E. Young, *The Texture of Memory: Holocaust Memorials and Meaning* (New Haven, Conn.: Yale University Press, 1993), pp. 288–90; Rebecca Read Shanor, *The City That Never Was* (New York: Viking, 1988), p. 219.

18. Publicity materials, "American Memorial to Six Million Jews of Europe, Inc.," in YIVO 1206, box 1, file 1.

19. Clipping, *New York Times*, January 18, 1950, p. 9, in YIVO 1206, box 2.

20. Advertising material, in YIVO 1206, box 1, files 1 and 3; Obituary, Eric Mendelsohn, *New York Times*, October 16, 1953.

21. "Six Million Jews Slain by the Nazis," in YIVO 1206, box 1, file 3.

22. Thomas E. Dewey, press release, in YIVO 1206, box 1, files 1 and 2.

23. Israel Tabak, "The Tenth Yahrtzeit," in *The Rabbinical Council Manual of Holiday and Sabbath Sermons, 5714–1953*, ed. Solomon J. Sharfman (New York: Rabbinical Council Press, 1953), pp. 235–36. In his own Rosh Hashanah sermon, published in the same volume, Sharfman noted that many American Jews speak "even of the land of Israel, in terms of our dead six million" (p. 325).

24. Saidel, *Never Too Late*, 56–67. See also "Statement Made by Dr. Joachim Prinz: Chairman of the Committee for the Six Million," in AJA, Hebrew Union College, collection 673, box 1, folder 3; Letter of September 28, 1966, "Committee to Commemorate the Six Million Martyrs," in Tamiment Library, Wagner Labor Archives, NYU, Edward S. Goldstein Papers, box 2, file 10.

25. Jacob Katzman to Joachim Prinz, February 9, 1966, in AJA, Hebrew Union College, collection 673, box 1, folder 4.

26. Bernard G. Richards, "A Jewish Memorial Library as an Adjunct to Lincoln Center," *Congress Bi-Weekly* 28, no. 16 (November 13, 1961), pp. 8–9; Letter, Hugo Stansky, "A Jewish Memorial Library," *Congress Bi-Weekly* 28, no. 18 (December 11, 1961), p. 14. See also Mrs. Moses Epstein to Bernard Richards, January 10, 1962, in Ratner Center, Jewish Theological Seminary of America, Bernard Richards Papers, archive 96, box 12.

27. On Schneersohn's successful fundraising efforts with the American Jewish Committee, see Laura Jockusch, " 'Collect and Record! Help to Write the History of the Latest Destruction!' Jewish Historical Commissions in Europe, 1943–1953," Ph.D. diss., New York University, 2007.

28. This material is drawn from the Administrative Archives of the Centre de Documentation Juive Contemporaine in Paris. That material has not been cataloged and lacks box and folder numbers. Thanks to Laura Jockusch for bringing these documents to my attention. See also Ronald W. Zweig, *German Reparations and the Jewish World: A History of the Claims Conference* (London: Frank Cass, 2001), pp. 158–59; material on the Claims Conference and its funding of the Paris memorial and documentation center is in AJHS, I-319, particularly box 1; much of the funding for the Paris project came from the Conference of Jewish Material Claims Against Germany, but the majority came from American Jewry.

29. *American Jewish Year Book: 1952*, p. 285; "Editorial," *Jewish Spectator* 16, no. 2 (February 1951), p. 19.

30. *American Jewish Year Book: 1953*, pp. 261–62.

31. Catherine Poujol, *L'affaire Finaly* (Paris: Berg International, 2006); Michael R. Marrus, "The Missing: The Holocaust, the Church, and Jewish Orphans," *Commonweal* 133, no. 1 (January 13, 2006), pp. 11–12, 14–16.

32. Both quoted and cited in Deborah Lipstadt, *Denying the Holocaust: The Growing Assault on Truth and Memory* (New York: Plume, 1994), pp. 51–63.

33. "Between You and Me," December 25, 1959, in AJHS, P-588, Boris Smolar Papers, box 11. After Nixon's visit to Warsaw and to the Ghetto monument, the Club of Polish Jews in New York commissioned Rapoport to make a bust of the vice president, "in appreciation of the latter's visit to the Warsaw Ghetto."

34. Cover of *Furrows* 15, no. 6 (April 1960).

35. *American Jewish Year Book: 1953*, p. 321.

36. *American Jewish Year Book: 1961*, p. 270.

37. "Department of Defense Urged to Put Directional Markers on Road to Army Base in Dachau," August 10, 1961, in Tamiment Library, Wagner Labor Archives, NYU, Julius Bernstein Papers, box 13.

38. Minutes, Board Meeting, Synagogue Council of America (SCA), February 5, 1947, in AJHS, I-68, SCA Papers, "1947" folder.

39. Arieh Tartakower to Kalman Stein, March 17, 1947, in Yad Vashem Administrative Archives, AM.1, 141; A. Tartakower to Israel Goldstein, August 6, 1947, in Yad Vashem Administrative Archives, AM.1, 233; AM.1, 90.

40. Z. Warhaftig to Philip Goodman, March 23, 1948, in Yad Vashem Administrative Archives, AM.1, 421 II.

41. Notes of Meeting, July 22, 1947, in Yad Vashem Administrative Archives, AM.1, 233.

42. A. Tartakower to J. Tenenbaum, July 28, 1947; "Notes of meeting," February 10, 1947; and Letter from Moshe Shifriss to Members, December 15, 1947—all in Yad Vashem Administrative Archives, AM.1, 213; AM.1, 233.

43. Letter to Max Grünewald, *Aufbau* editor, August 2, 1946, and *Aufbau*, October 25, 1946, both in Yad Vashem Administrative Archives, AM.1, 11.

44. A. Tartakower to Association of Yugoslav Jews in the United States, December 22, 1946, in Yad Vashem Administrative Archives, AM.1, 233.

45. Letter to Jewish Welfare Board, February 4, 1948, in Yad Vashem Administrative Archives, AM.1, 421 II.

46. Moshe Shifriss to Yad Vashem, October 18, 1947, in Yad Vashem Administrative Archives, AM.1 233.

47. *American Jewish Year Book: 1953*, p. 100.

48. These represent but a few examples of the ways in which local Jewish communities and organizations constructed physical reminders of the victims of the Holocaust. For more, see, for example, Bernard Postal and Lionel Koppman, *American Jewish Landmarks*, Vol. 1 (New York: Fleet Press, 1954), p. 126; Postal and Koppman, *A Jewish Tourist's Guide to the United States* (Philadelphia: Jewish Publication Society of America, 1954); "The Month in the Workmen's Circle," *Workmen's Circle Call* (September 1961), p. 22.

49. Clippings, *Wisconsin Jewish Chronicle*, January 8, 1954, November 30, 1956, October 11, 1957, November 30, 1962, in University of Wisconsin–Milwaukee, New Home Club Papers, manuscript 42.

50. Avram Kampf, *Contemporary Synagogue Art: Developments in the United States, 1945–1965* (New York: Union of American Hebrew Congregations, 1966), pp. 81–84.

51. Louise D. Kayser, *Light from Our Past: A Spiritual History of the Jewish People Expressed in Twelve Stained Glass Windows Designed by Louise D. Kayser for Har Zion Temple, Philadelphia* (New York: Shengold, 1959).

52. Mignon Rubenovitz, the wife of the rabbi of Boston's Mishkan Tefillah Congregation, created a small Jewish museum in the synagogue and in the late 1940s began to add Holocaust-related objects for display in the galleries, which served a broad public, including public school children and community groups. Clipping, *Jewish Advocate*, September 6, 1945, March 27, 1947, Scrapbook, "The Jewish Museum, Annual Report, 1948," "The Jewish Museum," *Bulletin of Temple Mishkan Tefilla*, 1953, in Ratner Center, Jewish Theological Seminary of America, archive 99, box 8; Mignon L. Rubenovitz, *Altars of My Father* (Boston: Jewish Museum, Temple Mishkan Tefilah, 1954), p. 21; Herman Rubenovitz and Mignon Rubenovitz, *The Waking Heart* (Cambridge, Mass.: Nathaniel Dame, 1967), pp. 258–59.

53. Simon Kramer to Ben Marcus, September 21, 1951, in AJHS, I-68, SCA Papers, box 27, "Jewish Cultural Reconstruction" folder.

54. "Dear Colleague," February 26, 1952, in AJHS, I-68, SCA Papers, box 38, "Service of Thanksgiving" folder.

55. Bernard Bamberger to Salo Baron, May 22, 1951, in box 27, "Jewish Cultural Reconstruction" folder; "Religious Objects Distribution," April 4, 1951, in box 1, "1950, 1951, 1952, 1958" folder—both in AJHS, I-68, SCA Papers. See also, for example, "Poetic Justice," *Jewish Spectator* 16, no. 4 (April 1951), p. 9.

56. Sanford Rosen to Bernard Bamberger, May 9, 1951, in AJHS, I-68, SCA Papers, box 27, "Jewish Cultural Reconstruction—Distribution of Ritual Objects from Germany; General Correspondence, and by State, California to New Jersey" folder.

57. William B. Helmreich, *The Enduring Community: The Jews of Newark and Metrowest* (New Brunswick, N.J.: Transaction, 1999), pp. 269, 287.

58. Joseph L. Fink to Bernard Bamberger, December 14, 1950, and Philon Wigder and Louis Feldman to Norman Salit, December 20, 1950, both in AJHS, I-68, SCA Papers, box 11, "Religious Objects Committee" folder. Quotation from Widger and Feldman to Salit.

59. *American Jewish Year Book: 1948–49*, p. 274, as just one example.

60. Many American Jewish texts of the postwar era referred to the Nazis' practice of using the fat of their Jewish victims in bars of soap. Recent scholarship indicates that this did not happen. I thank Marion Kaplan for drawing my attention to this.

61. All quotations in the preceding two paragraphs are from Alvin M. Poplack, *Carved in Granite: Holocaust Memorials in Metropolitan New York Jewish Cemeteries* (New York: Jay Street, 2003).

62. "This Week in Religion," December 28, 1952, in AJHS, I-68, SCA Papers, box 36, "This Week" folder.

63. Jewish National Fundletter, August 14, 1951, and "Minutes, Annual Meeting, 10/21/51," in University of Wisconsin–Milwaukee, New Home Club Papers, manuscript 42.

64. Trude Weiss-Rosmarin, "Memorials," *Jewish Spectator* 16, no. 5 (May 1951), p. 15.

65. Certificate, 1951, in University of Wisconsin–Milwaukee, New Home Club Papers, manuscript 42, box 2, file 2.

66. "Educational News and Notes," *Pedagogic Reporter* 5, no. 1 (September 1953), p. 13.

67. "Summary of Meeting with B'nai B'rith," March 30, 1947, in Yad Vashem Administrative Archives, AM.1 104.

68. *National Jewish Monthly* 69, no. 4 (December 1954), p. 20.

69. Minutes of Women's Auxiliary, B'nai B'rith Waukesha [Wisconsin] Chapter 156, in University of Washington–Milwaukee, New Home Club Papers, manuscript 138.

70. "The B'nai B'rith Martyrs Forest" and "Dedication of B'nai B'rith Martyrs Forest Memorial Shrine, May 29, 1959, Program," in AJHS, P-492, Label Katz Papers, box 1, "Election as President" folder.

71. Herman Weil to Melvin Zaret, November 18, 1956, in University of Wisconsin–Milwaukee, New Home Club Papers, manuscript 42, box 2, file 7. It would probably be impossible, and surely unnecessary, for a historian to document all the times, places, and ways in which American Jews made financial contributions in the postwar period in the name of the victims of the Holocaust. It would require an investigation into the

fundraising activities of synagogues, schools, federations, welfare funds, organizations, hospitals, and nearly every kind of Jewish charity that existed. The New Home example, as such, will have to suffice here.

72. "Temple Sholom Concert Forum, 5/6/59," in Chicago Jewish Archives, Spertus Institute of Jewish Studies (hereafter, Spertus), collection 94, Halevy Choral Society Papers, box 1, "Programs" folder.

73. Sholem Asch, *Tales of My People*, trans. Meyer Levin (New York: Putnam's, 1948).

74. Irving Howe and Eliezer Greenberg, *A Treasury of Yiddish Stories* (New York: Viking, 1954).

75. Emil J. Long, *2,000 Years: A History of Anti-Semitism* (New York: Exposition, 1953).

76. Dagobert D. Runes, ed., *The Hebrew Impact on Western Civilization* (New York: Philosophical Library, 1951).

77. Hayyim Schauss, *The Lifetime of a Jew: Throughout the Ages of Jewish History* (Cincinnati: Union of American Hebrew Congregations, 1950).

78. Rachel Wischnitzer, *Synagogue Architecture in the United States: History and Interpretation* (Philadelphia: Jewish Publication Society of America, 1955).

79. Malka Lee, *Durkh kindershe oygen* (Buenos Aires: Yidbukh, 1955).

80. H. S. Kaasdan, *Lerer yizker bukh: Teacher Memorial Book* (New York: Committee to Remember Forever the Murdered Teachers of the Tsisho Schools in Poland, 1952–1954). See also Aaron Tverski, *Ich bin der korben un der eydes* (New York: Shulsinger, 1947).

81. Jacob Sloan, ed., *Notes from the Warsaw Ghetto: The Journal of Emmanuel Ringelblum* (New York: McGraw-Hill, 1958), p. ix.

82. Simon Dubnow, *Nationalism and History*, edited with an introductory essay by Koppel S. Pinson (Philadelphia: Jewish Publication Society of America, 1958).

83. Abraham Joshua Heschel, *The Earth Is the Lord's: The Inner World of the Jew in Eastern Europe* (New York: Farrar, Straus, Giroux, 1949).

84. Ludwig Lewisohn, "A Panorama of a Half-Century of American Jewish Literature," *Jewish Book Annual: 5711, 1950–1951* (New York: National Jewish Welfare Board, 1952), p. 10. Hereafter cited with years only if no author is given.

85. Herman Kieval, "The Earth Is the Lord's," *Conservative Judaism* 7, no. 3 (April 1951), pp. 25–31.

86. Roman Vishniac, *Polish Jews: A Pictorial Record* (New York: Schocken, 1947).

87. *Jewish Book Annual: 5709, 1948–1949*, p. 44.

88. Jews from places other than Poland also participated in projects to write and publish volumes similar to the *yizker bikher*. For example, *Von Juden in Muenchen: Ein Gedenkbukh* (Munich: Ner-Tamid, 1959).

89. Robert Chazan, *God, Humanity and History: The Hebrew First Crusade Chronicles* (Berkeley: University of California Press, 2000).

90. For a listing of *yizker bikher*, see Zachary Baker, "Bibliography of Eastern European Memorial Books," in *From a Ruined Garden: The Memorial Books of Polish Jewry*, ed. Jack Kugelmass and Jonathan Boyarin (New York: Schocken, 1983), pp. 223–64; this number does not include an even larger trove of articles that appeared in the Yiddish press and in Yiddish magazines such as *Zukunft, Unzer Veg*, and *Yidisher Kempfer*.

91. Meeting announcement for a talk with the chairman of the Memorial Book Committee, November 14, 1959, in AJHS, I-125, Radomer Culture Center (New York) Papers. As YIVO amassed more and more material on these towns, memorial book committees turned to its archives to gather photographs and other kinds of documents. YIVO took tremendous pride in the number of *yizker bikher* that depended on its holdings, and considered this one of its key services to the Jewish public. This is discussed later in the chapter.

92. "Correspondence—Bialystok Book: 1958," in Tamiment Library, Wagner Labor Archives, NYU, Jacob Pat Papers, box 1.

93. The renowned artist Chaim Gross created the title page for *Pinkes Kolomey*, published in New York in 1957.

94. *News of Yivo* (December 1957), p. 1; H. Sabatka, ed., *Lomza: Ir oyfkum un untergang* (New York: American Committee for the Book of Lomza, 1957); A. Meyerowitz, ed., *Megilat Kurenits: Ayara be-hayeha u-ve-mota* (Tel Aviv: Former Residents of Kurzeniec in Israel and the USA, 1956).

95. Yudl Mark, "Among the Recent Yiddish Books," *Jewish Book Annual: 5708, 1946–1947* (New York: National Jewish Welfare Board, 1948), p. 54.

96. Reviewed in Shlomo Bickel, ed., *Pinkes Kolomey* (New York: Kolomeyer Memorial Book, 1957), pp. 112–13.

97. Review, Isaiah Trunk, *Yedios* 41 (1957), p. 359.

98. "Chapel of the Air: Mutual Broadcasting System," May 2, 1943, in AJHS, I-68, SCA Papers, box 10, "Radio Committee" folder.

99. Administrative Report, April 1946, in AJHS, I-68, SCA Papers, box 2, "Administrative Committee Meetings, 1940–1946" folder. While the Synagogue Council did not adopt this idea, it did send out missives to American rabbis asking them to "mention these martyrs at kaddish on that day."

100. This and the following discussion from "Meeting of the Board, Minutes, Synagogue Council of America," June 12, 1946, in AJHS, I-68, SCA Papers, box 1, "Days of Mourning" folder; "1946; Press Release," n.d., in AJHS, I-68, SCA Papers, box 22, "Days of Mourning" folder.

101. "Report on Camp Ramah Summer–1947" and "To Camp Ramah Directors," both in Ratner Center, Jewish Theological Seminary of America, Camp Ramah Papers, RG 28, box 34, file 19, and RG 28, box 10, file 5, respectively.

102. Ludwig Geismar, "A Scale for the Measurement of Ethnic Identification," *Jewish Social Studies* 16, no. 1 (January 1954), p. 48. This social-psychological article involved a study of the Ninth of Av incorporation of Holocaust material.

103. Manuel Saltzman, National Radio Show, in AJHS, I-68, SCA Papers, box 36, "This Week in Religion" folder.

104. Religious News Service, "Synagogue Council Sets Day of Mourning," March 8, 1945, and Rabbi Ahron Opuer, "March 14th Proclaimed Day of Mourning," press release, n.d., both in AJHS, I-68, SCA Papers, box 22, "Days of Mourning" folder.

105. Bernard Bamberger to Leo Jung, November 23, 1949, in AJHS, I-68, SCA Papers, box 22, "Days of Mourning" folder. To get around any problems as the Orthodox might have seen it vis-à-vis the fixed liturgy of the Tenth of Tevet, the Synagogue Council actually designated that evening as the period within the day for memorializing the six million rather than the entirety of the day. Thus they could not be accused of

violating established practice. The council may very well have turned to Jung, an Ortho-dox rabbi, to deflect any criticism that by linking the Tenth of Tevet to the Holocaust, they were violating Jewish tradition.

106. "Service of Memorial for Six Million Jewish Martyrs of Nazi Tyranny," in AJHS, I-68, SCA Papers, box 35, "Service of Memorial" folder.

107. Letter from Simon Konovitch to SCA, December 19, 1950, in AJHS, I-68, SCA Papers, box 38, "Service of Memorial" folder.

108. Abraham I. Katsch, ed., *Bar Mitzvah: Illustrated* (New York: Shengold, 1955), pp. 84–87. This same material appeared several years later in a companion volume: Meyer Waxman, Sulamith Ish-Kishor, and Jacob Sloan, *Blessed Is the Daughter* (New York: Shengold, 1959). Both books also included a photograph of Isaac Herzog, the chief rabbi of Israel, "Planting the First Tree in the Forest of the Six Million Martyrs" and a selection from the diary of a young boy in the Warsaw Ghetto, Hillel Seidman, titled "Last Dance," and the words and music to "Ani Maamin."

109. "Prospective Program for TV-WABD, February 2, 1951," in AJHS, I-68, SCA Papers, box 35, "Radio-TV" folder. This example was typical of the kind of media pro-gram in which the SCA linked itself, American Jews, and the memorialization of the Holocaust.

110. In 1956, a letter came to the council from France asking that the SCA partici-pate in an international interfaith Day of Remembrance. The council informed them, "we have already established Asarah B'Teveth [Tenth of Tevet] as such a day of memo-rial" (Minutes, April 11, 1956, in AJHS, I-68, SCA Papers, box 2, "Plenum Meetings: 1949–1959" folder).

111. "News Releases, 1955–1958," in AJHS, I-68, SCA Papers, box 50.

112. *SAJ Bulletin* 42, no. 13 (April 13, 1962), p. 2.

113. The Israeli rabbinate seemed to have preferred the Tenth of Tevet and actually opposed the Twenty-seventh of Nisan and the creation of Yom Hashoah.

114. Yael Zerubavel, *Recovered Roots: Collective Memory and the Making of the Israeli National Tradition* (Chicago: University of Chicago Press, 1995), p. 75.

115. Ironically, despite the amount of publicity generated by the Synagogue Council on the Tenth of Tevet, Louis Finkelstein, chancellor of the Jewish Theological Seminary, claimed in a 1950 magazine article that "the cremation of six millions of our brethren and the destruction of their communities in our time is recalled by no day of sorrow" (Finkelstein, "The Jew in 1950," *Conservative Judaism* 6, no. 4 [May 1950], p. 3).

116. "Rosh Hashanah, 5707: New Horizons," *Kolbuszower Clarion* 2, no. 1 (October 1946), n.p., in YIVO 858.

117. Martin Kessler, "Confidential Note: To the Jewish Women of Oak Ridge, Tenn., Concerning Candle Lighting on the Eve of the Jewish New Year, on Erev Rosh Hashanah, September, 1955," *Conservative Judaism* 10, no. 1 (Fall 1955), pp. 28–29. That *Conservative Judaism* reprinted the letter gave it a wider audience than just the women of the Tennessee congregation and may indeed have meant that other rabbis incorporated elements of the letter in their sermons, congregational newsletters, and other modes of communication with members.

118. Leonard Gewirz, "How Quickly We Forget," in *The Rabbinical Council Manual*

of Holiday Sermons, 5711–1950, ed. Abraham Kellner (New York: Rabbinical Council Press, 1950), p. 29.

119. Moshe Weiss, "Self-Sacrifice," in *The Rabbinical Council Manual of Holiday and Sabbath Sermons,* ed. Samuel J. Fox (New York: Rabbinical Council Press, 1959), p. 140.

120. Jewish Reconstructionist Foundation, *High Holiday Prayerbook* (New York: Jewish Reconstructionist Foundation, 1948), pp. 387, 396.

121. Morris Silverman, *United Synagogue of America High Holiday Prayer Book* (Hartford, Conn.: Prayer Book Press, 1951), p. 386a.

122. Clipping, *The Diamondback,* December 16, 1960, in AJHS, P-358, Meyer Greenberg Papers, box 3, "Program Reports, 1959" folder. See also, for example, Philip Goodman, *The Purim Anthology* (Philadelphia: Jewish Publication Society of America, 1949), pp. 483, 384–85.

123. Scattered through the American Jewish press and through books written for Jewish and general audiences, as well as in the archival material of many Jewish organizations, is in fact a good deal of evidence that Hanukkah and Purim also served as holiday vehicles to focus on the Holocaust. Purim generally got associated with focusing on the perpetrators. For example, the Zionist Organization of Chicago staged an annual Hanukkah festival, for many years filling that city's large Civic Opera House. Repeatedly in the speeches offered at these holiday celebrations, the Holocaust surfaced as a point of reference. In 1949, as one example, President Max Bressler reminded all those assembled that "on this festive occasion, we remember our martyrs who died at the hands of their persecutors." In 1951 at the same event, the speaker intoned, "Antiochus, the madman was defeated by the flames that came from Sinai. But Antiochus never died. In every generation, he arises under a different name—Titus, Haman, Torquemada, Tsar, Hitler" (in Chicago Jewish Archives, Spertus, collection 19, Labor Zionist Organization of Chicago Papers, box 1).

124. As with the Synagogue Council and the Tenth of Tevet, the author of the Ritual of Remembrance wanted the text to operate around the Jewish world. Learsi communicated with Jewish writers, journalists, and rabbis in Italy, South Africa, France, and elsewhere to get the text adopted outside of the United States and to have a universal Jewish text (in AJHS, I-50, Seder Ritual of Remembrance, "Correspondence" folder).

125. Rabbi Joseph B. Soloveitchik, considered by many the seminal figure in modern Orthodoxy in the twentieth century, bitterly opposed the Passover reading, partly because it came from "a group whose philosophy is diametrically opposed to Torah and tradition and which does not accept the authority of Halakah [Jewish law] as a Divine . . . guide." He also reacted against the text because it "was written as a declaration addressed to ourselves and not a supplication and prayer addressed to the Almighty." And while he made it clear that he did not oppose "a new memorial for the martyrs of the most recent catastrophe," he considered this one to be too secular (Soloveitchik, "On Inserting Memorial Prayers for Holocaust Victims on Passover Night at the Seder," in *Community, Covenant and Commitment: Selected Letters and Communications: Rabbi Joseph B. Soloveitchik,* ed. Nathaniel Helfgot [New York: Toras Horav Foundation, 2005], pp. 119–21). I thank Yigal Sklarin for bringing this text to my attention.

126. Samson Weiss to Rufus Learsi, December 7, 1962, in AJHS, I-50, Rufus Learsi Papers, box 1, "Correspondence, 1962–63" folder.

127. Hershel Lookstein and David da Sola Pool, "Lest We Forget," *Jewish Forum* 37, no. 3 (March 1955), p. 35.

128. David Rudavsky to Editor, *Congress Weekly*, April 1, 1952, in AJHS, I-50, box 1, "Ritual of Remembrance" folder.

129. This and the following quotes from I. Usher Kirshblum to the Editor, *Congress Weekly*, April 22, 1952, in AJHS, I-50, box 1, "Ritual of Remembrance" folder.

130. Rabbi Isaac Klein to Learsi, April 18, 1957, in AJHS, I-50, Seder Ritual Committee, "Reaction" folder.

131. March 6, 1962, in AJHS, I-50, box 1, "Organizational Memoranda" folder; Martha Marenoff, *Haggadah for the Seder Service* (Detroit: DOT Publications, n.d.), n.p.

132. Menachem Kasher, *The Israel Passover Haggadah: Supplemented by One Hundred Chapters* (New York: Shulsinger, 1950), p. 93.

133. Sidney B. Hoenig, ed., *The Haggadah of Passover* (New York: Shulsinger, 1950), p. 80.

134. Isidore Krakower, *Haggadah for Young American Jews* (Philadelphia: Bernard Malerman, 1951), pp. 34–35, 41.

135. Shlomo Kahn, *From Twilight to Dawn: The Traditional Pesach Hagadah* (New York: Scribe, 1960), pp. 132, 151.

136. There is no way to know how many third seder participants used these same booklets at home.

137. Mikhl Gelbert, *A naye haggadah shel Pesach* (New York: Building Committee of the Arbeiter Ring, 1958), pp. 25–27.

138. The full run of the third seder *haggadot* is in the Chicago Jewish Archives, Spertus, collection 17, Labor Zionist Organization of America Papers, box 9. This 1959 *haggadah* contained numerous other references to the catastrophe, and at various points during the third seder ritual, the memory of the Holocaust was included.

139. Bernard Berzon, "When Moses Wept," in *The Rabbinical Council Manual of Holiday and Sabbath Sermons, 5714–1953*, ed. Solomon J. Sharfman (New York: Rabbinical Council of America, 1953), p. 269; Philip Goodman, *The Passover Anthology* (Philadelphia: Jewish Publication Society of America, 1961), pp. viii, 54–59, 80, 82, 264–65, 383.

140. Rufus Learsi, "We Must Remember," *Congress Weekly* 22, no. 13 (March 17, 1958), p. 8.

141. The Jewish Labor Committee (JLC), in conjunction with the Workmen's Circle and the Congress of Jewish Culture, estimated that it held commemorations in 1953 in New York, Miami, Chicago, Los Angeles, and "other cities around the country" (JLC, *Reports to NYC-E-S Division Workmen's Circle, Branch Bulletin Supplement* 2 [May 1953], in Tamiment Library, Wagner Labor Archives, NYU, Julius Bernstein Papers, box 31, file 14).

142. Morris Blumenstock to Fiorello LaGuardia, April 12, 1945, American Federation of Polish Jews, in YIVO 1015, box 2, file 2.

143. Thomas E. Dewey to Joseph Tenenbaum, April 12, 1945, in YIVO 1015, box 2, file 2. In his telegram to the American Federation of Polish Jews, for that second anniversary, Mayor Robert F. Wagner asserted his horror at "the most gruesome crime in history, the annihilation of more than 3 million Jews in Poland. . . . The revival of Jewish

culture in Poland will be a suitable tribute to the memory of the martyrs who died in Warsaw two years ago" (Wagner to Tenenbaum, in ibid.).

144. These programs are scattered throughout the papers of the Chicago Council of the American Jewish Congress, in Chicago Jewish Archives, Spertus, collection 14.

145. Quoted in Eli Lederhendler, *New York Jews and the Decline of Urban Ethnicity* (Syracuse, N.Y.: Syracuse University Press, 2001), p. 37.

146. "For Release, April 18, 1952," in Tamiment Library, Wagner Labor Archives, NYU, Julius Bernstein Papers, box 13.

147. "Report, April 1953," and "Harvard, Radcliff, Lesley, MIT, Wellesley Program Reports, 1946–1963," both in AJHS, P-112, Maurice L. Zigmond Papers, box 19.

148. "Massapequa Jewish Center," April 14, 1961, in AJHS, I-50, box 1, "clippings" folder. The synagogue announcement pages erroneously described "Ani Maamin" as the song sung by the "D.P.s" on their way to the crematoria.

149. Fanny Licht to Morris U. Schappes, March 25, 1947, in Tamiment Library, Wagner Labor Archives, NYU, Morris U. Schappes Papers, box 1, "Correspondence" folder.

150. The papers of the Chicago Council of the American Jewish Congress are in the Chicago Jewish Archives, Spertus, collection 14. The material on the Warsaw Ghetto memorial programs is scattered throughout the collection through the date-appropriate boxes and folders.

151. Mid-West Jewish Council Collection in Chicago Jewish Archives, Spertus, collection 175, box 1.

152. American Jewish Congress, Executive Committee Meeting, February 23, 1953, in Chicago Jewish Archives, Spertus, collection 14, box 21, file 4.

153. "10th Anniversary Commemoration of the Warsaw Ghetto," April 7, 1953, in YIVO 1258, Philip Friedman Papers, box 918.

154. Jewish Community Council of Greater Washington, Executive Committee, May 11, 1955, in Marvin Gelman Library, George Washington University, manuscript 2012/002, box 4, folder 17.

155. "Atlanta Jewish Community Council," in Tamiment Library, Wagner Labor Archives, NYU, Isaiah Minkoff Papers, box 2, file 26; Pittsburgh Jewish Community Relations Council, Meeting, April 23, 1958, in AJA, Hebrew Union College, collection 283, box 11, folder 4; Milton Speizman to Herman Weil, February 22, 1956, in University of Wisconsin–Milwaukee, New Home Club Papers, manuscript 42, box 2, file 9.

156. Bernice Green, *Resistance and Redemption: A Narrative Script with Musical References* (New York: National Jewish Welfare Board, 1960), p. 2.

157. Around 1948, the Farband-Labor Zionist Order put together a sixty-three-page pamphlet for its chapters to adapt for their local programming. In this organizational booklet, *The Battle of the Warsaw Ghetto,* Jacob Katzman noted the experimental nature of the collection to be appropriate inasmuch as "we are still too close in point of time to the unforgettably epic events . . . for the proper assimilation of the battle of the Warsaw Ghetto." Katzman described what he accomplished here as "fumblings in the right direction" (Farband-Labor Zionist Order, *The Battle of the Warsaw Ghetto* [New York: Farband, n.d.], p. 1).

158. "Despite Its Serious Theme, Play About Warsaw Ghetto Uprising Captures Audience," *Jewish Forum* 43, no. 11 (December 1960), p. 208.

159. Notably, the calling together of large Jewish gatherings to commemorate the Warsaw Ghetto uprising began immediately after the ghetto was liquidized in 1943. In large meetings, like the one held in New York's Madison Square Garden and in the many local Jewish communities around the country, the Warsaw Ghetto immediately came to symbolize the devastation taking place in Europe, told in the context of the valiant fight. In Buffalo, New York, for example, six weeks after the fall of the ghetto, Jews from across the denominational spectrum joined together at Temple Beth El, to mourn collectively that the ghetto fight had ended in its inevitable failure. At that meeting, as described in 1960, the Jews had memorialized the event, which they considered the greatest "monument to human dignity" (Selig Adler and Thomas E. Connolly, *From Ararat to Suburbia: The History of the Jewish Community of Buffalo* [Philadelphia: Jewish Publication Society of America, 1960], p. 399). The Synagogue Council of America issued a call to remember the first anniversary of the uprising in April 1944, asking "all the Rabbis of the country to convoke their communities for special Services on the evening of April 19th to honor and mourn the heroes and martyrs" ("Warsaw Ghetto: First Anniversary," in box 47, "Dear Colleague" folder; Israel Goldstein to American rabbis, April 4, 1944, in box 44, "Warsaw Ghetto" folder—both in AJHS, I-68, SCA Papers). Also during the war, Jewish publications began to publish eyewitness accounts and assessments of the meaning of the uprising (Shlomo Mendelsohn, "The Battle of the Warsaw Ghetto," *Menorah Journal* 32, no. 1 [Spring 1944], pp. 5–25).

160. Victoria Secunda, *Bei Mir Bist Du Schön: The Life of Sholom Secunda* (New York: Magic Circle Press, 1982), pp. 200–201.

161. "Martyrs and Heroes of the Ghettos," in YIVO 1206, box 1, file 1.

162. "The Work of Arthur Szyk: A Memorial Exhibition of Original Miniatures and Paintings," in Ratner Center, Jewish Theological Seminary of America, RG 25, box 7, "Szyk Exhibit" folder.

163. The radio play had aired earlier than its first *Eternal Light* broadcast. NBC "Red" had broadcast it in 1943 (David Weinstein, "Maintaining Neutrality: NBC and the Holocaust," unpublished manuscript, p. 2).

164. Script for "The Battle of the Warsaw Ghetto," *Eternal Light* (radio script) (New York: Jewish Theological Seminary of America). "The Ballad of the Warsaw Ghetto" was not the only *Eternal Light* drama to tackle the Warsaw Ghetto. It also used it for "The Last Rabbi" in 1954 and "In the Beginning" in 1956 ("In the Beginning," September 23, 1956, in Ratner Center, Jewish Theological Seminary of America, RG 19, box 4, file 71).

165. Report, in AJHS, P-112, Maurice L. Zigmond Papers, box 10, "Smith Program Reports, 1951–1957" folder.

166. *Proceedings of the Seventeenth Biennial Assembly: National Federation of Temple Sisterhoods, Hotel Cleveland, Cleveland, Ohio, November 12–15, 1950,* p. 25, in AJA, Hebrew Union College, collection 73, box 4, folder 3; "Sales Brochure," in collection 73, box 39, folder 2.

167. Michael Strasser, "'A Survivor from Warsaw' as Personal Parable," *Music and Letters* 76, no. 1 (1995), pp. 60–61. I thank Jeremy Eichler for pointing me to this source and for his insights on "Survivor from Warsaw," in his unpublished paper, "Exile Beneath the Palms: Arnold Schoenberg in Los Angeles," delivered at the Center for Jewish History Graduate Fellows Seminar, December 10, 2007.

168. "Reviews of Films and Filmstrips," *Pedagogic Reporter* 6, no. 2 (November

1954), p. 5; because of its lack of a Warsaw connection, Strasser has defined the place name as a "symbolic Holocaust parable.".

169. Salo Baron, *Steeled by Adversity: Essays and Addresses on American Jewish Life* (Philadelphia: Jewish Publication Society of America, 1971), p. 546.

170. Flyers, in Chicago Jewish Archives, Spertus, collection 124, Sholem Aleichem Folk Institute Papers, box 2.

171. "Warsaw Ghetto Memorial Meeting, Saturday April 28, 1951," in YIVO 1015, box 3, file 5.

172. "Let Us Light Six *Yahrtzeit* Candles on April 19," March 26, 1951, in YIVO 1148, "World Congress for Jewish Culture," box 3, "AR, 1948–1951" folder.

173. World Jewish Congress, "Survey and Analysis of the Eleventh Anniversary Commemorations," in YIVO 1148, box 2.

174. Announcement, in University of Wisconsin–Milwaukee, New Home Club Papers, manuscript 42.

175. These memorial events were generally advertised in the *landsmanshaft* magazine, if such existed, or were announced at the monthly meetings and then postcards were sent to members. For example, *Kolbuszower Echo* 5, no. 1 (October 1948), p. 6.

176. "A Memorial Service," in YIVO 1148, box 2.

177. Bernard Carp, ed., *The Jewish Center Songster* (New York: National Jewish Welfare Board, 1949), p. 91.

178. Harry Coopersmith, *The Songs We Sing—U'leshonenu rena* (New York: United Synagogue of America, 1950), p. 149.

179. United Synagogue of America, *P'tsah b'zemer: A Basic Selection of Hebrew and Yiddish Folk Songs* (New York: United Synagogue of America Youth Commission, 1959), p. 34.

180. New England Zionist Youth Commission, *Young Judea Songster* (Boston: New England Zionist Youth Commission, 1953).

181. Young Zionist Action Committee, *Songs of Israel / Sheray Yisrael* (New York: Young Zionist Action Committee, 1949), p. 9.

182. Emma Schaver and Lazar Weiner, *Songs of the Concentration Camps* (New York: Transcontinental Press and Union of American Hebrew Congregations, 1960).

183. Chemjo Vinaver, ed., *Anthology of Jewish Music* (New York: Edward B. Marks Music, 1955), song no. 95.

184. Ruth Rubin, *A Treasury of Jewish Folksong* (New York: Schocken, 1950), pp. 12, 175–85.

185. Clipping, *Milwauker Wocheblatt*, September 26, 1947, in YIVO RG 380, ORT Papers, box 30, file 33.

186. Speech, December 21, 1951, in AJHS, I-68, SCA Papers, box 15, "25th Anniversary Dinner" folder.

187. *Morning Freiheit*, April 10, 1954, in Tamiment Library, Wagner Labor Archives, NYU, Morris U. Schappes Papers, box 1, "Correspondence" folder.

188. Louis I. Newman, *Pangs of the Messiah and Other Plays, Pageants and Cantatas* (New York: Bloch, 1957), pp. 153, 358.

189. Samuel J. Citron, *Dramatics the Year Round* (New York: United Synagogue Commission on Jewish Education, 1956), p. 171.

190. *SAJ Bulletin* 35, no. 12 (June 17, 1955), n.p.

191. Louis Horst, "Two Premieres at Festival: Group Composition and Solo," August 17, 1949, in New York Public Library (NYPL) for the Performing Arts, Sophie Maslow Clipping Files, Dance Collection; "Dudley, Bales, Maslow and Co. Perform Sun.," *Y Bulletin* 52, no. 17 (January 24, 1951); "Sophie Maslow and Company," *Dance Observer* 23, no. 10 (December 1956), pp. 152–53. My thanks to Joshua Perelman for the Sophie Maslow citations.

192. David M. Schiller, *Bloch, Schoenberg, and Bernstein: Assimilating Jewish Music* (New York: Oxford University Press, 2003), pp. 74–125; Irene Heskes, *Passport to Jewish Music: Its History, Traditions, and Culture* (Westport, Conn.: Greenwood, 1994), pp. 274–76; Arthur Holde, *Jews in Music: From the Age of Enlightenment to the Present* (New York: Philosophical Library, 1959), p. 85; Albert Weisser, *The Modern Renaissance of Jewish Music: Events and Figures of Eastern Europe and America* (New York: Bloch, 1954), pp. 158–59; *American Jewish Year Book: 1951*, p. 230. *A Survivor from Warsaw* was recorded by the Vienna Symphony in 1952, under the Columbia Records label.

193. Linenthal, *Preserving Memory*, p. 8.

194. Susannah Heschel, "Imagining Judaism in America," in *The Cambridge Companion to Jewish Literature in America*, ed. Michael P. Kramer and Hana Wirth-Nesher. (Cambridge: Cambridge University Press, 2003), p. 41.

Notes to Chapter 2

1. Shlomo Katz, "Ben Hecht Rides," *Midstream* 8, no. 1 (Winter 1962), p. 101.

2. Yossel Ostrover, "I Believe with Perfect Faith," *Jewish Spectator* 18, no. 4 (April 1953), p. 10.

3. Rufus Learsi, *Fulfillment: The Epic Story of Zionism* (Cleveland: World, 1951), p. 314; Leibush Lehrer, "A yizkor bukh voss iz andersh: *Lehrer yizkor-bukh*," *YIVO Bletter* 39 (1955), p. 355.

4. Harry Golden, "Modern Jewish Writing," *Jewish Spectator* 22, no. 4 (April 1957), p. 17.

5. Samuel Charney Niger, "Trends in Yiddish Literature," *Jewish Spectator* 24, no. 2 (February 1959), p. 17. Niger had died three years earlier, but the *Spectator* reprinted his earlier article; his reference to those "who had not been in Treblinka" pointed to a lengthy poem (discussed later in this chapter) by Hayim Leivik, "In Treblinka bin ikh nit geven" [I was not in Treblinka].

6. Max Grünewald, "Dedication Address," *Leo Baeck Institute Newsletter* 3, no. 1 (March 1962), p. 3.

7. Peter Novick, *The Holocaust in American Life* (Boston: Houghton Mifflin, 1999), p. 103.

8. David M. Schiller, " 'My Own Kaddish': Leonard Bernstein's Symphony No. 3," in *Key Texts in American Jewish Culture*, ed. Jack Kugelmass (New Brunswick, N.J.: Rutgers University Press, 2003), p. 188.

9. Alfred Werner, "The Children of Terezin," *Congress Bi-Weekly* 28, no. 16 (November 11, 1961), pp. 13–14.

10. Leo Shpall, "The Library Table," *Jewish Forum* 51, no. 4 (April 1958), p. 61.

11. "Book Reviews," *Jewish Forum* 42, no. 11 (November 1959), p. 1188.

12. Isaac I. Schwarzbart, *The Story of the Warsaw Ghetto Uprising: Its Meaning and Message* (New York: World Jewish Congress Organization Department, 1953).

13. Jodfred Tash to WCPO-TV, n.d., 1962, in AJA, Hebrew Union College, collection 202, box 35, folder 9.

14. Solomon Bloom, "Dictator of the Lodz Ghetto," *Commentary* 7 (February 1949), pp. 111–12.

15. Philip Friedman, "Reitling, Gerald, *The Final Solution: The Attempt to Exterminate the Jews of Europe, 1939–1945*," *Jewish Social Studies* 16, no. 1 (January 1954), pp. 186–89.

16. Only in 2007, for example, did the twenty million meters of archival material collected by the Germans and housed in the town of Bad Arolsen become available to the public; the opening of the Bad Arolsen archives to researchers was covered in the press. For example, Andrew Curry, "The Nazi Chronicles: Closed for Decades, the World's Largest Holocaust Archive Now Reveals Its Secrets," *U.S. News and World Report* (May 13, 2007).

17. Jacob Lestchinsky, *Balance Sheet of Extermination* (New York: Institute for Jewish Affairs, 1946); Jacob Lestchinsky, *Crisis, Catastrophe, and Survival* (New York: American Jewish Congress, 1948); Anatole Goldstein, *From Discrimination to Annihilation* (New York: Institute for Jewish Affairs, 1952); Institute for Jewish Affairs, *European Jewry Ten Years After the War: An Account of the Development and Present Status of the Decimated Jewish Community of Europe* (New York: World Jewish Congress, 1956).

18. Paul Massing, *Rehearsal for Destruction: A Study of Political Anti-Semitism in Imperial Germany* (New York: Harper Brothers, 1949); Nathan W. Ackerman and Marie Jahoda, *Anti-Semitism and Emotional Disorder: A Psychoanalytic Interpretation* (New York: Harper Brothers, 1950).

19. Selma G. Hirsh, *The Fears Men Live By* (New York: Harper Brothers, 1955).

20. Leon Poliakov, *Harvest of Hate: The Nazi Program for the Destruction of the Jews of Europe* (Syracuse, N.Y.: Syracuse University Press, 1954). Text quotation from "Why Study Post-War Problems," vol. 1, p. 7; *American Jewish Year Book: 1955*, p. 642.

21. On the American Jewish Committee and Schneersohn, see Laura Jockusch, "'Collect and Record! Help to Write the History of the Latest Destruction!' Jewish Historical Commissions in Europe, 1943–1953," Ph.D. diss., New York University, 2007, pp. 374–75.

22. Ibid., pp. 181–82.

23. "JLC Summary of Activities, December, 1946," in Tamiment Library, Wagner Labor Achives, NYU, Julius Bernstein Papers, box 13.

24. Joseph Kissman, "A Record to Remember," *Jewish Labor Commission Outlook* 1, no. 1 (Summer 1954), pp. 9–10.

25. *Jewish Book Annual: 5712, 1951–1952*, p. 55.

26. Clipping, "Two LaMed Prize Yiddish Books," *Congress Weekly*, in YIVO 526, box 7, file 189; Philip Goodman to Louis Lamed, April 19, 1945, box 6, file 170; *Der Tog*, May 7, 1958, clipping, in box 7, file 189; Aharon Kessler to Louis Lamed, May 28, 1948, in box 5, file 164—all in YIVO 526, Louis Lamed Papers. See also Shmuel Charney Niger, *Kiddush hashem* (New York: Central Yiddish Culture Organization, 1947).

27. On the involvement of YIVO with media presentations of the Holocaust, see, for example, *Yedios* 75 (July 1960), p. 4. The *Yedios* headline reads, "YIVO Pictures

Help Win Award," and the article noted that, in 1959, CBS used YIVO's material for a program, "The Warsaw Ghetto." In 1963, *Yedios* reported that NBC "presented a YIVO program on the Warsaw Ghetto and the Uprising," with a script by novelist Howard Fast and starring Celeste Holme and Dana Clark (*Yedios* 86 [June 1963], p. 5).

28. Fruma Mohrer and Marek Webb, *Guide to YIVO Archives* (New York: YIVO Institute for Jewish Research, 1998), p. xiii.

29. "Jews in Europe, 1939–1946," *Yedios* 17 (November 1946), p. 1.

30. *Yedios* 18 (December 1946), p. 6.

31. Max Weinreich, *Hitler's Professors: The Part of Scholarship in Germany's Crimes Against the Jewish People* (New York: YIVO Institute for Jewish Research, 1946).

32. *Yedios* 52 (March 1954), p. 7.

33. *Yedios* 46 (September 1952); *Yedios* 49 (June 1953), p. 7; *Yedios* 50 (September 1953), p. 8.

34. *Yedios* 69 (December 1958), pp. 4–5; *Yedios* 70 (April 1959), p. 472; *Yedios* 73 (January 1960), p. 7. Other exhibitions on the Lithuanian city of Vilna, where YIVO had been before its flight to New York, on the historian Simon Dubnow, and on the Yiddish language all provided opportunities for YIVO to tell about the Holocaust, using its materials, through a specific angle or context.

35. Joshua L. Liebman to Fanny Goldstein, June 6, 1945, in AJA, Hebrew Union College, collection 205, Fanny Goldstein Papers, box 2, folder 7.

36. Ronald W. Zweig, *German Reparations and the Jewish World: A History of the Claims Conference*, 2nd ed. (London: Frank Cass, 2001), pp. 222–23, 157.

37. "Report of the Study Committee, 1958," in AJHS, I-319, Claims Conference Papers, box 1, in particular, p. 69.

38. "World Congress for Jewish Culture, 1948–1956," in Tamiment Library, Wagner Labor Archives, NYU, Jacob Pat Papers, box 1, "World Congress for Jewish Culture" folder; Boris Smolar, "Between You and Me, September 25, 1959," in AJHS, P-588, Boris Smolar Papers, "Between You and Me, 1957–1960" folder; Jewish Labor Committee, "The Jewish Labor Committee and a Quarter-Century of Human Rights Progress, March, 1960," in Tamiment Library, Wagner Labor Archives, NYU, Edward S. Goldstein Papers, box 2, file 23; "Hebraica," Library of Congress, *Quarterly Journal of Current Acquisitions* 17, no. 2 (February 1960), pp. 111–12.

39. Henry Shoskes, *No Traveler Returns: The Story of Hitler's Greatest Crime* (Garden City, N.Y.: Doubleday, Doran, 1945), p. 267.

40. Helen Waren, *The Buried Are Screaming* (New York: Beechhurst, 1948), pp. 9, 185.

41. Bernard Goldstein, *The Stars Bear Witness*, trans. Leonard Shatzkin (New York: Viking, 1949).

42. Joseph Tenenbaum, *Underground: The Story of a People* (New York: Philosophical Library, 1952).

43. Joseph Tenenbaum, *Race and Reich: The Story of an Epoch* (New York: Twayne, 1956); Boris Smolar, "JTA Features: Between You and Me," March 2, 1956, in AJHS, P-588, Boris Smolar Papers, box 10. Reviewers differed about this and all the other books. They differed not over the issue of whether the material should be made available and be discussed widely but on which books did a better job. Koppel Pinson reviewed the Tenenbaum book for *Jewish Social Studies*, and while he found it a

"worthwhile addition," he opined that it added little "new to the materials already available. . . . But it is a more comprehensive synthesis of Nazi racial policies than any . . . other existing volumes" (Koppel Pinson, "Tenenbaum, Joseph, *Race and Reich: Story of an Epoch*," *Jewish Social Studies* 18, no. 4 [October 1956], p. 309).

44. Gerda Weissman Klein, *All but My Life* (New York: Hill and Wang, 1957).

45. Jacob Sloan, ed., *Notes from the Warsaw Ghetto: The Journal of Emmanuel Ringelblum* (New York: McGraw-Hill, 1958).

46. Randolph L. Braham, *Eichmann and the Destruction of Hungarian Jewry* (New York: Twayne, 1961).

47. Elie Weisel, *Night* (New York: Hill and Wang, 1960).

48. Kitty Hart, *I Am Alive* (New York: Coward-McCann, 1960); Andre Schwarz-Bart, *The Last of the Just* (New York: Bantam, 1961).

49. Raul Hilberg, *The Destruction of the European Jews* (Chicago: Quadrangle, 1961). Hilberg's book received mixed but extensive reaction in Jewish publications. Saul Esh, writing in *Judaism*, noted that, despite some reservations he had about the book, "I must acknowledge the indebtedness that I and everyone else engaged in research on the Nazi period owe to him" (Saul Esh, "Review: Raul Hilberg, *The Destruction of the European Jews*," *Judaism* 12, no. 1 [Winter 1963], pp. 113–18).

50. Meyer Barkai, *Fighting Ghettos* (New York: Lippincott, 1962).

51. The other two full-length historical works on the Holocaust of this period were American editions of books initially published elsewhere, particularly Leon Poliakov, *Breviarire de la Haine: Le IIIe Reich et les Juifs* (Paris: Calmann-Levy, 1951), published in the United States as *Harvest of Hate: The Nazi Program for the Destruction of the Jews of Europe* (Syracuse, N.Y.: Syracuse University Press, 1954), and Gerald Reitlinger, *The Final Solution: The Attempt to Exterminate the Jews of Europe, 1939–1945* (London: Valentine, Mitchell, 1953), published in the United States the same year by Beechhurst. Reitlinger's American Jewish commentators lamented the lack of a single general history of the "destruction of nearly all European Jews," as Solomon F. Bloom referred to the Holocaust in a review essay in *Commentary* 10 (January 1955), pp. 89–91, which considered Reitlinger and Poliakov, as well as two other books.

52. John Hersey, *The Wall* (New York: Knopf, 1950).

53. Anne Frank, *The Diary of a Young Girl*, intro. Eleanor Roosevelt, trans. B. M. Mooyaart (New York: Bantam, 1952).

54. Sloan, *Notes from the Warsaw Ghetto*; Leon Uris, *Exodus* (Garden City, N.Y.: Doubleday, 1958), and *Mila 18* (Garden City, N.Y.: Doubleday, 1961); Meyer Levin, *Eva* (New York: Simon and Schuster, 1959); and Albert C. Todd, ed., *The Collected Poems of Yevgeny Yevtushenko* (New York: Holt, 1991), pp. 102–4.

55. For just a smattering of these, see Joel Carmichael, "The Phenomenon Leon Uris," *Midstream* 7, no. 4 (Autumn 1961), pp. 86–90; Eugene Lyon, "Russia's Megaton Poet," *Midstream* 7, no. 4 (Autumn 1961), pp. 7–17; Boris Smolar, "Babi-Yar Reverberations: JTA, Between You and Me," October 13, 1961, and Boris Smolar, "Contemporary History: JTA, Between You and Me," August 21, 1959—both in AJHS, P-588, Boris Smolar Papers, box 10, p. 1, and box 11, p. 1, respectively.

56. Harold U. Ribalow, "Do Jews Read?" *Congress Weekly* 18, no. 25 (October 8, 1951), pp. 10–12.

57. Aaron Zeitlin, "Letter," *Jewish Spectator* 18, no. 4 (April 1953), p. 29.

58. Marie Syrkin, *Blessed Is the Match: The Story of Jewish Resistance* (New York: Knopf, 1947); Rachmil Bryks, *A Cat in the Ghetto: Four Novelettes* (New York: Bloch, 1959). The reviews and advertisements for *A Cat in the Ghetto* are in the New York Public Library (NYPL), Rare Books and Manuscripts Division, Bloch Publishers, box 1, file 18. The importance of the Eleanor Roosevelt letter was demonstrated by a clipping included in the papers of Bloch Publishers and taken from the *Bulletin* of the East Midwood Jewish Center of January 1960. The "Booknotes" section included a lengthy review of *A Cat in the Ghetto*, which noted that reading the book required "a courageous strong heart" and the characters "become part of our memory-family." This congregational booknote also reprinted in its entirety the Roosevelt letter and added, "I do not disagree with Mrs. Roosevelt. But I must warn our readers that her attitude is an understatement," as to the difficulty of the book.

59. Boris Smolar, "Between You and Me," June 6, 1959, in AJHS, P-588, p. 622.

60. Shmuel Lapin, "An Era That Must Be Remembered," *Farband News* 5, no. 1 (November–December 1959), p. 5.

61. Philip Goodman, "A Chronicle of the Jewish Book Council of America," *Jewish Book Annual* 25 (New York: National Jewish Welfare Board, 1967–1968), pp. 366–89.

62. *Jewish Book Annual: 5709, 1948–1949*, p. 3.

63. Ibid., pp. 19–23. In addition, Bloch described Meyer Levin's *In My Father's House*, Zelda Popkin's *Small Victory*, and Arnold Zeig's *The Axe of Wandsbeck* as pieces of fiction which, while focusing on the illegal immigration to Palestine, the Displaced Persons camps, and the Nazis, respectively, pivoted around the Holocaust narrative (ibid.).

64. *Jewish Book Annual: 5709, 1948–1949*, pp. 23–42.

65. Ibid., pp. 58–62. The Yiddish and Hebrew essays are paginated by means of Hebrew letters.

66. *Jewish Book Annual: 5711, 1950–1951*, pp. 12–14.

67. *Jewish Book Annual: 5714–5715, 1953–1955*, p. 91.

68. *Jewish Book Annual: 5720, 1959–1960*, pp. 98, 103, 104, 106.

69. *Jewish Book Annual: 5721, 1960–1961*, pp. 158–60.

70. *Jewish Book Annual: 5712, 1951–1952*, p. 32; *Jewish Book Annual: 5720, 1959–1960*, p. 131; *Jewish Book Annual: 5715–5716, 1955–1956*, p. 109; *Jewish Book Annual: 5722, 1961–1962*, p. 171.

71. "Summary: Yiddish Section—A Review of B. I. Bialosotzky, *Yiddish Literature After the Hitler Tragedy*," in *Jewish Book Annual: 5709, 1948–1949*, pp. 114–15.

72. Ibid., p. 114.

73. B. I. Bialosotzky, "American Yiddish Literature," in *Jewish Book Annual: 5714–5715, 1953–1955*, pp. 43–44.

74. "Schwarz," in NYPL, Rare Books and Manuscripts Division, Farrar, Straus and Giroux Papers, box 316.

75. This aspect of Jewish organizational "human relations" work of the postwar period is well documented in Stuart Svonkin, *Jews Against Prejudice: American Jews and the Fight for Civil Liberties* (New York: Columbia University Press, 1997).

76. Jewish Community Relations Committee, Regular Meeting Minutes, November 10, 1958, in AJA, Hebrew Union College, collection 283, box 11, folder 4.

77. For example, Leon I. Feur, *On Being a Jew* (New York: Bloch, 1947), pp. 3, 14–15, 24, 101, 269, 276; Morris N. Kertzer, *What Is a Jew?* (Cleveland: World, 1960), pp. xxi–xxii, 45, 48, 178–79, 190–91; Maxwell D. Silver, *The Way to God* (New York: Philosophical Library, 1950), pp. 3–4. See also Will Herberg, *Judaism and Modern Man: An Interpretation of Jewish Religion* (Philadelphia: Jewish Publication Society of America, 1951), p. 3; Eric Gutkind, *Choose Life: The Biblical Call to Revolt* (New York: Harry Schuman, 1952), pp. 12–13, 33–34, 62, 69. As well, references to the Holocaust, the Nazis, and Hitler appear in nearly every chapter of Joachim Prinz, *The Dilemma of the Modern Jew* (Boston: Little, Brown, 1962).

78. David da Sola Pool, *Why I Am a Jew* (Boston: Beacon, 1957), p. 190.

79. Robert Gordis, *Judaism for the Modern Age* (New York: Farrar, Straus, and Cudahy, 1955), pp. 20, 70–71, 95, 109–10.

80. Philip Bernstein to Roger W. Straus, January 18, 1960, in NYPL, Rare Books and Manuscripts Division, Farrar, Straus and Giroux Papers, box 25, "Bernstein" folder.

81. Philip S. Bernstein, *What the Jews Believe* (New York: Farrar, Straus and Young, 1951), pp. 40, 96. It is worth noting that Jewish organizations and Jewish communities hailed the Bernstein book. The Jewish Community Relations Committee of Cincinnati placed copies in the city's public libraries and sent copies to key individuals, with the "compliments of the Community Relations Committee in cooperation with the Cincinnati Chapter of the American Jewish Committee. Your name was suggested to us as a key person in our community who might be interested in reading this informative material" (in AJA, Hebrew Union College, collection 202, box 31, folder 2).

82. Reuben Wallenrod, *The Literature of Modern Israel* (New York: Abelard-Schuman, 1956), pp. 1, 5.

83. Leo Schwarz, ed., *Great Ages and Ideas of the Jewish People* (New York: Modern Library, 1956), p. xviii; see also pp. 286, 313–486.

84. Bernard Postal and Samuel H. Abramson, *The Landmarks of a People: A Guide to Jewish Sites in Europe* (New York: Hill and Wang, 1962), pp. vi, 127, 129.

85. Ibid., p. 4. The authors included this kind of material for every relevant country. Harry Simonhoff in *Under Strange Skies* (New York: Philosophical Library, 1953), in his section on Denmark, noted how "the traveler is constantly reminded of the contrast between the Scandinavians and the Germans. Historians say both are of the same Teutonic stock. Yet the former are peaceful and human . . . the Germans acted more like beasts than human beings" (p. 31).

86. Meyer Waxman, Sulamith Ish-Kishor, and Jacob Sloan, *Blessed Is the Daughter* (New York: Shengold, 1959), p. 10. See also Abraham L. Katsh, ed., *Bar Mitzvah: Illustrated* (New York: Shengold, 1955), pp. 2984–87, 151; Azriel Eisenberg, ed., *The Bar Mitzvah Treasury* (New York: Behrman House, 1952), pp. 98–102, 144–50, 205–12, 234–36, 297–300.

87. Nathan Ausubel, *Pictorial History of the Jewish People* (New York: Crown, 1953), pp. 254–69. Bernard Richards of the Jewish Information Bureau expressed concern to Arthur Hayes Sulzberger that the Ausubel book, in which "unfortunately the treatment of the Jews under the Soviets and satellite countries is written from a distinctly pro-Soviet attitude," would be "put across on a large scale" by the publisher (Bernard

Richards to Arthur Sulzberger, December 17, 1953, in Ratner Center, Jewish Theological Seminary of America, Bernard Richards Papers, archive 96, box 12).

88. Gerald Sorin, in *Tradition Transformed: The Jewish Experience in America* (Baltimore: Johns Hopkins University Press, 1997), p. 217, labeled the Holocaust "taboo" in the years before 1967.

89. One medium of communication within the American Jewish world that cannot be adequately treated here is synagogue bulletins, the hundreds of weekly or monthly newsletters issued by synagogues to their members. A suggestive example of what might be learned is drawn from the *SAJ Bulletin*, of New York's Reconstructionist congregation, the Society for the Advancement of Judaism. Not only did the *SAJ Bulletin* inform members where and how, in the late 1940s, to contribute money for the "Support Overseas Survivors" project, but it also published letters that congregants had received about their relatives in Europe. In February 1946, synagogue members could read the following letter: "I have been in touch with a distant relative who was in a German concentration camp for over a year and seems to be in desperate need of help." The relative needed someone to furnish an affidavit, and the SAJ member asked if anyone in the congregation could help. Likewise, this very small publication tracked books being published on the subject of the Holocaust, suggesting that members read them. In the September 8, 1950, issue, it highlighted Marie Syrkin's *Blessed Is the Match*. This small publication suggests a potential source for studying the ways in which the Holocaust got discussed and disseminated among American Jews in the postwar period. If multiplied by the number of congregations that had such bulletins, it can be an illuminating source.

90. These numbers are based on the 1950 and 1959 volumes of the *American Jewish Year Book*, which annually listed all Jewish publications, worldwide.

91. Elliott Cohen, "An Act of Affirmation: Editorial Statement," *Commentary* 1, no. 1 (November 1945), p. 1; Salo Baron, "The Spiritual Reconstruction of European Jewry," ibid., pp. 4–12.

92. Shlomo Katz, "Statement of Purpose," *Midstream* 1, no. 1 (Autumn 1955), p. 1.

93. Julius Horowitz, "Dachau—1955," *Midstream* 1, no. 1 (Autumn 1955), pp. 2–4; Ben Halpern, "America Is Different," ibid., pp. 39–52 .

94. Norman Lamm, "The Need for Tradition: The Editor's Introduction to a New Journal," *Tradition* 1, no. 1 (Fall 1958), p. 10.

95. Emanuel Rackman, "Arrogance or Humility in Prayer," *Tradition* 1, no. 1 (Fall 1958), p. 23; "Book Review: Arthur Gilbert and Oscar Tarcov, *Your Neighbor Celebrates*," ibid., p. 130. See also "Book Review: *Joseph Carlebach and His Generation*," p. 95, and "Review of Halakhic Periodical Literature," p. 80—both in *Tradition* 3, no. 1 (Fall 1960).

96. It would be quite useful to also scan articles in general American magazines in which Jewish writers presented the Holocaust to a wide readership. As a suggestion for the availability of this kind of magazine, Andrew R. Heinze notes that Boston rabbi Joshua Loth Leibman speculated about the Holocaust in a 1948 article in *Ladies' Home Journal*; *Newsweek* then reprinted it (Heinze, *Jews and the American Soul: Human Nature in the Twentieth Century* [Princeton: Princeton University Press, 2004], pp. 213–14). Several articles by American Jews in general magazines also tackled the Holocaust: a small sample includes Saul Padover, "And the Germans Jeered," *Saturday Review* 30, no.

31 (August 2, 1947), pp. 9–10; William Zuckerman, "They Found Friends," *Readers Digest* 50, no. 299 (March 1947), pp. 102–4; Harold U. Ribelow, "Reading for Jews," *Saturday Review* 37, no. 10 (March 6, 1954), pp. 49–51; Charles Angoff, "John Hersey's Ghetto," *American Mercury* 70, no. 317 (May 1950), pp. 623–31; and Alfred Kazin, "The Least of These," *Reporter* 23, no. 7 (October 27, 1960), pp. 54–56. Indeed, a thorough and creative investigation would yield many more.

97. These titles by no means exhaust the Jewish magazines published at the time or consulted for this book.

98. Trude Weiss-Rosmarin, "Comments and Opinions," *Jewish Spectator* 18, no. 4 (April 1953), p. 4.

99. Trude Weiss-Rosmarin, "Lest We Forget," *Jewish Spectator* 19, no. 5 (May 1954), pp. 27–29.

100. Joseph Schechtman, "My Visit to Babi Yar," *Midstream* 5, no. 4 (Autumn 1959), pp. 49–57.

101. Andre Ungar, "Hungarian Memories," *Jewish Spectator* 24, no. 8 (June 1959), pp. 10–14, and *Jewish Spectator* 24, no. 10 (October 1959), pp. 21–24.

102. Charles Angoff, "In the Margin," *Jewish Spectator* 24, no. 2 (February 1959), pp. 21–24. For analysis of Leivik's work, see Sol Liptzin, *The Flowering of Yiddish Literature* (New York: Thomas Yoseloff, 1963), p. 230. See also "Comments and Opinions," *Jewish Spectator* 24, no. 5 (May 1959), pp. 7, 19.

103. Rachmil Bryks, "Rivka'le's kiddush hashem," *Jewish Spectator* 21, no. 6 (June 1956), pp. 19–20; A. Sutzkever, "Short Tales," *Jewish Spectator* 19, no. 1 (January 1954), pp. 14–16. See also K. Tzetnik, "On the Road to the Crematorium," *Jewish Spectator* 19, no. 5 (May 1954), pp. 18–19.

104. Fishel Shneirsohn, "Ani Ma'amin—I Believe," *Conservative Judaism* 12, no. 3 (Spring 1958), pp. 20–30.

105. Aharon Megged, "The Name," *Midstream* 6, no. 2 (Spring 1960), pp. 61–71.

106. Marie Syrkin, "My Uncle in Treblinka," *Jewish Frontier* 12, no. 6 (June 1945), p. 16.

107. Elaine Toby Kaplan, "Poems," *Jewish Spectator* 21, no. 10 (December 1956), p. 12.

108. Harold Shapiro, "The Six Million Speak!" *Jewish Spectator* 22, no. 4 (April 1957), p. 6; Hilda Marx, "The Six Million to Job," *Jewish Spectator* 24, no. 6 (June 1959), p. 15.

109. Kadya Molodowsky, "Premier Yiddish Books," clipping, *Der Kempfer*, in YIVO 526, Louis Lamed Papers, box 7, file 189. A monumental but crucial research project awaits the scholar who would study the daily Yiddish press of the postwar years and uncover patterns of engagement with the "hurban."

110. *American Jewish Year Book: 1958*, p. 147.

111. Ibid., pp. 147–53, 250–55, 286–302, 504.

112. Ibid., pp. 294–95.

113. *American Jewish Year Book: 1955*, pp. 355–56.

114. The American Jewish Historical Society I-61 is a major collection of Jewish student periodicals and contains full runs of *Furrows*, the magazine of Habonim; *Youth and Nation*, the official publication of Hashomer Hatzair; and *The Senior*, Young Judea's newsletter.

115. Speech, Annual Meeting of Habonim, *Furrows* 5, no. 9 (October 1947), p. 8; David Halperin, *Furrows* 11, no. 4 (April 1954), p. 14; Carole Weiss, *Furrows* 13, no. 11 (May 1956), p. 8.

116. *Youth Leader: A Magazine for Jewish Youth Groups* 9, no. 3 (Spring 1948), p. 28, in AJA, Hebrew Union College, collection 266, box 1, folder 6.

117. Dozens of Jewish communities had a weekly newspaper, like Boston's *Jewish Advocate*, Chicago's *Jewish Sentinel*, and Milwaukee's *Wisconsin Jewish Chronicle*. These newspapers deserve a full-length treatment in terms of their dealing with the details of the Holocaust, both as history and as a factor in the contemporary lives of the local Jewish public.

118. Philip Friedman, "American Jewish Research and Literature on the Jewish Catastrophe of 1939–1945," *Jewish Social Studies* 13, no. 3 (July 1951), pp. 235–50; Joseph Tenenbaum, "Auschwitz in Retrospect: The Self-Portrait of Rudolf Hoess, Commander of Auschwitz," *Jewish Social Studies* 15, nos. 3–4 (July–October 1953), pp. 203–36; Joseph Tenenbaum, "Einsatzgruppen," *Jewish Social Studies* 17, no. 1 (January 1955), pp. 43–64; Julius S. Fisher, "How Many Jews Died in Transnistria," *Jewish Social Studies* 20, no. 1 (January 1958), pp. 95–101; Bernard Klein, "The Judenrat," *Jewish Social Studies* 22, no. 1 (January 1960), pp. 27–42.

119. Salo Baron, "Problems of Research in the Study of the Jewish Catastrophe 1939–1945," *Jewish Social Studies* 12, no. 1 (January 1950).

120. "Tentative List of Jewish Cultural Treasures in Axis-Occupied Countries," *Jewish Social Studies* 8, no. 1 (suppl.) (January 1946), pp. 5–9; "Tentative List of Jewish Cultural Treasures in Axis-Occupied Countries," *Jewish Social Studies* 10, no. 1 (suppl.) (January 1948), pp. 3–16; "Tentative List of Jewish Educational Institutions in Axis-Occupied Countries," *Jewish Social Studies* 8, no. 3 (suppl.) (July 1946), pp. 5–8; "Tentative List of Jewish Publishers of Judaica and Hebraica in Axis-Occupied Countries," *Jewish Social Studies* 10, no. 2 (suppl.) (April 1948), n.p. The "treasures" listing was also published in the special January 1950 issue and in the *Joshua Starr Memorial Volume*.

121. *Publications of the American Jewish Historical Society*, founded in 1892, dealt exclusively with American Jewish history.

122. Dora Edinger, "Bertha Pappenheim (1859–1936)," *Jewish Social Studies* 20, no. 3 (July 1958), pp. 180–86. Another example is Samuel Gringauz, "Jewish National Autonomy in Lithuania (1918–1925)," *Jewish Social Studies* 14, no. 3 (July 1952), pp. 225–46.

123. Yudl Mark, "Philip Friedman," *Jewish Book Annual* 18 (1960–61), p. 80.

124. Edward Sachar to Philip Friedman, November 27, 1951, in YIVO 1258, I-380, Philip Friedman Papers.

125. American Academy for Jewish Research, "Twenty-First Annual Meeting, December 26, 1948," in YIVO 1258, Philip Friedman Papers, box 36, file 687.

126. *Jewish Book Annual: 5721, 1960–1961*, p. 81.

127. Philip Friedman, "The Jews of Greece During the Second World War," in *The Joshua Starr Memorial Volume: Studies in History and Philology*, ed. Conference on Jewish Relations (New York: Conference on Jewish Relations, 1953), pp. 241–48; Philip Friedman, "American Jewish Research and Literature on the Jewish Catastrophe of 1939–1945," *Jewish Social Studies* 13, no. 3 (July 1951), pp. 235–50.

128. For example, Philip Friedman to Dr. Neiman, January 13, 1958, in YIVO 1258, I-284; P. Friedman to Riverdale Temple, September 13, 1955, in YIVO 1258, I-285.

129. Friedman's most notable English books were *Martyrs and Fighters: The Epic of the Warsaw Ghetto* (New York: Praeger, 1954), *Their Brother's Keepers* (New York: Crown, 1957), and, with Jacob Robinson, *Guide to Jewish History Under Nazi Impact* (New York: YIVO Insitute for Jewish Research, 1960).

130. Koppel S. Pinson, *Modern Germany: Its History and Civilization* (New York: Macmillan, 1954). For reviews and clippings about the reaction to this book, see NYPL, Rare Books and Manuscripts Division, Koppel S. Pinson Papers.

131. Simon Dubnow, *Nationalism and History: Essays on Old and New Judaism*, ed. Koppel S. Pinson (Philadelphia: Jewish Publication Society of America, 1958). For extensive and positive reviews and clippings, see NYPL, Rare Books and Manuscripts Division, Koppel S. Pinson Papers. Pinson wrote the entry on Dubnow for the *Encyclopedia Britannica*, stating succinctly that Dubnow had lived in Berlin "until the advent of Hitler forced him . . . into exile and he went to Riga in Latvia. Here he remained until he met his tragic end at the hands of the Nazis when they liquidated the Jewish population of Riga in December, 1941" (Pinson Papers, box 1).

132. Salo Baron, "The Modern Age," in *Great Ages and Ideas of the Jewish People*, ed. Leo Schwarz (New York: Modern Library, 1956), pp. 312–486. On Baron and his ideas of Jewish history, see Robert Liberles, *Salo Wittmayer Baron: Architect of Jewish History* (New York: New York University Press, 1995).

133. Dagobert D. Runes, ed., *The Hebrew Impact on Western Civilization* (New York: Philosophical Library, 1951), p. ix. See also Emil Bernhard Cohn, *This Immortal People: One Hour of Jewish History* (New York: Behrman House, 1945), pp. 116–17; Solomon Landman and Benjamin Efron, *Story Without End: An Informal History of the Jewish People* (New York: Holt, 1949), pp. 234–35.

134. Uriel Weinreich, ed., *The Field of Yiddish: Studies in Yiddish Language, Folklore, and Literature* (New York: Linguistic Circle of New York, 1954), p. v. See also Joseph Leftwich, *The Golden Peacock: A Worldwide Treasury of Yiddish Poetry* (New York: Thomas Yoseloff, 1961), p. 18. In *Treasury of Jewish Folklore* (New York: Crown, 1948), Nathan Ausubel anticipated the emergence of a folklore of the Holocaust: "It is perhaps too early for the emergence of a legend out of the staggering tragedy of the six million Jews murdered in the charnel houses of Hitler. . . . Yet that time will surely come" (p. xxi).

135. It is beyond the scope of this book to systematically examine several other vehicles by which American Jews presented the Holocaust, including radio and television, film, and museum exhibitions. Suffice it to say here that such radio shows as *The Eternal Light*, sponsored by the Jewish Theological Seminary of America, and the weekly Yiddish broadcasts of actress Molly Picon narrated the details of the Holocaust extensively. Similarly, the United Jewish Appeal made several fundraising films that told of the Holocaust, focusing particularly on the needs of the survivors, and the Jewish Museum, also a project of the Jewish Theological Seminary, displayed the artistic works of Holocaust survivors depicting the memories of their experiences. In addition, various Jewish organizations used the medium of radio to address primarily Jewish audiences. The Synagogue Council of America, for example, issued numerous messages over the radio, and these remarks often included Holocaust references. In 1963, as one of many

examples, Rabbi Julius Mark delivered a "Purim Message," presumably to America's Jews, and he noted in describing the holiday that "many scholars of the Bible regard this story as fictional rather than factual. They claim that none of the figures portrayed in this ancient tale ever existed. There is nothing fictional about a plot to destroy a Jewish community. Pharaoh and Torquemada tried it. So did Hitler who, alas, was more successful in carrying out his barbarous intentions than was Haman" (Julius Mark, "A Purim Message," in AJHS, I-68, SCA Papers, box 50, "New Releases 1961–1964" folder).

136. AAUW Speech, October 20, 1948, in AJHS, P-678, Robison Family Papers, box 14, file 3.

137. All of these, and dozens of other talks by Pinson on the Holocaust, are in NYPL, Rare Books and Manuscripts Division, Koppel S. Pinson Papers, box 4.

138. American Jewish Committee, *Proceedings of the Fiftieth Anniversary Observance of the American Jewish Committee, April 10–14, 1957: The Pursuit of Equality at Home and Abroad* (New York: American Jewish Committee, 1958), pp. xi, 3, 27, 40, 133, 140–41, 199, 226, 228.

139. For example, "Transactions of the XVI Biennial Assembly, National Federation of Temple Sisterhoods [hereafter, NFTS], March, 1946," in AJA, Hebrew Untion College, collection 73, box 5, folder 4, pp. 18–22, 93–102, 185.

140. Isaac Neuman, "Transactions of the XXI Biennial Assembly, NFTS, April 27–May 2, 1957," in ibid., pp. 33, 36.

141. "Transactions of the XXII Biennial Assembly, NFTS, November 15–19, 1959," in ibid., p. 6.

142. "Transactions of the XXIII Biennial Assembly, NFTS, November, 1961," in ibid., n.p.

143. Isaiah Minkoff, "What Is Our Stake in the American Jewish Community?" speech at Annual Conference, Workmen's Circle Division of the Jewish Labor Commission, September 19, 1954, in Tamiment Library, Wagner Labor Archives, NYU, Isaiah Minkoff Papers, box 12, file 9. See also "Remarks at Jewish War Veterans Convention, 10/24/55," December 10, 1955, and "Speech Plenary, 1954, National Community Relations Advisory Committee," both in ibid.

144. "Jewish Youth at Midcentury," Camp Wel-Met, Narrowsburg, New York, August 30, 1951–September 7, 1951, in AJA, Hebrew Union College, collection 266, box 2, folder 8, p. 12.

145. Bicentennial Committee, *The Souvenir Book of the Bicentennial: The Story of the Celebration of the Bicentennial of the Charleston Jewish Community November 19 Through November 26, 1950* (Charleston, S.C.: Bicentennial Committee, 1951), p. 123.

146. No archival holdings have collected these lectures. Rather, they show up almost randomly in the papers of individuals who gave them or in the archival materials and printed newsletters of the organizations that sponsored them. By definition, all the material included here is ad hoc and can be assumed to represent a mere fraction of such presentations.

147. Hans Morgenthau, *The Tragedy of German-Jewish Liberalism*, Leo Baeck Memorial Lecture 4 (New York: Leo Baeck Institute, 1961), pp. 5–6, 10, 11.

148. An entire world of Yiddish lectures also existed around the country, and

many of these talks either presented the Holocaust as the theme or drew implications from it. Samuel Charney Niger offered three talks in Yiddish at the Jewish Theological Seminary between 1946 and 1951 and then published them together. Each talk extensively explored aspects of the Holocaust. In the second of these lectures, given in 1950, he invoked the familiar Yiddish phrase "der dritten hurban" (the third destruction) as "the conventional way in which we refer to the destruction of European Jewry" (Samuel Charney Niger, Yisrael: Folk un land—Drei redes [Chicago: L. M. Stein, 1952], p. 28).

149. In University of Wisconsin–Milwaukee, Wisconsin Society for Jewish Learning, manuscript 132, box 1, files 1 and 9; box 2, file 4.

150. "Annual Reports," in AJHS, I-240, Young Israel Papers, box 1.

151. College of Jewish Studies, Annual Bulletin, 1947–1948, 1948–1949, 1951–1952, 1959–1960, 1964–1965, in Chicago Jewish Archives, Spertus.

152. "The Contribution of Jewish Composers to the Music of the Modern World," in AJA, Hebrew Union College, collection 73, box 35, folder 1; "Program and Study Materials, 1945–1946," 1947–1948, in ibid., box 36, file 1.

153. Sarah Kussy, Handbook and Guide for Jewish Women's Organizations (New York: National Women's League of the United Synagogue of America, 1947), pp. 37, 41, 52, 54, 70–71.

154. Simon Noveck, ed., Contemporary Jewish Thought: A Reader (New York: B'nai B'rith Department of Adult Jewish Education, 1963), p. 177; Simon Noveck, ed., Great Jewish Thinkers of the Twentieth Century (Washington, D.C.: B'nai B'rith Department of Adult Jewish Education, 1963), pp. 133–57.

155. Sidney L. Markowitz, What Do You Know About Jewish Religion, History, Ethics and Culture? A Comprehensive Book Covering Every Phase of Jewish Life for the Past 3500 Years (New York: Saphrograph, 1954), pp. 39–43, 47, 88.

156. In the pedagogic journal Jewish Education of 1960, Harold Margolin, reviewing M. H. Lewittes's "student version" of the Diary of a Young Girl, suggested that this might provide a beginning of the study of the Holocaust in public schools. While the reviewer thought the material was pitched a bit too low for high school students and that it did not include enough "on the nature of Hitlerism and its relationship to the Jews," the book still should be applauded because "the important thing is that schools can now introduce their students to this book; that greater numbers will have an opportunity to get to know Anne, her family and friends; that her life and her death will continue to influence those who follow her" (Margolin, Jewish Education 31, no. 1 [Fall 1960], p. 64).

157. The topic of Jewish education and the Holocaust has been excellently treated in Rona Sheramy, "Defining Lessons: The Holocaust in American Jewish Education," Ph.D. diss., Brandeis University, 2001. Sheramy emphasized the degree to which Jewish educators told (or, better, "overtold") the story of Jewish heroism and resistance in their curricular materials in order to provide a more palatable message to American Jews. This is a somewhat limited view and does not stand up fully to the broad sweep of the evidence. The discussions in textbooks and magazines like World Over, published throughout this period by the Jewish Education Committee, set the material on heroism against the larger and deeper context of the massive Jewish death toll and the destruction of most of European Jewish communal life.

418   Notes to Chapter 2

158. Flyer, "You Can Have a Happy School," 1953, in AJA, Hebrew Union College, collection 73, box 39, folder 2.

159. Michael Stavitsky, "Jewish History Week: Survival and Revival," in AJHS, I-68, SCA Papers, box 27, "Jewish History Week" folder, p. 2.

160. Emanuel Gamoran, "The Role of Jewish Education in Developing a Creative Jewish Center in America," *Jewish Education* 19, no. 1 (Fall 1947), p. 24.

161. Uriah Zevi Engelman, "Educating the Jewish Child," *Jewish Affairs* 1, no. 11 (November 1, 1946), p. 25.

162. In at least one case, the Jewish Education Committee of New York published a book of Holocaust scholarship. In 1964, it released Solomon Colodner's study *Jewish Education in Germany Under the Nazis* (New York: Jewish Education Committee Press, 1964), a work a reviewer for *Jewish Education* described as "a moving and authentic account of Jewish education during the Nazi era. . . . He has succeeded in portraying how our people taught Jewish youth to identify itself with the fate and destiny of our people under the most adverse and degrading setting in the history of mankind. The book should serve as an excellent source, both to the historian and educator" (Samuel Dinsky, "Jewish Schools in Nazi Germany," *Jewish Education* 36, no. 2 [Winter 1966], pp. 124–25). Colodner had first presented his work on Jewish education in Germany under the Nazis as a Ph.D. dissertation at Dropsie College for Hebrew and Cognate Learning in Philadelphia in 1954.

163. For example, Israel Kazis, "Informal Youth Education Through the Synagogue Youth Organization," in *Proceedings of the Second Annual Rabbinical Assembly Conference on Jewish Education, "The Structure of Jewish Education in Conservative Judaism," December 22–23, 1947*, ed. Jewish Theological Society (New York: Jewish Theological Society, 1947), p. 71.

164. Clipping, May 4, 1956, "Passover Celebration in the Y. L. Peretz A. R. School 20," in YIVO 1258, box 2, file 916.

165. Saul Goodman, ed., *Our First Fifty Years: The Sholem Aleichem Folk Institute—A Historical Survey* (New York: Sholem Aleichem Folk Institute, 1972), p. 153.

166. Alfred Friedman, "Providing Meaningful Experiences in History for the Ten to Twelve Group," *Synagogue School* 14 (November 1955), pp. 17–18; Freida Clark Hyman, "Living History," *Synagogue School* 14 (March 1955), pp. 15–17; Deborah Pessin, "The Teaching of Jewish History," *Synagogue School* 13 (September 1954), pp. 5–9; Milton Plesur, "Correlation in the Teaching of Jewish History," *Synagogue School* 11 (February 1953), pp. 3–9.

167. American Association for Jewish Education, "Holocaust Curriculum Project," *Pedagogic Reporter* 3, no. 3 (March 1949), p. 7, cited in Joshua M. Zeitz, *White Ethnic New York: Jews, Catholics and the Shaping of Postwar Politics* (Chapel Hill: University of North Carolina Press, 2007), pp. 188–89 (originally Ph.D. diss., Brown University, 2002).

168. Listings in *Jewish Education* 17, no. 1 (November 1945), p. 44; *Jewish Education* 18, no. 2 (February–March 1947), p. 61; *Jewish Education* 19, no. 3 (Summer 1948), p. 57; *Jewish Education* 30, no. 3 (Spring 1960), pp. 30–31. *Pedagogic Reporter* of May 1952 drew educators' attention to Joanna Strong and Tom B. Leonard's book, *A Treasury of the World's Greatest Heroines*, which included a chapter on Hannah Senesh (*Pedagogic Reporter* 3, no. 5 [May 1952], p. 19).

169. *Pedagogic Reporter* 3, no. 1 (September 1951), p. 13; *Pedagogic Reporter* 6, no. 2 (January 1954), p. 7; *Pedagogic Reporter* 7, no. 3 (January 1956), p. 22; *Pedagogic Reporter* 7, no. 1 (September 1955), pp. 10–11.

170. "Reviews of Films and Filmstrips," *Pedagogic Reporter* 6, no. 2 (November 1954), p. 5.

171. "Musico-Dramatic Materials," *Pedagogic Reporter* 4, no. 3 (January 1953), p. 5.

172. "U.A.H.C." [Union of American Hebrew Congregations], *Jewish Education* 19, no. 3 (Summer 1948), p. 62.

173. Several magazines published specifically for Jewish children also carried voluminous material on the European catastrophe. In English, *World Over*, given out free every week to every child in a Hebrew school or synagogue school, abounded with small news pieces, short stories, and biographical sketches focused on the Holocaust. For a sampling of material from before 1952, see Norton Belth, ed., *The World Over Story Book: An Illustrated Anthology for Jewish Youth* (New York: Bloch, 1952). After that, issue by issue, the editors of the magazine made the European catastrophe and its aftermath a subject for children. Several Yiddish publications went home with children from school, including *Kinder zhurnal*, which began publication in 1920 for pupils in the Sholem Aleichem schools, and *Kinder tsaytung,* which started in 1935 to serve those in the Arbeiter Ring schools. They contain a massive trove of Holocaust material, way beyond this study and worth analysis in themselves. Finally, *Hadoar*, the premier Hebrew-language magazine published in the United States, offered a supplementary, *Hadoar Lanoar,* for young readers. In addition, regular issues of *Hadoar* randomly contained a "pinah layeled," or children's corner, or a "mussaf l'korey hatzair," an addition for the young reader. Here again Holocaust material appeared often. For example, in the January 23, 1959, youth supplement, young readers learned about the recent publication of a Holocaust diary, that of Moshe Flinker, which had appeared the year before in Hebrew, published in Israel. See H. Leaf, "Yomano ha-ivri she hanaar Moshe," *Hadoar* 39, no. 11 (January 23, 1959), pp. 195–96. In addition, Histadruth Ivrith of America published *Hadoar*-issued books for young readers, among them Holocaust texts, like the 1963 *Giborah ha-getto: Pirkay kreah l'kitot givohot,* a book for upper-grade classes on "the heroes of the ghetto."

174. Roland B. Gittelsohn, *Modern Jewish Problems: A Textbook for High School Classes and Jewish Youth Groups,* 5th ed. (Cincinnati: Union of American Hebrew Congregations, 1949), pp. 114–28, 205; Roland B. Gittelsohn, *Little Lower Than the Angels* (New York: Union of American Hebrew Congregations, 1955), pp. 67, 74–75, 127.

175. Deborah Pessin, *The Jewish People: Book Three* (New York: United Synagogue Commission on Jewish Education, 1953), pp. 277–89, 293. Pessin's fourth volume, on American Jewish history, also managed to tell bits of the Holocaust story. Writing about the efforts of American Jews from 1933 onward to rescue Jews from Europe and to stem the tide of Nazism, she noted how ineffective these measures had been and also how militarily weak the Allies had been at the beginning: "The Jews, whom the Nazis wished to destroy completely, suffered the worst devastation they had ever known in their long history. Six million Jews were cold-bloodedly murdered by the men who called themselves the 'master race'" (Pessin, *History of the Jews in America* [New York: United Synagogue Commission on Jewish Education, 1957], pp. 233–35).

176. The archival material had no date attached to these Yiddish essays, and they

seem to have come from several years worth of classroom work. The fact that some refer to the movie version of *The Diary of Anne Frank* places some of them in 1959, the year the film was released.

177. In YIVO 1148, box 4.

178 "Evaluation, 1959, Intermediate Session," in AJA, Hebrew Union College, collection manuscript-648, Olin-Sang-Ruby Papers, box 4, folder 7, p. 2.

179. "The Educational Principles of Camp 'Hemshekh,'" 1962, in YIVO, RG 1400, ME 18, file 121.

180. *Yeshivah Flatbush Yearbook: 1953*, pp. 28, 30, 34, 36; in addition, the Hebrew section is numbered by Hebrew letters.

181. William Chomsky, *Hebrew: The Eternal Language* (Philadelphia: Jewish Publication Society of America, 1957), p. 11.

182. Judah Pilch, "Education for Halutziut," *Jewish Education* 32, no. 2 (1962), cited in Judah Pilch, *Between Two Generations: Selected Essays by Judah Pilch* (New York: Bloch, 1977), p. 162.

183. "Hear O Israel: A Sabbath Service Dedicated to Israel: The People, Land, and Faith," in AJA, Hebrew Union College, collection 266, box 1, folder 6.

184. "The Twelfth Principle," in Ely E. Pilchik, *Jeshurun Sermons* (New York: Bloch, 1957), pp. 220–25.

185. "Resolution of the 20th Anniversary Conference of the Yiddish Scientific Institute-YIVO," *News of the YIVO* 13 (February 1946), p. 1.

186. Louis Barish and Rebecca Barish, *Basic Jewish Beliefs* (New York: Jonathan David, 1961), p. 135.

187. Gertrude Hyman, "A Leader's Discussion Guide for a Purim Workshop," in AJA, Hebrew Union College, collection 73, box 39, folder 2.

188. Philip Goodman, *The Passover Anthology* (Philadelphia: Jewish Publication Society of America, 1961), p. viii.

189. Address, September 26, 1959, in AJHS, P-92, Label Katz Papers, box 2, "Speeches by date (1)" folder.

190. Ben Stern, "Solidarity," *Young Zionist* 1, no. 1 (August 1959), p. 6.

191. Samuel Rosenbaum, "President's Annual Report," in *Proceedings of the Eleventh Annual Conference-Convention of the Cantors Assembly of America and the Department of Music of the United Synagogue of America, April 21, 22, 23, 24, 1958*, ed. United Synagogue of America (New York: United Synagogue of America, 1958), p. 23.

192. Simon Dolgin, "Selichot 1953: Arise, Sing in the Night," in Simon Dolgin, *The Rabbinical Council Manual of Holiday Sermons, 5725–1954* (New York: Rabbinical Council Press, 1954), p. 19.

193. H. Mahlerman, "Purim Thoughts 5714," *Jewish Spectator* 37, no. 2 (February 1954), p. 48.

194. Morgenthau, *Tragedy of German Jewish Liberalism*, pp. 5, 16.

195. Anita Libman Lebeson, *Pilgrim People* (New York: Harper Brothers, 1950), pp. 4, 409–10, 444–45, 455, 476, 460–61,480–87. See also Lee M. Friedman, *Pilgrims in a New Land* (Philadelphia: Jewish Publication Society of America, 1948), pp. 9, 113, 365, 367, 374–75; Rufus Learsi, *The Jews in America: A History* (Cleveland: World, 1954), 291, 293, 295, 297–98, 301–5, 312; Oscar Handlin, *Adventure in Freedom: Three Hundred Years of Jewish Life in America* (New York: McGraw-Hill, 1954), pp. vii–viii, 260;

Morris U. Schappes, *The Jews in the United States: A Pictorial History, 1654 to the Present* (New York: Citadel, 1958), pp. 219–81.

196. Elma Ehrlich Levinger, *Jewish Adventures in America: The Story of 300 Years of Jewish Life in the United States* (New York: Bloch, 1954), pp. 233–35, 238–40, 277.

197. For example, Nathan Abrams, "America Is Home: *Commentary* Magazine and the Refocusing of the Community of Memory, 1945–60," *Jewish Culture and History* 3, no. 1 (Summer 2000), pp. 65–74. Abrams asserted with complete certainty that "the recent history of the Holocaust was not allowed to mar the festivities" (p. 67).

198. Israel Goldstein, *American Jewry Comes of Age: Tercentenary Addresses* (New York: Bloch, 1955), pp. 74, 90, 97, 127, 192–93, 246.

199. Salo Baron had linked the Nazi campaign against the Jews and American Jewish history in 1942 when in his presidential address to the American Jewish Historical Society he called for American Jews to invest in the writing of their own history, since, he noted, "the fate of the Jewish people is being decided now for generations to come" (Baron, *Steeled by Adversity: Essays and Addresses on American Jewish Life* [Philadelphia: Jewish Publication Society of America, 1971], p. 15).

200. Jacob Rader Marcus, "The Program of the American Jewish Archives," *American Jewish Archives* 1 (1948), p. 2. Marcus continued into the 1950s to refer to the destruction of the larger portion of European Jewry as one—although certainly not *the* —reason to study American Jewish history. In one of his writings during the tercentenary year, he noted that "sometimes . . . in the quiet and the solitude of our thoughts, we lift up our eyes and we recall what has happened abroad since 1939, particularly in central Europe. We are disturbed by the fact that a Jewry that we thought was secure has been destroyed; that five million Jews have been destroyed. We sometimes ask ourselves, How can we attain security? How can we survive as Jews and as an integral part of this great American Republic?" (Marcus, "Three Hundred Years in America," in *The Dynamics of American Jewish History: Jacob Rader Marcus's Essays on American Jewish History*, ed. Gary P. Zola [Waltham, Mass.: Brandeis University Press, 2004], p. 124).

201. Committee for the 300th Anniversary of Jewish Settlement in the U.S.A., "Declaration: 300 Years of Jewish Life in America," adopted June 19, 1954, by the Preliminary Conference of the Committee for the 300th Anniversary of Jewish Settlement in the U.S.A., in AJHS, I-11, American Jewish Tercentenary Celebration Papers, box 6, folder 8. A dissident group, representing Jews further to the left than the "official" planning committee, also made use of the Holocaust in their "Declaration": "When we draw upon the bloody reckoning of World War II, of the numberless victims exacted from the Jewish People, we remember not only the martyrs murdered in the ghettoes and Hitler's slaughter camps, but also those Jews who wrote a chapter in the book of Jewish heroism. . . . We remain true to the watchword: 'Never to forgive, Never to forget.' " They continued: "On this solemn occasion we recall with deepest pain the memory of the six million Jews who perished at the hands of the Nazis."

202. "The Sisterhood Caravan Rolls On," "Transactions of the Biennial Assembly, NFTS, February 13–17, 1954," in AJA, Hebrew Union College, collection 73, box 5, folder 4, p. 53.

203. Jewish Labor Committee, *Scope and Theme: American Jewish Tercentenary 1654–1954*, November 1953, in Tamiment Library, Wagner Labor Archives, NYU, Julius Bernstein Papers, box 8, "American Jewish Tercentenary" folder. See also

speeches by Isaiah Minkoff for the Tercentenary in ibid., Isaiah Minkoff Papers, box 11, file 5.

204. Abraham Menes, "The East Side Matrix of the Jewish Labor Movement," *Judaism* 3 (Fall 1954), pp. 366–80.

205. Schappes, *Jews of the United States*, pp. 219, 225, 271. Given his Communist sympathies, Schappes could not resist using this history book—in particular, the matter of the "six million"—to venture out in a distinctive and combative mode. He used his book to condemn the American Jewish "plutocracy," the American Jewish Committee, and the B'nai B'rith during the Hitler years for their inaction: "Organizations like the B'nai B'rith were virtually paralyzed by this approach, and bestirred themselves mainly, as did the American Jewish Committee, with vain programs of research and publications" (p. 225).

206. Alfred Werner, "Remember? Ten Years Ago War Ended, Along with Nazis Who Started It," *National Jewish Monthly* 69, no. 9 (May 1955), pp. 3, 33.

207. Edward E. Grusd, "Book Review: The Horror of Nazism," *National Jewish Monthly* 69, no. 4 (December 1954), pp. 42–43.

208. Judah Nadich, "Review: *Dr. Goebbels: His Life and Death*," *Jewish Social Studies* 24, no. 2 (April 1962), p. 114.

209. Deborah Lipstadt, *Denying the Holocaust: The Growing Assault on Truth and Memory* (New York: Plume, 1994).

210. Letter from Bob Johnson, n.d., in Tamiment Library, Wagner Labor Archives, NYU, Julius Bernstein Papers, box 5, file 10; this letter appeared in a folder of material from the middle of the 1950s.

211. "Report of Activities," July 1955, American Jewish Congress, Chicago Council, Commission on Law and Social Action, in Chicago Jewish Archives, Spertus, collection 14, box 1, file 7.

212. Alfred Werner, "The Roots of Nazism," *Congress Weekly* 21, no. 27 (October 11, 1954), pp. 5–7.

213. Isaac Franck, "Teaching the Tragic Events in Jewish History," *Jewish Education* 34, no. 3 (Spring 1964), pp. 173–80. Two other articles in this 1964 issue of the journal also addressed the place of the Holocaust in the Jewish school, including Judah Pilch, Sara Feinstein, and Zalman Ury, "The 'Shoah' and the Jewish School," pp. 162–72, and William Glicksman, "Bias Against Whom? A Reply to Rabbi Harold M. Schulweis," pp. 181–86. Schulweis had had an article in the fall issue of the publication titled "The Bias Against Man," in which he encouraged more attention to "The Third Destruction" in the Jewish school. Glicksman, "a witness and a victim of the Hitler era," offered some vigorous objections to *how* Schulweis proposed to present the Holocaust but declared, "It is the wish of every Jew who cherishes the Jewish group entity that Rabbi Schulweis' efforts may be crowned with success."

214. Novick, *Holocaust in American Life*, p. 104.

Notes to Chapter 3

1. Ira A. Hirschmann, *Life Line to a Promised Land* (New York: Jewish Book Guild of America, 1946), p. 205.

2. This number appeared in *American Jewish Year Book: 1946–1947*, p. 202. The

number varied a bit over time but importantly always excluded the Jews in the Soviet Union, many of whom also fell into the category of "survivor" as understood by American, and world, Jewry.

3. Peter Novick, *The Holocaust in American Life* (Boston: Houghton Mifflin, 1999), p. 69.

4. William B. Helmreich, *Against All Odds: Holocaust Survivors and the Successful Lives They Made in America* (New York: Simon and Schuster, 1992), p. 38.

5. According to Novick, "the most common postwar term, 'displaced person,' or 'DP,' was . . . nonspecific" and as such without specific Jewish or even Holocaust connotations. Only in "recent years has 'Holocaust survivor' " become "an honorific term" (Novick, *Holocaust in American Life*, pp. 67–68).

6. Simon H. Rifkind, *The Disinherited Jews of Europe Must Be Saved* (New York: American Jewish Conference, 1946), p. 3.

7. On an institutional level, projects and organizations applied to the Claims Conference for funding. Each year the Claims Conference issued a report on the successful and unsuccessful applications, the number of such applications, and the like. The reports and other materials of the Claims Conference are in AJHS, I-319.

8. The most important book on the Claims Conference is Ronald W. Zweig, *German Reparations and the Jewish World: A History of the Claims Conference*, 2nd ed. (London: Frank Cass, 2001).

9. Allan Nevins, *Herbert H. Lehman and His Era* (New York: Scribner's, 1963), pp. 300–301.

10. Bernard Richards to Herbert Lehman, January 29, 1946, in Ratner Center, Jewish Theological Seminary of America, Bernard Richards Papers, archive 96, box 5.

11. Quoted in Leonard Dinnerstein, *America and the Survivors of the Holocaust: The Evolution of a United States Displaced Persons Policy* (New York: Columbia University Press, 1982), p. 109.

12. Yehuda Bauer, *Out of the Ashes: The Impact of American Jews on Post-Holocaust European Jewry* (Oxford: Pergamon, 1989), p. 39.

13. For the fullest and more thorough depiction of this encounter, see Alex Grobman, *Rekindling the Flame: American Jewish Chaplains and the Survivors of European Jewry, 1944–1948* (Detroit: Wayne State University Press, 1993).

14. Bernstein's speech is in AJHS, P-290, Celia Razovsky Papers, box 4, file 4.

15. Roger Daniels, *Guarding the Golden Door: American Immigration Policy and Immigrants Since 1882* (New York: Hill and Wang, 2004), p. 103.

16. David Kenney has written a full-length biography of Stratton in which he admitted that he could not explain the onetime anti-immigrant, isolationist's change of heart (Kenney, *A Political Passage: The Career of Stratton of Illinois* [Carbondale: Southern Illinois University Press, 1990], pp. 52–53). Roger Daniels also noted that no scholar has figured out Stratton's motives (Daniels, *Guarding the Golden Door*, pp. 105–6).

17. Dinnerstein, *America and the Survivors of the Holocaust*, pp. 137–82.

18. On the active collaboration of eastern Europeans with the Germans in the slaughter of the Jews, see Martin Dean, *Collaboration in the Holocaust: Crimes of the Local Police in Belorussia and Ukraine, 1941–1944* (New York: St. Martin's, 2000).

19. Will Maslow and George J. Hexter, "Immigration—Or Frustration?" *Jewish Community* 3 (September 1948), p. 17.

20. On the details of the legislation, see Daniels, *Guarding the Golden Door,* pp. 98–112.

21. Quoted in ibid., p. 106.

22. "Draft Jewish War Veterans to Harry Truman," in NYPL, Rare Books and Manuscripts Division, Hyman Schulson Papers, box 1, file 10.

23. Jacob Pat to Harry Truman, July 23, 1948, in Tamiment Library, Wagner Labor Archives, NYU, Jacob Pat Papers, box 2, "Immigration: 1948" folder.

24. Joseph Baron to Alexander Wiley, January 12, 1949, in University of Wisconsin–Milwaukee, manuscript 173, box 9, file 4.

25. *Current Copy* (August–September 1947), pp. 2–3, in AJA, Hebrew Union College, collection 73, box 35, folder 2.

26. Ibid.

27. "Youth Speaks Its Mind," *Senior* 5, no. 1 (November 1946), p. 2, in AJHS, I-61, box 30.

28. Haim Genizi, in *America's Fair Share: The Admission and Resettlement of Displaced Persons, 1945–1952* (Detroit: Wayne State University Press, 1993), treats this issue in great detail. He reiterates on pp. 203–4 the fact that, at the time, American Jews understood the discriminatory nature of the DP legislation and the irony that many of the non-Jews who benefited from the legislation had been Nazi collaborators.

29. "Address Delivered at National Conference of Board of Directors United Service for New Americans by Arthur Greenleigh, Executive Director," 1951, in Tamiment Library, Wagner Labor Archives, NYU, Isaiah Minkoff Papers, box 11, file 18. The number dropped off after the end of 1948 as Jewish displaced persons could go to Israel, as most then did en masse.

30. The amount of money raised by American Jews in order to help the survivors, community by community, and the actual on-the-ground work of American Jewish organizations in Europe, in the United States, and in various other places around the world is a topic somewhat different from this one here. In fact, we do not have a systematically researched history of this subject, although bits and pieces have been written. I am more interested here in the ways in which American Jewish organizations and organs of public opinion narrated this phenomenon and how telling the story of the survivors constituted a core part of postwar American Jewish life and, at the same time, how speaking on behalf of the survivors and their needs allowed—or forced—American Jews to revisit the Holocaust.

31. *American Jewish Year Book: 1945–1946,* p. 310.

32. *American Jewish Year Book: 1948–1949,* p. 141. These figures do not include money that went directly, for example, from *landsmanshaftn* and individuals to family and friends who they had established contact with or who had come to the United States or Israel. Notably, in addition, the money that went to Israel was to help settle Holocaust survivors; in campaigns for fundraising for Israel, this point was made repeatedly.

33. Bauer, *Out of the Ashes,* p. xxi.

34. "To All Friends," n.d., in Tamiment Library, Wagner Labor Archives, NYU, Jacob Pat Papers, box 1, file 2.

35. *SAJ Bulletin* 25, no. 10 (January 11, 1946), p. 1; *SAJ Bulletin* 25, no. 15 (March 3, 1946), p. 1; *SAJ Bulletin* 26, no. 18 (June 20, 1947), p. 1.

36. New York League of NFTY Affiliates, "An Urgent Appeal to Youth," *Bulletin* 1, no. 4 (March 1946), p. 4.

37. Oscar Handlin, *A Continuing Task: The American Jewish Joint Distribution Committee, 1914–1964* (New York: Random House, 1964), pp. 90–106; Tom Schachtman, *I Seek My Brethren: Ralph Goldman and "The Joint"* (New York: Newmarket Press, 2001), pp. 20–47; Women's Division, Jewish Welfare Board, *Bulletin* 7, no. 2 (Winter 1949), p. 6; Joseph Levine, "Synagoges I Remember," *Jewish Spectator* 23, no. 3 (March 1958), pp. 19–22.

38. Jack Rader, *By the Skill of Their Hands: The Story of ORT* (Geneva: World ORT Union, 1970); Leon Shapiro, *The History of ORT* (New York: Schocken, 1980).

39. Koppel S. Pinson, "Jewish Life in Liberated Germany: The Story of the Jewish DP's," *Jewish Social Studies* 9, no. 2 (April 1947), pp. 101–26. For his lectures and public speaking schedule, see NYPL, Rare Books and Manuscripts Division, Koppel S. Pinson Papers. See also Zeev W. Mankowitz, *Life Between Memory and Hope: The Survivors of the Holocaust in Occupied Germany* (New York: Cambridge University Press, 2002).

40. Joseph J. Schwartz, "On the Road to Recovery," "Workbook," 34th Annual Meeting, Joint Distribution Committee (JDC), October 30–31, 1948, in AJA, Hebrew Union College, collection 73, box 34, folder 1. JDC reports can also be found in the papers of the Jewish Labor Committee. The Joint Committee also published monthly bulletins, giving the specifics of its work with survivors; its publications, such as *This Month* and *JDC Digest*, were circulated around the country.

41. Flyers, "You Saved Him from Dying," box 142; "What ORT Offers Its Membership? Education and Program Kit," box 6; Pamphlet: "Exhibition of Articles Made by Students of ORT Vocational Schools," folder 142; Women's ORT, "Weekly Summary," April 9, 1948, box 144—all in YIVO 380, ORT Collection.

42. "Minutes, Delegate Assembly," April 27, 1949, in Marvin Gelman Library, George Washington University, Jewish Community Council of Greater Washington Papers, MS2012, box 1, folder 3.

43. "Minutes," B'nai B'rith Women's Auxiliary, August 1947; November 17, 1947; December 3, 1947—all in University of Wisconsin–Milwaukee, manuscript 138.

44. Abraham J. Karp, *To Give Life: The UJA in the Shaping of the American Jewish Community, 1939–1978* (New York: Schocken, 1980).

45. Quoted in William B. Helmreich, *The Enduring Community: The Jews of Newark and Metrowest* (New Brunswick, N.J.: Transaction, 1999), p. 217.

46. Motion picture, *Passport to Nowhere*, in YIVO 380, box 6; Alvin H. Marill, *The Complete Films of Edward G. Robinson* (New York: Citadel, 1990), p. 241. Evidence of the showing of these films at Jewish community gatherings runs through the archival material and publications of Jewish institutions around the country. For example, Southern New England Federation of Temple Youth, North Madison, Connecticut, in AJA, Hebrew Union College, collection 266, box 1, folder 8.

47. "Statement for Radio Interview by Dr. Greengaus," "Greengaus Speech Before Philadelphia Chapter," in YIVO 380, Part 1, file 6.

48. "Hadassah Program Committee: *How Can I Tell It?*" in NYPL for the Performing Arts, Paul Muni Papers, box 1, file 35.

49. "Operation *Nissim venifloos!*" "Radio Sermons," "Message of Israel" folder; "NBC Chapel of the Air," "This Week in Religion," and "Radio Broadcasts," box 36,

"Radio Broadcasts" folder—all in AJHS, P-327, William Franklin Rosenblum Papers. See also Roberta Newman, "Delayed Pilgrims: The Radio Programs of the United Service for New Americans, 1947–48," M.A. thesis, Gallatin Division, New York University, 1966. This thesis provides an even larger number of examples of radio programs of various kinds about the survivors who had come to the United States.

50. Jeffrey Shandler, *While America Watches: Televising the Holocaust* (New York: Oxford University Press, 1999), pp. 28–37. The HIAS film *Placing the Displaced* was also shown in movie theaters.

51. David Crystal, *The Displaced Person and the Social Agency: A Study of the Casework Process in Its Relation to Immigrant Adjustment* (New York: United HIAS Service and Jewish Social Service Bureau of Rochester, N.Y., 1958), pp. 12–13. Jewish social service agencies produced a voluminous professional literature on these issues for various professional journals, most notably, the *Jewish Social Service Quarterly*, which, well into the 1960s, published scores of articles on social work with Holocaust survivors, and these articles also played a role in keeping the events surrounding the Holocaust prominent in American Jewish life.

52. *Masada* 1, no. 6 (May 1946), p. 3.

53. Clipping, *Simmons News*, March 17, 1947, in AJHS, P-112, Maurice L. Zigmond Papers, "Simmons-Tufts Scrapbook," box 3, 1947 folder.

54. Jacob Pat to Israel Feinberg, November 7, 1945, in Tamiment Library, Wagner Labor Archives, NYU, Jacob Pat Papers, box 2, file 12.

55. *The Link* 4 (May 7, 1949), in AJA, Hebrew Union College, collection 266, box 1, folder 8.

56. "Invitation to Dinner," 1946, in YIVO 380, box 141.

57. JLC Women's Division, *Bulletin* (October 1956), pp. 11–12. Children from the Workmen's Circle schools also raised money by selling stamps, a project described as "their holy work." The stamp-selling project of the schools fit into their pedagogic project as well. Printing the names of the schools that had collected the most money in the foreword, in the spring of 1945, the article asserted that "the children in the Arbeiter Ring schools heard from their teachers about the horrible conditions of the children in Europe. They know what is going on with all their heart and soul" (JLC, Workmen's Circle Division, May 29, 1945, in Tamiment Library, Wagner Labor Archives, NYU, Jacob Pat Papers, box 2, file 47).

58. David Saltz to David Polimer, October 30, 1946; *Kolbuszower Echo* (December 1946), p. 1; *Kolbuszower Clarion* 2, no. 1 (October 1946)—all in YIVO 888, box 2. The minutes of the Kolbuszowa Relief Society, like those of all the *landsmanshaftn*, contained personal details about the survivors. Individual survivors who arrived in New York came to the meetings, where they were greeted and where they told their stories of suffering and survival. They also reported on other townspeople, describing where they were and what relief they needed.

59. Minutes, New Home Club, January 27, 1950; "Correspondence, 1947," in University of Wisconsin–Milwaukee, New Home Club Papers, manuscript 42, box 1, file 29; Manfred Swarensky to Joseph Baron, May 17, 1946, in University of Wisconsin–Milwaukee, Joseph Baron Papers, manuscript 173, box 8, file 11.

60. At present, there is no history of the Jewish Labor Committee. Judah J. Shapiro, *The Friendly Society: A History of the Workmen's Circle* (New York: Media Judaica, 1970),

provides some background information, as well as some details of the JLC's orphan program. See also Robert D. Parmet, *The Master of Seventh Avenue: David Dubinsky and the American Labor Movement* (New York: New York University Press, 2005), pp. 241–42.

61. Jewish Labor Committtee, Child "Adoption" Program, "Our Children," Julius Bernstein Papers, box 15, file 14; *Voss ess tut der Yidisher Arbeter-Comitet* (New York: Jewish Labor Committee, 1954), Isaiah Minkoff Papers, box 5, file 27; Julius Bernstein to Philip Kramer, December 2, 1953, JLC Boston Papers, box 15, file 9—all in Tamiment Library, Wagner Labor Archives, NYU. See also "Bazaar by Women," *JLC Outlook* 1, no. 2 (Autumn 1954), pp. 3–4.

62. *Youth Leader: A Magazine for Jewish Youth Groups* 9, no. 1 (Spring 1948), p. 9, in AJA, Hebrew Union College, collection 266, box 1, folder 6.

63. Child Rescue Fund of the Pioneer Women to Hasye Cooperman, n.d., in YIVO 398, box 151; "Please Bring to Attention of Your Organization," September 1949, in YIVO 1015, box 3, file 5.

64. "Cultural Cooperation with Jewish Communities Abroad," *Jewish Education* 18, no. 1 (November 1946), pp. 63–65.

65. Marie Syrkin, *The State of the Jews* (Washington, D.C.: New Republic, 1980), pp. 11–54; the original articles appeared in the *Jewish Frontier.*

66. For a brief description of the Hillel project, see *American Jewish Year Book: 1964*, p. 142; "Speakers' Briefs: Hillel Helps," n.d., AJHS, Label Katz Papers, box 2, "Notes for Speeches" folder. On Hillel assistance to survivor college students vis-à-vis their immigration status, see Marilyn Tallman to John Frank, AJHS, P-92, box 1, "Correspondence—Re: John Frank" folder.

67. The papers of the Jewish Central Orthodox Committee are in the Yeshiva University Archives. This organization was in conflict with the older Vaad Hatzala, which after the war created the Vaad Hatzala Rehabilitation Committee. The papers of the Vaad Hatzala are in this same archive, Vaad Hatzala Papers, box 7, file 61. The Vaad Hatzala competed with the Jewish Central Orthodox Committee in providing for the religious needs of the survivors. Both organizations prepared material, including flyers and posters, to raise funds for the survivors.

68. "Appeal," n.d., Tamiment Library, Wagner Labor Archives, NYU, Jacob Pat Papers, box 1, file 2.

69. "Special Report of Committee on European Jewish Blind Survivors of the Palestine Lighthouse," box 39, file 1; "To Members of the NFTS Executive Board," April 29, 1948, box 37, file 2; "The Work of the Committee of the Palestine Lighthouse for European Jewish Blind Survivors of World War II," box 36, file 2; Freda Rosett, "To Members of the NFTS Board," March 5, 1948, box 37, file 2; "NFTS, Committee on Jewish Literature for the Blind," February 15, 1954, box 40, file 1; "NFTS Calendar of Events, 1955–56," box 39, file 2—all in AJA, Hebrew Union College, collection 73.

70. "Meeting of the Board, Minutes," June 6, 1945; April 10, 1946; February 5, 1947; February 9, 1949—all in AJHS, I-68, SCA Papers, box 1, "1945" folder, "1946" folder, "1949" folder; various materials, box 10, "Religious Rehabilitation" folder.

71. Ibid. In addition, in 1949, the National Federation of Temple Sisterhoods launched a special effort to pay the salary of Rabbi Steven Schwarzchild to minister to the needs of the Reform congregation in Berlin, a congregation by definition made up

of those who had endured the Nazi era ("Dear Uniongram Chairman," March 28, 1949, in AJA, Hebrew Union College, collection 73, box 37, folder 1).

72. "Report of the Cultural Committee of the Jewish Labor Committee," n.d., Tami-ment Library, Wagner Labor Archives, NYU, Jacob Pat Papers, 2, 46.

73. "40th Anniversary Presentation," in AJA, Hebrew Union College, National Fed-eration of Temple Sisterhoods (NFTS) Collection, box 41, folder 2, p. 3; "Transactions of the XXI Biennial Assembly, NFTS, April 27–May, 2, 1957," in AJA, Hebrew Union College, collection 73, box 41, folder 2, pp. 33, 36.

74. Elma Ehrlich Levinger, *Jewish Adventures in America: The Story of 300 Years of Jewish Life in the United States* (New York: Bloch, 1954), pp. 233–38.

75. Herman Stein, "Jewish Social Work in the United States, 1920–1955," in *The Jews: Social Patterns of an American Group,* ed. Marshall Sklare (Glencoe, Ill.: Free Press, 1958), pp. 173, 192–95.

76. Nathan Glazer, "Social Characteristics of American Jews," in *The Jews: Their His-tory, Culture and Religion,* ed. Louis Finkelstein (New York: Harper and Row, 1960), vol. 2, p. 1729.

77. Thomas Kolsky, *Jews Against Zionism: The American Council for Judaism* (Phila-delphia: Temple University Press, 1990).

78. Joseph Tenenbaum, *Peace for the Jews* (New York: American Federation for Pol-ish Jews, 1945), pp. 6, 57, 159. That year the federation passed a resolution at its annual convention calling for the "establishment of Palestine as a Jewish State," in light of the fact that "the Jews of Europe have been the chief object of Nazi brutality" (Resolutions, June 29–30 Convention, in YIVO 1150, box 3, file 1).

79. Milton Steinberg, "A Voice from the Grave," *Senior* (April 1945), p. 2.

80. *Mizrachi Jubilee Book: Thirty-Five Years of Mizrachi in the United States of America (1911–1946)* (Pittsburgh: Mizrachi Tri-State Region, 1947), frontispiece, in AJHS I-400, box 1, "Mizrachi Organization of America, Publications" folder.

81. "Open Door," May 1946, in AJHS, I-71, Jewish Reconstructionist Foundation Papers, box 43, "Cantata" folder.

82. *Israel Is Born: The Return to the Jewish Homeland—A Documentary Record,* 33 ⅓ rpm LP record sleeve (New York: Caedmon Records, n.d.). Jewish education publications hailed this record for pedagogic uses and for school assemblies (*Pedagogic Reporter* 5, no. 2 [November 1953], p. 22).

83. On the workings of the White Paper vis-à-vis the survivors of the Holocaust, see Arieh J. Kochavi, *Post-Holocaust Politics: Britain, the United States, and Jewish Refu-gees, 1945–1948* (Chapel Hill: University of North Carolina Press, 2001), pp. 60–86.

84. Joseph Baron to James F. Byrnes, November 9, 1945, in University of Wiscon-sin–Milwaukee, collection 173, box 4, file 7; "Conduct of British Assailed by Cincinnati Jewish Group," clipping, in AJA, Hebrew Union College, collection 202, box 28, folder 5; "Resolution Passed at Quarterly Meeting of Delegates of Jewish Community Council of Washington," April 28, 1947, in Marvin Gelman Libary, George Washington Univer-sity, Jewish Community Council of Greater Washington Papers, manuscript 2012, box 1, folder 3.

85. Simon Rifkind et al., *The Basic Equities of the Palestine Problem: A Memorandum by Simon H. Rifkind, Chairman, Jerome N. Frank, Stanley H. Fuld, Abraham Tulin, Hilton Handler, Murray I. Gurfein, Abe Fortas, Lawrence R. Eno* (New York, 1947).

86. I. F. Stone, *Underground to Palestine* (New York: Boni and Gaer, 1946). For one of many reviews, see Carl Alpert, "Stone, I. F., *Underground to Palestine*," *Jewish Education* 18, no. 3 (Summer 1947), p. 56.

87. Meyer Levin, *My Father's House* (New York: Viking, 1947); Meyer Levin, *If I Forget Thee: A Picture Story of Modern Palestine Based on the Film "My Father's House"* (New York: Viking, 1947). Levin also made a film, *The Illegals*, depicting the harrowing experiences of Polish Holocaust survivors trying to reach Palestine.

88. Ben Hecht, *A Flag Is Born* (New York: American League for a Free Palestine, 1946), pp. 2–4; Samuel L. Leiter, *Encyclopedia of the New York Stage, 1940–1950* (New York: Greenwood, 1992), pp. 204–6, which includes some comments from the reviews of the play from the New York press.

89. "Henrietta Szold," *Eternal Light* (radio script) (New York: Jewish Theological Seminary, April 22, 1945); "The Lantern in the Inferno (A Story of a Modern Maccabee)," *Eternal Light* (radio script) (New York: Jewish Theological Seminary, December 22, 1946); "To the Disinherited," *Eternal Light* (radio script) (New York: Jewish Theological Seminary, June 30, 1946).

90. "Appeal to the President of the United States," in AJHS, P-359, box 2, "1946–1947" folder.

91. The *Eternal Light* broadcast hundreds of radio dramas that conjoined the survivors of the Holocaust and Israel as their place of refuge, both physically and culturally. For example, "These Rocks Are Mine," *Eternal Light* (radio script) (New York: Jewish Theological Seminary, April 27, 1952), p. 14; "Lullaby for Ruth," *Eternal Light* (radio script) (New York: Jewish Theological Seminary, January 11, 1959); for other examples, see "A Duty of Conscience," *Eternal Light* (radio script) (New York: Jewish Theological Seminary, October 8, 1950); "A New Beginning," *Eternal Light* (radio script) (New York: Jewish Theological Seminary, October 21, 1956); "Children of Liberty," *Eternal Light* (radio script) (New York: Jewish Theological Seminary, April 7, 1956); "Take with You Words," *Eternal Light* (radio script) (New York: Jewish Theological Seminary, September 22, 1957).

92. "For Release On or Before 9/7/48," in AJHS, I-68, SCA Papers, box 37, "Rosh Hashanah" folder.

93. I. F. Stone, *This Is Israel* (New York: Boni and Gaer, 1948), pp. 9, 35, 54, 76, 119.

94. *Pedagogic Reporter* 6, no. 2 (November 1954), p. 7.

95. "Nine Years of Jewish Statehood," *Jewish Spectator* 22, no. 6 (June 1957), p. 6; *Jewish Spectator* 23, no. 5 (May 1958), p. 5; *Jewish Spectator* 20, no. 5 (May 1955), p. 2.

96. "A Decade of Growth," *Senior* 16, no. 6 (April 1958), p. 3.

97. Ruth Gruber, *Israel Without Tears* (New York: A. A. Wyn, 1950), pp. 13, 18, 20–21, 77, 89.

98. See also the much less popular works of this genre, for example, Zelda Popkin, *Quiet Street* (Philadelphia: Lippincott, 1951). Popkin's autobiography, *Open Every Door* (New York: Dutton, 1956), tells of her work with the Joint Committee in a Displaced Persons camp; she also wrote *Small Victory* (Philadelphia: Lippincott, 1947), set among a group of Jewish survivors in a German DP camp, where the talk among the survivors was about Palestine. This type of fiction also includes Michael Blankfort, *The Juggler* (Boston: Little, Brown, 1952), the story of a concentration camp survivor who experienced personal restoration in Israel, where he overcame the psychological

torment inflicted on him. *The Juggler* became a Hollywood movie in 1953, starring Kirk Douglas.

99. Leon Uris, *Exodus* (New York: Doubleday, 1958).

100. Leo W. Schwarz, *The Root and the Bough: The Epic of an Enduring People* (New York: Rinehart, 1949), pp. xv–xvii, 93.

101. In the text and the notes here, it is not possible to list, let alone comment on, the vast outpouring of articles about the survivors in the American Jewish press, whether in English, Hebrew, or Yiddish and whether in the daily Yiddish newspapers, the weekly local community newspapers, or the magazines that circulated nationally as independent publications or as the official publications of organizations. For a listing, though incomplete, of some English articles, see Special Subcommittee of the Committee on the Judiciary, House of Representatives, *Report: The Displaced Persons Analytical Bibliography* (Washington, D.C.: U.S. Government Printing Office, 1950).

102. Jacob Pat, *Ash un fayer* (New York: Central Yiddish Culture Organization, 1946). For the Efros book, see *Jewish Book Annual: 5708, 1947–1948*, p. 55. Efros also published a series of reports from his journey in *Hadoar,* as did Moshe Frager and Moshe Braver.

103. Quoted in Joseph Leftwich, "Leivik," *Jewish Spectator* 24, no. 5 (May 1959), pp. 15–17.

104. Hayim Leivik, *Di Khasene in Fernwald: Dramatishe poeme in elf stsenes* (New York: Central Yiddish Culture Organization, 1949), p. 119. See also Hayim Leivik, *Mit der sheyres ha-pleyteh* (New York: Central Yiddish Culture Organization, 1947). English readers who could not access Leivik in Yiddish could read about his poetry and survivor accounts in the Anglo-Jewish press (Charles Angoff, "In the Margin," *Jewish Spectator* 24, no. 2 [February 1959], pp. 21–24). Angoff translated sections of *Di Khasene* and commented on them. Likewise, the *Jewish Book Annual* and the *American Jewish Year Book* listed and described Leivik's work in the years that they appeared. Finally, English-language books about Yiddish literature considered Leivik, his work, and the impact of the survivors on his vision. For example, Sol Liptzin, *The Flowering of Yiddish Literature* (New York: Thomas Yosellof, 1963). According to Liptzin, in *Di Khasene* Leivik "tried to free himself from the Nazi nightmare. . . . He sought to symbolize the beginning of a new life that would again blossom over the ruins of the old." As a result of his visit to the "American Zone of Occupation," Leivik "discovered among them [the survivors] an indestructible will to rebuild their shattered existences. This enabled him to sing again of new hopes and of Israel's eternal regeneration after historic catastrophes" (pp. 230–31). Liptzin's book in the early 1960s functioned, then, not just as a source of information about Leivik and other Yiddish writers but as a postwar-era text that testified to the continuing interest in both the catastrophe and the ability of the survivors to re-create their lives.

105. For one example, see AJHS, P-678, Robison Family Papers. Anne Robison gave radio speeches and lectures on her travels in Germany in the late 1940s to chapters of the National Council of Jewish Women and to the American Association of University Women, in which she was also active.

106. Information on this organization is best accessed from three books based on these trips, all by its president, Joseph Tenenbaum, including *The Road to Nowhere: An Indictment and a Challenge* (New York: American Federation for Polish Jews, 1947);

Let My People In (New York: American Federation for Polish Jews, 1947); and, with Sheila Tenenbaum, *In Search of a Lost People* (New York: Beechhurst, 1948). Tenenbaum addressed a June 1946 rally at Madison Square Garden, at which he described the twinned crisis of Polish Jewry, the legacy of "ruin and devastating" caused by the legacy of the "Nazi occupation," and the continuing violence being perpetrated on the "remaining Jews . . . the pitiful remnants" (Tenenbaum, "Address at Madison Square Garden," in YIVO 1015, box 4).

107. "Excerpts from the Annual Report on the House of Living Judaism—NFTS Victory Project," in AJA, Hebrew Union College, collection 73, box 41, folder 1.

108. *Tzukunft* 26, no. 6 (October 1946), pp. 18–19; clipping, in YIVO 526, Louis Lamed Papers, box 7, file 187; S. Margoshes, "My Friend Louis Segal," in *Louis Segal: In Memoriam,* ed. Mordecai Strigler (New York: Farband-Labor Zionist Order, 1965), pp. 29–31; Louis Segal, *Bei unzere sheeris hapletah in poilin un maarv-airope* (New York: Farband, 1947). The World Jewish Congress was one key organization that monitored the plight of the survivors. It published a steady stream of booklets, like Zorach Warhatg, "Where Shall They Go" *Jewish Affairs* 1, no. 7 (May 1, 1946), and Gerhard Jacoby, "The Story of the Jewish 'DP,'" *Jewish Affairs* 2, no. 6 (November 15, 1948).

109. "Press Release," July 10, 1946, in AJA, Hebrew Union College, collection 73, box 37, folder 1. The National Federation of Temple Sisterhoods also provided a stipend for Emanuel Gamoran, a Jewish educator, to travel to Europe and report back on the spiritual and educational needs of the Displaced Persons ("Press Release," May 28, 1948, in AJA, Hebrew Union College, collection 73, box 37, folder 1).

110 Naomi W. Cohen, *Not Free to Desist: The American Jewish Committee, 1906–1966* (Philadelphia: Jewish Publication Society of America, 1972), pp. 265–93; American Jewish Committee, ed., *Proceedings of the Fiftieth Anniversary Observance of the American Jewish Committee, April 10–14, 1957: The Pursuit of Equality at Home and Abroad* (New York: American Jewish Committee, 1958), pp. 133–36.

111. *American Jewish Year Book: 1951,* p. 225.

112. "Soldiers Write," *Youth and Nation* 14, no. 3 (December 1945), pp. 22–23.

113. Ira A. Hirschmann, *The Embers Still Burn: An Eye-Witness View of the Postwar Ferment in Europe and the Middle East and Our Disastrous Get-Soft-with-Germany Policy* (New York: Simon and Schuster, 1949). Hirschmann had been in Germany as a worker for the War Refugee Board, and he went to Europe and the DP camps as the personal representative of Fiorello LaGuardia, director general of the United Nations Relief and Rehabilitation Administration.

114. Leo W. Schwarz, "How the DPs Rose Above Adversity," in Jewish Welfare Board, *In Jewish Bookland* (December, 1954), p. 2. See also Leo W. Schwarz, *The Redeemers: A Saga of the Years 1945–1952* (New York: Farrar, Straus and Young, 1953); clipping, *Philadelphia Jewish Exponent,* March 5, 1954, in NYPL, Rare Books and Manuscripts Division, Farrar, Straus, Giroux Papers, box 316, "Schwarz, Leo, The Redeemers" folder.

115. *Congress Weekly* 13, no. 1 (January 4, 1946), p. 5.

116. Zachary Serwer, *Creative Dramatics in the Jewish Club* (New York: Jewish Welfare Board, 1946), pp. 6–7.

117. *Jewish Education* 20, no. 2 (Spring 1949), p. 56.

118. Ben Edidin, *Jewish Community Life in America* (New York: Hebrew Publishing, 1947), pp. 23, 115–17, 161, 175–80.

119. "An Interesting Episode in My Life," in YIVO 1148, box 4.

120. Flyer included in "40th General Assembly: Boston: 1948—Union of American Hebrew Congregations, National Federation of Temple Sisterhoods, National Federation of Temple Youth, National Association of Temple Secretaries," in AJA, Hebrew Union College, collection 266, box 1, folder 4.

121. National Federation of Temple Youth (NFTY), "Mimeo-Messenger," May 1952, in AJA, Hebrew Union College, collection 266, box 2, folder 5, p. 1.

122. In 1948, the Union of American Hebrew Congregations sponsored a radio dramatization of Baeck's life, "Unconquerable Soul: Dr. Leo Baeck Speaks to America." In telling Baeck's life, this program told as well the bigger Holocaust story. So, as the drama brought Baeck into Theresienstadt, the commentator declared, "Yes, it happened. The aged, venerable, rabbi was taken to Theresienstadt, a camp of death. They sent him with 2,000 other believers. Four survived. Four survived that trip. Four out of 2,000. They locked him in Theresienstadt. They locked in 60,000 sons and daughter of the covenant." For the script, see "40th General Assembly," in AJA, Hebrew Union College, collection 266, box 1, folder 4.

123. For the Baeck play, see Olin-Sang-Ruby, Leadership Conclave 1962, in AJA, Hebrew Union College, collection 266, box 5, folder 8. By the early 1950s, the Reform movement also launched a "Bricks-for-Baeck" project, this time to help build a Reform school in Israel.

124. Ely E. Pilchik, "The First Commandment," *Jeshurun Sermons* (New York: Bloch, 1957), pp. 41–49.

125. The narrative of Baeck as a Holocaust hero who symbolized Jewish endurance went beyond the Reform movement, although it claimed him first and foremost. The Jewish Theological Seminary offered him an honorary degree in 1946, and several *Eternal Light* dramas told his story. For example, "The Man Who Remembered Lincoln," *Eternal Light* (radio script) (New York: Jewish Theological Seminary, February 10, 1957).

126. Alfred Kazin, *A Walker in the City* (New York: Grove, 1951), pp. 51–52.

127. Trude Weiss-Rosmarin, "The Talmud and the U.S. Army," *Jewish Spectator* 16, no. 3 (March 1951), p. 26. On the printing of this edition of the Talmud by the survivors, see Sharon L. Mintz and Gabriel Goldstein, *Printing the Talmud: From Bomberg to Schottenstein* (New York: Yeshiva University Museum, 2005), pp. 294–95.

128. Moses A. Leavitt to Fanny Goldstein, December 28, 1950, in AJA, Hebrew Union College, collection 205, Fanny Goldstein Papers, box 5, folder 13.

129. Beth R. Cohen, *Case Closed: Holocaust Survivors in Postwar America* (New Brunswick, N.J.: Rutgers University Press, 2007). Cohen takes a critical look at American Jewish services for survivors, emphasizing that agencies rushed through the cases, eager to declare the survivors fit and settled. According to Cohen, they did not provide enough services at a sophisticated-enough level to really meet the needs, particularly, of orphans and those suffering trauma.

130. Clipping, *Wisconsin Jewish Chronicle,* November 16, 1945, in University of Wisconsin–Milwaukee, manuscript 87, box 1, file 3. This collection contains clippings from the local Jewish newspaper and the general city press on the activities of the Jewish Social Service agency and its various subsidiaries, like the Jewish Family and Children's Service, vis-à-vis the survivors who came to Milwaukee.

131. Clippings, *Milwaukee Journal*, May 20, 1949, and November 29, 1956, in University of Wisconsin–Milwaukee, manuscript 87, box 1, file 4. This collection is full of press releases issued by the Jewish Family and Children's Service and clippings from newspapers.

132. "Clipping, *Indianapolis Star*, 3/13/48," in YIVO 380, box 135.

133. Nora Faires and Nancy Hanflik, *Jewish Life in the Industrial Promised Land, 1855–2005* (East Lansing: Michigan State University Press, 2005), pp. 87–88.

134. "Employment for Refugees," Executive Committee, September 14, 1950, in Marvin Gelman Library, George Washington University, Jewish Community Council of Greater Washington Papers, manuscript 2012, box 3, folder 12.

135. Discussion in this and the next paragraph (*Those Who Live in the Sun*) from Bicentennial Committee, *The Souvenir Book of the Bicentennial: 1750–1950—The Story of the Celebration of the Bicentennial of the Charleston Jewish Community, November 19 Through November 26, 1950* (Charleston, S.C.: Bicentennial Committee, 1951), pp. 29, 83, 87, 91–92, 99, 103, 141. The official program book for the bicentennial included an address by the head of the local Jewish Community Center on the need to donate money in order to assist the survivors who were coming to Charleston.

136. "JLC July–December, 1947," in Tamiment Library, Wagner Labor Archives, NYU, Julius Bernstein Papers, box 13. The JLC also brought its message of the need to admit Displaced Persons to the United States and the particular plight of the Jews to the various city and state labor conferences and to both the American Federation of Labor and the Congress of Industrial Organizations at the national level. In November 1946, Rottenberg asked the head of the Rhode Island State Industrial Union Council for permission to "address the delegates for about 10 minutes on the subject of admitting European displaced persons to the United States" (Rottenberg to Frank Benti, November 26, 1946, in ibid.).

137. "Annual Report, 1946," p. 1, box 1, file 9. See also "Annual Report, 1945," Committee on Service for Foreign Born, New York Section, p. 1, box 1, file 8; "Annual Report, 1948," p. 1, box 10–13, file 1, folder 10—all in Yeshiva University Archives, National Council of Jewish Women Papers.

138. Clipping, *Wisconsin Jewish Chronicle*, February 10, 1950, September 20, 1957, University of Wisconsin–Milwaukee, manuscript 87, box 1, file 4.

139. Jack Fischel and Sanford Pinsker, eds., *Jewish-American History and Culture: An Encyclopedia* (New York: Garland, 1992), p. 251. See also Dorothy Rabinowitz, *New Lives: Survivors of the Holocaust Living in America* (New York: Knopf, 1976).

140. "Monument to Destroyed Synagogue," *Jewish Spectator* 16, no. 3 (March 1951), p. 10. The *Jewish Spectator* also provided a venue for the publication of translations of Yiddish works by Holocaust survivors about that experience. Among others, Abraham Sutzkever, Rachmil Bryks, and K. Tzetnik got their first non-Yiddish readership in this magazine. *Midstream* also published this kind of work. In 1962, it published a "condensation of a full-length play" based on Rachmil Bryks's *A Cat in the Ghetto*, interpreted by Shimon Wincelberg (Bryks, "The Window of Heaven: A Condensation of a Full-Length Play," *Midstream* 8, no. 4 [December 1962], pp. 44–65).

141. "Laughter Through Tears: A New American Who Arrives in Pittsburgh This Week Relates the Incredible Story of His Survival," *Pittsburgh Criterion* (March 31, 1950).

142. "Transactions of the XXI Biennial Assembly, NFTS, April 27–May 2, 1957," in AJA, Hebrew Union College, collection 73, box 5, folder 4, p. 6.

143. I thank Naomi Sage for this reference (Sage, "A Memorial Culture: The American Jewish Joint Distribution Committee [JDC] and Its Relationship with the Holocaust and Holocaust Survivors," unpublished manuscript).

144. Transcript of Proceedings of the XXIV Biennial Assembly, NFTS, 1963, in AJA, Hebrew Union College, collection 73, box 7, folder 3.

145. Chicago Yizkor Committee for Six Million Martyrs, Minutes, Meeting, March 7, 1957, in Chicago Jewish Archives, Spertus, collection 14, box 5, file 2, p. 6.

146. Minutes, Jewish Community Council of Pittsburgh, April 23, 1958, in AJA, Hebrew Union College, collection 283, box 11, folder 4.

147. National Federation of Temple Youth (NFTY), *Mimeo-Messenger* 2, no. 4 (February 1951), in AJA, Hebrew Union College, collection 266, box 2, folder 4; *Senior* 20, no. 1 (November 1961), pp. 2, 30, AJHS I-161; Society for the Advancement of Judaism, *Bulletin* 42, no. 12 (March 23, 1962), p. 12.

148. "Chaike Grossman," *Youth and Nation* 14, no. 8 (June 1946), pp. 2, 10–13; Labor Zionist Organization of America, Chicago Chapter, *Bulletin* 5 (January 1, 1958), n.p., in Chicago Jewish Archives, Spertus, collection 17, box 22.

149. *Mir Zeinen Doh* 1 (April 1951), p. 4.

150. Farband fun Gevezene Yidishe Katzetler un Partizaner in New York, *Calendar for 1953*, in YIVO 918, p. 2.

151. Clipping, *Forward*, n.d.; clipping, *Morgen Zhurnal*, in YIVO, RG 1400, ME-18–29, folder 121.

152. Biographical and autobiographical fragments in the printed programs of communal events, in magazines, and the like also turned attention to the centrality of Germany to the Nazi narrative. For an example of this nearly boundless genre of material, in 1958 the Chicago chapter of the American Jewish Congress sent out press releases to all the local papers informing them that Joachim Prinz, its newly elected president, would be in Chicago, speaking to various groups. The press release stated simply, "As Rabbi of the Jewish community of Berlin from 1925 to 1937, Dr. Prinz was one of the first Jewish leaders to speak out against the rising tide of Nazism. Hitler's rise to power only intensified Dr. Prinz's warnings from the pulpit until he was forced to flee Germany in 1937." In addition, the press release let the city papers know that Prinz served on the board of the Conference of Jewish Material Claims Against Germany and that a recent book which Prinz had just written, *We Jews*, had been "a continental best seller—remained a clear analysis of the plight of Europe's doomed Jewish communities and a call to action against the Nazi regime," referring to his 1934 book *Wir Juden* ("Press Release," October 24, 1958, in Chicago Jewish Archives, Spertus, collection 14). Similarly, the National Federation of Temple Sisterhoods issued a set of materials on "The Contribution of Jewish Composers to the Music of the Modern World," complete with recorded music and booklets for use by its chapters at their meetings. The materials had been prepared by Eve Landau. As the brochure accompanying the material read, she had been born in Germany, and after "escaping Hitler Germany, Dr. Landau found refuge in England and then, in America" ("Brochure," in AJA, Hebrew Union College, collection 73, box 35, folder 1).

153. This and the following discussion from University of Wisconsin–Milwaukee,

New Home Club Papers, manuscript 42, particularly boxes 1,4, 1,17, 1,22, 1,30, 2,1, 2,4, 2,7, 2,11, 2,12. In 1965, the New Home Club spearheaded an effort to abort Milwaukee's adoption of Munich as its sister city.

154. For one analysis of Jewish hometown associations and their place in American Jewish history, see Daniel Soyer, *Jewish Immigrant Associations and American Identity in New York, 1880–1939* (Cambridge: Harvard University Press, 1997).

155. Flyer, March 4, 1958, in YIVO 1148, box 3, "Youth Section" folder; "Turkoff," in AJHS, P-38, Molly Picon Papers, box 36, file 681. Picon frequently devoted her radio show to memoirs by survivors, as well as the publication of *yizker bikher*. In 1947, for example, she spent the broadcast reading from Aaron Tverski's *Ikh bin der korben un der eydes* [I am the victim and the witness] (New York: Shulsinger, 1947) (in AJHS, P-38, Molly Picon Papers, box 32, file 551).

156. Tverski, *Ikh bin der korben un der eydes*; Shlomo Brynski, *Vehn fundamentn traislin zikh* (Chicago: International Press, 1951); Committee to Perpetuate the Memory of the Fallen Teachers from the Tsisho Schools in Poland, *Lerer-yizkor-bukh: Di umgekummene lerer fun Tzishe shuln in Poilin* (New York: Marstin, 1952–1954). In 1961, Dina Abramowicz, essaying Yiddish writing in America for the *Jewish Book Annual: 5721, 1961*, commented that "numerous . . . personal memoirs and diaries of the . . . Hurban . . . were added to the vast body of documentation of the catastrophe" (p. 171).

157. Gerda Weissman Klein, *All but My Life* (New York: Hill and Wang, 1957).

158. Kitty Hart, *I Am Alive* (New York: Coward-McCann, 1960); Earl Weinstock, *The Seven Years* (New York: Dutton, 1959).

159. S. B. Unsdorfer, *The Yellow Star* (New York: Thomas Yoseloff, 1961); David Wdowinski, *And We Are Not Saved* (New York: Philosophical Library, 1963). See also Sarah Bick Berkowitz, *Where Are My Brothers?* (New York: Helios, 1965).

160. Abraham Fuksman, "My Life Story," *Yeshivah Yearbook: 1953*, p. 36. Fuksman also contributed a version of this same life story in the Hebrew section of the yearbook.

161. For example, Rachmil Bryks, *Oyf kidesh hashem: Un andere dertseylungen* (New York: Yerahmiel Briks Bukh-Komitet, 1952); Rachmil Bryks, *A Cat in the Ghetto: Four Novelettes* (New York: Bloch, 1959), see p. 7.

162. Ilona Karmel, *Stephania* (Boston: Houghton Mifflin, 1953); Herman Taube, *Empty Pews: A Novel of World War II Based on the Life of Immigrants Who Found Hope, Love, and Happiness in America*, trans. Sarah Chodosh Lesser (Baltimore: Gossman, 1958); Norman Lipschutz, *Victory Through Darkness* (New York: Vantage, 1960); Elie Weisel, *Night* (New York: Hill and Wang, 1960).

163. "In Commemoration of the Tenth Anniversary," Exhibition Catalog, JLC, 2, YIVO 1148.

164. *Mir Zeinen Doh* 1 (April 1951), p. 4.

165. *American Jewish Year Book: 1961*, pp. 105–7.

166. "Memo," January 25, 1961, in Tamiment Library, Wagner Labor Archives, NYU, Julius Bernstein Papers, box 1, "American Nazi Party, 1961–1965" folder.

167. Clipping, January 16, 1961, in Tamiment Library, Wagner Labor Archives, NYU, Julius Bernstein Papers, box 1, "American Nazi Party, 1961–1965" folder.

168. "Transcript of Radio show, WEEI 1/21/61," in Tamiment Library, Wagner Labor Archives, NYU, Julius Bernstein Papers, box 1, "American Nazi Party, 1961–1965" folder.

169. Robert Segal, clipping, in Tamiment Library, Wagner Labor Archives, NYU, Julius Bernstein Papers, box 1, "American Nazi Party, 1961–1965" folder.

170. Clipping, February 6, 1961, in Tamiment Library, Wagner Labor Archives, NYU, Julius Bernstein Papers, box 1, "Co-ordination Committee, Jewish Culture Clubs" folder.

171. "Editorial," *Jewish Advocate*, in Tamiment Library, Wagner Labor Archives, NYU, Julius Bernstein Papers, box 1, "American Nazi Party, 1961–1965" folder. Similar confrontations between organized survivor groups and local Jewish community councils took place in Washington, D.C., Pittsburgh, and Cincinnati. The records of other Jewish communities would very likely reveal such clashes there, as well. *American Jewish Year Book: 1961* reported on this exact struggle in New York (p. 108).

172. Emanuel Muravchik to JLC Field Staff, August 3, 1960, in Tamiment Library, Wagner Labor Archives, NYU, Julius Bernstein Papers, box 1, "Co-ordination Committee, Jewish Culture Clubs," folder.

Notes to Chapter 4

1. Discussion in this and the next paragraph from Trude Weiss-Rosmarin, "Auf Wiedersehen!" *Jewish Spectator* 18, no. 1 (January 1953), pp. 3–4.

2. Peter Novick, *The Holocaust in American Life* (Boston: Houghton Mifflin, 1999), p. 96.

3. Leo W. Schwarz, *The Redeemers: A Saga of the Years 1945–1952* (New York: Farrar, Straus and Young, 1953), p. ix.

4. Labor Zionist Organization (LZO) Branch Meetings, April 1965, in Chicago Jewish Archives, Spertus, collection 17, box 12; Annual Dinner, Pittsburgh Jewish Community Council, May 14, 1951, in AJA, Hebrew Union College, collection 283, box 11, folder 1.

5. Gerald Krefetz, "Nazism: The Textbook Treatment," *Congress Bi-Weekly* 28, no. 16 (November 13, 1961), pp. 5–6. The author described the treatment of "German war crimes" in one of the textbooks as cast in language so bland that it could be used to describe "salmon fishing in Canada" (p. 5).

6. So irrelevant was Dachau to the history of the Holocaust that it merited no entry in either the *Encyclopedia Judaica* (Jerusalem: Encyclopedia Judaica, 1972) or the *Encyclopedia of Jewish Life Before and During the Holocaust*, ed. Shmuel Spector (New York: New York University Press, 2001).

7. Shlomo Katz, "Symbol of Terror," *Midstream* 8, no. 3 (September 1962), pp. 56–59.

8. Shlomo Katz, "Self-Portrait of an American Jew," *Jewish Frontier* 21, no. 8 (August 1954), pp. 12–13.

9. Clipping, *Boston Globe*, 1959, in Tamiment Library, Wagner Labor Archives, NYU, Julius Bernstein Papers, box 5, file 9.

10. Henry Morgenthau Jr., *Germany Is Our Problem* (New York: Harper Brothers, 1945), p. 105.

11. Quoted in Naomi W. Cohen, *Not Free to Desist: The American Jewish Committee, 1906–1966* (Philadelphia: Jewish Publication Society of America, 1972), p. 480. For a

local report on negative reactions by non-Jews to the Morgenthau Plan, see "Survey of Anti-Semitism Cincinnati Area," in AJA, Hebrew Union College, collection 202, box 3, folder 1.

12. "Request for a Senate Investigation," in Chicago Jewish Archives, Spertus, collection 14, box 11, file 2.

13. "Dare We Forget . . . ? Can We Forget?" December 23, 1949, in Chicago Jewish Archives, Spertus, collection 14, box 3, file 5; "You Must Stop the Renazification of Germany," in Tamiment Library, Wagner Labor Archives, NYU, Julius Bernstein Papers, box 9.

14. "Headquarters Release No. 176," December 29, 1949, in AJHS, I-32, box 1, "JWV Conventions" folder.

15. *American Jewish Year Book: 1953*, p. 106.

16. "Resolution on Germany," in Tamiment Library, Wagner Labor Archives, NYU, Isaiah Minkoff Papers, box 7, file 41.

17. "Senate Body Will Discuss Failure of Denazification in U.S. Zone, Jews Urge Investigation," in Tamiment Library, Wagner Labor Archives, NYU, Julius Bernstein Papers, box 9, "Germany-Denazification, 1949–1963" folder.

18. American Jewish Committee, *Proceedings of the Fiftieth Anniversary Observance of the American Jewish Committee, April 10–14, 1957: The Pursuit of Equality at Home and Abroad* (New York: American Jewish Committee, 1958), pp. 226–27.

19. Joshua M. Zeitz, *White Ethnic New York: Jews, Catholics, and the Shaping of Postwar Politics* (Chapel Hill: University of North Carolina Press, 2007), p. 198 (originally, Ph.D. diss., Brown University, 2002); American Jewish Committee, *Proceedings of the Fiftieth Anniversary Observance*, pp. 228–29.

20. Robert Segal to Abraham Alper et al., June 6, 1949, in Tamiment Library, Wagner Labor Archives, NYU, Julius Bernstein Papers, box 12.

21. Adolph Held to John Foster Dulles, March 30, 1955, in Tamiment Library, Wagner Labor Archives, NYU, Edward S. Goldstein Papers, box 4, file 56. Held not only sent the letter to Dulles but also issued it as a press release.

22. Proceedings, 1950 Assembly, National Jewish Youth Conference, Camp Wel-Met, Narrowsburg, New York, August 31–September 8, 1950, in AJA, Hebrew Union College, collection 266, box 2.

23. "For the Sake of Humanity," *Furrows* 15, no. 5 (June 1959), pp. 3–4.

24. Meetings of Executive Council, American Jewish Congress Chicago Chapter, December 5, 1950, in Chicago Jewish Archives, Spertus, collection 14.

25. "On German Rearmament," *Furrows* 8, no. 5 (January 1951), pp. 11–12.

26. Quoted in Jeffrey Herf, *Divided Memory: The Nazi Past in the Two Germanys* (Cambridge: Harvard University Press, 1997), p. 282. See also Elazar Barkan, *The Guilt of Nations: Restitution and Negotiating Historical Injustices* (New York: Norton, 2001).

27. Clipping, *Der Tog*, September 29, 1951, in NYPL, Rare Books and Manuscripts Division, Koppel S. Pinson Papers, box 8; "Toward a Settlement with Germany," *Congress Bi-Weekly* 18, no. 25 (October 8, 1951), p. 3; Mordecai Shtrigler, "Less Enthusiasm, Please," *Jewish Frontier* 19, no. 10 (November 1952), pp. 10–11.

28. *American Jewish Year Book: 1953*, p. 584.

29. Adolph Held, typescript of *New Leader* article, "A First-Hand Report for the

Israel-German Negotiations: European Labor's Support Is Secured," in Tamiment Library, Wagner Labor Archives, NYU, Edward S. Goldstein Papers, box 4, file 58.

30. "For Publication at Will," 1952, in AJHS, I-68, SCA Papers, box 10, "Press Release" folder. "The German Amends to Jews," *Congress Weekly* 19, no. 23 (September 22, 1952), p. 3. The article, it should be noted, went on to remark that two other countries had not yet come forward to behave in such a contrite and impressive manner: the Communist German Democratic Republic and Austria. As to the former, this article, like so many of its kind, could have been an occasion for indulging in anti-Communist rhetoric, and it would have been perfectly consistent for the American Jewish Congress, a foe of Communism, to do so. But in fact, at least in this article, it devoted much more space to criticizing Austria, "which was formerly part of Hitler's domain," than it did to East Germany, which it merely described in neutral and empirical terms as "Soviet-controlled" and "which must be held responsible for its proportionate share of the debt" to the victims: "The claim against it remains outstanding and the bill should be pressed for payment."

31. Aaron Aronin to Joseph Brumberg, March 31, 1955, in Tamiment Library, Wagner Labor Archives, NYU, Jewish Labor Committee Chicago Collection, box 1, file 5.

32. One statement of the "blood money" argument is found in an article by the Yiddish poet Hayim Leivik, "No Blood Money from Germany," *Jewish Frontier* 17, no. 5 (May 1950), pp. 14–15; see also Hayim Leivik, "Take with You Words," *Eternal Light* (radio script) (New York: Jewish Theological Seminary of America, September 22, 1957).

33. The small revisionist Zionist group in the United States and its youth movement Betar demonstrated against the agreement because the political party in Israel which it supported, Herut, led by Menachem Begin, opposed it in the parliament. So, too, Jewish Communist groups spoke out and demonstrated against the agreement in line with the stance taken by the Soviet Union, as did the Communists in Israel. On the revisionists, see Ronald W. Zweig, *German Reparations and the Jewish World: A History of the Claims Conference* (London: Frank Cass, 2001), p. 28; on Communists, see Barkan, *Guilt of Nations.* No scholar has as yet written a full history of Jewish Communists in the United States or on the Revisionists in America after 1948.

34. Trude Weiss-Rosmarin, "Israel Still Debates Ban on Germany," *Jewish Spectator* 16, no. 3 (March 1951), p. 24.

35. Ben Halpern, "The Nuremberg Trial," *Jewish Frontier* 12, no. 2 (October 1945), pp. 30–32. The American Jewish press, as well as rabbis in their sermons and organizations in their meetings, devoted vast attention to the Nuremberg trials and other less-famous legal proceedings against Nazis.

36. "A Feather in Hitler's Cap," *Furrows* 8, no. 7 (March 1951), pp. 4–5.

37. Trude Weiss-Rosmarin, "Comments and Opinions," *Jewish Spectator* 16, no. 3 (March 1951), pp. 5–6.

38. A full study of American Jewish discourse and programming around the Eichmann trial should be undertaken to analyze the range of reactions.

39. Harry Golden, foreword to Henry A. Zeiger, *The Case Against Adolf Eichmann* (New York: Signet, 1960), pp. vi–x. The cover of the paperback also highlighted the fact of the Jewishness of Eichmann's victims and the Germans as the perpetrators. On the front cover, the book enticed readers with the words "THE FULLY DOCUMENTED STORY

of the infamous Nazi captured in Argentina to stand trial for the murder of 6,000,000 Jews," while the back cover, with Eichmann's photographs from 1943 in his uniform and his "ordinary" photo of 1960, quoted him: "'I do not care if I die, for 5,000,000 Jews will have jumped into the grave ahead of me,' boasted ADOLF EICHMANN shortly before the defeat of Germany. Now this former Nazi colonel is to be tried in Israel for the murder of 6,000,000 Jews."

40. Boris Smolar, "The Eichmann Trial," January 13, 1961, in AJHS P-588, Boris Smolar Papers, box 11, "Between You and Me" folder. The issue of the need for the Eichmann trial and the denying of the fact of the Holocaust was also reported in the *American Jewish Year Book* of 1962, which noted that a number of "hatemongers" in the United States were spreading the line that "Adolf Eichmann was a martyr and six million Jews never died in the holocaust" (*American Jewish Year Book: 1962*, p. 196).

41. "The Labor Zionist Organization of Chicago, Third Seder, 1961," in Chicago Jewish Archives, Spertus, collection 17, Labor Zionists of Chicago Records.

42. Max Gottschalk, Abraham Duker, and Michael Alper, eds., *Jewish Post-War Problems: A Study Course—Relief, Reconstruction and Migration* (New York: Research Institute of Peace and Post-War Problems of the American Jewish Committee, 1943), p. 28.

43. Clipping, November 6, 1957, Marvin Gelman Library, George Washington University, Jewish Community Council of Greater Washington Papers, manuscript 2012.

44. Hayim Leivik, "No Blood Money," *Jewish Forum* 17, no. 5 (May 1950), pp. 14–15; "Program and Study Materials, 1945–1946," in AJA, Hebrew Union College, collection 73, box 36, folder 1; CLSA *Reports* (March 1950), in Chicago Jewish Archives, Spertus, collection 14, box 10, file 1.

45. *American Jewish Year Book: 1953*, p. 303.

46. National Community Relations Advisory Committee (NCRAC), Report of the Fourth Plenary Session, June 15–17, 1946, p. 7.

47. "Report of the Executive Director," April 11, 1960, in Marvin Gelman Library, George Washington University, Jewish Community Council of Greater Washington Papers, manuscript 2012, box 6, folder 6. See also "Report: The Meaning of the Swastika," April 20, 1960," in AJA, Hebrew Union College, collection 202, box 38, folder 1, p. 6; JCRC Meeting, April 27, 1960, in AJA, Hebrew Union College, collection 283, box 11, folder 5; Harry Miller to Burton Hirsch, October 24, 1966, in Chicago Jewish Archives, Spertus, collection 14, box 6, file 1; Boris Smolar, "American Moods," March 30, 1962, in AJHS, P-588, Boris Smolar Papers, box 11, "Between You and Me" folder.

48. "First National Jewish Leader to Visit Germany on Official Invitation in Twenty Years Leaves Today with Eight U.S. Clergymen," in AJHS, I-68, SCA Papers, box 50, "Press Release" folder.

49. Arno Herzberg to Norman Salit, December 1, 1953, in AJHS, I-68, SCA Papers, box 25, "Germany-Salit" folder.

50. Boris Smolar, "Mission to Germany," March 26, 1954, in AJHS, P-588, Boris Smolar Papers, box 10, "Between You and Me" folder. Material on Isaac Frank's Germany trip is in Marvin Gelman Library, George Washington University, Jewish Community Council of Greater Washington Papers, manuscript 2012, box 5, folder 9; box 11, folders 5–6.

51. The full history of American Jewish institutional monitoring and involvement with postwar Germany cannot be treated here, given the enormity of both the work undertaken and the commentary on it at the time. At the institutional level, see Shlomo Shafir, *Ambiguous Relations: The American Jewish Community and Germany Since 1945* (Detroit: Wayne State University Press, 1999).

52. Alexander Miller to Label Katz, January 6, 1961, and report, "Mission to Germany," in AJHS, P-92, Label Katz Papers, box 12, "Germany" folder. In 1956, leaders of the B'nai B'rith Youth Organization (BBYO) had also gone to Germany as part of a larger European mission intended to evaluate the possibility of its establishing European clubs. The report written by Max Baer, BBYO's national director, took a decidedly pessimistic view of this possibility, in light of "the one central brutal fact which underlies Jewish community life in virtually every country on the Continent. Six million Jews were murdered by the Nazi hordes," leaving few Jewish youth alive to belong (Baer, "Memo," February 21, 1956, in AJHS, P-92, box 10, "BBYO, 1956–1964" folder).

53. Tony Judt, *Postwar: A History of Europe Since 1945* (New York: Penguin, 2005), pp. 59–60, 85–86, 122–23, 220.

54. *American Jewish Year Book: 1953*, p. 301.

55. Harry C. Schnur, "Nazism Documented," *Youth and Nation* (December 5, 1955), in I-61, AJHS.

56. Steve Orlow, "Forgive and Forget?" *Senior* 20, no. 2 (December 1961), p. 2, in AJHS, I-161, box 30.

57. Lillian Friedberg, Executive Director Report, May 14, 1951, in AJA, Hebrew Union College, collection 283, box 11.

58. Press release, April 20, 1949, in YIVO 1015, box 2, file 2.

59. Ibid.

60. Clipping, *Jewish Times*, Tamiment Library, Wagner Labor Archives, NYU, Edward S. Goldstein Papers, box 4, file 5.

61. Julius Bernstein Papers, box 30, file 14; Marvin Gelman Library, George Washington University, Jewish Community Council of Greater Washington Papers, manuscript 2012, box 1, file 7, and box 4, files 16–17. For more extensive treatment of this subject, see David Monod, *German Music, Denazification, and the Americans, 1945–1953* (Chapel Hill: University of North Carolina Press, 2005). Similarly, Arnold Forster, a longtime staff member of the Anti-Defamation League, covered the matter of the German pianist Walter Gieseking in *A Measure of Freedom: An Anti-Defamation League Report* (New York: Doubleday, 1950), pp. 95–96.

62. Material on the Chicago reaction to *The Desert Fox* is in Chicago Jewish Archives, Spertus, collection 14, box 3, file 7. The Jewish War Veterans were also quite active in the anti–"Desert Fox" effort ("It's Action That Counts," in AJHS, I-31, box 3, "Printed Material" folder). The same files contain letters written to the local distributor of the film, who happened to be Jewish, demanding that he refuse to show the film in Chicago.

63. *American Jewish Year Book: 1950*, p. 113.

64. Anti-Defamation League, *Anti-Semitism in the United States in 1947* (New York: Anti-Defamation League, 1947), p. 92; "Report of Activities: American Jewish Congress Chicago Council Commission on Law and Social Action," July 1955, in Chicago Jewish Archives, Spertus, collection 14, box 1, file 7.

65. Memo, "Information Re: The Work of the Cincinnati Jewish Community Relations Committee," 1952, in AJA, Hebrew Union College, collection 202.

66. "Monthly Reports, Committee on Law and Social Action," December 1955, in Chicago Jewish Archives, Spertus, collection 14, box 1, file 7.

67. Boris Smolar, "Washington Sidelights," October 6, 1957, in AJHS P-588, Boris Smolar Papers, box 11, "Between You and Me" folder.

68. Hasia R. Diner, *Fifty Years of Jewish Self-Governance: The Jewish Community Council of Greater Washington, 1938–1988* (Washington, D.C.: Jewish Community Council of Greater Washington, 1989).

69. Executive Committee Minutes, May 9, 1951, in Marvin Gelman Library, George Washington University, Jewish Community Council of Greater Washington, manuscript 2012.

70. Ibid.

71. Ibid.

72. Judah Nadich, *Eisenhower and the Jews* (New York: Twayne, 1953), p. 245.

73. Max Weinreich, *Hitler's Professors: The Part of Scholarship in Germany's Crimes Against the Jewish People* (New York: YIVO Institute for Jewish Research, 1946); Antatole Goldstein, *Operation Murder* (New York: Institute for Jewish Affairs, 1949); Antatole Goldstein, *From Discrimination to Annihilation* (New York: Institute for Jewish Affairs, 1952); Eva Reichmann, *Hostages of Civilization: The Social Sources of National Socialist Anti-Semitism* (Boston: Beacon, 1951); Eugen Kogon, *The Theory and Practice of Hell: The German Concentration Camps and the System Behind Them* (New York: Berkeley, 1950); Joseph Tenenbaum, *Race and Reich: The Story of an Epoch* (New York: Twayne, 1956); Leon Poliakov, *Harvest of Hate: The Nazi Program for the Destruction of the Jews of Europe* (Syracuse, N.Y.: Syracuse University Press, 1954); Gerald R. Reitlinger, *The Final Solution: The Attempt to Exterminate the Jews of Europe, 1939–1945* (New York: Beechhurst, 1953); Gerald R. Reitlinger, *The SS: Alibi of a Nation* (New York: Viking, 1957); Randolph Braham, *Eichmann and the Destruction of Hungarian Jewry* (New York: Twayne, 1961); Raul Hilberg, *The Destruction of the European Jews* (Chicago: Quadrangle, 1961).

74. American Jewish publications also paid a great deal of attention to the publication of William Shirer's *The Rise and Fall of the Third Reich: A History of Nazi Germany* (New York: Simon and Schuster, 1960). *Jewish Book Annual: 1961* gave high marks of praise for Shirer's *The Rise and Fall of Adolf Hitler* (New York: Random House, 1961), an illustrated version of the above-mentioned book, aimed at readers twelve to fifteen years old, "a dispassionate documented account which proves that truth can be more dreadful than fiction" (p. 155).

75. Nathan Zuckerman, *The Wine of Violence: An Anthology of Anti-Semitism* (New York: Association Press, 1947), p. xv.

76. Ben Edidin, *Jewish Community Life in America* (New York: Hebrew Publishing, 1947), pp. 158, 161, 175–80.

77. Milton Mayer provides an interesting example here. Born and raised as a Jew in Chicago, Mayer embraced the Quaker tradition in 1945. He did not have a doctorate, nor did he hold any long-term academic appointments. His 1954 *They Thought They Were Free: The Germans, 1933–45* (Chicago: University of Chicago Press, 1955) did gain the attention of Jewish publications, however, and as a work of history, it paid

attention not just to the persecution of the Jews in Germany but to Germany's undertaking of the "final solution to the Jewish problem." *Jewish Spectator* found it particularly
enlightening because it "highlights the way 'the little people' became Nazis" and as such
showed how the German masses played a key role in the destruction of European Jewry
("Review of *They Thought They Were Free," Jewish Spectator* 20, no. 7 [July 1955], p. 27).

78. Koppel S. Pinson, *Modern Germany: Its History and Civilization* (New York:
Macmillan, 1954). Shortly after Pinson's book came out, he reviewed one German
and two American books on the history of Germany and National Socialism in *Jewish
Social Science,* and he concluded his review with the importance of studying the topic,
organizing more archives, and publishing more works on the subject of "the recent Jewish Catastrophe." Pinson ended his review with the observation that "this is a task that
should not be delayed too long and it is one for which only American Jewish scholarship has the means and the facilities" to undertake (Koppel S. Pinson, *Jewish Social
Studies* 17, no. 1 [January 1955], pp. 81–82). Listings and the texts of some of Pinson's
speeches are in NYPL, Rare Books and Manuscripts Division, Koppel S. Pinson Papers,
boxes 1 and 4.

79. Boris Smolar, clipping, *Jewish Exponent,* September 3, 1954, in NYPL, Rare
Books and Manuscripts Division, Koppel S. Pinson Papers, box 14. Smolar's piece was
syndicated around the country and did not appear in just the Philadelphia newspapers.

80. Alfred Werner, "The Roots of Nazism," *Congress Weekly* 21, no. 27 (October 11,
1954), pp. 5–7.

81. Robert W. Kempner, "Blueprint for Murder," *Congress Weekly* 17, no. 10 (March
6, 1950), pp. 7–9.

82. Trude Weiss-Rosmarin, "Lest We Forget," *Jewish Spectator* 19, no. 5 (May 1954),
p. 27.

83. Abraham Micarmel to Philip Slomowitz, May 30, 1954, *Detroit Jewish News,*
in AJHS, P-841, "Correspondence as Jewish News Editor, 1950–1958" folder; Trude
Weiss-Rosmarin, "Comments and Opinions," *Jewish Spectator* 23, no. 9 (November
1958), p. 7.

84. Charles Chavel, "From Rephidim to Sinai," in *The 5708–1947 Manual of Holiday Sermons,* ed. Charles Chavel (New York: Rabbinical Council of America Press,
1947), p. 101.

85. "This Week in Religion: Radio Broadcasts," in AJHS, I-68, SCA Papers, box 36,
"This Week" folder.

86. "The Nazis in Retrospect," *Jewish Spectator* 22, no. 1 (January 1957), p. 29.

87. Adolf Leschnitzer, *The Magic Background of Modern Anti-Semitism: An Analysis of the German-Jewish Relationship* (New York: International Universities Press,
1956).

88. *Jewish Book Annual 5717, 1957,* p. 90.

89. Hayim Greenberg, *The Inner Eye* (New York: Jewish Frontier Association,
1953), pp. 103, 111.

90. Julius Guttmann, "The Principles of Judaism," *Conservative Judaism* 14, no. 1
(Fall 1958), pp. 22–23.

91. Alan Miller, "Letter to the Readers," *SAJ Bulletin* 43, no. 6 (December 21,
1962), pp. 2–3.

92. Boris Smolar, "Dictators and Jews," May 14, 1954, in AJHS, P-588, Boris Smolar

Papers, "Between You and Me" folder, box 10, file 2. Solomon Landman and Benjamin Efron, *Story Without End: An Informal History of the Jewish People* (New York: Holt, 1949), p. 234.

93. "Role of German Scholarship in Annihilation of Jews Analyzed," *News of YIVO* 10 (September 1945), pp. 1–2.

94. L. G. Kay, "Extermination Was a German Cartel: Recent Trials Reveal How All Classes of German Society Participated," News Release, Office of Jewish Information, 1949, NYPL, Rare Books and Manuscripts Division, Koppel S. Pinson Papers, box 8; *Yedios* 10 (September 1945), p. 8; Morris Janowitz, "German Reactions to Nazi Atrocities," *American Journal of Sociology* 52, no. 2 (September 1946), pp. 141–46.

95. References to this kind of material could be drawn from every volume of the *American Jewish Year Book*, as it annually included lengthy sections of Jewish news from around the world. See, as just two examples, *American Jewish Year Book: 1958*, pp. 250–51, 258–59. France received the most attention, and books like William Herzog's *From Dreyfus to Petain* (New York: Creative Press, 1947) were lauded in American Jewish publications.

96. *Congress World* 5, no. 2 (September 1951), p. 2.

97. Boris Smolar, "The Untold Story: Between You and Me," April 3, 1959, in AJHS, P-588, Boris Smolar Papers, box 11, "Between You and Me" folder.

98. "For Release: Thursday, November 20, 1952," in Tamiment Library, Wagner Labor Archives, NYU, Jewish Labor Committee Papers, box 11, "Immigration: McCarran Act" folder; "JTA News: 3/4/49," in YIVO 380, ORT Papers, box 139.

99. Jacob R. Marcus to Richard Bluestein, May 31, 1949, in AJA, Hebrew Union College, collection 202, box 3, folder 10. The same file that contains the material on the Flagstad affair also details the activities of the Cincinnati Jewish Community Relations Committee and the matter of Walter Gieseking, a German pianist who was a member of the Nazi Party and had performed for Hitler.

100. For some of the Austrian material, see Plenum Meeting, Synagogue Council of America, February 9, 1955, in AJHS, I-68, SCA Papers, box 2, "Plenum Meetings: 1949–1959" folder; Boris Smolar, "Washington Moods, Between You and Me," January 1, 1954, in AJHS, P-588, Boris Smolar Papers, box 10, "Between You and Me" folder; Committee for Restitution in Austria to Jewish Labor Committee, February 29, 1952, in Tamiment Library, Wagner Labor Archives, NYU, Edward S. Goldstein Papers, box 4, file 56; clipping, "American Fed. of Labor Backs Jewish Claims Against Austria," January 29, 1954, in ibid., Julius Bernstein Papers, box 13.

101. Clipping, "The Austrian Settlement," April 1957, in Tamiment Library, Wagner Labor Archives, NYU, Edward S. Goldstein Papers, box 4, file 56; *American Jewish Year Book: 1958*, pp. 305–6; "Ungenerous Austria," *Congress Bi-Weekly* 33, no. 14 (November 7, 1966), p. 8; "Austrian Claims," in Chicago Jewish Archives, Spertus, collection 14, box 21, file 5.

102. "Ungenerous Austria," *Congress Bi-Weekly* 33, no. 14 (November 7, 1966), p. 8; clipping, "The Austrian Settlement," April 1957, in Tamiment Library, Wagner Labor Archives, NYU, Edward S. Goldstein Papers; *American Jewish Year Book: 1958*, pp. 305–6; "Austrian Claims," in Chicago Jewish Archives, Spertus, collection 14, box 21, file 5.

103. Trude Weiss-Rosmarin, "The Nations Against Israel," *Jewish Spectator* 21, no. 2 (February 1956), p. 6.

104. On the Grand Mufti's pro-Nazi, pro-German speeches, see Jeffery Herf, "The Classic Case: Nazi Germany, Anti-Semitism, and Anti-Zionism During World War II," *Journal of Israeli History* 25, no. 1 (March 2006), pp. 63–83.

105. Henry Atkinson, "Shall International Promises Be Kept?" in Zionist Organization of Chicago, *Yearbooks: 5707, 1946–47*, pp. 18, 151, in Chicago Jewish Archives, Spertus, collection 19; "History in the Making," *Masada* 1, no. 6 (May 1946), p. 3; Jesse Calmenson to Harry Truman, March 21, 1948, in AJHS-359, Jesse Calmenson Papers, box 6; Trude Weiss-Rosmarin, "The Great Western Folly," *Jewish Spectator* 21, no. 2 (February 1956), p. 3.

106. Irving Kane, "Speech," November 16, 1957, in Tamiment Library, Wagner Labor Archives, NYU, Isaiah Minkoff Papers, box 12, file 12; Rabbi Israel Breslau, "Letter to the Editor, *Washington Star,* December 23, 1953," in AJHS, P-507, box 4; Weiss-Rosmarin, "Great Western Folly," p. 3.

107. These writers obviously had no access to Vatican archives, many of which have not even been opened at the beginning of the twenty-first century.

108. Clipping, "Reviews of Essays on Antisemitism," in NYPL, Rare Books and Manuscripts Division, Koppel S. Pinson Papers, box 14.

109. Boris Smolar, "Contemporary History, Between You and Me," March 2, 1956, in AJHS, P-588, Boris Smolar Papers, box 10, "Between You and Me" folder.

110. Leon Poliakov, "The Vatican and the Jewish Question," *Commentary* 10, no. 5 (November 1950), pp. 439–49.

111. "The Pope and Jewry," *Jewish Forum* 41, no. 12 (December 1958), pp. 192–95; Rabbi Philip W. Zimmerman, and Hirsch Loeb Gordon, Ph.D., M.D., letters to editor, *Jewish Forum* 42, no. 2 (February 1959), pp. 32–33; "Editorial: Saving Jewish Dignity —and the Swastika," *Jewish Forum* 43, no. 2 (February 1960), p. 16; Dr. Jacob B. Glenn, "Re: Religion in Public Life" and "Catholic Sins of Omission," letters to the editor, *Jewish Forum* 43, no. 10 (October 1960), p. 181 (first appeared in *New York Times,* February 1, 1960).

112. Glenn, "Re: Religion in Public Life" and "Catholic Sins of Omission."

113. See also Marie Syrkin, *Jewish Forum* 17, no. 1(January 1950), p. 27, in which the author reviewed Erick H. Boehm's *We Survived,* narratives of fourteen Germans who had to go into hiding because of their opposition to Nazism. Syrkin praised the book for helping Jews to become "aware of the Christian Germans who opposed Hitler and who aided Jews at great personal risk."

114. "The Dark Places," *Eternal Light* (radio script) (New York: Jewish Theological Seminary of America, February 7, 1957).

115. Philip Friedman, *Their Brothers' Keepers* (New York: Crown, 1957). The 1978 reprint published by the Holocaust Library included information on the Anti-Defamation League ceremony, as well as a reprint of a letter of support for the book written to Friedman by Eleanor Roosevelt in 1957, just after the book came out, in which she commented, "I have come through with a feeling that if all of us had the courage to protest immediately when we felt something was wrong, we could perhaps prevent the tragedies that Hitler brought."

116. Other texts of this period that looked specifically at Germans who defied Hitler and his Jewish policies in Germany include C. C. Aronsfeld, "Not All Germans Are Guilty," *Jewish Spectator* 20, no. 2 (February 1955), pp. 9–11. In 1962, the Leo Baeck

Institute held a public ceremony to honor Heinrich Grueber of Berlin, a Protestant minister "who saved many Jewish lives during the darkest days of the Nazi period." One of those aided by him, Mrs. Jesse Vorst, a member of the board of the Leo Baeck Institute's Women's Auxiliary, spoke at the ceremony in "a short and moving speech, expressing her gratitude to Probst Grueber for saving her life by providing her with a permit to go to Holland where she survived and worked in the underground movement for many years" (*Leo Baeck Institute Newsletter* 3, no. 2 [Fall 1962], p. 1).

117. "One Man," *Eternal Light* (radio script) (New York: Jewish Theological Seminary of America, April 21, 1957); Julius Fisher, "Not a Minor Saint," *Jewish Spectator* 22, no. 7 (September 1957), pp. 14–16.

118. The Jewish Education Committee of New York issued a drama, "suitable for children in the upper grades," with a similar title, *His Brothers Keeper,* in 1951. The play by Samuel Citron told "the story of Sally Mayer who saved 200,000 Bulgarian Jews from the Nazi Death Camps, at the risk of his own life, because of his belief that he was his brothers' keeper" (*Pedagogic Reporter* 2, no. 3 [January 1951], p. 10).

119. Aronsfeld, "Not All Germans Are Guilty," pp. 9–11.

120. Ibid.

121. *American Jewish Year Book: 1945–1946,* p. 148.

122. Aage Bertelsen, *October '43* (New York: Putnam's, 1954).

123. Samuel Sandmel, "Religion and Good Will," in AJHS, I-68, SCA Papers, box 36, "Radio Chapel: Radio Broadcast" folder.

124. Clipping, "Synagoguge Council Honors Danish Underground Heroes," in AJHS, I-68, SCA Papers, box 50, "New Releases, Undated, and 1941–1954" folder.

125. "The House with the Blue Curtains," *Eternal Light* (radio script) (New York: Jewish Theological Seminary of America, May 26, 1957).

126. On the speech by Henrik Kauffman, Denmark's ambassador to the United Nations, to "Jewish leaders in Cincinnati," see *Congress Weekly* 25, no. 6 (March 17, 1958), p. 16.

127. Script, September 5, 1948, in AJHS, P-327, William Franklin Rosenblum Papers, box 6, "Television Scripts" folder; "The Pastor of Eindhoven," *Eternal Light* (radio script) (New York: Jewish Theological Seminary of America, February 17, 1946).

Notes to Chapter 5

1. Norman Finkelstein, *The Holocaust Industry: Reflections on the Exploitation of Jewish Suffering* (London: Verso, 2000), p. 13.

2. For some of the most recent statements on continued Jewish liberalism and activism for liberal causes in the postwar years, see Marc Dollinger, *Quest for Inclusion: Jews and Liberalism in Modern America* (Princeton: Princeton University Press, 2000); Cheryl Lynn Greenberg, *Troubling the Waters: Black-Jewish Relations in the American Century* (Princeton: Princeton University Press, 2006); Joshua M. Zeitz, *White Ethnic New York: Jews, Catholics and the Shaping of Postwar Politics* (Chapel Hill: University of North Carolina Press, 2007).

3. Lawrence H. Fuchs, *The Political Behavior of American Jews* (Glencoe, Ill.: Free Press, 1956), pp. 172–76.

4. Alan Mintz, *Popular Culture and the Shaping of the Holocaust Memory in America* (Seattle: University of Washington Press, 2001), pp. 5–6.

5. Hasia R. Diner, *In the Almost Promised Land: American Jews and Blacks, 1915–1935* (Westport, Conn.: Greenwood, 1977).

6. Mintz, *Popular Culture,* p. 7.

7. The tendency of postwar Jews, even the unaffiliated, to see American life through a Holocaust prism has been finely portrayed in Kirsten Fermaglich's *American Dreams and Nazi Nightmares: Early Holocaust Consciousness and Liberal America, 1957–1965* (Waltham, Mass.: Brandeis University Press, 2006). Fermaglich explores the use of Holocaust analogies in the works of four intellectuals, all Jews, including Betty Friedan, Stanley Elkins, Stanley Milgram, and Robert J. Lifton.

8. "WTMJ, December 15, 1946," in University of Wisconsin–Milwaukee, Joseph Baron Papers, box 7, file 1, folder 173.

9. *American Jewish Year Book: 1950,* pp. 551, 556.

10. Press release, February 21, 1956, in Tamiment Library, Wagner Labor Archives, NYU, Julius Bernstein Papers, box 11, "Immigration 1955–1957" folder.

11. American Jewish Committee, Discussion Guide, September 1960, in Tamiment Library, Wagner Labor Archives, NYU, Julius Bernstein Papers, box 17, file 12.

12. "Censorship," *Teller* (August 21, 1961), in AJA, Hebrew Union College, Olin-Sang-Ruby Union Institute Papers, manuscript 648, box 5, folder 1.

13. Statement by William Stern, in Tamiment Library, Wagner Labor Archives, NYU, Julius Bernstein Papers, box 13, "1952" folder.

14. Women's Division of the Jewish Labor Committee, *Bulletin* (Spring 1960), in Tamiment Library, Wagner Labor Archives, NYU, Julius Bernstein Papers, box 17, file 8.

15. JCRC, Memorandum on Meeting with Dr. Calvin E. Gross, Schools Committee, February 1, 1960, in AJA, Hebrew Union College, collection 283, box 11, folder 5; "The Meaning of the Swastikas," Cincinnati, April 20, 1960, in ibid., collection 202, box 38, file 1; Executive Committee Report, April 11, 1960, in Marvin Gelman Library, George Washington University, Jewish Community Council of Greater Washington Collection, manuscript 2012/002, box 6, folder 6.

16. Material on the *Merchant of Venice* controversy is in AJHS, P-71, Rufus Learsi Papers, box 4, "Merchant of Venice" folder.

17. Discussion in this and the next paragraph from Annual Report, Isaac Franck, January 22, 1961, in Marvin Gelman Library, George Washington University, Jewish Community Council of Greater Washington Collection, manuscript 2012, box 1, folder 11.

18. The first full-length book on the subject appeared in 1968: Arthur Morse, *While Six Million Died: A Chronicle of American Apathy* (New York: Random House, 1968).

19. Gerald Gamm, *Urban Exodus: Why the Jews Left Boston and the Catholics Stayed* (Cambridge: Harvard University Press, 1999).

20. "Excerpts from President's Remarks," *Bulletin* 1, no. 4 (March–April 1946), p. 3, in AJA, Hebrew Union College, collection 266, box 1, folder 3.

21. Anti-Defamation League, *Anti-Semitism in the United States in 1947* (New York: Anti-Defamation League of B'nai B'rith, 1947), p. 69; Melissa Fay Greene, *The Temple Bombing* (Reading, Mass.: Addison-Wesley, 1996), p. 158. On Jesse B. Stoner, see Raymond A. Mohl, *South of the South: Jewish Activists and the Civil Rights Movement in Miami, 1945–1960* (Gainesville: University Press of Florida, 2004), p. 16.

22. *American Jewish Year Book: 1953*, pp. 92, 97; *American Jewish Year Book: 1954*, p. 77.

23. Anti-Defamation League, *Anti-Semitism in the United States*, p. 70; *American Jewish Year Book: 1952*, pp. 97, 92; *American Jewish Year Book: 1954*, pp. 77–78; *American Jewish Year Book: 1958*, p. 149.

24. David Caplowitz and Candace Rogers, *Swastika 1960: The Epidemic of Anti-Semitic Vandalism in America* (New York: Anti-Defamation League, 1961), p. 40; *American Jewish Year Book: 1963*, p. 144; *Headquarters Letter* 4, no. 1 (November 1961), p. 1, in AJHS, I-32, box 1, "Printed Matter" folder. See also Arnold Forster, *A Measure of Freedom: An Anti-Defamation League Report* (Garden City, N.Y.: Doubleday, 1950), pp. 36–79, which describes many anti-Semitic groups and their uses of pro-Nazi rhetoric, which at times validated the Holocaust.

25. *American Jewish Year Book: 1963*, pp. 120–21.

26. "Report of the Plenary Session, June 16–19, 1955," in Tamiment Library, Wagner Labor Archives, NYU, Isaiah Minkoff Papers, box 8, file 2.

27. Herman Wouk, *This Is My God* (Garden City, N.Y.: Doubleday, 1959), p. 281; Nina Alderblum, "The Common Denominator Between the American and the Jewish Outlook," *Jewish Forum* 37, no. 5 (June 1954), p. 96.

28. "First National Jewish Leader to Visit Germany on Official Invitation in Twenty Years Leaves Today with Eight U.S. Clergymen," Press Release, October 13, 1953, in AJHS, I-68, SCA Papers, box 50, "Press Release" folder.

29. A vast literature on this subject exists, and, regardless of the particular context in which it has been studied or the assessment of the nature of the Cold War, the various aspects of the conflict between the Soviet Union and the United States, or the legitimacy of domestic anti-Communism, historians agree that all institutions and sectors of American life were touched by this issue. On the impact of the Cold War on the premier civil rights organization in the United States, see, for example, Manfred Berg, *"The Ticket to Freedom": The NAACP and the Struggle for Black Political Integration* (Gainesville: University Press of Florida, 2005), pp. 116–39. On academia in the Cold War years, see, for example, Ellen Schrecker, *No Ivory Tower: McCarthyism and the Universities* (New York: Oxford University Press, 1986).

30. All quoted in *Jewish Labor Fights Communism* (New York: Jewish Labor Committee, n.d.), in AJS 1145, Judah Pilch Papers, box 3.

31. Clipping, *Jewish Civic Leader*, December 9, 1954, in Tamiment Library, Wagner Labor Archives, NYU, Julius Bernstein Papers, box 5, file 28; "The Voice," *Eternal Light* (radio script) (New York: Jewish Theological Seminary, December 26, 1954), pp. 2, 14–15. *The Eternal Light* also aired an episode in April 1957 about Raoul Wallenberg, the Swedish diplomat who rescued many Hungarian Jews from the Nazis. Wallenberg ended up in Soviet custody and died in a Moscow prison. Word came to the Swedish government about his death a few months before the broadcast. This play would have been a natural device to confront Stalinism, the evils of Communism, and the like, but it did not. Rather, the drama focused on the events of "the last months of 1945, when the Nazis saw the Third Reich collapsing, they organized deportations from Budapest, from every city in Hungary, to feed the death camps of Poland" ("One Man," *Eternal Light* [radio script] [New York: Jewish Theological Seminary, April 21, 1957], p. 3).

32. Trude Weiss-Rosmarin, "Thinking About Germany," *Jewish Spectator* 20, no. 2 (February 1955), pp. 3–5.

33. Leo Heiman, "Khrushchev and the Jews," *Jewish Spectator* 24, no. 3 (March 1959), p. 9. On the collaboration between the "local Ukrainian population" with the Germans in the "massacres of Jews carried out with . . . energetic participation," see Reuben Ainsztein, "The Bandera-Oberlaender Case," *Midstream* 6, no. 2 (Spring 1962), pp. 17–25.

34. *American Jewish Year Book: 1947–1948*, pp. 394–95.

35. "How Many Jews Survived in the Soviet Union?" n.d., in Tamiment Library, Wagner Labor Archives, NYU, Julius Bernstein Papers, box 27, file 8.

36. "Press Release: Jewish Life Abroad Surveyed, Free World and Slave Compared," March 27, 1960, in Tamiment Library, Wagner Labor Archives, NYU, Edward S. Goldstein Papers, box 2, file 24.

37. *American Jewish Year Book: 1961*, p. 287.

38. *American Jewish Year Book: 1962*, pp. 370–71; "Babi-Yar Reverberations," "Khruschev's Pledge," October 13, 1961, in AJHS, P-583, Boris Smolar Papers, box 11, "Between You and Me" folder.

39. Mordechai Altshuler, *Soviet Jewry Since the Second World War: Population and Social Structure* (Westport, Conn.: Greenwood, 1987).

40. It would be nearly impossible to list all of the details of this reportage in the *American Jewish Year Book* alone.

41. Administrative Committee Reports, American Jewish Congress, January 30, 1952, in Chicago Jewish Archives, Spertus, collection 14, box 21, file 2, p. 5.

42. *American Jewish Year Book: 1954*, p. 502.

43. Hayim Leivik, "Who Are the Guilty?" in World Congress for Jewish Culture, *A Decade of Destruction: Jewish Culture in the USSR, 1948–1958* (New York: World Congress for Jewish Culture, 1958), pp. 25–27. Variants on Leivik's phraseology showed up randomly in American Jewish writings and speeches about Stalin. In 1953, for example, the Jewish Labor Committee held a protest rally in front of the Soviet embassy in Washington, and, as reported in its bulletin, speakers "accused the Kremlin of a deliberate plan to complete the destruction of the Jewish people which Hitler began" (in Tamiment Library, Wagner Labor Archives, NYU, Edward S. Goldstein Papers, box 1, file 2).

44. *American Jewish Year Book: 1954*, p. 146.

45. Mrs. Abram V. Goodman to Co-Workers, February 18, 1953, in AJA, Hebrew Union College, collection 73, box 40, folder 1.

46. Jack Winocur, "Genocide—1953," *Senior* 9, no. 4 (January–February 1953), p. 1; Joseph Leftwich, *The Golden Peacock: A Worldwide Treasury of Yiddish Poetry* (New York: Thomas Yoseloff, 1961), p. 18; Jewish Labor Committee, "Memorandum Documentation: Soviet Liquidation of Jewish Culture," February 10, 1958, in Tamiment Library, Wagner Labor Archives, NYU, Julius Bernstein Papers, box 13.

47. Israel Goldstein, *American Jewry Comes of Age: Tercentenary Addresses* (New York: Bloch, 1955), p. 114.

48. Press Release, n.d., World Federation of Bessarabian Jews—American Section, in Tamiment Library, Wagner Labor Archives, NYU, Jacob Pat Papers, box 1, "Bessarabian Jewry" folder.

49. Speech, 1953, and "Soviet Anti-Semitism," September 14, 1963, both in Tami-

ment Library, Wagner Labor Archives, NYU, Isaiah Minkoff Papers, box 12, files 8 and 17.

50. Maurice Lamm, "'Red or Dead'? An Attempt at Formulating a Jewish Attitude," *Tradition* 4, no. 2 (Spring 1962), pp. 165–97.

51. Trude Weiss-Rosmarin, "Soviet Anti-Semitism in Historic Perspective," *Jewish Spectator* 18, no. 2 (February 1953), p. 5.

52. Speech, Pittsburgh, May 12, 1954, in Tamiment Library, Wagner Labor Archives, NYU, Isaiah Minkoff Papers, box 12, file 19.

53. "A Study on Soviet Jews," Leadership Conclave, 1962, in AJA, Hebrew Union College, Olin-Sang-Ruby Union Institute Papers, collection 266, box 5, folder 8.

54. Chaim Fabrikant, "Where Do We Go from Here?" *Sixtieth Jubilee of the Labor Zionist Organization of America—Poale Zion,* in Chicago Jewish Archives, Spertus, collection 17, box 1, file 12.

55. One of the few English-language literary engagements with Soviet anti-Semitism to posit a connection between it and "Nazi Anti-Semitism" was Aaron Schmuller's *Treblinka Grass: Poetical Translations from the Yiddish and with an Introductory Essay and Notes on Nazi and Soviet Anti-Semitism* (New York: Shulsinger, 1957). In addition, one of the few scholarly books on the subject written in this period—Peter Meyer, Bernard Weinryb, and Eugene Duschinsky's *Jews in the Soviet Satellites* (Syracuse, N.Y.: Syracuse University Press, 1953)—provided almost as much space to the liquidation of the Jewish communities by the Nazis as it did to the status of the survivor communities under Communism.

56. *American Jewish Year Book: 1952,* p. 135.

57. Clipping, *Metropolitan Star,* September 1950, in Tamiment Library, Wagner Labor Archives, NYU, Isaiah Minkoff Papers, box 2, file 12.

58. Adolph Held to John Foster Dulles, March 30, 1955, in Tamiment Library, Wagner Labor Archives, NYU, Edward S. Goldstein Papers, box 4, file 56.

59. Howard Fast, "A Matter of Validity," in *The Midstream Reader,* ed. Shlomo Katz (New York: Thomas Yoseloff, 1960), p. 176.

60. Gennady Estraikh, "Metamorphoses of *Morgen-Frayheyt,*" in *Yiddish and the Left: Papers of the Third Mendel Friedman International Conference on Yiddish,* ed. Gennady Estraikh and Mikhail Krutikov (Oxford: University of Oxford, European Humanities Research Centre, 2001), pp. 144–45.

61. On the role of the national Jewish organizations in the struggle with Jewish Communist groups, see Dollinger, *Quest for Inclusion,* pp. 133–37; on Holocaust imagery as employed by the Jewish left in relationship to the trial of Ethel and Julius Rosenberg, see Peter Novick, *The Holocaust in American Life* (Boston: Houghton Mifflin, 1999), p. 94.

62. Clipping, *Daily Worker,* 1954. A group, the American Committee of Jewish Writers, Artists and Scientists, Inc., issued a statement that claimed that all charges of anti-Semitism in the Soviet Union were an "outright falsification" ("Anti-Semitism in the Soviet Union," n.d., in YIVO 1015, American Federation of Polish Jews, box 2, file 2; *American Jewish Year Book: 1954,* p. 262).

63. "Statement of Dr. Louis Harap in Connection with His Appearance Before the House Committee on Un-American Activities in Washington D.C. on June 29, 1953," in AJA, Hebrew Union College, collection 683, box 25, folder 7.

64. Simon Federman, "The Role of the American Federation for Polish Jews on the Present Crisis in America," May 14, 1950, in YIVO 1015, box 2, file 2.

65. To be sure, as American Jewish organizations on the pro-Soviet left engaged in this rhetoric, references in the Soviet Union to Jews as the victims of the Nazis had become virtually taboo. Public programs, textbooks, and memorial markers in the Ukraine, where millions of Jews perished, labeled the victims as "Russians" or "Soviets," effacing their Jewishness.

66. American Federation of Polish Jews to B'nai B'rith, February 2, 1950, in YIVO 1015, box 3, file 7.

67. Morris Schappes to Herbert Lehman, March 23, 1950, in Tamiment Library, Wagner Labor Archives, NYU, box 1, "Correspondence" folder.

68. In some of the larger Jewish communities, left-leaning groups sponsored their own Warsaw Ghetto memorial programs, which differed little in format from the memorial programs sponsored by the mainstream non-Communist groups, in particular, by the Jewish Labor Committee, the Workmen's Circle, the American Jewish Congress, and the Jewish Community Councils. In addition, on specific issues, such as the involvement of American Jewish organizations in the creation of and support for the Claims Conference agreement with the West German government, the Communist groups maintained the position that this constituted an act of forgiving Germany for its crimes against the Jewish people. In articulating this position, the Communist groups and publications in the American Jewish world echoed the position of the Soviet Union against the restitution agreement. This same position was adopted as well by the Communists in West Germany and in Israel. Similarly, the American Jewish left made frequent reference to the imagery of Nazism and the catastrophe when protesting against the trial and execution of Ethel and Julius Rosenberg on espionage charges in the early 1950s.

69. Clipping, *Common Cause,* July 1946, in Tamiment Library, Wagner Labor Archives, NYU, Julius Bernstein Papers, box 12, "JLC July–September, 1946" folder.

70. Quoted in Zeitz, *White Ethnic New York* (originally Ph.D. diss., Brown University, 2002), pp. 75, 196.

71. Fuchs, *Political Behavior of American Jews,* p. 176.

72. Discussion in this and the next two paragraphs from Arthur Plaut, "Community Relations Committee Report," in AJA, Hebrew Union College, collection 202, box 31, folder 4.

73. Salo Baron, *Steeled by Adversity: Essays and Addresses on American Jewish Life* (Philadelphia: Jewish Publication Society of America, 1971), p. 483.

74. "Memorandum to Chapter Presidents," March 12, 1947, in AJHS, I-57, Intercollegiate Zionist Federation of America Papers, "Memos" folder, pp. 2–3.

75. Adolph Held to Irving Salert, National Field Director to National Executive Committee, JLC, September 30, 1946, in Tamiment Library, Wagner Labor Archives, NYU, Julius Bernstein Papers, box 12, "JLC July–September, 1946" folder.

76. "Statement by William Stern . . . at the United States Senate Labor-Management Subcommittee Hearings on a Fair Employment Practices Legislation on Tuesday May 6th, 1952," in Tamiment Library, Wagner Labor Archives, NYU, Edward S. Goldstein Papers, box 1, file 91; clipping, *Boston Jewish Advocate,* in ibid., Julius Bernstein Papers, box 17, file 6.

77. "There Is Happiness in Numbers," March 24, 1950, in AJHS, P-327, William Franklin Rosenblum Papers, box 6, "Radio Sermons and Sermonettes" folder.

78. Louis Ruchames, "Parallels of Jewish and Negro History," *Journal of Negro History* 19, no. 3 (December 1955), p. 63.

79. Handbill, "The Truth About Jewish-Negro Relations," in Tamiment Library, Wagner Labor Archives, NYU, Morris U. Schappes Papers, box 1, "1952" folder.

80. Otto Kleinberg, "Equality of Opportunity," in *Proceedings of the Fiftieth Anniversary Observance of the American Jewish Committee, April 10–14, 1957: The Pursuit of Equality at Home and Abroad,* ed. Jewish Publication Society of America (Philadelphia: Jewish Publication Society of America, 1958), pp. 40–41.

81. Abraham Feinberg, "Why We Must Never Forget the 6,000,000," *National Jewish Monthly* 73, no. 4 (January 1959), pp. 10–11.

82. "The Jewish Labor Committee and a Quarter-Century of Human Rights Progress," in Tamiment Library, Wagner Labor Archives, NYU, Julius Bernstein Papers, box 12, file 13, p. 1, "JLC 1960" folder.

83. Session, 1961, in AJA, Hebrew Union College, Olin-Sang-Ruby Union Institute Papers, manuscript 648, box 4, folders 14–15.

84. "Editorially Speaking," *Senior* 18, no. 4 (February 1960), p. 2.

85. Speech, William Haber to Hillel, University of Michigan, Kol Nidre, 1962, part II, in YIVO, file 141, folder 380.

86. "*For Release*: May 27, 1961," in Tamiment Library, Wagner Labor Archives, NYU, Julius Bernstein Papers, box 21, file 31.

87. *American Jewish Year Book: 1958,* p. 112.

88. Label Katz, "The State of the Bigot," *Anti-Defamation League Bulletin* (June 1958), in AJHS, P-92, Label Katz Papers, box 7, "ADL-U.S.C.R." folder.

89. "Hate Propaganda," in AJHS, I-32, box 1, "Printed Material" folder. On *The Thunderbolt* and the Eichmann trial, which it claimed Jews took on only "to secure the worldwide ratification of the Genocide convention," see Tamiment Library, Wagner Labor Archives, NYU, Julius Bernstein Papers, box 7, "Eichmann Trial" folder.

90. Roger Daniels, *Guarding the Golden Door: American Immigration Policy and Immigrants Since 1882* (New York: Hill and Wang, 2004), pp. 113–28. The quote is from Press Release, "Jewish Labor Committee Calls for Revision of McCarran Immigration Law Permitting Nazis to Enter the United States," November 20, 1952, in Tamiment Library, Wagner Labor Archives, NYU, Julius Bernstein Papers, box 11, "Immigration: McCarran Act" folder.

91. Clipping, *Boston Jewish Advocate,* January 15, 1953, and "Fact Sheet on the McCarran-Walter Immigration Law, Prepared by the Boston Section, National Council of Jewish Women, for the Jewish Community Council of Metropolitan Boston"—both in Tamiment Library, Wagner Labor Archives, NYU, box 11, "Immigration: McCarran Act 1951–53" folder.

92. See, for example, Irving Kane, "Domestic Issues in America Today," November 1957, in Tamiment Library, Wagner Labor Archives, NYU, Isaiah Minkoff Papers, box 8, file 2.

93. "A Statement of Principles in Regard to American Immigration and Naturalization Policies Including Some Suggestions for Basic Revision of the Immigration and

Nationality Act of 1952," in Tamiment Library, Wagner Labor Archives, NYU, Isaiah Minkoff Papers, box 8, file 2.

94. Statement of Rabbi Simon G. Kramer before the President's Commission on Immigration and Naturalization, September 30, 1952, and Statement of Hon. Simon H. Rifkind before Joint Subcommittees of Senate and House Judiciary Committees, March 21, 1951—both in Tamiment Library, Wagner Labor Archives, NYU, box 11, "Immigration: McCarran: 1951–1953" folder; *American Jewish Year Book: 1953*, p. 85; "Editorial," *Jewish Forum* 38, no 3 (March 1955), p. 33.

95. I thank Michael Galchinsky for drawing my attention to the Declaration of Human Rights and the American Jewish role in it.

96. On the activities of Proskauer and the AJC at the San Francisco meeting of the United Nations, see Naomi W. Cohen, *Not Free to Desist: The American Jewish Committee, 1906–1966* (Philadelphia: Jewish Publication Society of America, 1972), pp. 272–73; "Declaration of Human Rights Submitted by the American Jewish Committee," Joseph L. Baron, 1894–1960, Papers, 1910–1960, in University of Wisconsin–Milwaukee, collection 173, Wisconsin Historical Society, Milwaukee Area Research Center, box 4, file 7. The AJC incorporated its own history of involvement with drafting the declaration in the context of the Holocaust. In 1957, at its Jubilee banquet, Proskauer wove these two together. He noted in one paragraph that the organization had been involved in sponsoring research on the causes of prejudice such as that which led to "the Hitler holocaust." In the very next paragraph, he moved on to the San Francisco Conference and the AJC's vision for the declaration. By his decision to place these two items one after the other, Proskauer made the connection obvious (in American Jewish Committee, *Proceedings of the Fiftieth Anniversary Observance of the American Jewish Committee: April 10–14, 1957: The Pursuit of Equality at Home and Abroad* [New York: American Jewish Committee, 1958], p. 3; see also Michael Galchinsky, *Jews and Human Rights: Dancing at Three Weddings* [Lanham, Md.: Rowman and Littlefield, 2008], pp. 29–34).

97. "Report of Jacob Pat, Secretary of the Jewish Labor Committee," 1959, in Tamiment Library, Wagner Labor Archives, NYU, Jacob Pat Papers, box 2, file 46, p. 4.

98. "Memorandum to the American Delegates to the United Nations Conference of San Francisco," adopted April 11, 1945; "Report on San Francisco Conference," box 38, "San Francisco Conference" folder; clipping, "Proposals for Frisco Conference," *Chicago Jewish Chronicle* (April 20, 1945), box 47, "Press Clipping" folder—all in AJHS, I-68, SCA Papers.

99. On Lemkin and the origins of the Genocide Convention, see Lawrence J. LeBlanc, *The United States and the Genocide Convention* (Durham, N.C.: Duke University Press, 1991), pp. 17–19.

100. Clipping, Gertrude Samuels, "U.N. Portrait of Raphael Lemkin," *New York Times Magazine*, March 20, 1949, in Marvin Gelman Library, George Washington University, Jewish Community Council of Greater Washington Papers, manuscript 2012, box 83, folder 2, p. SM20; clipping, *Council Woman*, n.d., in AJHS, P-678, Robison Family Papers, box 15, file 3.

101. "Honored for Genocide Fight," *Jewish Spectator* 16, no. 3 (March 1951), p. 12; "Press Release," American Jewish Congress, January 19, 1951, in Marvin Gelman Library, George Washington University, Jewish Community Council of Greater

Washington Papers, manuscript 2012, box 83, folder 3; "B'nai B'rith Lodge, No. 1, New York," January 1953, in Tamiment Library, Wagner Labor Archives, NYU, Isaiah Minkoff Papers, box 3, file 29. As was reflective of American Jewish concerns in the 1950s, when the American Jewish Congress decided to honor Lemkin in 1951, it also honored at the same ceremony Abba Eban, Israel's ambassador to the United Nations, the American Association for Jewish Education, and the National Association for the Advancement of Colored People, for its work in "the extension of civil rights in the United States" (Executive Director's Report for National Administrative Meeting, March 27, 1951, in Chicago Jewish Archives, Spertus, collection 14, box 12, file 2).

102. *Current Copy* (February–March 1953), p. 3; *Current Copy* (December 1953–January 1954), p. 3.

103. "Confidential Daily Events Bulletin," April 20, 1953, in Tamiment Library, Wagner Labor Archives, NYU, Julius Bernstein Papers, box 15, file 18.

104. For just a few citations on this subject, see Jewish War Veterans, "For American Unity," n.p., in AJHS, I-32, Jewish War Veterans Papers, box 3, "Printed Material" folder; "The Work of the CLSA: A Bibliography of Representative Publications of the Commission on Law and Social Action: American Jewish Congress," August 1945–June 1957, in Chicago Jewish Archives, Spertus, collection 14, box 10, file 1, p. 53; American Jewish Committee, *Who Is Holding Up the Genocide Convention?* cited in *American Jewish Year Book: 1954*, p. 503.

105. Cohen, *Not Free to Desist*, p. 364; "NCRAC: Sub-Committee on Genocide," October 20, 1948, in Marvin Gelman Library, George Washington University, Jewish Community Council of Greater Washington Papers, manuscript 2012, box 83, folder 1.

106. "There Are Things to Do! *To Prevent Mass Murder*," *Current Copy* (May–June 1949), p. 4; *Current Copy* (August–September 1949), pp. 3, 4. On American Jewish remonstrances to the American Bar Association, see "The Genocide Convention: Plain Talk from American Lawyers," a lengthy pamphlet put together by NCRAC which quoted lawyers and legal scholars on why the Genocide Convention did not violate American law (Isaiah Minkoff Papers, box 1, file 48; "Branch Bulletin Supplement, Jewish Labor Committee," March 1953, Julius Bernstein Papers, box 31, file 14; Jewish Community Relations Committee Cincinnati to "Chairman of Community Organizations," February 18, 1952, in ibid., n.p.—all in Tamiment Library, Wagner Labor Archives, NYU).

107. Lawrence LeBlanc claimed in *The United States and the Genocide Convention* that Jewish groups, as well as Jews who served in the U.S. Senate, like Jacob Javits, "always took pains to rebut the notion that the issue of ratification was a 'Jewish' issue." LeBlanc offers no evidence of this claim, nor does his otherwise dense and well-researched book indicate that he examined the archives of the Jewish organizations that wrote, testified, and spoke out on this matter (p. 22).

108. Jacob Blaustein, " 'The Eyes of the World Are upon Us . . .': The Case for Ratification by the United States of the Convention on the Prevention and Punishment of Genocide," copy in Marvin Gelman Library, George Washington University, Jewish Community Council of Greater Washington Papers, manuscript 2012, box 83, folder 2.

109. "Statement of National Community Relations Advisory Committee in Support of Ratification by the United States Senate of the United Nations Genocide Convention," January 24, 1950, in Marvin Gelman Library, George Washington

University, Jewish Community Council of Greater Washington Papers, manuscript 2012, box 83, folder 2.

110. My thanks to Marc Saperstein for sharing this document with me: Leo Jung to "My Dear Colleague," December 22, 1949.

111. Hirsch E. L. Freund to Leo Jung, December 16, 1949, in AJHS, I-68, SCA Papers, box 22, "Days of Mourning" folder; SCA Statement, January 4, 1950, March 3, 1950, in ibid., box 1, "1950, 1951, 1952, 1958" folder; "News Release: Synagogue Council of America Calls for Ratification of Genocide Convention," December 29, 1949, in ibid., box 50, "Press Releases" folder.

112. American Jewish Congress, "To Presidents of Jewish Communal Organizations," September 10, 1951, in Chicago Jewish Archives, Spertus, collection 14, box 12, file 2.

113. Ad Hoc Committee on the Human Rights and Genocide Treaties, in Tamiment Library, Wagner Labor Archives, NYU, Julius Bernstein Papers, box 9, "Genocide Treaties: 1953–1966" folder.

114. "Resolution: Genocide," 1955, in Tamiment Library, Wagner Labor Archives, NYU, Julius Bernstein Papers, box 15, file 21.

115. "NCRAC/CRC Programming," February 20, 1961, in Marvin Gelman Library, George Washington University, Jewish Community Council of Greater Washington Papers, manuscript 2012, box 83, folder 5; "Eichmann Echoes: Between You and Me," April 7, 1961, in AJHS, P-588, box 11, "Between You and Me" folder.

116. Clipping, June 1961, in Tamiment Library, Wagner Labor Archives, NYU, Julius Bernstein Papers, box 7, "Eichmann Trial" folder.

117. "Eichmann Echoes: Between You and Me," June 9, 1961, in AJHS, P-588, Boris Smolar Papers, box 11, "Between You and Me" folder.

118. For example, Michelle Mart, *Eyes on Israel: How Americans Came to See Israel as an Ally* (Albany: State University of New York Press, 2006).

119. Trude Weiss-Rosmarin, "Israel—Five Years Old," *Jewish Spectator* 18, no. 5 (May 1953), p. 3.

120. Isaac Lewin, *Noch'n Hurban: Collected Essays* (New York: Research Institute for Post-War Problems of Religious Jewry, 1950), p. 259. See also Israel Tabak, "The Tenth Yahrtzeit," in *The Rabbinical Council Manual of Holiday and Sabbath Sermons, 5714–1953*, ed. Solomon J. Sharfman (New York: Rabbinical Council Press, 1953), pp. 235–36. In his Rosh Hashanah sermon, published in the same volume, Sharfman noted that many American Jews speak "even of the land of Israel, in terms of our dead six million" (p. 325).

121. The two exceptions to the communal consensus included the very small American Council for Judaism, a group that broke off from Reform Judaism, on the one extreme, and the small knots of ultra-Orthodox Jews representing some of the Hasidic communities who asserted that only with the coming of the Messiah could a Jewish sovereignty be reestablished in the ancestral land.

122. Marshall Sklare and Marc Vosk, *The Riverton Study: How Jews Look at Themselves and Their Neighbors* (New York: American Jewish Committee, 1957), pp. 21–22, 30.

123. Yaacov Shelhav, "The Holocaust in the Consciousness of Our Generation," *Yad Vashem Bulletin* 3 (July 1958), p. 3.

124. The image of Israel in liberal American discourse in the postwar period deserves a full-length historical study.

125. "Service of Thanksgiving," in AJHS, I-68, SCA Papers, box 38, "Service of Thanksgiving" folder.

126. Radio Sermon, "The Words We Live By," July 20, 1952, in AJHS, I-68, SCA Papers, box 35, "SCA-Activities-Radio Broadcasts: Faith in Our Time" folder.

127. Nahum Goldman, "Towards Peace in the Middle East," *Jewish Spectator* 20, no. 10 (December 1955), p. 10.

128. Sidney B. Hoenig, ed., *The Haggadah of Passover* (New York: Shulsinger, 1950), p. 80.

129. "Press Release," November 29, 1948, in AJHS, I-68, SCA Papers, box 50, "Press Releases, Undated and 1941–1954" folder.

130. "The Hour of Forgiveness," *Eternal Light* (radio script) (New York: Jewish Theological Seminary of America, September 25, 1955), p. 13.

131. Benny Silver, "A halber yohr hundert," *Fiftieth Jubilee: Branch 244—Workmen's Circle*, in AJHS, P-712, Shloyme Rosenberg Papers, "The Shtetl" folder.

132. Ed Greene, "On Redefining Chalutziut," *Ha-Oleh* 3, no. 4 (June 1950), p. 8.

133. Trude Weiss-Rosmarin, "Comments and Opinions," *Jewish Spectator* 24, no. 10 (December 1959), pp. 3–4; quoted in review, "The Library Table," *Jewish Spectator* 43, no. 7 (July 1960), p. 115.

134. Sermon, October 1, 1955, Temple Emeth, South Brookline, in Ratner Center, Jewish Theological Seminary, archive 99, "Sermons" folder.

135. Labor Zionist Organization of Americas, "Hagadah for the Third Seder, 1954," pp. 9–10, and 1959, p. 3, both in Chicago Jewish Archives, Spertus, collection 17, box 9, "Third Seder Haggadot" folder.

136. Program, "Geto Yizker Ovent," April 13, 1957, in YIVO 1148, box 1, "JLC" folder; Bernice Green, *Resistance and Redemption: A Narrative Script with Musical References Commemorating the Uprising in the Warsaw Ghetto and Israel Independence* (New York: National Jewish Welfare Board, 1960); see also Minutes, April 18, 1953, in Chicago Jewish Archives, Spertus, collection 17, box 3, "Brenner Branch" folder; *SAJ Bulletin* 38, no. 15 (May 2, 1958), n.p.

137. "Editorial Comment," *Jewish Frontier* 19, no. 11 (December 1952), pp. 5–6; *American Jewish Year Book: 1955*, p. 355.

138. National Federation of Temple Sisterhoods, *Current Copy* (January–February 1955), p. 3.

139. "Hate Literature and the U.N.," *Jewish Forum* 42, no. 4 (April 1959), p. 48; Boris Smolar, "Arab Poison: Between You and Me," August 25, 1961, in AJHS, P-588, Boris Smolar Papers, box 11, "Between You and Me: 1961–1962" folder. Various volumes of the *American Jewish Year Book* from the middle of the 1950s onward pointed the finger of blame at the Arabs for collaborating with pro-Nazi groups in the United States as they disseminated anti-Semitic and anti-Israel material. In 1958, for example, the yearbook reported that "official Arab sources welcomed" the efforts of "James Madole's openly Nazi National Renaissance Party in New York City which sold and distributed official Arab propaganda in bulk. The material included the writings of Nasser and *Zionist Espionage in Egypt*, an anti-Jewish pamphlet originating in Egypt.... Madole's *National Renaissance Bulletin* for March–April, 1957 viciously attacked Israel

as 'the vampire state' which drained other countries of its resources" (*American Jewish Year Book: 1958*, p. 110).

140. *American Jewish Year Book: 1955*, p. 356.

141. "From the President," *Senior* 31, no. 7 (May 1963), p. 2.

142. On the expulsion of Egyptian Jewry, see Michael M. Laskier, *The Jews of Egypt, 1920–1970: In the Midst of Zionism, Anti-Semitism, and the Middle East Conflict* (New York: New York University Press, 1992).

143. American Jewish Congress, *The Black Record: Nasser's Persecution of Egyptian Jewry* (New York: American Jewish Congress, 1956), p. 26

144. Letter to President Eisenhower, November 27, 1956, in Tamiment Library, Wagner Labor Archives, NYU, Julius Bernstein Papers, box 20, file 30.

145. *Let's Talk About Arab Propaganda*, October 1955, in Tamiment Library, Wagner Labor Archives, NYU, Isaiah Minkoff Papers, box 1, file 7; letter to the editor, *Milwaukee Journal* (November 2, 1956), in University of Wisconsin–Milwaukee, collection 173, Joseph Baron Papers, box 7, file 10; Boris Smolar, "Washington Talks: Between You and Me," in AJHS, P-588, Boris Smolar Papers, box 10, "Between You and Me: 1956–1957" folder; "An Ominous Anschluss," *Congress Weekly* 25, no. 4 (February 17, 1958), p. 3.

146. Speech by Emanuel Neumann, December 30, 1956, in NYPL, Rare Books and Manuscripts Division, Hyman Schulson Papers, box 5, file 1; Harold Debrest, "Remark-Ables," *Jewish Forum* (October 1956), p. 142.

147. Trude Weiss-Rosmarin, "The Nations Against Israel," *Jewish Spectator* 21, no. 2 (February 1956), p. 5; "American Support of Arab Violence," *Jewish Spectator* 21, no. 10 (December 1956), p. 5.

148. Office of Public Information, Jewish War Veterans of the U.S.A. to Post, County, Department Commanders, et al., February 2, 1957, in AJHS, I-32, box 4, folder 3.

Notes to Chapter 6

1. Mrs. Sheldon Black, "The Child in the Jewish Home," in AJA, Hebrew Union College, collection 273, box 36, folder 2.

2. William Berkowitz, ed., *I Believe: The Faith of a Jew* (New York: B'nai Ishurun, Institute of Adult Jewish Studies, 1961), pp. 2–3.

3. Hasia R. Diner, *The Jews of the United States, 1654–2000* (Berkeley: University of California Press, 2004), pp. 259–304; Arthur A. Goren, "A 'Golden Decade' for American Jews: 1945–1955," in *A New Jewry: America Since the Second World War*, ed. Peter Y. Medding (New York: Oxford University Press, 1992), pp. 3–20; Jonathan D. Sarna, *American Judaism: A History* (New Haven, Conn.: Yale University Press, 2004), pp. 272–315.

4. *American Jewish Year Book, 1955*, p. 646.

5. Horace Kallen, introduction to A. Raymond Katz, *Synagogue Art* (New York: Jewish Theological Seminary, 1953), n.p.

6. Max Lerner, "Role of the American Jew," *Congress Weekly* 17, no. 3 (January 16, 1950), p. 9.

7. Stuart Koff, quoted in "Memo," Max F. Baer, National Director, B'nai B'rith Youth

Organization (BBYO), February 21, 1956, in AJHS, P-92, box 10, "BBYO, 1956–1964" folder.

8. Bernard Lander and Nathan Lander, paper, March 24, 1957, in AJHS, I-68, SCA Papers, box 16, "2nd General Assembly: Speeches, Papers" folder.

9. Albert I. Gordon, *Jews in Suburbia* (Boston: Beacon, 1959), pp. 137, 139, 165–66.

10. Morris U. Schappes, *The Jews in the United States: A Pictorial History, 1654 to the Present* (New York: Citadel, 1958), p. 281.

11. C. Bezalel Sherman, *The Jew Within American Society: A Study in Ethnic Individuality* (Detroit: Wayne State University Press, 1965), p. 213.

12. Label Katz, "Acceptance Speech," 1959, in AJHS, P-492, Label Katz Papers, box 1, "Election as President—1959" folder.

13. Nathan Glazer, *American Judaism* (Chicago: University of Chicago Press, 1957), pp. 114–15. In fact, Glazer's only piece of evidence on why "Hitler" was not responsible for the skyrocketing synagogue membership was that the increase did not begin until the war had come to an end.

14. Milton H. Polin, "A Cup of Wine and Jewish Self-Acceptance," in *The Rabbinical Council: Manual of Holiday and Sabbath Sermons, 5717–1956,* ed. Solomon Freilich (New York: Rabbinical Council Press, 1956), p. 135.

15. "Educational News and Notes," *Pedagogic Reporter* 4, no. 1 (September 1952), p. 12.

16. For example, Alan Silverstein, *Alternatives to Assimilation: The Response of Reform Judaism to American Culture, 1840–1930* (Hanover, N.H.: University Press of New England, 1994); David Kaufman, *Shul with a Pool: The "Synagogue-Center" in American Jewish History* (Hanover, N.H.: University Press of New England, 1999).

17. This point runs deeply through the literature on modern Jewish history and on the ways in which European Jews, the intellectuals in particular, viewed America. It was true for the Orthodox leadership in Europe that opposed the migration of Jews to the United States because of the shallowness of the religious culture and also for the radicals who believed that the lures of economic success and integration would dilute political commitments, national identification, and cultural authenticity (Sarna, *American Judaism*, p. 155; see also Tony Michels, *A Fire in Their Hearts: Yiddish Socialists in New York* [Cambridge: Harvard University Press, 2005], p. 143).

18. Isaiah Minkoff, National Executive Conference of the Jewish Labor Committee, Text of Address [Yiddish], February 16–18, 1951, in Tamiment Library, Wagner Labor Archives, NYU, Isaiah Minkoff Papers, p. 2.

19. Trude Weiss-Rosmarin, "Aaron Zeitlin: Jewish Poet," *Jewish Spectator* 24, no. 5 (May 1959), p. 7.

20. Trude Weiss-Rosmarin, "America Is Not Babylon," *Jewish Spectator* 18, no. 3 (March 1953), p. 3.

21. Trude Weiss-Rosmarin, "The American Jewish Revival," *Jewish Spectator* 24, no. 7 (September 1959), p. 4.

22. National Federation of Temple Youth, Fifth Annual Leader Training Institutes Handbook, 1952, Course 3, in AJA, Hebrew Union College, collection 266, box 2, folder 5.

23. "The Little Shoemaker," *Eternal Light* (radio script) (New York: Jewish Theological Seminary of America, May 1, 1955), p. 13.

24. Herman Kieval, "The Earth Is the Lord's," *Conservative Judaism* 7, no. 3 (April 1951), pp. 25–30.

25. Label Katz, "Keynote Address," June 1956, in AJHS, P-92, Label Katz Papers, box 2, "Speeches by date (1)" folder.

26. Shlomo Katz, ed., *The Midstream Reader* (New York: Thomas Yoseloff, 1960), pp. 5–6.

27. Maurice Samuel, *Prince of the Ghetto* (New York: Knopf, 1948), pp. 7–8; Maurice Samuel, *The World of Sholom Aleichem* (New York: Knopf, 1962), pp. 3–6.

28. Abraham Joshua Heschel, *The Earth Is the Lord's: The Inner World of the Jew in Eastern Europe* (New York: Farrar, Straus, Giroux, 1949), p. 7.

29. Mark Zborowski and Elizabeth Herzog, *Life Is with People: The Culture of the Shtetl* (New York: International Universities Press, 1952), p. 34.

30. Isaac Bashevis Singer, *The Family Moskat* (New York: Knopf, 1950); Isaac Bashevis Singer, *Gimpel, the Fool* (New York: Noonday, 1952); Isaac Bashevis Singer, *Satan in Goray* (New York: Noonday, 1955); Isaac Bashevis Singer, *The Magician of Lublin* (New York: Farrar, Straus, Giroux, 1960); Isaac Bashevis Singer, *Spinoza of Market Street* (New York: Farrar, Straus, Cudahy, 1961).

31. "Book Review," *Furrrows* (December 12, 1955), p. 5.

32. "Oneg Shabbat: The Chagall Windows," Mid-Atlantic Federation of Temply Youth (MAFTY) Leadership Institute, August 20–30, 1962, in AJA, Hebrew Union College, collection 266, box 3, folder 5.

33. "Recent Audio-Visual Materials," *Pedagogic Reporter* 5, no. 5 (May 1954), p. 21.

34. Trude Weiss-Rosmarin, "Inscribe Us in the Book of Life," *Jewish Spectator* 19, no. 7 (September 1954), p. 5.

35. The popularity of Roman Vishniac's photographs, as in *Polish Jews: A Pictorial Record* (New York: Schocken, 1947), also points to this shift in American Jewish culture.

36. Israel Goldstein, "The Organization of the American Jewish Community: Address Delivered Before Rabbinical Assembly of America Convention, Grossinger's, New York, May 9, 1960," in Israel Goldstein, *The American Jewish Community: Trends, Potentials, Leadership and Organization* (New York: Bloch, 1960), p. 15.

37. Arthur Green, "New Directions in Jewish Theology," David W. Belin Lecture in American Jewish Affairs, Jean and Samuel Frankel Center for Judaic Studies, University of Michigan, 1994, p. 1. By the middle of the 1960s, theologians like Irving Greenberg, Emil Fackenheim, and Richard Rubenstein began to engage in the kind of systematic theological work that had previously not been present. These three in particular placed the Holocaust into the center of their theologies. See, for example, their contributions to "Symposium Toward Jewish Religious Unity," *Judaism* 15, no. 2 (Spring 1966), pp. 131–63; see also Robert G. Goldy, *The Emergence of Jewish Theology in America* (Bloomington: Indiana University Press, 1990).

38. Glenn T. Miller, "JTS and Other Forms of American Ministerial Preparation," in *Tradition Renewed: A History of the Jewish Theological Seminary of America—Beyond the Academy*, ed. Jack Wertheimer (New York: Jewish Theological Seminary of America, 1997), vol. 2, pp. 658–59.

39. Quoted in Jason Kalman, "'With Friends Like These': Turning Points in the

Jewish Interpretation of the Biblical Book of Job," unpublished ms. (Montreal: McGill University, 2005), pp. 262–63.

40. Quoted in Goldy, *Emergence of Jewish Theology*, pp. 37, 66.

41. Morton M. Applebaum, *What Everyone Should Know About Judaism: Answers to the Questions Most Frequently Asked About Judaism* (New York: Philosophical Library, 1959), pp. 26–27.

42. Quoted in Sidney Greenberg, ed., *A Modern Treasury of Jewish Thoughts* (New York: Thomas Yoseloff, 1960), p. 433.

43. Zvi Kolitz, *Tiger Under the Skin: Stories and Parables of the Years of Death* (New York: Creative Age, 1947).

44. Quoted in Greenberg, *Modern Treasury of Jewish Thoughts*, pp. 67, 91–97.

45. Steve Rosenberg, "A Concept in the Religion of Judaism," Mimeographed Newsletter, Torah Session, 1962, in AJA, Hebrew Union College, Olin-Sang-Ruby Union Institute Papers, manuscript-648, box 5, folder 7.

46. "God on Trial," High School Session newspaper, 1962, in AJA, Hebrew Union College, Olin-Sang-Ruby Union Institute Papers, manuscript 648, box 5, folder 6.

47. Alan Luger, "Dean Speaks Out," *Dilly Daily* (August 22, 1962), in AJA, Hebrew Union College, collection 266, box 3, folder 5.

48. David Petegrosky, "Report of Executive Director to Chairman of Executive Committee," May 1946, in AJHS, I-77, American Jewish Congress, box 13, file 186, p. 1. Thanks to Beth Halpern for this citation.

49. Jewish Publication Society of America, "Press Release," 1948, in NYPL, Rare Books and Manuscripts Division, Farrar, Straus Papers, box 107, "Friedman, Lee" folder.

50. Abraham Neuman, "The Evolving American Jewish Community," *Journal of Jewish Social Service Quarterly* 31, no. 1 (Fall 1954), p. 10.

51. Israel Goldstein, "Some Current Problems of Jewish Life in the United States," January 24, 1951, in Tamiment Library, Wagner Labor Archives, NYU, Isaiah Minkoff Papers, box 7, file 33.

52. Trude Weiss-Rosmarin, "Living by Jewish Law," *Jewish Spectator* 24, no. 10 (December 1959), p. 3.

53. Sol Liptzin, ed., *Peretz* (New York: YIVO Institute for Jewish Research, 1947), p. 11.

54. Press Release, March 4, "Jewish Community Must Learn Hebrew to Survive, Says Nahum Goldmann: Columbia University Cited for Role in Promoting Hebrew Culture," in AJA, Hebrew Union College, collection 683, box 21, folder 2.

55. Suggested Basic Speech, 1946, House of Living Judaism: NFTS Victory Project, in AJA, Hebrew Union College, collection 73, box 41, folder 1.

56. Abraham Scheinberg, *American Jews: Their Lives and Achievements—A Contemporary Biographical Record* (New York: Golden Book Foundation of America, 1947), p. viii.

57. Philip Goodman to Bernard Bamberger, November 17, 1949, in AJHS, I-68, SCA Papers, box 27, "Jewish History Week" folder.

58. "Press Release," in AJA, Hebrew Union College, collection 266, box 1, folder 5. Hebrew Union College also connected the founding of the American Jewish Archives

on its Cincinnati campus with the "Hitlerian catastrophe of the 1930's and 1940's" (Jacob R. Marcus, "Important Historic Records," Jewish Publication Society of America, *Bookmark* 2, no. 4 [December 1955], p. 4).

59. Publicity, 1954/1955, 4, 63; Program Notes, "A Concert to Jewish Music Dedicated to the Cantors Institute of the Jewish Theological Seminary of America," in Ratner Center, Jewish Theological Seminary, RG 19, archive 1, box 23.

60. For the Holocaust and the projects undertaken by the Jewish Music Council, see "First Draft of a Proposed Handbook on Commissioning Jewish Musical Works," January 4, 1956, National Jewish Music Council, "Commission a Jewish Musical Work," September 1956; A. W. Binder and Avraham Soltes, "Progress Report on Commissioning," 1959, in AJHS, 331, National Jewish Music Council, box 1, file 6. "The Last Sabbath" was performed in 1960 at the 92nd Street YM–YWHA and received a review in *Dance Observer*, a magazine of note for the world of American dance (clipping, *Dance Observer* 27, no. 3 [March 1960], p. 44).

61. Ira Eisenstein, *Creative Judaism* (New York: Jewish Reconstructionist Foundation, 1953), p. vi.

62. Joachim Prinz, "Creative Catastrophe," *Conservative Judaism* 12, no. 2 (Winter 1958), p. 23.

63. C. Bezalel Sherman, "Three Generations," *Jewish Frontier* 21, no. 7 (July 1954), p. 15.

64. On that crisis, see James B. Gilbert, *A Cycle of Outrage: America's Reaction to the Juvenile Delinquent in the 1950s* (New York: Oxford University Press, 1986).

65. Graenum Berger, "The World of the Young Adult and the YM–YWCA," May 17, 1959, in Berger, *Graenum Berger Speaks on the Jewish Community Center: A Fourth Force in American Jewish Life* (New York: Jewish Education Committee Press, 1966), pp. 246–47.

66. Z. Szakowski, "Review, *Blessed Is the Match*," *Jewish Social Studies* 11, no. 2 (April 1949), p. 165.

67. Discussion in this and the next paragraph from Albert Vorspan, *Giants of Justice* (New York: Union of American Hebrew Congregations, 1960), pp. 39, 74, 121–26, 111–16, 186–87, 209, 241, 253. See also Philip Klutznick, *No Easy Answers* (New York: Farrar, Straus and Cudahy, 1961), pp. 7, 9, 39, 67, 111.

68. Abraham E. Millgram, "The Objectives of Jewish Education," *Jewish Education* 18, no. 2 (February–March 1947), p. 23. See also "U.S. Jewry's Role in Jewish History Discussed at Education Session," *Jewish Education Newsletter* 30 (March 1947), n.p.; Noah Nardi, "The Growth of Jewish Day Schools in America," *Jewish Education* 20, no. 1 (February 1948), p. 32.

69. Salo Baron, "Communal Responsibility for Jewish Education," *Jewish Education* 19, no. 2 (Spring 1948), p. 9.

70. Meir Ben-Horin, "Jewish Education: The Deeper Challenge," *Jewish Spectator* 24, no. 7 (September 1959), p. 309.

71. Berkowitz, *I Believe*, pp. 2–3.

72. Discussion in this and next paragraph from Simon Rawidowicz, "On Jewish Learning," College of Jewish Studies, Chicago, 1950, pp. 19, 23–24.

73. "Chicago Councilor," February 1951, in AJA, Hebrew Union College, collection 266, box 2, folder 4.

74. "B. A. P.," "The Fear of Spiritual Devastation," in *Manual of Holiday and Sabbath Sermons*, ed. Samuel J. Fox (New York: Rabbinical Council Press, 1959), pp. 347–48.

75. Yudl Mark, "The Yiddish Schools in America in the Past Thirty Years," *Jewish Review* 5 (1948), pp. 115–16.

76. Yudl Mark, "Changes in the Yiddish School," *Jewish Education* 19, no. 1 (Fall 1947), pp. 34, 38.

77. Mark Millstone, "Trends in American Yiddish Education," *Jewish Spectator* 18, no. 8 (October 1953), p. 26.

78. "Send Your Child to One of the 145 AR Schools," "Jewish Education for Your Child," in YIVO 1148, box 2, "Shul Propaganda" folder.

79. N. Chanin, Workman's Circle, "An Appeal to the Parents of Our School Children," n.d., in YIVO 1148, Jewish Labor Committee Papers, box 2.

80. Saul Goodman, ed., *Our First Fifty Years: The Sholem Aleichem Folk Institute—A Historical Survey* (New York: Sholem Aleichem Folk Institute, 1972), pp. 158–59, 45.

81. Discussion in this and the next paragraph from Jewish Labor Committee Research Department, "Jewish Culture and the American Jewish Community," *JLC Outlook* 3, no. 1 (February 1959), pp. 6–7.

82. Isaac Franck, "Changes in American Jewish Life," National Association of Temple Educators, *News* 4, no. 2 (March 30, 1959), n.p.

83. "Problems Worrying Our Youth," *Jewish Forum* 42, no. 7 (July 1959), p. 107.

84. Quoted in Henry Lurie and Max Weinreich, eds., "Jewish Social Research in America: Status and Prospects—A Symposium," *YIVO Annual* 4 (1949), p. 178.

85. Label Katz, "Jewish Survival," in AJHS P-492, Label Katz Papers, box 2, "Undated Speeches by Title" folder. The speech referred to the "large numbers of Jews languishing in D.P. camps," putting this talk no later than the early 1950s and probably the late 1940s.

86. Israel Tabak, "The Tenth Yahrtzeit," in *The Rabbinical Council Manual of Holiday and Sabbath Sermons: 5714–1953*, ed. Solomon Sharfman (New York: Rabbinical Council Press, 1953), p. 236; Julius Hoffman, "Lest We Forget," in *The Rabbinical Council Manual of Holiday Sermons: 5715–1954*, ed. Simon Dolgin (New York: Rabbinical Council Press, 1954), p. 156.

87. "Let's Avoid Being Normal! Some Vignettes from the World Zionist Congress," *Council News* 10, no. 6 (June 1956), pp. 5–7.

88. Leibush Lehrer, *Camp Boiberik: The Growth of an Idea* (n.p., 1959), p. 37.

89. Solomon F. Bloom, "The Great Unsolved Crime," *Commentary* 19, no. 1 (January 1955), pp. 89–93.

90. Berger, *Graenum Berger Speaks*, pp. 110–11, 116, 143, 157–58.

91. David Ulman, "How the Climate Was Altered," National Community Relations Advisory Committee, *Report of the Plenary Session, May 17–19, 1959*, in Tamiment Library, Wagner Labor Archives, NYU, Isaiah Minkoff Papers, box 8, file 9.

Notes to the Conclusion

1. The Library of Congress did not have a designation "Holocaust" until 1968, according to Gerd Korman, "The Holocaust in American Historical Writing," *Societas* 2, no. 3 (Summer 1972), p. 261.

2. Susannah Heshel, "Imagining Judaism in America," in *The Cambridge Guide to Jewish American Literature*, ed. Michael P. Kramer and Hana Wirth-Nesher (Cambridge: Cambridge University Press, 2003), p. 43.

3. Ruth Wisse, "Jewish American Renaissance," in ibid., p. 192; in the same volume, Alan Mintz noted that "American Jewry was reluctant to dwell on the victimization of Jews in the Holocaust" (Mintz, "Hebrew Literature in America," in ibid., p. 92).

4. Political scientist Daniel Elazar claimed that in Habonim, as he remembered it from his Detroit years in the movement, the Holocaust played no role. The publications and the programs of its meetings tell a very different story. For example, Daniel J. Elazar, "Detroit, the Early 1950s: 'Habonim Was Looked at as a Bit Wild,'" in *Builders and Dreamers: Habonim Labor Zionist Youth in North America*, ed. J. J. Goldberg and Elliott King (New York: Habonim, 1993), pp. 172–74.

5. Thomas D. Fallace, "The Origins of Holocaust Education in American Public Schools," *Holocaust and Genocide Studies* 20, no. 1 (2006), pp. 80–102.

6. See, for example, the website of the March of the Living, which started sending teenagers to Auschwitz-Birkenau in the 1990s, at http://www.marchoftheliving.org.

7. Sybil Milton, "The Memorialization of the Holocaust: Museums, Memorials, and Centers," in *Genocide: A Critical Bibliography*, ed. Israel Charney (New York: Facts on File, 1991), vol. 2, pp. 299–320.

8. On the Holocaust museum, see Edward T. Linenthal, *Preserving Memory: The Struggle to Create America's Holocaust Museum* (New York: Columbia University Press, 1995); on the successful effort to build a museum in New York, see Rochelle G. Saidel, *Never Too Late to Remember: The Politics Behind New York City's Holocaust Museum* (New York: Holmes and Meier, 1996).

9. Lawrence Baron, *Projecting the Holocaust into the Present: The Changing Focus of Contemporary Holocaust Cinema* (Lanham, Md.: Rowman and Littlefield, 2005). As an example of the critique that late-twentieth- and early-twenty-first-century America and American Jews give too much prominence to the Holocaust, see Tony Judt, "The 'Problem of Evil' in Postwar Europe," *New York Review of Books* 55, no. 2 (February 14, 2008).

10. Lucia Meta Ruedenberg, "'Remember 6,000,000': Civic Commemoration of the Holocaust in New York City," Ph.D. diss., New York University, 1994.

11. For example, J. J. Goldberg, *Jewish Power: Inside the American Jewish Establishment* (Reading, Mass.: Addison-Wesley, 1996); Charles Silberman, *A Certain People: American Jews and Their Lives Today* (New York: Summit Books, 1988); Leonard Fein, *Where Are We? The Inner Life of America's Jews* (New York: Harper and Row, 1988).

12. Hasia R. Diner, *The Jews of the United States, 1654–2000* (Berkeley: University of California Press, 2005), pp. 324–25.

13. Leon Jick, ed., *The Teaching of Judaica in American Universities* (Waltham, Mass.: Association for Jewish Studies, 1970); for current numbers, see the Association for Jewish Studies website, at http://www.ajs.org.

14. *World Directory of Jewish Museums* (Jerusalem: Hebrew University, 1991).

15. On the "missions" to Israel, see Jonathan Woocher, *Sacred Survival: The Civil Religion of American Jews* (Bloomington: Indiana University Press, 1986).

16. Hasia R. Diner, *Lower East Side Memories: The Jewish Place in America* (Princeton: Princeton University Press, 2000).

17. James T. Patterson ended his prize-winning book *Grand Expectations* in 1974 with the observation that "many goals of postwar American liberalism, notably the dismantling of Jim Crow and the rise of federal standards in social policy, especially for the disabled and the elderly, were far closer to realization in 1974 than they had been in 1945.... Greater personal choice, also advanced with special speed.... Age-old stigmas seemed to collapse.... Liberating forces in personal life had been rapid and dramatic, more so than in most eras of comparable length" (Patterson, *Grand Expectations: The United States, 1945–1974* [New York: Oxford University Press, 1966], p. 788).

18. Michael E. Staub, *Torn at the Roots: The Crisis of Jewish Liberalism in Postwar America* (New York: Columbia University Press, 2002).

19. For example, Maurice Isserman and Michael Kazin, *America Divided: The Civil War of the 1960s* (New York: Oxford University Press, 1999); Alexander Bloom and Wini Breines, eds., *"Takin' It to the Streets": A Sixties Reader* (New York: Oxford University Press, 1995); Donald Alexander Downs, *Cornell '69: Liberalism and the Crisis of the American University* (Ithaca, N.Y.: Cornell University Press, 1999).

20. Todd Gitlin, *The Twilight of Common Dreams: Why America Is Wracked by Culture Wars* (New York: Holt, 1995), pp. 70–73.

21. One example is William Wei, *The Asian American Movement* (Philadelphia: Temple University Press, 1993).

22. Quoted in Cheryl Lynn Greenberg, *Troubling the Waters: Black-Jewish Relations in the American Century* (Princeton: Princeton University Press, 2006), p. 229.

23. For the Sonny Carson quote, see Marvin Perry and Frederick M. Schweitzer, *Anti-Semitism: Myth and Hate from Antiquity to the Present* (New York: Palgrave Macmillan, 2002), p. 219; *American Jewish Year Book: 1969*, p. 84.

24. Greenberg, *Troubling the Waters,* p. 231; Deborah Lipstadt, *Denying the Holocaust: The Growing Assault on Truth and Memory* (New York: Free Press, 1993).

25. On the inner-Jewish turbulence commencing in the late 1960s, see Michael E. Staub, *The Jewish 1960s: An American Sourcebook* (Waltham, Mass.: Brandeis University Press, 2004); on the breakdown of an inner-Jewish consensus, see Staub, *Torn at the Roots.*

26. Riv-Ellen Prell, *Prayer and Community: The Havurah Movement in American Judaism* (Detroit: Wayne State University Press, 1989); Mark Oppenheimer, *Knocking on Heaven's Door: American Religion in the Age of Counterculture* (New Haven, Conn.: Yale University Press, 2003), pp. 95–129.

27. Arthur I. Waskow, *The Freedom Seder: A New Haggadah for Passover* (New York: Holt, Rinehart and Winston, 1969), p. 19.

28. Sherman Rosenfeld, "The Struggle for Shalom," in *Jewish Radicalism: A Selected Anthology,* ed. Jack Porter and Peter Drier (New York: Grove, 1973), pp. 222–28.

29. Jack Porter and Peter Dreier, eds., *Jewish Radicalism: A Selected Anthology* (New York: Grove, 1973); James A. Sleeper and Alan L. Mintz, eds., *The New Jews* (New York: Vintage, 1971); Janet L. Dolgin, *Jewish Identity and the JDL* (Princeton: Princeton University Press, 1977).

30. Sleeper and Mintz, *New Jews,* pp. 3, 29.

31. Meir Kahane, *Never Again! A Program for Survival* (Los Angeles: Nash, 1971), pp. 11–12, 244; Meir Kahane, *Why Be Jewish? Intermarriage, Assimilation and Alienation* (New York: Stein and Day, 1977), p. 156; quoted in Dolgin, *Jewish Identity,* p. 67.

32. Elma Ehrlich Levinger, *Jewish Adventures in America: The Story of 300 Years of Jewish Life in the United States* (New York: Bloch, 1954), pp. 233–35.

33. Kahane, *Never Again!*, pp. 68–69.

34. Jews for Urban Justice, "The Oppression and Liberation of the Jewish People in America," in *Jewish Radicalism: A Selected Anthology*, ed. Jack Porter and Peter Drier (New York: Grove, 1973), p. 331.

35. Aviva Cantor Zuckoff, "The Oppression of America's Jews," in ibid., p. 37.

36. M. J. Rosenberg, "To Uncle Tom and Other Jews," in ibid., p. 10.

Bibliography

Archives

American Jewish Archives (AJA), Hebrew Union College, Cincinnati, Ohio
    Abelson, Paul
    Friedberg, Lillian
    Goldstein, Fanny
    Harap, Louis
    Hirsch, Rhea
    Jewish Community Relations Committee (JCRC)
    Jewish Telegraphic Agency News
    National Federation of Temple Sisterhoods (NFTS)
    National Federation of Temple Youth (NFTY)
    Olin-Sang-Ruby Union Institute
    Prinz, Joachim
    Tucker, Sophie
    Women of Reform Judaism

American Jewish Historical Society (AJHS), Center for Jewish History,
    New York City
    American Jewish Congress (AJC)
    American Jewish Tercentenary Celebration
    B'nai B'rith Hillel Foundation at Harvard
    Board of Jewish Education, New York
    Breslau, Rabbi Isador
    Calmenson, Jesse
    Cohen, Jacob X.
    Conference on Jewish Material Claims Against Germany (Claims Conference
        Papers)
    Debrest, Harold
    Goldberg, Israel
    Greenberg, Meyer
    Intercollegiate Zionist Federation of America
    Jewish Community Council of Metropolitan Boston
    Jewish Labor Committee (JLC)
    Jewish Music Forum
    Jewish Reconstructionist Foundation
    Jewish Student Organization Collection
    Jewish Theological Seminary of America

Jewish War Veterans
Katz, Label
National Community Relations Advisory Committee
National Jewish Music Council
Picon, Molly
Pilch, Judah
Radomer Culture Center
Razofsky, Cecilia
Religious Zionists of America
Robison Family Papers
Rosenberg, Shloyme
Rosenblum, William Franklin
Scharry, Dore
Seder Ritual Committee / Seder Ritual of Remembrance
Smolar, Boris
Society for the Advancement of Judaism
Synagogue Council of American Papers (SCA Papers)
Weinstein, Lewis H.
Workmen's Circle
Young Israel
Zigmond, Maurice L.
Zionist Collegiate Organization

Chicago Jewish Archives, Spertus Institute of Jewish Studies (Spertus), Chicago
    Chicago Jewish Academy
        American Jewish Congress, Chicago Council
        Anti-Defamation League, Chicago Chapter
    Chicago YIVO
    Halevy Choral Society
    Labor Zionist Organization of America, Chicago
    Mid-West Jewish Council
    Sholem Aleichem Folk Institute
    Spertus College
    Workmen's Circle

Fales Library and Special Collections, Bobst Library, New York University (NYU),
    New York City
    Secunda, Shalom

Marvin Gelman Library, George Washington University, Special Collections,
    Washington, D.C.
    Jewish Community Council of Greater Washington

New York Public Library (NYPL) for the Performing Arts, New York City
    Irene Heskes Collection of Jewish Songs
    Muni, Paul

New York Public Library (NYPL), Rare Books and Manuscripts Division,
    New York City
  Bloch Publishers
  Farrar, Straus and Giraux
  Hirschmann, Ira
  Pinson, Koppel
  Raphael Lemkin
  Schulson, Hyman

Ratner Center for the Study of Conservative Judaism, Jewish Theological Seminary of
    America, New York City
  Camp Ramah
  Cantor's Institute
  Jewish Museum
  Levitsky, Louis
  O'Dwyer, Paul
  Richards, Bernard
  Rubenovitz, Herman
  Synagogue Bulletins
  Teachers Institute

Tamiment Library, Robert F. Wagner Labor Archives, New York University (NYU),
    New York City
  Bernstein, Julius
  Goldstein, Edward S.
  Jewish Labor Committee
  Jewish Labor Committee, Chicago
  Minkoff, Isaiah
  Pat, Jacob
  Schappes, Morris U.

University of Wisconsin–Milwaukee, Archives and Special Collection Division
  American Jewish Tercentenary Committee of Wisconsin
  B'nai B'rith Waukesha Chapter
  Baron, Joseph
  Jewish Community Center of Wisconsin
  Jewish Family and Children's Services
  Milwaukee Area Research Center
  New Home Club
  Weinshel, Howard
  Wisconsin Society for Jewish Learning

Yad Vashem Administrative Archives, Jerusalem

Yeshiva University Archives, New York City
  Benjamin and Pearl Koenigsberg

Central Orthodox Committee
National Council of Jewish Women
Vaad Hatzala

YIVO Institute for Jewish Research (YIVO), Center for Jewish History,
    New York City
Adel, Bessie
American Federation for Polish Jews
American Jewish Historical Society (AJHS)
American Memorial to Six Million Jews of Europe
Belarsky, Sidor
Bonus, Ben
Breziner Sick and Benevolent Society
Busker Society
Cogan, Edna
Congregation Tifereth Joseph, Anshei Prezemysl
First Klimontover Sickness and Benevolent Society
First Zbarozer Relief Society
Friedman, Philip
Greenberg, Eliezer
Jewish Labor Bund
Jewish Labor Committee
Kolbuszowa Relief Association
Lamed, Louis
Minkoff, Nahum, and Cooperman, Hasye
ORT (Organization for Rehabilitation Through Training)
Przemysler Society
Records of the United Service for New Americans
Schwarz, Leo
Sholem Aleichem Folk Institute
Sholem Aleichem Folk Institute, Camp Boiberik
Tenenbaum, Joseph
United Radomer Society
Workmen's Circle Branch 42
World Congress for Jewish Culture
YIVO

Selected Sources

Ackerman, Nathan W., and Marie Jahoda. *Anti-Semitism and Emotional Disorder: A Psychoanalytic Interpretation*. New York: Harper Brothers, 1950.

Adler, Selig, and Thomas E. Connolly. *From Ararat to Suburbia: The History of the Jewish Community of Buffalo*. Philadelphia: Jewish Publication Society of America, 1960.

Agar, Herbert. *The Saving Remnant: An Account of Jewish Survival*. New York: Viking, 1960.

Alexander, Edward. *The Resonance of Dust: Essays on Holocaust Literature and Jewish Fate.* Columbus: Ohio State University Press, 1979.

Altshuler, Mordechai. *Soviet Jewry Since the Second World War: Population and Social Structure.* Westport, Conn.: Greenwood, 1987.

American Jewish Committee. *Neo-Nazi and Nationalist Movements in West Germany.* New York: American Jewish Committee, 1952.

———, ed. *Proceedings of the Fiftieth Anniversary Observance of the American Jewish Committee, April 10–14, 1957: The Pursuit of Equality at Home and Abroad.* New York: American Jewish Committee, 1958.

American Jewish Congress. *The Black Record: Nasser's Persecution of Egyptian Jewry.* New York: American Jewish Congress, 1957.

———. *In Everlasting Remembrance: A Guide to Memorials and Monuments Honoring Six Million.* New York: American Jewish Congress, 1969.

———. *Nazi Germany's War Against the Jews.* New York: American Jewish Conference, 1947.

American Jewish Year Book: 1945–1946 Through 1969. Philadelphia: Jewish Publication Society of America and American Jewish Committee.

American Jews: Their Lives and Achievements—A Contemporary Biographical Record. Vol. 1. New York: Golden Book Foundation of America, 1947.

Angress, Ruth K. Afterword to Ilona Karmel, *An Estate of Memory* (pp. 445–57). New York: Feminist Press, 1969.

Annual Assembly Workbook: Jewish Youth at Midcentury. Narrowsburg, N.Y.: Camp Wel-Met, 1951.

Anti-Defamation League. *Anti-Semitism in the United States in 1947.* New York: Anti-Defamation League of B'nai Brith, 1947.

Apenszlak, Jacob. *The Black Book of Polish Jewry.* New York: American Foundation for Polish Jews in Cooperation with Association of Jewish Refugees and Immigrants from Poland, 1943.

Applebaum, Morton M. *What Everyone Should Know About Judaism: Answers to the Questions Most Frequently Asked About Judaism.* New York: Philosophical Library, 1959.

Aronson, Arnold. "Organization of the Community Relations Field." *Journal of Intergroup Relations* 1, no. 2 (Spring 1960). [Reprint, no pp.]

Asch, Shalom. *Tales of My People.* Trans. Meyer Levin. New York: Putnam's, 1948.

Ausubel, Nathan. *Pictorial History of the Jewish People.* New York: Crown, 1953.

———. *Treasury of Jewish Folklore.* New York: Crown, 1948.

Baker, Zachary. "Bibliography of Eastern European Memorial Books." In *From a Ruined Garden: The Memorial Books of Polish Jewry,* ed. Jack Kugelmass and Jonathan Boyarin (pp. 223–64). New York: Schocken, 1983.

Bamberger, Bernard. *The Story of Judaism.* New York: Union of American Hebrew Congregations, 1957.

Bamberger, Fritz. *Leo Baeck: The Man and the Idea.* Leo Baeck Memorial Lecture 1. New York: Leo Baeck Institute, 1958.

Barish, Louis, and Rebecca Barish. *Basic Jewish Beliefs.* New York: Jonathan David, 1961.

Barkai, Meyer. *The Fighting Ghettos.* New York: Lippincott, 1962.

Barkan, Elazar. *The Guilt of Nations: Restitution and Negotiating Historical Injustices*. New York: Norton, 2001.

Baron, Lawrence. "The Holocaust and American Public Memory, 1945–1960." *Holocaust and Genocide Studies* 17, no. 1 (Spring 2003), pp. 62–88.

———. *Projecting the Holocaust into the Present: The Changing Focus of Contemporary Holocaust Cinema*. Lanham, Md.: Rowman and Littlefield, 2005.

Baron, Salo. "The Modern Age." In *Great Ages and Ideas of the Jewish People*, ed. Leo Schwarz (pp. 312–486). New York: Modern Library, 1956.

———. *Steeled by Adversity: Essays and Addresses on American Jewish Life*. Philadelphia: Jewish Publication Society of America, 1971.

Bauer, Yehuda. *Out of the Ashes: The Impact of American Jews on Post-Holocaust European Jewry*. Oxford: Pergamon, 1989.

Bell, Daniel, ed. *The Radical Right*. Garden City, N.Y.: Anchor Doubleday, 1964.

Belth, N. C. *Barriers: Patterns of Discrimination Against Jews*. New York: Friendly House, 1958.

Belth, Norton, ed. *The World Over Story Book: An Illustrated Anthology for Jewish Youth*. New York: Bloch, 1952.

Berg, Manfred. *"The Ticket to Freedom": The NAACP and the Struggle for Black Political Integration*. Gainesville: University Press of Florida, 2005.

Berger, Graenum. *Graenum Berger Speaks on the Jewish Community Center: A Fourth Force in American Jewish Life*. New York: Jewish Education Committee Press, 1966.

Berger, Zdena. *Tell Me Another Morning*. New York: Harper Bros., 1959.

Berkowitz, Sarah Bick. *Where Are My Brothers?* New York: Helios, 1965.

Berkowitz, William, ed. *I Believe: The Faith of a Jew*. New York: B'nai Ishurun, Institute of Adult Jewish Studies, 1961.

———, ed. *Ten Vital Jewish Issues*. New York: Thomas Yoseloff, 1964.

Berman, Aaron. *Nazism, the Jews, and American Zionism, 1933–1948*. Detroit: Wayne State University Press, 1990.

Bernstein, Philip S. *What the Jews Believe*. New York: Farrar, Straus and Young, 1951.

Bertelsen, Aage. *October '43*. New York: Putnam's, 1954.

Berzon, Bernard. "When Moses Wept." In *The Rabbinical Council Manual of Holiday and Sabbath Sermons, 5714–1953*, ed. Solomon J. Sharfman. New York: Rabbinical Council of America, 1953.

Bicentennial Committee. *The Souvenir Book of the Bicentennial: The Story of the Celebration of the Bicentennial of the Charleston Jewish Community November 19 Through November 26, 1950*. Charleston, S.C.: Bicentennial Committee, 1951.

Bickel, Shlomo, ed. *Pinkes Kolomey: Geshikhte, Zihroyness, Geshtaltn, Hurban*. New York: Kolomeyer Memorial Book, 1957.

Bickel, Shlomo, and Leibush Lehrer, eds. *S. Niger Memorial Volume*. New York: YIVO, 1958.

Blakher, Shabtai. *One and Twenty and One: Twenty-Two Discourses About the Murdered Jewish Actors in the First Year of the Nazi Rule in Vilna, 1941–1942*. (Words, Abraham Marovsky and Leizer Ran). New York: Vilner, 1962.

Blankfort, Michael. *The Juggler*. Boston: Little, Brown, 1952.

Blaustein, Jacob. *The Eyes of the World Are upon Us . . .* New York: American Jewish Committee, 1950.

Bloom, Alexander, and Wini Breines, eds. *Takin' It to the Streets: A Sixties Reader.* New York: Oxford University Press, 1995.

Boder, David P. "The Displaced People of Europe: Preliminary Notes on a Psychological and Anthropological Study." *Illinois Tech Engineer* (March 1947). [Reprint, pp. 2–7, no orginal page numbers.]

———. *I Did Not Interview the Dead.* Urbana: University of Illinois Press, 1949.

———. "The Impact of Catastrophe: I. Assessment and Evaluation." *Journal of Psychology* 38 (1954), pp. 3–50.

Boehm, Eric H. *We Survived: The Stories of Fourteen of the Hidden and the Hunted of Nazi Germany as Told to Eric H. Boehm.* New Haven: Yale University Press, 1949.

Boyarin, Jonathan, and Daniel Boyarin, eds. *Jews and Other Differences: The New Jewish Cultural Studies.* Minneapolis: University of Minnesota Press, 1997.

Braham, Randolph L. *Eichmann and the Destruction of Hungarian Jewry.* New York: Twayne, 1961.

———. *The Hungarian Jewish Catastrophe: A Selected and Annotated Bibliography.* New York: YIVO Institute for Jewish Research, 1962.

Braiterman, Zachary. (*God*) *After Auschwitz: Tradition and Change in Post-Holocaust Jewish Thought.* Princeton, N.J.: Princeton University Press, 1998.

Breslau, David, ed. *Adventures in Pioneering: The Story of Twenty-Five Years of Habonim Camping.* New York: Chay Commision of the Labor Zionist Movement, 1957.

Brettschneider, Marla. *The Narrow Bridge: Jewish Views on Multiculturalism.* New Brunswick, N.J.: Rutgers University Press, 1996.

Bryks, Rachmil. *A Cat in the Ghetto: Four Novelettes.* New York: Bloch, 1959.

———. *Oyf kidesh hashem:Un andere dertseylungen.* New York: Yerahmiel Brike Bukh-Komitet, 1952.

Brynski, Shlomo. *Vehn fundamentn traislin zikh.* Chicago: International Press, 1951.

Budish, J. M., ed. *Warsaw Ghetto Uprising, April 19th, 10th Anniversary.* New York: United Committee to Commemorate the Tenth Anniversary of the Warsaw Ghetto, 1953.

Bugatch, Samuel. *Songs of Our People: A Collection of Hebrew and Yiddish Songs.* New York: Farband, 1961.

Bugatch, Shmuel. *Doros Zingen: B'Shirat Hadorot.* New York: Farband, 1961.

Cantor, Eddie. *Take My Life.* New York: Doubleday, 1957.

Caplowitz, David, and Candace Rogers. *Swastika 1960: The Epidemic of Anti-Semitic Vandalism in America.* New York: Anti Defamation League, 1961.

Carp, Bernard, ed. *The Jewish Center Songster.* New York: National Jewish Welfare Board, 1949.

Central Conference of American Rabbis Yearbook, 1946–1962. New York: Central Conference of American Rabbis, 1946–1962.

Central Yiddish Culture Organization. *The Jewish People: Past and Present.* 3 vols. New York: Jewish Encyclopedic Handbooks, 1946, 1949, 1952.

Chalmers, David. *And the Crooked Places Made Straight: The Struggle for Social Change in the 1960s.* Baltimore: Johns Hopkins University Press, 1991.

Chang, Gordon H., ed. *Asian Americans and Politics: Perspectives, Experiences, Prospects.* Washington, D.C.: Woodrow Wilson Center Press, 2001.

Chavel, Charles. "From Rephidim to Sinai." In *The 5708–1947 Manual of Holiday*

Sermons, ed. Charles Chavel (pp. 94–102). New York: Rabbinical Council of America Press, 1947.

Chavel, Charles. "The Storms in Modern Man's Soul." In *The Rabbinical Council Manual of Holiday and Sabbath Sermons: 5714–1953,* ed. Solomon J. Sharman (pp. 162–63). New York: Rabbinical Council of America Press, 1953.

Chazan, Robert. *God, Humanity and History: The Hebrew First Crusade Chronicles.* Los Angeles: University of California Press, 2000.

Chomsky, William. *Hebrew: The Eternal Language.* Philadelphia: Jewish Publication Society of America, 1957.

Choper, Carl Samuel. "Tisha B'Av and Holocaust Commemoration: A Study of Observances in American Jewish Summer Camps, 1985." M.A. thesis, University of Maryland, 1986.

Citron, Samuel J. *Dramatics the Year Round.* New York: United Synagogue Commission on Jewish Education, 1956.

Cohen, Beth R. *Case Closed: Holocaust Survivors in Postwar America.* New Brunswick, N.J.: Rutgers University Press, 2007.

Cohen, Naomi W. *Not Free to Desist: The American Jewish Committee, 1906–1966.* Philadelphia: Jewish Publication Society of America, 1972.

Cohn, Emil Bernhard. *This Immortal People: One Hour of Jewish History.* New York: Behrman House, 1945.

Cole, Tim. *Images of the Holocaust: The Myth of the "Shoah" Business.* London: Duckworth, 1999.

———. *Selling the Holocaust: From Auschwitz to Schindler—How History Is Bought, Packaged and Sold.* New York: Routledge, 1999.

Colodner, Solomon. *Jewish Education in Germany Under the Nazis.* New York: Jewish Education Committee Press, 1964.

Committee to Perpetuate the Memory of the Fallen Teachers from the Tsycsho School in Poland. *Lerer-yizkor-bukh: Di umgekummene lerer fun tzishe shuln in Poilin.* New York: Marstin, 1952–1954.

Cooperman, Hasye. "Yiddish Literature in the United States." In *The American Jew: A Reappraisal,* ed. Oscar I. Janowsky, pp. 193–209. Philadelphia: Jewish Publication Society of America, 1964.

Coopersmith, Harry. *The Songs We Sing—U'leshonenu rena.* New York: United Synagogue of America, 1950.

Cronbach, Abraham. *Judaism for Today: Jewish Thoughts for Contemporary Jewish Youth.* New York: Bookman Associates, 1954.

Crystal, David. *The Displaced Person and the Social Agency: A Study of the Casework Process in Its Relation to Immigrant Adjustment.* New York: United HIAS Service, and Jewish Social Service Bureau of Rochester, N.Y., 1958.

Curry, Andrew. "The Nazi Chronicles: Closed for Decades, the World's Largest Holocaust Archive Now Reveals Its Secrets." *U.S. News and World Report* (December 11, 2007), www.usnews.com/usnews/news/article/070513/21archives.

Daniels, Roger. *Asian America: Chinese and Japanese in the United States Since 1850.* Seattle: University of Washington Press, 1988.

———. *Guarding the Golden Door: American Immigration Policy and Immigrants Since 1882.* New York: Hill and Wang, 2004.

Dean, Martin. *Collaboration in the Holocaust: Crimes of the Local Police in Belorussia and Ukraine, 1941–1944*. New York: St. Martin's, 2000.

Deloria Jr., Vine. *Custer Died for Your Sins: An Indian Manifesto*. London: Collier-Macmillan, 1969.

———. *We Talk, You Listen: New Tribes, New Turf*. New York: Macmillan, 1970.

Deutsch, Babette. *The Collected Poems of Babette Deutsch*. Garden City, N.Y.: Doubleday, 1969.

Diner, Hasia R. *Fifty Years of Jewish Self-Governance: The Jewish Community Council of Greater Washington, 1938–1988*. Washington, D.C.: Jewish Community Council of Greater Washington, 1989.

———. *In the Almost Promised Land: American Jews and Blacks, 1915–1935*. Westport, Conn.: Greenwood, 1977.

———. *The Jews of the United States, 1654–2000*. Berkeley: University of California Press, 2005.

———. *Lower East Side Memories: The Jewish Place in America*. Princeton: Princeton University Press, 2000.

Dinnerstein, Leonard. *America and the Survivors of the Holocaust: The Evolution of a United States Displaced Persons Policy*. New York: Columbia University Press, 1982.

Dolgin, Janet L. *Jewish Identity and the JDL*. Princeton: Princteon University Press, 1977.

Dolgin, Simon, ed. *The Rabbinical Council Manual of Holiday Sermons, 5715–1954*. New York: Rabbinical Council Press, 1954.

Dollinger, Marc. *Quest for Inclusion: Jews and Liberalism in Modern America*. Princeton: Princeton University Press, 2000.

Downs, Donald Alexander. *Cornell '69: Liberalism and the Crisis of the American University*. Ithaca, N.Y.: Cornell University Press, 1999.

Drachler, Norman, ed. *A Bibliography of Jewish Education in the United States*. Detroit: Wayne State University Press, 1996.

Dubnow, Simon. *Nationalism and History: Essays on Old and New Judaism*. Ed. Koppel S. Pinson. Philadelphia: Jewish Publication Society of America, 1958.

Duker, Abraham G. *Jewish Community Relations: An Analysis of the MacIver Report*. New York: Jewish Reconstructionist Foundation, 1952.

Dushkin, Alexander M., and Uriah Z. Engelman. *Jewish Education in the United States: Report of the Commission for the Study of Jewish Education in the United States*. New York: American Association for Jewish Education, 1959.

Ebenstein, Ruth. "Remembered Through Rejection: *Yom Hashoah* in the Ashkenazi Haredi Press, 1950–2000." *Israel Studies* 8, no. 3 (Fall 2003), pp. 141–67.

Edidin, Ben. *Jewish Community Life in America*. New York: Hebrew Publishing, 1947.

Eichler, Jeremy. "Exile Beneath the Palms: Arnold Schoenberg in Los Angeles." Paper presented at the Center for Jewish History Graduate Fellows Seminar, December 10, 2007.

Eisenberg, Azriel, ed. *The Bar Mitzvah Treasury*. New York: Behrman House, 1952.

———. *Modern Jewish Life in Literature*. New York: United Synagogue Commission on Jewish Education, 1948.

Eisenstein, Ira. *Creative Judaism*. New York: Jewish Reconstructionist Foundation, 1953.

Elazar, Daniel J. "Detroit, the Early 1950s: "Habonim Was Looked At as a Bit Wild." In

Builders and Dreamers: Habonim Labor Zionist Youth in North America, ed. J. J. Goldberg and Elliott King (pp. 172–74). New York: Habonim, 1993.

Encyclopedia Judaica. Jerusalem: Keter, 1972.

Encyclopedia of Jewish Life Before and During the Holocaust. Ed. Shmuel Spector. New York: New York University Press, 2001.

Estraikh, Gennady. "Metamorphoses of *Morgn-Frayhayt*." In *Yiddish and the Left: Papers of the Third Mendel Friedman International Conference on Yiddish*, ed. Gennady Estraikh and Mikhail Krutikov (pp. 144–45). Oxford: University of Oxford, European Humanities Centre, 2001.

Faires, Nora, and Nancy Hanflik. *Jewish Life in the Industrial Promised Land, 1855–2005.* East Lansing: Michigan State University Press, 2005.

Fallace, Thomas D. "The Origins of Holocaust Education in American Public Schools." *Holocaust and Genocide Studies* 20, no. 1 (2006), pp. 80–102.

Farband-Labor Zionist Order. *The Battle of the Warsaw Ghetto.* New York: Farband, n.d.

Farber, David. *The Age of Great Dreams: America in the 1960s.* New York: Hill and Wang, 1994.

Fast, Howard. "A Matter of Validity." In *The Midstream Reader*, ed. Shlomo Katz (pp. 166–81). New York: Thomas Yoseloff, 1960.

Fein, Leonard. *Where Are We? The Inner Life of America's Jews.* New York: Harper and Row, 1988.

Fermaglich, Kirsten. *American Dreams and Nazi Nightmares: Early Holocaust Consciousness and Liberal America, 1957–1965.* Waltham, Mass.: Brandeis University Press, 2006.

Feur, Leon I. *On Being a Jew.* New York: Bloch, 1947.

Finkelstein, Norman G. *The Holocaust Industry: Reflections on the Exploitation of Jewish Suffering.* London: Verso, 2000.

Fischel, Jack, and Sanford Pinsker, eds. *Jewish-American History and Culture: An Encyclopedia.* New York: Garland, 1992.

Forster, Arnold. *A Measure of Freedom: An Anti-Defamation League Report.* Garden City, N.Y.: Doubleday, 1950.

Forster, Arnold, and Benjamin R. Epstein. *Cross-Currents.* Garden City, N.Y.: Doubleday, 1956.

———. *The Trouble-Makers.* Garden City, N.Y.: Doubleday, 1952.

Fox, Samuel J., ed. *The Rabbinical Council Manual of Holiday and Sabbath Sermons.* New York: Rabbinical Council Press, 1959.

Frank, Anne. *The Diary of a Young Girl.* Intro. Eleanor Roosevelt. Trans. B. M. Mooyaart. New York: Bantam, 1952.

Fraser, Steve, and Gary Gerstle. *The Rise and Fall of the New Deal Order, 1930–1980.* Princeton: Princeton University Press, 1989.

Freed, Morris. *The Survivors: Six One Act Dramas.* Cambridge, Mass.: Sci-Art, 1956.

Freilich, Solomon, ed. *The Rabbinical Council Manual of Holiday and Sabbath Sermons 5717–1956.* New York: Rabbinical Council Press, 1956.

Fried, Richard M. *Nightmare in Red: The McCarthy Era in Perspective.* New York: Oxford University Press, 1990.

Friedlander, Saul. *Pius XII and the Third Reich: A Documentation.* New York: Knopf, 1966.

Friedman, Lee M. *Pilgrims in a New Land*. Philadelphia: Jewish Publication Society of America, 1948.

Friedman, Philip. "The Jews of Greece During the Second World War." In *The Joshua Starr Memorial Volume: Studies in History and Philology*, ed. Conference on Jewish Relations (pp. 241–48). New York: Conference on Jewish Relations, 1953.

———. *Martyrs and Fighters: The Epic of the Warsaw Ghetto*. New York: Praeger, 1954.

———. *Their Brothers' Keepers*. New York: Crown, 1957.

Friedman, Philip, and Jacob Robinson. *Guide to Jewish History Under Nazi Impact*. New York: YIVO Insitute for Jewish Research, 1960.

Friends of Bialystok Club. *Lieder un bilder fun Bialystoker Ghetto*. New York: Friends of Bialystok Club, 1948.

Frisch, Daniel. *On the Road to Zion: Selected Writings of Daniel Frisch*. New York: Zionist Organization of America, 1950.

Fuchs, Lawrence H. *The Political Behavior of American Jews*. Glencoe, Ill.: Free Press, 1956.

Gaddis, John Lewis. *We Now Know: Rethinking Cold War History*. Oxford: Clarendon, 1997.

Galchinsky, Michael. *Jews and Human Rights: Dancing at Three Weddings*. Lanham, Md.: Rowman and Littlefield, 2008.

Gamm, Gerald. *Urban Exodus: Why the Jews Left Boston and the Catholics Stayed*. Cambridge: Harvard University Press, 1999.

Ganin, Zvi. *An Uneasy Relationship: American Jewish Leadership and Israel, 1948–1957*. Syracuse, N.Y.: Syracuse University Press, 2005.

Gar, Joseph. *Bibliografye fun yidishe bikher vegn hurbn un gvure / Fun Yosf Gar un Filip Fridman*. New York: YIVO Institute for Jewish Research, 1962.

Gebirtig, Mordecai. *Lider*. New York: Workmen's Circle, 1948.

Gelbert, Mikhl. *A neye haggadah shel Pesach*. New York: Building Committee of the Arbeiter Ring, 1958.

Genizi, Haim. *America's Fair Share: The Admission and Resettlement of Displaced Persons, 1945–1952*. Detroit: Wayne State University Press, 1993.

Gersh, Harry. *Minority Report*. New York: Collier, 1961.

———. *These Are My People: A Treasury of Biographies of Heroes of the Jewish Spirit from Abraham to Leo Baeck*. New York: Behrman House, 1959.

Gerstein, Israel, ed. *The 5708–1947 Manual of Holiday Sermons*. New York: Rabbinical Council Press, 1947.

Gilbert, James B. *A Cycle of Outrage: America's Reaction to the Juvenile Delinquent in the 1950s*. New York: Oxford University Press, 1986.

Gitlin, Todd. *The Twilight of Common Dreams: Why America Is Wracked by Culture Wars*. New York: Holt, 1995.

Gittelsohn, Roland B. *Little Lower Than the Angels*. New York: Union of American Hebrew Congregations, 1955.

———. *Modern Jewish Problems: A Textbook for High School Classes and Jewish Youth Groups*. 5th printing. Cincinnati: Union of American Hebrew Congregations, 1949.

Glazer, Nathan. *American Judaism*. Chicago: University of Chicago Press, 1957.

———. "Hansen's Hypothesis and the Historical Experience of Generations." In *American Immigrants and Their Generations: Studies and Commentaries on the Hansen Thesis*

After Fifty Years, ed. Peter Kvisto and Dag Blanck. Urbana: University of Illinois Press, 1990.

Glazer, Nathan. "Social Characteristics of American Jews." In *The Jews: Their History, Culture and Religion*, ed. Louis Finkelstein (vol. 2). New York: Harper and Row, 1960.

Goldberg, I. *Our Dramaturgy*. New York: Yidisher Kultur Farband and Yechiel Lewenstein Book Committee, 1961.

Goldberg, J. J. *Jewish Power: Inside the American Jewish Establishment*. Reading, Mass.: Addison-Wesley, 1996.

Golden, Harry. Foreword to Henry A. Zeiger, *The Case Against Adolf Eichmann* (pp. vi–x). New York: Signet, 1960.

Goldstein, Anatole. *From Discrimination to Annihilation*. New York: Institute for Jewish Affairs, 1952.

———. *Operation Murder*. New York: Institute for Jewish Affairs, 1949.

Goldstein, Bernard. *The Stars Bear Witness*. Trans. Leonard Shatzkin. New York: Viking, 1949.

Goldstein, Israel. *The American-Jewish Community: Trends, Potentials, Leadership and Organization*. New York: Block Publishing, 1960.

———. *American Jewry Comes of Age: Tercentenary Addresses*. New York: Bloch, 1955.

———. *Trends and Potentials in American Jewish Life*. New York: Bloch, 1960.

Goldy, Robert G. *The Emergence of Jewish Theology in America*. Bloomington: Indiana University Press, 1990.

Goodman, Philip. *The Passover Anthology*. Philadelphia: Jewish Publication Society of America, 1961.

———. *The Purim Anthology*. Philadelphia: Jewish Publication Society of America, 1949.

Goodman, Saul, ed. *Our First Fifty Years: The Sholem Aleichem Folk Institute—A Historical Survey*. New York: Sholem Aleichem Folk Institute, 1972.

Gordis, Robert. *Jewish Learning and Jewish Existence: Retrospect and Prospect*. Leo Baeck Memorial Lecture 6. New York: Leo Baeck Institute, 1963.

———. *Judaism for the Modern Age*. New York: Farrar, Straus, and Cudahy, 1955.

Gordon, Albert I. *Jews in Suburbia*. Boston: Beacon, 1959.

Goren, Arthur A. "A 'Golden Decade' for American Jews: 1945–1955." In *A New Jewry: America Since the Second World War*, ed. Peter Y. Medding (pp. 3–20). New York: Oxford University Press, 1992.

Gottschalk, Max, and Abraham G. Duker. *Jews in the Post-War World*. New York: Dryden Press, 1945.

Gottschalk, Max, Abraham Duker, and Michael Alper, eds. *Jewish Post-War Problems: A Study Course—Relief, Reconstruction and Migration*. New York: Research Institute of Peace and Post-War Problems of the American Jewish Committee, 1943.

Green, Bernice. *Resistance and Redemption: A Narrative Script with Musical References Commemorating the Uprising in the Warsaw Ghetto and Israel Independence*. New York: National Jewish Welfare Board, 1960.

Greenberg, Cheryl Lynn. *Troubling the Waters: Black-Jewish Relations in the American Century*. Princeton: Princeton University Press, 2006.

Greenberg, Hayim. *The Inner Eye*. New York: Jewish Frontier Association, 1953.

Greenberg, Sidney, ed. *A Modern Treasury of Jewish Thoughts*. New York: Thomas Yoseloff, 1960.

Greenberg, Simon. *Israel and Zionism: A Conservative Approach*. New York: United Synagogue of America, 1956.

Greene, Melissa Fay. *The Temple Bombing*. Reading, Mass.: Addison-Wesley, 1996.

Gritz, Linda. "Commemorating the Uprising: Challenges Throughout the History of Warsaw Ghetto Uprising Observances." *Jewish Currents* (March–April 2006), pp. 23–27.

Grobman, Alex. *Rekindling the Flame: American Jewish Chaplains and the Survivors of European Jewry, 1944–1948*. Detroit: Wayne State University Press, 1993.

Grossman, Kurt R. "Zionists and Non-Zionists Under Nazi Rule in the 1930's." In *Herzl Year Book: Essays in Zionist History and Thought*, ed. Raphael Patai (vol. 4, pp. 329–44). New York: Herzl Institute, 1961–62.

Gruber, Ruth. *Destination Palestine: The Story of the Haganah Ship Exodus 1947*. New York: Current Books, 1948.

———. *Israel Without Tears*. New York: A. A. Wyn, 1950.

Gubar, Susan. *Poetry After Auschwitz: Remembering What One Never Knew*. Bloomington: Indiana University Press, 2003.

Gutkind, Eric. *Choose Life: The Biblical Call to Revolt*. New York: Harry Schuman, 1952.

Handlin, Oscar. *Adventure in Freedom: Three Hundred Years of Jewish Life in America*. New York: McGraw-Hill, 1954.

———. *A Continuing Task: The American Jewish Joint Distribution Committee, 1914–1964*. New York: Random House, 1964.

Handlin, Oscar, and Mary F. Handlin. *Danger in Discord: Origins of Anti-Semitism in the United States*. New York: Anti-Defamation League of B'nai B'rith, 1948.

Harap, Louis, ed. *"Jewish Life" Anthology, 1946–1956*. New York: Jewish Life, 1956.

Hart, Kitty. *I Am Alive*. New York: Coward-McCann, 1960.

Hashomer Hastzair Zionist Youth Organization. *Haggadah shel Pesach*. New York: Hashomer Hastzair Zionist Youth Organization, n.d.

Hebrew Union College. *Reform Judaism: Essays by Hebrew Union College Alumni*. Cincinnati: Hebrew Union College, 1949.

Hebrew Union College Annual, 1945–1962. New York: KTAV, 1945–1962.

Hecht, Ben. *Child of the Century*. New York: Simon and Schuster, 1954.

———. *A Flag Is Born*. New York: American League for a Free Palestine, 1946.

Heimler, Eugene. *Concentration Camp*. New York: Pyramid, 1959.

Heinze, Andrew R. *Jews and the American Soul: Human Nature in the Twentieth Century*. Princeton, N.J.: Princeton University Press, 2004.

Heller, Joseph. *The Zionist Idea (ZOA)*. New York: Schocken, 1949.

Hellerstein, Kathryn, ed. and trans. *Paper Bridges: Selected Poems of Kadya Molodowsky*. Detroit: Wayne State University Press, 1999.

Helmreich, William B. *Against All Odds: Holocaust Survivors and the Successful Lives They Made in America*. New York: Simon and Schuster, 1992.

———. *The Enduring Community: The Jews of Newark and Metrowest*. New Brunswick, N.J.: Transaction, 1999.

Herberg, Will. *Judaism and Modern Man: An Interpretation of Jewish Religion*. Philadelphia: Jewish Publication Society of America, 1951.

Herberg, Will. *Protestant, Catholic, Jew: An Essay in American Religious Sociology*. Garden City, N.Y.: Doubleday, 1955.

Herf, Jeffrey. *Divided Memory: The Nazi Past in the Two Germanys*. Cambridge: Harvard University Press, 1997.

Hersey, John. *The Wall*. New York: Knopf, 1950.

Hershman, Abraham. *Religion in the Age and of the Ages*. New York: Bloch, 1953.

Herzog, William. *From Dreyfus to Petain*. New York: Creative Press, 1947.

Heschel, Abraham Joshua. *The Earth Is the Lord's: The Inner World of the Jew in Eastern Europe*. New York: Farrar, Straus, Giroux, 1949.

Heschel, Susannah. "Imagining Judaism in America." In *The Cambridge Companion to Jewish American Literature*, ed. Michael P. Kramer and Hana Wirth-Nesher. Cambridge: Cambridge University Press, 2003.

Heskes, Irene. *Passport to Jewish Music: Its History, Traditions, and Culture*. Westport, Conn.: Greenwood, 1994.

Heydrick, Benjamin A. *Americans All: Stories of American Life*. New York: Harcourt Brace, 1941.

Hilberg, Raul. *The Destruction of the European Jews*. Chicago: Quadrangle, 1961.

———. *The Politics of Memory: The Journey of a Holocaust Historian*. Chicago: Ivan R. Dee, 1996.

Hirschmann, Ira A. *The Embers Still Burn: An Eye-Witness View of the Postwar Ferment in Europe and the Middle East and Our Disastrous Get-Soft-with-Germany Policy*. New York: Simon and Schuster, 1949.

———. *Life Line to a Promised Land*. New York: Jewish Book Guild of America, 1946.

Hirsh, Selma G. *The Fears Men Live By*. New York: Harper Brothers, 1955.

Hoenig, Sidney B., ed. *The Haggadah of Passover*. New York: Shulsinger, 1950.

Hoffman, Julius. "Lest We Forget." In *The Rabbinical Council Manual of Holiday Sermons: 5715–1954*, ed. Simon Dolgin (pp. 155–58). New York: Rabbinical Council Press, 1954.

Holde, Artur. *Jews in Music: From the Age of Enlightenment to the Present*. New York: Philosophical Library, 1959.

Hollander, Paul. *Anti-Americanism: Critiques at Home and Abroad, 1965–1990*. New York: Oxford University Press, 1992.

Howe, Irving, and Eliezer Greenberg. *A Treasury of Yiddish Stories*. New York: Viking, 1954.

Institute of Jewish Affairs. *European Jewry Ten Years After the War: An Account of the Development and Present Status of the Decimated Jewish Community of Europe*. New York: World Jewish Congress, 1956.

Israel Is Born: The Return to the Jewish Homeland—A Documentary Record. 33 ⅓ RPM LP record sleeve. New York: Caedmon Records, n.d.

Isserman, Maurice, and Michael Kazin. *America Divided: The Civil War of the 1960s*. New York: Oxford University Press, 1999.

Janowsky, Oscar I. *The American Jew: A Reappraisal*. Philadelphia: Jewish Publication Society of America, 1964.

Jeansonne, Glen. *Gerald L. K. Smith: Minister of Hate*. New Haven, Conn.: Yale University Press, 1988.

Jewish Academy of Arts and Sciences. *Jews in the Arts and Sciences*. New York: Herald Square Press, 1955.

Jewish Black Book Committee. *The Black Book: The Nazi Crime Against the Jewish People*. New York: Jewish Black Book Committee, 1946.

Jewish Book Annual: 1945 Through 1962. New York: National Jewish Welfare Board, 1948–1969.

Jewish Labor Committee. *The Jewish Labor Committee and a Quarter-Century of Human Rights Progress*. New York: Jewish Labor Committee, 1960.

———. *Yiddisher Arbeter Komittet*. New York: Jewish Labor Committee, 1950.

Jewish Life Anthology, 1946–1956. New York: Progressive Jewish Life, 1956.

Jewish Social Studies. *The Joshua Starr Memorial Volume: Studies in History and Philology*. New York: Conference on Jewish Relations, 1953.

Jewish Theological Society, ed. *Proceedings of the Second Annual Rabbinical Assembly Conference on Jewish Education, "The Structure of Jewish Education in Conservative Judaism, December 22–23, 1947."* New York: Jewish Theological Society, 1947.

Jewish War Veterans. *Fifty Years of the J.W.V.* New York: Jewish War Veterans, 1946.

Jews for Urban Justice. "The Oppression and Liberation of the Jewish People in America." In *Jewish Radicalism: A Selected Anthology*, ed. Jack Porter and Peter Drier (pp. 323–46). New York: Grove, 1973.

Jick, Leon. "The Holocaust: Its Uses and Abuses in the American Public." *Yad Vashem Studies* 14 (1981), pp. 303–18.

———, ed. *The Teaching of Judaic in American Universities*. Waltham, Mass.: Association for Jewish Studies, 1970.

Jockusch, Laura. "'Collect and Record! Help to Write the History of the Latest Destruction!' Jewish Historical Commissions in Europe, 1943–1953." Ph.D. diss., New York University, 2007.

Joint Distribution Committee. *The Joint Distribution Committee Album: 1914–1954*. New York: Joint Distribution Committee, 1954.

Judt, Tony. *Postwar: A History of Europe Since 1945*. New York: Penguin, 2005.

Jung, Leo, ed. *Guardians of Our Heritage (1724–1953)*. New York: Bloch, 1958.

———, ed. *Israel of Tomorrow*. New York: Herald Square Press, 1946.

Kaasdan, H. S. *Lerer yizker bukh: Teacher Memorial Book*. New York: Committee to Remember Forever the Murdered Teachers of the Tsisho Schools in Poland, 1952–1954.

Kaczerginski, Shmerke. *Destruction of Jewish Vilna*. New York: Futuro, 1947.

———. *Lider fun di getos*. New York: Central Yiddish Culture Organization, 1948.

Kaganovich, Moshe. *The Participation of Jews in the Partisan Movement of Soviet Russia*. Rome: Central Historical Commission at the Union of Partisans, 1948.

Kahane, Meir. *Never Again! A Program for Survival*. Los Angeles: Nash, 1971.

———. *Time to Go Home*. Los Angeles: Nash, 1972.

———. *Why Be Jewish: Intermarriage, Assimilation and Alienation*. New York: Stein and Day, 1977.

Kahn, Shlomo. *From Twilight to Dawn: The Traditional Pesach Hagadah*. New York: Scribe, 1960.

Kalman, Jason. "With Friends Like These: Turning Points in the Jewish Interpretation of the Biblical Book of Job." Ph.D. diss., McGill University, 2005.

Kampf, Avram. *Contemporary Synagogue Art: Developments in the United States, 1945–1965.* New York: Union of American Hebrew Congregations, 1966.

Karff, Samuel E., ed. *Hebrew Union College–Jewish Institute of Religion at One Hundred Years.* New York: Hebrew Union College Press, 1976.

Karmel, Ilona. *Stephania.* Boston: Houghton Mifflin, 1953.

Karp, Abraham J. *To Give Life: The UJA in the Shaping of the American Jewish Community, 1939–1978.* New York: Schocken, 1981.

Kasher, Menachem. *The Israel Passover Haggadah: Supplemented by One Hundred Chapters.* New York: Shulsinger, 1950.

Katsh, Abraham I., ed. *Bar Mitzvah: Illustrated.* New York, Shengold, 1955.

———, ed. and trans. *Scroll of Agony: The Warsaw Diary of Chaim A. Kaplan.* New York: Macmillan, 1965.

Katz, A. Raymond. *Synagogue Art.* New York: Jewish Theological Seminary, 1953.

Katz, Shlomo, ed. *The Midstream Reader.* New York: Thomas Yoseloff, 1960.

Katzenelson, Yitzhak. *Dos lied funm oisgehargeten Yiddishe Folk.* Brooklyn, N.Y.: Hakibbutz Hameuchad, 1948.

———. *Elegy.* Trans. Rose Freeman-Ishill. Berkley Heights, N.J.: Oriole, 1948.

Katzman, Jacob, and Mordecai Strigler, eds. *Louis Segal, 1884–1964.* New York: Farband-Labor Zionist Organization, 1965.

Kaufman, David. *Shul with a Pool: The "Synagogue-Center" in American Jewish History.* Hanover, N.H.: University Press of New England, 1999.

Kayser, Louise D. *Light from Our Past: A Spiritual History of the Jewish People Expressed in Twelve Stained Glass Windows Designed by Louise D. Kayser for Har Tzion Temple, Philadelphia.* New York: Shengold, 1959.

Kayser, Stephen S. *Jewish Ceremonial Art.* Philadelphia: Jewish Publication Society of America, 1955.

Kazin, Alfred. *A Walker in the City.* New York: Grove, 1951.

Kazis, Israel. "Informal Youth Education Through the Synagogue Youth Organization." In *Proceedings of the Second Annual Rabbinical Assembly Conference on Jewish Education, "The Structure of Jewish Education in Conservative Judaism," December 22–23, 1947,* ed. Jewish Theological Society (pp. 67–75). New York: Jewish Theological Society, 1947.

Kellner, Abraham, ed. *The Rabbinical Council Manual of Holiday Sermons, 5711–1950.* New York: Rabbinical Council Press, 1950.

Kennedy, John F. *A Nation of Immigrants.* New York: Harper and Row, 1964.

Kenney, David. *A Political Passage: The Career of Stratton of Illinois.* Carbondale: Southern Illinois University Press, 1990.

Kertzer, Morris N. *What Is a Jew?* Cleveland: World, 1960.

Kessner, Carole S., ed. *The "Other" New York Jewish Intellectuals.* New York: New York University Press, 1994.

Klein, Gerda Weissman. *All but My Life.* New York: Hill and Wang, 1957.

Kleinberg, Otto. "Equality of Opportunity." In *Proceedings of the Fiftieth Anniversary Observance of the American Jewish Committee, April 10–14, 1957: The Pursuit of Equality at Home and Abroad,* ed. Jewish Publication Society of America (pp. 40–41). Philadelphia: Jewish Publication Society of America, 1958.

Klutznick, Philip M. *No Easy Answers.* New York: Farrar, Straus and Cudahy, 1961.

Kochavi, Arieh J. *Post-Holocaust Politics: Britain, the United States, and Jewish Refugees, 1945–1948.* Chapel Hill: University of North Carolina Press, 2001.

Kogon, Eugen. *The Theory and Practice of Hell: The German Concentration Camps and the System Behind Them.* New York: Berkeley, 1950.

Kolitz, Zvi. *Tiger Beneath the Skin: Stories and Parables of the Years of Death.* New York: Creative Age, 1947.

Kolsky, Thomas. *Jews Against Zionism: The American Council for Judaism.* Philadelphia: Temple University Press, 1990.

Kon, Henryk. *Songs from the Ghetto and Uprising: Twentieth Anniversary of the Uprising in the Warsaw Ghetto: 1942–1963.* New York: Universal [Allvelltlecher] Jewish Culture Congress, 1963.

Korman, Gerd. "The Holocaust in American Historical Writing." *Societas* 2, no. 3 (Summer 1972), pp. 251–69.

Krakower, Isadore. *Haggadah for Young American Jews.* Philadelphia: Bernard Malerman, 1951.

Kramer, Aaron, ed., and trans. *A Century of Yiddish Poetry.* New York: Cornwall, 1989.

Kramer, Michael P., and Hana Wirth-Nesher, eds. *The Cambridge Companion to Jewish American Literature.* Cambridge: Cambridge University Press, 2003.

Krop, J. F. "The Jews Under the Nazi Regime." *Annals of the American Academy of Political and Social Science* 245 (May 1946), pp. 28–32.

Kugelmass, Jack, and Jonathan Boyarin, eds. and trans. *From a Ruined Garden: The Memorial Books of Polish Jewry.* New York: Schocken, 1983.

Kussy, Sarah. *Handbook and Guide for Jewish Women's Organizations.* New York: National Women's League of the United Synagogue of America, 1947.

Kuznitz, Cecile Esther. "The Origins of Yiddish Scholarship and the YIVO Institute for Jewish Research." Ph.D diss., Stanford University, 2000.

Landman, Solomon, and Benjamin Efron. *Story Without End: An Informal History of the Jewish People.* New York: Holt, 1949.

Lang, Berel. "On Peter Novick's *The Holocaust in American Life.*" *Jewish Social Studies* 7, no. 3 (Spring/Summer 2001), pp. 149–58.

Laskier, Michael M. *The Jews of Egypt, 1920–1970: In the Midst of Zionism, Anti-Semitism, and the Middle East Conflict.* New York: New York University Press, 1992.

Layman, Richard, ed. *American Decades: 1960–1969.* New York: Thomson International, 1995.

Learsi, Rufus. *Fulfillment: The Epic Story of Zionism.* Cleveland: World, 1951.

———. *The Jews in America: A History.* Cleveland: World, 1954.

———. *A Study Guide in Jewish History.* Cleveland: World, 1949.

Leavitt, Moses. *The JDC Story, 1914–1952.* New York: Joint Distribution Committee, 1952.

Lebeson, Anita Libman. *Pilgrim People.* New York: Harper Brothers, 1950.

LeBlanc, Lawrence J. *The United States and the Genocide Convention.* Durham, N.C.: Duke University Press, 1991.

Lederhendler, Eli. *New York Jews and the Decline of Urban Ethnicity.* Syracuse: Syracuse University Press, 2001.

———. "On Peter Novick's *The Holocaust in American Life.*" *Jewish Social Studies* 7, no. 3 (Spring/Summer 2001), pp. 159–68.

Lee, Malka. *Durkh kindershe oygen.* Buenos Aires: Yidbukh, 1955.

Leftwich, Joseph. *The Golden Peacock: A Worldwide Treasury of Yiddish Poetry.* New York: Thomas Yoseloff, 1961.

Lehrer, Leibush. *Camp Boiberik: The Growth of an Idea.* N.p., 1959.

Lehrman, Irving, and Joseph Rappaport. *The Jewish Community of Miami Brochure.* New York: Jewish Theological Seminary, American Jewish History Center, 1954.

Leiter, Samuel L. *Encyclopedia of the New York Stage, 1940–1950.* New York: Greenwood, 1992.

Leivik, Hayim. *Di hasene in Fernvald: Dramatische poeme in elf stsenes.* New York: Central Yiddish Culture Organization, 1949.

———, ed. *Lieder fun di getos un lagern: Zog nit keinmol az du geist dem letzen veg!* New York: Central Yiddish Culture Organization, 1948.

———. *Mit der sheyres ha-pleteh.* New York: Central Yiddish Culture Organization, 1947.

———. "Who Are the Guilty?" In World Congress for Jewish Culture, *A Decade of Destruction: Jewish Culture in the USSR, 1948–1958* (pp. 25–27). New York: World Congress for Jewish Culture, 1958.

Lengyl, Olga. *Five Chimneys: The Story of Auschwitz.* New York: Ziff-Davis, 1947.

Leschnitzer, Adolf. *The Magic Background of Modern Anti-Semitism: An Analysis of the German-Jewish Relationship.* New York: International Universities Press, 1956.

Lestchinsky, Jacob. *Balance Sheet of Extermination.* New York: Institute for Jewish Affairs, 1946.

———. *Crisis, Catastrophe, and Survival.* New York: American Jewish Congress, 1948.

Levin, Meyer. *Eva.* New York: Simon and Schuster, 1959.

———. *If I Forget Thee: A Picture of Modern Palestine Based on the Film "My Father's House."* New York: Viking, 1947.

———. *My Father's House.* New York: Viking, 1947.

Levinger, Elma Ehrlich. *Jewish Adventures in America: The Story of 300 Years of Jewish Life in the United States.* New York: Bloch, 1954.

Levinthal, Israel H. *Point of View: An Analysis of American Judaism.* London: Abelard-Schuman, 1958.

Lewin, Isaac. *Noch'n hurban: Collected Essays.* New York: Research Institute for Post-War Problems of Religious Jewry, 1950.

Lewisohn, Ludwig. *The American Jew: Character and Destiny.* New York: Farrar, Straus, 1950.

Lewittes, Mendel, ed. *The 1945 Manual of Holiday and Occasional Sermons.* New York: Rabbinical Council Press, 1945.

Liberles, Robert. *Salo Wittmayer Baron: Architect of Jewish History.* New York: New York University Press, 1995.

Linenthal, Edward T. *Preserving Memory: The Struggle to Create America's Holocaust Museum.* New York: Columbia University Press, 1995.

Lipschutz, Norman. *Victory Through Darkness.* New York: Vantage, 1960.

Lipset, Seymour Martin, and Earl Rabb. *Jews and the New American Scene.* Cambridge: Harvard University Press, 1995.

Lipstadt, Deborah. "America and the Memory of the Holocaust, 1950–1965." *Modern Judaism* 16, no. 3 (1996), pp. 195–214.

———. *Denying the Holocaust: The Growing Assault on Truth and Memory*. New York: Plume, 1994.

Liptzin, Sol. *The Flowering of Yiddish Literature*. New York: Thomas Yoseloff, 1963.

———. *Generation of Decision: Jewish Rejuvenation in America*. New York: Bloch, 1958.

———. *Germany's Stepchildren*. New York: Meridian, 1961.

———, ed. *Peretz*. New York: YIVO Institute for Jewish Research, 1947.

Long, Emil J. *2,000 Years: A History of Anti-Semitism*. New York: Exposition, 1953.

Louis LaMed Literary Foundation. *Kidush hashem*. New York: Central Yiddish Culture Organization, 1948.

Lytle, Mark Hamilton. *America's Uncivil Wars: The Sixties Era from Elvis to the Fall of Richard Nixon*. New York: Oxford University Press, 2006.

Macedo, Stephen, ed. *Reassessing the Sixties: Debating the Political and Cultural Legacy*. New York: Norton, 1997.

Mankowitz, Zeev W. *Life Between Memory and Hope: The Survivors of the Holocaust in Occupied Germany*. New York: Cambridge University Press, 2002.

Marcus, Jacob R. "Important Historic Records." *JPS Bookmark* (December 1955), pp. 4–6.

———. "Three Hundred Years in America." In *The Dynamics of American Jewish History: Jacob Rader Marcus's Essays on American Jewish History*, ed. Gary P. Zola (pp. 116–26). Waltham, Mass.: Brandeis University Press, 2004.

Marenhof, Martha. *Haggadah for the Seder Service*. Detroit: DOT Publications, n.d.

Margoshes, S. "My Friend Louis Segal." In *Louis Segal: In Memoriam*, ed. Mordecai Strigler (pp. 29–31). New York: Farband-Labor Zionist Order, 1965.

Marill, Alvin H. *The Complete Films of Edward G. Robinson*. New York: Citadel, 1990.

Mark, Julius. *Reaching for the Moon and Other Addresses*. New York: Farrar, Straus and Cudahy, 1959.

Markowitz, Sidney L. *What Do You Know About Jewish Religion, History, Ethics and Culture? A Comprehensive Book Covering Every Phase of Jewish Life for the Past 3500 Years*. New York: Saphrograph, 1954.

Marrus, Michael R. *The Holocaust in History*. New York: Penguin, 1987.

Mart, Michelle. *Eyes on Israel: How Americans Came to See Israel as an Ally*. Albany: State University of New York Press, 2006.

Martin, James J. *The Man Who Invented "Genocide": The Public Career and Consequences of Raphael Lemkin*. Torrance, Calif.: Institute for Historical Review, 1984.

Massing, Paul W. *Rehearsal for Destruction: A Study of Political Anti-Semitism in Imperial Germany*. New York: Harper Brothers, 1949.

Matusow, Allen J. *The Unraveling of America: A History of Liberalism in the 1960s*. New York: Harper and Row, 1984.

Mayer, Milton. *They Thought They Were Free: The Germans, 1933–45*. Chicago: University of Chicago Press, 1955.

McWilliams, Carey. *Brothers Under the Skin*. Boston: Little, Brown, 1943.

Meyer, Peter, Bernard Weinryb, and Eugene Duschinsky. *Jews in the Soviet Satellites*. Syracuse: Syracuse University Press, 1953.

Meyerowitz, A. ed. *Megilat kurenits: Ayara be-hayeha u-ve-mota*. Tel Aviv: Former Residents of Kurzeniec in Israel and the USA, 1956.

Michels, Tony. *A Fire in Their Hearts: Yiddish Socialists in New York.* Cambridge: Harvard University Press, 2005.

Miller, Glenn T. "JTS and Other Forms of American Ministerial Preparation." In *Tradition Renewed: A History of the Jewish Theological Seminary of America—Beyond the Academy,* ed. Jack Wertheimer (vol. 2, pp. 658–59). New York: Jewish Theological Seminary of America, 1997.

Miller, Israel, ed. *The Rabbinical Council Manual of Holiday Sermons 5712–1951.* New York: Rabbinical Council Press, 1951.

Milton, Sybil. "The Memorialization of the Holocaust: Museums, Memorials, and Centers." In *Genocide: A Critical Bibliography,* ed. Israel Charney (vol. 2, pp. 299–320). New York: Facts on File, 1991.

Minkoff, Nochum. "Artists and Scholars View Jewish Art." *Jewish Art Center: Aims and Aspirations* (n.d.), pp. 8–16.

Mintz, Alan. "Hebrew Literature in America." In *The Cambridge Guide to Jewish American Literature,* ed. Michael P. Kramer and Hana Wirth-Nesher (pp. 92–109). Cambridge: Cambridge University Press, 2003.

———. *Popular Culture and the Shaping of the Holocaust Memory in America.* Seattle: University of Washington Press, 2001.

Mintz, Sharon L., and Gabriel Goldstein. *Printing the Talmud: From Bomberg to Schottenstein.* New York: Yeshiva University Museum, 2005.

Mohl, Raymond A. *South of the South: Jewish Activists and the Civil Rights Movement in Miami, 1945–1960.* Gainesville: University Press of Florida, 2004.

Mohrer, Fruma, and Marek Webb. *Guide to YIVO Archives.* New York: YIVO Institute for Jewish Research, 1998.

Monod, David. *German Music, Denazification, and the Americans, 1945–1953.* Chapel Hill: University of North Carolina Press, 2005.

Moore, Deborah Dash. *To the Golden Cities: Pursuing the American Jewish Dream in Miami and L.A.* New York: Free Press, 1994.

Morgan, Michael L. "To Seize Memory: History and Identity in Post-Holocaust Jewish Thought" (pp. 151–81). In *Thinking About the Holocaust: After Half a Century,* ed. Alvin H. Rosenfeld. Bloomington: Indiana University Press, 1997.

Morgenthau, Hans. *The Tragedy of German-Jewish Liberalism.* Leo Baeck Memorial Lecture 4. New York: Leo Baeck Institute, 1961.

Morgenthau Jr., Henry. *Germany Is Our Problem.* New York: Harper Brothers, 1945.

Moyn, Samuel. *A Holocaust Controversy: The Treblinka Affair in Postwar France.* Waltham, Mass.: Brandeis University Press, 2005.

Morse, Arthur. *While Six Million Died: A Chronicle of American Apathy.* New York: Random House, 1968.

Nadich, Judah. *Eisenhower and the Jews.* New York: Twayne, 1953.

Nathan, Robert R., Oscar Glass, and Daniel Creamer. *Palestine: Problem and Promise—An Economic Study.* Washington, D.C.: American Council on Public Affairs, Public Affairs Press, 1946.

National Jewish Music Council. *Bibliography of Jewish Recordings.* New York: National Jewish Music Council, 1948.

Neusner, Jacob. *Death and Birth of Judaism: The Impact of Christianity, Secularism, and the Holocaust on Jewish Faith.* New York: Basic Books, 1987.

———. "How the Extermination of European Jewry Became 'The Holocaust.'" In *Stranger at Home: "The Holocaust," Zionism, and American Judaism,* ed. Jacob Neusher (pp. 82–91). Chicago: University of Chicago Press, 1981.

Nevins, Allan. *Herbert H. Lehman and His Era.* New York: Scribner's, 1963.

New England Zionist Youth Commission. *Young Judea Songster.* New England Zionist Youth Commission, 1953

Newman, Louis I. *Biting on Granite: Selected Sermons and Addresses.* New York: Bloch, 1946.

———. *Pangs of the Messiah and Other Plays, Pageants and Cantatas.* New York: Bloch, 1957.

———. *Trumpet in Adversity and Other Poems.* New York: Renascence Press, 1948.

Newman, Roberta. "Delayed Pilgrims: The Radio Programs of the United Service for New Americans, 1947–48." MA thesis, Gallatin Division, New York University, 1996.

Niger, Samuel Charney. *Yisrael: Folk un land—Drei redes.* Chicago: L. M. Stein, 1952.

———. *Kiddush hashem.* New York: Central Yiddish Culture Organization, 1947.

Noveck, Simon, ed. *Contemporary Jewish Thought: A Reader.* New York: B'nai B'rith Department of Adult Jewish Education, 1963.

———. ed. *Great Jewish Personalities in Modern Times.* Washington D.C.: B'nai B'rith Department of Adult Jewish Education, 1960.

———, ed. *Great Jewish Thinkers of the Twentieth Century.* Washington, D.C.: B'nai B'rith Department of Adult Jewish Education, 1963.

Novick, Peter. *The Holocaust in American Life.* Boston: Houghton Mifflin, 1999.

———. "Response to Lederhendler and Lang." *Jewish Social Studies* 7, no. 3 (Spring/Summer 2001), pp. 169–79.

Nussbaum, Max, and Wm. M. Kramer. *Temple Israel Pulpit: A Selection of Published Sermons, Speeches and Articles.* Los Angeles: College of Jewish Studies Under the Patronage of the Union of American Hebrew Congregations, 1957.

Ofer, Dalia. "Mah v'ad kama lezkor mean hashoah: Zikaron hashoah b'medinat Yisrael b'assor harishon l'kiyuma." In *Atzmaut: 50 shanim harishonim,* ed. Anita Shapira. Jerusalem: Mercaz Zalman Shazar L'Toldot Yisrael, 1998.

Olsvanger, Immanuel, ed. *Royte Pomerantsen: Jewish Folk Humor.* New York: Schocken, 1947.

Oppenheimer, Mark. *Knocking on Heaven's Door: American Religion in the Age of Counterculture.* New Haven, Conn.: Yale University Press, 2003.

Ortner, Sherry B. *New Jersey Dreaming: Capital, Culture, and the Class of '58.* Durham, N.C.: Duke University Press, 2003.

Our Story . . . Atlanta: A Panorama of Israel. White Plains, N.Y.: Monde, 1957.

Parmet, Robert D. *The Master of Seventh Avenue: David Dubinsky and the American Labor Movement.* New York: New York University Press, 2005.

Pat, Jacob. *Ash un fayer* [*Ashes and Fire*]. New York: Central Yiddish Culture Organization, 1946.

Patterson, James T. *Grand Expectations: The United States, 1945–1974.* New York: Oxford University Press, 1966.

Perry, Marvin, and Frederick M. Schweitzer. *Anti-Semitism: Myth and Hate from Antiquity to the Present.* New York: Palgrave Macmillan, 2002.

Pessin, Deborah. *History of the Jews in America*. New York: United Synagogue Commission on Jewish Education, 1957.

———. *The Jewish People: Book Three*. New York: United Synagogue Commission on Jewish Education, 1953.

Phayer, Michael. *The Catholic Church and the Holocaust, 1930–1965*. Bloomington: Indiana University Press, 2000.

Pilch, Judah. *Between Two Generations: Selected Essays by Judah Pilch*. New York: Bloch, 1977.

Pilch, Judah, and Meir Ben-Horin. *Judaism and the Jewish School: Selected Essays on the Direction and Purpose of Jewish Education*. New York: Bloch, 1966.

Pilchik, Ely E. *Jeshurun Sermons*. New York: Bloch, 1957.

Pinson, Koppel S. *Modern Germany: Its History and Civilization*. New York: Macmillan, 1954.

———. *Nationalism and History*. New York: Jewish Publication Society of America, 1958.

Poliakov, Leon. *Harvest of Hate: The Nazi Program for the Destruction of the Jews of Europe*. Syracuse, N.Y.: Syracuse University Press, 1954.

Polin, Milton H. "A Cup of Wine and Jewish Self-Acceptance." In *The Rabbinical Council: Manual of Holiday and Sabbath Sermons, 5717–1956*, ed. Solomon Freilich (pp. 132–36). New York: Rabbinical Council Press, 1956.

Pool, David da Sola. *Why I Am a Jew*. Boston: Beacon, 1957.

Popkin, Zelda. *Open Every Door*. New York: Dutton, 1956.

———. *Small Victory*. Philadelphia: Lippincott, 1947.

———. *Quiet Street*. Philadelphia: Lippincott, 1951.

Poplack, Alvin M. *Carved in Granite: Holocaust Memorials in Metropolitan New York Jewish Cemeteries*. New York: Jay Street, 2003.

Porter, Jack Nusan, and Peter Dreier, eds. *Jewish Radicalism*. New York: Grove Press, 1973.

Postal, Bernard, and Samuel H. Abramson. *Landmarks of a People: A Guide to Jewish Sites in Europe*. New York: Hill and Wang, 1962.

Postal, Bernard, and Lionel Koppman. *American Jewish Landmarks*. Vol. 1. New York: Fleet Press, 1954.

———. *A Jewish Tourist's Guide to the United States*. Philadelphia: Jewish Publication Society of America, 1954.

Poujol, Catherine. *L'affaire Finaly*. Paris: Berg International, 2006.

Poupko, Rabbi Bernard A., ed. *The Rabbinical Council Manual of Holiday and Sabbath Sermons, 5716–1955*. New York: Rabbinical Council Press, 1955.

Prell, Riv-Ellen. *Prayer and Community: The Havurah Movement in American Judaism*. Detroit: Wayne State University Press, 1989.

Prinz, Joachim. *The Dilemma of the Modern Jew*. Boston: Little, Brown, 1962.

Proskauer, Judge Joseph M. *In Peace and Dignity: Testimony of the American Jewish Committee for the Rehabilitation of Jews in Europe and the Palestine Question as Presented by Judge Joseph M. Proskauer, President, Before the Anglo-American Committee of Inquiry on Palestine*. New York: American Jewish Committee, 1946.

Rabinowitz, Dorothy. *New Lives: Survivors of the Holocaust Living in America*. New York: Knopf, 1976.

Rabinowitz, Stanley. *The Assembly: A Century in the Life of the Adas Israel Congregation of Washington, D.C.* Hoboken, N.J.: KTAV, 1993.

Rader, Jack. *By the Skill of Their Hands: The Story of ORT.* Geneva: World ORT Union, 1970.

Raskas, Bernard S. *Heart of Wisdom.* New York: Burning Bush, 1962.

Rawidowicz, Simon. *On Jewish Learning: Address Delivered at the Opening Convocation of the College of Jewish Studies, September, 1948.* Chicago: College of Jewish Studies, 1950.

Reichmann, Eva. *Hostages of Civilization: The Social Sources of Nazi Anti-Semitism.* Boston: Beacon, 1951.

Reiss, Lionel. *New Lights over Old Shadows.* New York: Reconstructionist, 1954.

Reitlinger, Gerald R. *The Final Solution: The Attempt to Exterminate the Jews of Europe, 1939–1945.* New York: Beechhurst, 1953.

———. *The S.S.: Alibi of a Nation.* New York: Viking, 1957.

Ribalow, Harold U., ed. *This Land, These People.* New York: Beechhurst, 1950.

Ricoeur, Paul. *Memory, History, Forgetting.* Chicago: University of Chicago Press, 2004.

Rifkind, Simon H., et al. *The Basic Equities of the Palestine Problem: A Memorandum by Simon H. Rifkind, Chairman, Jerome N. Frank, Stanley H. Fuld, Abraham Tulin, Hilton Handler, Murray I. Gurfein, Abe Fortas, Lawrence R. Eno.* New York, 1947.

———. *The Disinherited Jews of Europe Must Be Saved.* New York: American Jewish Conference, 1946.

Robinson, Jacob, and Philip Friedman. *Guide to Jewish History Under Nazi Impact.* Yad Vashem Martyrs' and Heroes' Memorial Authority and YIVO, Joint Documentary Projects Bibliographical Series No. 1. New York: YIVO, 1960.

Robinson, Nehemiah. *Ten Years of German Indemnification: Memorial Edition.* New York: Conference of Jewish Materials Claims Against Germany, 1964.

Rogow, Arnold A., ed. *The Jew in the Gentile World: An Anthology of Writing About Jews, by Non-Jews.* New York: Macmillan, 1961.

Rosenbaum, Samuel. "President's Annual Report." In *Proceedings of the Eleventh Annual Conference-Convention of the Cantors Assembly of America and the Department of Music of the United Synaogue of America, April 21, 22, 23, 24, 1958,* ed. United Synagogue of America (pp. 20–24). New York: United Synagogue of America, 1958.

Rosenberg, M. J. "To Uncle Tom and Other Jews." In *Jewish Radicalism: A Selected Anthology,* ed. Jack Porter and Peter Drier (pp. 5–10). New York: Grove, 1973.

Rosenberg, Stuart, E. *A Time to Speak: Of Man, Faith and Society.* New York: Bloch, 1960.

Rosenfeld, Alvin H. "The Assault on Holocaust Memory." In *American Jewish Yearbook: 2001* (pp. 3–20). New York: American Jewish Congress, 2001.

———, ed. *Thinking About the Holocaust After Half a Century.* Bloomington: Indiana University Press, 1997.

Rosenfeld, Sherman. "The Struggle for Shalom." In *Jewish Radicalism: A Selected Anthology,* ed. Jack Porter and Peter Drier (pp. 222–28). New York: Grove, 1971.

Roskies, Diane K. *Teaching the Holocaust to Children: A Review and Bibliography.* New York: KTAV, 1975.

Rothfels, Hans. *The German Opposition to Hitler: An Appraisal.* Hinsdale, Ill.: Regnery, 1948.

Rozenblit, Marsha. "The Holocaust During the Seminary Years." In *Tradition Renewed: A History of the Jewish Theological Seminary of America,* ed. Jack Wertheimer (vol. 2, pp. 273–308). New York: Jewish Theological Seminary of America, 1997.

Rubenovitz, Herman, and Mignon Rubenovitz. *The Waking Heart.* Cambridge, Mass.: Nathaniel Dame, 1967.

Rubenovitz, Mignon L. *Altars of My Fathers.* Boston: Jewish Museum, Temple Mishkan Tefilah, 1954.

Rubin, Ruth. *A Treasury of Jewish Folksong.* New York: Schocken, 1950.

Ruchames, Louis. "Parallels of Jewish and Negro History." *Negro History Bulletin* 19, no. 3 (December 1955), pp. 63–65, 66.

Ruedenberg, Lucia Meta. "'Remember 6,000,000': Civic Commemoration of the Holocaust in New York City." Ph.D. diss., New York University, 1994.

Runes, Dagobert D., ed. *The Hebrew Impact on Western Civilization.* New York: Philosophical Library, 1951.

Sabatka, H. ed. *Lomza: Ir oyfkum un untergang.* New York: American Committee for the Book of Lomza, 1957.

Sage, Naomi. "A Memorial Culture: The American Jewish Joint Distribution Committee (JDC) and Its Relationship with the Holocaust and Holocaust Survivors." Unpublished ms.

Saidel, Rochelle G. *Never Too Late to Remember: The Politics Behind New York City's Holocaust Museum.* New York: Holmes and Meier, 1996.

Samuel, Maurice. *The Gentleman and the Jew.* New York: Knopf, 1950.

———. *Level Sunlight.* New York: Knopf, 1953.

———. *Prince of the Ghetto.* New York: Knopf, 1948.

———. *The World of Sholom Aleichem.* New York: Knopf, 1962.

Saperstein, Harold I. *Witness from the Pulpit: Topical Sermons, 1933–1980.* Ed. Marc Saperstein. Lanham, Md.: Lexington Books, 2000.

Sarna, Jonathan D. *American Judaism: A History.* New Haven, Conn.: Yale University Press, 2004.

Schachtman, Tom. *I Seek My Brethren: Ralph Goldman and "The Joint."* New York: Newmarket Press, 2001.

Schappes, Morris U., ed. *Jewish Currents Reader: A Selection of Short Stories, Poems and Essays from Jewish Currents, years 1956–1966.* New York: Jewish Currents, 1956–1966.

———. *The Jews in the United States: A Pictorial History, 1654 to the Present.* New York: Citadel, 1958.

Schauss, Hayyim. *The Lifetime of a Jew: Throughout the Ages of Jewish History.* Cincinnati: Union of American Hebrew Congregations, 1950.

Schaver, Emma, and Lazar Weiner. *Songs of the Concentration Camps.* New York: Transcontinental Press and Union of American Hebrew Congregations, 1960.

Scheinberg, Abraham. *American Jews: Their Lives and Achievements—A Contemporary Biographical Record.* New York: Golden Book Foundation of America, 1947.

Schiller, David M. *Bloch, Schoenberg, and Bernstein: Assimilating Jewish Music.* Oxford: Oxford University Press, 2003.

———. "'My Own Kaddish': Leonard Bernstein's Symphony No. 3." In *Key Texts in*

American Jewish Culture, ed. Jack Kugelmass (pp. 185–96). New Brunswick, N.J.: Rutgers University Press, 2003.

Schmaltz, William H. *Hate: George Lincoln Rockwell and the American Nazi Party*. Washington, D.C.: Brassey's, 1999.

Schmuller, Aaron. *Treblinka Grass: Poetical Translations from the Yiddish and with an Introductory Essay and Notes on Nazi and Soviet Anti-Semitism*. New York: Shulsinger Brothers, 1957.

Schnabel, Ernst. *Anne Frank: A Portrait in Courage*. New York: Harcourt, Brace, 1958.

Schneider, Gertrude. *Mordechai Gebirtig: His Poetic and Musical Legacy*. Westport, Conn.: Praeger, 2000.

Schneiderman, Harry, and Itzhak J. Carmin, eds. *Who's Who in World Jewry: A Biographical Dictionary of Outstanding Jews*. New York: Monde, 1955.

Schneiderman, S. L. *Between Fear and Hope*. New York: Arco, 1947.

———, ed. *Warsaw Ghetto: A Diary by Mary Berg*. New York: L. B. Fischer, 1945.

Schnitzer, Henry R. *Thy Goodly Tent: The First Fifty Years of Temple Emanu-El, Bayonne, N.J.* Bayonne, N.J.: Temple Emanu-El, 1961.

Schrecker, Ellen. *No Ivory Tower: McCarthyism and the Universities*. New York: Oxford University Press, 1986.

Schulman, Elias. *The Fate of Soviet Jewry*. New York: Jewish Labor Committee, 1948.

Schwartz, David. *Bitter Herbs and Honey*. New York: Silver Palm, 1947.

Schwarz, Karl. *Jewish Artists of the Nineteenth and Twentieth Centuries*. New York: Philosophical Library, 1949.

Schwarz, Leo W. *Enduring Ideas in the Jewish Heritage: A Discussion Guide for Youth and Adults Based on Feast of Leviathan—Tales of Adventure, Faith and Love from Jewish Literature*. New York: Rinehart, 1956.

———, ed. *Great Ages and Ideas of the Jewish People*. New York: Modern Library, 1956.

———, ed. *The Menorah Treasury: Harvest of Half a Century*. Philadelphia: Jewish Publication Society of America, 1964.

———. *The Redeemers: A Saga of the Years 1945–1952*. New York: Farrar, Straus and Young, 1953.

———. *The Root and the Bough: The Epic of an Enduring People*. New York: Rinehart, 1949.

Schwarz-Bart, Andre. *The Last of the Just*. New York: Bantam, 1961.

Schwarzbart, Isaac I. *The Story of the Warsaw Ghetto Uprising: Its Meaning and Message*. New York: World Jewish Congress Organization Department, 1953.

Secunda, Victora. *Bei Mir Bist Du Schön: The Life of Sholom Secunda*. Weston, Conn.: Magic Circle Press, 1982.

Segal, Charles M. *Fascinating Facts About American Jewish History*. New York: Twayne, 1955.

Segal, Louis. *Bei unzere sheeris hapletah in poilin un maarv-airope*, New York: Farband, 1947.

Serwer, Zachary. *Creative Dramatics in the Jewish Club*. New York: National Jewish Welfare Board, 1946.

Shachtman, Tom. *I Seek My Brethren: Ralph Goldman and "The Joint."* New York: Newmarket Press, 2001.

Shafir, Shlomo. *Ambiguous Relations: The American Jewish Community and Germany Since 1945*. Detroit: Wayne State University Press, 1999.

Shandler, Jeffrey. *While America Watches: Televising the Holocaust*. Oxford: Oxford University Press, 1999.

Shapira, Anita, ed. *Atzmaut: 50 Hashanim Harishonot*. Jerusalem: Zalman Shazar Center, 1998.

Shapira, Anita. "Hashoah: Zikaron prati v'zikaron tzibui." In *Atzmaut: 50 shanim harishonim*, ed. Anita Shapira (pp. 527–40). Jerusalem: Mercaz Zalman Shazar L'Toldot Yisrael, 1998.

Shapiro, Edward S. *A Time for Healing: American Jewry Since World War II*. Baltimore: Johns Hopkins University Press, 1992.

Shapiro, Judah J. *The Friendly Society: A History of the Workmen's Circle*. New York: Media Judaica, 1970.

Shapiro, Leon. *The History of ORT*. New York: Schocken, 1980.

Sharfman, Benjamin, ed. *The Rabbinical Council Manual of Holiday and Sabbath Sermons*. New York: Rabbinical Council Press, 1957.

Sharfman, Solomon J., ed. *The Rabbinical Council Manual of Holiday and Sabbath Sermons, 5714–1953*. New York: Rabbinical Council Press, 1953.

Sheramy, Rona. "Defining Lessons: The Holocaust in American Jewish Education." Ph.D. diss., Brandeis University, 2001.

Sherman, C. Bezalel. *The Jew Within American Society: A Study in Ethnic Individuality*. Detroit: Wayne State University Press, 1965.

Shirer William. *The Rise and Fall of Adolf Hitler*. New York: Random House, 1961.

———. *The Rise and Fall of the Third Reich: A History of Nazi Germany*. New York: Simon and Schuster, 1960.

Shoskes, Henry. *No Traveler Returns: The Story of Hitler's Greatest Crime*. Garden City, N.Y.: Doubleday, Doran, 1945.

Sieve, Asher, ed. *The Rabbinical Manual of Holiday Sermons, 5710–1949*. New York: Rabbinical Council Press, 1949.

Silberman, Charles. *A Certain People: American Jews and Their Lives Today*. New York: Summit Books, 1988.

Silver, Abba Hillel. *Therefore Choose Life: Selected Sermons, Addresses and Writings of Abba Hillel Silver*. Cleveland: World, 1967.

———. *Where Judaism Differed: An Inquiry into the Distinctiveness of Judaism*. New York: Macmillan, 1956.

Silver, Maxwell D. *The Way to God*. New York: Philosophical Library, 1950.

Silverman, Morris. *United Synagogue of America High Holiday Prayer Book*. Hartford, Conn.: Prayer Book Press, 1951.

Silverstein, Alan. *Alternatives to Assimilation: The Response of Reform Judaism to American Culture, 1840–1930*. Hanover, N.H.: University Press of New England, 1994.

Simon Dubnow, 1860–1941: The Life and Work of a Jewish Historian. New York: YIVO Institute for Jewish Research, 1961.

Simonhoff, Harry. *Under Strange Skies*. New York: Philosophical Library, 1953.

Singer, Isaac Bashevis. *The Family Moskat*. New York: Knopf, 1950.

———. *Gimpel, the Fool*. New York: Noonday, 1952.

———. *The Magician of Lublin*. New York: Farrar, Straus, Giroux, 1960.

———. *Satan in Goray*. New York: Noonday, 1955.

———. *Spinoza of Market Street*. New York: Farrar, Straus, Cudahy, 1961.

Sklare, Marshall, ed. *The Jews: Social Patterns of an American Group*. Glencoe, Ill.: Free Press, 1958.

Sklare, Marshall, and Marc Vosk. *The Riverton Study: How Jews Look at Themselves and Their Neighbors*. New York: American Jewish Committee, 1957.

Slawson, John. *Realities of Jewish Integration*. New York: American Jewish Congress, 1961.

Sleeper, James A., and Alan L. Mintz, eds. *The New Jews*. New York: Vintage, 1971.

Sloan, Jacob, ed. *Notes from the Warsaw Ghetto: The Journal of Emmanuel Ringelblum*. New York: McGraw-Hill, 1958.

Smith, Judith E. *Visions of Belonging: Family Stories, Popular Culture, and Postwar Democracy, 1940–1960*. New York: Columbia University Press, 2004.

Soloveitchik, Haym. "Rupture and Reconstruction: The Transformation of Contemporary Orthodoxy." In *Jews in America: A Contemporary Reader*, ed. Roberta Rosenberg Farber and Chaim I. Waxman (pp. 320–76). Hanover, N.H.: University Press of New England, 1999.

Soloveitchik, Joseph B. "On Inserting Memorial Prayers for Holocaust Victims on Passover Night at the Seder." In *Community, Covenant and Commitment: Selected Letters and Communications: Rabbi Joseph B. Soloveitchik*, ed. Nathaniel Helfgot (pp. 119–21). New York: Toras Horav Foundation, 2005.

Sorin, Gerald. *Tradition Transformed: The Jewish Experience in America*. Baltimore: Johns Hopkins University Press, 1997.

Soyer, Daniel. *Jewish Immigrant Associations and American Identity in New York, 1880–1939*. Cambridge: Harvard University Press, 1997.

Special Subcommittee of the Committee on the Judiciary, House of Representatives. *Report: The Displaced Persons Analytical Bibliography*. Washington, D.C.: U.S. Government Printing Office, 1950.

The Standard American-Jewish Directory. New York: Barkai and Hudes, 1960.

Staub, Michael E. *The Jewish 1960s: An American Sourcebook*. Waltham, Mass.: Brandeis University Press, 2004.

———. *Torn at the Roots: The Crisis of Jewish Liberalism in Postwar America*. New York: Columbia University Press, 2002.

Stein, Herman. "Jewish Social Work in the United States, 1920–1955." In *The Jews: Social Patterns of an American Group*, ed. Marshall Sklare (pp. 173–204). Glencoe, Ill.: Free Press, 1958.

Stitskin, Leon D., ed. *The Rabbinical Council Manual of Holiday Sermons, 5709–1948*. New York: Rabbinical Council Press, 1948.

———, ed. *The Rabbinical Council Manual of Holiday Sermons, 5713–1952*. New York: Rabbinical Council Press, 1952.

Stone, I. F. *This Is Israel*. New York: Boni and Gaer, 1948.

———. *Underground to Palestine*. New York: Boni and Gaer, 1946.

Strasser, Michael. "'A Survivor from Warsaw' as Personal Parable." *Music and Letters* 76, no. 1 (1995), pp. 60–61.

Svonkin, Stuart. *Jews Against Prejudice: American Jews and the Fight for Civil Liberties*. New York: Columbia University Press, 1997.

Syrkin, Marie. *Blessed Is the Match: The Story of Jewish Resistance.* New York: Knopf, 1947.

———. *The State of the Jews.* Washington, D.C.: New Republic, 1980.

Tabak, Israel. "The Tenth Yahrtzeit." In *The Rabbinical Council Manual of Holiday and Sabbath Sermons, 5714–1953,* ed. Solomon J. Sharfman (pp. 235–36). New York: Rabbinical Council Press, 1953.

Takaki, Ronald. *Strangers from a Different Shore: A History of Asian Americans.* New York: Penguin, 1989.

Taube, Herman. *Empty Pews: A Novel of World War II Based on the Life of Immigrants Who Found Hope, Love, and Happiness in America.* Trans. Sarah Chodosh Lesser. Baltimore: Nicholas A. Gossmann, 1958.

Tenenbaum, Joseph. *Let My People In.* New York: American Federation for Polish Jews, 1947.

———. *Peace for the Jews.* New York: American Federation for Polish Jews, 1945.

———. *Race and Reich: The Story of an Epoch.* New York: Twayne, 1956.

———. *The Road to Nowhere: An Indictment and a Challenge.* New York: American Federation for Polish Jews, 1947.

———. *Underground: The Story of a People.* New York: Philosophical Library, 1952.

Tenenbaum, Joseph, with Sheila Tenenbaum. *In Search of a Lost People.* New York: Beechhurst, 1948.

Todd, Albert C., ed. *The Collected Poems of Yevgeny Yectushenko.* New York: Holt, 1991.

Trepp, Leo. *Eternal Faith, Eternal People: A Journey into Judaism.* Englewood Cliffs, N.J.: Prentice Hall, 1962.

Trunk, Isaiah. *Lodzsher Geto: A Historishe Un Sotsiologishe Shtudye, Mit Dokumenten, Taveles Un Mape.* New York: YIVO Institute for Jewish Research, 1962.

Tussman, Malka Heifetz. *With Teeth in the Earth: Selected Poems of Malka Heifetz Tussman.* Ed. and trans. Marcia Falk. Detroit: Wayne State University Press, 1992.

Tverski, Aaron. *Ikh bin der korben un der eydes.* New York: Shulsinger, 1947.

United Synagogue of America, ed. *Proceedings of the Eleventh Annual Conference-Convention of the Cantors Assembly of America and the Department of Music of the United Synagogue of America, April 21, 22, 23, 24, 1958.* New York: United Synagogue of America, 1958.

———. *P'tsah b'zemer: A Basic Selection of Hebrew and Yiddish Folk Songs.* New York: United Synagogue of America Youth Commission, 1959.

Unsdorfer, S. B. *The Yellow Star.* New York: Thomas Yoseloff, 1961.

Unterman, Isaac. *The Jewish Holidays.* New York: Bloch, 1950.

Uris, Leon. *Exodus.* Garden City, N.Y.: Doubleday, 1958.

———. *Mila 18.* Garden City, N.Y.: Doubleday, 1961.

———. "The Most Heroic Story of Our Century." *Coronet* (November 1960), pp. 170–78.

Vinaver, Chemjo, ed. *Anthology of Jewish Music.* New York: Edward B. Marks Music, 1955.

Vishniac, Roman. *Polish Jews: A Pictorial Record.* New York: Schocken, 1947.

Von Juden in Muenchen: Ein Gedenkbuch. Munich: Ner-Tamid, 1959.

Vorspan, Albert. *Giants of Justice.* New York: Union of American Hebrew Congregations, 1960.

Wallenrod, Reuben. *The Literature of Modern Israel*. New York: Abelard-Schuman, 1956.

Waren, Helen. *The Buried Are Screaming*. New York: Beechhurst, 1948.

Warhaftig, Zorach. *Relief and Rehabilitation: Implications of the UNRRA Progam for Jewish Needs*. From War to Peace, vol. 1. New York: Institute of Jewish Affairs of the American Jewish Congress and World Jewish Congress, 1944.

———. *Uprooted: Jewish Refugees and Displaced Persons After Liberation*. From War to Peace, vol. 5. New York: Institute of Jewish Affairs of the American Jewish Congress and World Jewish Congress, 1946.

Waskow, Arthur I. *The Freedom Seder: A New Haggadah for Passover*. New York: Holt, Rinehart and Winston, 1969.

Waxman, Meyer, Sulamith Ish-Kishor, and Jacob Sloan. *Blessed Is the Daughter*. New York: Shengold, 1959.

Wdowinski, David. *And We Are Not Saved*. New York: Philosophical Library, 1963.

Wei, William. *The Asian American Movement*. Philadelphia: Temple University Press, 1993.

Weinreich, Max. *Hitler's Professors: The Part of Scholarship in Germany's Crimes Against the Jewish People*. New York: YIVO Institute for Jewish Research, 1946.

Weinreich, Uriel, ed. *The Field of Yiddish: Studies in Yiddish Language, Folklore, and Literature*. New York: Linguistic Circle of New York, 1954.

Weinstein, David. "Maintaining Neutrality: NBC and the Holocaust." Unpublished ms.

Weinstock, Earl. *The Seven Years*. New York: Dutton, 1959.

Weintraub, Ruth G. *How Secure These Rights? Anti-Semitism in the United States in 1948: An Anti-Defamation League Survey*. Garden City, N.Y.: Doubleday, 1948.

Weisel, Elie. *Night*. New York: Hill and Wang, 1960.

Weiss, Moshe. "Self-Sacrifice." In *The Rabbinical Council Manual of Holiday and Sabbath Sermons*, ed. Samuel J. Fox (pp. 140–43). New York: Rabbinical Council Press, 1959.

Weisser, Albert. *The Modern Renaissance of Jewish Music: Events and Figures of Eastern Europe and America*. New York: Bloch, 1954.

Wertheimer, Jack. *A People Divided: Judaism in Contemporary America*. Hanover, N.H.: University Press of New England, 1993.

———. *Tradition Renewed: A History of the Jewish Theological Seminary of America*. Vol. 2: *Beyond the Academy*. New York: Jewish Theological Seminary of America, 1997.

White, Lyman Cromwell. *300,000 New Americans: The Epic of a Modern Immigrant-Aid Service*. New York: Harper Brothers, 1957.

Whitfield, Stephen J. "The Jews." In *The Encyclopedia of American Cultural and Intellectual History*, ed. Mary Kupiec Cayon and Peter W. Williams (vol. 2, pp. 375–84). New York: Scribner's, 2001.

———. "Value Added: Jews in Postwar American Culture." In *A New Jewry: America Since the Second World War*, ed. Peter Medding (pp. 68–84). New York: Oxford University Press, 1992.

Whitman, Ruth, ed. *An Anthology of Modern Yiddish Poetry*. New York: October House, 1966.

Wischnitzer, Rachel. *Synagogue Architecture in the United States: History and Interpretation*. Philadelphia: Jewish Publication Society of America, 1955.

Wise, Judah L. *On This Day: Brief Bar Mitzvah Addresses Based on the Portion of the Week [Sidrot] for Each Sabbath of the Year.* New York: Bloch, 1954.

Wisse, Ruth. "Jewish American Renaissance." In *The Cambridge Guide to Jewish American Literature,* ed. Michael P. Kramer and Hana Wirth-Nesher (pp. 190–211). Cambridge: Cambridge University Press, 2003.

Woocher, Jonathan. *Sacred Survival: The Civil Religion of American Jews.* Bloomington: Indiana University Press, 1986.

Wouk, Herman. *This Is My God.* Garden City, N.Y.: Doubleday, 1959.

Yeruchem, Ahron. *Lo tishkach [Don't Forget].* New York: Sinai, 1949.

Yeshiva Yearbook, 1953. Brooklyn, N.Y.: Yeshiva of Flatbush, 1953.

Yidisher Kultur Farband. *100 Contemporary American Jewish Painters and Sculptors.* New York: Yidisher Kultur Farband, Art Section, 1947.

YIVO. *Life Struggle and Uprising in the Warsaw Ghetto.* New York: YIVO Institute for Jewish Research, 1963.

———. *Vilna, the Jerusalem of Lithuania, in Times of Glory and in Its Destruction.* New York: YIVO Institute for Jewish Research, 1960.

———. *YIVO Annual of Jewish Social Science.* New York: YIVO Institute for Jewish Research, 1946–1962.

Young Zionist Action Committee. *Songs of Israel / Sheeray Yisrael.* New York: Young Zionist Action Committee, 1949.

Young, James E. *The Texture of Memory: Holocaust Memorials and Meaning.* New Haven, Conn.: Yale University Press, 1993.

Zborowski, Mark, and Elizabeth Herzog. *Life Is with People: The Culture of the Shtetl.* New York: International Universities Press, 1952.

Zeiger, Henry A., ed. *The Case Against Adolf Eichmann.* New York: Signet Books / New American Library, 1960.

Zeitz, Joshua M. *White Ethnic New York: Jews, Catholics, and the Shaping of Postwar Politics.* Chapel Hill: University of North Carolina Press, 2007.

Zerubavel, Yael. *Recovered Roots: Collective Memory and the Making of the Israeli National Tradition.* Chicago: University of Chicago Press, 1995.

Zimmels, H. J. *The Echo of the Nazi Holocaust in Rabbinic Literature.* New York: KTAV, 1977.

Zola, Gary Phillip, ed. *The Dynamics of American Jewish History: Jacob Rader Marcus's Essays on American Jewry.* Hanover: University Press of New England, 2004.

Zuckerman, Nathan. *The Wine of Violence: An Anthology of Anti-Semitism.* New York: Association Press, 1947.

Zuckoff, Aviva Cantor. "The Oppression of America's Jews." In *Jewish Radicalism: A Selected Anthology,* ed. Jack Porter and Peter Drier (pp. 29–49). New York: Grove, 1973.

Zumoff, Barnett, trans. *I Keep Recalling: The Holocaust Poems of Jacob Gladstein.* New York: KTAV, 1993.

Zweig, Ronald W. *German Reparations and the Jewish World: A History of the Claims Conference.* 2nd ed. London: Frank Cass, 2001.

Index

495

About the Author

HASIA R. DINER is Paul S. and Sylvia Steinberg Professor of American Jewish History and the Director of the Goldstein-Goren Center for American Jewish History at New York University. She is the author or editor of numerous books, including *The Jews of the United States, 1654–2000; Hungering for America: Italian, Irish, and Jewish Foodways in the Age of Migration; Her Works Praise Her: A History of Jewish Women in America from Colonial Times to the Present* (with Beryl Lieff Benderly); and *From Arrival to Incorporation: Migrants to the U.S. in a Global Era* (available from New York University Press), among others.

D 804.3 .D58 2009

Diner, Hasia R.

We remember with reverence
  and love

GAYLORD